An Inconvenient History

Japan's Dark Shadow on Asia

Charles Park

East Asian History and Peace Institute

CONTENTS

Contents

Contents

PREFACE

History is accompanied by both light and shadow. People tend to be interested in and remember the light of history. On the other hand, people feel rather uncomfortable regarding the shadow of history and easily turn away from it. The light of history shines brighter due to its shadow. However, the shadow, which is cast by the light of history, is another name for tragedy and suffering. Thus, an authentic development of history can be expected when people confront the shadow head-on while still feeling uncomfortable about it. Germany initiated two World Wars in the early 20th century. It had grown its power to conquer Europe twice and Germany's national power at the time was considered as a light. However, the two wars that Germany initiated were tragedies that brought many deaths and destruction in Europe. Such acts of Germany in boasting its power cast a dark shadow not only across Europe but on itself as well. Nevertheless, after World War II, Germany and Europe faced the uncomfortable shadow and sought to change it to light. Therefore, as Germany and Europe increased their economic cooperation and advanced their integration, they were able to form the European Union (EU).

Japan was the first non-Western country to achieve a high level of modernization during the late 19th century and early 20th century. Based on this, Japan increased its national power by invading, colonizing, and occupying Asian countries. Such events at the time were considered as a light for Japan but it was a huge tragedy and a dark shadow cast over Asian countries. At the time, as Western countries were also governing the world through imperialism, such development of Japan was astonishing to them and was applauded by them. As a result, the suffering and tragedy of Asian countries was considered uncomfortable and ignored by the Western countries. When focusing on Japan at the time, Japan's modernization and external expansion was considered as a light that raised self-esteem as Asia's leading country for the military authorities and the ruling powers, but it cast a shadow on the Japanese people because their thoughts were suppressed and they were mobilized to the war. After the war, Japan did not put in effort to change such shadow into light. Therefore, the shadow that was cast from the light of Japan's history in the early 20th century is still hanging over Asia today in the 21st century.

This book straightforwardly depicts the light shined by Japan's history and the shadow cast from that light. It particularly focuses on the facts and causes of the shadow of Japan's history, which has been neglected so far. Thus, when people learn and hear candidly about the shadow cast by Japan's history, many of them will feel uncomfortable and be astonished. Since Western people have known mostly about the light of Japan's history, they may feel very uncomfortable when they learn about the true character of the shadow cast by it. The Japanese ruling powers, which have tried to hide and prevent such shadow from emerging, will feel even more uncomfortable. Since the Japanese people had been brainwashed that Japan was a country chosen by god during the late 19th century and early 20th century and have considered Japan as the best country through national pride in being an economic power after the war, they will also feel uncomfortable about the shadow as well. Asian people, who had suffered under Japan's colonial rule and from war of aggression in the first half of the 20th century, will also have uncomfortable feelings, when recalling the scars. However, if such uncomfortableness is not confronted and overcome, reconciliation in Asia and Japan's genuine development cannot be sought. Therefore, by revealing the true character of the shadow cast by Japan's history, this book seeks to confront head-on the uncomfortableness that has been avoided to this day and tries to find a method of resolution. Franz Kafka said, "A book must be the axe that breaks the frozen sea inside us." The author wishes this book to become 'Kafka's axe' that breaks the uncomfortableness of the shadow of Japan's history and allows future-oriented reconciliation and development. So, in a sense, it can be said that 'To study history is to prepare for a better future.'

Modern Japan (1868-1945) not only put Taiwan and Korea under colonial rule and invaded Asian countries in the early 20th century through its development strategy of foreign expansion, but also waged the Pacific War against the United States. Modern Japan's expansionism brought about a major disaster to Asian countries and their people. However, Japan did not properly repent and apologize for its historical wrongdoings after the war, and the necessary reparations were not made for the victims. As the right-wing forces gain more power, Japan is attempting to commemorate its history of colonization and invasion as a glorious history, which is acting as an impediment to reconciliation and mutual coexistence with Asian countries. Economic interdependence between Japan and other Asian countries is growing stronger but political and military conflict is increasing due to Japan's rightward shift and rise in military power. Meanwhile, Germany has conducted postwar settlements in a relatively exemplary manner and has become the cornerstone of European integration. Then, why has Japan become an impediment to reconciliation and peace in Asia? For what reason had modern Japan committed such brutal acts without hesitation to Asian countries and their people? What correlation was there between the development of modern Japan and the pain of Asian countries? Why is Japan reluctant to truly reconcile with neighboring countries and denying historical facts? What should be done in order to change Japan's attitude and establish peace in Asia and in the world? The author has prepared for approximately ten years in order to respond to such questions through this book.

Modern Japan had developed through the foreign expansion strategy of invading, occupying and colonizing Asian countries. The foreign expansion development strategy of modern Japan caused a tragic history by bringing immense pain and damage to Asian countries and their people. However, postwar Japan did not take on its war responsibility properly and returned to the international society through the San Francisco Peace Treaty under the protection of the United States amidst the Cold War and the Korean War. Furthermore, Japan succeeded in achieving economic revival and growth through the Korean War and the Vietnam War. Then, Japan faced the end of the Cold War without properly repenting and apologizing for its historical wrongdoings in the early 20th century nor making the necessary reparations. As the Cold War ended and the democratization and economic growth of Asian countries made progress, problems regarding Japan's past affairs began to rise to the surface. In response, Japan showed efforts to repent and apologize to some degree in the early 1990s. However, due to the loss of self-confidence resulting from long-term economic recession, Japan has been pursuing historical revisionism and making conservative swings starting from the late 1990s, and thus becoming the epicenter of conflict in Asia. What is worse, the right wing of Japan came to assert that the Nanjing Massacre was a made-up incident and comfort women were nothing more than prostitutes. In particular, this tendency has been growing stronger since the appearance of the Abe administration, and the prospect of historical reconciliation with Asian countries is becoming more remote.

This book, which integrates the field of international politics with historical studies, shows Japan's development and the resulting damages and sufferings of Asian countries from it. Furthermore, it offers an opportunity to understand Japan and Asia's past, present, and future from diverse angles, since it comprehensively encompasses history, economy, society, culture, and psychology. Going beyond criticism toward Japan, this book will contribute in finding a reasonable and constructive way forward and on what to do in order to promote reconciliation between Japan and other Asian countries and to build a more peaceful regional community. In order to achieve these goals, this book utilizes a unique structure and various useful perspectives. First of all, in the introduction, the author imagines an alternate reality that Japan was not occupied solely by the United States but, like Germany, by both the United States and the Soviet Union when World War II ended, and correspondingly, divided into West and East Japan. Under this assumption, the author exercises his imagination and makes a reconstruction on how the history of Japan and East Asia would have unfolded, indirectly showing what benefits Japan has enjoyed after World War II. Through this illustration, the reader will be able to realize the copious benefits that Japan received not only during the Cold War but also in the post-Cold War era, and this history of imagination will leave the reader in fresh shock.

In particular, this book examines in detail the damages and sufferings of Asian countries and their people in the development process of modern Japan. This book also attempts to analyze the reasons why modern Japan followed this trajectory, in various aspects such as history, society, culture, institutions, psychology, and so forth. Furthermore, this book investigates the reason why 'Japan's war problems' (abbreviation: 'Japanoblems') remained dormant in the Cold War era and how the problems rose to the surface after the end of the Cold War. Moreover, this book criticizes the attitude of Japan in comparison to Germany which has made postwar settlements in a relatively exemplary manner, and discusses how international society should respond to such issues in the future. Furthermore, this book suggests what Japan and Asian countries should do in order to accomplish reconciliation, peace, and mutual prosperity in the region.

INTRODUCTION:

RETHINKING HISTORY OF JAPAN AND ASIA

What if Japan had been divided into East Japan and West Japan after World War II? 'The Japanese War' broke out five years after the division of Japan into East and West. On June 25, 1950, the troops of East Japan, a communist state, made a westward invasion and captured Osaka, the capital of West Japan, within three days. The troops of East Japan gained the momentum to advance westward with irresistible force and within two months, seized almost the entire region of West Japan except for the Kyushu region. The United States convened the United Nations Security Council and passed a resolution for the United Nations forces to participate in the Japanese War, and as a result, 16 countries (the United States, the United Kingdom, Australia, New Zealand, France, Canada, South Africa, Turkey, Thailand, Greece, the Netherlands, Colombia, Ethiopia, the Philippines, Belgium, and Luxembourg) participated in the war as the United Nations forces, siding with West Japan. Due to the participation of the United Nations forces, the troops of West Japan started to turn the tide of war and engaged in an offensive and defensive battle of alternately advancing and retreating in the Hiroshima and Shikoku region. In the midst of all this, on September 28, 1950, MacArthur, the commander of the Allied Forces, succeeded in the Yokohama Landing Operations and occupied Tokyo, the capital of East Japan. This further turned the tide of war and MacArthur started to push the troops of East Japan toward the northeast. Within two months, the United Nations forces and the troops of West Japan continued eastward and had their sights on Hokkaido. The Soviet Union and China felt threatened by this advance, which resulted in their engagement in the war, sending troops to East Japan. Accordingly, troops of West and East Japan engaged in fierce battles near longitude 139° and continued the fighting for over two years, and on July 27, 1953, reached a ceasefire agreement at Kanagawa.

As a result of this Japanese War, both East and West Japan were reduced to ashes and many lives were lost. West Japan, which had just been established as an independent state after the occupation period of the United States and had been reconstructing its economy, suffered a tremendous blow from this war. As a result, the economy of West Japan was almost completely destroyed and its economic development was severely delayed. On the other hand, East Japan accelerated socialist economic reconstruction after the war and achieved a certain level of results, but after experiencing the oil shock of the 1970s, it faced great difficulties in its economic development as well. Furthermore, the one-party rule system of the Communist Party and the social system of a garrison state obstructed the economic development of East Japan. Most of all, the conflict structure and the arms race between East and West Japan incurred enormous socioeconomic costs to both countries.

Japan built the foundation for modernization through the Meiji Restoration, and in the late 19th and early 20th century, made use of the '*Datsua Nyuo* (脫亞入歐, Leave Asia, enter Europe)' strategy to colonize Taiwan and the Korean Peninsula. Based on this strategy, Japan accelerated its imperialistic expansion of territory and occupied Manchuria, the northeast region of China. Furthermore, Japan invaded China and even occupied Southeast Asia, disguising its imperialistic intention as liberating Asia from the West. Such imperialistic expansion inevitably caused conflict with the United States, now the most powerful country in the world. Thus, Japan made a surprise attack on Pearl Harbor and the Pacific War broke out. Although Japan lost the war against the United States eventually, it was the only non-Western country to succeed in modernization and increase its national power to the point of invading many countries abroad and engaging in global warfare with the United States.

When defeat seemed certain for Germany in Europe, in order to bring the Soviet Union into the war against Japan, the United States presented a proposal to divide and rule Japan jointly with the Soviet Union. The United States and the Soviet Union concluded an agreement for the Soviet Union to occupy East Japan and for the United States to occupy West Japan, setting longitude 139° as the border. The Soviet forces, which had been fighting against Japan's Kwantung Army in Manchuria, rapidly occupied Hokkaido and the region east of longitude 139°, once Japan surrendered on August 15, 1945. By occupying East Japan, the Soviet Union was able to repay the disgrace of Imperial Russia's defeat in the Russo-Japanese War in the early 20th century.

Initially, West Japan's Kyushu was supposed to be occupied by the United Kingdom and Shikoku was supposed to be occupied by China. However, the United Kingdom was too far away and engrossed in postwar economic reconstruction, and China was not able to participate in the Japanese occupation due to internal conflicts between the Chinese Nationalist Party (Kuomintang) and the Chinese Communist Party. Therefore, West Japan came under the sole occupation and direct rule of the United States.

After dividing Japan into East and West, the Soviet Union and the United States initially agreed to undergo a certain period of trusteeship over Japan and then eventually re-establish a single independent country later. But due to opposition within Japan and discord during the negotiation process between the United States and the Soviet Union, East Japan and West Japan ended up establishing their own respective governments. With the support of the United States and the United Nations, West Japan conducted a general election and on August 15, 1948, established the 'Democratic Republic of

Japan' based on the parliamentary system. Soon afterward, on September 9, 1948, East Japan established the 'Democratic People's Republic of Japan' with support from the Soviet Union. As the Soviet Union occupied Tokyo where the imperial palace was located, and refused to acknowledge the emperor system, the Japanese Emperor fled to Kyoto where the imperial palace used to be for approximately 1,000 years up until the Meiji Restoration. However, situations in West Japan were not promising for the Japanese Emperor either. In West Japan which was under the direct rule of the United States, the Japanese Emperor's responsibility for the Asian invasion and the Pacific War was considered to be the greatest and voices were raised to put the Emperor to trial and execute him. Fortunately, MacArthur, the Supreme Commander for the Allied Powers, attempted to use the Japanese Emperor as a means of appeasing the opposition against the occupation rule. As a result, the Japanese Emperor was able to retain his position in West Japan as a constitutional monarch like that of the United Kingdom. The Japanese Emperor, who led the modern Japan at the height of power through the Meiji Restoration, lost his power and degraded into just a symbolic figure, just like back in the Middle Ages, during which they barely maintained the imperial family by legitimizing the power of the shogunate generals. Such symbolic authority of the Japanese Emperor was only effective in West Japan in an indirect manner, and did not have any influence whatsoever in East Japan.

Meanwhile, the Korean Peninsula was divided and ruled by the United States and the Soviet Union with latitude 38° as the border. However, as a divide and rule agreement was settled for Germany and Japan, the Soviet forces withdrew from the northern areas of the Korean Peninsula, and in the end, the Korean Peninsula came under the sole occupation of the United States. In particular, as the Communist government came into power in China after the civil war between Nationalist and Communist forces, the United States decided to make Korea the last bastion of capitalism to prevent the communization of East Asia. Accordingly, when the Japanese War broke out, Korea was used as the rear base for war supplies. Initially, the United States planned to convert the Korean Establishment Preparation Board led by Lyuh Woon-hyung or the Provisional Government of the Republic of Korea led by Kim Koo, which had been making preparations even before the occupation rule of the United States, to a government to rule over the Korean Peninsula. However, under the judgment that the nationalist colors of these organizations were too strong, the United States supported Rhee Syngman, who had studied abroad in the United States, and established a pro-American government. Korea, which established the independent sovereignty as a unitary state, made every effort to achieve economic development with the full support and protection of the United States. It also had the opportunity of groundbreaking growth through increased demands resulting from the 'Japanese War' in the early 1950s and the Vietnam War from the mid-1960s to the early 1970s. Based on such economic development, Korea stepped into the ranks of a semi-developed country by the 1960s and held the Seoul Olympic Games in 1964. Afterward, Korea grew even more and in the early 1980s joined the OECD, the club of advanced countries, and became one of the seven largest economies in the 1990s.

In the case of China, which suffered greatly from Japan's invasion with approximately 10 million casualties, the Communist Party led by Mao Zedong won the civil war between the Nationalist and Communist forces, establishing a totally different sociopolitical system compared to Korea or West Japan. After the establishment of a communist government, China went through a tumultuous period up until the early 1970s, mainly caused by the costly aftermath of participating in the 'Japanese War', the failure of the Great Leap Forward, the destruction of its soft power through the Cultural Revolution, and so on. However, as the idea of détente spread in the 1970s, China sought to restore its relations with the United States, West Japan, and Korea. After the death of Mao Zedong, Deng Xiaoping came into power, adopted the capitalist economic system outright, and strengthened exchange and cooperation with countries in the capitalist bloc. In particular, by establishing diplomatic relations with West Japan and Korea in 1978, China attracted capital from Korea and West Japan, which provided momentum for its rapid economic growth. China recorded high-speed growth marking an annual average growth rate of 8% in the 1980s and stepped up as the world's second largest economy just below the United States in 2010. Based on such economic development, China hosted the Beijing Olympic Games in 2008 and has been leading cooperation communities within the region, such as APEC, ASEAN+3 (ASEAN Plus Three, APT), and so on.

West Japan had a difficult time in the 1950s due to the calamity of the 'Japanese War' but slowly started to revive its economy starting from the 1960s, with the help of the United States' strategic support to prevent the communization of East Asia as well as increased demands due to the Vietnam War. After overcoming the oil shock of the 1970s, West Japan took a giant leap forward in its economy. As a result, West Japan joined the OECD in the late 1980s and hosted the 'Osaka Olympic Games' in 1988. Above all, during this period, West Japan genuinely reflected upon its past, made sincere apologies, and made sufficient reparations to its neighboring countries that had suffered due to Japan's colonization and invasion in the past. Moreover, West Japan underwent a thorough trial against war criminals, punishing not only the inner circles of the Army and Navy but also war collaborators within the government and the private sector. Even to this day, West Japan continues to track people with war responsibility and punish people who glorify the war. Most of all, Emperor Hirohito himself, who was recognized as the one with the greatest war responsibility, made a heartfelt apology not only to the Japanese people but also to the people of Asian countries. He

4

even visited Asian countries to give words of apology and comfort, in order to set an example of taking responsibility for the war. Emperor Akihito, who had newly succeeded to the throne after the death of Emperor Hirohito, visited China and Korea, which suffered greatly from modern Japan's invasion and colonization, and continued the atmosphere of reconciliation and cooperation. Following the actions of the Japanese Emperors, government officials and the people of West Japan reinforced the specific practice of legislative enactment and reparations regarding the damages that Imperial Japan had caused to Asian countries. Such actions moved the hearts of the people in each Asian country and their descendants, who had suffered damage from modern Japan, and peace and cooperation in Asia advanced even more.

Meanwhile, East Japan, which had an almost equal economic level with West Japan in the 1960s, is facing continuous stagnation and retrogression due to the limits of a socialist planned economy and closed market. In particular, the aftermath of the collapse of Eastern European socialist governments and the dissolution of the Soviet Union starting from the late 1980s aggravated the economic regression of East Japan. Today, East Japan still continues to struggle due to negative economic growth rates accompanied by famine and earthquakes.

After the dismantling of the Cold War system, East and West Japan adopted the 'Inter-Japanese Basic Agreement' in 1991 and reinforced exchanges and economic cooperation between each other. East and West Japan also have been advancing discussions on reunification since the 'Inter-Japanese Summits' in 2000. West Japan's economic development and exemplary international relations is decreasing East Japan's fear of absorption unification, and many people expect that East and West Japan may accomplish reunification in the near future. In particular, West Japan has been thoroughly apologizing and making sufficient reparations and compensations to neighboring countries which suffered from colonization and war, just as postwar Germany did. As a result, Asian countries do not feel that the reunification of East and West Japan will be a threat to them and show great support toward the reunification movements of East and West Japan. If East and West Japan achieve reunification and cooperation in Asia is strengthened accordingly, it may be possible to envision the formation of a community of countries ('Asian Union' or 'East Asian Union') such as the European Union.

The above scenario is a rough imaginary picture of how things would have been had the history of Japan and Asia developed in a commonsensical and generally forecastable way, as in the history of Germany and Europe after World War II. Making assumptions on past history cannot turn back the past. However, when reflecting and contemplating on history, it becomes possible to understand the reason why history flowed in a certain way and consider if there could have been a better path to avoid something or bring about better outcomes. Such rumination of history can be an important means to heal historical wounds among countries or people and induce future-oriented cooperation and coexistence. Germany, which initiated wars in Europe, spent roughly half a century as a divided country after being divided and ruled by the Allied Forces, and paid the price for its crimes to some degree. In particular, Germany thoroughly apologized for and reflected upon its acts of crime such as invading neighboring countries and the Holocaust, and made payments of immense reparations or compensations, leading to genuine reconciliation and cooperation in Europe.

In this respect, the history of Asia after World War II developed in a different way from the common notion of justice or values. Japan gave a tremendous amount of pain and damage to Asian countries and their people through colonization and massive invasions, but as Japan was put under the sole occupation of the United States, Japan avoided division and punishment from the Allied Forces or Asian countries. The Japanese Emperor, the one with the greatest war responsibility, was exempted, and except for a small minority of war criminals, the majority of war leaders escaped responsibility and rather reassumed their positions in the process of postwar administration and economic restoration. In addition, in the midst of the Korean War, Japan concluded the Treaty of San Francisco with capitalist countries including the United States to its great favor, and officially made a comeback as a member of the international society. Due to concerns that it could affect Japan's economic revival, the United States urged countries that suffered from the war to adhere to the 'minimum reparation, in-kind reparation' principle. Thus, victim countries who had been put under Japan's colonial rule and had suffered from Japan's invasion could not receive a penny in cash for war reparations and only received reparations in the form of in-kind or services which was actually more beneficial to Japan's economic growth. As a result, in the situation where the Cold War became aggravated, Japan restored its international relations and enjoyed rapid economic growth through the Korean War and Vietnam War under active support and protection of the United States. This whole situation acted as a factor that prevented Japan not only from reflecting on its colonization and war of aggression but from making a proper apology and compensation for the damage of neighboring countries, and Japan used this situation to its own advantage.

In this way, Japan was able to easily escape from war responsibility and achieve rapid economic growth under the protection of the United States amid the Cold War. During this process, Korea, which groaned under Japan's colonization, experienced the tragedy of being divided instead of Japan. All of this is another benefit granted to Japan by the international society as well as Japan's liability. Japan has already had a tremendous historical liability by inflicting a great amount of pain on neighboring Asian countries, but Japan greeted a new era without settling this liability. In other words, a new liability had been added without settling existing liabilities. Originally, liabilities can be settled when the principal and interest are all paid off. But Japan did not settle the principal of its historical liabilities, which made the liability bigger, and a new liability was added on top of this, which made its settlement even worse. Historical liabilities require an even greater repayment effort and must come with sincerity. However, Japan has not properly made an attempt to settle its historical liability, and as time goes on and the memory of war fades, Japan strives not to acknowledge such liabilities and rather, the voices of the rightwing forces, which try to remember Japan's war of aggression and colonization as a history of glory, are becoming louder and louder. Therefore, if Japan continues to take the stance as it is taking today, there is an extremely high possibility that Japan will fail to escape from the fetters of the past even in the 21st century and be incapable of creating a genuine future.

What if Japan had done its best to pay back its historical liability as Germany did in Europe? Then Japan would probably have become a respected leader in the international society and established more peaceful and intimate relations with Asian countries. This is a kind of assumption of recent history. Some assumptions can be drawn from speculating Japan's history shortly after the Meiji Restoration. Modern Japan's development can be evaluated as successful for a non-Western country in terms of the materialistic aspect, such as an increase in national wealth and expansion of military power. Modernization was a Western model of development, but it included not only material abundance but also factors such as improvement of human rights and expansion of democracy. However, Japan's modernization was an unbalanced type of modernization that sacrificed such factors. It is a pity that Japan did not put in any effort to learn and develop such positive factors of modernization while adopting the strategy of '*Datsua Nyuo* (Leave Asia, enter Europe).' Was the course taken by modern Japan an inevitable choice? What if Japan had attempted an approach to genuinely heighten its national status and seek true development? Japan's Iwakura delegation was sent to the United States and Europe between 1871 and 1873. Japan later on made great reference to the Constitution and institutions of Prussia, a militaristic nation, which had accomplished unification of Germany shortly before Japanese delegates visited. If Germany had not been unified in 1871 and had been unified after the Japanese delegation had visited (or if the Japanese delegation had visited Germany before unification), Japan's footsteps would have advanced toward the direction of imitating the institutions of the United Kingdom or the United States. In that case, there was a high probability that the freedom and civil rights movement under the flag of enactment of a Constitution and establishment of a parliament during the 1870s and 1880s would have succeeded, forming a constitutional monarchy similar to the United Kingdom and developing democracy, instead of forming militarism and causing for Asian invasion and the Pacific War.

As examined above, the development of history becomes clearly different depending on what choice is made at a turning point in history. From a historical standpoint, Japan could have maintained internal stability and external peace by adopting a closed-door policy rather than foreign expansion. In other words, Japan adopted a closed-door policy when authority and power was shared between the Japanese Emperor and the government and the two parties showed mutual respect. However, Japan pushed ahead with foreign expansion and war when authority and power was integrated into one or when a sole power exercised centralized power as in the case of modern Japan. The choices of Japan, which gave birth to the historical tragedies of modern and contemporary history, were fundamentally made by Japan itself, but it is also the result of a certain degree of toleration by international society. Therefore, Japan's choice on whether it will take the path to historical justice or not becomes more important. In addition, the solidarity of international society to exercise pressure on Japan to make a more righteous decision is crucial.

This book will first illustrate the fact that modern Japan chose to achieve development through foreign expansion and war of aggression, and contemplate how much pain and damage this strategy caused to Asian countries. In addition, this book will examine from various angles as to why this tragedy, by modern Japan's choice, occurred and specifically how it came about. By considering the social and cultural characteristics of Japan as well as the Janus that supported modern Japan, namely, the Constitution and the Japanese Emperor system, it will be possible to decipher the cause of the tragedy to some extent. Next, this book will critically review how modern Japan's foreign expansion and war of aggression developed and how postwar settlements were made. Furthermore, this book will look into Japan's development and foreign relations during the Cold War era and examine why the so-called 'Japan's war problems' (abbreviation: 'Japanoblems') lay dormant. In addition, this book will inspect the phenomena in which 'Japan's war problems,' such as war responsibilities and reparations, the comfort women issue, distortion of history textbooks, territorial disputes, war damage and lack of healing, and so on, newly surfaced after the end of the Cold War, and comparatively analyze Germany's exemplary postwar settlements and Japan's poor postwar settlements. Furthermore, based on the above, this book will make recommendations on how the international society can induce Japan to a desirable direction and what choices Japan needs to make in order to accomplish reconciliation and cooperation in Asia.

CHAPTER 1

DEVELOPMENT OF MODERN JAPAN AND DAMAGES OF ASIAN COUNTRIES

"I know not where to end. Never I have heard or read such brutality. Rape! Rape! Rape! We estimate at least 1,000 cases a night and many by day. In case of resistance or anything that seems like disapproval, there is a bayonet stab or a bullet. Women are being carried off every morning, afternoon and evening. The whole Japanese army seems to be free to go and come as it pleases, and to do whatever it pleases" (James M. McCallum's diary, 19 December 1937).[1] "On 14 December 1937, the Tokyo Nichi Nichi Shimbun carried a series of reports by Asami Kazuo and Suzuki Jiro on the 'Contest to kill 100 Chinese using a sword between Noda Tsuyoshi and Mukai Toshiaki' at the foot of Purple Mountain in Nanjing. By that time, Mukai Toshiaki had slaughtered 105 Chinese and Noda Tsuyoshi 106. Their failure to judge who had first killed 100 people pitted them against each other in 'extra innings' for a new aim of 150 kills".[2] Modern Japan (1868-1945) committed such brutal acts without hesitation to Asian countries and their people during the early 20th century. This chapter will illustrate the fact that modern Japan chose to achieve development through foreign expansion and war of aggression, and contemplate how much pain and damage this strategy caused to Asian countries.

1. Development of Japan through Foreign Expansion and War

In the first administrative policy address of the Imperial Diet in 1890, Japan's Prime Minister Yamagata Aritomo (山縣有朋, 1838-1922) stressed that in order to protect Japan's 'zone of sovereignty' (主權線), which is Japan's territory, it is necessary to protect Japan's 'zone of interest' (利益線),[3] which is the region closely related to the protection of Japan's 'zone of sovereignty.'[4] At the time, Japan's 'zone of interest' was the Korean Peninsula, but after Taiwan and the Korean Peninsula was annexed by Japan and incorporated into Japan's 'zone of sovereignty,' the eastern region of China and Manchuria became the new 'zone of interest.' After Manchuria was included in Japan's 'zone of sovereignty' through the Manchurian Incident, the entire country of China became the new 'zone of interest' and Japan came to invade China outright. After invading China, Japan's 'zone of interest' was expanded to the Southeast Asian region, in which Japan carried out an invasion, and at last, Japan invaded the governmental territory of the United States in the Pacific Ocean. Such concepts of 'zone of sovereignty' and 'zone of interest' acted as the logic for Japan's Asian invasion, and the series of invasions and war, such as the colonization of Taiwan and Korea, establishment of the Republic of Manchukuo, invasion of China, invasion of Southeast Asia, and provocation of the Pacific War, were a process of expanding its 'zone of sovereignty' and 'zone of interest.' In other words, it can be said that Japan managed to succeed in the Meiji Restoration and accomplish modern development despite internal and external difficulties through foreign expansion and war of aggression.

Modern Japan's growth and development through war of aggression is called 'military developmentalism,' and so modern Japan is also called a 'warfare state.'[5] The fundamental reason why modern Japan waged frequent wars is related to Japan's foreign perception. The Japanese understood international relations mainly as the relationship between subordinates and superiors, and they had a strong sense of consciousness that the relationship between subordinates and superiors was determined by power (military power). As Japan went through the age of civil wars and the era of *samurai* rule, it began to regard the relationship of power, in which a strong organization or country succeeds and a weak organization or country declines, as its major epistemological framework. The Western modern state which Japan imitated was a 'garrison state' in that it was formed through military competition, and it was a 'nation state' and 'economic state' in that mobilization of the people and economic resources was key. Based on this perception, modern Japan's leaders reinforced military power and prioritized national development through foreign expansion and war of aggression.[6]

Japan won the First Sino-Japanese War in 1895 (Meiji Year 28) and received war reparations[7] amounting to at least 4 years of government budgets of Japan at the time. With this money, Japan created an education fund, and as state subsidies increased, primary school tuition was abolished in 1900.[8] Furthermore, with the war reparations, Japan not only expanded armaments but also promoted industries, such as the construction of the Yawata Steel Works, and the expansion of railway, telegraph, and telephone projects. Japan did not receive war reparations from the Russo-Japanese War, but instead gained part of the Liaodong Peninsula and southern region of Sakhalin by cession, and most importantly, established control over Korea. When World War I broke out in 1914, Japan declared war against Germany, secured concessions in China's Shandong Peninsula, occupied several islands in the southern region of the Pacific Ocean, and dominated the Asian market instead of Europe, which resulted in immense economic growth. Thus, Japan, which was a debtor nation in 1914 transformed into a creditor nation of JPY 2.7 billion in 1920.[9]

Furthermore, Japan not only attempted to overcome its economic recession but also sought to expand its political and military power through the Manchurian Incident, the Second Sino-Japanese War, and the Pacific War. After the Second World War, Japan did not directly engage in war, but restored its impoverished postwar economy in a short period of time through the Korean War. It also accelerated its path toward an economic power by benefiting from increased demands from the Vietnam War. Due to the Korean War, there were increased demands for war supplies totaling USD 1,618 million for Japan, which revived Japan's stagnant economy.[10] In addition, amidst the Korean War, Japan came to possess its own military (the Self Defense Forces), which was prohibited by the Constitution, and was able to make an easy comeback to international society by concluding the Treaty of San Francisco. Furthermore, under the umbrella of national security provided by the United States, Japan reduced defense expenditures and concentrated on economic development to become a global economic power. In this sense, it can be strongly argued that Japan was able to expand and develop through wars with other countries or wars that broke out in other countries. Of course, there were benefits that Japan earned through wars, but there were also massive casualties and the aftermath of war. The most representative cases are the Russo-Japanese War and the Pacific War, after which Japan went through severe economic recession and other difficulties. However, Japan managed to revive its economy through World War I as well as the Korean War and Vietnam War which occurred afterward.

The concepts of 'zone of sovereignty' and 'zone of interest' were theories of expansion that Japan was forced to give up after World War II, but the strategy of 'Datsua Nyuo (脱亞入歐, Leave Asia, enter Europe)' which was based on Fukuzawa Yukichi's 'Datsuaron (脱亞論, Escape from Asia)' still exercises its power to this day by being transformed into the form of 'Leave Asia, enter the United States (脱亞入美).' As China lost the Opium War and signed a humiliating one-sided treaty, Asia shriveled under the power of the West. Amid this situation of crisis, the issue of what kind of relationship to build with Asia was a difficult task for Japan, which was pushing ahead with modernization. An idea of 'Pan-Asian solidarity' was raised, which meant standing up to the Western forces by banding together with Asian countries. However, the 'Datsuaron (Escape from Asia),' which meant escaping from less advanced Asia and becoming an advanced civilization like Europe, became modern Japan's key strategy. On March 16, 1885, Fukuzawa Yukichi wrote an editorial[11] in the *Jiji Shinpo* (時事新報), on 'Datsuaron (Escape from Asia)' asserting that 'Japan must escape from Asia,' clearly showing Japan's direction of choice. Fukuzawa urged the necessity to become 'an invading country' rather than 'an invaded country' by spreading Western civilization to the Japanese people as soon as possible, and wrote a book called *Recommendation of Learning*, to assert that Japan should increase its competitiveness through 'learning' or 'scholarship.' And so Fukazawa personally founded Keio Gijuku (慶應義塾), and the Meiji government also built many schools and introduced the compulsory education system for primary school. When Japan succeeded in modernization after the Meiji Restoration, this '*Datsuaron* (Escape from Asia)' functioned as a theory to justify the invasion of Asia and led to contempt for and feelings of superiority over Asian countries, triggering Japan to commit terrible acts of brutality without reserve toward Asian people. In this sense, a key motive for modern Japan's ambitious external expansion was the belief of the Japanese people in their destiny as a superior country. This was reflected in fictitious ideas and ideologies such as *Kokutai no Hongi* (*Cardinal Principles of the National Entity of Japan*), Asia's liberation from Western imperialist powers.[12]

Japan needed a strong, nationwide, centralized political system in order to overcome the external threats from the Western world and maintain its national survival. Thus, Japan dissolved the Bakuhan System (幕藩體制, the government system of the Tokugawa period – literally a combination of 'bakufu' (the shogunate) and 'han' (the domains of daimyos)) and successfully executed the Meiji Restoration, the key of which was to establish a unified nation with the Emperor at its center. The main objective of the Meiji government was to gain industrial power and military force to stand up against Western nations through modernization. The problem was that Japan tried to meet the need for resources and markets required for modernization by invading and controlling neighboring Asian countries. The external expansion of modern Japan helped solve other challenges of the Meiji government, which were to resolve the complaints of the warrior class (士族, *samurai*) that had fallen from the ruling class due to the abolition of the old system through the Meiji Restoration, and to obtain national independence from external pressure. In this situation, the Seikanron (argument to invade Korea) and the invasion of Taiwan were executed in the 1870s. The Meiji government later dominated the Korean Peninsula as a colony but, as immediate measures to resolve internal disintegration, executed the invasion of Taiwan in order to prevent the revolt of those asserting Seikanron and suppress antigovernment uprisings.

With the victory of the First Sino-Japanese War in 1895, Japan received enormous war reparations from China and acquired the territories of Taiwan and the Liaodong Peninsula[13] by cession. This was an opportunity to imprint the superiority of Japan both internally and externally, by tearing down the traditional East Asian order centering on China. This became a decisive event that justified Fukazawa Yukichi's '*Datsuaron* (Escape from Asia),' and strengthened Japan's contempt against the Chinese,[14] as well as Japan's contempt against Asians. This contempt against the Chinese led to the massacre of innocent civilians during the First Sino-Japanese War, and when the Japanese military occupied Port Arthur in November 1894, they butchered 60,000 civilians in four days.[15] This massacre was the beginning of the brutality of the Japanese, in which they butchered numerous human lives, exploited human rights, and looted property in the course of Japan's colonial domination and invasion of Asia.[16]

Japan gained much recognition by dispatching 22,000 of the 47,000 military troops of the 8 nations' alliance to suppress China's Boxer Rebellion in August 1900. Through this incident, Japan was designated by the Western imperialists as the 'Far East Military Police' that could protect their interests, and was incorporated as a member of advanced imperialistic nations. In particular, Japan formed close ties with the United Kingdom during the negotiation process of the military expedition, and by proving its capability during the suppression of the Boxer Rebellion, Japan laid the foundations for the Anglo-Japanese Alliance, which later became the basis of international support for victory in the Russo-Japanese War. The Boxer Protocol between the Allied Forces and the Qing Empire in 1901 regulated the forfeiture of incomes, such as tariffs and salt taxes, and the stationing of foreign troops in addition to war reparations of 450 million taels of silver. Pursuant to this protocol, Japanese troops were stationed in China's Tianjin, Beiping, etc., and these stationed forces[17] were later involved in triggering the Second Sino-Japanese War.

Japan won the Russo-Japanese War and concluded the Treaty of Portsmouth through the arbitration of the United States but did not manage to receive war reparations from Russia and only ended up acquiring the southern region of Sakhalin (Karafuto) by cession. However, by winning a victory against Russia, a global power, Japan not only strengthened its position as the leader of East Asia but also expanded its market by securing supremacy over the Korean Peninsula and extending its influence in South Manchuria, which was a large gain. Afterward, Japan annexed Joseon of the Korean Peninsula and incorporated it as part of its own territory, and ameliorated its unequal treaties with Western powers, completing the 'independent state of Japan,' true to the name.

Japan's external military expansion policy, combined with its capitalistic system which was dependent on overseas markets, accelerated external invasion. As the Great Depression that began in the US impacted the global economy, Japan attempted to respond by sacrificing neighboring East Asian nations. As a result, in 1931, Japan occupied Manchuria and established Manchukuo (滿洲國, the State of Manchuria), with Puyi (溥儀, 1906-1967), the last emperor of the Qing Dynasty, as its leader (the Manchurian Incident), and at last in 1937, Japan full-fledgedly invaded China. Furthermore, Japan invaded Southeast Asia in order to create a self-sufficient system independent from the Western world. This continuous aggression of Japan, especially the expansion of its influence in the Pacific and Southeast Asia created conflicts with the United States in many areas, resulting in the Pacific War and the defeat of Japan.

As illustrated above, it can be acknowledged that Japan succeeded in the aspect of material civilization as a modern nation, but most of the 'success' was achieved through expansion in the manner of invading neighboring nations. Also, regarding Japan's economic success after World War II, the groundwork was granted from the outside, and a considerable part of the executing ability came from the experience and accumulation of capital through external expansion.[18] In other words, the successful economic policy of postwar Japan was based on experience accumulated through the implementation process of external expansion policies and domestic policies from the depression era to the defeat in the war. During this period, bureaucrats and political leaders established the institutional foundation to guide and control the private economy. Wartime experiences acted as a core factor in achieving economic prosperity after the war.[19] After the defeat, Japan did not directly engage in any wars, but Japan gained great profits through wars in the East Asian region. First, as the Cold War intensified and the Korean War broke out, Japan signed the Treaty of San Francisco under the support of the US, and was easily freed from the war responsibilities, such as paying enormous amounts of war reparations, and set the foundation to recover a position in the higher ranks of the capitalist world. Also, profits from the Korean War revitalized Japan's economy which had become stagnant due to defeat in the war. Especially, Japan's high economic growth rates since the mid-1960s was largely due to an increase in exports to the US based on Vietnam War demands[20] and an increase in exports to pro-American countries in Asia.[21]

The reason Japan was able to focus on economic growth without the burdens of national security after World War II was that the US provided full-fledged support to Japan as the bastion to prevent the proliferation of Communism in East Asia as its international policy, and that neighboring nations covered a considerable portion of Japan's military burden. The size of military troops in the 1950-1970s was 500,000 in Taiwan, 600,000 in South Korea, and 250,000 in the case of the Japanese Self Defense Forces. It can then be said that the burden on Taiwan and South Korea was extremely large, considering population size and economic scale. Also, the ground combat forces of the US moved to Okinawa and Korea, and due to the discomfort of the Japanese people toward nuclear weapons, the nuclear weapons positioned in mainland Japan were transferred to these regions in the late 1950s. In other words, due to the progression of demilitarization or reduction of military burden in mainland Japan, the number of nuclear weapons and military bases decreased, but the burden was posed on neighboring nations.

Also, dictatorships or military governments were maintained in these regions, due to the military power of the US and the economic support of Japan.[22]

In the case of Japan, it was the increase of military power and war that led the industry during the period from the First Sino-Japanese War to World War II. However, after achieving dazzling economic growth during the Cold War, it is now industry and economy that are leading military reinforcement in the post-Cold War Era and the 21st century.[23] Modern Japan's industrial revolution and economic development was inseparable with military necessity, and was interlocked with external invasion led by military needs.[24] If the modernization strategy of modern Japan was '*Datsua Nyuo* (Leave Asia, enter Europe),' the strategy during the Cold War after being defeated in the war was 'Leave Asia, enter the United States,' focusing on economic growth without the burdens of security and diplomacy, by joining the capitalist bloc under the security umbrella of the US. With this strategy, in the circumstances of the Cold War, Japan was able to easily free itself from compensation responsibilities and grew into a major economic power. In this sense, it can be said that the greatest beneficiary of the Cold War was Japan. However, as the Japanese economy went into a long-term depression after rising up as the world's second economic power, and as China emerged as a new power with the evolvement of the post-Cold War Era, Japan is making efforts to resolve this crisis by pursuing to become a great political and military power. The actions of Japan attempting to distort the history of East Asia and deny the suffering and damage it caused to neighboring countries are rising as the main cause of the regional conflicts in the present day. Now Japan is standing at the crossroad of deciding whether to become a peaceful nation leading peace and cooperation in East Asia as the first country with a Peace Constitution, or cause various types of conflict and war with neighboring countries by pursuing external expansion once again and becoming an imperialist country.

As explained above, it is recognized that Japan succeeded in modernization and economic development through external expansion such as the invasion of neighboring countries and stepped up as a modern state dominating East Asia, in response to the external pressure of the Western world. During this process, neighboring countries and their people greatly suffered from material, human, and mental agony and damage. The Japanese military which invaded China, Korea, and the Asian region committed brutalities such as merciless massacre, looting, and rape, and stripped victims of various economic resources, and mobilized numerous young people into forced labor and the military.[25] Japan brought forth tragedies beyond description, such as uncountable atrocities in China including the Nanjing Massacre, and massacres in Singapore and the Philippines. Furthermore, they killed 36,000 US and UK prisoners of war, which amounted to over a quarter of all captured soldiers.[26] Even more tragic was that countless young girls or women of Asia were forcefully dragged to comfort stations in the battlefields and became sex slaves. Some women from European nations, such as the Netherlands, were included. The recruiters lured the women in by saying that they could make money or dragged them in at gunpoint. Most of the women were not paid, and some women were given military tickets which could be used for purchasing daily necessities such as soap or food. Therefore, they cannot be seen as prostitutes, but as a type of sex slaves that were forced to give sexual comfort to the Japanese military. These comfort women and comfort stations were approved and regulated by Japan's state officials, ranging from Japanese cabinet officials to the local commanders, and in some cases, they operated the stations themselves. The number of the women who lived as sex slaves for the Japanese military is estimated to range from 100,000 to 200,000.[27]

The number of Asians sacrificed by the Japanese in the 1930s and 1940s by country is approximately 10 million Chinese (the Chinese government claims that the number is over 20 million), 2 million Indonesians (the Indonesian government claims that the number is over 4 million), 2 million Vietnamese, 1 million Filipinos, 80,000 Singaporeans, 50,000 Myanmarese, and 50,000 Malaysians.[28] Prior to this, in the process of external expansion and colonization, modern Japan killed countless natives in Hokkaido and Okinawa, mobilized the innocent residents of Taiwan and Korea in forced labor, and killed hundreds of thousands of people in these colonies. Furthermore, the war that Japan triggered left great pain and scars on the Japanese themselves. 1.7 million Japanese soldiers died from 1937 to 1945, and numerous Japanese prisoners of war captured by the Soviet Union died in Soviet detention camps. 9 million people lost their homes to air raids of the US on mainland Japan, and 200,000 civilians lost their lives. Due to the atomic bombs dropped on Hiroshima and Nagasaki by the US forces, over 200,000 were killed on the spot, and over 100,000 died due to the aftermath of exposure to radiation. As millions died through the war, the Japanese people developed a deep revulsion towards wars, which led them to resist movements of political leaders to amend the Peace Constitution after the war. On the other hand, the unprecedented experience of atomic bombing gave the Japanese the perception that they were not the perpetrators of war, but the victims.[29] In the next sections, we will examine such damages done not only to Asian nations and their people but also to Japanese people due to modern Japan's external expansion and war of aggression in more detail. Without concretely being aware of the ravages caused by Japan's external expansion and war of aggression, one cannot properly feel the full weight of responsibility.

2. Damages on China: Nanjing Massacre and other Atrocities

After Japan started the Second Sino-Japanese War in July 1937 and occupied Shanghai, it continued to proceed southwest, and on December 13, 1937 occupied Nanjing, the capital of the Chinese Nationalist Party government. Over the next six weeks, the Japanese military committed the so-called 'Nanjing Massacre,' in which it brutally killed Chinese people. The Japanese military that entered Nanjing executed a 'surround and eliminate operation' in order to thoroughly attack and kill all Chinese troops. Through this operation, the Japanese violated the 'International Humanitarian Law (Jus in bello, Hague Regulation on Ground Combat)' which prohibits the killing of enemies who throw away their weapons or surrender, by collectively killing surrendering soldiers, injured soldiers, and prisoners of war. Chinese men became the object of bayonet exercise for Japanese soldiers and were even sacrificed as objects of decapitation contests.[30] Also, tens of thousands of Chinese women were raped by Japanese soldiers.[31] After raping Chinese women, the Japanese soldiers would sometimes cut open their stomachs so that their intestines would pour out or cut out their breasts.[32] As Japanese soldiers with low military discipline were stationed in Nanjing, brutalities such as raping of Chinese women, looting of food and supplies, arson and destruction of civilian homes were committed all over the place. The Japanese commanders merely watched with folded arms believing that such actions resolved the discontent and raised the morale of the soldiers.[33] In a situation where it was difficult to conclude favorable negotiations with China, the top leaders of the Japanese military may have wanted to break the will of the Chinese to resist by setting an example through the massacre. If this were the case, the Japanese were not only abominably brutal but also made a misjudgment.[34]

In this manner, for six weeks, the Japanese military committed a large-scale massacre, rape, looting, and arson in Nanjing and recorded loss of human lives amounted to approximately 300,000. In the verdict of the International Military Tribunal for the Far East held in Tokyo after the war, it is stated that after the Japanese military occupied Nanjing, approximately 20,000 rape incidents occurred within the Nanjing Fort, and over 200,000 civilians and prisoners of war were killed for six weeks in the Nanjing Fort and its surrounding area. Also, in the Nanjing Military Tribunal held in Nanjing, it was revealed that the number of victims in the massacre was 190,000 and the number of sporadically killed people whose bodies were recovered by private charities was approximately 150,000, and thus the total number of victims was well over 300,000.[35] It was possible to obtain these statistics because a military tribunal in which China participated as a victor country was held after the war. If the casualties that have not actually been verified are added, then the number of victims will increase. The details of a letter which a German national, John H. D. Rabe, sent to the chief of the Board of Directors in Shanghai, reveals that he personally witnessed approximately 20,000 rapes.[36] Japanese soldiers not only made little of raping women, but believed they became even stronger in the war if they raped virgins. Furthermore, they even believed that if they made and kept a talisman with a virgin's pubic hair, they would mystically avoid getting injured at war.[37] As rape was prohibited under military law, Japanese soldiers sometimes killed the women they raped in order to destroy the evidence. Japanese military officers did not restrain soldiers from raping women, and sometimes advised soldiers to 'appease raped women by giving them money or take them far away and quietly kill them.'[38] Considering this brutal nature of the Japanese military, it is safe to assume that there would have been other actions of brutality tantamount to these in other regions as well. However, at the time, as the Japanese military continued to be stationed, they would have tried not to leave any relevant evidence behind, and as China did not have an administrative system to systematically collect this data, it is difficult to specifically identify the status of damage in other regions.

Other than the ones mentioned above, there are many other pieces of evidence regarding the Nanjing Massacre. There is video footage of some of the atrocities in Nanjing,[39] and there are many remorseful testimonies of the Japanese soldiers who took part in the massacre.[40] After the war, a doctor named Hakudo Nagatomi lived a life of repentance for the acts he had committed as a soldier in Nanjing. He recalled that at the time, Japanese soldiers would stab newborn babies with bayonets and throw them in boiling water, and rape and kill numerous women regardless of age. He reproached himself for being the terrible devil rather than a human being, as he had personally decapitated, burnt or buried alive more than 200 Chinese people.[41] The commander at the time of Nanjing occupation was General Matsui Iwane (松井石根, 1878-1948), who was greatly tormented by a guilty conscience regarding the Nanjing Massacre. Thus, after the Nanjing Massacre, he resigned from his post as general, shaved his head, and retired to a temple. After being defeated in the war, at the Tokyo Trial, he regretted that the Nanjing Massacre was a 'national disgrace' but was eventually condemned to execution by hanging.[42] Emperor Hirohito's younger brother, Prince Mikasa was in Nanjing at the time, and he admitted that the massacre had actually occurred in an interview with *Yomiuri Shimbun* after the war.[43] Books have been published containing detailed testimonies and photographs regarding the horrible situation of people who were on the scene.[44] In particular, Iris Chang vividly portrays the horrors of brutalities, such as carnage and rape, that unfolded in Nanjing in 1937, in her book *The Rape of Nanking* (1997), which was written based on thorough data research, interviews with victims or perpetrators, and data photos. She referred to the Nanjing Massacre as the forgotten holocaust. Even so, some Japanese people view the Nanjing Massacre as a trivial incident, or deny the fact itself altogether.[45] For instance, Ishihara Shintaro (石原慎太郎), who is the bestselling author of *The Japan That*

Can Say No and a politician of the Liberal Democratic Party, stated in an interview with *Playboy* in 1990 that the Nanjing Massacre is not true and that it is merely a lie fabricated by China.[46]

The story of Oscar Schindler, a Nazi party member during World War II, saving 1,200 Jewish people from Auschwitz was made into a movie and is now widely known by many people around the world. In the late 1930s, amid the massacre in Nanjing, some westerners saved the lives of numerous Chinese people. Some westerners, such as German businessman John Rabe, American surgeon Robert Wilson, and American president of Jinling Art Science College for Women Wilhelmina Vautrin, did not leave the city during the terrible carnage and established safe zones, protecting numerous Chinese people from being murdered or raped by Japanese soldiers.[47] However, it was common for Chinese people who were outside of such safe zones to become victims of ruthless massacre or rape by Japanese soldiers. In particular, the Japanese military committed brutal medical experiments on Chinese people in Nanjing. In April 1939, the Japanese military converted a hospital in Nanjing into a medical laboratory, named 'Unit 1644' and conducted research on epidemics. Researchers in this laboratory conducted cruel experiments on Chinese prisoners of war or convicts using viruses, toxic chemicals and poison gas, and every week approximately 10 people died, and their bodies were incinerated.[48]

When the Japanese troops occupied Nanjing, the Japanese people held a celebration ceremony and ran out into the streets, excited by the ambience of complete victory. However, most of the Japanese did not know that the horrible Nanjing Massacre was being committed in China. This was because the Japanese military and government controlled information and executed a media blackout so that only articles that were favorable to Japan would be reported. In other respects, Japanese people, who were already brainwashed by the government's propaganda and intoxicated with the joy of victory, may have intentionally ignored the dark side of the victory.

When the Chinese Kuomintang government transferred the capital to Wuhan following the fall of Nanjing, the Japanese troops attacked for four and a half months and managed to occupy Wuhan. In this process, the Japanese troops used poisonous gas 375 times and fired at least 40,000 poisonous gas shells, violating the international law prohibiting the use of chemical weapons.[49] In order to bring the Chinese Kuomintang government to their knees, the Japanese troops heavily bombed Chongqing which was the political and military center of China at the time. On June 5, 1941, approximately 1,200 residents had escaped into the Great 18th Tunnel in order to avoid air raids but suffocated to death. This is the so-called 'Great Tunnel Tragedy of June 5th.'[50] In commemoration of this horrendous incident, a ceremony is held in Chongqing every year on the 5th of June.

The Japanese troops launched the Sanguang (三光) Operations to annihilate anti-Japan bases in the northern region of China by burning down villages that acted as bases of resistance (燒光, Shaoguang), killing all their residents (殺光, Shaguang), and looting all the goods (搶光, Qingguang).[51] A representative example of damage done by the Sanguang Operations is the Beitan Tragedy, in which 500 soldiers of the Japanese Military Division 110 suddenly made a surprise attack on Beitan in May 1942. In this village, there were 1,227 residents with 220 families, and in order to evade the Japanese troops, they built an underground passage penetrating the whole village. However, the Japanese troops fired poisonous gas shells into this underground passage and 1,100 people were killed by gas and shooting. Women who escaped gas poisoning were raped by the Japanese troops, houses were burnt down, and food and supplies were all looted. In addition, the Japanese troops forcefully collected grains from the Manchurian region, and established a regulation prohibiting the Chinese from eating rice, punishing them as economic criminals when caught.[52]

The brutality of the massacre the Japanese troops committed in Nanjing is explicitly shown in the letter that Jiang Jieshi published on July 7, 1938, *An Appeal to the Japanese People*.[53] Also, the horrors caused by the Sanguang Operations are being vividly conveyed through the testimonies of the Japanese troops who took part in these operations. Japanese war criminals who were held in China until 1956, were influenced by the Tolerance Policy of the Chinese government and recognized their past faults and crimes. Consequently, after returning to Japan, in 1957, they created 'the Association of Returnees from China (中歸連)' and traveled all around Japan to testify about the acts of murder, looting, rape, arson and destruction, and engaged in anti-war and peace activities as well as promoting friendly relations between China and Japan.[54]

The atrocities committed in China by Japanese soldiers and Japanese people of various ranks during the Second Sino-Japanese War are minutely described in a total of 45 written confessions of war criminals that the Chinese government made public from July to August 2014. At the time, a written confession was made public each day through a website managed by the Chinese government authorities. There were specific details, such as the photos of the war criminals, their individual introductions, and confession statements of their crimes by date. The people who wrote the disclosed written confessions were mostly soldiers, but also included Japanese people of various ranks, including public officials, employees of state-owned companies, police officers, and military police officers. On the first day, the written confession of division commander Suzuki Keiku (鈴木啓久) was made public, and according to his confession, he killed 5,470 Chinese people. His written confession describes in detail acts of killing pregnant women by cutting open their stomachs and committing genocide burying people alive. Fujita Shigeru (藤田茂), who first participated in the war as a colonel in 1938 and then was promoted to division commander in 1945, stated that in 1939 he made his subordinates conduct bayonet exercises on prisoners by telling them "Killing people strengthens courage." Taiji Ohno (大野泰治), who was a police officer in charge of public order, confessed that he ate the brain of a Chinese person he had killed. Yuichi Kashiwaba (柏葉勇一), who was a squad commander of the military police, confessed that he killed workers who could not work anymore by throwing them in the furnace. Yoshio Mizoguchi (溝口 嘉夫), who was a public prosecutor of Manchuria, wrote in his written confession that he had killed dozens of anti-Japanese figures.

Japan, which prepared for biological and chemical warfare since after World War I, established a military unit called the 'Epidemic Prevention and Water Purification Department of the Kwantung Army' in Pingfang (平房) of Harbin, China, and Isii Shiro (石井四良, Army Medic, Medical Doctor, 1892-1959)[55] became the commander. This unit was the only unit to be founded through the imperial order of the Japanese Emperor, and the budget of this unit was assigned according to a written order with the Imperial Seal of Japan engraved, within the defense budget of 1936. The budget was assigned on the grounds of being an 'Epidemic Prevention and Water Purification Unit,' but the actual usage of the budget was unknown to the National Diet.[56] This unit was called the 'Manchurian Unit 731' after 1941. This unit undertook germ experiments, using diseases such as bubonic plague, typhoid fever, and cholera on anti-Japan figures (so-called, *maruta*) who were captured, and conducted human experiments such as frostbite, exchange of human blood with horse blood and poisonous gas experiments. Through these experiments, it is said that at least 3,000 people died brutally.[57] Furthermore, approximately 90,000 Chinese were harmed due to the use of chemical weapons in approximately 2,000 instances and countless Chinese were killed or injured from biological warfare and the number of casualties in Changde of Hunan alone amounted to 7,463 people.[58] After the war ended, Lieutenant General Isii Shiro, following the orders of the Japanese military authorities, erased the trace of Unit 731 by blowing up the laboratories in which virus and chemical weapons had been experimented with and produced and by burying alive the *marutas* who had served as guinea pigs of the experiments. However, as these laboratories, which had been scattered across China, were blown up, the viruses spread about and in the following years epidemics occurred in the regions where the medical experiment troops had been stationed, killing tens of thousands of people.

It had already been rooted in the international society that prisoners of war or civilian residents should be treated humanely. Accordingly, Japan had once been praised by the international society for treating prisoners of the enemy country relatively humanely during the military expedition to suppress the Boxer Rebellion in 1900, the Russo-Japanese War, and World War I. When declaring war in the First Sino-Japanese War, Russo-Japanese War, and

World War I, the Japanese Emperor ordered in an Imperial Edict that troops should not violate international laws and should act within the boundary of international acceptance. However, in the Manchurian Incident, the Second Sino-Japanese War and the Pacific War, which occurred after the 1930s, Japan engaged without even declaring war and committed actions violating international laws without hesitation in the battlefields. Therefore, Japanese soldiers killed prisoners by decapitating them with swords and firing machine guns at them. Furthermore, it was common for Japanese troops to order new recruits to stab prisoners of war to death with bayonets as part of their training. The new recruits were hesitant in the beginning, but as their minds became paralyzed after the demonstrations and commands of their superiors, they became murder weapons, killing nonchalantly with smiles on their faces. The atrocities of Japanese soldiers were not only toward prisoners but also toward civilians including elderly people and women. These facts have been thoroughly confirmed not only through testimonies of Chinese people but also through diaries and testimonies of Japanese soldiers who were present at the time.[59] In particular, Mikasa Takahito, the youngest sibling of Emperor Hirohito, who acted as an advisor at the Nanjing headquarters in 1943, considered the act of Japanese officers ordering new recruits to conduct bayonet practice on Chinese prisoners of war as a gruesome massacre. Thus, he prepared a lecture criticizing Japan's invasion of China and drafted a report titled 'Reflection of a Japanese person on the Second Sino-Japanese War.'[60]

After occupying China's eastern region, Japan achieved great profits by smuggling large quantities of opium through the Manchurian region which was under its rule and this eventually led many Chinese people to become addicted to opium. This was similar to the case in the mid-19th century in which the United Kingdom gained great profits and made numerous Chinese people ill by smuggling opium into China. Furthermore, Chinese people were blackmailed or enticed to work for Manchukuo which Japan established in the Manchurian region, or other puppet governments in new occupied territories, which resulted in people betraying their own country. It is undeniable that such acts of Japan were against human dignity in that Japan encouraged enmity and conflict among Chinese people and forced individuals to live lives that went against their conscience.

Even before the Second Sino-Japanese War, the Japanese troops likewise revealed their brutal side. In September 1932, when the Mushun Coal Mine operated by the South Manchuria Railway Company was attacked by anti-Japan guerrillas, the Japanese troops brutally killed approximately 3,000 civilians living near Pingdingshan as revenge. This is called the Pingdingshan Massacre (平頂山事件). In the Siberian Intervention (1918-1920) to prevent the proliferation of the Russian Revolutionists, Japan dispatched far more troops (71,000) than other allied nations (US 9,000, UK 6,000), and even after the troops of the allied nations failed in the joint intervention on the Russian

Revolution and withdrew, the Japanese troops remained until 1922 when international criticism heightened. By taking part in the Siberian Intervention on the Russian Revolution, Japan lost approximately 3,500 soldiers for 5 years, and many more soldiers were injured. Above all, the Japanese troops killed numerous Russian residents during that period and the number of casualties is said to be over 80,000.[61]

The Russo-Japanese War was not fought in the territory of the two parties engaging in war, but was fought in Korea and China, which resulted in many Koreans and Chinese being killed. The damage was especially large in Manchuria which was the main battlefield of Japan and Russia. According to *Eastern Miscellany* (東方雜誌), the number of civilian deaths in China, a nation that had stayed neutral between Russia and Japan, reached hundreds of thousands, which was more than the total number of Russian and Japanese soldiers killed on the battlefield. Japan mobilized 1,090,000 soldiers during the Russo-Japanese War, which was over four times the number during the First Sino-Japanese War. The number of Japanese soldiers who died in this war amounted to 81,000, which was six times the number in the First Sino-Japanese War.[62]

The eight allied nations, including Japan, Russia, and the UK dispatched troops to resolve the Boxer Rebellion in 1900 and after occupying Beijing, committed murder, arson, and looting without hesitation in various places. The Japanese troops, which comparatively refrained from these actions, made up half of the allied forces, and Russia occupied Manchuria with approximately 100,000 troops in the name of protecting the Chinese Eastern Railway. In September 1901, the Qing Empire signed the Boxer Protocol (辛丑條約, 北京議定書) and paid war reparations of 450 million taels of silver (980 million taels of silver including interest) to the Allied Forces.[63] It was the Chinese who actually suffered damages throughout the war, but since they were defeated, they had to pay enormous war reparations. In the end, the Qing Empire dissolved into the dust of history ten years later.

In the First Sino-Japanese War, the Japanese troops occupied Qing's strategic locations, Dalian and Lushun. When entering the urban district of Lushun, the Japanese soldiers brutally killed not only the defeated soldiers and prisoners of war, but also civilians such as women, children and the elderly.[64] In Manchuria and northern Korea which had become the main battlefields, countless fallen soldiers were left out in the open without a proper burial. This caused contagious diseases such as dysentery and cholera which numerous people died from.[65] After the First Sino-Japanese War, China signed the Shimonoseki Treaty (April 17, 1895) and handed over the Liaodong Peninsula, Taiwan, and the Punghu Islands to Japan and paid war reparations tantamount to three times the national budget of Qing.[66] Hereby, Qing lost its position as the leading power of the East Asian region, and it served as momentum for Qing's national finances to drastically go downhill.

On the other hand, Japan established a foothold to advance into the continent, such as the Korean Peninsula and Manchuria. It also used war reparations to establish the foundation for educational finance and industrial development.

As examined above, China suffered from immense human and material losses through the First Sino-Japanese War, the Manchurian Incident, the Second Sino-Japanese War, and the Pacific War triggered by Japan. It is difficult to calculate the exact amount of damages, but according to Lin Zhe Fen (林則芬)'s *History of Sino-Japanese Relations* (中日關係史) which was published in Taiwan in 1970, there is a record of 4,150,000 casualties among Chinese soldiers, 20,000,000 casualties among civilians and 100,000,000 civilians who roamed around homeless.[67] US representative Dulles, who participated in the San Francisco Peace Conference after the war, stated that Japan's invasions caused extremely great harm and suffering and that the adequate amount of war reparations which China could demand amounted up to 100 billion USD.[68] In the 1970s, China relinquished war reparations from Japan and received economic cooperation aid, but the actual amount of damage to China in monetary terms was incalculable, and in particular, the mental agony that the Chinese people suffered could not be compensated by anything.

3. Japanese Military Sexual Slavery and Abuse of Female Human Rights

After the Manchurian Incident in 1931, comfort women began to emerge overtly, as the Japanese troops installed and operated comfort stations to prevent the rape of Chinese women, resolve stress and enhance the morale of soldiers. During the thirteen years from 1932 to 1945, women from various countries, such as China, Korea, the Philippines, Taiwan, Indonesia, Timor, Burma, Malaysia, the South Pacific Islands, and the Netherlands, were seized and raped as sex slaves and became subjects of abuse and exploitation at comfort stations in Japanese military posts located in various regions. The comfort women, who were used to fulfill the sexual needs of millions of Japanese troops, were forcefully mobilized by Japanese troops and regional leaders of occupied territories, or were dragged from other places such as China or Korea. Women from various regions, including girls who had not yet experienced their first menstruations, were locked up for long periods of time and became subjects to sexual slavery and suffered from sexual abuse in which sometimes one comfort woman had to deal with over 50 Japanese soldiers in one day.[69]

In the sense that they provided comfort to the Japanese troops in occupied territories, they are often referred to as comfort women, but it is rather more appropriate to call them 'sex slaves' as they were systematically raped by the Japanese troops after being seized through force or enticement. Particularly, Japan uses the expression, 'comfort women who followed the military troops (從軍慰安婦),' which implies the sense of voluntary participation. However, this term is adopted in the standpoint of the Japanese soldiers who received 'sexual comfort' and does not consider at all that these women's actions were not voluntary but all too inhumane and painful. In this respect, it is very appropriate that the term 'sexual slavery by Japan' was used in the report (1996) of Radhika Coomaraswamy, Special Rapporteur on Violence against Women of the United Nations Human Rights Commission. However, it is said that the actual victims themselves prefer to be called 'comfort women' rather than 'sex slaves.'[70] This is probably because there is a highly negative connotation in the term 'slave'. Therefore, the terms 'comfort women' or 'sex slaves' will be used in this book, but even if the term 'comfort women' is used, it will mean 'sex slaves' which connotes that they were forcefully mobilized.

The history of the Japanese military sexual slave system can be traced back to the period of the Siberian Intervention. At the time, the Japanese troops that occupied the Siberian region committed brutal looting and rape on local women, and so there was an epidemic of sexually transmitted diseases among the soldiers and there was a severe loss in combat force. In response, to resolve the sexual needs of the soldiers and maintain combat force, the head of the military government created the 'Prostitute and Hostess Regulation Rules (藝妓酌婦取締規則)' in September 1, 1920, so that the military police could control prostitutes (藝妓) and hostesses (酌婦).[71] It is presumable that such phenomena consistently occurred prior to and posterior to this event, but it is merely difficult to find evidence in official documents, as the Japanese troops may not have officially produced documents that disgraced themselves or may later have destroyed such documents. When the Japanese troops triggered the Shanghai Incident in January 1932, there were frequent rape incidents targeting Chinese women, and in response, General Okamura invited military comfort women through his request to the Governor of Nagasaki, installing the first Japanese comfort station. The Nanjing Massacre, which the Japanese troops committed in 1937 and which included large-scale rape, heightened international criticism and hostility of the Chinese. After this incident, the Japanese troops installed comfort stations in a more systematic manner. The 'solution' that the Japanese government and troops came up with in order to prevent the deterioration of international reputation and to maintain the safety of the Japanese troops was the installation of comfort stations. Therefore, from that point on, in almost every location the Japanese troops were stationed, comfort stations were installed.[72]

Based on various data from the military, Professor Yoshimi Yoshiaki, an authority on Japanese military comfort women research, provided four reasons as to why the Japanese troops systemically established the comfort women system. First, to prevent rape committed by Japanese troops, second, to prevent the diffusion of sexually transmitted diseases, third, to provide sexual comfort to the soldiers, and fourth, to prevent espionage. Among the four reasons, the goals of preventing rape and sexually transmitted diseases were not effectively accomplished, and it is said that the biggest motive was to provide sexual comfort to the soldiers. Japan's war of aggression became a murky war without a clear prospect of victory. There were no clear standards on the replacement and return regulations or vacation policies for the soldiers. Welfare was poor, and infringement of soldiers' rights was severe, leading the soldiers into despair. Thus, the Japanese military authorities provided sexual comfort to the soldiers in order to prevent soldiers from giving themselves up in despair, exploding their anger towards the military, or disobeying the commands of their superiors.[73]

As the war expanded, it became difficult to meet the demands for Japanese military comfort women with only Japanese women. Therefore, women from colonies such as Korea and Taiwan were mobilized and it eventually led to the forceful mobilization of the local Chinese, Filipino, and Indonesian women from the territories the Japanese troops occupied throughout the war. Many young women in the Southeast Asian region were seized as comfort women and suffered from sexual violence from Japanese soldiers. In the Japanese Army Conference of June 1942, it was reported that 400 comfort stations had been established in China and the Southeast Asian region. In Indonesia, approximately 200-300 Dutch women who had been held in captivity by Japanese soldiers, were mobilized as comfort women. Professor Yoshimi Yoshiaki, who was the Japanese historian to discover an official document proving that the Japanese military was involved in the installation of comfort stations and conscription of 'comfort women,' provided a momentum for the Japanese government to release a statement that admitted and apologized for the fact that the Japanese military was involved in the 'comfort women' issue. He estimated that approximately 80,000 to 200,000[74] women were mobilized as comfort women.[75]

There were many cases in which victims who were mobilized as comfort women were tricked into going to comfort stations by being told that they could make money or get a job at a factory. In addition, there were cases where they were kidnapped and trafficked by comfort station dealers or recruiters, and sometimes they were forcefully kidnapped by officials, police, and soldiers. In occupied territories such as China or Southeast Asia, the Japanese troops sometimes assigned village chiefs the number of women to mobilize or kidnapped the women themselves. Even when civilian dealers recruited women, they were under the management and supervision of the Japanese troops, and military trucks, trains, and warships were used when transporting them to comfort stations. This usage of military transportation would not have been possible without the cooperation and approval of military officers.[76] Even the postwar Japanese government admitted and apologized through the statement of Chief Cabinet Secretary Kono Yohei in August 1993 for not only the existence of Japanese military 'comfort women,' but also the fact that the Japanese military was directly and indirectly involved and that there was compulsory mobilization.

Let us bring up some specific cases of rape or forced labor as comfort women by the Japanese troops. Shanshi in China was a place where the Sanguang Operations (operations to burn to the ground) were committed, and 15-year-old Liu Xiu Mei (李秀梅), who lived there, was suddenly approached by Japanese troops with guns, was gagged and tied by her hands, loaded on a donkey, and was raped as a comfort woman for five months at the Japanese military base. She was hit in the eye with a belt while resisting and lost her sight and was not able to move due to severe beating. Her mother paid 600 taels of silver to the Japanese troops to save her daughter, but hanged herself to death in despair, upon hearing that it was not enough. When Liu returned home as she became useless as a comfort woman, she could do nothing but cry in sorrow upon hearing the sad news of her mother's death. Liu Mian Huan (劉面煥) was also dragged to a cave by the Japanese troops at the age of 15 and was raped for approximately 40 days. She could not easily move her left shoulder which was fractured by a gunshot and she could not move her legs freely either. Due to the pain of being infected by a sexually transmitted disease, she had to crawl to the toilet, and her father brought her back home with the promise that he would cure her and bring her back, but she was sick in bed for a year and just barely held on to her life. Afterwards, the two of them lived in agony from serious pain and aftereffects.[77] Such brutalities of the Japanese troops in Shanshi were disclosed by the vivid testimony of 83-year-old former Japanese soldier, Gondo Hajime on November 17, 2003 at the Tokyo High Court. According to his testimony, Japanese troops freely looted Shanshi, and committed rape and gang rape against the women without hesitation, and brutally killed people.[78]

Mardiem was seized by Japanese troops in Indonesia and was raped by six Japanese soldiers that very day and became a sex toy for the soldiers every day afterwards. When she resisted, she was kicked by Chikada, the head of the comfort station, and the aftermath led to growth abnormalities in her legs and she ended up having lopsided legs. Also, five months into her pregnancy, the heads of the comfort station forcefully pressed her abdomen and pulled out the fetus, so that she could keep working as a comfort woman, and it is said that she was raped for more than ten hours a day without rest, every day for three years.[79]

The comfort stations installed by Japanese troops can be classified into three categories. First, comfort stations that were directly operated by

Japanese troops; second, comfort stations that were exclusively for soldiers and civilians attached to the military, operated by civilian dealers but under the supervision and control of Japanese troops; and third, comfort stations that were originally civilian brothels but designated for military use for a certain period of time. Even when the Japanese military did not directly operate the comfort stations, the locations, buildings, workers and comfort women were all subject to the approval and regulation of the logistics officer in the region.[80]

The Army Penal Code of the Meiji Period stipulated regulations to punish soldiers who committed rape, but there were instances where the commanding officer would overlook these incidents in order to boost the morale of the soldiers. Some soldiers killed the women they raped, for fear of being punished pursuant to the Penal Code. Under such circumstances, comfort stations started to appear around the time of the Manchurian Incident and were fully operational and systematized after the Second Sino-Japanese War and continued to expand after the beginning of the Pacific War. The expansion of the comfort stations was in sync with the expansion of the war of aggression. In the *Wartime Service Summary* (戰時服務提要) published by the Japanese Army's Training and Doctrine Command in May 1938, there were regulations on methods to prevent sexually transmitted diseases, equipment of sanitary facilities in comfort stations, prohibition of contact with prostitutes or locals other than those who were designated by the military. In other words, the ability to manage comfort stations was also one of the essential virtues of a Japanese army officer. Through this, it is possible to get a peep into the fact that the Japanese military system itself structurized and internalized sexual violence against women.[81]

In general, comfort women had to deal with enlisted soldiers during the daytime, non-commissioned officers in the early evening, commissioned officers in the late hours, and commissioned officers could spend the night. When several units were stationed in the same area, sometimes they took turns using the comfort stations on different days of the week. Comfort women had to deal with at least five to six, and sometimes up to 40-50 Japanese soldiers a day. On weekends, they were subject to fulfilling the lust of even more Japanese soldiers. Also, in locations without comfort stations, they sometimes had to deal with all the soldiers in that unit in temporary barracks. If they were to refuse, they were heavily beaten or tortured by electrification.[82]

The Japanese troops forced sexual slavery on comfort women by dragging them along even to the front lines and made them die in US troop attacks. Also, comfort women were abandoned or killed by Japanese soldiers who retreated after losing the battle. Even if these women survived, they chose to commit suicide or remain in foreign lands, as they could not return home due to the shame. Even if they managed to find their way home, they were not able to erase the traumatic memories of the past, always feared social negligence and exclusion, and were thoroughly ostracized by the society. Furthermore, the social atmosphere of the East Asian region, which places importance on a woman's virginity, looked coldly upon these victimized women. Therefore, the victims of sexual slavery could not confide in anyone about their pain and suffering and were forced to remain quiet for half a century. Most of the victims, whose human rights were violated and whose lives were completely trampled on as Japanese military sexual slaves, passed away after living in indescribable pain, and the few surviving victims are still suffering from mental and physical pain even to this day.[83] So far, the victims of sexual slavery have been erased from the memories of the people in their home countries due to prejudice and indifference. Even Japan, who is the perpetrator, is denying the historical fact itself and evading the problem of solving the sexual slavery issue. In the early 20th century, forced sexual slavery by the Japanese military was a discrimination against ethnicities, discrimination against women, and annihilation of human dignity, but the physical and mental wounds are yet to be healed in the 21st century.[84]

4. Colonization of Taiwan, Massacre and Exploitation of Asians in Japan

Japan, which was victorious in the First Sino-Japanese War, signed the Treaty of Shimonoseki and consequently, Qing ceded Taiwan to Japan. When the residents of Taiwan learned about the decision to cede Taiwan, they were furious that the Qing government had abandoned Taiwan and started a movement against the cession. Therefore, in May 1895, the Taiwanese declared independence and established the Republic of Formosa, adopting the republic system. Tang Jingsong (唐景崧), who was the Taiwan governor (臺灣巡撫), was recommended as the president, and Liu Yongfu was appointed as the commanding general. When the Treaty of Shimonoseki was ratified, Japan appointed Kabayama Sukenori, a navy admiral as the governor of Taiwan, and ordered him to lead Japanese troops to occupy Taiwan. It is estimated that the number of Taiwanese killed by Japanese troops in the occupation process was well over 14,000. Japan dispatched approximately 76,000 troops in order to suppress Taiwan's fierce resistance, among which approximately 5,000 died on the battlefield or of disease. The residents of Taiwan continued to resist even after the occupation, but due to Japan's coercive occupation policy, it is said that a total of 10,950 people were executed or killed between 1898 and 1902.[85] After Taiwan was occupied and colonized by the Japanese military, the school education of Taiwan was proceeded in Japanese, and the use of Chinese was prohibited.[86]

On October 27, 1930, the Formosan people (Gao Shan Zu, 高山族), who were the locals of Taiwan killed 134 Japanese and wounded 26 in the mountain area called Wushe (霧社) located in the central area. In the backdrop of this incident was Japan's coercive domination. Japan's forceful migration of villages and coercive rice farming destroyed the livelihoods of the locals. Furthermore, starting from the 1920s, Japan deprived the locals of their identity and forced them to use Japanese and revere the Japanese Emperor. In particular, the locals were greatly discontented by the increase in forced labor and the tyranny of the supervising police. In order to retaliate against the Wushe incident, Japan deployed the police and the military, and executed operations to subdue the people using machine guns, cannons, and aircraft. In this process, incendiary bombs and gas bombs were dropped from the aircraft, and according to data compiled by the Taiwanese government, the gas bombs were not tear gas, but poison gas. As a result of such attacks, numerous locals, including women and children, were slaughtered.[87]

As Japan triggered the Second Sino-Japanese War and continued to expand the war, Japan used not only Korea but also Taiwan as its logistics bases, and freely exploited large amounts of resources and manpower. Japan strongly pushed forward the Loyal Imperial Subject Policy in Taiwan, such as forcing daily usage of the Japanese language and shrine worship, and young Taiwanese men were drafted to serve in the military in Malaysia and the Philippines. Japan also organized the 'Takasago Volunteer Corps' consisting of Taiwanese locals, and forced them to fight in the southern lines. Through the special voluntary service system from 1942 to 1943 and the introduction of the draft system in January 1945, numerous Taiwanese men were forcefully mobilized by the Japanese troops and faced death or injury up until Japan's surrender.[88] According to statistics provided by Japan's Ministry of Health, Labor and Welfare, approximately 207,000 Taiwanese were drafted as soldiers and civilians attached to the military, more than 30,000 of which were estimated to have died.[89] Two-thirds of the dead were locals affiliated to the Takasago Volunteer Corps. As education under the Loyal Imperial Subject Policy was conducted for over 40 years, the locals were indoctrinated with a Japanese mindset and were deployed to the most dangerous battlefields in the front line jungle areas, such as the Philippines and New Guinea. Thus, it was inevitable that the death toll of Taiwanese locals was high.

Due to the Great Kanto Earthquake, which occurred on September 1, 1923, the dead and missing were estimated to be between 100,000 and 200,000, and 570,000 dwellings were destroyed.[90] The Great Kanto Earthquake of 1923 brought great damage to the Japanese, and on the other hand, it presented an unforgettable tragedy to ethnic immigrants, especially the Koreans. At the time, the Koreans faced racism and discrimination by the Japanese, and the Japanese hated the Koreans even more as they thought that the Koreans were taking away their jobs. Such prejudice and racial discrimination of the Japanese brought upon a more tragic incident during the Great Kanto Earthquake of 1923. A few hours after the earthquake, rumors began to spread that the Koreans and socialists set fires and poisoned wells. As a response to this, the Japanese organized vigilante groups to indiscriminately assault and kill the Koreans and the Chinese. Instigated and supported by the media, police and soldiers, collective madness engulfed the earthquake-stricken area like wildfire. They addressed passers-by on the streets and murdered them at random if they seemed to be Korean or Chinese. To some extent, it can be said that the Japanese authorities tried to resolve the anxiety of Japanese people by utilizing the prejudice and discrimination that the Japanese people had against Asians. It is difficult to determine an accurate death toll, but by and large, it is said that approximately 3,000 to 6,000 people were killed during this massacre.[91]

In the 1940s when Japan's Militarism was in full swing, 1.5 million Korean laborers were conscripted, and in August 1945, the number of Koreans in Japan increased to 2.4 million. The number of Koreans in Japan amounted to 10% of the total population of the Korean Peninsula at the time. The Koreans dragged over to Japan were engaged in civil works, construction, coal mine labor, harbor loading and unloading, odd jobs, and day labor, which the Japanese avoided. Their wage was less than half the wage of Japanese workers in almost all fields and their living conditions were worse than the lowest Japanese class.[92]

One of the places with the most severe working conditions that Koreans were drafted to work was Hashima (端島)[93] in the Nagasaki Prefecture. In Hashima, coal reserves were confirmed to be discovered in the 19th century, and the Mitsubishi *zaibatsu* acquired ownership of the island in 1890. Reclamation work was done for coal mining and after the Taisho Period, houses of reinforced concrete structures were constructed. As a result, the shape of the island from a distance seemed like a battleship, and so it was also called Gunkanjima (軍艦島), literally, Battleship Island. In terms of size, it is a very small island, approximately 160m from east to west and 480m from north to south, with an area of roughly 6.3 hectares and a coastline length of about 1.2km. As Japan ran out of manpower and resources by provoking the Second Sino-Japanese War and the Pacific War, Japan came to stage a total war through the National General Mobilization Law. As the front line expanded, manpower and resources from Taiwan and Korea were mobilized and plundered, and in particular, many Korean people were drafted to Japan. As demand for coal, an important war material at the time, soared, manpower from Korea or China were deployed to the coal mine in Hashima. In the case of Koreans, approximately 500 to 600 people were forced to bear the inferior and harsh working conditions of this island for many years. They were sent to do mining work for over 12 hours a day, and there were many cases where they died from coal mine accidents, malnutrition, disease, brutal treatment or drowned to death in the sea while attempting to escape. After the war ended, they were excluded from obtaining Japanese nationality and most of them went back to their countries without even receiving proper compensation for their labor. Of course, they did not receive any type of indemnification or compensation from Mitsubishi or the Japanese government after the war. Due to a decline in demand for coal, the mine was abandoned in the early 1970s and the island was neglected as a deserted island, until the southern part of the island was cleaned up and opened to tourists in 2009. Japan promoted this island to be registered as a UNESECO World Heritage Site as part of 'modernization industry heritage of Kyushu and Yamaguchi,' but faced strong opposition from Korea and other countries. Eventually, this island was registered as a World Heritage Site in 2015, as Japan accepted the condition that Japan would indicate the fact[94] that forced labor took place. However, as Japan did not properly implement the condition that UNESCO had put up at the time of registration, which was to clearly state the fact of forced labor, UNESCO World Heritage Committee called upon Japan in 2018 to properly report the 'entire history,' including forced labor which had been conducted at industrial facilities such as Hashima which was registered as a UNESCO World Heritage Site three years ago.

During World War II, countless Koreans were forcefully seized and dragged by the Japanese government to Sakhalin, which is now Russian territory, and were forced into harsh labor in coal mines or munitions factories. In an investigation conducted in 1946, the number of Koreans remaining in Sakhalin amounted to approximately 43,000 people.[95] These people were engaged in hard labor, which was a living hell, and most of them ended up dying in the process or dying after the war without being able to return home, but the reality is that Japan is not uttering a single word of apology or compensation for these people.

As Japan could not fill the necessary manpower with Koreans only, the Japanese government decided to bring in Chinese workers into Japan in 1942. The number of Chinese people forcefully seized and dragged over to Japan after 1944 amounted to approximately 40,000 people, and among them, approximately 7,000 people lost their lives while suffering from severe labor and dismal conditions. In the Hanaoka (花岡) region of Akita Prefecture (秋田縣), Kajima Gumi (鹿島組, present day Kajima Construction Corporation) was in charge of the betterment of the Hanaoka River. During this construction, 986 Chinese were mobilized after July 1944, and due to heavy labor, 137 lost their lives by June 1945. Unable to stand this cruel heavy labor, 800 Chinese rose in rebellion on the night of June 30, 1945, killing four Japanese guards and attempted to run away. On July 1, the military police were dispatched to suppress them violently. The Chinese were tied up, tortured and interrogated under the burning sun of July without any water, for three days and 282 people died or were killed in the process. As many people died until June, the death toll amounted to 419, which means that more than 40% of the Chinese who were forcefully mobilized in the construction work of Hanaoka River died.[96]

5. Massacre and Brutality in Southeast Asia and the Pacific

As Japan was not able to gain a certain victory in the Second Sino-Japanese War and as pressure from the US heightened, Japan invaded and dominated Southeast Asia for the purpose of securing a supply route of resources and forming a self-sustaining economic bloc. Prior to Japan's invasion, most of the Southeast Asian countries were colonized by Western powers, and Japan advanced its troops on the grounds of liberating them from Western colonization and pursuing coexistence and co-prosperity of Asian nations. Thus, at first, the Southeast Asian people, who longed for liberation and independence, welcomed the Japanese troops and had high hopes, but they soon realized that it had been a mere illusion. The Japanese troops established military governments in occupied territories in various Southeast Asian countries and directly ruled the territories, and in various places, they exploited resources required for war, such as food, crude oil and rubber, and forcefully drafted countless laborers to build railroads, roads, airports and mines. For example, in Indonesia, approximately 4 million laborers were forcefully mobilized, and they had to work in conditions in which meals were not properly provided and safety was not guaranteed. Also, Japan pushed ahead with the Loyal Imperial Subject Policy by banning national flags and songs native to each region and instead forcing use of the Japanese Hinomaru (national flag of Japan) and Kimigayo (national anthem of Japan), and forced the construction of and worship in shrines in various regions.[97]

In addition, the Japanese troops that occupied Southeast Asia committed massacres, looting, and rape, and in Singapore and Malaysia, numerous Chinese immigrants were brutally killed under the allegation that they were engaged in anti-Japanese activities. The Japanese troops shot to death 1,474 residents of Jelulung village, located approximately 50km southeast of Kuala Lumpur, Malaysia. [98] Furthermore, after the Japanese troops occupied Singapore on February 15, 1942, they set up checkpoints in various areas, arrested all male adults, killed on the spot those who appeared to be against the Japanese, and also brutally killed those who resisted or attempted to escape. The death toll of the Chinese immigrant massacre in Singapore, amounted to approximately 5,000 people according to the number acknowledged by Japan, and 40,000-50,000 people according to the assertions of the locals.[99] Also, Japanese troops seized the Pacific Timor Island and Macau, which were the colonies of the neutral country of Portugal, and on Timor Island, they killed numerous Portuguese and natives.

After the Japanese troops occupied the Philippines, they habitually committed aggressive actions, such as kicking and striking passers-by for no reason. Furthermore, as the Japanese troops cruelly committed rape, torture, looting and murder, fear spread throughout various regions of the Philippines. Therefore, resistance groups such as the 'Huks' or 'Free Philippines' increased, and the guerilla attacks of these organizations led to even more brutal retaliations, murders and rape by the Japanese troops. Due to the genocide by the Japanese troops, many lives were lost in the Philippines and the national territory was burnt down to the ground. As a result, the economy was devastated, and the social infrastructure and cultural traditions were heavily damaged.[100] Furthermore, as the war situation went from bad to worse for Japan and the Japanese military faced defeat after defeat, Japanese soldiers' actions became even more atrocious in various regions of Southeast Asia. In particular, the retaking of Manila by US troops became rather a tragedy to the native residents. As the attack of the US troops became more severe, the 20,000 Japanese troops which were like rats in a trap became even more brutal at the risk of their lives. Although it is relatively not well known, the atrocities of the Japanese troops in the Philippines, such as rape, looting, and murder were almost equivalent to the Nanjing Massacre. During the month before the city was retaken by US troops, an estimated number of approximately 100,000 civilians were killed. Even the Japanese civilians living in the Philippines suffered hardships due to the Japanese troops. In May 1945, retreating Japanese soldiers killed approximately twenty Japanese children, fearing that they might expose military locations.[101]

Thus, the Philippines can be seen as one of the Southeast Asian countries that suffered the most during the war. According to the estimation of President Elpidio Quirino's Advisory Council after the war, the Japanese troops incurred loss of lives amounting to approximately USD 1.67 billion, loss of property amounting to approximately USD 810 million, and cost of mobilized supplies and manpower amounting to approximately USD 5.52 billion, adding up to a total of USD 8 billion. The Indonesian representative mentioned that their losses were 4 million lives and several billion dollars of material losses.[102] As the Japanese troops occupied Southeast Asia and caused great damage to lives, properties, and native culture, anti-Japanese movements actively rose up in various Southeast Asian countries. In each country, various resistance groups were organized to give a difficult time to the Japanese through guerilla warfare, and in response to Japan's Loyal Imperial Subject Policy, the native languages, songs, and histories of the nation were taught and newspapers were published to raise anti-Japanese awareness.[103]

Numerous soldiers of the Allied Powers that became prisoners of war to the Japanese troops in Southeast Asia were mobilized for forced labor and were abused to death. An accurate representation of it is what happened to the Allied prisoners of war while constructing the Thai-Burma Railway. The Thai-Burma Railway, which was a railway connecting Kanchanaburi in Thailand and Tanbijaya in Burma, was constructed to furnish supplies to Japanese troops stationed in Burma. However, during the construction of this railway, many people died, giving this railway the nickname 'the railway of death.' It is said that approximately 13,000 of 60,000 Allied prisoners of war and approximately 40,000-60,000 of the 100,000-200,000 Asian laborers died. This Thai-Burma Railway became the venue for the famous movie, 'the Bridge on the River Kwai.' Approximately 22,000 Australian troops were held prisoner by the Japanese troops, and one-third of them died due to forced labor and brutalities.[104]

It is said that the brutalities of the Japanese troops towards the Allied prisoners of war who were captured in Southeast Asia or Pacific regions were extremely severe. This is clearly presented by the fact that the death rate of the Allied prisoners of war captured by the Japanese was 30%, while that of prisoners of war captured by the Germans or Italians was less than 5%.[105] Many Japanese believed that death was comparatively less painful, because they would be brutally tortured by the enemy if they were caught as prisoners. This was mainly due to the brainwashing of the Japanese military authorities, but other than that, the Japanese preferred death, as they thought surrendering was considered a shameful act and would even be a dishonor to the family when they later returned to Japan.[106] As the Japanese possessed this kind of perception about becoming prisoners of war, in a way, it was natural for them to neglect and abuse the Allied prisoners of war. Regardless of nationality, it is inevitable that one becomes weak and shivers in fear when becoming a prisoner, and so the Japanese troops who had distorted views on prisoners would have viewed them with contempt rather than pity.

The Japanese troops, which occupied Burma, incorporated the Indian soldiers they had captured in Singapore into the India National Army and persuaded an Indian nationalist, Subhas Chandra Boss, to command the army under the guise of helping India escape from the British colonial rule. In the spring of 1944, these Indian troops of approximately 10,000 men and Japanese troops of approximately 80,000 men joined forces and marched into India from Burma, but they were heavily defeated by the British troops in the Imphal Campaign. Japan could not manage to provide proper logistical support in this battle, and it is estimated that approximately 75,000 Indian and Japanese troops were either killed in battle or died from sickness. Vietnam, which was under French colonial rule, fell under double suppression when it was seized by Japanese troops in 1941 to secure Southeast Asia's underground resources and military outpost. France, which was under the Vichy puppet government after surrendering to Germany, was providing military convenience to Japanese troops in Vietnam. The Japanese troops, which seized southern Vietnam in May 1941, were provided with rice, rubber, underground resources such as coal, and even received warfare expenses from the Vietnam Bank. However, as the war intensified, the Japanese troops that occupied Vietnam intensified their exploitation, and brutally suppressed the Vietminh nationalist movement. Even worse, Japanese troops stationed in Vietnam confiscated most of the rice that had been harvested in Vietnam in 1944 and supplied it to the Japanese troops stationed in the Philippines as military provisions. As famine occurred in Vietnam, this confiscation of rice directly led to almost one million people starving to death.[107]

Guam of the Mariana Islands, which used to be US territory, was occupied by Japanese troops during the Pacific War, and the native Chamorros were either forced to labor or killed by the Japanese troops. Even worse, the Chamorro women were sometimes forced to serve as sexual slaves for the Japanese troops.[108] On December 10, 1941, which was right after the Pearl Harbor attack, approximately 5,000 Japanese troops occupied Guam. US prisoners of war were sent off to concentration camps on mainland Japan, and Japan ruthlessly ruled over Guam for 2 years and 7 months. The Japanese troops forced the island residents to use Japanese, and conducted the Loyal Imperial Subject Policy as in colonies such as Korea and Taiwan. Chamorro women were subjects of rape by Japanese soldiers. It is said that Maria Aguon Perez (also known as Mariquita), a Chamorro woman who was married to a US marine, rejected the sexual advances of a Japanese officer and was murdered for it. Her son Chris Perez Howard wrote the book *Mariquita*, which describes the actualities of Guam under Japanese occupation, including his mother's tragedy.[109]

During Japan's colonial rule and occupation period of Asian countries, Japanese troops committed large-scale massacres, assaults, and rape of Asians. In the backdrop of such acts was an attitude of contempt toward Asia, which began to become stronger while going through the First Sino-Japanese War and Second Sino-Japanese War. Furthermore, the local procurement policy of the Japanese military fueled Japan's cruel treatment of residents of occupied territories. Japan incorporated the vast Asia region into its sphere of influence, and troops were required to procure rations and necessary resources from the local areas due to lack of supplies. When the United States denounced the US-Japan Treaty of Commerce and Navigation in 1939 and it became even more difficult to secure war supplies, Japan's mobilization and exploitation of occupied territories intensified. This situation led Japanese troops to enforce food quota collection and plunder in occupied territories, and as a result, local residents suffered from severe food shortage and starved to death. Local residents who resisted were subject to massacres, arson, and even sexual violence towards women. In resistance against such cruel acts by Japanese troops, anti-Japanese movements arose in various regions of

Southeast Asia. Ironically, the development of such anti-Japanese organizations and movements became the foundation on which Southeast Asian people achieved independence after the end of World War II.

6. Massacre and Colonial Exploitation on the Korean Peninsula

The Korean Peninsula was not only the route for pre-modern Japan to adopt China's advanced culture but was also a gateway that Japan had to pass in order to advance into the continent. Therefore, it can be said that the states that historically existed on the Korean Peninsula during the pre-modern period were culturally more advanced than Japan. The Japanese invasion of this Korean Peninsula goes up until the 13th century. It was the plundering of the southern regions and islands of the Korean Peninsula by the so-called Japanese pirates. There had been invasions by Japanese pirates several centuries before, but it became more large-scale in the 13th century and in the mid-14th century, the Japanese pirates wielded more power, taking advantage of the instability of Japan and the international situation in East Asia. Since these invasions were mainly led by pirates from Japan's southwest region,[110] it can be said that the first invasion by the Japanese central government was the Imjin War (Japanese invasion of Korea in 1592) which broke out in the late 16th century. Toyotomi Hideyoshi (豊臣秀吉, 1536-1598) unified Japan and invaded the Korean Peninsula (the Joseon Dynasty) in 1592. As a result of this invasion, numerous lives were lost and many people were dragged to Japan as prisoners, which led to a sharp decrease in Korea's population. Furthermore, due to seven years of war, supplies were looted, farmland was wasted, and many of Korea's cultural artifacts were burnt down or looted.[111] More specifically, according to Japanese researchers, the number of Koreans forcefully abducted by the Japanese troops is estimated to be about 20,000-30,000, and Korean researchers estimate that 100,000 male and females, young and old, were abducted and taken to various regions of Japan.[112] The Korean potters that Japan abducted at the time produced the porcelain called Imari ware (伊万里焼, Imari-yaki, present day Arita-yaki, 有田焼). During the chaotic transition period from the Ming Dynasty to Qing Dynasty, when Chinese pottery was difficult to come by, Imari ware was even exported to Europe through Dutch merchants. On the other hand, prior to the war caused by Japan's invasion, the total area of farmland in Korea was 1,510,000 Gyul (1 Gyul = 10,000 ha), but three years after the end of the war in Year 34 of King Seonjo (1601), it decreased to one-fifth, becoming only 300,000 Gyul.[113] At that time, in Korea, there was a great naval admiral, Yi Sun-shin (李舜臣, 1545-1598), who is highly appreciated in world naval history. Therefore, even though Korea experienced horrible defeats on land as illustrated above, it was able to have dominance over the sea.

The brutality of the Japanese troops to the Korean people in the Imjin War can be glimpsed through the following two cases. In *Joseon Inikki* (朝鮮 日日記, *Korea Day by Day*), written by monk Keinen (慶念) who served as a medical monk for the Japanese troops, there is a depiction of the Japanese troops brutally killing the people of the Korean Peninsula, looting supplies, and burning houses. Also, Kang Hang, who was abducted in 1597 at the Battle of Namwon Castle and dragged to Japan but managed to return to Korea after all sorts of hardships, wrote a book called *Kanyangrok (Prisoner's record of the Imjin War*, 看羊錄) describing the events he experienced in Japan. In this book, it is written that the Japanese troops cut off the noses of the Korean people as a booty of war and sent them to Hideyoshi. At the time, the Japanese troops sent 50,000 noses marinated in salt in 15 large wooden crates, and they were buried in Daibutsuji (大佛寺) of Kyoto and named 'Ear Grave (Mimizuka, 耳塚).' It is said that this was because Japanese people were ashamed to call it Nose Grave, since their acts were too diabolic. In the current signboard of the Nose Grave, the date of renovation is written as May 30, Meiji Year 5, and it is said to be because the Meiji government found the grave as educational material for external invasion and renovated it.[114]

Using the Nose Grave, which was a historical tragedy, as a means of educating its people was an imperialistic idea that was willing to pursue national interests by invading other countries and sacrificing other people. It can also be interpreted that the Japanese have an inhumane side as to openly use the past brutalities for means of education. We can only be petrified by Japan's acts in the modern times: colonizing Taiwan and Korea and committing all sorts of atrocities; invading China and committing the massacre of brutally killing approximately 300,000 people in Nanjing; executing the Sanguang Operations without hesitation, burning down houses, looting, and killing people all throughout China. Furthermore, dragging Asia's young women to the battlefields and using them as comfort women, or in other words, sexual slaves, was an infringement of human rights and abuse of women, an inhumane crime which cannot be forgiven. Just as Japan didn't hesitate to expose the wrongdoings during the Imjin War for use as an education material for external invasion during the Meiji Period, it may be possible for Japan to use the atrocities of the 20th century for educational purposes today in the 21st century, as Japan is burning with ambition to once again become a militaristic nation. To a certain degree, such signs can be seen in the actions of Japanese right-wingers who are striving to remember and teach the history of invasion and wrongdoings in the early 20th century as a history of glory.

After the Imjin War, the Tokugawa Shogunate came into power and implemented the Closed Country Policy, so there were no more political and military conflicts caused by Japan for the next 250 or so years in East Asia. However, after Qing China was defeated by the UK in the Opium War and

Japan opened doors due to the pressure of the fleet of Commodore Perry in 1853, Japan came to actively push ahead with foreign expansion policies. The Korean Peninsula, which was the gateway for Japan to the continent, became the first target and in 1876, Japan was able to sign the Treaty of Kanghwa (Japan-Korea Treaty of 1876), which was a favorable treaty to Japan, by imitating the Americans. With the excuse of suppressing the Tonghak Revolution which occurred in Korea in 1894, Japan dispatched troops to the Korean Peninsula, occupied Korea's palace (Kyeongbok Palace) and drove out all Korean military forces stationed in Seoul to the outskirts. This was a measure to provoke the Qing troops and find an excuse to attack.[115] After the Tonghak Revolution was suppressed, the Japanese troops attacked the Qing troops and was victorious (the First Sino-Japanese War), expanding their influence over Korea. In the process of suppressing the Tonghak Revolution, the Japanese troops not only brutally killed the revolutionists but also killed normal farmers in the vicinity, under the policy of wiping out the enemy. According to the records of the Korean government at the time and Oh Ji-yeong's *Tonghak History* (1940),[116] the death toll of the revolutionists directly killed in battle and suppression was at least 30,000 and other casualties were estimated to be 300,000-400,000.[117]

In the early stages of the First Sino-Japanese War, the Korean Peninsula was the main battlefield of Qing China and Japan, and the Japanese troops forcefully mobilized food, supplies, manpower and horses necessary for war from all throughout Joseon Korea. Even though Korea was undoubtedly an independent nation, it became the battlefield of the two nations and was degenerated into the status of a subject state supporting Japan's war. When Japan returned the Liaodong Peninsula, which it had acquired through victory in the First Sino-Japanese War, to Qing due to the Tripartite Intervention led by Russia, pro-Russian groups centering on Empress Myeongseong of the Joseon Dynasty gathered strength and attempted to keep the Japanese forces in check. In response, in October 1895, Miura Koro, the Japanese minister to Korea, mobilized the members of the Japanese legation, the Japanese guards, the Japanese councilors, and the Japanese *samurais* residing in Korea to infiltrate Kyeongbok Palace to murder Empress Myeongseong and burn her body (Eulmi Incident and Assassination). Japan did not punish one single Japanese national involved in this assassination. Despite the fact that the Joseon Dynasty of Korea experienced the brutality of having its queen assassinated, Korea, whose national power had declined, was not able to make a proper protest to Japan and responded only with the Korea Royal Refuge at the Russian legation.[118]

As the war sentiment was rising between Russia and Japan, Korea (Joseon) declared neutrality in January 1904, but Japan ignored this declaration, dispatched troops to Hansung (present Seoul), and occupied Kyeongun Palace. And when war broke out, Japan signed the Japan-Korea Treaty of

1904, forcing Korea to fully cooperate during Japan's war.[119] Hence, Japan forcefully occupied land all throughout the Korean Peninsula for military use, forcefully mobilized countless civilians to construct railways, transport war supplies, and build military bases, and looted rations and livestock. In this situation, Japan incorporated Dokdo (Liancourt Rocks), which had historically been affiliated to Korea, into Japanese territory under the name of Takeshima (竹島) through a Cabinet resolution on January 28, 1905.[120] Those who sabotaged military lines or railways to stand up against the brutalities and abuse of the Japanese troops were brutally killed.[121] As a victor of the Russo-Japanese War, Japan treated Korea, which had not even been a party in the war, as a trophy of war, forcefully signed the Japan-Korea Treaty of 1905 (Eulsa Treaty) and made Korea a protectorate of Japan. Japan installed the Office of Resident General (統監府), which took over the politics, administration, judiciary, education, diplomacy, and national defense, and ruled Korea through this organization.

As Korea lost its sovereignty as an independent country through the Japan-Korea Treaty of 1905 (Eulsa Treaty), Righteous Army Movements (the Eulsa Righteous Army) spread all throughout the nation. From 1907 to 1910, the Korea Righteous Army fought in approximately 2,819 battles with Japanese troops, and the total number of the Righteous Army troops amounted to 140,000. The Japanese troops mobilized one infantry division, one cavalry regiment, and approximately 6,000 military police to execute brutal suppression on the Righteous Army. The Japanese troops burnt down the villages and houses which had a possibility to become bases for the Righteous Army, and the continued oppression and suppression by the Japanese troops caused many casualties of Righteous Army soldiers and Korean civilians. According to data from Japan, the death toll between 1906 and 1910 exceeded 17,000.[122]

During the Russo-Japanese War, Japan stated that it needed to pursue an agricultural colonial policy in Korea to gain reclaimed land and fill the shortage of food for the excess population. As the resistance of the Righteous Army continued incessantly in the Honam area of Korea, Japanese troops executed the 'Military Operation to Subjugate Honam of Korea'. For two months starting from September to October 1909, Japan brutally suppressed the Righteous Army. In the following year, one-fourth of the Japanese officials added to the Office of Resident General and agricultural immigrants were moved to this area. This was a typical Japanese method of colonization, in which Japanese troops invaded a certain area, suppressed the resisting forces, and implemented immigration.[123]

On August 22, 1910, with thousands of Japanese troops surrounding the palace of Korea, Resident General Terauchi Masatake and Prime Minister Lee Wanyong signed a merger treaty and announced it one week later, and thus, Korea became a colony of Japan. The merger treaty and colonial rule by Japan was procedurally unjust and illegal,[124] but Korea could not complain about it as it was a weak nation. Japan set up the Japanese Government General of Korea (總督府) to dominate Korea as a colony, and the Governor General had all authority over colonial rule. Japan stationed two divisions to forcefully suppress the resistance of the Korean people and stationed approximately 16,000 military police all throughout the country to carry out oppressive governing. After this tyrannical colonial rule began, many Korean people moved to Manchuria. Not only did they lose a lot of land due to the Land Survey Project of the Japanese Government General of Korea, but the unstable situation of the Korean Peninsula due to Korea's degeneration as Japan's colony triggered the emigration of Korean people. The number of Koreans who moved to Manchuria up until 1919 exceeded 400,000.[125]

As Japan's tyrannical rule intensified after Japan took over Korea, dissatisfaction piled up among the Korean people, and from March to May 1919, approximately 1,500 peaceful independence demonstrations were held all through the Korean Peninsula, and approximately 2 million people participated in the demonstrations (March 1 Movement). The Japanese Government General of Korea mobilized troops and military police to mercilessly suppress the movement. Japan condemned the Korean people who came out for the peaceful demonstrations as rioters and reported that many Japanese people were harmed, but in reality, there were almost no Japanese civilians killed by the demonstrators.[126] The death toll due to the suppression of the Japanese troops and police was 7,645, the number of injured people was 45,562, and the number of imprisoned people was 49,811, which added up to a total number of 103,018 people victimized by the Japanese.[127] Especially, in Jeam-ri of Suwon, a city nearby Seoul, a heinous incident occurred in which approximately 30 people who participated in the demonstrations were forced into a church building and the building was blindly fired at with guns and then burnt down.[128]

Other countries that were being invaded or put under colonial rule, such as China and India, showed great interest in the March 1 Movement in colonial Korea. The March 1 Movement was especially a stimulation to Chinese students and intellectuals. In *Meizhou Pinglun* (每週評論, *Weekly Review*) published on March 23, 1919, Chen Du Xiu (陳獨秀, 1879-1942) highly praised the March 1 Movement as a nonviolent movement and as a movement which opened a new paradigm of world revolutions. In the magazine *Xin Chao* (新潮), the March 1 Movement was highly rated in that it did not use weapons, that it was implemented despite the fact that it was practically impossible, and that it was led by students.[129] During the May Fourth Movement, Beijing academics highly appreciated the will of the Korean people for independence, and the Kwangtung Government of Sun Wen sent its support for the March 1 Movement, strongly criticizing the violent and bloody suppression of the Japanese Government General of

Korea.[130]

When the Treaty of Versailles was signed in June 1919, the countries that participated in the Siberia Intervention withdrew their troops, as the cause was weak and the burden of war expenses was high, but the Japanese troops remained. Japan sought to take possession of Siberia and create a favorable environment in securing influence over Manchuria using this opportunity. However, the resistance of the Korean Independence Army engaged in activities in this region and the increasing public opposition in Japan worked as obstacles. In response, starting from October 1920, the Japanese military moved the troops that had participated in the Siberia Intervention and the troops that had been stationed in colonial Korea to the northern part of the Korean Peninsula near Baekdu Mountain in order to eliminate the Korean Independence Army troops. However, they failed due to the strong resistance of the Korean Independence Army troops in battles such as the Battle of Cheongsanri. To retaliate for consecutive defeats in the Battle of Fengwudong in June 1920 and the Battle of Cheongsanri in October 1920, the Japanese troops committed the Kando Massacre to weaken the support base of the Independence Army troops, killing approximately 5,000 Korean people living in Manchuria and burning down approximately 3,500 houses.[131]

By causing the Manchurian Incident in 1931, Japan established Manchukuo, a puppet state, and provoked the Second Sino-Japanese War in 1937. Furthermore, to support this war, Japan made the Korean Peninsula into a logistics base, and mobilized a great deal of supplies and manpower for the war. In order to enforce the Loyal Imperial Subject Policy, Japan emphasized the 'Japan and Korea are one' policy, and every day at noon, everyone was forced to bow in the direction of Tokyo, where the Emperor was, and during events everyone had to recite the 'Oath as Subjects of the Imperial Nation'. Using the Korean language was prohibited in schools and everyday life, and people were forced to worship shrines.[132] People were forced to change their names to Japanese names, and if they did not comply, they were not even allowed to attend school. Various resources were mobilized as war supplies, and food was confiscated, and most Korean people suffered from hunger as the rice consumption per capita was only one-fifth of that of the Japanese. Fania Isaakovna Shabshina, in the book *In Colonial Korea,*[133] vividly described the shocking situation of the time.[134]

Japan continued to expand the war after the breakout of the Second Sino-Japanese War, and in 1939, Japan enacted the National Draft Order and applied this to Korea as well, forcefully mobilizing countless Korean people in mines, civil works and construction sites, and munitions factories. Approximately 1.5 million Korean people were forcefully drafted, and they were dragged not only to mainland Japan, but also to Japanese occupied territory such as Okinawa, Manchuria, Pacific Islands, and even to southern Sakhalin to engage in hard labor under poor conditions.[135] Korean people who had been drafted to construct military airports or military fortresses would sometimes all be killed en masse by the Japanese authorities who were concerned about leakage of military secrets once the construction was completed. Also, several hundreds of thousands of Korean people were forcefully mobilized in the construction of the Continental Logistics Base in the northern region of the Korean Peninsula. The women of Korea were also forcefully mobilized to work in munitions factories in Japan and Korea, and some women were dragged to battlefields in various places to serve as sex slaves for the Japanese troops. Japan implemented the draft system in Korea in 1944, and mobilized countless Korean people as soldiers.[136] The number of Korean people mobilized in the wars triggered by Japan amounted to 7,320,000 forced laborers and 614,000 military personnel and civilian workers in the military, adding up to 7,940,000, which was nearly one-third of the population of Korea at the time.[137]

After the war, the Rhee Syngman government, established in the southern part of the Korean Peninsula, created a committee to request compensation from Japan. It collected data to request compensation and announced the 'Reparation Demands of South Korea against Japan.' This committee calculated the damage caused by Japan's colonial rule in Japanese yen, and the total amount excluding payment in kind was JPY 31,400,975,503. Despite the fact that it was reasonable to demand that Japan compensate for the material, human, and mental damage inflicted on Korean people during Japan's colonial rule, the US was keen on enhancing Japan's economic power and using it as a counterforce against the proliferation of Communism in a situation where the Cold War intensified, so the US was not enthusiastic about the Rhee Syngman government's reparation demands against Japan and excluded South Korea from participating in the peace treaty.[138]

7. Tragedy Caused by Modern Japan's Development

The development strategy of modern Japan through foreign expansion and invasion, as illustrated above, inflicted great damage and immeasurable agony to various Asian countries. Japan's victory in the Russo-Japanese War and easy victories in the early stages of the Pacific War encouraged overconfidence about Japan's superiority over the West, especially its spiritual superiority, and enforced a sense of ethnic and racial superiority over Asian countries. It can be said that this aggravated the merciless abuse and murder, looting, and rape by Japanese troops against the residents of occupied territories and colonies as well as the prisoners of war. The damage and suffering inflicted by Japan did not end with the war. Japan's colonial rule and war of aggression led to negative ramifications in all aspects of each country, including politics, society, economy, and culture, and the scars of the 20th century caused by Japan did not properly heal and are still bringing pain in the 21st century. Furthermore, Japan's conservative right-wingers wish to remember the early 20th century, a period of Japan's colonization and invasion of Asian countries, as a glorious history of wielding power internationally and raising national status. As the far-rights of Japan are expanding their influence in the 21st century, opposition and conflicts among the Asian countries over territory and history issues are becoming acute. There are rising concerns that the tragic history of the 20th century brought forth by Japan has failed to have proper closure even in the 21st century and may be galloping towards another tragedy.

Each Asian country suffered damage and pain inflicted by Japan, and the negative impacts continued even after the end of the war. For example, in Korea, Indonesia, and Myanmar (Burma), dictatorships continued for a long time, and this was a strong influence of the negative legacy of domination by Japanese troops, as it was the soldiers who had been affiliated with the Japanese troops or had been influenced by the Japanese military during the Japanese rule that seized power and maintained dictatorships.[139] Let us examine in more detail the Korean Peninsula which was strongly and directly influenced by Japan compared to other Asian countries due to geopolitical factors. Joseon Dynasty (朝鮮, 1392-1910) of the Korean Peninsula was able to create a flourishing culture in the first half of the dynasty as there was a great king called Sejong, and in the second half of the dynasty, there were difficulties due to the invasion by Japan and Qing China, but politics and society became somewhat stabilized during the reign of King Yeongjo and Jeongjo. Especially in the 18th century, some scholars of Korea keenly realized the limitations of the doctrines of orthodox Neo-Confucianism (by Zhu Xi) and began Silhak (Korean Pragmatic Philosophy) which pursued practicality. These Realists can be viewed as the modern enlightenment thinkers of Korea, and their activities had sufficient potential to lead to Korea's autonomous modernization. Thus, it can be said that Japan's influence over Korea during the late 19th century and colonization in the early 20th century, had taken the opportunities for Korea to seek autonomous modernization and even greatly hampered the historical development on the Korean Peninsula.[140] Furthermore, if Japan had accepted the Potsdam Declaration earlier and surrendered, US troops would have taken the Korean Peninsula and the Soviet troops would not have come to this peninsula, and thus, Korea would not have been divided into north and south.[141] In a way, the Korean Peninsula, which had been tormented under Japan's colonial rule, came under the yoke of being divided in Japan's stead due to Japan's bad decision. In the end, after having suffered colonial rule, the Korean Peninsula was divided into north and south instead of Japan, which should have taken responsibility for the colonial rule and war of aggression. Taking advantage of the Korean War, Japan was not only able to easily restore its economy, backed by the US, but was also able to make a comeback to international society by signing the Treaty of San Francisco.[142]

The Korean Peninsula, which had been a colony of Japan, was divided into north and south by the US and the Soviet Union after the surrender of Japan. These superpowers established governments in accord with their ideologies. In North Korea, the Kim Il-sung government, backed by the support of the Soviet Union and armed with the ideology of Communism, was established. The US troops which came into South Korea imposed military rule against the will of the Korean people, using the institutions and ruling powers of the Japanese colonial times, and on this basis, established the pro-American Rhee Syngman government.[143] Thus, the economy was severed as the northern part of the Korean Peninsula, which was reliant on heavy industry, and the southern part, which was reliant on agriculture and light industry, and even this economic foundation was burnt to ashes due to the Korean War. The governments of North Korea and South Korea stood face to face until the Korean War broke out due to North Korea's invasion, in which 150,000 South Korean troops, 520,000 North Korean troops, 35,000 UN troops, and approximately 1 million civilians were killed, and the entire Korean Peninsula fell into ruins.[144] China dispatched over 1 million troops to support North Korea, which led to casualties of at least half a million.[145] Due to the division of Korea into north and south as well as the Korean War, the Korean Peninsula went through harsh ideological conflicts and the enmity within the nation intensified. This situation is causing both North Korea and South Korea to bear the opportunity costs of excessive military expenditures and declined vitality in the society due to ideological rigidity. After the end of the Cold War, through the adoption of the Inter-Korea Basic Agreement in 1991, realization of mutual visiting between North Korea and South Korea on several occasions, and the first ever summit meeting between North Korea and South Korea in June 2000, there are higher hopes of reconciliation and cooperation between North and South Korea, but there is still a long way to go in order to resolve conflicts between the ideological systems. After a conservative right-wing government came into office in 2008, the relationship between North Korea and South Korea became tense. After President Park Geun-hye was impeached and the Moon Jae-in government came to power, the relationship between North Korea and South Korea has taken a favorable turn, with several Inter-Korean summits and the United States-North Korea summits.

The people who had been dragged to Japan from colonies such as Korea and Taiwan during the war were put into a worse position after the end of the war. On September 1, 1945, before the US troops full-fledgedly implemented the occupation policy in Japan, the Japanese government decided on a policy to prioritize the repatriation of Korean laborers who had been forcefully mobilized by Japan from mainland Japan to Korea.

Furthermore, in December, the political rights of the Korean people and Taiwanese people who had gained Japanese citizenship during the colonial period were suspended and a political expulsion was carried out.[146] In the midst of all this, the ship Fujimaru which had been heading to Korea loaded with Korean people suddenly exploded and sunk, killing numerous Koreans, and up to this day, the cause and the number of victims has not been clarified.[147] The Korean people and Chinese people who remained in Japan lived in discrimination and contempt, such as being excluded from the GI Bill of Rights even after falling victim to atomic bombs. Why did Japanese people continue such harsh discrimination and contempt after the war against the Korean people and Chinese people, whom Japan had forcefully mobilized to carry out their war and had inflicted much pain to? It is necessary to deeply investigate what type of mentality and thought of the Japanese worked to bring about this result.

As mentioned above, atrocities as in the case of Unit 731 in China's Manchuria were committed in various forms within Japan's colonies and occupied territories. Furthermore, the Japanese military often executed Allied prisoners of war who had been captured in the Pacific regions, considering them as criminals instead of treating them according to international law. In particular, crew members of US war planes that had been shot down while attacking mainland Japan were brutally executed, to the point of being excessive. There were instances that even civilians stabbed them to death with bamboo spears. The most brutal incident is known as the vivisection incident[148] committed by doctors of Kyushu University School of Medicine. Eight crew members of a US war plane that had been shot down after attacking mainland Japan were captured as prisoners and were murdered through live dissection over four occasions conducted by professors of Kyushu University School of Medicine in May and June 1945. Medical experiments performed on living bodies included surgical removal of a lung, injection of diluted seawater into a vein, cardiac standstill experiments, surgical removal of the brain, experiment of critical condition due to bleeding, etc. Such acts were as horrendous as the experiments of Unit 731 in Manchuria, since doctors with the duty to save lives dissected prisoners alive and killed them in order to satisfy their passion for research.

Modern Japan's foreign expansion and war of aggression did not only harm neighboring countries and their people. The Japanese people who had been mobilized and had to back up Militarist Japan's foreign expansion also suffered damage, and furthermore, the national image of Japan was tarnished. After the Manchurian Incident occurred in 1931, nationalist education was reinforced, the note of Militarism became stronger, and the suppression of ideology and academics increased in Japan. Especially, after Japan started the Second Sino-Japanese War and the Pacific War, Japanese society was converted into a wartime mobilization system, forcing the sacrifice of all the people.[149]

Japanese society was reorganized into a structure for war, and a war collaboration system was established with approximately 1.3 million *tonarigumis* (Neighborhood Associations), each of which consisted of approximately ten households. The number of soldiers, which had been 310,000 in 1931 when the Manchurian Incident began, consistently increased to approximately 7,190,000 in 1945. In schools, it was compulsory to worship the Emperor and sing the Kimigayo, and contempt and sense of superiority over Asians was encouraged in classes, teaching students that it was natural for Japan, 'God's Nation,' to dominate other Asian countries. Forcing nationalism on the Japanese people and compelling the whole nation to participate in the war ultimately caused loss of lives and property. Beginning with the Tokyo Bombing in March 1945, approximately 150 cities including Yokohama and Osaka were bombarded, and Hiroshima and Nagasaki became targets of atomic bomb attacks.[150] The number of civilians sacrificed by the bombings and nuclear attacks was approximately 380,000, and over 2.4 million houses were burnt down. Especially, due to the heat rays and storms caused by the atomic bomb explosions, buildings were destroyed, and many people were killed on the spot. Countless people died with symptoms of fever, diarrhea, hemoptysis, and hypodermal bleeding, due to radiation, and even the survivors had to live miserably with the aftereffects. In the Battle of Okinawa[151] between April and June of 1945, there was a great number of victims, including approximately 94,000 Japanese soldiers, 12,500 US soldiers, and 94,000 residents. As the war took a turn against Japan's favor nearing the end of the war, the Japanese military operated a suicide aviation commando unit,[152] through which 2,443 aircraft were lost and 3,940 pilots, including student soldiers in the commando unit, were sacrificed. As for Japanese women, some women were mobilized as comfort women, but the main role assigned to women due to the war was to become the 'mother of the military nation' who produced the human resources for the war by marrying at an early age and giving birth to five children, and also to become industrial warriors in the absence of men.[153]

The Japanese troops resisted fiercely in Okinawa, far away from the mainland, in order to gain more time to prepare for the battle against the US on the mainland. However, the Battle of Okinawa was hopeless from the start, and since Okinawa was not even considered a true part of Japan, the Japanese troops were not interested in protecting the residents of Okinawa. In bombardments by US warships and on ground combat, not only were Japanese troops killed but also people of Okinawa, and one quarter of the people of Okinawa died during the war. In particular, the people of Okinawa were mobilized to transport weapons and procure food for the Japanese troops, they were taught that 'it is better to die than to become prisoners,' and were forced to commit 'group suicide' worrying that they might provide military secrets to the US troops.[154] The Japanese troops killed many people in Okinawa, suspecting that they were spies of the enemy, and also killed people of Okinawa who attempted to surrender to the US troops to save their lives. Also, wherever Japanese troops were stationed, so-called 'comfort women' or 'Japanese military sexual slaves' were mobilized, and Okinawa was no exception. In the many islands where the Japanese troops were undergoing defensive battles, there were over 130 comfort stations.[155] In these comfort stations, there were not only women from Okinawa but also women dragged from Korea, China, and various Southeast Asian countries. Countless people among them died during the battles. Okinawa, which suffered from the devastation of the Pacific War, remained under US occupation for 27 years after the end of the war until it was returned to Japan in 1972. Even now the territory has been returned, 10% of Okinawa's area is occupied by the US military base,[156] which makes up 75% of the area occupied by all US military bases in Japan. This situation not only causes discomfort in the lives of the people of Okinawa, but also causes many socioeconomic problems.[157]

Japanese soldiers were taught that the greatest honor of a soldier was to die on the battlefield, because the obligation of loyalty was as heavy as a great mountain and an individual's life was as light as a feather. Therefore, dying for the Japanese Emperor was the greatest honor, but becoming a prisoner of the enemy was the worst shame. As Japanese soldiers regarded their own lives so lightly, they were able to commit atrocities to enemy soldiers or civilians without constraint. During the war, beatings were an everyday occurrence in the barracks of the Japanese troops and soldiers in the ranks had to suffer from severe training and hard labor. In this environment, the soldiers were ordered to stab swords into prisoners, being trained to become 'murderers.' Then when a fellow soldier died, the soldiers who used to be good turned into devils and came to think they had paid their fellow soldier's revenge by brutally killing Chinese prisoners of war or civilians. In short, the Japanese troops in the battlefields experienced ruin in their minds and lost their basic humanity, literally creating their own living hell. It is estimated that the number of Japanese soldiers who died on the battlefield, driven in this inhumane environment, was approximately 2.12 million. As for the causes of death, disease and malnutrition, or in a wider sense, death from famine amounted to approximately 1.28 million, which was over 60% of all deaths. Almost half of the 460,000 deaths of the Japanese troops on the Chinese front was due to death from disease caused by malnutrition, whereas in the Philippines, at least 400,000 out of the 500,000 deaths were due to famine. Ironically, more than half of the deaths of the Japanese troops was not due to the artillery and guns of the enemies, but by the Japanese government and the Japanese troops themselves.[158]

In 1945, around when Japan was facing defeat, a considerable portion of

Japan's population were soldiers, with 5.5 million in the army and 1.7 million in the navy. This number shows how fanatic Japan was about the war.[159] Japan started a hopeless war from the outset, considering its national power and external conditions, and Japan lost the opportunity to reduce the immense damage which followed, when former Prime Minister Konoe Fumimaro advised Emperor Hirohito to negotiate surrender in February 1945 but the Emperor refused by saying, 'It is difficult to discuss such matters without achieving another victory.'[160] In the Pacific War alone, Japan suffered from approximately 1,840,000 deaths of military personnel and civilians attached to the military, 660,000 civilian deaths, and 2,360,000 houses were burnt down. Thus, after the war, the Japanese people came to cultivate an abhorrence of war and yearning for peace, which ironically became the foundation on which the Peace Constitution was established and maintained.[161]

Many Japanese people resided in overseas areas occupied by Japanese troops, but after being defeated in the war, many of them were killed in attacks from enemy soldiers or local residents or died of famine or disease while fleeing for refuge. Among the various regions overseas, the largest damage was done in Manchuria, which was dominated by Japan's Kwantung Army. The Soviet Union dragged approximately 600,000 disarmed Japanese troops and civilians from Manchuria to Siberia for forced labor. Due to forced labor of 2 to 11 years, approximately 68,000 people died of malnutrition, overwork, and the cold temperature. The Japanese victims who were detained in Siberia later demanded compensation from the Japanese government, but in 1997, the Supreme Court of Japan dropped the case with the reason that 'The Japanese people must endure it together.'[162]

The Japanese people did not suffer damage only from the wars in the 1930s and 1940s. As Japan started the First Sino-Japanese War and the Russo-Japanese War in order to advance onto the continent, countless Japanese young men ended up dying in the battlefields. In the First Sino-Japanese War, 13,311 Japanese soldiers died, among which 1,417 died in combat and 11,894 died of disease. In the Russo-Japanese War, the battles were more heated and as many as 82,847 Japanese soldiers died, among which 55,655 died in combat and 27,192 died of disease. The number of troops Japan mobilized for the Russo-Japanese War was approximately 1 million, among which 470,000 died or were injured. In particular, in January 1905, when Japan captured Lushun of Qing which had been occupied by Russian troops, the Japanese Army suffered massive casualties and approximately 60,000 soldiers died or were injured. In March 1905, in Fengtian (奉天), approximately 370,000 Russian and 250,000 Japanese troops fought a ferocious battle, in which the Japanese troops claimed victory, but suffered approximately 70,000 casualties.[163] In the Russo-Japanese War, the Russian troops suffered as many casualties as the Japanese troops.[164]

As a result of the 15 or so years of war beginning with the Manchurian Incident in 1931, Japan lost approximately 3 million troops and half a million civilians. Most of the deaths occurred during the four years of the Pacific War. Despite this enormous casualty rate, Japan was defeated in war for the first time in history and was put under the occupation of external forces. In his letter to his son in September 1945, Emperor Hirohito attributed the defeat in war to an underestimation of the US and the UK, overreliance on spirit rather than science, and the arrogance of military leaders who knew only of advancing forward.[165]

Japan faced the risk of extermination due to the war that it had provoked, losing millions of military personnel and civilians and becoming the first ever target of an atomic attack in the history of humankind. Many people of the Allied Powers who had fought in World War II believed that the Japanese race should be annihilated for the safety of humankind. Even humanitarians such as Franklin Roosevelt (1882-1945) seemed to think that ethnic cleansing could be beneficial in various aspects.[166] Modern Japan had not only caused immense losses in human lives and property and inexpungible agony to various Asian countries through colonial rule and war of aggression, but it also threw themselves into an indescribable abyss of tragedy.

After a short-lived predominance in the early stages of the Pacific War, Japan was subject to defeat after defeat all throughout the war and surrendered only after suffering a massive loss of lives and property from the two atomic bombings by the US troops. Ironically, due to the atomic attack, the Japanese people came to think of themselves as victims, not perpetrators. Therefore, Japan stresses that it was the only country in the world to be hit by atomic bombs and pushes ahead with movements against atomic experiments and movements for peace. If the US had not dropped the atomic bomb, it would have been difficult for the Japanese to nurture this victim mentality. It can be said that as opposed to the Germans, who are conscious of the fact that they were perpetrators that caused damage to neighboring countries, the Japanese were given justification to avoid this perpetrator mentality by the US.[167] Japan caused immeasurable agony and casualties by colonizing and invading neighboring Asian countries. Japan had also brought calamity upon itself in the final year by not surrendering earlier. Therefore, it is nonsensical for Japan to regard itself as a victim. It is shameless to mention its own loss, without prioritizing enough remorse and apology regarding the perpetration committed by Japan and the Japanese and the damage that neighboring countries and their people suffered from.

The scars of colonial rule and war of aggression toward Asian countries caused by modern Japan's external expansionism policy goes beyond its time. Japan's invasive occupation and colonial rule eventually caused division in neighboring countries such as Korea, China, and Vietnam. Furthermore, as Japan leaned against the US, one axis of the Cold War, and focused on promoting its national interest such as economic development without properly taking responsibility for the war and colonial rule, the historical scars among countries grew deeper. Even if they had survived the war, Asians were forced to live with the torment of having lost their families and those who were injured could not but live in agony with disability for the rest of their lives. Japanese people were also not able to escape from the aftermath of war. First and foremost, victims of atomic bombs or air raids had to live in suffering beyond description after the war. Furthermore, as more than half of the war dead were single men of marriageable age, it caused a gender imbalance, which made it difficult for some women to find spouses and as a result they had to remain singles throughout their lives. Therefore, the tragedy caused by the development of modern Japan continued beyond the end of the war, and as Japan failed to properly apologize to Asian countries and avoided responsibility after the war, the historical settlement of the tragedy still remains as a task to be solved. Furthermore, Japan has not taken responsibility for the agony inflicted on the Japanese people through the war, which prevented Japanese people from being conscious of the responsibility that they themselves either actively supported or failed to block the war.

CHAPTER 2

CHARACTERISTICS OF JAPANESE SOCIETY
AND JAPANESE PEOPLE

1. Influence of Geographical Environment

Geographically, Japan consists of several thousand islands situated on the eastern end of the Asian continent. When the Japanese archipelago was formed through severe orogenic movement and volcanic activity approximately 200 million years ago at the end of the Paleozoic era, it was connected to the Asian continent. It was at the end of the diluvial epoch of the Cenozoic era, approximately 20,000 years ago, that the Japanese archipelago was completely separated from the continent. Such separation from the continent acted as a factor which deterred the advancement of Japanese history, but on the other hand, it was the background for forming a unique and distinctive culture. Japan's territory is mainly composed of 4 large islands, Hokkaido (北海道), Honshu (本州), Shikoku (四國), and Kyushu (九州), but there are several thousand other big and small islands. Today, the big four islands are all connected through submarine tunnels or bridges. As Japan extends on the Circum-Pacific volcanic belt, it has frequent damage from volcanic activities and earthquakes and has many hot springs. Japan has many high mountains, including approximately 70 mountains reaching higher than 2,000m. These high mountains form mountain ranges and rivers are formed in between. Geographical isolation due to mountain ranges and rivers was also a factor that caused distinct regional features in politics and culture during the ancient and medieval times.

The geographic environment of Japan influenced the history of Japan in many ways. The distance between Kyushu Island on the southern part of Japan and the Asian continent was close enough to sail across even two thousand years ago but was far enough to be extremely risky when actually sailing across. Therefore, before the modern ages, it was not easy for the continental countries to engage in military aggression toward Japan nor for Japan to conquer the continent. This appropriate distance allowed the Japanese people to selectively accept relationships with the various cultures of the continent and to search an independent path, which made it possible for them to develop a culture influenced by China but with their own distinct color. The leaders of Japan hesitated to accept the subordinate position in the Chinese tributary system. Fortunately, thanks to the appropriate distance and the barrier of the sea, they were able to successfully resist requests for tributes or threats of invasion. Also, due to the many islands and the rugged mountainous terrain of Japan, it was difficult to have a nationwide central power in the pre-modern era, and even in the Tokugawa Period when there was political order and peace, regional leaders still had considerable autonomy. Therefore, the common people did not share the identity of common Japanese culture. In this sense, the concept of Japan being an ethnically homogenous nation can be said to have been created in the modern age. The concept of 'Japanese-ness' was an identity made in order to overcome geographic difficulties that hindered integration and to respond to external pressures.[168]

As Japan is an island country, it has both various strengths and weaknesses. Japan has strengths such as being protected from external invasion and being able to selectively accept foreign culture since it is far from the continent. Japan also has weaknesses such as being exclusive and closed. The thought of being isolated from the continent is helpful in creating a sense of homogeneity, but when this homogeneity becomes stronger, it leads to an exclusive nature.[169] This geographic environment is what creates the uniqueness of Japan, but sometimes it goes as far as to lead to consecration of Japanese history, showing a tendency to distort the general and universal perspective on the history of mankind. Due to geographically unfavorable factors, Japan suffers from frequent earthquakes and typhoons and the Japanese people live in anxiety. When this anxiety becomes stronger, it often leads to the perspective of nihilism in the present life. The obsession due to anxiety sometimes works as a factor to make the Japanese people save a lot. Furthermore, in Japan, as high mountains and rivers divide the regions distinctively, social structures and traditions vary by region. After the establishment of ancient countries, there were 65 'Kunis', and in Japan, 'Kunis' (國) usually refer to regions with different traditions rather than countries.[170]

As each region of Japan is separated by high and rugged mountains, Japan was placed in an unfavorable geographic environment to have centralized power in the pre-modern era. Also, as an island country with a certain distance from the continent, it was difficult for the continental countries to invade Japan, so Japan lacked the need to unite national power. Hence, it can be said that this was why it was difficult to strengthen the power of the king and why a social system was created in which regional lords or *samurais* ruled. Also, as Japan was an island country with a moderate distance from the continent, it was able to selectively accept continental culture based on its needs and circumstances. Even for ideology and religion, Japan was able to select only the parts that were suitable for Japan's circumstances, without the need to understand the essence and spirit. Therefore, as seen in the examples of Buddhism and Christianity, it was difficult for foreign religions or ideologies to take root in Japan.

If Japan had been connected to the Korean Peninsula by land, would the above phenomena have happened? In other words, would there have been large regional differences, and would Japan have realized a decentralized political order centering on the *samurais*? Japan's history and culture probably would have taken a different path. Sudden changes in politics and military on the continent or the Korean Peninsula would have directly influenced Japan, and a sense of crisis in foreign relations derived from this would have led Japanese history in the direction of pursuing a powerful king and a centralized government in order to aggregate the strength of Japanese society.[171]

In the case of Japan, farmlands were small, and typhoons and earthquakes were frequent, so it was inevitable to have a strong order of social status for many people to coexist with little food. Since this hierarchical order of social status was maintained through heredity, the position of each individual was fixed. Therefore, what individuals could do was to do their best within the hierarchy or group to which they belonged. It can be said that Japan's thorough craftsmanship and work ethic to become the best in one's field was created amid the hierarchical order of social status in which social mobility was impossible. Japan was the only East Asian country not to adopt the state examination system, since the idea of rising in status through a state examination was not suitable for a country where hereditary status order was strong and firm. Such characteristics were first pointed out by sociologist David Riesman.[172] Based on Riesman's idea, historian Edwin Reischauer[173] defined Japan as a goal-oriented society, while defining China or Korea as a status-oriented society. As it was impossible to rise in status in Japan, individuals pursued goals within one's social stratum, making it possible to accumulate technology, which later contributed to Japan's modernization. On the other hand, in societies that adopted the state examination system, individuals focused on one's studies in order to rise in status, which made it difficult to accumulate technology though craftsmanship.[174]

The Japanese flag Hinomaru, represents Japan (日本), or 'the place where the sun rises.' 'Ni (日) hon (本)' means 'a place that is to the east of a certain place,' and that 'certain place' is China. Therefore 'Japan' means 'a country that is to the east of China,'[175] and it is the same logic as calling Vietnam 'the country of Viet people living in the south (越南).' Therefore, at the late Tokugawa period, Sato Tadamitsu, a nationalist, asserted that the country name of 'Japan' should be changed as it represented a subject country. The geographic location of Japan influenced not only the historical name of the country but also the mentality of the people. Furthermore, Japanese people,

54

who have lived on islands, view that the center of the world is not here but somewhere in the outside world, and determine their thoughts and actions based on their sense of distance from that place. Uchida Tatsuru calls such people 'marginal people (邊境人).' As marginal people, the Japanese always are interested in what happens in the center. They endlessly peek towards the center and fail to develop the ability to think independently. The Japanese people, who are harassed with a sense of cultural inferiority compared to the center, struggle to catch up with changes in the center. To the Japanese, the center was China in the pre-modern age, the UK and Western powers in the modern age, and the US after being defeated in the war.[176]

2. Structure and Characteristics of Japanese Society

After living over 250 years under the closed hierarchical order of the Tokugawa Period, Japanese people became accustomed to obeying authority and taking collective responsibility. Confucianism, which idealized harmony, order, and knowing one's place, played an important role in creating this attitude of the Japanese people during the Tokugawa Period. Professor Ito Chosei (伊藤長正), in his book *Rediscovering Collectivism,* describes Japanese society as an extremely closed society with a strong sense of unity based on the same values.[177] The social class that led changes in the history of Japan was always the ruling class that dominated power. The general public sometimes temporarily resisted the ruling class, but eventually embraced the ideology of being dominated. As such, the idea of integration of the ruling class was always victorious, and the idea of resistance by the general public was easily succumbed by the ruling power. In this process, Japanese society naturally formed the social value of avoiding total destruction even if there were conflicts and opposition due to changes in forces leading integration, and therefore ordinary Japanese people adhered to the attitude of conforming and adapting to the general trend. Chaos in Japanese society was resolved through integration, and integration led to the unification of ideology and social systems. This aspect can be viewed in recent discussions to amend the Constitution in Japanese society which is taking a conservative swing. In the past several decades, the right-wing leaders have continued working under the table to weaken the overwhelming public opposition against amending the Constitution. In this process, the groups opposing the amendment of the Constitution have become 'resistance groups', and these groups have become too small to stand up against the integration logic. The right-wing is currently trying to amend the Constitution to enable the regal rearmament and the dispatch of Japanese military overseas. But the fact that there are almost no parties or groups to keep the right-wing in check against committing such actions is showing that Japanese society is once again forming ideological unification. This allows us to anticipate that Japan will intensify conflicts and enmity in the East Asian region in the future by pursuing military hegemony and by not yielding in historical issues and territorial disputes.[178]

In Japan, any benefit or debt from another person is called 'on (恩).' This 'on' must be repaid, does not disappear or decrease with time, and rather interest is added. When one receives great benefits from another, one sometimes responds by saying 'katajikenai (かたじけない),' and this expression means both grateful and being demeaned. This statement expresses shame for owing something to someone, and this shame, or 'haji (恥)' is one of the things that Japanese people wish to avoid the most. Also, Japanese people feel great shame in the case of being helped by their subordinate or someone who is inferior to them.[179] This is the reason that Japan refused to acknowledge the benefits it received from Korea or China which it regarded as inferior, during the process of rising as a modern country. However, Japan took a submissive attitude towards the US, which it regarded as superior, and actively sought benefits in national security and the economy from the US. Through exploitation of manpower and resources and expansion of markets, Japan received an immense amount of help from the Korean Peninsula, Taiwan, and China in growing and developing into a modern country. It can be said that Japan received 'on' from the Korean Peninsula and Taiwan, which it colonized, and from Manchuria, which it made into a puppet nation, and from China, whose rights it took possession of through invasion. Based on Japan's concept of 'on' and concept of honor, Japan needs to pay back these countries. However, Japan is either trying to deny such facts, is not aware of the debt, or is deliberately trying not to acknowledge it at all. Therefore, it can be said that Japanese people as individuals feel the burden of 'on' and wish to repay it, but collectively as a country or society, Japan has a nature of trying to avoid reciprocation of 'on (恩).'

Japanese people consider honor as one of the most important aspects of life. Their reputation being harmed or slandered or insulted in any way is unacceptable for the Japanese people. They take revenge on the person that harms or slanders their reputation, or even commit suicide to recover their honor. If they cannot take their revenge, Japanese people quietly refrain themselves as they consider keeping their face very important. According to Okakura Yoshisaburo's *The Life and Thought of Japan*,[180] Japanese people are trained to accept unavoidable stains or wounds when they cannot make an excuse to clear away an insult to their family's honor or country's pride. In other words, they do their best to keep their honor, but if the situation changes, they give up the effort to recover their honor or avoid dishonor by changing their mindset and attitude.[181] This can be clearly seen from the fact that when Japan was defeated by the US in the Pacific War, Japan advocated for the victor the US and gained benefits in terms of the economy and national security, while turning away from the less developed countries in Asia, which it had dominated. Despite the fact that the honor of Japan as a country and as a people was tarnished because Japan was criticized for failing to take responsibility for the harm it caused to the Asian countries through colonization and war of aggression, Japan did not try to recover its honor, but rather, opted to head towards the direction of damaging its honor even more, which can be understood in this context.

Another major characteristic of Japanese society is that it considers 'wa (和, harmony)' to be very important. Therefore, knowing one's place is important, and knowing where to draw the line became a basic virtue for Japanese people. Crossing the line meant death in the past, and even nowadays, it means that one must endure social treatment such as bullying and alienation. If one does not know one's place and does not do one's part, this causes harm to others and this is called '*meiwaku* (迷惑)'. In Japanese society, if one causes harm to others by failing to do one's part, one is branded as incompetent. This sort of person is considered as a person with no shame. In order to maintain a proper relationship without causing harm to others, or *meiwaku*, it is important to preemptively catch what the other party wants in advance and fulfill that need, which is called '*kikubari* (氣配り)'. What the Japanese people have in mind and what they actually say are often the opposite, and this is called '*honne* (本音, thoughts inside)' and '*tatemae* (建前, what they say)'. This two-sided attitude of Japanese people is a consideration so that other people don't feel embarrassed (*kikubari*), but is also a factor that makes it difficult to know their true thoughts. However, the attitude above of Japanese people does not consistently apply to Asian nations and their people. How could Japanese people, who consider the rule of not causing inconvenience to others as an inviolable rule, cause so much harm as to invade Asian countries and put their people in agonizing pits of hell? Also, why is it that Japanese people, who consider fathoming what the other party wants and doing it for them in advance as a virtue, do not fathom what Asian people want them to do and take necessary measures about their historical wrongdoings?

Japan emphasized 'wa (和)' in historically critical moments. During the 7th century, Prince Shotoku announced the Seventeen-Article Constitution to strongly promote centralization and the first article emphasized 'wa.' At that time on the Korean Peninsula, war among the three countries of Koguryo, Baekje, and Shilla intensified and China was unified by the Sui Dynasty which invaded Koguryo frequently. Due to these political changes in the continent, the Japanese court could not but emphasize internal harmony and unity amidst the sense of crisis that these continental countries might invade them. Even the opening words of the Imperial Rescript on Education, which was announced after the success of the Meiji Restoration, emphasized national harmony. Also, it can be considered that the Japanese Emperor's declaration of surrender after being defeated in the Pacific War was an emphasis of 'wa.' However, Japan's concept of 'wa' was an Emperor-centric ideology for the Japanese people, and the power created through this 'wa' sometimes led to actions of external invasion. The sense of superiority or hostility toward the outside world brought forth 'wa' and solidarity within Japan, but when this was expressed externally, it made it extremely easy to despise and exploit others.[182]

The spirit of 'wa' and the culture of collectivism in Japanese society can be said to be a Japanese value that was formed on the basis of being an agricultural nation centered on paddy fields. In terms of the basic characteristics of Japanese society, Kato Shoichi (加藤周一) cites competitive collectivism, secularism, and putting emphasis on the present. He says that when these characteristics turn outwards, the distinction between friend and foe becomes strong, and they become extremely exclusive. Therefore, it becomes difficult to communicate with people other than those who belong to one's own group and when a sense of superiority is added on top of it, it leads to contempt and discrimination against the outsiders.[183] A clear example of this would be modern Japan's contempt for Asian people and contemporary Japan's discrimination against Korean residents in Japan. This collectivism silences the minority voices in a group and emphasizes the common goal of the group as the most important. Thus, the sense of belonging in a group strongly dominates the mentality of its members.[184]

Due to this strong sense of belonging to groups, it is said that in Japanese society there is a sense of shifting responsibility to others, or buck-passing. As social mobility is restricted and order of rank between the upper and lower class is strictly sustained, individuals in a certain group or hierarchy only need to do one's part and the group does not ask for the individual to make autonomous decisions or take any responsibility. This is, in a sense, exemption of responsibility for individuals and buck-passing to the group. Therefore, this is considered to be a formation of an irresponsible system lacking a sense of responsibility. Since members of a group are given this exemption of responsibility, individuals are able to mechanically execute what the group asks of them towards other groups, without the independent and autonomous judgment of their actions. The reason behind why Japanese troops were so cruel in the colonies or occupied territories in Asia can be understood in this context. The merciless and cruel acts of the Japanese troops occurred because they lacked an autonomous sense of responsibility. Their deep sense of belonging and loyalty toward the group paralyzed the individuals' sense of ethics and responsibility.[185] In a sense, it can be said that this analysis is similar to Arendt's definition of the brutalities of Nazis as 'the banality of evil.'[186]

This aspect can also be examined from the perspective of a state leader's responsibility. Japan introduced Confucianism from Korea and China, but since it failed to learn about the core concept of Confucianism on the leader's 'benevolence (仁)', a political culture in which the ruler's responsibility was not questioned came to settle for a long period of time. Historically, Japan's rulers adopted an obscurantist policy, preventing ordinary people from being involved in politics, and as the people also wished to avoid resisting against power, the government's irresponsibility system was condoned and maintained.[187]

High importance is put on 'wa (和)' in Japanese society. On the other hand, it seeks to find an external scapegoat to unite the Japanese people. Such an aspect can be found in cases where medieval Japanese warriors and gangs during the modern and contemporary era killed prisoners and hostages in order to consolidate internal solidarity and raise the will to fight ahead of decisive battles. Modern Japan sacrificed countless prisoners during the war by making them subjects of bayonet or shooting drills in order to raise the will of new recruits to fight and to consolidate internal solidarity. In short, there were many cases where Japan's 'wa' or group solidarity was based on sacrifices of others.[188] Furthermore, if one fails to contribute to the 'wa' of the group and is pushed out of the group, one must bear heavy collective restrictions, and therefore individuals often show extreme exclusiveness to prove that one is a loyal member of the group. During the Kanto Earthquake, the Japanese people of that region actively participated in the massacre of Koreans and Chinese to prove that they were proper Japanese. The crueler they were to the Korean and Chinese people, the more they could prove they belonged to the group of Japanese people and feel a sense of relief, which led to more ruthless killings.[189]

As high importance was placed on 'wa,' Japanese people went to the extremes within the boundary allowed to them, at extent of not harming 'wa.' As a result, the cultures of 'mania (マニア)' or 'otaku (オタク, お宅)' came to be formed in the Japanese society.[190] Also, there are many Japanese people who give their full loyalty to one workplace, and 'itshokenmei (一生懸命),' which means giving one's entire life to a single job, is a word describing these people. This attitude of Japanese people was established in the Tokugawa Period, when the chaos of the warring state ended and a strong social status order came to rule. As a hierarchical social status order took root, it was impossible to think little of the upper class which possessed the power of the sword, and the general public who were suppressed by power, sought beauty, which was irrelevant to the ruling system, or pursued to become the best in one's field. In order to become the best in Japan or the best in the world, it was important to put all effort into trying one's best. This is why the Japanese people devoted their entire lives to their jobs, and sometimes committed suicide to prove that they had committed all their strength and mind. Thus, the social trend to discover beauty was created through the phenomenon of laying down one's life and striving to do one's best. Just as a blacksmith strived night and day to be the best in the world in making agricultural tools, a servant showed his utmost loyalty towards his master by being prepared to lay down his life. Through this social custom, the aesthetics of death came to emerge.[191]

In 1871, after the Meiji Restoration, Japan sent an observation group with Iwakura Domomi (岩倉具視, 1825-1883) as the leader to Western countries for approximately two years, to benchmark advanced institutions in order to achieve national prosperity and military power. Japan imitated and applied the institutions of Prussia, which unified Germany in 1871, and was later successful in reaching modernization under the administrative guidance of bureaucrats. Germany broke away from the bureaucrat-led system after its defeat in World War II, but Japan has maintained the bureaucrat-led socio-economic system. Western societies such as the United States and Germany put emphasis on 'equal opportunity' based on the autonomous competition of individuals and development of democracy. However, Japanese society, where bureaucracy is rampant, aimed for 'equal result' by preventing unnecessary competition and by regulating equal opportunity. Equal result ultimately means standardizing all people, and such equalization of people created human beings that focused only on their jobs and obeyed their superiors, allowing the state and society to move like the military or a factory. This social system was effective until the late 1980s, contributing in making Japan the second largest economic power in the world. However, this was no longer effective starting from the early 1990s, as the Cold War thawed and the world became globalized, and Japan has suffered from the ordeal of the 'lost 30 years.'

Japan had benchmarked the laws and institutions of the Western powers and applied them to Japanese society in the late 19th century and early 20th century in an effort to catch up with the more advanced Western nations. However, after World War II, Japan no longer followed the new stream. The new stream refers to emphasis on individuals, proliferation of democracy, increase of mutual dependence and seeking for co-existence and co-prosperity among countries. But it appears as though Japan still cannot escape much from the way of thinking of the late 19th and early 20th century. This phenomenon seems to be a result of the internal and external situation in which demilitarization and democratization, which were the basic goals after the war, could not be thoroughly implemented due to the Cold War and the Korean War. In particular, the major cause was that the figures who had led political parties, the military, the government, and industries during the militaristic period of war once again played key roles in politics, administration, economy, and business. Despite the accomplishments made so far, this will act as an obstacle for Japan's long-term growth in the future.

3. Cultural Traits of Japan

In cultural anthropologic research, cultures are divided into types based on shame (humiliation) and types based on sin. A society that sets absolute moral standards and emphasizes conscience is based on the 'culture of sin.' A person who sins can take the heavy load off one's heart by confessing one's sin instead of hiding it. The Western world falls into this category. On the other hand, in a society that is dominated by shame, a person does not feel forgiven even after one confesses one's mistake or fault and repents. As long as one's fault does not come to light, there is no need to worry, thus repentance through confession is rather an act of asking for trouble. Japan falls into the typical category of a 'culture of shame.' People who are in a society where the culture of sin is dominant tend to practice virtue as they acknowledge sin, but in the culture of shame, it is force in an external form that induces virtuous actions. Therefore, Japanese people, who belong to a culture of shame, speculate how others would judge them and decide their course of action based on the judgment of others. In short, the differences between Japanese and Western cultures are 'shame' and 'sin,' where the shame of Japanese people is an external ethic which is conscious of the public eye, and the sin of Westerners is internal.[192] We can apply this analysis of culture by Ruth Benedict to war-defeated Japan. It can then be said that Japanese people would have thought that if they were to confess their faults and crimes of colonization and war of aggression, their conscience would be burdened and more difficulties would follow in the future, which is why they are not apologizing. Despite mounting criticism from Asia and the world towards this attitude of Japan, Japan does not appear to be concerned and acts even more shamelessly. Japanese people are overlooking the fact that this attitude and behavior will further damage their national honor and bring about even greater shame.

Today's Japanese culture went through a lot of change during the course of modernization, but it can be said that its basis was made in the Tokugawa Period. In the Tokugawa Period when the warriors ruled, the sword defined not only general society but also the mental world, creating a unique culture. Therefore, a rigid and self-tormenting culture was created, in which one-sided command and obedience, stern laws, secluded hobbies restricted to one's immediate surroundings, and degenerated brothels were widespread. Just as a sword cuts through a straight line, a social system regulated by the sword has a clear line, so Japanese culture can be called a linear culture. Therefore, Japan is a rigid society that does not allow the line of hierarchical order to be disturbed. In this stern hierarchical society, Japan's literary activity lacked serious cognition on ideology, life, or society, and only sought life experiences or artistic stimulation. The only way to assuage fear and emptiness in the heart was to seek beauty in the delicate change of seasons, or croon about the futility of life. When one believes that these things allow people to realize the value of human beings, one receives self-consolation that one's life is no different from the life of a man of power, and that people are all similar. Furthermore, Japanese literature considers superbly cutting off someone's head with a sword and beautifully committing suicide to be worthwhile and has no interest in the suffering of the victim that groans in pain covered in blood. Therefore, there is no sympathy for the weak under suppression, and only the strong who suppresses and rules over others is praised.[193] This way of thinking by the Japanese people is linked to their distorted historical consciousness, which is indifferent to and refuses to acknowledge the pain of Asian countries and their people who were invaded by Japan, and furthermore, strives to remember the period in which they wielded influence based on strong power as a history of glory.

Kokugaku, the study of culture and national heritage of the island state Japan, was a discipline in the 18th century that strived to seek for the pure spirit of ancient Japan by researching Japanese classical literature. This Kokugaku was put together by Motoori Norinaga (本居宣長, 1730-1801), who strongly rejected Confucianism and Buddhism which came from China or the Korean Peninsula, and sought to find the purest Japanese spirit. *Nihongi* (*Nihon Shoki*, 日本書紀, *Chronicles of Japan*) and *Kojiki* (古事記, *Record of the Ancient Things*) are history books written during the 8th century to glorify Japanese history and raise the prestige of the Japanese Emperor. Based on these books, Motoori claimed that the existence of the sun goddess Amaterasu Omikami proved that Japan was a nation selected by god, and therefore, the Japanese people were the most superior beings in the world. This was a foolish assertion that considered legendary myth to be a historical truth and he was engrossed in fictional ethnocentrism. Motoori's ideology and Shinto (神道), the representative religion of Japan which encourages the thought that Japan is superior, were accepted by many Japanese people in order to overcome internal and external crises of the modern age and later became the ideological basis of the Meiji Restoration and invasion of the continent. Shinto, combined with the Japanese Emperor System, created the basic primal emotions of Japanese people and played a key role in unifying modern Japanese society to advance down the path of militarism.

On the other hand, when accepting foreign cultures, Japan has shown the capability to adopt the strengths of foreign cultures and make them more Japanese. Even the food introduced from China or Korea were adapted into Japanese style. For example, Chinese dumplings, which are made of vegetables or meat inside, were passed on to Japan and transformed into 'Manju' with Anko (sweet red beans) inside. Also, after the 6th century, Mahayana Buddhism was introduced to Japan, but combined with folk religion, it was changed into a new form. As for Confucianism, the theory of neo-Confucianism was introduced, but the essential logic and philosophy was eliminated and it only played the role of supplementing practical laws and ethics and influencing the creation of Kokugaku, the study of culture and national heritage of Japan. In short, difficult and logical ideologies and philosophies were introduced, but in the process of being spread and applied to Japanese society, the contents were altered by being fused with Japan's unique features. In other words, the outer shell was from China and other countries, but the core contents inside were structured as Japanese. The Japanese called this 'Wakon Hosai (和魂漢才, 'Japanese Spirit, Chinese learning'),' meaning that they utilized the studies or arts from China based on Japanese tradition and spirit. In the modern age, Japan actively introduced Western culture, which was more advanced than Eastern culture. This concept was called 'Wakon Yosai (和魂洋才, 'Japanese spirit, Western learning'),' meaning that they developed Japanese society by utilizing the science and technology of the West based on Japanese tradition and spirit. This way of thinking and attitude of the Japanese people became the driving force of further developing the existing Japanese culture and also creating a new Japanese culture. This greatly contributed to Japan's leap from a peripheral nation to a central nation in Asia. Furthermore, it played a crucial role in post-war Japan's revival of its economy and achievement of high economic growth.[194]

The cultural characteristics of Japanese society is often described as having 'a tendency to reduce.' However, this is not applicable to politics and religion since political leaders and religious authority have a tendency to expand. As the status and authority of a leader expands, the position of the ordinary people inversely shrinks. As shown through the great tombs of ancient Japanese kings and noblemen, political power and religious authority tended to expand. When a superior rose to the status of being a god, the ordinary people would consider themselves as dust or rubbish and even considered dying for the god as something trivial. It is inevitable that when the status and authority of the Japanese Emperor and high nobleman rises, the general public is reduced to an even lower status.[195]

The life curve of Japanese people is in a wide U-shape, in which newborn babies and the elderly are granted maximum freedom and indulgence. Adults teach children that they will be subject to ridicule if they act wrong. We can call this etiquette. Children must learn how to control themselves. As they become older, Japanese people are demanded more and more to obey the duties to their family, neighbors, society, and nation. The benefits they have received from other people, society, and nation are interpreted as 'on (恩 =favor)' and from it, they have a sense of repaying that debt. In Japanese society where returning a favor is considered most important, spiritual favors must be repaid throughout one's entire life and material favors must be repaid immediately. Therefore, in order to pay such debt, Japanese people have to be careful of the world and work hard as debtors for life.[196] However, when considering the manner in which the Japanese had treated the Asian countries and their people after the Meiji Restoration, such an attitude and behavior seems to apply only among Japanese people and not apply outside Japan.

Japanese people have a culture that is extremely devoted to record-keeping. During World War II, US troops discovered many memos and diaries within the belongings of fallen and captured Japanese soldiers and were able to figure out the psychology of Japanese soldiers or their military operations by reading and analyzing them. Japanese soldiers recorded even the smallest things in great detail, sometimes including military secrets. This habit of leaving detailed records has to do with the attitude of doing one's best even with the smallest things. This appears to be rooted in the animistic tendencies believing that there is a god in even the smallest things. An interesting fact is that during the 9th century when Chang Bogo (張保皐), a General of Shilla in the Korean Peninsula, grasped maritime power in East Asia, Yenjin (Jikaku-daiji, 慈覺大師) kept an extremely detailed description of Chang in his diary, while he traveled back and forth between Japan and Tang China with Chang's help.[197] In this regard, during the early 20th century when Japan colonized and invaded other nations, Japanese government officials, soldiers, and many civilians would presumably have left extremely detailed records of even their faults, but few records have been revealed. Rather, before the occupation of US troops, Japanese people burnt many government documents and records that would have been unfavorable to Japan and tried to hide their shame. Furthermore, nowadays, they are denying or distorting historical facts that include their faults.

There is a saying in Japan, 'If something smells fishy, cover it up (臭い物 に蓋をする),' which shows that Japanese people have a mindset of believing that settling a matter in accordance to one's convenience is enough. The saying, 'Crossing a red light is not scary if everyone crosses together', can be understood in the same context. After being defeated in the war, the Prime Minister of the Cabinet suggested the 'All 100 Million People Repent' campaign, which implied that if Japanese people shouted once in unison 'I am sorry' for the crimes that Japanese people extensively committed together, then everything would be resolved. Also, 'wa (和),' which has been regarded as important in Japanese history since the ancient times, means that one should accept reality as it is and refrain from words or actions that cause trouble.[198] In this aspect, Japan did not truly repent or apologize for the past colonization or invasions. There were instances where Japan reluctantly apologized when pressured by circumstances, but soon after, rightwing politicians would make reckless remarks, making the world doubt Japan's sincerity.

As Japanese people lived in a strict hierarchical order of rank during the Tokugawa Period and the modern era under the Japanese Emperor's rule, they became accustomed to believing that the world was beyond their control. In a sense, Japanese society has suppressed personal emotions in order to enforce hierarchical public order and eliminated affection among families, which led to the formation of a unique culture of 'loyalty' in Japan. As Japanese people have lived believing that absolute obedience to hierarchical organizations and power is a virtue, having conversations is not thought to be of importance. The Japanese etiquette of not talking or making sounds while eating is related to the social atmosphere that considers accepting one's fate and being silent a virtue. The Japanese saying, 'The eye speaks as much as the mouth,' means that one can grasp the will of others through intuition rather than through conversation. Well-planned order is important in Japan and as the order of external appearance and inner thoughts exist separately, figuring out this invisible thinking of other person is a key factor in social and organizational life.[199]

The characteristics of the lives and culture of Japanese people can be understood through community lifestyles and practical ethics such as frugality, honesty, respect for the elderly, and harmony. These practical ethics have influence on not only the everyday lives of individuals, but also the characteristics of groups and business management. In Japanese society, there is a communication culture of tacit understanding based on mutual trust. The sentiment of 'wa,' which backs up the collectivism of Japanese society, is reflected in the everyday life and culture, including food. Both community lifestyle and tradition of collectivistic culture based on such lifestyle has contributed to the establishment of a monolithic ideology which makes it easier to integrate an organization or nation. For example, the ideology of the Emperor System was established in the mid to late 19th century in order to overcome internal and external troubles and lead the creation of a modern nation. Ever since, the Japanese Emperor has dominated the spiritual domains of Japanese people, reigning at the height of the state governance system. It is true that after being defeated in the war, the status of the Japanese Emperor was converted to 'Symbolic Emperor' and its position as a governance ideology was weakened, but even to this day, the Japanese Emperor remains as an ideological subject of worship in the minds of Japanese people. This sentiment is one of the reasons why the conservative swing of Japanese society nowadays is gaining acceptance. Meanwhile, the practical ethics mentioned above focuses more on the value of self-discipline in order to overcome crises, rather than the expression of critical views on social structure. Therefore, it is difficult to display patterns of social criticism within the Japanese society and the top-down integration ideology is easily accepted under the pretext of filial obedience and harmony. As a result, there are few extreme conflicts within Japanese society and the culture of 'managed society' or 'enterprise society' was able to be easily formed.[200]

4. The Samurai Tradition and Traits of Japanese People

The biggest characteristic that differentiates Japan from other Asian nations is the *samurai* (侍) culture. This is because the warrior groups ruled the land for over 700 years and this has had a huge impact on not only the domains of daily life but also the spiritual area of Japanese society. As the governing power of the central government was no longer influential in the provincial areas due to the collapse of the centralized political system after the Heian Era in Japan, influential people within the provincial areas armed themselves to protect their lives and land, which was how warriors, or *samurais*, came to emerge. A master-servant relationship was formed between landlords and *samurais*, and although a certain level of practical calculations was inherent in the loyalty and valor of *samurais*, there was a certain level of morality as well. In the *samurai* society, social cohesion and bonding based on loyalty towards the lord often took precedence over familial relationships. In other words, loyalty to the group, including the lord, was glorified as a necessity for the maintenance of society and was considered as the greatest value of *samurai* society. Hence, death was the best way to show loyalty and *samurais* became as brave as to think lightly of death on the battlefield, and sometimes took their own lives to protect their honor. As death was recognized as the expression of the greatest loyalty and valor and a means of raising honor, *harakiri* became a ritual to prove this. *Harakiri* is committing suicide by cutting one's abdomen with the sword and is accompanied by immense pain as it does not lead to immediate death. It was a method of death that required extreme courage. Therefore, *harakiri* received the highest praise within *samurai* society, and the honorable death of a *samurai* became an object of art and rose to the level of aesthetics. Therefore, literary works about *samurais* often depicted stories where a main character with fault or a moral defect was able to erase his fault by gallantly meeting his end and leaving behind a sorrowful beauty that his heroic death brought.

All *samurais* were taught to have loyalty and a sense of duty to their lord or warrior group according to their hierarchical status. Therefore, *samurais* possessed a much stronger concept of 'loyalty' and 'shame' compared to ordinary people. As Confucianism was introduced to the ruling class during the Tokugawa Period, loyalty and shame, strong sense of duty, and sense of honor became more universal throughout the entire society than before and it even developed to becoming legislated into law beyond the level of ethical behavior. As *samurai* ethics took root within the entire society in such a way, it has still been acknowledged as holding an important value even until the modern and contemporary Japan era.

However, an ideology or ethic only applies to the specific period it is in

66

and as time and society changes, its legitimacy becomes weaker in most cases. If certain ethic or life attitudes that had been appropriate and popular during the time when *samurai* groups ruled is still widely adopted in today's society, which has gone through cataclysmic change, then it may require going over the concept once again and seeing if it is appropriate to be still applied in today's society. Let us examine a case under such perspective. In 1701, Asano Naganori (淺野長矩, 1667-1701), the lord of Ako Castle living in Edo (today's Tokyo) due to the *Sankin Kotai* (參勤交代, alternate attendance), was under the command of Kira Yoshinaka (吉良義央, 1641-1703), a high official of the Shogunate. However, due to quarrel caused by a conflict of opinion, Asano wounded Kira with his sword. At that time during the Tokugawa Period, in order to establish peace, warriors were forbidden from drawing their swords within the castle walls and the law stipulated that one must perform *harakiri* if this were to be violated. According to the law, Asano was ordered to commit suicide and he eventually died unfairly, whereas there was no punishment for Kira. The 47 men of Asano (浪人, ronin), who lost their master, elaborated a plan to attack Kira to avenge their master. They attacked Kira's house in 1703 and after beheading him offered it in front of their master's grave. In respect to the punishment of these 47 men, there was a debate within the Shogunate of the time over whether it should be considered as an act of loyalty to their master or a violation of law, but eventually they were all ordered to perform *harakiri*. Their actions gained much sympathy among the general public, and this incident was made into a work of art and was performed in the Kabuki (歌舞伎) under the name of 'Jushingura (忠臣藏).'

Loyalty and fidelity shown in this incident is based on the relationship and promise between the master and the vassal, and does not consider whether the master was right or wrong. The concept of duty, honor, fidelity, and shame of *samurais*, which were developed through Confucianism adopted during the Tokugawa Period, did not have universal characteristics that can be accepted in any society, but rather, was merely a group ethic which existed only in the *samurai* society. In this context, the remark made by the famous Japanese ideologist Maruyama Masao (丸山眞男, 1914-1996)[201] that 'There have been many Japanese politicians or businessmen who laid down their lives for groups such as their political party or company but not many who died for universal truths or justice,' is quite appropriate. Although Japan caused much pain and suffering to Asian nations through colonization and invasion, due to the fact that Japan suffered from two atomic bombings and millions of Japanese troops and civilians were sacrificed in the war, Japanese people seem to think that they have already paid the price and everything has been settled. Japan sets no account on the violence it caused and the immense damage it brought forth, and only places importance on the damage it experienced at the later stage of war. In other words, it seems that Japan is not concerned about the fundamental justification and matter of universality that its action itself holds.

During the Medieval and Warring States period, surviving was important for the *samurais*, due to the frequent warfare and chaos. However, during the Tokugawa period, since peace and order had been settled, the manner of death became more important for the *samurais*.[202] Therefore, *harakiri*, which demonstrated a *samurai*'s utmost loyalty, was praised and eventually, specific rules for *harakiri* were made. As *samurais* always carried a sword, strict discipline was crucial in minimizing conflicts and friction, as a trivial remark or action could cause misunderstanding and lead to a swordfight. This may be the reason as to why abusive language against another person is not well-developed in Japan.[203] When Japanese people actually do use insulting language, they use words such as 'Baka' (馬鹿, Stupid), or 'Manuke' (間抜け, Idiot), which is not that heavy. It may be due to the fact that in a strict hierarchical society ruled by the sword, a clumsy joke or insulting language could lead to a huge misfortune.[204]

In this regard, if the *samurai* code makes further progress, the reason for martial arts could change from winning over an opponent with the sword to not making enemies in the first place. In a broad sense, if the 'enemy' is defined as everything that causes harm to one's mind and body, then everything surrounding oneself and even oneself can become an enemy, making it become impossible to defeat. Therefore, it can be said that being invincible in martial arts refers to a person who does not make enemies at all.[205] However, it is doubtful whether Japan's *samurai* code has sublimated to such dimension. Chivalry, which emerged during the feudal society of medieval Europe, embraced Christianity while going through the modern era, and was reborn as gentlemanship (紳士道), which later came to lead European society. However, in Japan, there were no religions providing a cultural and ideological basis such as Christianity. Therefore, Japan's warrior code that considers loyalty as the greatest virtue, could not escape the boundaries of the military or ruling group, and during the process of modernization, it degenerated into a sub-ideology to serve nationalism. Therefore, modern Japan imposed a distorted concept of the warrior code, forcing people to lay down their lives for the Japanese Emperor and state and try their best to repay the grace of the Emperor at the risk of their lives. In other words, the idea of the *samurai*'s warrior code had changed from showing loyalty towards one's master being the regional lord, to showing loyalty towards the Japanese Emperor, who was the symbol of nationalism.[206]

The role of *samurais* was immense in leading the Meiji Restoration to success and propelling modernization in Japan. In the backdrop was the influence of the status and nature of *samurais*. *Samurai* was a hereditary status, but under the system in which *shoguns* and *daimyos* ruled, *samurais* lived on stipends paid in compensation for the bureaucratic work that they performed.

Therefore, unlike literary noblemen in China or Korea, *samurais* did not own fixed property (恒産) such as land and as they left the rural areas and resided in urban areas they became the consumer class. Accordingly, as the socio-economic foothold of *samurais* was unstable and vulnerable, they were directly affected by and had to respond sensitively to changes in the outside world. Such socio-economic status and background of *samurais* became the driving force behind dreaming of a new society and pushing for revolution during the mid-19th century when Tokugawa Japan was suffering from internal and external issues. In particular, low class *samurais* of the Satsuma domain (薩摩藩) and Choshu domain (長州藩) in the southwest region of Japan actively participated in the reform of their domains and paid sharp attention to the international situation. They played a key role in forming a new modern state system centering on the Japanese Emperor under the flag of Sonno Joi (尊王攘夷, 'Revere the Emperor, Expel the Barbarians'). However, despite the positive role of *samurais* in the formation of modern Japan, the negative historical legacy put at the root of the *samurai* spirit cannot be overlooked. The greatest achievement that a *samurai* could achieve prior to the modern times was being ready to die for one's lord, and if a *samurai* failed to achieve one's mission, he would prove his loyalty by committing suicide. After the Meiji Restoration, the *samurai's* loyalty not only shifted towards the Japanese Emperor, but also shifted towards the modern state of Japan as well. As the Japanese people were ready to lay down their lives to prove loyalty, when it comes to the act of massacring or raping Asians, who were considered uncivilized, the Japanese people considered it insignificant.[207]

Japan went through an age governed by the *samurai* ideology and culture. Therefore, since utmost importance was placed on 'wa' and top-down hierarchy was strictly implemented in Japan, anyone who violated this 'wa' was ostracized. In this kind of social environment, a person that stands out from the crowd suffers consequences such as bullying. Therefore, Japanese people strictly align their outward appearance and behavior in conformity to the organization or society's expectation and conceal their inner thoughts. In relation to this behavior, the so-called Syncretism (習合思想), which was to learn, master and internalize things that are useful to oneself and the society without hesitation, settled into Japan. It became a characteristic of Japanese people to openly adopt a new idea as long as it is good regardless of its origin and modify it to fit their circumstances. Such characteristic is called Iitokotori (良いとこ取り).

It is said that Japanese people do not question why things are the way they are. They are merely not interested in knowing when things came to be and accept things the way they are already. They also have the tendency to submissively accept an already solidified fact. Therefore, in Japan, a policy is accepted without much differentiation, whether it is a policy just enacted or a policy made one hundred years ago. According to Uchida, Japanese people, as marginal people, show the behavioral tendencies of dependence, reliance, variability, lack of centrality, realism, compliance with the general trend, and blindly following. Therefore, it is difficult to find autonomous and independent individuals in Japan, whereas the power of the group that puts forward harmony and integration is extremely strong. There are few cases in which an individual opposes the general trend for the sake of his or her name. Japanese people are used to following the surrounding atmosphere or trend rather than making an independent decision and they avoid trying to change a situation upon their own will. Accordingly, Japanese people show high effectiveness and great capability when emulating previous successful cases as a latecomer, but reveal a vulnerability when they are taking the lead in a certain field.[208]

It is said that the men of modern Japan became different men and turned into reckless nationalists after receiving severe and offensive military training. This was, on the one hand, influenced by the indoctrination of collectivist state theory and stressing of loyalty towards the Japanese Emperor, but the biggest reason appears to have been the experience of humiliating punishments and beatings from the military. When young men who had received strict education in the family and had been obsessed with 'self-esteem (amour-propre)' or honor were faced with such humiliating situations, they were prone to losing their mind and turning into beasts. Since they could not directly respond to the humiliation on the spot, they waited until they became superiors and treated new recruits more harshly than they themselves had been treated, and this even led to abusing prisoners or killing them mercilessly.[209] In other words, the less power a person has, the more sadistic a person can become, when given the power. Japanese soldiers who had been in the lowest ranks of power used Asian people as an outlet for all the humiliation they had experienced so far and became that much more brutal. Such attitude of the Japanese people has not changed much after being defeated in the war and has influenced Japanese society by continuing to exist within companies and various social organizations. It is said that Japanese people consider recovering their honor by taking revenge on the indignity they suffered as a lifelong task. It is then justifiable for China, Taiwan, Korea, and other Asian countries that suffered from national and ethnic ridicule and indignity to take revenge. Despite this fact, since these countries have not taken revenge on Japan, it is reasonable to say that Japan received 'on (恩)'. If so, it is reasonable for Japan to repay for this 'on' that they have received. If this is not repaid, it becomes a shame for Japan as well. Furthermore, why is it that Japan is enduring the ridicule from other countries by failing to take responsibility over colonization and invasion wars? Are Japanese people truly unaware of the fact that the best way to escape from such shame is to look squarely at the problem, honestly admit it, and apologize for it, rather than evading it?

Historically, in Japan, incidents among the ruling class, such as a power shift, usually took place without any connection with the general public. The reason why the Meiji Restoration was able to instantly get rid of over 300 regional political bodies was largely due to the fact that the general public considered this sort of restoration as a matter concerning the *samurai* or men of power, having absolutely nothing to do with them. Similar to the Meiji Restoration, the Battle of Sekigahara that triggered the launch of the Tokugawa military government and the struggles of political factions for political power during modern Japan, both achieved a shift of power through the same pattern without involving the general public. Therefore, in Japan, there have been many cases of regime change within the ruling power, but there have been no cases in which the ruling power itself changed nor so much as an attempt to do so. In this sense, be it Toyotomi, Tokugawa, MacArthur, Koizumi, Abe, or Suga, it did not matter to the general public who reigned. Consequently, as it was an issue irrelevant to them and only concerned the top authorities, the general public were in no environment to dream of a revolution. Therefore, the Japanese people have worked themselves to death in their own fields with such fervor.[210]

Unlike in Western society, it is difficult for the Japanese to persuade others or come up with a rational solution through a form of discussion or debate. The method of rational persuasion of one's logic shows 'You can reach the same conclusion if you were to use rational reasoning with the same given information as myself.' However, in Japanese society and political atmosphere, such method of persuasion is not used. The widely used method is the type of argument showing 'I have more information than you and I can reason more rationally than you can, therefore my conclusion is correct and yours is wrong.' If one can merely prove that one is superior to the other, then the authenticity or legitimacy of the logic or message one wishes to convey no longer matters. What takes precedence is not what is right, but who appears more likely to be right. The purpose of question and answer among the Japanese people is not to arrive at the right answer, but to show that there exists an asymmetric relationship between the one questioning and the one being questioned. Therefore, the characteristic of communication within Japanese society shows that the determination of who is superior between the sender and the receiver takes priority over the message itself.[211] In this sense, Japan remained silent and took on a submissive attitude towards international society regarding its historical wrongdoings such as colonization and war of aggression. However, as Japan rose to be an economic power and gained the means of becoming a military power, the attitude of Japan began to change by starting to deny or distort historical facts and avoiding apology and responsibility. It can also be interpreted that these aspects are displayed due to the Japanese people having dual personalities, both as individuals and as a group. They sugarcoat this with specious concepts such as *tatemae* (建前,

façade, lip service) and *honne* (本音, inner thoughts). However, in reality, Japanese people only show *tatemae* when they are powerless and feel constrained towards their counterpart. Then, when they gain power and no longer need to stoop low, Japanese people reveal their *honne*.[212]

CHAPTER 3

THE TWO-FACED JANUS SUSTAINING JAPAN: CONSTITUTION AND EMPEROR SYSTEM

The Meiji Constitution, along with the Japanese Emperor system, acted as a stepping stone for Japan to rise as a modern state after the Meiji Restoration. After the Meiji Restoration, modern Japan had debates on how to form the state system. This came down to two key tasks of what form the constitution, the fundamental law of a state, should take and what position the Japanese Emperor should take. The leaders of the Meiji government tried to learn advanced culture and institutions by dispatching large delegations to advanced nations such as the United States, United Kingdom, and Germany. After 20 years of heated debate, they furnished the foundation for a modern state system by announcing a Constitution mainly emulating the German model and by placing the Japanese Emperor in a position of the bearer of sovereignty and owner of divine power. However, modern Japan's Constitution and the Japanese Emperor System showed the aspects of Janus, as they greatly contributed to Japan's successful modernization in material terms but also played the role of locomotive in causing immense pain and damage to Asian countries through colonization and invasion.

1. The Japanese Constitution

After the Meiji Restoration, amidst the Jiyu Minken Undo (自由民權運動, Freedom and Civil Rights Movement) in the civilian sector, Japan proceeded with the establishment of the constitution and the modern Japanese Emperor system as a constitutional monarchy. In 1874, the Jiyu Minken Undo took place, requesting the Meiji government for land tax reduction, establishment of the parliament and enactment of the constitution. Former *samuris*, landlords, merchants, industry workers and the poorest farmers participated in the Jiyu Minken Undo which had been triggered by the submission of the 'White Paper for Establishing National Diet (民選議院設立建白書)' by Itagaki Taisuke (板垣退助, 1837-1919) and others. In 1880, this movement expanded into the entire nation and various first drafts of the constitution were presented. In response to the Jiyu Minken Undo, in 1881, there were conflicts within the Meiji government between Okuma Shigenobu (大隈重信, 1838-1922), who sought for the British constitutional monarchy centered on the parliament, and Iwakura Domomi (岩倉具視, 1825-1883) and Ito Hirobumi (伊藤博文, 1841-1909), who pursued the establishment of the German constitutional system with a strong monarchy. However, in October of the same year, Ito Hirobumi, backed by the Japanese Emperor, promised to establish a constitution by 1889 and launch a parliament by 1890 through the Imperial Order (勅諭, an announcement made by the monarch himself), and settled the heated debate on the enactment of a constitution by expelling Okuma from the Meiji government.[213]

Detailed preparations for the establishment of the constitution on the part of the Meiji government began at the initiative of Ito Hirobumi in 1882. In order to prepare a draft constitution, Ito Hirobumi visited major European countries with a large delegation to study European constitutions for 18 months starting from March 1882. After his visit to Europe, Ito decided to establish a constitution based on the German model, reflecting the opinions of constitutional scholars, such as Rudolf von Gneist and Lorenz von Stein. Thus, Ito drafted a constitution through consultations with German advisors, Hermann Roesler and Alfred Mosse.[214] In June 1886, the draft constitution went through the assessment of the Privy Council, and in February 1889, the Meiji Constitution (The Constitution of the Empire of Japan) was established and announced in the form of the Japanese Emperor having created and bestowed it. The Meiji government attempted to establish the constitution with the intent of pacifying the request of the Jiyu Minken Undo (Freedom and Civil Rights Movement), but the contents did not take the form that the movement intended. The Meiji Constitution stipulated that the Japanese Emperor was the sole sovereign power and all government agencies were placed under the Japanese Emperor. Takashiro Koichi summarizes the characteristics of this Meiji Constitution into six features. First, the Meiji Constitution simultaneously contained the factors of centralized nationalism and constitutionalism. Second, the Japanese Emperor (天皇, Tenno) dominated sovereign power and all state power. Third, civil liberties guaranteed by the constitution were merely a 'right of a subject' granted by the Japanese Emperor. Fourth, the House of Lords, which consisted of members appointed by the Japanese Emperor, were able to keep the elected House of Representatives in check and balance. Fifth, the Japanese Emperor had the power to declare an order without Parliament's deliberation and could issue an urgent imperial order. Sixth, the Japanese Emperor had an independent prerogative of supreme command to order the military without consultation with Parliament or the government.[215]

The constitutions of Western nations basically had the purpose of checking and balancing the power abuse of the monarch or leader, protecting the lives and properties of the general public, and guaranteeing their political participation. In contrast, the Meiji Constitution put the Japanese Emperor in the position of a sovereign ruler and allowed him to exercise supreme power over the legislative, judicial, and executive branches of the state. Despite this fact, according to the tradition of keeping his distance from power and limiting his role in justifying power, the Japanese Emperor did not properly exercise this absolute power. As a result, the powers of each sector were not properly controlled or coordinated and as Japan was at that time being led by external expansionists such as the military authorities, it was inevitable for modern Japan to strengthen its policy of militarism and accelerate colonization and war of aggression against Asian countries. In that sense, if Japan's Jiyu Minken Undo of the 1870s and 1880s had been successful and a model of the British parliamentary democracy had been settled, modern Japan would have been able to free itself from its history of invasion and grow as the true leading country of Asia.

British history after the 13th century can be summarized as limitation of the monarch's power, enforcement of parliamentary power, and expansion of political rights of the people. The French Revolution in the late 18th century and the Napoleon Wars in the early 19th century intensified criticism and offense on monarchism. As a reaction to this, a system of cooperation among the monarch nations in Europe was reinforced at the instigation of Metternich. However, this cooperation system among the monarch nations met its greatest crisis in the early 20th century due to various incidents. The fall of the Qing Dynasty in China due to the Xinhai Revolution in 1911 and the emergence of a republic, the fall of Czarist Russia following the Bolshevik Revolution in 1917, and the fall of the German Empire due to defeat in World War I showed that monarchy was confronted with a crisis all throughout the world. Even in Japan, the Taisho Emperor, who emerged after the death of the Meiji Emperor, had a dwindling influence as an absolute monarch due to the lack of governing capacity and physical health problem. Also, during this period in Japan, there was a boost in civil movements and a stronger tendency to value parliamentary and party politics, leading to the development of democracy (Taisho Democracy).[216] Amidst these internal and external circumstances, there were no modifications or amendments to the Meiji Constitution, but the power of political parties and the authority of the Parliament became stronger, weakening the despotic forces centered on the Japanese Emperor. What reflected the trend of such Taisho Democracy was the Emperor Organ Theory (天皇機關說) by Professor Minobe Tatsukichi (美濃部達吉, 1873-1948) of Tokyo Imperial University. Through the *Constitutional Speech* (憲法講話) in 1912 and *Constitutional Requirement* (憲法撮要) in 1923, Tatsukichi presented a theory of constitution interpretation that sovereign power belongs to the state, which is a corporate body, and that the Japanese Emperor merely executes sovereign power as the highest organ of the state. This Emperor Organ Theory became the dominant constitutional theory in Japan during the 1910s and 1920s.[217]

However, as Japan triggered the Manchurian Incident and enforced the militarist system, the rightwing forces strongly criticized Minobe and aggression intensified in Parliament as well. Eventually, in 1935, a publication ban was placed on his books. Now that the Emperor Organ Theory was banished from the academic world and even the constitutional theory centered on the Parliament was denounced, the Japanese Emperor was elevated to a godlike figure under the Meiji Constitution and Emperor Showa was revered as a human god (現人神, Arahitogami). Since the Japanese Emperor institutionally possessed absolute power and was also recognized as a godlike figure, the Japanese Emperor could not be free from the responsibility of the war which Japan waged during his reign. Japan continued the war under the motto of 'death and no surrender', but eventually ended the war with the Japanese Emperor's declaration of surrender. In this sense, the Emperor was responsible for not having ended the war earlier and preventing further damage. The fact that he had the power to end the war ultimately meant that he was in a position to prevent the war. Therefore, he had the responsibility of failing to prevent the war. Even though it was difficult to make the Japanese Emperor take responsibility for the war due to America's governing strategy of occupied territories later on, it can be said that he would have been required to make Japan bear the full responsibility of apologizing and making reparations for the damages caused to Asian countries and their people through war of aggression. After the defeat in war, as the symbolic Japanese Emperor under the new constitution, he should have made the Japanese government do that at the very least. Also, he had the responsibility to correct the distorted historical perceptions that the Japanese government and its people ceaselessly pursue and enhance peace and collaboration with neighboring countries. Considering the Japanese Emperor's enormous power stipulated by the Constitution and the divine authority that was formed during the 1930s and 1940s, comments such as the ones above may be raised.

The ruling powers of Japan wished to maintain the Japanese Emperor system after being defeated in World War II and MacArthur wished to use the Japanese Emperor to enable stable occupational rule. As mutual interests matched, the Japanese Emperor system continued to exist in the new constitution in the form of a symbol figure. Therefore, postwar Japan established the so-called 'Peace Constitution,' which gave sovereignty, something that used to solely belong to the Japanese Emperor in the old constitution, back to the people, enhanced basic human rights, and gave up on war. However, with the intensification of the Cold War and the breakout of the Korean War, requests to amend this constitution poured out not only from the United States, which had initially presented a draft of this constitution, but also from the Japanese government and political parties. But, this triggered the efforts of the Japanese people, who had gone through the wretchedness of war, to protect the Peace Constitution even more. Japanese people proceeded with movements against the expropriation of land near US military bases and movements to ban atomic or hydrogen bomb experiments in the 1950s. In particular, there was a large-scale demonstration against the amendment of the US-Japan Security Treaty in 1960, leading the Japanese government to assume a passive attitude toward constitutional amendment. As a result, Japan has attempted to achieve the effect of amending the Constitution through the interpretation and application of the Constitution. However, since the 1990s when the Cold War thawed, arguments supporting constitutional amendment have built up under the grounds that there have been amplified requests from the United States for Japan to reinforce its defense capacity and internal voices within Japan that Japan should contribute to international society.

After the emergence of the Abe government, Japan has actively contributed to the security cooperation between the US and Japan by allowing the right of collective self-defense and has pushed ahead with various measures, including constitutional reform, to expand its military influence. Self-defense can be categorized into individual self-defense and collective self-defense, in which individual self-defense can be understood as 'the right of a state to defend itself with military power, in the case of a pressing invasion from other state'. It is considered that Japan not only holds but can also exercise this right of individual self-defense. Collective self-defense is generally defined as 'the right of a state with a close relationship with an invaded state to come forward in joint defense when the other state has been hit by a military attack.' With respect to this collective self-defense, the established interpretation has been that Japan 'holds this right but its exercise is prohibited by the Constitution.' There could be three ways in which the exercise of this right of collective self-defense could be possible. In other words, these could be alteration in the interpretation of the Constitution, enactment of a basic law on national security, and amendment of the Constitution. The Japanese government is currently pushing ahead with all three measures, although there is a difference in time. Of course, the ultimate goal of right wing conservatives is to amend the Peace Constitution so that Japan can legitimately hold military power and actively wield it on the international stage.

2. The Emperor System of Japan

Many people consider the Japanese Emperor system as the most unique feature among Japan's institutions. Even when excluding the fictional age of myths, the Japanese Emperor system historically existed for at least 1300 years. It is especially astonishing that Emperors of the same bloodline continued to succeed throughout that period. Above all, the geographical factor of being an island nation played a big role. The Mongolian Empire, which had coerced the Goryeo Dynasty of the Korean Peninsula into submission, invaded Japan twice during the 13th century but it was easy for Japan to defend itself thanks to climatic factors such as the typhoon. The second instance of invasion from external forces was during the mid-20th century, when the Allied Forces led by the United States attacked and occupied mainland Japan in the process of ending World War II. At that time, MacArthur's plan to use the Japanese Emperor for a smooth execution of the occupation policy and the objective of Japan's ruling powers to maintain the Japanese Emperor System coincided. Therefore, Japan managed to survive its biggest crisis in history by transfiguring the godlike Japanese Emperor with absolute power into a symbolic figure of national unity and adopting the Peace Constitution. In the history of Japan, the Japanese Emperor did not directly have or exercise power, with the exceptions of the 200 years from the Taika Reforms (大化改新, 645) when royal authority was strengthened to the start of 'Sekkan (攝關) Politics' by the Sessho (攝政) or Kanpaku (關白) during the mid-9th century and 77 years after the Meiji Restoration. In other words, the Japanese Emperor was merely a source of authority to give legitimacy to the power of the Sekkan (攝關) or Shogun (將軍). Therefore, as the Japanese Emperor did not exist as the absolute power holder in most of Japanese history, he was not a target to be overthrown by men of actual power, such as the Shogun and was rather utilized as a factor to justify their power. Perhaps due to this tradition, there were hardly any cases where the Japanese Emperor in modern Japan directly exercised substantial power, even though he gained absolute power pursuant to the Meiji Constitution. These factors came into play to maintain the bloodline of the Japanese Emperor for over 1,300 years.

Up until the early 6th century, Japan consisted of many regional states, among which the 'Yamato State,' which was an alliance of clans surrounding Yamato (大和, present day Nara (奈良)), dominated most of the regional states during the mid-6th century. The king of the Yamato State was called the Great King (大王) as he reigned over other regional states. However, as the royal authority was not strong, politics was at the mercy of powerful families such as Soga (蘇我) or Mononobe (物部). The period between 672 and 710, when Emperors Tenmu (天武), Jito (持統), and Monmu (文武) reigned, was the time when the state system centered around the Japanese Emperor system was completed. It was also during this time that the country name of 'Nihon or Nippon (日本, Japan)' started to be used instead of 'Wa (倭)' as well as the deified title 'Tenno (天皇, Japanese Emperor)' instead of Great King. As Japan is divided into several regions by high and rugged mountains, it was not suitable to have a nationwide system of centralized power. However, at the time, Baekje of Korea was overthrown by the combined forces of Shilla of Korea and Tang of China and the backup forces deployed by Japan to aid Baekje suffered a big defeat. Furthermore, the combined forces of the two nations had also overthrown Gogureo in Korea and this sparked a sense of crisis to the Japanese. Accordingly, Japan could not but push ahead with centralization of power and focused all authority into one place. In order to raise the authority of the Japanese Emperor and to establish the legitimacy of the nation, Japan moved its capital by creating the Heijokyo (平城京) in the Nara (奈良) region in 710 and officialized the title of 'Tenno (天皇, Japanese Emperor)' and the country name of 'Nihon or Nippon(日本, Japan)'. The period between 710 and 794 is called the Nara Period and during this period, Japan published *Kojiki (Record of the Ancient Things,* 古事記, 712) and *Nihongi (Nihon Shoki, Chronicles of Japan,* 日本書紀, 720), which contained mythical stories about the Japanese Emperor's ancestors, in order to show the authority of the Japanese Emperor and Japan both internally and externally. During the Nara Period, rather than going through the Korean Peninsula that had been the intermediary of civilization, Japan sent missions to Tang of China and directly brought in China's advanced culture and institutions that later furnished the basis in creating a unique Japanese culture. However, royal authority weakened as the need for centralization of power decreased with the fading threat of external invasion and as the power of noblemen and temples became stronger. Therefore, in 794, Emperor Kanmu (桓武) moved Japan's capital to Heian (平安, present day Kyoto) to overcome the situation.[218]

After moving the capital to Heian, there was less need for the Japanese Emperor to intervene in politics since the system of the royal court was sorted out and the authority of the Japanese Emperor was reinforced. Hence, the Fujiwara (藤原) family became the maternal relatives of the Japanese Emperor for generations and substantially conducted state affairs as a Sessho (攝政, role of assisting an underage Emperor) or Kanpaku (關白, role of assisting an adult Emperor). This political situation that lasted from the mid-9th century to the late 11th century was called Sekkan (攝關) politics. Subsequently, during the 100 years starting from the late 11th century, 'Insei politics (院政, politics led by the father of the Emperor)' was implemented in which the Japanese Emperor abdicated the throne to his young son and exercised power as the father and guardian of the Emperor (上皇). Amidst this situation, there was a fierce struggle between two influential families - the Daira (平, also known as 'Hei') family and the Minamoto (源, also known as Kenji) family. The Daira family was later eliminated by the Minamoto family, which effectively gathered and commanded the regional warriors. When Minamoto Yoritomo (源頼朝, 1147-1199) was appointed as the Seiitai-shogun (征夷大將軍) by the Japanese Emperor in 1192, the Kamakura (鎌倉) Shogunate, which was the first military regime in Japan, was established and lasted for over 140 years (Kamakura Period, 1192-1333). During this period, there were two invasions by Mongolia (1274, 1281) and when the Kamakura Shogunate fell, there was a temporary period in which the Japanese Emperor himself governed Japan (1333-1335). The power void after the fall of the Kamakura Shogunate was filled by Ashikaga Takauji (足利尊氏) when he was appointed as the Seiitai-shogun in 1338 and this began the period of the Muromachi (室町) Shogunate.

When Ashikaga Yoshimitsu (足利義滿, 1358-1408), the third generation shogun, died, the power of the Muromachi Shogunate gradually went over to Shugodaimyo (守護大名). Then in the late 15th century, Senkokudaimyos (戰國大名) emerged and created their own governing system in the local regions. The strongest among Senkokudaimyos, Oda Nobunaga (織田信長, 1534-1582) kicked out the shogun of the Muromachi Shogunate in 1573. Furthermore, he attempted to establish a new order based on power without relying on the authority of the Japanese Emperor. Therefore, Oda Nobunaga was given a government post from the Japanese Emperor but he soon returned the post and attempted to establish a new power which was free from the limitations of a granted post.[219] After Oda Nobunaga died from the betrayal of his subordinate, Toyotomi Hideyoshi (豊臣秀吉, 1537-1598) succeeded him to unify Japan. Toyotomi was appointed as the Kanpaku and the Daijo-daijin (Chancellor of the Realm) by the Japanese Emperor and as a result, he was entrusted with the power to rule over the entire nation of Japan. Once Toyotomi Hideyoshi died without achieving meaningful results in the war to invade Korea, Tokugawa Ieyasu (德川家康, 1542-1616) dominated Japan after winning the Battle of Sekigahara (關ヶ原). After winning this battle, Ieyasu was appointed the Seiitai-shogun by the Japanese Emperor in 1603 and he established a shogunate in Edo (江戶, present day Tokyo). The Edo Shogunate kept a tight rein on Japan through the Closed Door Policy and the *Sankin Kotai* (參勤交代) system, and surveillance and control over the Japanese Emperor was stronger than ever. However, as Western invasion of East Asia became conspicuous, lower class warriors brought down the Edo Shogunate under the flag of *Sonno Joi* (尊王攘夷, Revere the Emperor, Expel the Barbarians) and handed power over to the Japanese Emperor, completely disintegrating the dualistic governance system of the shogun's power and the Japanese Emperor's authority that had existed for over 700 years.

As seen above, in the long history of pre-modern Japan, the period in which the Japanese Emperor personally ruled was not that long. For most of the time, there was the dualistic structure in which the Japanese Emperor and the royal court had the spiritual authority and the shogun and the shogunate had the political and military power.[220] In other words, the practical ruler was the shogun, not the Japanese Emperor. This dualistic structure of authority and power was able to function properly when the Closed Door Policy was in place and internal politics was stable. But since power is dispersed in a dualistic structure, it was difficult to effectively respond to the growing threat of the external forces. Therefore, when China, the leading power in the East, was defeated in the Opium War and was forced to sign an unfair treaty with the United Kingdom and when Perry's fleet came to Japan from the United States to demand the opening of ports, Japan became keenly aware of limitations in responding to external pressure and sought for a strong state system based on centralization of power. These efforts of modern Japan manifested in the form of the Meiji Restoration, which centralized political power in the Japanese Emperor who was the source of authority.

The factor that had the greatest influence on modern Japan was the Japanese Emperor System. Prior to the Meiji Restoration, the Japanese Emperor simply played the role of a tool in justifying the power of warrior groups or the ruling class. Therefore, the general public barely perceived the existence of the Japanese Emperor. As the Japanese Emperor himself was content with having authority instead of power, there was no reason for the ruling class, who sought for power, to get rid of the Japanese Emperor. For this reason, the Japanese Emperor System continued to exist for a long time. However, with the Meiji Restoration as momentum, the existence of the Japanese Emperor rose to the surface. It was not that the Japanese Emperor himself sought to gain power, but the reformist lower class warriors of the Choshu and Satsuma domains used the Japanese Emperor as a means to gain power, which resulted in a situation where the Japanese Emperor came to possess power in addition to his inherent authority. The new Meiji government that created a centralized government with the Japanese Emperor in the backdrop dispatched large delegations to America and Europe to actively introduce Western civilization and institutions and became the first Asian country to succeed in modernization. However, this success in modernization was limited to the materialistic aspect and the government did not place much value in liberty or democracy, as can be seen in the suppression of the Jiyu Minken Undo (Freedom and Civil Rights Movement). Rather, the government established a Constitution that granted sovereignty to the Japanese Emperor, instead of the people, and created the Imperial Rescript to Soldiers and Sailors (軍人勅諭, Gunjin Chokuyu, 1882) and the Imperial Rescript on Education (教育勅語, Kyoiku Chokugo, 1890) to brainwash the people within the military and schools to become loyal subjects of the Japanese Emperor. The Japanese government used shrines (神社) as a method to promote the Japanese Emperor and induce loyalty towards the Japanese Emperor since shrines were familiar to ordinary people. The government merged all the shrines throughout the nation with the Ise Grand Shrine (伊勢神宮), which enshrined Amaterasu and the ancestors of the Japanese Emperor, and put the shrines under the control of the government. In addition, high importance was placed on the Yasukuni Shrine (靖國神社) that enshrined people who had given their lives for the Japanese Emperor. Yasukuni Shrine served them as national gods and performed ancestral rites for them. While the power of the king had been usurped or limited through revolutions or reforms in the United Kingdom and France, Japan's Meiji Restoration and its constitution enhanced the power of the Japanese Emperor and the government supporting him. A constitution ought to play the role of limiting a ruler's exercise of power and protecting and enhancing the rights of the people, but the Meiji Constitution was a contradiction to such a concept.[221]

It can be said that the Meiji government internalized the Japanese Emperor System within the modern institution - the constitution. Let us take a closer look into it. The leaders of the Meiji Restoration put forward *Sonno Joi* (尊王攘夷, 'Revere the Emperor, Expel the Barbarians') in order to unite around the Japanese Emperor as the pivotal figure and respond to Western powers and they eventually brought down the Tokugawa Shogunate. The new government established by the Meiji Restoration borrowed the authority of the Japanese Emperor to establish a centralized modern nation and overcome internal and external crisis. This process was accompanied with the reinforcement of the Japanese Emperor's power. Consequently, the Japanese Emperor was stipulated in the Constitution of the Empire of Japan (Meiji Constitution) as the sole sovereign power and sacrosanct figure in Japan and the government strived to instill loyalty toward the Japanese Emperor into the people through various moral codes.[222] The Constitution of the Empire of Japan (Meiji Constitution), which was created at Ito Hirobumi's lead, was announced in 1889 and put into effect in 1890. It enabled the Japanese Emperor to dominate all authority over the legislative, judiciary, and executive branches. As all authority was concentrated on the Japanese Emperor pursuant to the Meiji Constitution, anything could be done without Parliament's intervention through the Japanese Emperor.[223]

The traditional state governance structure of dualizing of the Japanese Emperor's authority and the ruling group's power was transformed into a centralized dictatorship system integrating authority and power to the Japanese Emperor through the Meiji Restoration and the Meiji Constitution. Emperor Mutsuhito (睦仁, 1852-1912), who reigned during the First Sino-Japanese War, stayed at the headquarters in Hiroshima (廣島) and commanded the entire army. Each of the respective Japanese Emperors during the Meiji

(明治), Taisho (大正), and Showa (昭和) Periods of modern Japan directly and indirectly participated in important policy decisions or declaration and execution of war. In reality, the Japanese Emperor had absolute power only on the surface and he governed with assistance from the Cabinet, elder statesmen, and military authorities. If an issue occurred regarding an act of the state, it became the responsibility of the one who had assisted the Japanese Emperor, and the Emperor could avoid responsibility. Under the Meiji Constitution, the judiciary, executive, and military branches only took responsibility over the Japanese Emperor. Therefore, except for the Japanese Emperor, it was difficult to control each state institution, especially the army and the navy. In this Meiji Constitution system, the Japanese Emperor, who held sovereign power and was the owner of absolute power, should have exercised strong leadership. However, unable to escape from the traditional political culture in which the Japanese Emperor remained reluctant in possessing or exercising power, locus of responsibility became ambiguous and as a result, conflicts and interests among state institutions were not properly managed.[224]

The ideology of the Japanese Emperor System was supported by the three pillars of the Meiji Constitution, 'Imperial Rescript on Education', and 'Imperial Rescript to Soldiers and Sailors.' The Imperial Rescript on Education became the basis of school education and functioned as a norm that publicly regulated national morality. When examining the contents of the Imperial Rescript on Education, in that it only emphasized compliance to the national law and failed to mention the rights of the people and that it forced certain morals on the people by relying on the authority of the Japanese Emperor, it does not correspond to the modern nation's principle of popular sovereignty.[225] Modern Japan instilled the ideology of the Japanese Emperor System into the people through such means as the Imperial Rescript on Education. The ideology of loyalty to the Emperor and devotion to the nation was widely spread all throughout the nation through the school education and various forms of social education. The establishment of modern Japan's centralized governance system with the Japanese Emperor at the top allowed Japan to repel external threats and furnish the basis of a wealthy and strong nation. But it also had the side effects of spiritually and ideologically devastating Japanese society and eventually leading Japan towards the path of colonization and wars of aggression. These side effects ended up bringing damage and suffering to Asian countries and their people. Such pain and suffering have not healed even to this day and even Japan itself failed to avoid the calamities of war.[226]

After Japan succeeded in the Meiji Restoration and introduced modern institutions of Europe, Japanese people considered themselves as proud subjects of the Japanese Emperor through winning victories in the First Sino-Japanese War and the Russo-Japanese War and justified colonization and invasion by looking down on other Asians as barbarians. Modern Japan's invasion and colonization was led by the military authorities but they would not have been possible without the connivance or approval of the Japanese Emperor, who had sovereignty and absolute authority pursuant to the constitution. The Japanese Emperor did not prevent these wars of aggression but rather praised the outcomes. When the tide of the Pacific War turned completely against Japan and some people voiced proposals to end the war earlier, the Japanese Emperor held out saying that such discussion was not to take place until achieving certain outcomes. This caused Japan to additionally suffer from the damage of the bombing of Tokyo, occupation of Okinawa, and atomic bombing of Hiroshima and Nagasaki. After suffering this damage, the Japanese Emperor, who had sovereignty and absolute power, eventually surrendered and ended the war. The Japanese Emperor, who can be considered to have the greatest war responsibility as he had sovereignty and absolute power, benefited from MacArthur's occupation policy and was exempted from war responsibilities and lived a full life. After being defeated in the war, on January 1, 1946, Emperor Hirohito (裕仁) proclaimed the Declaration of Humanity through the 'Imperial Rescript on the Construction of a New Japan.' This meant that the Japanese Emperor denied his own divinity. The newly prepared Japanese Constitution stipulated the Japanese Emperor, who had been worshipped as a divine figure with absolute power, as a symbol of the state of Japan and a symbol of unity of the Japanese people. This eventually led to the launching of the Symbolic Emperor System.

Once the Symbolic Emperor System took root after the war, it was rare for the Japanese Emperor to be exposed to the public unless there were special occasions such as his death, a new Emperor's accession to the throne, or the marriage of a prince. Emperor Hirohito, who avoided war responsibilities and maintained his status as Japanese Emperor, consistently assumed the attitude of avoiding war responsibilities after the war. For instance, at a press conference on October 31, 1975, to the question, "What does Your Highness think about war responsibilities?" posed by a journalist, Emperor Hirohito replied, "As I have not studied literature, I do not know words of such expressions, so I cannot answer that question." [227] In September 1987 Emperor Hirohito underwent surgery on his swollen pancreas, and in September 1988 eventually collapsed due to internal bleeding. He suffered from months of hemorrhage and blood transfusion before his death. During the period Emperor Hirohito was in suffering, Japanese government officials encouraged the people to refrain from daily celebrations. Expressions of happiness disappeared from television commercials and Japanese society was dominated by an atmosphere that regarded any criticism on the Japanese Emperor's role during the war as a taboo. As a consequence, Motoshima Hitoshi (本島 等), the Mayor of Nagasaki who spoke up saying that 'The Japanese Emperor also has war responsibility' on December 1989, was met with harsh criticism from advocates of the Japanese Emperor and was even wounded by gunshot.[228] However, even in this solemn atmosphere, a considerable number of people did not conform to it. When all the television networks were covering the Japanese Emperor's funeral, many people went to video rental shops to find something else to watch. Some people criticized the excessive stance of the government forcing the atmosphere of self-discipline and others protested about spending government budget on a funeral that had strong religious overtones. The 'Nagasaki Citizens' Committee to Seek Free Speech' defended the Mayor of Nagasaki who had been attacked for criticizing the Japanese Emperor and it presented a petition calling upon an end to the practice of suppressing criticism toward the Japanese Emperor, receiving over 400,000 signatures within months.[229]

After Emperor Hirohito died in 1989, his son Crown Prince Akihito (明仁) succeeded to the throne and the Japanese government named this new age the Heisei (平成, meaning 'achieving peace'). In November 1990 the accession ceremony of the new Japanese Emperor, Akihito, once again triggered the dispute on the extent of government support for imperial ceremonies with religious character. Government officials and conservatives had a positive stance toward expanding the role of the government related with imperial ceremonies, but liberals and leftists asserted that the role of the government should be limited, due to the possibility of the reintegration of the state and the religion of Shinto (神道). The new Emperor took an oath that he would respect the symbolic role stated in the Peace Constitution and opinion polls showed that most of the people supported the Japanese Emperor as a symbolic monarch. In June 1993 Crown Prince Naruhito (徳仁) married Owada Masako (小和田雅子), the daughter of a high ranking diplomat, following the suit of his father in marrying a woman outside the court aristocracy. It is said that the Crown Prince had tried to win her heart for over 7 years. She was an elite who had studied at Harvard, Oxford, and Tokyo University and had worked as a diplomat in the Foreign Ministry for over 7 years prior to their engagement. The state put a lot of effort into the wedding ceremony but it did not attract as much attention as the wedding of Crown Prince Akihito and Shoda Michiko (正田美智子) in 1959. Many young women criticized that giving up an excellent career by marrying the Crown Prince was a 'waste,' and others worried whether the Crown Princess could endure the confining palace life. In 2001 when the Crown Princess gave birth to a baby girl, Princess Aiko, the question of an eligible successor surfaced as an immediate issue. This was because the Imperial Household Law limited successors of the imperial throne only to males and the younger brother of the Crown Prince also only had two daughters. Therefore, there were active discussions that the imperial throne should be open to females as well and there were movements to amend the relevant law. However, when the wife of the Crown Prince's brother, Princess Kiko (紀子), gave birth to a boy in 2006, such discussions no longer continued.[230]

Recently, the Japanese politic world was in a state of confusion from the issue of Emperor Akihito's abdication. In August 2016, Emperor Akihito announced that he would abdicate the imperial throne to his eldest son, Naruhito, as he could no longer perform the tasks of an emperor due to his old age and health issues. The political world, including the Abe government, did not welcome this announcement since there were no regulations on abdication. The Abe government expressed its reluctance and did not wish to accept the emperor's abdication. However, with the will of Emperor Akihito's being strong, the government had to adopt a new law to allow the emperor's abdication before his death. Eventually, Japan's National Diet passed the Special Law for the Japanese Emperor's Abdication in June 2017. Thus, Emperor Akihito formally abdicated on April 30, 2019, and his eldest son Crown Prince Naruhito succeeded to the throne as Japanese Emperor. The Japanese government named this new age the 'Reiwa (令和, meaning beautiful peace or harmony).'

This chapter examined Japan's Constitution and the Japanese Emperor System, which are evaluated as having double-sided aspects, such as Janus, and as having had the most crucial influence in the history of modern Japan. The leading forces of the new Meiji government from the Choshu and Satsuma domains, which had overturned the Tokugawa Shogunate by setting ahead the Japanese Emperor who had been behind veils for hundreds of years, were engrossed in how to constitute the new state system. Therefore, after sending a large-scale delegation to advanced countries in America and Europe and benchmarking modern institutions, they came up with the Meiji Constitution based on the German model and a new Japanese Emperor System that integrated authority and power. The Meiji Constitution stipulated the Japanese Emperor as a bearer of sovereignty and a sacrosanct being. The Meiji Constitution and the Japanese Emperor system played a locomotive role in the development of modern Japan. In other words, these two things not only concentrated power in order to respond to external pressure from the West and changes in the international situation, but also acted as the foundation to allow Japan to become the first country in Asia to achieve modernization by rapidly absorbing the modern institutions and culture of the West. Of course, the Western modernization that Japan accomplished mainly meant growth in terms of industry and military as a means to achieve *fukoku kyohei* (富國强兵, rich country, strong army). Therefore, values such as freedom, democracy, and human rights were neglected and values such as efficiency and pursuit of national interest dominated Japanese society. Based on the national power that Japan built through Western modernization, Japan pursued militaristic external expansion, which led to colonizing, invading, and plundering Asian countries. In this manner, Japan boosted national power and wealth through the colonization and invasion of Asian countries and even started the Pacific War. However, when defeated in the war, Japan gave up the colonies and regions that it had acquired over the years of invasion and was subject to the judgment of the Allied Powers. Under the Meiji Constitution, by participating in militaristic expansion and war, with political parties, zaibatsu, and the people constituting a harmonious whole, centering on the Japanese Emperor and the military authorities, Japan came upon an unavoidable collapse. Eventually, Japan accomplished modernization and became a strong nation based on the Meiji Constitution and the absolute Japanese Emperor System, but on the reverse side, this accomplishment was accompanied by the suffering of the Japanese people, and furthermore, cruel sacrifices of Asian countries and their people. However, after the war, Japan lightened its war responsibility and made a speedy comeback to international society, backed by the US in the confusion of the Cold War. Then it emerged as a major economic power by focusing on economic development without going through proper reflection, apology, indemnification or compensation. Alleviating domestic and international concerns of nationalism and war, by including an article giving up war in the new postwar constitution and by returning the Japanese Emperor's sovereignty to the people and converting the Japanese Emperor into a symbolic figure of the state, played a crucial factor. In other words, it can be said that the so-called Peace Constitution and the symbolic Japanese Emperor System became the foundation on which Japan was able to newly develop after the war. However, after the end of the Cold War, there is a possibility that the spirit of militarism of the past may revive, as the voice of Japan's rightwing forces becomes louder and as politics in Japan takes a rightward shift. The current situation is that the Peace Constitution and the symbolic Japanese Emperor System, which soundly supported the Japanese society and acted as the balanced weight after the war, is wavering. Furthermore, the Hinomaru and Kimigayo, which were national symbols in the historical period of war of aggression, were legalized at the end of the 20th century, and recently, there have been movements to elevate the Japanese Emperor to the head of state. In particular, since the Abe government came into power, tenacious efforts to accomplish the goal of amending the Peace Constitution and becoming a strong military power have been made. If such efforts further advance, tension and conflict with Asian countries will heighten, and this cannot but act as a burden to the Japanese people. Japan is on the verge of becoming oblivious to the historical lessons it learned in the past century at a high and cost and sinking into a pit of tragedy once again. It looks as though whether the Peace Constitution and the symbolic Japanese

Emperor System is substantially maintained or not will be the touchstone of whether this tragedy can be prevented or not.

CHAPTER 4

AGITATION OF THE TRADITIONAL ORDER IN EAST ASIA AND CHANGES IN JAPAN

1. The Traditional Order in East Asia and Japan

The East Asian region, to which Japan belongs, has traditionally shared politics, culture, and values for a long period of time. Typically, the traditional order of civilization in this region was called the Chinese world order (Sino-centric order). This traditional Chinese world order was hierarchically organized with China, the advanced civilized nation in the East Asian region, at the top. Thus, the advanced culture and system of China was propagated to surrounding nations at different points in time depending on the distance from China and such underdeveloped regions sought modes of survival under the influence of China. The so-called tributary system (tributary and investiture relationship) was the key mechanism which sustained the Chinese world order. The underdeveloped nations in the surrounding region paid tribute to China, the main country of civilization, and in return, the developed nation of China recognized the kings of surrounding nations and provided standards of culture and civilization. The Chinese Emperor did not intervene in domestic affairs or diplomacy as long as the tributary state observed diplomatic protocols and accepted the standards of civilization. Therefore, it can be said that paying tributes was a diplomatic strategy of the small states bordering China to protect their independence and identity from China, the superpower of the pre-modern society. Such a relationship not only reinforced the political authority and legitimacy of both China and surrounding nations, but also had the effect of promoting a certain degree of trade among the nations.

In addition, the traditional Chinese world order had been established on the Confucian thinking system, which was fundamentally reality-oriented and focused on 'human beings.' Confucianism had a twofold characteristic which aimed for self-perfection in terms of moral philosophy and promoted order within relationships with others in terms of political philosophy. Therefore, Confucianism could be considered as a thinking system which essentially emphasized mutual balance and harmony between the individual and various communities, while denouncing individualism and collectivism in the extremes. Within this traditional order in the East Asian region, in which the tributary system and Confucian thinking paradigm was predominant, Japan accepted China's civilization as the standard on the one hand and created its own history by digesting China's civilization in an autonomous manner on the other.

Up until the last glacial period 13,000 years ago, Japan was connected to mainland Asia, where China was located, through several overland routes. Three major routes were formed through Sakhalin on the north, Tsushima (對馬) Island on the west, and the Ryukyu (琉球) Islands on the South. This tells us that immigration of the people through these regions was not a difficult task at the time.[231] The Jomon Period,[232] which was formed by these immigrating people, showed traces of earthenware and farming in some regions, but the main livelihood of the Jomon people largely depended on hunting and gathering. Therefore, it can be said that rice cultivation that mainly appeared within the Asian region started from China, the most advanced nation at the time, and traveled to the Korean Peninsula and was introduced to Japan in the end.[233] This shows the typical form of creation and dissemination of ancient civilization and this form can be regarded as a pattern which continued for a long period of time, with the exception of the 9th century when Japan strived to create its own capability for adaptation and development as well as the modern period in which Japan came to accept the culture and system of Western powers.

According to the findings of anthropological studies, the Jomon people are said to be close to the Ainu tribe of today's Hokkaido and far from people of mainland Japan. Modern and contemporary Japanese people are more similar, in terms of appearance and culture, to immigrants who came from the Asian continent, such as China or Korea, after 4 BC, rather than the Ainu tribe.[234] These immigrants expanded their dominance in Japan on the basis of well-developed technology, such as bronze ware and ironware, and advanced rice cultivation technology. These immigrants came to create the Yayoi culture and during the Yayoi Period, the Jomon people being former indigenous people, were crowded out to the northeast region of mainland Japan. In the modern world, the Jomon people are barely maintaining their meager existence in the Hokkaido region.

The ancient myths of Japan first began to be recorded at the end of the 7th century, leaving records such as *Kojiki (Record of Ancient Things)*, which was written in 712, and *Nihongi* or *Nihon Shoki (Chronicles of Japan)*, which was written in 720. These mythical chronicles were initiated by Emperor Temmu (reign period, 673-86), who aimed to secure the supremacy and legitimacy of the imperial family, by creating a mythical origin of his family line. Some of these works cannot be trusted as historical facts. It was during the mid-5ᵗʰ century that letters began to be used as a means for keeping records in Japan, which meant that historical facts which occurred before that period could not be recorded. Therefore, we cannot take at face value the assertion that the first Japanese emperor existed in 660 BC and that a definite genealogical record of the family line was presented without over one thousand years of written records to support its authenticity. However, a close examination of such mythical works can be helpful in understanding the ancient times of Japan. In other words, we can deduce that there was a conflict between the imperial family based on Amaterasu's lineage and the Izumo family based on Susanoo's lineage, and that in the end, the imperial family was able to secure its legitimacy when its supremacy was recognized.[235]

Japan first appeared in history books through *Han Shu* (漢書, *History of Han*) of China, which was completed at the end of the 1ˢᵗ century. *Han Shu* described Japan as the land of Wa or Wo (倭),[236] which consisted of approximately 100 small kingdoms, and recorded that Japan regularly dispatched an envoy to pay its tribute to China. A more detailed description is shown in the section on 'Eastern Barbarians' of *Wei Shu* (魏書, *History of Wei*), which was completed in 297.[237] The *Wei Shu* treated the journey of Chinese people to Japan in 240, and mentioned Yamatai (邪馬台),[238] the most powerful state among the 100 small kingdoms. Yamatai was ruled by Himiko (卑弥呼), an unmarried Shaman queen, who was a mythical figure that assumed power through years of war and solidified her position by dazzling people with magic.[239] In 238, Himiko dispatched a tributary delegation to the Chinese emperor, in accordance with the customs of other small kingdoms in Japan which had begun at around 57. As a result, her legal position was formally recognized by China. Himiko died in 248 at the age of 65, and it is recorded that approximately 100 slaves were buried alive with her.

The fact that approximately 100 people were buried alive when Himiko died implies that a correspondingly large tomb was necessary. As society became more and more stratified, people in the high class desired to reveal their high position even after their death. Consequently, for hundreds of years, huge tombs such as ancient Egyptian pyramids were built. These tombs assumed the shape of heaps of earth, or *kofun* (古墳, ancient grave) which was a raised mound. The Kofun / Yamato Period (250-710) is symbolized by *kofuns*, but the most distinguishing feature was that Yamato (大和) state started to emerge, centering on the Yamato of the Nara basin.[240] Some scholars believe that the ruling class of Yamato was a group of conquerors known as 'horse-riders' who came from the Korean Peninsula in the 4ᵗʰ century.[241] Even if there had been no substantial conquests of horse-riders, there were very strong relationships between the Yamato State of ancient Japan and Baekje (百濟) or Goguryeo (高句麗) of the Korean Peninsula. For example, as we can see through the Soga family and Prince Shotoku, an extremely strong relationship was formed between the Yamato State and the aristocratic class and ruling class of Baekje. Just like many aristocratic families at the time, the Soga family was of Korean descent (from Baekje in the Korean Peninsula) and had a much stronger affinity for Buddhism than the native Japanese. Consequently, the Soga family accepted Buddhism from Baekje in the mid-6th century, utilizing it as the new state ideology of unification as well as a means to raise the authority of the imperial family. The introduction of the Chinese character and Chinese Buddhism eventually made the newly emerged state assume a Chinese-style tinge to a certain degree in terms of authority and culture. [242] Japan did not have an amicable relationship with Silla (新羅) of the Korean Peninsula, and when Baekje called for help in the face of danger by the combined forces of Silla and Tang China, Japan dispatched 800 ships and military forces on a large scale. However, despite their advantage of ship numbers, Baekje and Japan suffered a crushing defeat in the battle which took place at the mouth of Geum River (the so-called Battle of Baekgang) due to failure in strategy and the poor condition of the ships.[243] Fortunately, Silla was not interested in invading Japan after unifying the Korean Peninsula, and Japan's relationship with the Korean Peninsula followed a road of decline with the collapse of its close ally Baekje.

Japan's endeavor to imitate China was characterized by Prince Shotoku (聖德太子, Shotoku Taishi, 574-622), the second son of Emperor Yomei (用明). Prince Shotoku was partly of Soga family descent and acted as the regent of Empress Suiko (推古, reign period, 593-628) from 594 to his death in 622. He spread Buddhism by building a countless number of temples and made a huge contribution to promoting all forms of Chinese things. Prince Shotoku enacted the so-called Seventeen Article Constitution in 604 in order to reinforce the power of the central government. The constitution had a strong Chinese-style tinge including Confucianism, and stressed harmony (wa) and loyalty toward the imperial family. The Soga family had a key influence on the early royal court of the Yamato State, and even controlled the imperial family itself. However, in 645, a coup d'état was staged by Fujiwara Kamatari (藤原鎌足, 614-699), and the Fujiwara family seized control of the Japanese royal court for many centuries afterward. Despite this fact, the Fujiwara family inherited the Chinese style policies, adopted by the Soga family, and implemented various ambitious reformations based on the Chinese model for the central administration system. These series of reformations are collectively known as the Taika Reforms (大化改新) of 645. Hereby, a central administration system which imitated the legal system of Tang China was created.

Yamato State needed a capital in order to reinforce the system of centralized power, and built a new capital in 710 at Heijo, the current region of Nara, by imitating Tang China's capital city of Chang-an. In this period, which is called the Nara Period (710-794), buildings such as the Todaiji Temple (東大寺) were constructed and a large bronze statue of Buddha was built inside that temple. Also, in the Nara Period, renowned books such as *Kojiki* (712), *Nihon Shoki* (720), and *Manyoshu* (萬葉集, Collection of Ten Thousand Leaves, 759), were written. In 794, Emperor Kanmu (桓武, reign period, 781-806) transferred the capital to Heian (the current region of Kyoto), which was a short distance north of Heijo, in the attempt to check the Buddhist temple forces and the existing aristocratic forces, as they became stronger. Heian was also built in the Chinese style as was Heijo, and remained as Japan's official capital for over one thousand years afterward. In this Heian Period (794-1185), court culture came to its climax in terms of refined beauty and artistic exploration. In particular, in 1004, Murasaki Shikibu (紫式部), a lady of the court, wrote *Genji Monogatari* (源氏物語, *The Tale of Genji*), which is considered to be the first novel ever written.

As the power of the central government became weaker and the power of the warrior groups in provincial areas became stronger, prominent figures began to appear in such areas. Minamoto no Yoritomo (源頼朝, 1147-1199), who rose as the strongest force, seized nationwide ruling power in 1185, but did not make himself the king or eliminate the emperor system itself. Instead, he secured the legitimacy of his power by being titled as *Seiitai-shogun* (征夷大将軍, 'barbarian-subduing great general)[244] from the imperial family in 1192. This type of *samurai* governments substantially ruled Japan for approximately 700 years until modern Japan emerged, in which the Emperor came forward to rule. A dual governing system was formed, in which the *samurai* could secure legitimacy by being granted the title of shogun (将軍) from the Emperor, who had the traditional authority, and the imperial family could receive protection from the *samurai*. The place in which the shogun lived was called the *bakufu* (幕府, tent headquarters), and Japan's first *bakufu*, or shogunate, was located in Kamakura (鎌倉) of the Kanto region. Consequently, this period is called the Kamakura Period (1185-1333). Of course, the royal court formed by the Emperor and aristocrats was situated in Kyoto. The greatest incident which occurred in the Kamakura Period was the invasion of Mongolia. Mongolia had formed a worldwide empire and invaded Japan, the last remaining nation in East Asia, across two occasions, in November 1274 and June 1281. However, the Mongolian military was defeated due to the active response of the Japanese, the neglectful preparation of the Mongolian military which included Goryeo (高麗) Korea and Song (宋) China troops, and above all, the decisive impact of the typhoon. Unskilled technicians who were mobilized from Goryeo and Song at Khubilai's urgent demand could not build proper ships, and the Mongolian military which had next to no experience in naval battles could not supervise the technicians either, which resulted in ships that were easily overturned by typhoons. Therefore, the

Japanese people call the wind that blew at the time *Shinpu* or *Kamikaze* (神風, divine wind), and have believed that Japan is the land of the gods and has been protected by the gods.[245]

As the control of the Kamakura Shogunate rapidly weakened in the 14th century, Emperor Go-daigo (後醍醐, 1288-1339) attempted to directly govern the state, and anti-shogunate forces began to emerge from various parts of the country. The figure that formed the strongest force at the time was Ashikaga Takauji (足利尊氏, 1305-1358). Ashikaga Takauji overset the Kamakura Shogunate along with Nitta Yoshisada (新田義貞, 1301-1338) in 1333 and enabled Emperor Go-daigo to establish himself. But when the Emperor refused to grant him the position as a shogun, he helped a new Emperor to the throne, namely Komyo (光明, 1322-1388, reign period, 1336-1348). In this process, Emperor Go-daigo was thrown out to Yoshino (吉野), a mountainous region 100 km south of Kyoto, and Nitta Yoshisada, who sided with Emperor Go-daigo, was defeated and killed. Through these series of events, Ashikaga Takauji was granted the title of shogun, and a new shogunate was established in Muromachi (室町). This period is called the Muromachi Period (1333-1568). Japan still kept its distance with the East Asian continent but showed slightly different attitudes in this period. Takauji's grandson, Yoshimitsu (義満, 1358-1408) sent a correspondence to the royal court of Ming China in 1403, and called himself the King of Japan (Your subject, the King of Japan). It can be viewed that the shogun sought to compromise with the traditional tributary order centered on China, and laid the foundation for dealing with external forces independently from the royal court of the imperial family.[246] However, in this period, forces from various parts of the country continued meeting and parting as the power of the shogun was not very strong. After the Onin Civil War (應仁之亂, 1467-1477), Japan eventually stepped into the Sengoku-Warring State Era (戰國時代), in which there were movements to unify Japan by absorption. This era lasted for approximately 100 years.[247] During this period, Europeans appeared in Japan for the first time and introduced Christianity. In particular, there were three Portuguese traders who drifted ashore on a Chinese boat in Tanegashima (種子島), south of Kyushu, in 1534. It was through these traders that firearms were introduced into Japan, which changed the game of the Sengoku-Warring State Era and were effectively used in the invasion of Korea several decades later.[248]

At the end of the 16th century, Japan was unified sequentially through the fierce struggle for supremacy in the Sengoku-Warring State Era, and the three figures that played the most significant roles were Oda Nobunaga (織田信長, 1534-1582), Toyotomi Hideyoshi (豊臣秀吉, 1536-1598) and Tokugawa Ieyasu (德川家康, 1542-1616).[249] The unification of Japan made progress through these people, and the period up to the point when Ieyasu finally installed a new shogunate is called the Azuchi-Momoyama (安土桃山) Period

(1568-1600). Nobunaga, who was highly reputed for being merciless, built a temple celebrating himself and designated his birthday a national day. In particular, he trusted his own absolute supremacy and made no attempt to secure his legitimacy by being titled as a shogun by the Emperor. His rationale was that if one were to receive such a title, then logically the person who grants the title is a more supreme being.[250] In this perspective, if Nobunaga had not died at an early age and had unified Japan and continued to hold the reigns, he might have abolished the emperor system itself. At any rate, Nobunaga implemented various systems that were succeeded even after his death, such as farmland investigation, confiscation of weapons from peasants, standardization of scales and rulers. He also built huge castles and several temples in Azuchi (安土), but he committed suicide when he was trapped in the burning temple of Honnoji (本能寺), due to the betrayal of his subordinate Akechi Mitsuhide (明智光秀, 1526-1582). And so, Nobunaga's plan for the unification of Japan was implemented by Hideyoshi, his successor. Like Nobunaga, Hideyoshi did not become a shogun, but he received several of the most significant positions as a regent in order to secure his legitimacy. In 1588, he implemented a nationwide policy of confiscating weapons from peasants, called the Sword Hunt (Katanagari). The purpose of this policy was to prevent the danger of a peasant uprising as well as the possibility that rival *samurai* groups might utilize the military force of peasants. The result of this Sword Hunt was that peasants and the *samurai* were completely separated in terms of social class.[251] Hideyoshi made the vision of conquering China and constructing a pan-Asian empire and invaded Joseon in the Korean Peninsula in 1592 as the first step (the Japanese invasions of Korea of 1592-1598 or Imjin War). When the Sengoku-Warring State Era, which was the arena of the struggle for supremacy among groups of warriors, had come to an end, as Japan became integrated by force of arms, the accumulated energy and impulse for foreign expansion led to a challenge toward the traditional Chinese world order. However, the Japanese military could not but experience defeat, as Japan fell behind the combined forces of Joseon Korea and Ming China. In particular, Japan's naval forces continuously met with disastrous defeats (23 defeats in 23 battles) against Joseon's Admiral Yi Sun-shin (李舜臣), who achieved a prominent record in the world history of naval warfare. After Hideyoshi died in 1598, Ieyasu smashed the camp of Hideyori (秀頼), the successor of Hideyoshi, at the Battle of Sekigahara near Nagoya in October 1600, and opened the new Tokugawa Period (1603-1868).

The Tokugawa Shogunate succeeded the policies of Nobunaga and Hideyoshi for the most part and formed a society that was both internally and externally exclusive and operated through strict order of rank. First of all, the Chinese-style social order of rank, namely Shi-no-ko-sho (士農工商, meaning 'warrior-peasant-artisan-merchant') was established. Court aristocrats and Buddhist monks did not belong to this social order of rank, and under these four social ranks were eta (穢多, 'great filth'), burakumin (部落民, 'hamlet people') and hinin (非人, 'non-persons'), who were treated inhumanely. In order to control the *daimyo*, the system of *sankin kotai* (參勤交代, alternate attendance) was operated, in which the *daimyo* had to alternately live one year in Edo (江戶, today's Tokyo) and one year in their territory and their family had to live in Edo perpetually. Since the *daimyos* were obliged to maintain households in two locations and had to travel each year, they were forced to bear considerable expenses, which lowered the possibility that they could strengthen their forces. In addition, the Tokugawa Shogunate limited the mobility of ordinary people, and prepared various devices to control unstable factors, such as issuance of travel permits, imposition of curfew, and adoption of a mutual surveillance system. Ordinary people who did not abide by the many social rules were sentenced to death. In the case of *samurais* or aristocrats who committed crimes, they were granted the privilege to take one's own life through the ritual disembowelment, known as *seppuku* (切腹) or *harakiri* (stomach cutting). For a while, there was tolerance toward Christianity, but the Tokugawa Shogunate eventually prohibited Christianity and persecuted Christians, because some *daimyos* became involved in Christianity and the shogunate felt the threat of European powers in the background of missionary work. Such acts of the Tokugawa Shogunate were manifested in the Shimabara Massacre, at a region located near Nagasaki in 1638. A total of 35,000 people were killed regardless of age or gender in this massacre, most of whom were Christians. Starting from 1640, all Japanese people were required to register at Buddhist temples in order to provide evidence that they were non-Christians, through which the Tokugawa Shogunate were able to identify and control the overall population. All Westerners, with the exception of the Dutch who were permitted to reside in Deshima, a small island of Nagasaki Harbor, were thrown out of the country. Of course, Chinese people and Korean people were able to trade with Japan restrictively, but now Japan was to experience the so-called Sakoku Jidai (鎖國時代, 'Closed Country Period') for the coming 200 years. Within this closed society, the life of the *samurai* was idealized and standardized as bushido (武士道, 'way of the warrior'), in the process of which the spiritual value of Confucianism was utilized and education was proliferated, bringing about the emergence of nationalism through *Kokugaku* (國學, 'national learning'). It can be said that these factors played a role in the formation of modern Japan to a certain degree.[252]

Affluent farmhouses supported schools (*deragoyas*, 寺小屋), which were operated by Buddhist temples, and peasants who received education at these schools came to follow scholars who formed a new trend of thought called *kokugaku* (national learning). Motoori Norinaga (本居宣長, 1730-1801), one of the pioneers of this trend of thought argued that scholars should focus on the historical chronicles or fictions of ancient Japan, such as *Kojiki* (712) or

Genji Monogatari (11th century), rather than unfamiliar scriptures from China. One of Norinaga's students, Hirata Atsutane (平田篤胤, 1776-1842) politicized his ideas in the early 1800s, and presented the ideal of loyalty toward 'Japan' as a whole, moving beyond the narrow sense of loyalty toward *daimyos* and their territory. At the time, most Japanese people regarded the territory they belonged to as their country (國, *guni*). The ideas presented by Hirata transcended loyalty toward segmented territories and moved toward a sort of nationalism which characterized the reaction of the Japanese toward the pressure of Western power that became stronger.[253]

Meanwhile, the Tokugawa Shogunate actively utilized the diplomatic envoys of Joseon Korea and the Ryukyu Islands in order to reinforce its political legitimacy. When the diplomatic relations recommenced, after being severed by the Japanese invasion of Korea, Joseon Korea dispatched twelve major delegations to Japan from 1610 to 1811. Each delegation consisted of 300 to 500 people, and sometimes the visits were timed at the birth of a shogunal heir or inauguration of a new shogun. Japan actively welcomed the visit of the Korean people, but Joseon Korea did not invite the Japanese to visit Joseon, and even disregarded Japan's intention to make a visit. Similarly, the Ryukyu Islands dispatched twenty-one delegations to Japan from 1610 to 1850. The Tokugawa Shogunate utilized these visits of foreign delegations to show influential *daimyos* and high ranking *samurais* that the political order of the time was respected by foreign states. Yet, the Tokugawa Shogunate did not establish official diplomatic ties with China, which can be interpreted as Japan's intention to avoid having to acknowledge Chinese superiority by refusing to be incorporated into the tributary relationship of the Chinese world order.[254]

2. Agitation of International Order in East Asia and Japan's Crisis

The traditional order of the East Asian region was a tributary system centering on China, but the Ming-Qing transition in the 17th century was an event which shook Sinocentrism and had an impact on the perception of neighboring nations about regional world order. The idea of 'Small China' or 'Little Sinocentrism' was enhanced in Joseon of the Korean Peninsula as well as Vietnam, and a consciousness was formed in Japan that Japan, being the 'land of the gods,' was the most superior nation in the world. In other words, the traditional idea Sinocentrism, which regarded China as the origin of values, began to be relativized by nations surrounding China. In this process, Japan realized that it was a small state, but on the other hand, Japan also formed the fictional concept that Japan was the most superior nation in the world through the instillation of the idea that it was the land of the gods.[255]

Meanwhile, the Sakoku Policy (Closed Country Policy) of the Tokugawa Period enabled Japan to manage its foreign relations in an autonomous manner on the fringe of the Chinese world order centering on China. In this environment of the Closed Country Policy, the threats of Western forces encouraged the sprouting of anti-alien liberation against the West and the notion of the Japanese empire, and went further to unleash the creation of a scientific world view and modern knowledge. In other words, by the threats of Western forces, the external subject against which Japan measured its identity gradually changed from China to the Western powers.[256]

As Western powers started to assume an imperialistic character in the 19th century, the traditional world order in the East Asian region faced a crisis. The 19th century was a transitional period in which the traditional Chinese world order collapsed and the world order became reorganized to a modern Western world order. This meant that the relationship among nations in the East Asian region moved away from the tributary system under the Chinese world order and transformed into a modern world order in which importance was placed on sovereignty and territory. Each nation coped with the situation differently in terms of degree and measures of response, depending on the intensity, nature, and timing of the foreign pressure imposed on each nation, in response to the impact that Western powers gave to the East Asian region based on the supremacy of modern civilization. Since China had been the standard of civilization in the East Asian region for thousands of years in the pre-modern period, it was difficult for China to actively accept the Western civilization as the new standard. China had been the center of the world for a long period of time, and it was not an easy task to dismiss the idea of Sinocentrism in a short period of time and accept that China was one of many other nations. On the other hand, in the period when Western powers advanced toward East Asia, Japan had kept an adequate distance with Chinese civilization and established a new political system pivoted around the Japanese emperor, for the exclusion of foreign forces and pursuit of strong leadership. In other words, modern Japan was born amidst the disintegration of the traditional world order in the East Asian region which had been provoked by the Western powers.

Since the late 18th century, Japanese people experienced an increasing sense of crisis as more and more Westerners appeared on the shores of Japan and, in particular, as Russia's demand for commerce became stronger.[257] Meanwhile, the Tokugawa Shogunate had immense difficulties in resolving Japan's economic crisis as well as the socioeconomic discontent of peasants and *samurais*.[258] On top of such domestic issues, the strong demand of Western powers for new international relations made the people doubt the legitimacy of the Tokugawa Shogunate. The Tokugawa Shogunate experienced hardships in ruling due to the frequent occurrence of drought and famine as well as the failure of various efforts for reform, and when

China was forced to open its doors through the Opium War, Japan's ruling powers became more strained. In the process of responding to such situations, there were attempts to block all discussions on Western powers, and radical nationalists conceived plans to actively stand up against foreign forces by creating a new system centering on the Japanese emperor, under the slogan of *Sonno Joi* (尊王攘夷, 'Revere the Emperor, Expel the Barbarians').

The greatest moment of external crisis experienced by the Tokugawa Shogunate was when Commodore Matthew Perry (1794-1858) of the United States appeared on Edo Bay in 1853 with four ships. Perry demanded humanitarian treatment toward castaways, use of ports for rations and fuel, and the opening of ports for commerce. Perry, who was a man of decision, assumed that the Japanese sufficiently comprehended his intentions as well as the power of weapons, and handed over a white flag as a gesture of urging surrender. Perry delivered a letter written by Millard Fillmore, the President of the United States to the Japanese Emperor, and left Japan with the promise to return the following year to hear Japan's answer. Japan fell into a state of confusion after Perry's departure. The rulers of the Tokugawa Shogunate were seized by fear that Japan may degenerate to a wretched situation like China, which had been downtrodden by Western powers such as the United Kingdom. The Tokugawa Shogunate reported the demand of the United States to the Japanese Emperor and even asked for advice from *daimyos* (大名), which was an unprecedented act of humiliation. This served as momentum for the Japanese Emperor and *tozama daimyos* (外様大名, outside daimyos who became hereditary vassals of the Tokugawa after the Battle of Sekigahara), who had been excluded from the process of political decision-making in the Tokugawa Period, to step up to the forefront of history. When Perry came back in February 1854 with nine ships, the Tokugawa Shogunate had no choice but to enter into a treaty. In accordance with the Treaty of Kanagawa, settled in March 1854, Japan accepted the demands of the United States including the installation of a consul, and Townsend Harris (1804-1878) established the first consulate in the port of Shimoda in 1856 after his appointment as the first United States consul to Japan. Thus, the strong and firm doors of the Closed Country were forced open. After the settlement of the Treaty of Kanagawa, Japan successively entered into similar treaties with Western powers, such as the United Kingdom, Russia, France, and the Netherlands.[259]

In this process, the Tokugawa Shogunate damaged its legitimacy and caused its demise by failing to respond to foreign forces on its own and drawing in various political forces. In 1853, Abe Masahiro (阿部正弘, 1819-1857), the chief councilor of the Tokugawa Shogunate asked the opinion of *daimyos* on how to respond to Perry's demand. This signified a domestic political opening, which was equivalent to an opening to the West. This opening exposed the vulnerability of the Tokugawa Shogunate, and it served as momentum for the rulers of strong domains (雄藩) to dream of new political ambitions. Abe Masahiro, who was criticized for inappropriately responding to Perry's demand, resigned in 1855, and the urgent priority of his successor, Hotta Masayoshi (堀田正睦, 1810-1864), was to solve the issue of concluding the commercial treaty with the United States that Townsend Harris was pressing for and the issue of selecting a new successor of the shogun. Harris, the consulate general appointed by the United States, came to Shimoda in 1856, and urged the settlement of a commercial treaty with the United States, by raising the issue of the Arrow War in China. Consequently, Hotta broke the precedents and travelled to Kyoto with gifts in an attempt to receive permission to enter into a commercial treaty with the United States from the Japanese emperor. However, Emperor Komei (孝明, 1831-1867) intervened in the diplomatic and domestic policy decisions, and took measures which were different from the request of the shogunate. Thus, the Japanese Emperor, who had been influenced by court officials and reformist *daimyos* and had a strong propensity for exclusionism of Westerners, told Hotta that he would prohibit the commercial treaty, and sternly declared that he recommended Yoshinobu (慶喜, 1837-1913), the son of Tokugawa Nariaki, a *daimyo* of Mito (水戸) domain, as the next shogun, instead of the figure recommended by the Tokugawa Shogunate.[260]

However, when consulate general Harris threatened that fleets of Western powers that had defeated Qing through the Arrow War were making preparations to conquer Japan, the rulers of the Tokugawa Shogunate became disconcerted and fearful, and entered into the Treaty of Amity and Commerce between Japan and the United States in June 1858, without the royal sanction of the Japanese Emperor. Consequentially, the United States was able to exercise extraterritoriality and an unequal treaty was concluded in which Japan was deprived of its tariff autonomy, which provided a reason for opponents to attack the Tokugawa Shogunate. The Tokugawa Shogunate appointed Tokugawa Yoshitomi (慶福) as the new shogun instead of Tokugawa Yoshinobu, who was supported by the opponents of the commercial treaty, and oppressed the opponents on a large scale. Through this incident, which is called the Ansei Daigoku (安政大獄), more than a hundred opponents were executed.

The Tokugawa Shogunate entered into commercial treaties of similar content with four other Western powers after the conclusion of the commercial treaty with the United States. For ten years after Japan was semi-colonialized through the Ansei treaties with five nations in 1858, there were a myriad of factors that hindered Japan from maintaining national independence. There was every possibility that Japan could be divided into districts and ruled by several Western powers both in terms of economy and politics. The decentralized political system of the Tokugawa Period was reason enough for division into districts. Despite the circumstances, the reason that the Meiji Restoration was possible was that external factors took a favorable turn to Japan. In other words, the time was ripe for revolution in China and there were vigorous national liberation movements in India, as a result of the Taiping Rebellion (1851-1864) and the Sepoy Rebellion (1857-1859) which occurred in resistance to the Asian invasion of Western powers. Western powers, which had experienced opposition and resistance of Asian nations, implemented policies toward Japan with intentions to not bring about national resistance in Japan. In this sense, the national resistance movements which occurred in China and India provided the foundation on which the Meiji Restoration could spontaneously progress in Japan.[261]

A plan to respond to Western pressures and to transform Japan into a powerful nation like the Western powers was actively propelled by *tozama* domains, which had been given unkind treatment by the Tokugawa Shogunate all the while. Satsuma, which was located south of Kyushu, and Choshu, which was located west of Honshu, became the spearhead. In particular, nationalists of Choshu were especially passionate, one of whom was Yoshida Shoin (吉田松陰, 1830-1859). Yoshida Shoin attempted to stow away on one of Perry's ships in order to learn the ways of the West to make Japan into a powerful nation only to fail. As a consequence, Yoshida was put into confinement in a prison in his hometown for one year, and when he was under house arrest, he trained patriots at his house by holding Shoka Sonjuku (松下村塾).[262] Later, Yoshida was executed in the Ansei Daigoku for the offense of planning the assassination of Manabe Akikatsu (間部詮勝, 1804-1884), an official of the Tokugawa Shogunate, and became a martyr for the cause of *Sonno Joi*. In particular, Yoshida Shoin asserted that it was necessary to invade East Asia, including Korea, in order to offset what Japan had been deprived of by the Western powers, and this idea was inherited by the forces that led the Meiji Restoration. Thus, Yoshida's argument was continued by Seikanron (征韓論, Advocacy of a punitive expedition to Korea) in the early Meiji period and Yamagata Aritomo's 'zone of interest theory.' Choshu, being disappointed with the Tokugawa Shogunate which did not appropriately cope with the Western powers, attacked foreign ships on the Strait of Shimonoseki in July 1863 and September 1864. As a result of the retaliation of the United Kingdom and United States fleets, Choshu lost many of its ships and military forts. The Tokugawa Shogunate dispatched armed forces in order to punish Choshu, but was defeated by Choshu's troops. One of the factors behind the defeat was that Satsuma, who was in a competitive relationship against Choshu, did not side with the Tokugawa Shogunate, and later the influential domains in the southwest region formed a close union of forces. In the background of this union of forces was the arrangement and role of Sakamoto Ryoma (坂本龍馬, 1836-1867), a patriot of the Tosa (土佐) domain.[263]

3. Japan's Meiji Restoration and Modernization

When Yoshinobu (慶喜) assumed power in January 1867 as a new shogun, the *Sonno Joi* forces felt a sense of crisis and rushed to obtain an imperial rescript that ordered the abolition of the shogunate. Based on this authority, the *Sonno Joi* forces occupied the imperial palace and declared imperial restoration on January 3, 1868. There was resistance from some shogunate forces afterward, but a new system commenced without heavy scenes. The Japanese emperor at the time of the imperial restoration was the 15-year-old Mutsuhito (睦仁, 1852-1912), whose period was called Meiji (明治, 'enlightened rule'). Mutsuhito succeeded the imperial throne one year before the imperial restoration when his father Komei (1831-1867) died in January 1867. Komei's death has been caught up in controversy, and there are possibilities that he was poisoned to death.[264] Komei preferred the *Kobu gattai* (公武合體), which was a union of the royal court and the shogunate, to the imperial restoration. At any rate, the death of Komei, who was reluctant toward the imperial restoration and was difficult to deal with, enabled the *Sonno Joi* forces to easily obtain an imperial rescript from his son, the new underage emperor who was easy to deal with, and it became possible for *Sonno Joi* forces to coordinate the Meiji Restoration.

Mutsuhito, the first emperor after the imperial restoration, had no choice but to be guided by many advisors because he was only 15 years old at the time. The advisors and main figures of the new government were mainly from the southwest region of Japan.[265] The key issue of the new Meiji government for achieving national development was to figure out how to respond to the Western powers. The new government discarded the exclusive catch phrase of *Sonno Joi* (尊王攘夷, 'revere the emperor and expel the barbarians') that had been used in the process of coming into power, and selected a new slogan which was constructive and practical, namely *Wakon Yosai* (和魂洋才, 'Japanese spirit, Western learning'). The new Meiji government's approach towards the West was similar to the approach of Yamato and Nara in ancient Japan towards China. In addition, it can be said that Japan was fortunate in imitating the West at its own pace and method, without being swayed under the control of Western powers. This was because the United Kingdom and other Western powers were engrossed in the colonization and acquirement of rights in China, India, and the New Continent and did not have much interest in colonializing the island country of Japan which was located in the Far East.

As a matter of fact, nothing much had changed in 1868 when the Tokugawa Shogunate collapsed and imperial restoration was achieved, with the exception of the political upheaval in Kyoto and Edo. Each domain, which was relatively autonomous, maintained its own treasury and army, and *samurais* still received stipends and perceived the stipends as a hereditary birthright. However, after this situation in 1868, there had been an immense change in all aspects, such as politics, the economy, society, and culture, and considering the situation ten years afterward, it was no exaggeration to call it a revolution. The revolution that commenced at the end of the 1860s could be called a Japanese variation of revolution for modernization, which was a universal goal. However, the revolution in Japan was somewhat different in its process from the revolution which occurred in Europe at the end of the 18th century and 19th century. In Europe, the urban bourgeoisie, which had newly taken the reins, challenged and even abolished the privileges that aristocrats had enjoyed for a long period of time. In contrast, low class *samurais* which constituted the ruling class in the Tokugawa Period led the attack against the old order in Japan's Meiji Period. Due to this role of the *samurais*, some historians refer to Japan's Meiji Restoration as the 'revolution from above' or 'aristocratic revolution.'[266] The reason that it was possible for the elite class, or *samurais*, to take the lead in revolution in Japan can be found in the hierarchical characteristics of *samurais*. First of all, *samurais* did not own any land and were fundamentally salaried employees of *daimyos*. Therefore, although their social status was hereditary, *samurais* did not have much to lose in comparison to the elite class of Europe, China, or Korea, since they did not own private property such as land. It can then be said that they did not have a strong resistance against change. In addition, low class *samurais*, who longed for change, had the sense of duty to construct the new nation of Japan, transcending from the narrow realms called domains.[267]

The new Meiji government pushed ahead with manifold groundbreaking reformations of policies one after the other, in order to accomplish the top priority of the nation, which was *Fukoku Kyohei* (富國強兵, 'rich country and strong army'). First of all, in August 1871, the Meiji government abolished domains, which had been the major administrative districts in the Tokugawa Period, and newly established prefectures (廢藩置縣, *hihanchiken*).[268] In addition, the new Meiji government reformed the taxation system on land in 1873, as a part of significant financial reform, in order to secure stable tax income. The new government invested the funds from this income in public projects and system improvement in order to build infrastructure for the industrial economy of capitalism. In particular, the new Meiji government abolished the strict class system that could hinder modernization, and the classes were changed from Shi-no-ko-sho to *kazoku* (nobles) which included *daimyos*, *shizoku* (*samurai*), and *heimin* (commoners). The imperial family formed the *kazoku* which was a separate class in itself, and in 1870, commoners were officially able to have names. The lowest classes of people, *eta*, *burakumin*, and *hinin*, were abolished in 1871 and could have the same rights as commoners, but discrimination continued afterward. Furthermore, universal education was declared in 1872 under the pretext of equality, and as the years passed, enforcement of universal education began to spread. In addition, compulsory military draft was introduced in 1873, and men who reached a certain age were obligated to serve in the military. This draft system was promoted by Yamagata Aritomo, and the conscripted military troops became the foundation for protecting the country against foreign forces and also a good instrument for integrating the people.[269] The new government dispatched the Iwakura Delegation to the West from 1871 to 1873 in order to systematically understand and adopt Western law and systems.[270] Thus, the new government had considered Westernization as the key factor of modernization.

The greatest material symbol of Japan's modernization was probably the railway.[271] From 1870 to 1874, one-third of government investments were spent on the construction of the railway.[272] The development of public transportation within and between cities facilitated urbanization and changed the mindset of the Japanese people. At the time, concepts such as 'self-help' and 'survival of the fittest' took center stage, and there was a thread of connection with the arguments of Fukuzawa Yukichi (福澤諭吉, 1835-1901),[273] who was the most influential educationalist and pioneer of Westernization in Meiji Japan. In his book, *Gakumon no Susume (An Encouragement of Learning*, 1872), Yukichi argued that there was no inherent difference between aristocrats and commoners, and that the mere difference was whether one studied hard or not. In this atmosphere, Darwin's theory of evolution and natural selection as well as Herbert Spencer (1820-1903)'s Social Darwinism was extremely popular. The Japanese government asked for a lot of advice on its national policies from Spencer and invited Western experts in various fields. At around 1875, there were approximately 520 foreigners employed by the Japanese government, and employment of foreigners gradually spread to the private sector as well.[274] Approximately five percent of all government expenditure in Meiji Japan was spent on the wages and other expenses related to foreign employees.[275] On the one hand, Japan learned from Westerners by inviting them to Japan, and on the other hand, Japan dispatched many people to the United States and Europe and sent many people to study abroad in order to actively learn the civilization and systems of the West. The most representative example was the Iwakura Delegation in 1871-1873 which was mentioned above.

In the early years of Meiji Japan, nationalism was an ideal cause, and catch phrases such as *Oitsuke, Oikose* ('catch up, overtake') and *Fukoku Kyohei* (富國強兵, 'rich country, strong army') were promoted. To achieve this, universal education was declared in 1872, and by 1879, two-thirds of boys and one-fourth of girls received elementary education at the very least. Many of the textbooks used in the early years were Japanese translations of Western books, which allowed students to naturally learn about concepts such as individual rights and democracy. The Japanese government expanded its influence in the selection of textbooks and at the end of the Meiji Period, the government was able to assume complete control over textbooks. Accordingly, Western heroes were replaced with Confucian Japanese figures in school textbooks, and the flag of Japan was printed in every textbook. Furthermore, in 1890, the *Imperial Rescript on Education* (教育勅語, Kyoiku Chokugo)[276] was publicly announced and students were to learn it by heart and read it aloud at every major event of the school. The Imperial Rescript, the purpose of which was to maintain the order of rank centering on the Japanese emperor, was not easily accepted from the beginning, but it eventually settled as the virtue which regulated not only the school but society as a whole.[277] Thus, the young people of the time were indoctrinated that they should be diligent, respect their elders, work for public interests, and serve their nation and the Japanese emperor.

As Japan pushed ahead with modernization, or Westernization, Western concepts such as human rights and democracy were introduced, and in the 1870s and early 1880s, the Jiyu Minken Undo (自由民権運動, Freedom and Human Rights Movement) was actively deployed.[278] Thus, at around 1880, approximately 150 civil rights social groups were active in each region, and in 1881, the first major political party, *Jiyuto* (the Liberal Party) was formed. These civil rights groups made requests for the establishment of a national diet and the enactment of a constitution and even presented proposals for the constitution, but the free ideological activities of the private sector were not an easy factor for the new government to control, as the Meiji government had a vulnerable hold of power as of yet.[279] Accordingly, Ito, who had been leading the new government, could not but promise to establish a national diet and enact a constitution within ten years. Ito visited Europe in order to study various constitutions, and prepared the initial draft for the constitution with aid from various German scholars. Eventually, Japan imitated the Constitution of Germany (then Prussia), which granted powers and prerogatives to the emperor. The Prussian model of the constitution, which was announced in 1889, was far from the pro-British constitution that the civil rights activists had in mind. A broad scale civil rights movement served as a momentum for the government to introduce an oppressive censorship system, and brought about the negative outcome of establishing a constitution which was counter to the arguments of the civil rights activists. Accordingly, the Japanese Emperor came to reign over all of the Japanese people as the supreme ruler and commander-in-chief of the nation's forces. The nation's armed forces had a responsibility solely toward the Japanese Emperor and were free from the controls of the administration and national diet, which became the beginning of modern Japan's step toward militarism.

As the new Meiji government pushed ahead with various reformations, many incidents occurred in fierce opposition. Ordinary Japanese people who opposed to the military draft destroyed the registration centers in each region, and people who were enraged due to the imposition of an education tax for universal education and the establishment and operation of provincial schools demolished many newly established schools. Moreover, former *samurais*, who had enjoyed many privileges in the Tokugawa Period, stirred revolts in the mid-1870s. The Satsuma Rebellion (Seinan War) which was led by Sigo Dakamori (西鄉隆盛, 1827-1877), was the largest in size but was eventually suppressed by the government forces. In addition, new religions, which delivered the message that one could be liberated from this world through *yonaoshi* (world rectification) which could distribute wealth equally, were founded in the 1870s.[280]

In 1880, some of the government-run industries were sold to the private sector, which became the foundation of future *zaibatsu* or conglomerates in Japan. In addition, Japan established a strong financial system with low interest rates in 1886, which enabled the economy to grow and develop afterward. From this period up until the end of the Meiji Period, Japan continuously achieved an average annual growth rate of 3% in terms of gross national product. Despite advances in industrialization, the proportion of agriculture in the economy of the Meiji Period was high, but owing to consistent efforts for industrialization, the proportion of agriculture in gross domestic product dropped from 42% in 1885 to 31% at the end of the Meiji Period. The light industry and textile industry were especially important in manufacturing, and in the last ten years of the Meiji Period, electric products developed as a significant industry field. At the end of the Meiji Period, heavy industries achieved great developments in connection with Japan's reinforcement of military activities. The shipbuilding industry, which was strategically important, was vigorously promoted during the 15 years before the end of the Meiji Period.[281]

In short, the new Meiji government built economic infrastructure, and played a leading role for providing the foundation for *zaibatsu* (conglomerates) in the 1870s and early 1880s. Afterward, the Meiji government actively implemented policies to promote and nurture high technology industries which were capital intensive. Thus, conglomerates such as Mitsui (三井) and Mitsubishi (三菱) enjoyed prosperity in a wide range of industries, such as trade, marine transport, finance, and steel. The growth of Japanese conglomerates can be explained in connection with the relative lateness of Japan's economic development. According to this perspective, late developers had to expand their organization and rapidly mobilize scarce resources, such as capital, skilled laborers, and technology, into new industries, in order to narrow the gap with early developers and achieve global competitiveness. In the case of some late developers, the nation played the role of providing resources. Also, in the case of Japan, it can be said that Japan reaped success through the system in which the government took the initiative and private conglomerates responded to the government.[282]

A turbulent social response to the Meiji Restoration and rapid modernization included the issue of a conservative conception of gender roles. The Meiji government declared an ordinance in 1871 which recommended that men adopt Western hair styles, and when the Japanese emperor set an example, most of the *samurais* followed suit. Some women in Tokyo organized societies which recommended short and practical hair styles and cut their own hair. Accordingly, the government took measures to prohibit women from getting short hair cuts in 1872. Moreover, the Meiji government limited the imperial succession to males, and prior to the public announcement of the Constitution in 1889, the Meiji government prohibited women from joining political organizations, participating or making speeches at political rallies, and observing national diet in audience seats, through various legislations. Even most men in the people's rights movements showed discomfort over political rights for women and sympathized with the government's stance. When the industrial revolution advanced in Japan, tens of thousands of young women engaged in agonizing labor at low wages in sewing factories, textile factories, matchstick factories, etc. In addition, many young women worked in the red-light district, and women engaged in prostitution received relatively higher pay in comparison to those who worked in factories. In the 19th century, the largest number of women were engaged in the sex industry after the textile industry, and at the time, prostitution was legal and brothels (遊廓) were subject to authorization and regulation from the government. Of course, there were many brothels which were operated without receiving authorization. In the early 20th century, there were approximately 50,000 licensed prostitutes, which was second only to female laborers working at cotton spinning mills at the time. These women received relatively high wages, but they had to pay the price of losing their health, being unable to maintain their dignity, and being deprived of their freedom. In the case where a girl's parents sold their daughter to a brothel, they received a considerable amount of money in advance, and the girl could not quit for about 3 to 5 years until the money was repaid. Meanwhile, it was in 1899 that the Meiji government finally made it mandatory to establish at least one higher school for girls in each prefecture, but the most prestigious higher schools were eight public schools for boys. Moreover, at the pinnacle of the education system were the seven imperial universities, the admission to which was only permitted to boys, and the Tokyo Imperial University was the shortcut to entering the upper echelon of the bureaucracy or the business world. In addition, the Meiji government presented the ideal of the 'good wife and wise mother' (賢母良妻) as the gender role of females and attempted to restrict the existence of women to nurturing children and caring for the family. Thus, women's role was extremely limited during the Meiji Period, and women were excluded from politics, inheritance, and almost all legal positions under the civil law.[283]

As illustrated above, Meiji Japan was a male-oriented society in which females suffered from oppression. Women suffered from low wages and hard labor on the industrial site, such as textile factories, and sexual harassment and mistreatment were commonplace without any restraint. In particular, as brothels were prevalent and young women were driven to prostitution, the general perception of women did not get any better. After all, women in the Meiji Period were nothing more than complementary goods or playthings of men, and lived lives which were far from self-realization, tied down by the ideal of the 'good wife and wise mother' who served the family. It can be conjectured that this reality easily led to the brutalities committed without hesitance by Japan, such as raping and cruelly killing women from the countries which Japan invaded or colonialized and regarded as uncivilized countries, and manipulating women from other countries as sexual slaves at comfort facilities, in the process of modern Japan's expansion toward the Asian continent.

Modernization also had a huge impact on religion. In 1873, the Meiji government withdrew the anti-Christian laws enacted under the Tokugawa Shogunate, but the government did not make special efforts to protect religious activities, either. Thus, the Constitution newly enacted in 1889 restrictively permitted freedom of religion within the boundaries of maintaining peace and observing duties as citizens. Furthermore, the Meiji government actively controlled all religions so that they would be advantageous to the establishment of the nation's legitimacy. In the Tokugawa Period, the Shinto existed for the purpose of worshipping community deities at local shrines and was not closely connected with the central government. However, the Meiji government established the Jinkikan (神祇官, the Department of Divinity) in 1868, declared that Japanese people would be guided by Shinto in 1869, and established a national organization of Shinto shrines. The government consistently supported the Shinto shrines, and Shinto was upgraded to a national religion in close association with the emperor system. In particular, a Shinto shrine was established in 1869 for the 7,700 soldiers who had died for the Japanese Emperor in the war which collapsed the Tokugawa Shogunate. At first, this Shinto shrine was named the Tokyo Shrine, and it was renamed the Yasukuni Shrine (靖國神社) in 1879.[284] This preferential treatment toward Shinto led to criticism and persecution of Buddhist monks and Buddhism. In 1868, the Meiji government ordered the Separation Edict (神佛分離令) and deprived

Buddhist temples of the semi-official status that had been recognized in the Tokugawa Period. Thus, the custom of the Tokugawa Period, in which all individuals were obligated to register at a local Buddhist temple, was converted to an obligation to register at a Shinto shrine. As a certain religion was promoted by the government and closely associated with the emperor system, the religious diversity of Japanese people was infringed upon, and this naturally led to suppression of freedom of thought and ideology.[285]

In short, the Meiji Restoration was stirred by an interaction between the international pressure of Western powers (external pressure) and the sociopolitical power that internally demolished the Tokugawa Shogunate (internal pressure), and furthermore, it was a transformational process in which Japan created a nation-state by imitating the modern state systems of Western countries and formed modern thoughts and policies in order to achieve civilization and enlightenment as well as a rich country and strong army. The political process of imperial restoration in which the principal agents of the Meiji Restoration overthrew the Tokugawa Shogunate and established a new government was a coup d'état. However, the coup was a remarkable revolution that innovated the society at large, by reorganizing the political system, abolishing the class system, reforming the military system, reorganizing the school system, and establishing the Constitution. The Meiji Restoration was the light of modernization in that it laid the foundation for modern and contemporary Japan's national development and status. However, the Meiji Restoration was also accompanied by a shadow behind the light. Due to the inherent characteristic of the Meiji Restoration, which was to respond to the threat of external forces, the new government was obsessed about *Fukoku Kyohei* (rich country and strong army), and created sociopolitical systems in which the nation strongly regulated the society and individuals. Also, the Meiji Restoration opened the possibility of despotism through the fixation of major forces, such as the Japanese emperor, rulers and officials of the new government, and military authorities, and the *Fukoku Kyohei* policy permitted coalition between politicians and capitalists. After the emperor system was established through the enactment of the Constitution which recognized the sovereign power of the Japanese Emperor, Japan started the First Sino-Japanese War and the resulting Nationalism of 'national unity' overwhelmed liberalism and reinforced chauvinism.[286]

After the Meiji Restoration, Japan imitated Western powers and made countless endeavors to achieve modernization. However, the Japanese version of modernization was a materialistic version which was centered on pragmatism and was limited to industrialization and capitalization. In other words, Japan neglected modern values and ideology which were sought after by Western countries with high regard. In short, it can be said that in the process of pushing ahead with modernization after the Meiji Restoration,

Japan did not substantially adopt democratic values and ideologies such as human rights, the right of freedom, and rights to equality, which had been pursued in major modernized Western countries such as the United Kingdom and France.[287]

CHAPTER 5

FOREIGN EXPANSION OF MODERN JAPAN

1. Initiation of Territorial Expansion by Modern Japan

Prior to modernization, a generally decentralized political system had been formed in Japan, which meant Japan did not have the will or power to push ahead with external expansion, so there were barely any acts of aggression toward surrounding regions or countries. After finishing the Warring State period, Toyotomi Hideyoshi had invaded the Korean Peninsula, but in the pre-modern era, Japan did not have the practical power to spread out abroad, even when it had a centralized state system. In particular, the Tokugawa Ieyasu government, which was formed after Toyotomi Hideyoshi's death, had a decentralized political system, but as it put forth a thorough Closed Country Policy based on strong control over local lords, it was forbidden for domains in remote areas to expand territory externally and even engaging in external relationships and trade required permission from the Tokugawa government. However, at the end of the Tokugawa Period, Japan reinforced its defensive posture to guard the country as Western powers attempted to influence the East Asian region, and after the Meiji Restoration, Japan started to expand its external relations actively. As a result, modern Japan gradually began to incorporate surrounding regions into Japanese territory, and starting from the First Sino-Japanese War, Japan vigorously pushed forward with expanding its territory with a more aggressive attitude.

The Ainu people, whose origins can be traced to the indigenous people of the Japanese Islands, led their lives with a relatively independent culture in the northern region of Honshu and Ezo Island (today's Hokkaido) prior to the Tokugawa Period. During the Tokugawa Period, there were approximately 25,000 people in the Ainu tribe, who managed their livelihood mostly through hunting and gathering. The *daimyo* in the Matsumae (松前) domain, which was the northern most region of Honshu, was in charge of trading with and controlling the Ainu tribe. The Ainu tribe continued to exist on the margins of society with an ambiguous social status during the Tokugawa Period. They were not completely incorporated into the civilized world of Japan, but they were not considered to be part of the barbarous foreigners.[288] The Ainu people had a unique culture and language, and historically resided in the Tohoku region of Honshu, Hokkaido (北海道),

Karafuto (樺太, Sakhalin), and Chishima Islands (千島, Kuril Islands). From the late 18th century, Japan started to be wary of losing the land where Ainu people resided to Russia which moved southward. The Ainu people were doomed to fade into the mists of history when Japan succeeded in the Meiji Restoration and aimed to become a modern territorial state.[289]

The new Meiji government devoted itself to expanding the border of Japan during the first ten years after the construction of a new country. First of all, the northern island known as Ezo in the Tokugawa Period, which had been the home turf of the Ainu people, was renamed as the prefecture of Hokkaido in 1869 and was officially incorporated into the new Meiji government. Later, the rulers of the new Meiji government sent former *samurais* and prisoners to the region in order to reclaim arable land in their newly acquired territory. As a result, the Ainu people were mercilessly thrown out from their nest and kicked out to remote areas, and their number drastically decreased. In 1872, the Ainu people were included in the new family register system, and the government regulated them as Japanese people. However, since the Ainu tribe was marked as 'former natives' in the family register system, they were distinguished from the mainland Japanese people, and were not drafted into the army up until the 1890s.[290] Thus, the Ainu people lived a life full of ups and downs in modern Japan, and eventually assimilated with the Japanese and lost their unique language and customs.

Okinawa (沖繩), which currently makes up approximately 0.6% (2,274 ㎢) of the total area of Japan, is a region that is closer to China or Taiwan than Japan in terms of geography. Okinawa was called Ryukyu (琉球) prior to modern Japan. In 1429, the entire Ryukyu Islands were unified, and the Ryukyu Kingdom was officially established after being bestowed *Shoshi* (尚氏) and its control being recognized over the islands from the Ming Dynasty of China. In 1469, the second Shoshi Dynasty began, which prospered through intermediary trade with foreign countries. After the establishment of the Tokugawa Shogunate, the Satsuma domain invaded the Ryukyu Kingdom with approximately 3,000 armed forces and 100 warships. The cause for the invasion was to punish the Ryukyu Kingdom for defying the demands for obedience and offering of rice for military provisions in the Hideyoshi Period, but in reality, there was a political intention of converting the contradiction within the domain to external targets. The Ryukyu Kingdom externally had dual subordinate relationships with China (Ming, Qing) and Japan (Tokugawa Shogunate), but was actually suffering from the exploitation of the Satsuma domain. Even in this situation, the ruling elite of the Ryukyu Kingdom was still cultivated by studying abroad in China (Ming, Qing), and Ryukyu continued to send the children of officials to China's Guozijian (國子監) to study. The Tokugawa Shogunate, which heard the news of China's defeat in the Opium War, tried to stop the pressures of Western powers through the

Ryukyu Islands. Therefore, through the Satsuma domain, the Tokugawa government permitted commercial trade between the Ryukyu Islands and France as well as the United Kingdom, and the Ryukyu Kingdom opened a port in 1847.[291]

Mainland Japan's ports were opened through the fleets of Perry from the United States, and Japan began to grow ambitions of territorial expansion, along with the pursuit of modernization and aim for nation-state through the Meiji Restoration. Right after the Meiji Restoration, the rulers of the Meiji government and famous intellectuals had an ambiguous attitude toward Asia. On the one hand, they cried for a Pan-Asian solidarity to stand against the plunderous imperialism of the Western powers, and on the other hand, they thought that Japan, the leader of Asia, should lead the modernization of Asian countries and take action against the Western powers. However, as Meiji Japan gradually became industrialized and took the form of a modern nation, it became the common way of thinking to forget the former and focus on the latter. Some examples of this way of thinking were the conflict related to the *Seikanron* (征韓論, the argument that Japan must conquer Korea) and the Japanese invasion of Taiwan. Saigo Takamori, who had temporarily led the Meiji government in 1873 when the Iwakura Delegation was dispatched abroad, attempted to push ahead with an invasion against Korea. However, the members of the Iwakura Delegation, who thought that it was more important to accelerate the reformation of internal affairs by visiting countries abroad before Japan concentrated its energy on foreign expansion, were against the idea of invading Korea for strategic reasons. Kido and Okubo, who were members of the delegation, shortened their schedule and returned to Japan in order to abort Saigo's plan to invade Korea. Instead, they agreed to invade Taiwan the following year. The Japanese invasion of Taiwan originated from Meiji Japan's greed to obtain the territory of the Ryukyu Islands. The indigenous people of Taiwan had killed dozens of inhabitants of the Ryukyu Islands, who had drifted ashore in Taiwan when they were shipwrecked in 1871. As the Meiji government had intentions to incorporate these islands into Japanese territory, the government demanded compensation from China and dispatched armed forces of 3,000 men to Taiwan, despite the fact that three years had passed since the incident. Of course, it was a strategic measure to soothe the opponents within the government who had attempted to invade Korea in 1873 but were frustrated. The Japanese military dispatched to Taiwan lost over 500 men due to malaria, an endemic tropical disease, and did not make particular military gains. However, the Japanese government concluded a treaty through the mediation of a British minister with Qing China and received a certain amount of reparation (500,000 taels of silver or approximately 770,000 yen) from Qing. As a result, the Meiji government succeeded in building the necessary cause for subjugating the Ryukyu Islands in the future.[292]

Ryukyu was a tributary nation of Qing and Qing was the suzerain state of Ryukyu, but the new Meiji government, which had newly emerged after oversetting the Tokugawa Shogunate, had no relation with Ryukyu.[293] So, prior to the Japanese invasion of Taiwan, the new Meiji government changed the name of the Ryukyu Kingdom to the Ryukyu domain in 1872 and took direct control over the diplomatic affairs. King Shodai (尙泰) became the king of the Ryukyu domain, and was regarded as the court nobility of Meiji Japan. Furthermore, the new Meiji government mobilized armed forces and police forces to occupy the palace and forcibly hauled the Ryukyu King to Tokyo in 1879, despite the opposition of the Ryukyu Kingdom and Qing. Then, the Meiji government carried out its treatment for Ryukyu (琉球處分), namely, installing the prefecture of Okinawa and incorporating it into Japan.[294] As the Qing China strongly protested and international criticism arose, Qing and Japan agreed on a proposal for the division of the Ryukyu Islands. However, ratification was delayed due to circumstances in both countries and upon the settlement of the Treaty of Shimonoseki (April, 1895) after the First Sino-Japanese War, Japan's possession of Okinawa was finalized.[295] Also, with regard to the Diaoyu Islands (釣魚島, 尖閣列島 – Senkaku Islands), which had historically been recognized as Chinese territory, Japan watched for an opportunity and unilaterally annexed the islands to Japanese territory during the First Sino-Japanese War under the grounds of acquisition of ownerless land. In comparison to the Ainu tribe, the assimilation of the Okinawans was comparatively slow, which was due to concerns that broad scale programs of 'Japanization' might bring about conflict with Qing of China. Thus, it was only at the end of the 1890s and the early 20th century that policies such as the military draft and new land tax system were expanded to Okinawa.[296]

The Ogasawara Islands (小笠原諸島), which are approximately 1,000km south of Tokyo, were discovered by a Portuguese vessel in the 16th century, and officially discovered by a Japanese person in the 17th century, which led to the Tokugawa government sending officials to explore. However, the islands were neglected as deserted islands for a long time afterward until American or British whaling ships and Russian warships visited this group of islands in the 1820s, named each island, and claimed dominium. In 1830, approximately 20 Canadians who were living in Hawaii migrated to the islands, and so the Ogasawara Islands were inhabited for the first time. In 1862, the Tokugawa government sent officials to the islands to inspect the status of Westerners living on the islands and let them stay. But, in 1863, the government summoned the officials back to Japan and gave up developing the islands. However, in March 1876, the Meiji government declared dominium over the islands, by putting some of the islands under the jurisdiction of the Home Ministry. In response, the United Kingdom and the United States claimed dominium of the Ogasawara Islands, but in the end tolerated Japan's dominium, as the islands were far away from their countries and did not have great strategic value, and in order to establish a favorable relationship with Japan. Later, Japan continued to incorporate the remaining islands into Japanese territory, making the entire Ogasawara Islands into Japanese territory by the 1930s.[297]

In short, the forces that had formed a new government centered on the Japanese Emperor through the Meiji Restoration, escaping from the Closed Country Policy of the Tokugawa Period, started to pursue territorial expansion actively. Thus, the new Meiji government easily took possession of Hokkaido, which had been the base of the Ainu tribe, and as for the Ryukyu Islands, regarding which Japan engaged in a power struggle with China, Japan manipulated a past incident to its advantage and went so far as to dispatch military troops to Taiwan in order to secure a cause for subjugation. Modern Japan consistently repeated this type of conduct of manipulating or intentionally generating a certain incident to create a favorable situation or to obtain interests. This technique could also be found in prior provocations related to the settlement of the Treaty of Kanghwa (Japan-Korea Treaty of 1876) in the case of Korea and the Manchurian Incident and the Second Sino-Japanese War in the case of China.

2. Victories in the First Sino-Japanese War and Russo-Japanese War

The rulers of ancient Japanese nations set the goal of becoming No. 2 under the Asian world order centered on China or sought to escape from this world order and create their own unique culture. However, after the Meiji Restoration, Japan dreamed of becoming No. 1 in Asia, by aiming to establish a modern Western-style state system. Therefore, modern Japan's interest in *Theory of Small States* (小國論) by Yokoi Shonan (橫井小南) or small states such as Belgium or Switzerland, which a member of the Iwakura (岩倉) Delegation Kume Kunitake (久米邦武) was attracted by, was laid aside, and Japan came to tread the path of great power chauvinism under the slogan of 'civilization and enlightenment' as well as 'rich country and strong army.'[298]

As Japan succeeded in the Meiji Restoration and pushed ahead with modernization, it attempted to secure the physical base for modernization through foreign expansion. The logical consequence of these efforts was Fukuzawa Yukichi's *Datsuaron* (脫亞論, Escape from Asia) and Yamagata Aritomo's 'zone of sovereignty & zone of interest.' The meaning of 'Escape from Asia' was to create in Asia a Western-style modern state like the United Kingdom in order to form a relational structure of civilized nation versus uncivilized nation between Japan and other Asian countries. In this relational structure, which projected the concept of 'Oriental' in a stagnant sense in the historical philosophy of Hegel, Japan, which fancied itself as a civilized nation, defined all other Asian countries as stagnant Oriental nations outside the scope of civilization. In this sense, Fukuzawa's civilization theory defined China, the Oriental absolute monarchy, as a negative object, and established 'Datsua Nyuo' (脱亞入歐, Leave Asia, enter Europe) as the civilization process of modern Japan.[299] Modern Japan's notion of civilization represented as Datsuaron (Escape from Asia) was combined with 'zone of sovereignty & zone of interest' which was a logic for military expansion, creating the historical tragedy of colonization and invasion of Asian countries throughout the period from the end of the 19th century to the early 20th century.

The public law of all nations (萬國公法, international law) among the Western powers was an international order centered on the West, which aimed for an equal relationship between the so-called civilized nations. However, the Western powers did not apply the public law of all nations to uncivilized nations and considered it reasonable to limit the sovereignty of such uncivilized nations, and thought it was justifiable for unexplored lands 'with no owner' to be occupied by the nation that first discovered and pioneered them. This Western-oriented international law connoted a logic that justified the domination and subordination of Asian and African regions by Western powers. Japan, which had inevitably opened its doors to the Western powers, actively mastered the ambivalent characteristic of the public law of all nations and full-fledgedly started to tread the path toward becoming an imperialist nation. Thus, as Japan succeeded in achieving modernization after the Meiji Restoration, Japan forced the domination and subordination of Korea and China, which were underdeveloped neighboring countries, and went so far as to expand its forces to Southeast Asia and the Pacific.[300]

The focus of Japan's foreign expansion strategy was on the Korean Peninsula in the 1870s and 1880s. The reason behind this strategy was that Western powers were expanding their influence in Asia, and as the Western powers started to acquire various concessions in China, the Korean Peninsula which protruded from the Asian continent was like a knife pointing towards Japan's heart that could be utilized by the Western powers. Therefore, it was an urgent priority for Japan to incorporate Joseon, the nation on the Korean Peninsula, into its scope of influence. However, Joseon, which was incorporated within the traditional tributary relationship centering on China, was like a subordinate state of China (Qing) at the time. And so Japan attempted to exclude the influence of Qing on Joseon first of all. Therefore, Japan mobilized the gunboat diplomacy, which had been used on Japan by Commodore Perry of the United States in the 1850s and concluded the Treaty of Kanghwa with Joseon by force of arms in 1876. As a consequence of this treaty, Joseon of Korea opened three ports and Japan obtained extraterritoriality at these ports. In the 1880s, the Japanese government and Japanese people supported 'reformists' within Joseon of Korea, and Qing of China, which had acted as the patron of a tributary for a long period of time, was deeply involved in the domestic affairs of Joseon. The reformists within

Joseon, who had been supported by Japan, caused the Gapsin Coup (甲申政變) in 1884, but the revolt was easily subdued by the royal forces of Joseon and the military troops of Qing, and ten Japanese military advisors as well as 30 Japanese settlers in Joseon were put to death. In 1885, Japan's Ito Hirobumi and Qing's Li Hongzhang (李鴻章, 1823-1901) entered into the Convention of Tientsin (Li-Ito Convention), in which they agreed that the military forces of both countries would withdraw from Joseon, and if troops were to be dispatched in the future, each country would give prior notice to the other country. After this convention, Japan engaged in a fierce power struggle with Qing, which claimed suzerainty on Joseon, and the Japanese government made immense investments to reinforce its army and navy in order to prepare for a war with Qing. When the Tonghak Revolution was aroused by the peasants of Joseon in 1894, the royal court of Joseon requested that Qing dispatch armed forces, and Qing's intervention served as a momentum for Japan's wage of war. Under the cause of 'protecting Japanese settlers in Joseon,' Japan dispatched armed forces to Joseon in June 1894 and demanded equal rights to interfere in the domestic affairs of Joseon. Upon Qing's refusal, Japan attacked Qing's troops, and thus, the First Sino-Japanese War broke out.

The First Sino-Japanese War mainly consisted of naval battles, and the Japanese troops gained unilateral victory. After winning the war, Japan entered into the Treaty of Shimonoseki with Qing in April 1895, received huge war reparations, and obtained Taiwan and the Liaodong Peninsula in South Manchuria. Furthermore, Japan excluded Qing's influence on the Korean Peninsula, and was guaranteed the right to construct railroads in South Manchuria, securing a bridgehead for advancement into Manchuria. However, due to the Tripartite Intervention led by Russia, who had great interest in the Korean Peninsula and Manchuria, with Germany and France involved, Japan had no choice other than to return the Liaodong Peninsula to Qing.[301] Even so, Japanese people felt nationalist pride in the victory of the First Sino-Japanese War, which was a fight against the leader of Asia. In addition, the Japanese government, which realized that expansionism had a unifying effect that brought the Japanese people together, frequently went into warfare as a means of strengthening support from the Japanese people. More substantially, Japan received war reparations of 360,000,000 yen from Qing, which was a fortune equivalent to approximately 4.5 times the budget of the Japanese government in 1893. A considerable amount of the war reparations was used for military expenses, and it was partially invested in the state-run steel mill in Yahata. The Japanese government, which had a well-supplied budget due to the inflow of the war reparations, was able to grant large-scale subsidies to the marine transport industry and shipbuilding industry. In order to make the immense reparation payment to Japan, Qing China acquired 400 million franc loan from France and Russia in July 1895, and then borrowed 1.6 million pounds from the United Kingdom and Germany in 1896.

As a result of Japan's victory in the First Sino-Japanese War, the world order in the Asian region which had been centering on China for nearly two thousand years, finally collapsed. Consequently, Asian countries which lost their center came to be incorporated into the sub-system of the Western-oriented world order, and Japan harbored the ambition of standing shoulder to shoulder with Western powers and dominating Asia as the new center. Japan defined the First Sino-Japanese War as a war between the cultured and the savage, and as the war took a turn to its advantage, Japan raised its awareness as the leader of East Asia. Victory in the war was considered as a victory of civilization. This so-called victory of civilization formed a view that Chinese and Korean people were uncivilized, and furthermore, it justified discrimination, contempt, and even domination of China and Korea. [302] However, Japan's sense of superiority over other Asian countries was in fact a double-dealing with its sense of inferiority to Western powers. Japan's submission due to the Tripartite Intervention made Japan realize that there still existed a sense of inferiority to Western powers.

Upon victory in the First Sino-Japanese War, Japan made Qing of China recognize Joseon of Korea as an independent state through the Treaty of Shimonoseki. However, seizing the opportunity of Qing's decline, Russia expanded its influence on Joseon. In 1898, Russia hurt Japan's pride and made Japan feel humiliated by taking possession of the Liaodong Peninsula under the condition of leasing it for 25 years, which Russia had forced Japan to return to Qing through the Tripartite Intervention. It is also possible to glimpse Japan's sense of inferiority and crisis toward Russia in the Otsu Incident (大津事件) of 1891. In the spring of 1891, Russia's Crown Prince Alexandrovich (later Nicolai II) visited Japan on his way to attend the groundbreaking ceremony of the Siberian Railway in Vladivostok. When he was passing through Otsu (大津) in Shiga Prefecture (滋賀縣), he was attacked and injured by a police officer (津田三藏, Tsuda Sanzo) guarding the road. The Meiji government, which was conscious of the fact that Japan's power did not yet match that of Russia, was in uproar. Therefore, the Japanese Emperor himself expressed sympathy for the Russian Crown Prince and put pressure on the judicial branch to punish the criminal by death by applying a crime against the imperial family. [303] Japan took various measures to gain leadership in Asia, and dispatched armed forces amounting to more than 20,000 men in order to subdue the anti-foreign Boxer Rebellion in 1900-1901 in Qing, which was the largest scale of armed forces dispatched by a single nation. The Boxer Forces ended up submitting to the Allied Forces of eight nations. Later, Japan participated in the Peace Conference on the same footing with Western powers and acquired the right to station 'peace-keeping forces' near Beijing. Thus, the United Kingdom, which recognized the capability of Japan, considered Japan as its partner in cooperation in the East Asian region, and the United Kingdom officially allied with Japan in 1902. Russia also endeavored to acquire exclusive privileges from Qing by stationing its military troops in Manchuria. Japan indeed became a member of imperialist nations by colonializing Taiwan after the First Sino-Japanese War, stationing its military troops in Beijing after subduing the Boxer Forces, and allying with the United Kingdom.

Japan, which secured a reliable international support through the Anglo-Japanese Alliance, was ready to confront Russia taking advantage of public opinion that wanted war. And so, in 1904, the Japanese government declared war on Russia in order to solidify its leadership in Korea and Manchuria, and the Russo-Japanese War broke out. Japan won consecutive victories at the battlefield, and in January 1905, Japan captured Lushun (Port Arthur) in the southern region of the Liaodong Peninsula, after an enveloping attack that lasted for six months. Also, in May 1905, the Japanese navy, led by Togo Heihachiro (東郷平八郎, 1848-1934), sank Russia's Baltic Fleet which had entered the Straits of Korea after months of voyage. [304] However, the Japanese military did not manage to completely subdue the Russian military and suffered from great human and material losses. Both Japan and Russia were not in a situation to continue the war any longer, and in May 1905, the rulers of Japan requested US President Theodore Roosevelt mediate with utmost secrecy. Accordingly, a treaty of peace was settled in Portsmouth, New Hampshire on September 5, 1905. As a result of the Portsmouth Treaty, Japan obtained the right to manage the South Manchuria Railway Lines and even took over the leasehold rights to Lushun and Dalian from Russia. Also, Japan was acknowledged exclusive rights toward Korea. Meanwhile, Japan had spent huge expenses through the Russo-Japanese War and had borrowed a great deal of money from the United Kingdom and the United States to cover the expenses. Therefore, receiving war reparations from Russia was a critical issue, but Japan ended up obtaining only the southern region of the island of Sakhalin (Karafuto), an island north of Hokkaido. Moreover, war expenses in the Russo-Japanese War had been eight times as much the expenses in the First Sino-Japanese War and Japan had suffered from four times as many casualties. Such results aroused the indignation of the Japanese people, which acted as cause for a riot. Thus, many Japanese people held a rally at Hibiya Park in the central region of Tokyo in September 1905, and when the police prohibited the rally, the riot expanded nationwide. Despite the fact that Japan suffered from human and financial damage through the war, Japan's victory in the war led the international society, especially Western powers seeking imperialism, to highly regard the nation of Japan. Furthermore, the pride that Japan, so-called a civilized nation with a constitution, defeated Russia, a barbarous absolute monarchy, further strengthened Japan's scorn for Asia. Now that Qing (China) and Joseon

(Korea) were existences not worth saving, Japan had a prevalent sense of superiority that it was natural for Japan to dominate these countries.

Through victory in the Russo-Japanese War, Japan solidified exclusive control over Korea. However, Japan, which had tasted the bitter experience of the Tripartite Intervention after the First Sino-Japanese War, laid out the groundwork to appease, in advance, the opposition of the international society toward Japan's domination of Korea. Therefore, in July 1905, US Secretary of Army, William Howard Taft (1857-1930), and Japan's Prime Minister, Katsura Taro (桂太郎, 1848-1913) entered into the Taft-Katsura Agreement, agreeing to mutually respect their respective interests in the Philippines and Korea. Furthermore, in August, Japan and the United Kingdom entered into the second Anglo-Japanese Alliance, in which Japan's right over Korea was recognized. In the midst of the Russo-Japanese War, Japan coercively entered into the Japan-Korea Treaty of 1904 and acquired the right to randomly use Korea's territory during war. Furthermore, in February 1905, Japan incorporated Korea's Dokdo (Liancourt Rocks) into Japanese territory under the name of Takeshima (竹島), and quietly announced the fact in the official gazette of Shimane Prefecture in order to avoid a complaint from Korea. In November 1905, Japan seized the royal palace of Joseon of Korea, put Emperor Gojong into confinement, and threatened the Cabinet members into signing the Japan-Korea Treaty of 1905 (Eulsa Treaty). Thus, Japan took control of Korea's diplomatic rights through the Office of Resident General (統監府), and Korea degenerated into a Japanese protectorate. In fact, the government administration of Korea was at the mercy of Japan by and large, so it may safely be said that Korea was already Japan's colony from this point. In June 1907, Korea's Emperor Gojong sent three people, including Lee Jun, as a secret envoy to the International Peace Conference in Hague, the Netherlands, to reveal the illegality of the Japan-Korea Treaty of 1905 (Eulsa Treaty) and attempted to nullify the treaty, but failed due to Japan's interruption. As a result of this incident, Japan forced Emperor Gojong to abdicate the throne and put Sunjong in his stead, and forcibly concluded the Japan-Korea Treaty of 1907, through which Japan deprived Korea of both police power and judicial power and disbanded the Korean army. Eventually, Japan forcibly annexed Korea as a colony in 1910, and ruled Korea by installing the Office of Governor General (總督府). Now the Korean Peninsula became the territory of Japan, and shifted from the 'zone of interest' to the 'zone of sovereignty.' Thus, Japan came to pursue a new 'zone of interest' beyond the Korean Peninsula, and this logic of 'zone of sovereignty' and 'zone of interest' became the logic for modern Japan's infinite expansion. Now Japan solidified its position as an imperialist nation with supremacy in East Asia, by possessing Taiwan and the Korean Peninsula as colonies and dominating economic privileges in South Manchuria. In this way, Japan gained economic privileges beyond its national border and expanded the sphere of its political control by infringing upon and denying the sovereignty of other nations.

Owing to development in means of transportation, the speed and method in which people and objects moved changed dramatically. In particular, the railway acted as a catalyst for market expansion, human migration, and urban expansion in East Asia, and it also became the key means through which imperialist Japan colonialized and invaded Asia. Starting from the end of the 19th century, Japan fiercely struggled with Western powers for the railway rights in the Korean Peninsula. It was a necessity to secure the railway in Korea, since it was the gateway to the Asian continent. Prior to the First Sino-Japanese War in 1894, Japan, which had occupied the royal palace of Korea, demanded the Korean government hand over the right of construction for the Seoul-Incheon railroad and Seoul-Busan railroad. While the First Sino-Japanese War was in full swing, Army General Yamagata Aritomo submitted the 'Written Opinion on Korea's Reform' to the Meiji Japanese Emperor and suggested that Japan secure a railway running through Korea in order for Japan to conquer East Asia. Japan, which was in urgent need of a railway construction to transport war supplies, purchased the right of construction for the Seoul-Incheon railroad which had been secured by an American named James R. Morse, and opened the railroad in 1900. In the case of the Seoul-Busan railroad, construction began in 1901, but as relationships with Russia became aggravated in the autumn of 1903, Japan's military authorities deployed military forces in railway construction with the goal of completing the railway before the war started, in order to transport military men and war supplies. Finally, all sections of the Seoul-Busan railroad were completed in January 1905, and even during the Russo-Japanese War, Japan began constructions for the Seoul-Wonsan railroad and Seoul-Sinuiju railroad for military use and soon completed the railways. In the process of railway construction on the Korean Peninsula, Japan forcibly mobilized the labor of Korean people through military force and put various goods in requisition. Japan colonialized Taiwan, Korea, and the Manchurian region one after the other through the First Sino-Japanese war, Russo-Japanese War, and the Manchurian Incident, and reinforced its political control and military expansion as well as economic exploitation through the railway. In particular, the railway on the Korean Peninsula was not only used for controlling and plundering Korea but also enabled rapid transportation of military force and war supplies for invading the Asian continent. From the 1920s to the early 1930s, the railway on the Korean Peninsula was mainly utilized as a means of exploiting Korea's rations and resources. At the time, one to four million tons of rice was transported to Japan every year, which made up approximately 40-50% of rice production in Korea. As huge amounts of rice were shipped to Japan, the peasants of Korea had to live on substitutes such as millet or sorghum imported from Manchuria. Later, from the mid-1930s to 1945, Korea's railway was mainly used for transporting military men and war supplies as well as exploiting rations and resources.[305]

3. Japan's New Efforts for Change and Its Limitations

Emperor Mutsuhito, who had led modern Japan, died of diabetes on July 30, 1912, whose period named the Meiji (明治, 'enlightened rule') was over. On the day of Emperor Mutsuhito's funeral of the same year, General Nogi Maresuke (乃木希典, 1849-1912), a hero of the Russo-Japanese War, committed ritual disembowelment in order to follow the *samurai* tradition of junshi (following one's lord in death) and his wife Shizuko (1858-1912) also committed suicide. The death of Emperor Mutsuhito, who was the driving force behind the Meiji Restoration and Japan's modernization, signified the possibility that a new era would arrive. However, the most famous novelist in the Meiji Period, Natsume Soseki (1867-1916) felt that Westernization brought forth cold-hearted egoism and created lonely and rootless individuals. Furthermore, he forejudged in *Sore Kara* (*And Then*), a book he wrote in 1909, that Japan, which was at the height of international fame, would eventually burst in its attempt to grow large like a bull although it was an existence like a frog.[306]

When the Meiji Emperor's son, Yoshihito (嘉仁, 1879-1926) succeeded to the throne in 1912, various affairs were working out well in Japan. Taisho (大正), which meant 'Great Righteousness,' was selected as an auspicious name for the new era. However, the new emperor, who had suffered from meningitis in his childhood, had difficulties in walking and talking after his health started deteriorating in 1918. Thus, from 1919, he was unable to execute formal affairs, and the non-committal reign continued for many years until his son Hirohito (裕仁, 1901-1989) began to act as a regent in November 1921.[307]

The word Taisho became a term that indicated a spirit of liberalism, despite the infirmity and incompetence of Emperor Yoshihito. Thus, this era is called the period of 'Taisho democracy.' Considering the circumstances at the time, some people expand this era from 1905, when the riot broke out in protest to the insufficiency of the peace treaty resulting from the Russo-Japanese War, to 1932, when the party cabinet collapsed. During the Taisho period, members of the party became members of the National Diet through election and these diet members were composed of the Cabinet, which formed the system of party politics. However, at this period, people who defended democratic political order had the contradictory belief that loyalty to the emperor, support toward the empire, and public participation in politics could co-exist.

World War I, which broke out during the Taisho Period in Japan, inflicted immeasurable damage to Europe in terms of human lives and property, but gave unexpected opportunities to Japan. As it became inevitable for European traders to discontinue its trade relations with Asia due to war, the Japanese economy, which was going through industrialization, substituted that place. Industrial production of Japan from 1914 to 1918 rapidly increased from 1.4 billion yen to 6.8 billion yen, and export of cotton cloth increased by 185%.[308]

However, the economic boom of Japan came to an end in April 1920, stock prices plummeted, and many banks and companies went bankrupt. The Japanese economy was unable to escape from crisis all throughout the 1920s. Moreover, the Great Kanto Earthquake (關東大地震) that occurred in September 1923 paralyzed the economic activities of Tokyo, the greatest city in Japan, and fanned the flame of nationwide economic recession. In 1927, the weaknesses of Japan's financial system, which had been accumulated over the years, became worse and led to a financial crisis. However, the *zaibatsu* (conglomerates) strengthened their influence through the economic recession of the 1920s. In particular, the bank crisis of 1927 acted as a momentum for the *zaibatsu* banks to reinforce its dominance in the financial sector and control many small and medium-sized companies. Since the *zaibatsu* grew in the period of economic recession and social anxiety and colluded with political parties, top executives of large companies became the target of rightist assassins in the late 1920s and early 1930s.

As party politics became settled, many reformative measures were taken, such as the legislation of the general election law in 1925, which granted all men, who were at least 25 years old and did not receive public assistance, the right to vote for the House of Representatives. However, it was difficult for political democracy to take root in its entirety due to the emperor system with absolute power, the existence of *genros* (元老, the oligarchs or elder statesmen) who had continued to play a key role since the 1890s, and political terror which periodically flared up. In particular, it was difficult to cope with the Emperor-centered violent right-wing radicals and the ideological challenge and organized attacks of the social movement left-wing activists. Parliamentary democracy did not receive proper support even from the press or intellectuals. Therefore, each political party had to cooperate with the elite class, such as the military authorities, financial circles, and public authorities. Thus, the leaders of party politics could not but support the ideology in which the Emperor and the Empire was fundamentally the foundation of political order, while at the same time the democratic political participation of the public was pursued to some degree. Accordingly, Yoshino Sakuzo (吉野作造, 1878-1933), a professor at the Tokyo Imperial University and major advocate of parliamentary liberalism, criticized that major political parties had become morally depraved entities that could not perform public roles as they were stricken with egoistic and private interests like conglomerates.[309]

Such limitations of the Taisho Period were also reflected in the foreign policies of Japan. In the 1910s and 1920s, Japan's major political parties and elites in each field actively supported the foreign expansion of the Empire in order to join the ranks of the Western imperialist powers. World War I opened up to Japan a golden opportunity to expand its forces once more. Pursuant to the Anglo-Japanese Alliance of 1902, Japan declared war against Germany in August 1914 in favor of the United Kingdom, and occupied the railroad and military base on the Shandong Peninsula of China as well as several Pacific islands which were under Germany's control. Furthermore, the Japanese government presented the Twenty-one Demands under five articles to China's Yuan Shikai (袁世凱, 1859-1916) government in January 1915, and in particular, the content of the fifth article, which stated that the Chinese government must accept a Japanese advisor on military, political, and economic issues, was an insult to the Chinese. The Chinese people staged a boycott on Japanese goods and vehemently protested. Accordingly, Yuan Shikai refused to accept Japan's demands, and as the United Kingdom and the United States expressed objecting opinions, Japan withdrew the fifth article. Yuan Shikai accepted the other demands and acknowledged Japan's rights to former German possessions. Such conflicts continued at the peace negotiations of the Treaty of Versailles in 1919, which concluded World War I, and the Japanese delegates were anxious to clarify their control over the Shandong Peninsula which was formerly under Germany's control. Also, Japan claimed that the principle of racial equality should be included in the founding covenant of the League of Nations, which was an attempt to overcome the reality in which the Japanese were discriminated in the United States. The representatives of the Allied Powers acknowledged Japan's control over the territory formerly occupied by Germany but refused to include the principle of racial equality in the founding covenant of the League of Nations. The two opposing sides created a situation which was paradoxical for both, since Japan discriminated against the Chinese people, Korean people, and Taiwanese people, and Western powers claimed that equality and self-determinism should be the basis of international order after the war.[310]

The plenipotentiary of Japan at the peace negotiations of the Treaty of Versailles in 1919 was Saionji Kinmochi (西園寺公望, 1849-1940), who spoke nothing of peace and development of international society aside from the rights and interests of Japan. The majority of nations were disappointed with such attitude of the Japanese delegates, which eventually led to the breakup of the Anglo-Japanese Alliance in the early 1930s. The Japanese delegates had no thoughts whatsoever that a gruesome war like World War I should never happen again when they attended the peace negotiations. After the Meiji Restoration, Japan had not only expanded its territories through war, but also obtained various rights and interests, expanded its market, and created employment through war. This was why Japan could not readily consent to the demands of international society to stop war and seek peace. The Europeans, who had experienced the wretchedness of War World I in which ten million people died, felt a desperate need for international peace and disarmament, but the leaders of Japan, who had only suffered from a casualty of 1,250 people, did not feel this desperateness. Then British Ambassador to Japan, William Conyngham Greene, criticized in a report submitted to the United Kingdom, that in the situation where the paradigm of international order was moving toward a new direction in accordance with the principle of peace advocated by US President Wilson, Japan showed no interest whatsoever and was blinded by ambitions of imperialist expansion of the 19th century.[311]

Another one of Japan's bad moves appeared through the incident known as the Siberian Intervention, which occurred after Russia's success in the Bolshevik Revolution. In March 1918, the United Kingdom, France, and the United States agreed to send troops to Siberia in order to protect the war supplies of the Allied Powers and armed forces supporting Imperial Russia in Vladivostok. US President Wilson requested that Japan send a troop of 7,000 men. Japan dispatched a large force of 70,000 men with the intention to seize initiative in Siberia. However, the Japanese troops remained in Siberia even after the troops of the Western powers withdrew, and it was only in 1922 after suffering 3,000 casualties that Japanese forces finally withdrew amidst the suspicions of the Western powers and skepticism of the Soviet Union.

In the 1920s, the imperial powers were unstable but made efforts to establish a cooperation system of a sort. A representative case was the holding of the Washington Naval Conference (Nov. 12, 1921 – Feb. 6, 1922) in Washington D.C., which aimed to put the brakes on the competition between the United Kingdom, the United States, and Japan to reinforce naval power. As a result of the conference, the United Kingdom, the United States, and Japan concluded a treaty to maintain naval warship capacities at a proportion (a ratio by tonnage) of 5:5:3. Japan accepted the lower proportion as Japan was absorbed in an economic policy to reduce government expenditure, and because the United Kingdom and the United States promised not to build a naval base in the Western Pacific. In the 1920s, Japan downsized its military forces for economic and strategic reasons, and the military authorities supported this decision, reducing 34,000 soldiers in four divisions. Of course, the reduced budget was used to purchase modern weapons or to implement policies such as compulsory military education in middle and high schools. Furthermore, the Japanese government managed its foreign policies in a more prudent manner. One of the reasons behind this prudence was that hostility of Asian nations toward Japan had heightened due to the fact that Japan, which Asian nations had anticipated would act as a shield against the invasion of Western power, had not only colonialized and coercively ruled Korea but also showed ambitions toward China. On the Korean Peninsula, a nationwide peace demonstration demanding independence spread out from March 1, 1919, but the Japanese police killed thousands and arrested tens of thousands through violent suppression. After the March First Movement, Japan realized that simple repression was not the way to maintain colonial rule and converted to the so-called 'cultural rule.' Even so, the Japanese increased the number of police stations and substations by fourfold and established a nationwide intelligence network for strict censorship and inspection. When China's request for control over Shandong Peninsula was denied in the Treaty of Versailles, several thousand students held protests at Tiananmen (天安門) Square on May 4, 1919. This May Fourth Movement served as momentum for nationalism to become strengthened in China, and in particular, consistently expanded to anti-Japanese demonstrations, strikes, and boycotts of Japanese goods in the 1920s. As a result, Japan had no choice but to adopt appeasement policy to protect its economic interests in China. However, at the end of the 1920s, the solidarity of radical rightwing nationalistic political groups in Japan became stronger, and civilian expansionists as well as young action-oriented military men became more influential, and so, the appeasement policy of the cabinet on party lines started to lose its footing.[312]

Hirohito became the Japanese Emperor when his father died in December 1926. Hirohito was only in his mid-twenties but had gained a meaningful experience as a regent and had extensively traveled overseas. Influenced by the British monarchy and the ideas of Minobe Tatsukichi (美濃部達吉, 1873-1948), Hirohito was sensitive to functioning as a monarch pursuant to the Constitution. In addition, Hirohito grew up as a child under the military influence of generals such as Nogi and Togo. Hirohito's reign is called *Showa* (昭和) meaning 'Illustrious Peace,' which is paradoxical in that Militarism reached its climax and a gruesome war broke out during his reign.[313]

CHAPTER 6

DOMINATION OF JAPAN'S MILITARISM

1. Economic Depression and Formation of Japan's Militarism

As World War I ended in gruesome killing and destruction of humanity which lasted for a long period of time, discussions to consider war as illegal action came to the fore and the international society went on to settle the Kellogg-Briand Pact which agreed not to carry out war of aggression. Also, as the principle of national self-determination spread, colonialism lost its legitimacy and many ethnic groups became eager to establish independent nations. Thus, it was inevitable that imperialism and colonialism, which began to become ignited since the 19th century, needed to go through changes after World War I. Contrary to this new flow of world history, however, Japan and Germany strengthened their colonial policies and accelerated aggressive war.

In consequence to the collapse of the New York stock market in October 1929, a global economic crisis arose, and Japan also went through a mighty change in terms of politics and economy. In order to revive the stagnant economy, the Japanese government implemented retrenchment policies, such as tightening the money supply and cutting government expenditures in order to lower domestic prices and promote exports. Furthermore, the Japanese government aimed to stabilize international trade and investment through the fixed exchange rate based on the gold standard system. However, a deep global deflation counteracted the benefits of price drops and the fixed exchange rate prevented the devaluation of the yen, causing impediments to Japanese exports.[314] Under these circumstances, *zaibatsu* banks foresaw that it would eventually be inevitable to abandon the gold standard system and devalue the yen, and sold massive amounts of yen and bought dollars. These actions of foreign exchange speculation by capitalists brought about the sentiment that politicians who conspired with the capitalists took massive benefits in the midst of the economic crisis due to greed and selfishness.

Young military officers of Japan believed that the military became impotent and military families became impoverished as a result of the collusion between conglomerates and political parties, and came to take part in extreme actions. The Kwantung Army in Manchuria became a nest in which such military officers could act with full freedom outside of Japan. The Kwantung Army was established in 1906 under the pretext of protecting the leased territory and railways that Japan had acquired in South Manchuria, which Japan had obtained after winning a victory in the Russo-Japanese War in 1905. Aside from these duties, the Kwantung Army also believed that they had a duty to experiment on the construction of a new society in Manchuria. Furthermore, as the Chinese Nationalist Party (Kuomintang) led by Jiang Jieshi successfully performed the unification war in the northern regions of China, Japan's interests in Manchuria and Mongolia started to be threatened, and so Japan attempted to come up with a solution before China became stronger. In June 1928, Japan's Kwantung Army exploded a train near Mukden (today Shenyang) and killed Zhang Zuolin (張作霖, 1873-1928),[315] the warlord in the Manchurian region. The military officers that plotted the affair claimed that it was the work of the Chinese to unleash military action of the Japanese military in the area, but moderate forces within the Japanese military prevented the state of affairs from becoming aggravated. Emperor Hirohito was displeased with then Prime Minister Tanaka Giichi (田中義一, 1864-1929) for not taking firm action and deposed Tanaka from the position. However, the instigators of the incident only received light punishment.

Hamaguchi Osachi (濱口雄幸, 1870-1931) became the next Prime Minister to succeed Tanaka. Hamaguchi attempted to change the naval limitations agreement, which was settled in the Washington Conference, to Japan's favor, in the London Naval Conference in 1930, but to no effect. At the time, the Japanese cabinet announced that the naval warship capacities of Japan would be raised from 60% to 70% of the levels of the United Kingdom and the United States, but the plan failed due to the opposition of Western powers. In consequence, the Japanese people were enraged, and Prime Minister Hamaguchi was shot by a fanatic right-wing youth in November 1930, and eventually died the following August due to the wound. In the end, Japan opted out of all naval arms control agreements in 1934.

The officers of the Kwantung Army believed that it would be possible to resolve domestic and foreign difficulties through drastic military actions in Manchuria. In an extension of such beliefs, the Manchurian Incident (滿洲事變) was triggered on September 18, 1931. The Manchurian Incident occurred in a similar manner to the Zhang Zuolin train explosion in 1928. Japan's Kwantung Army destroyed the railway near Mukden (now Shenyang) and claimed that it was the conduct of the Chinese military. And then the Kwantung Army unilaterally attacked the Chinese military in order to strengthen its military status. This incident was executed by junior grade officers led by Colonel Ishiwara Kanji (石原莞爾, 1889-1949), and this time, the top leaders of the military condoned it.[316] The Wakatsuki Reijiro (若槻禮次郎, 1866-1949) cabinet had no power to apply restraint, and he resigned from the position without resolving the situation. His successor Inukai Tsuyoshi (犬養毅, 1855-1932) was inaugurated as Prime Minister and attempted to control the military authorities, but was assassinated several months later by extreme right navy officers in their youth. Inukai was the last

Prime Minister of party cabinets before War World II. There were warnings to Emperor Hirohito regarding the military action in Manchuria and an advice that it would be necessary to intervene through his brother Prince Chichibu (秩父, 1902-1953), but he disregarded those suggestions. [317] Emperor Hirohito's attitude and silence made the Japanese people to believe that the Emperor was in favor of the military action in Manchuria. When the Kwantung Army continued to expand war and conquered various regions of China, such as Jinzhou in January 1932, Emperor Hirohito issued an imperial rescript of reward to the Kwantung Army. Encouraged by the reward, the Kwantung Army captured Harbin on February 5 of the same year, and conquered 1,100,000 km² of Chinese territory (Manchuria region) which was equivalent to three times the size of mainland Japan, during the four months after the Manchurian Incident. [318]

The Kwantung Army, which had consistently expanded its territory after the Manchurian Incident and dominated Manchuria, eventually established Manchukuo (滿洲國, State of Manchuria, Empire of Manchuria after 1934) in March 1932. The puppet ruler of Manchukuo was Puyi (溥儀, 1906-1967), the last emperor of China's Qing Dynasty. Japan provoked the Shanghai Incident (January 28 Incident) in order to avert the eyes of international society, for the purpose of smoothly implementing the establishment of Manchukuo and the operation of bringing Puyi from Tianjin and enthroning him as the head. Thus, taking advantage of the incident, in which bribed Chinese people assaulted Japanese monks in January 1932, a battle broke out between Japanese troops and Chinese troops. The Manchurian Incident evoked strong opposition from the League of Nations, and an investigation team led by the United Kingdom's Lord Lytton was dispatched to Manchuria in early 1932. Based on the report of the investigation team, the General Assembly of the League of Nations denounced Japan, and Japan withdrew from the League of Nations immediately afterward. Various countries of the world criticized Japan's invasion of Manchuria through the League of Nations but did not actively deter Japan from its action because domestic situations were difficult due to economic crises. The lukewarm attitude of Western powers acted as a factor that fueled Japan's foreign invasions in the future, and Japan came to explicitly reveal its ambitions to invade China on the basis of Manchukuo. [319]

Due to unauthorized actions of some officers in Japan's Kwantung Army, the Kwantung Army came to dominate Manchuria more certainly and Japan's military authorities supported Japan's unilateral imperialism in Asia. For example, even General Ugaki Kazushige (宇垣一成, 1868-1956), who was a relatively moderate figure in Japan's military authority and a figure that experienced the post of Army Minister in the cabinet, considered that by implementing a more aggressive foreign policy and thereby securing foreign markets, Japan could enhance productivity and lower unemployment, which in turn would help avoid social tragedy.[320] With regard to Japan's invasion of Manchuria, most Japanese people welcomed and supported it, believing that it would be to the advantage of the whole nation.[321] Japan's takeover of Manchuria was the beginning of a new era of full-fledged expansionism which expanded the borders of the empire. Afterward, domestic politics was caught up in a whirlpool, and Imperial Japan's parliamentary politics came to an end when youth officers assassinated Prime Minister Inukai Tsuyoshi on May 15, 1932.

Japan's cabinet was led by five non-party prime ministers from 1932 to 1937, with an increasing number of bureaucrats and military men and the weakening position of professional politicians. As military men and bureaucrats took the top position of the political order, most politicians became in favor of foreign expansion. In addition, in order to preserve their positions and protect the interests of the *zaibatsus* and landlords, the politicians refrained from opposition against the new ruling class and trod the path of cooperation.

As Japan came to reign over Manchukuo, Japan's rulers regarded the colonies of Korea and Taiwan as strategic locations from which human and material resources were to be mobilized for the expanding empire. Ugaki Kazushige, the newly appointed Governor General of Korea in 1931, implemented harsh economic and social policies in Korea in order to meet these goals. Most businesses supplied agricultural products and raw materials to Japan, which was changing into a militaristic economy, on the basis of Korea's cheap labor. Furthermore, at schools, compulsory education of the Japanese language was expanded whereas education of Korean language was restricted, and in the late 1930s, use of the Korean language was banned altogether. Colonial policy in Taiwan was similar to that of Korea. Entering the 20th century, Western powers were converting their colonial policies into autonomism as they faced strong resistance from their colonies, and the principle of national self-determination emerged after World War I, but counter to this international trend, Japan implemented colonial rule based on the assimilation policy. While claiming to advocate assimilation in colonization, Japan maintained exclusion and discrimination, attempting to make colonial people into second-class or third-class Japanese citizens who supported first-class Japanese citizens. Furthermore, this discriminating structure became the background of reinforcing exploitation and suppression of colonies during the Second Sino-Japanese War and the Pacific War.

In the 1930s, Japan rapidly recovered from the economic crisis, industrial production increased explosively, and exports surged rapidly. Factors such as the plunge in the value of the yen and low domestic wages played a part, but the Japanese government's adequate use of policies had an effect as well. In the early 1930s, Japan implemented 'Keynesian economic policy' in order to bring about monetary inflation and deter economic recession, at the risk of deficit finance.[322] Since it was 1936 when renowned British economist John Maynard Keynes published *General Theory of Employment, Interest and Money*, it is highly laudable that Finance Minister Takahashi Korekiyo (高橋是清, 1854-1936) executed such a policy four years before the paper was published. Japan's annual economic growth rate in the 1930s was actually 5% as a result of the foreign exchange rate, low wages, and government policies.[323] Such economic growth signifies that Japan had alternatives to military expansionism in the 1930s.[324] However, Japan concentrated on developing military forces on the foundation of economic growth, in the attempt to dominate Asia and raise itself into a worldwide ruling country.

In the 1930s, the military authorities prevailed over the bureaucracy, the court, and the political parties. The military authorities were not controlled by any other than the Japanese Emperor, and it was considered that the Japanese Emperor himself did not object to the plans of the military authorities to push ahead with foreign expansion. Amidst this atmosphere, there was a fierce power struggle even within the military, and in particular, extremely radical military officers assembled as the Imperial Way Faction (皇道波, *kodo-ha*). The extreme rightists, centering on young military officers, clamored for 'Showa Restoration,' asserting that they should extricate themselves from Western and liberal thoughts and build a new Japan. The activities of these men led to terrorism or assassination of major figures in the government or business world. The climax of their activities was manifest in the so-called 'February 26 Incident' which took place in 1936. Military troops of approximately 1,400 men led by young military officers attacked the government buildings, killing or injuring many political leaders and imperial advisors. They attempted to establish a military government that sympathized with far-right nationalism and claimed to stand for absolute loyalty toward the Japanese Emperor. However, they did not receive support from the upper echelon of the military dominated by the Control Faction (統制波, *tosei-ha*)[325] and only gave rise to Emperor Hirohito's enragement. Emperor Hirohito was furious that his imperial advisors were attacked. So he ordered that since there was no relationship between the men and himself, they should be put on trial for treason. Emperor Hirohito even deprived the men of the right to commit suicide by disembowelment. Thus, the trial against the leaders of the rebellion progressed in secret, and 19 men were sentenced to death and 70 to penal servitude.

In the 1930s when the military authorities dominated power and tension mounted with China and Western nations, the leaders in the military and bureaucracy reinforced thought control with more severity toward the society. In the mid-1930s, even conservative ideas which had been extensively accepted in the past became targets of criticism. The Emperor Organ Theory (天皇機關設), proposed by Minobe Tatsukichi, a well-respected legal professor at the Tokyo Imperial University, was that the Japanese Emperor was merely an organ within the state structure since the Emperor's role was stipulated by the Constitution. Minobe's idea had been recognized without any problems up to the early 1930s. However, in 1935, some scholars, military men in the Imperial Way Faction, and representatives in the House of Peers, [326] severely criticized Minobe for slandering the Emperor by conducting treasonous research. As a result, several of Minobe's works were banned and Minobe resigned from his post as a representative in the House of Peers.[327]

In the Taisho Era, the time had been ripe for democracy on the foundation of political parties and parliamentary politics, but in the face of economic depression and international tension in the late 1920s and early 1930s, Japanese leaders and Japanese people came to select the Empire and Emperor over democracy. Finally, in the 1930s, the Japanese Emperor was revered as a transcendent being, and in 1937, the Ministry of Education promulgated a manifesto titled *Cardinal Principles of the National Entity of Japan* (*Kokutai no hongi*) which declared loyalty to the Emperor, military spirit, hierarchical family system and so forth as key values and institutions. Thus, the Japanese Emperor acquired an inviolable status and anything could be done under the Emperor's name. Under the political system created by the Meiji Constitution, it was difficult to arbitrate in conflicts between powerful actors, and in particular, there was a lack of political devices to apply restraint on the arbitrary actions of the military authorities. Only the Japanese Emperor who had the prerogative of supreme command of the military could control the military, but he did not attempt to play this role, and it was difficult to apply restraint in the midst of the domestic atmosphere that was fanatical about expanding the empire. A new era had arrived in which the military authorities could do as they wished by establishing a militaristic regime.[328]

It can be said that the aftermath of the failure of party politics to take root in Japan in the 1920s and 1930s, together with social factors (labor disputes, farm tenancy disputes) and economic instability (chronic recession), brought about the emergence of military power. According to this view, party politics started to collapse as the militarist and nationalist forces, which had fought to overthrow party politics, rapidly increased through the Manchurian Incident in 1931 and the 5.15 Incident in 1932. The view also holds that the system of Militarism, centering on the military authorities, dominated Japanese society until the end of the Pacific War.[329] In other words, if party politics had settled properly, domination of Japan's Militarism and the series of wars of aggression could have been prevented in advance. However, due to the existence of a solid Emperor system pursuant to the Japanese Constitution, it is judged that realization of representative democracy through party politics would have been realistically difficult. Considering the fact that even the contemporary Japanese society, which is governed by party politics, is becoming right-sided, it would be reasonable to say that party politics could not substantially have anchored in the 1920s and 1930s.

Japan's system of Militarism displayed some unique aspects, when compared with Fascism which rose at around the same time in Europe. Fascism is generally understood as dictatorship through public manipulation by those who have seized power by gaining support of the people. In other words, Hitler and Mussolini propagandized social anxiety in an exaggerated manner in the process of coming into power, but they did so by gaining consent of the people in a legitimate way. However, in the case of Japan, not only was there no change of ruling forces as in Fascist nations of Europe, but the colors of militarism became stronger through antidemocratic regulations such as the prerogative of supreme command of the military and the Japanese Emperor's governing power under the Meiji Constitution. After the economic boom during World War I, Japan felt a sense of crisis in foreign relations starting in the 1920s, due to problems such as excessive facilities and domestic economic recession, and insecure relationships with advanced Western nations, which brought forth militarism as a countermeasure. Furthermore, since the veterans of the Meiji Restoration who had played a role in balancing the establishment and management of domestic and foreign strategies had all passed away, and the system that the Defense Minister should be appointed with an incumbent general was introduced, Japan's politics was at the mercy of the military authorities. Thus, in order to hammer out a solution to domestic and foreign crises, modern Japan strengthened thought control under the pretext of concentrating national power domestically and made full-fledged invasions externally.[330]

2. Japan's Provocation of the Second Sino-Japanese War and the Pacific War

By using the situation that the Chinese Nationalist Party (Kuomintang) government led by Jiang Jieshi placed priority on stabilization of internal affairs by overthrowing warlords and the Chinese Communist Party over denouncement of foreign powers, Japan established Manchukuo led by a puppet government and strengthened its threat against mainland China. The Chinese Communist Party, which was confronted with such national crisis and threat to the party's existence, announced the Declaration of August 1 on August 1, 1935 and appealed for the formation of the anti-Japan national unification front. There was an incident (the so-called Xian Incident[331]) in which the warlord Zhang Xueliang (張學良, 1898-2001) confined Jiang Jieshi (蔣介石, 1887-1975), who visited Xian (西安) in December 1936, and demanded anti-Japanese struggle as the top priority. As a result, the Chinese Nationalist Party (Kuomintang) and the Chinese Communist Party began to work together again and collaborate in the anti-Japanese struggle. As the political forces within China formed a single line in this way, it became a burden to Japan, which aimed to expand its domination of China.

Amidst this situation, there was a gunfight between the Japanese military and the Chinese military on the evening of July 7, 1937, near Lugouqiao (盧溝橋, the Marco Polo Bridge), south of Beijing.[332] The Japanese military dispatched large scale troops, asserting that the Chinese military initiated the gunfight. The Japanese military seized Beijing and Tianjin, and within a month after the occurrence of the Lugouqiao Incident (the Marco Polo Bridge Incident), a full-scale war broke out between Japan and China. The expansionist forces within the Japanese military authorities, which led the war, probably wished to collapse the Chinese Nationalist Party (Kuomintang) government and invite a government which was more favorable to Japan. In the fall of 1937, the Japanese military moved south to occupy most of the Shandong Peninsula and the Yellow River (黃河) area, and occupied Shanghai in collaboration with the navy. Furthermore, in December the Japanese military occupied Nanjing (南京), which was the capital of the Chinese Nationalist Party (Kuomintang) government at the time, and this was where the Japanese committed horrible butchery and rape, which was called the massacre of the century. China lost its three major cities, but the Chinese Nationalist Party (Kuomintang) government led by Jiang Jieshi continued to resist while retreating toward the west. In the months that followed, the Japanese military continued to seize key cities and railway lines, but as they suffered from guerrilla attacks and as the Chinese Nationalist Party (Kuomintang) government retreated to Chongqing (重慶), the war front reached a deadlock.

As in the Manchurian Incident, Japan initiated the Second Sino-Japanese War through a unilateral attack without a declaration of war. This was influenced by Japan's judgment that the battle would end in a relatively short period of time, but more importantly, Japan took into account the protection of its rights and interests as well as the aggravation of international condemnation. In other words, if Japan were to declare war, there were many disadvantages, not only would Japan forfeit its rights pursuant to the treaty, such as extraterritoriality and international settlement that Japan enjoyed in China, but Japan would also have to endure international criticism for violating the renunciation of war treaty (the Kellogg-Briand Pact).[333] But most of all, there was a great tactical advantage to making a surprise attack without giving the counterpart any chance to prepare, and there would also have been a psychological factor of not wanting to publicly expose its self-fabricated pretext of war.

To make matters worse, while the China war front came to a deadlock, Japan engaged in a massive battle with the Soviet Union in Nomonhan, the border area between China and Mongolia, in the summer of 1939. This

Nomonhan Incident broke out because Japan's Kwantung Army attempted to unilaterally expand the territory of Manchuria without considering the historical border between Manchuria and Mongolia. The better equipped Soviet troops had a great victory against Japan's Kwantung Army. Japan suffered a humiliating defeat in this battle, where 20,000 out of Japan's 60,000 troops were killed in battle or died of disease.[334] Starting from the mid-1930s, some strategists attempted to restrain Japan's reckless military expansion. Ironically, Ishiwara Kanji, the mastermind behind the Manchuria takeover, asserted that since Japan did not have the resources and capacity to rule over the entire Chinese territory, Japan should concentrate on the development of Manchuria while building up national strength to respond to potential enemies such as the Soviet Union and the Western powers.

In March 1940, Japan established a puppet government in order to more efficiently rule over the Chinese people amounting to 300 million in its occupied regions of China. As the head of this government, Japan placed Wang Jingwei (汪精衛, 1883-1944), who had struggled with Jiang Jieshi for leadership of the Chinese Nationalist Party (Kuomintang). However, this puppet government was impotent because it could not gain support from the Chinese people. Unable to escape from the China stalemate, Japan fell into a state of confusion in which the prime minister was replaced several times. The Japanese government attempted to overcome the deadlock in China by taking various diplomatic strategies with Germany, the United States, the United Kingdom, the Soviet Union, and France, in order to isolate the Chinese Nationalist Party (Kuomintang) and destroy its will to survive. However, the Anti-Comintern Pact, which was settled in 1936 to keep the Soviet Union in check in Asia, was broken when Hitler's regime entered into a nonaggression treaty with Stalin in August 1939. Even so, when Hitler invaded Poland and France, the Japanese government adhered to neutrality and attempted to resolve the China stalemate with help from the United States and the United Kingdom. However, the military authorities asserted forming an alliance with Germany and Italy, and finally in September 1940, the Tripartite Pact was concluded between Japan, Germany and Italy. When Germany, which occupied Paris, established the collaborationist Vichy regime to rule over France, Japan was able to station its troops in the northern part of Indochina (Vietnam), which was a French colony, with connivance of the Vichy government. The motive behind Japan's expansion in Southeast Asia was to secure military resources such as oil, rubber, and tin, and to establish a base to siege the Chinese Nationalist Party (Kuomintang) government.

As European countries came to be occupied by Germany, the colonies of European countries in Southeast Asia were put into a defenseless state, and it was this absence of power that Japan targeted. In particular, Japan aimed to secure resources necessary for the execution of warfare by dominating

Southeast Asia. However, it was inevitable that Japan's expansion policy into Southeast Asia would be influenced by the response of the United States. In July 1939, the United States renounced the US-Japan commercial treaty, which meant that the United States could put an embargo on exports to Japan at any time, in order to make Japan abandon its expansion policy. When Germany invaded the Soviet Union in June 1941, the United States assumed a more aggressive stance toward Japan. In July 1941, when Japan advanced further south from Indochina, the United States froze Japanese assets within the United States and by and large prohibited exports to Japan. Among the prohibited items was oil. Japan had imported 90% or more of its oil consumption, three-fourths of which came from the United States.[335]

As the United States adhered to the position that Japan should withdraw from all of the regions in China with the exception of South Manchuria, which Japan had occupied prior to 1931, diplomatic negotiations were ruptured, and Japan sought expansion of war. Thus, in the meeting with the Japanese Emperor held on November 5, 1941, Japan decided to attack the colonies of Western powers in Southeast Asia as well as the United States military bases in the Philippines and Pearl Harbor, if the United States would not acknowledge Japan's status in Asia by all means. At the time, Japan's leaders were aware of the fact that Japan stood no chance in the war, considering the gap between Japan and the United States in terms of industries and armament. According to a study by Japan's Economic Planning Board in 1940, Japan depended on the United States for JYP 1.9 billion among its imports of JYP 2.1 billion, and the United States had higher production of goods, amounting to approximately 80 times that of Japan in 1941 and approximately 118 times that of Japan in 1944.[336] Japan was under the delusion that the United States would not engage in war in a faraway land, and proceeded with a chain of reckless military acts since 1931 without restraint. Thus, the Pacific War was the ultimate result of the continuous sedimentation of irrational and dreamlike decisions that started with the Manchurian Incident. Japanese society disregarded the immensely unfavorable reality and fell into a collective illusion of the superiority and confidence of Japan, a country ruled by a line of Japanese emperors unbroken for ages eternal.

Japan's attack on Pearl Harbor, the heart of the United States' Pacific fleet, on December 7, 1941 left six out of nine United States warships completely destroyed and two beyond repair. The United States' long-standing position of non-interventionism was neutralized by the Americans' rage due to Japan's cunning, sudden, and dishonorable attack. In fact, Japan's abrupt and ungentlemanly attack was not at all surprising. This was because Japan had often resorted to such tactics in the past against China and Russia. In addition, indications of Japan's attack had been detected to some extent through intercepted codes, radar signals, and information from American and Dutch intelligence personnel. Whatever the circumstances, Japan's attack on Pearl Harbor weakened the non-interventionist sentiment within the United States and served as momentum to draw the United States into war.[337] Later, President Roosevelt recollected that without Japan's attack on Pearl Harbor, there would have been great difficulties in bringing Americans to war.[338]

On the day Japan succeeded in making a surprise attack on Pearl Harbor, the Japanese military landed on the Malay Peninsula, continuously advanced southward pushing out the British military, and occupied Singapore in February 1942. In May, Japan won a victory in the battle in the Philippines, forcing the United States military led by General Douglas MacArthur to withdraw to Australia. Furthermore, the Japanese military occupied the British overseas territory of Burma and Dutch overseas territory of Indonesia, and went on to dominate many islands in the southern and central regions of the Pacific Ocean. Thus, the Japanese military suddenly came to form a vast empire, ranging 6,400km from north to south and 9,600km from east to west, through swift victories and occupations in the first six months of the war. Japan recovered in a single blow from the frustration and bruised ego it had suffered from deadlock in the China war front and pressure of the United States through the success of the surprise attack on Pearl Harbor and successive victories in Southeast Asia. During this period, Emperor Hirohito was overwhelmed by delight and euphoria at the news of the Japanese military's successive victories.[339]

It was only after the Japanese military made a surprise attack on Pearl Harbor and landed on the Malay Peninsula under British rule that Japan issued the Japanese Emperor's protocol for declaration of war against the United States and the United Kingdom. This sort of deceptive conduct was something that continued throughout modern Japan's foreign expansion process. Even in the First Sino-Japanese War and the Russo-Japanese War, Japan declared war only after making a preemptive strike against the counterpart, and in the vast areas of Manchuria and China, Japan expanded its domination step by step by fabricating various events. In June 1928, Japan's Kwantung Army assassinated Zhang Zuolin, the warlord of the Fengtian Army, by exploding a train which he was aboard. After creating confusion in this manner, Japan dispatched troops in an attempt to seize the northeastern region of China. In addition, in the late hours of September 18, 1931, the Kwantung Army detonated explosives in the South Manchuria Railway close to the Liutiao Lake (柳条湖) in Shenyang (瀋陽, 奉天, Manchu name Mukden), placed the blame on the Chinese troops, attacked the Chinese troops, and occupied cities along the railway one after the other (Manchurian Incident). Also, the Kwantung Army fabricated a false-flag operation with military officers in the Japanese consulate in Shanghai claiming that a mob had attacked Japanese monks. Using this as a pretext, on January 28, 1932, the Kwantung Army, along with the Japanese navy, attacked Chinese troops stationed in Shanghai (January 28 Incident). Furthermore, the Japanese military forged the Lugouqiao Incident (the Marco Polo Bridge Incident) in the outskirts of Beijing on the night of July 7, 1937, and began to attack by asserting that the Chinese military had commenced fire. Thus, the Second Sino-Japanese War began.

As a means of lowering its dependence on the United States for resources and to break through the deadlock in the China war front, Japan occupied Southeast Asia and attempted to form a self-sufficiency system. Also, in order to become a ruler instead of the Western powers, Japan needed the justification of liberating the yellow race from the domination of the white race. It was the 'Greater East Asia Co-Prosperity Sphere (大東亞共榮圈, Dai Toa Kyoei Ken)' that Japan set forth as the cause to disguise this realistic motive. Starting from the 1930s, Imperial Japan formed the concept of 'East Asia' as a region that it could reign as the leader, and in the 1940s, this concept was expanded into 'Greater East Asia' to include Southeast Asia.[340] The concept of Greater East Asia Co-Prosperity Sphere was based on 'Greater Asianism,' which could originally be seen as a conflicting concept with 'Datsua Nyuo' (Leave Asia, enter Europe). This is an idea of the Pan-Asian solidarity to stand against Asian invasion of Western powers, which originated from the idealism that 'Asia is one' which was proposed by Okakura Kakuzo (岡倉覚三, 1863-1913), a Meiji philosopher, in his book *The Ideals of the East* (1903). Japan's blatant foreign expansion policy after the Manchuria Incident, defying the United States and the United Kingdom, needed a just cause and ideology surpassing *Datsuaron* (Escape from Asia), and this was 'Greater Asianism.'[341]

The Japanese military claimed to stand for anti-colonialism in Burma, Thailand, and the Philippines by supporting the titular independent governments, while attempting direct rule in Indochina and Indonesia. In reality, however, governance was under the control of Japanese military commanders in each region. On the one hand, these commanders suppressed opposition movements against Japanese rule, and on the other hand, supported anti-West and pro-Japanese figures. In November 1942, Japan established a Greater East Asia Ministry (大東亞省) in order to group and collectively rule over its occupied territories. However, this new organization did nothing more than hold a single round of the Greater East Asia Conference in November 1943, by summoning to Tokyo the heads of Thailand, Burma, Wang Jingwei's puppet government of China, Manchukuo, and the Philippines, the five states constituting the Greater East Co-Prosperity Sphere (Dai Toa Kyoei Ken). The main discussions of the conference consisted of glorifying the Pan-Asian solidarity and criticizing Western imperialism. Eventually, the trust that the Japanese military had gained by banishing Western powers under the guise of Pan-Asian solidarity completely failed through brutal governance in occupied territories and rather, anti-Japanese movements heightened as time went by.

3. Social Suppression and Wartime Mobilization of Japan

The idea of an absolute and sacred Japanese Emperor was formed and diffused through the *Imperial Rescript on Education* (教育勅語) which was proclaimed in October 1890 under the name of the Japanese Emperor. The *Imperial Rescript on Education* stipulated the fundamental principles and practical morality of nationalistic education, and included the Confucian values of loyalty, filial duty, and obedience. This was an ideology used to reinforce the ruling system centering on the Japanese Emperor, by cultivating people who are loyal to the state, worship the Japanese Emperor as a god, and are willing to give up their lives for the Japanese Emperor in time of emergency, through borrowing Confucian ethics.[342] Therefore, all schools kept the *Imperial Rescript on Education* with the Japanese Emperor's portrait and recited it during the morning assembly. There was an incident where a teacher stuttered while reciting the *Imperial Rescript on Education* and committed suicide on the grounds of disgracing this great document.[343] This idea of worshipping the Japanese Emperor was strongly reinforced in the 1930s, and reached its climax in the *Cardinal Principles of the National Entity of Japan*, (*Kokutai no Hongi*) which is considered as the bible of the 'Emperor System (*Tennosei*).' This booklet which was published by the Ministry of Education in 1937 was distributed and taught not only in schools but also in various institutions. In the booklet, the Japanese Emperor was portrayed as a 'deity incarnate (現人神, Arahitogami),' the direct descendant of Amaterasu (天照), the sun goddess, and it was emphasized that showing loyalty to the Japanese Emperor was not an obligation or obedience toward authority, but a natural state occurring spontaneously from the heart.[344]

From 1925, Japan dispatched army officers at secondary schools and above to implement military drills, and after the Manchurian Incident in 1931, nationalist education was strengthened all throughout Japanese society. After the Second Sino-Japanese War in 1937, students were mobilized to worship and clean at shrines, participate in volunteer work for war-bereaved families, take part in farewell events for soldiers at the front, write letters of encouragement to soldiers, and do various types of labor service. After Japan started the Pacific War in 1941, Japan began to carry out full-fledged education for wartime mobilization and further strengthened education on militarism. Schools, which should have implemented education to build character and refine young students, were turning into military training camps, and education was conducted for the purpose of cultivating subjects that were loyal to the Japanese Emperor and the state and justifying war. As a consequence, the formation and content of school education changed in accordance with a war footing, textbooks emphasized the mental attitude of subjects of the Japanese Empire required for war, and Japan was depicted as a state of the god and the Japanese Emperor as a god. Even various school events outside of the classroom became characterized as wartime education, and extracurricular activities were focused on military training and physical education.[345]

As Japan was far off from victory in war and went through difficulties in governance in occupied territories, Japan externally claimed to advocate the establishment of a new order in East Asia and internally constructed a general wartime mobilization system. Accordingly, Japan denounced pluralism, as Nazi Germany and Fascist Italy did, and pursued an authoritarian political order and a society dominated by firm discipline based on a centrally-directed planned economy and a single unified political party. First of all, the National General Mobilization Law was passed by the Diet in 1938, pursuant to which the government could issue any necessary order to mobilize and control human and material resources without Diet approval in the case where a national emergency were to be proclaimed. In 1941, based on the Mobilization Law and the Important Industries Association Order, the Ministry of Commerce formed super cartels called 'Control Associations' which determined price, volume, market share, etc., in each industry. When the war became fierce in 1941 and adult male employees were drafted to the military causing a shortage of labor, bureaucrats assigned new graduates to war industries after discussions with school principals pursuant to the Mobilization Law. In order to supplement a shortage of labor, the Japanese government allowed the requisition of adult males from 16 to 40 and unmarried women from 16 to 25,[346] and from 1943 to 1945, three million Japanese schoolboys and schoolgirls were recruited by armaments factories. In late 1943, the final stage of the war, the government demanded that all single women from 12 to 39 should register for the so-called Women's Volunteer Labor Corps, and from 1943 to 1945, around 470,000 women were placed under requisition through this program. Furthermore, approximately a million Koreans and Chinese were placed under requisition by Japan, assigned to mines and armament factories, and suffered from heavy labor and abuse under strict surveillance.[347]

In the political arena, some bureaucrats and military officers deployed a movement to deconstruct existing political parties and create a new single mass party, which was patterned after Hitler's Nazis. Although a Nazi-style mass party was not established, Konoe, who assumed his second post as Prime Minister in July 1940, established the Imperial Rule Assistance Association (IRAA, 大政翼贊會). Accordingly, all political parties were pressured to voluntarily disperse, and the members of the House of Representatives were urged to join the IRAA respectively. The government intervened in every single aspect of society, and strict censorship and harsh measures were taken for political expression.

After 1937 when the Second Sino-Japanese War broke out, economic growth went through a sharp slowdown and the inflation rate rapidly rose in double-digit annual levels. Taxes were greatly increased after the late 1930s, and in 1938, military expenditures made up three-fourths of the government budget and 30% of gross national product. The consumer economy already froze in the early 1940s, the general mobilization system prevented raw materials and capitals from being invested in textiles and other consumer industries and encouraged companies in these fields to install war production lines. The real wages of Japanese people dropped by 60% between 1934 and 1945, during which time the figure increased by 20% in the United States and the United Kingdom and Germany maintained the status quo. As such, the lives of ordinary Japanese people were miserable due to the decrease in real wages and shortage of daily necessities, etc.[348]

As the production of daily necessities decreased due to the reshuffling of industrial productions centered on the military industry and defeats in the Pacific War continued, the lives of Japanese people were rapidly aggravated and nationwide agony was standardized. In the midst of universal agony, hatred toward war of the general public increased, but the dissatisfaction of the people was suppressed through strict control and manipulation of information and nationalistic education centered on the Japanese Emperor. Therefore, there were neither public displays of discontent or anti-war movements, nor were there insurgent activities such as assassination of war leaders. More and more, Japan was sinking into a pit of self-destruction, but surprisingly, Japanese society continued to worship the Japanese Emperor and persevered through all the agony. This shows that during the Pacific War era, modern Japan was seized with collective madness and reached the point in which all 100 million Japanese people were unable to judge and behave in a rational manner.

As the war was prolonged and the general mobilization system dominated the lives of the people, some cultural figures turned their interests to aesthetic or non-political areas as a means of self-protection or escape from reality. Of course, a very small minority managed to escape the vigilance of the censors and skillfully conveyed their critical views. However, the majority of intellectuals actively supported the war and joined government-sponsored associations. These intellectuals disguised wartime mobilization and reform as a mission to 'overcome the modern,' and concentrated on attacking modernity and Western culture. These anti-modernists defined rational science, which developed within Western traditions rooted in Hellenism and Hebraism, as the cultural enemy. The Western tradition postulates a conflict composition between Man and God, but the Japanese tradition sees no conflict between Man and God.[349] These anti-modernists evaluated the Meiji Restoration as a success in that Japan blocked the invasion of the West unlike

India or China, but considered that it was a mistake that Western materialism and selfishness became prevalent due to modernization during the Meiji Period. Thus, the war was extolled as a means of liberating Asians from Western-dominated modernism and enabling Asians to restore their true selves and live in harmony. This spirit was reflected in the policies of the Japanese government to reject the cultural influence of the West, banning American and British films and music and even prohibiting hair perms and baseball. However, the fact that there were such anti-modernist efforts shows that Japan was already modernized, and it can be said that Western trends, tastes, cultures, etc. were firmly rooted in Japanese society. Ironically, execution of war against the West required the utilization of rational science, the essence of modernity, in the production of advanced fighter planes and weapons. In fact, Japan had developed the zero fighter plane (零式艦上戰鬪機), which was a cutting-edge fighter at the time, by mobilizing the best technicians.

It is true that the military authorities fundamentally took the lead in the war under the emperor system, but various fields, such as politics, the economy, military, culture, mass media, and education, contributed to the execution of war in direct or indirect ways. As the party cabinet collapsed, politicians praised militarism under the emperor system and instigated war in order to maintain their influence. Various media, including newspapers, increased circulation by inciting war. As mass media and society were controlled, no brakes were put on militarism, and the situation was heated through the interaction of various fields, resulting in the expansion of war.[350] In particular, newspapers reported the news in accordance with false announcements of the Kwantung Army after the Manchurian Incident in 1931, and were intent on instigating hatred toward China and praising the victories of the Japanese army. After the Second Sino-Japanese War broke out in 1937, newspapers became even more engrossed in promoting war, to the extent that war correspondents described atrocious acts of killing during the war as heroic. Facts that were unfavorable to Japan were prohibited from being reported through censorship of the authorities, and in December 1940, an Information Bureau was installed within the Cabinet to control war-related coverage under a centralized system. The radio system, which first began broadcasting by transmitting the coronation ceremony of Emperor Hirohito in November 1928, was at the forefront of instigating the war sentiment along with newspapers.[351]

CHAPTER 7

JAPAN'S DEFEAT IN WORLD WAR II AND POSTWAR SETTLEMENTS

1. Japan's Defeat in World War II

In May 1942, the Japanese military failed to acquire the Coral Islands in the northeast coast of Australia, and during the battle of Midway Islands in June, the Japanese military suffered a crushing defeat in which four aircraft carriers, which were the principal axis of the Japanese navy, were destroyed. From this point on, the tide of war began to turn in the favor of the United States. After the United States built an air base in Szechwan (Sichuan), China, the United States forces were able to attack Japan with long-range B-29s. Furthermore, the loss of Saipan in July 1944 after a deadly battle was a big blow to Japan. Now the United States forces were able to directly attack Tokyo by utilizing Saipan as a bombing base. As a consequence, Tojo Hideki (東條英機, 1884-1948) resigned from his post as Prime Minister and General Koiso Kuniaki (小磯國昭, 1880-1950) became the new Prime Minister. One of the things that Japan devised as the tide of war became unfavorable was a suicide mission in which a pilot loaded a bomb on his plane and rushed toward a ship or target spot on the land, and these pilots were called *Kamikaze* or *Shinpu* (神風). The *Kamikaze* was named according to the 'divine wind' which was known to have protected Japan from Mongolian invasion in the 13th century. The suicide planes were designed to mount bombs on their wings, equipped with only simple control systems, and did not even have fuel for a return trip. These suicide planes, which were called 'baka bombs' by the United States forces, were mainly flown by teenagers who were assigned after receiving several weeks of training. The *Kamikaze* first emerged in the Battle of Leyte Gulf in the Philippines on October 25, 1944. However, the Allied Forces effectively subdued the Japanese navy in a full-fledged naval battle which lasted for four days (from October 23 to 26). As a consequence of losing the Battle of Leyte Gulf, Japan completely lost its capacity to engage in naval battles, and almost all of the 80,400 troops dispatched in ground combat in Leyte Island died on the battlefield.[352] The Allied Forces, which kept pushing out the Japanese military, regained the Corregidor region in February 1945, and occupied

Manila in mid-March. As Japan suffered from continuous defeats, it can be said that the rationale of expansionism of 'zone of sovereignty' and 'zone of interest' which modern Japan had pursued, turned into a trap that brought about a security crisis in Japan by losing the 'zone of interest' and threatening the 'zone of sovereignty.'[353]

Just as Japanese people in their homeland persevered all sorts of pain and did not hesitate to die without a word, the Japanese soldiers who faced defeat on the battlefields of Southeast Asia and the Pacific Ocean gallantly chose honorable death rather than suffering the humiliation of living as prisoners of war. The above-mentioned *Kamikaze* is the prime example of this tragic image of Japanese soldiers. Japanese newspapers photographed and reported the departure scenes of the *Kamikaze* rangers, and sometimes covered their courageous stories in the form of letters, wills, and songs. The Japanese military authorities propagandized the idea that if one died as a *Kamikaze* ranger, he would be buried in the Yasukuni Shrine and be praised as a national god. In the Japanese religion of Shinto at that time, there was a distinction between a higher god and a lower god when a person died and became a god, in which a higher god became a national god for which the Japanese Emperor performed ancestral rites, but an ordinary person could not become a national god. In other words, modern Japan proclaimed that even an ordinary person could become a national god if he died on the battlefield for the Japanese Emperor and cornered young men into a deadly situation. In this way, Japan's Emperor System and the Shinto religion dominated even the Japanese people's view of life and death and made them risk their lives in modern Japan's foreign invasion wars.

As the tide of the war became extremely unfavorable for Japan, some influential people in the Royal Court, the diplomatic circle, and the economic circle as well as some senior military officers came to think that it could be much better to surrender rather than being tragically defeated. In particular, they were most concerned that the Soviet Union might take part in the war and that the emperor system may collapse. Konoe Fumimaro (近衞文麿, 1891-1945), who had been the Prime Minister three times, submitted a plea called the Konoe Memorial (近衞上奏文) to the Japanese Emperor in February 1945. Konoe tried to persuade Emperor Hirohito that Japan must conduct a truce and peace negotiation with the United States even if it had to accept unconditional surrender, in order to save the people from the misery of war, to preserve the *kokutai* (國體, national entity, Japanese Emperor System), and to promote the safety of the imperial family.[354] Emperor Hirohito agreed with Konoe's views, but could not readily put it into practice.

Since early 1945, the American forces expanded their bombing raids on Japan with their long-range bombers (B-29s) over several months. These raids were more actively deployed after the American forces seized Iojima (硫

黄島) of the Ogasawara Islands (小笠原諸島) situated between Saipan and Japan in March and built an air base. At this point, Japan could only be helplessly attacked, whereas the United States lost only seventy-four B-29s in the 31,387 sorties from July 1944 to August 1945 when the war ended.[355] The largest air raid was targeted at Tokyo on March 10, when 100,000 Japanese people lost their lives. Aside from the cultural sites of Kyoto and Nara, 40-50% of urban infrastructure in Japan's major cities was destroyed.[356]

The attack of Okinawa by the Allied Forces began on April 1, 1945, and due to the Japanese military's strong resistance to defend the mainland of Japan, the fiercest battle during the final stages of the war took place. Four days after the battle began, Prime Minister Koiso Kuniaki resigned and Admiral Suzuki Kantaro (鈴木貫太郎, 1868-1948) became his successor. As Germany surrendered to the Allied Forces on May 8, the military power of the Allied Forces could now be focused on Japan, which made Japan plunge into an even more unfavorable situation. Eventually, after a fierce battle of nearly 3 months, the American forces secured Okinawa on June 21. Approximately 110,000 Japanese soldiers and 150,000 civilians died in this battle. The American forces also totaled 13,000 deaths and 40,000 injuries, suffering from the largest casualties in the Pacific War. Even more tragic was the fact that approximately 2,000 *Kamikaze* pilots lost their lives in the Okinawa battle, and numerous Japanese civilians, who were brainwashed to believe that the American forces were atrocious, committed mass suicides.[357]

Roosevelt from the United States, Churchill from the United Kingdom, and Jiang Jieshi (also known as Chiang Kai-shek) from China got together in November 1943 in Cairo, Egypt, to discuss the situation and joint operation in the Japan war front, and announced the so-called Cairo Declaration on December 1. The Cairo Declaration proclaimed that the Allied Forces would not delay attacks until Japan surrendered, would make Japan return all the territories that modern Japan occupied through foreign invasion, and would liberate Korea at an appropriate time in order to enable Korean people to escape from slavery. When the victory of the Allied Forces was anticipated in Europe, Roosevelt, Churchill, and Stalin congregated in Yalta, Soviet Union in February 1945, and discussed the Soviet Union's participation in the Japan operations as well as the new world order after the war. The United States and the United Kingdom accepted the Soviet Union's demand for concessions in Manchuria in China in order to induce the Soviet Union's participation in the war. Furthermore, it was decided that Japan's Kuril Islands would be ceded to the Soviet Union. The decision on the Kuril Islands in the Yalta Conference became the apple of discord in the territorial dispute between the Soviet Union (today's Russia) and Japan after the war.

On July 17, 1945, Truman, Stalin and Churchill met in Potsdam, Germany for a two-week discussion on the end of the war. China's Jiang Jieshi participated in the discussions over the phone. On July 26, the Potsdam

Declaration[358] was announced, and at the time, Stalin's name was omitted because the Soviet Union had not taken part in the war against Japan yet, but Stalin later signed the declaration. The Potsdam Declaration demanded Japan surrender unconditionally or suffer from prompt and utter destruction. Also, the Declaration included articles such as the occupation of the Allied Forces, the banishment of leaders of the military authorities, acknowledgement of Japan's sovereignty only within the border line formed at the beginning of the Meiji Period, etc.[359] Furthermore, the Declaration stipulated policies to severely punish all war crimes including abuse of prisoners of war. Fortunately for Japan, the declaration did not mention the Japanese Emperor.

As Japan would not accept the Potsdam Declaration, the United States, which succeeded in an atomic bomb experiment in July 1945, decided to use the bomb on Japan for the first time in history, in order to preferably end the war before the Soviet Union intervened. Ending the war as quickly as possible was beneficial for the United States in that it would reduce the casualties of American forces. In addition, the United States attempted to minimize the military role of the Soviet Union against Japan so as to take the initiative in East Asia. On August 6, an atomic bomb was dropped in Hiroshima (広島), killing 90,000 people and destroying at least 80% of the buildings in the city. When there was no response from Japan and the Soviet Union declared war on Japan, immediately attacking Manchuria on August 8, the United States dropped a second atomic bomb on Nagasaki (長崎) on August 9, killing approximately 50,000 people.

It was only after a series of big incidents, such as the United States' Hiroshima nuclear bombing on August 6 and Nagasaki nuclear bombing on August 9, the Soviet Union's declaration of war on August 8 and the Soviet invasion of Manchuria on August 9 that Japanese Emperor Hirohito decided to end the war. However, it took nearly a week to finally surrender as the military authorities were still against it. Emperor Hirohito decided to surrender under the sole condition that the emperor system would be maintained. Thus, on August 14, 1945, in the last meeting before the Emperor, the final resolution was made to surrender to the Allied Forces, mainly the United States, and the news was informed to all of the Japanese people the following day via radio broadcast. Finally, the Pacific War came to an end at the hands of Emperor Hirohito, which signifies that Emperor Hirohito could have prevented the commencement or expansion of the war and also could have ended the war at an earlier point. Therefore, this also means that the Japanese Emperor was not free from the issue of war responsibility. When Japan surrendered, the United States rejected the Soviet Union's request that they would occupy the northern region of Hokkaido and held fast to sole occupation of Japan. On September 2, the signing ceremony of the surrender documents was held on the American warship, the Missouri, which was docked on Tokyo Bay.[360]

Emperor Hirohito's declaration of surrender was something that was utterly unbearable to the Japanese people, who had endured the agony of war by worshipping the Emperor as a god. As a consequence, approximately 350 military officers committed suicide immediately after the announcement of the Imperial Rescript on the Termination of the War. However, most Japanese acknowledged that the war had been wrongful and realistically accepted defeat. As a result, bureaucrats, military officers, and businessmen promptly took extremely realistic and practical measures. Starting from the day the war ended on August 15 until the occupation army arrived in early September, there were flames of something burning all across Tokyo. Thousands of bureaucrats, businessmen and military officers incinerated and disposed of various types of documents and material, in order to destroy evidence of wartime activities that could cause retaliation by the occupation army or be unfavorable to Japan in the military court. Thus, Japan's ruling class incinerated important material in order to cope with the Allied Forces' policy to severely punish war criminals, which means that post-war Japan began with 'erasing the past' rather than 'overcoming the past.' In addition, the Japanese government made use of its experience during the war to promptly take another pragmatic measure, in which many women were recruited to work as prostitutes in dozens of Recreation and Amusement Centers built in cities all around Japan exclusively for the use of the occupation army.[361]

2. The Allied Occupation of Japan and Potential for Change in Japan

The Allied Forces had originally planned to divide and rule Japan among the four countries of the United States, the United Kingdom, the Soviet Union, and China, as was the case in Germany. Thus, the plan was for the Soviet Union to rule Hokkaido and the northeast region, the United Kingdom to rule Kyushu and the southwestern region of Honshu, China to rule Shikoku, the United States to rule the remainder, and the four countries would divide the capital of Tokyo, as in the case of Berlin.[362] If Japan had not surrendered and continued to put up a desperate resistance to protect its mainland, the war may have been extended by several months. However, when the United States dropped two nuclear bombs in early August 1945 and the Soviet Union declared war on Japan, Japan ended up accepting the Potsdam Declaration and surrendered.[363] As the war came to an end earlier than expected, it was possible for the United States, which had taken the lead in the war against Japan, to actually take over sole occupation. China could not dispatch troops due to domestic issues, and the Soviet Union refused to dispatch troops that would be assigned under an American commander, after the United States denied the Soviet Union rule over Hokkaido. The British troops mainly consisted of Australians, and only played a limited role in the western region of Honshu.[364]

The occupation policy on Japan was implemented by the Supreme Commander for the Allied Powers (SCAP),[365] with the advice and review of the Four-nation Allied Council for Japan and the Far Eastern Commission of 11 Victor Nations. In fact, the occupation policy was led by General Douglas MacArthur (1880-1964), the Supreme Commander, and the advisors receiving instructions from the United States government. Washington's policies were conceived by figures such as Hugh Burton and George Blakeslee, who were not widely known. These policies were presented as a directive toward MacArthur in October 1945, which was the *Basic Initial Post Surrender Directive to Supreme Commander for the Allied Powers for the Occupation and Control of Japan* (It was more conveniently known as JCS1380/15, in which JCS stands for Joint Chiefs of Staff).[366] SCAP, under the influence of the United States, attempted to implement policies in order to dismantle a militaristic and totalitarian Japan. Such policies can be summarized in two words: demilitarization and democratization.

First of all, SCAP officially dismantled the Japanese military on November 30, 1945, and from 1945 to 1948, SCAP banished from positions in the government and the business world at least 200,000 figures who were judged to have played a leading role in military expansion. Also, through the instruction SCAPIN-677 (Governmental and Administrative Separation of Certain Outlying Areas from Japan), SCAP returned Japan's territory to its condition before the First Sino-Japanese War of 1894-1895 broke out.[367] As a means of compensation to victim countries, a considerable number of Japan's ships were delivered to the Allied Forces, and war equipment and weapons, including nuclear particle accelerators which could be used to manufacture atomic bombs, were destroyed.[368]

Probably the most meaningful demilitarization measure was the inclusion of the 'no war' article in the new constitution. The draft of the new constitution was prepared by SCAP in early 1946, which went through the deliberation of the Imperial Diet and was passed in the spring of the same year. The new constitution went into effect in May 1947. The new constitution contains the three principles of popular sovereignty, renunciation of war and pacifism, and respect for fundamental human rights. Thus, this postwar constitution downgraded the Japanese Emperor from an absolute monarch with sovereignty to a 'symbol of the country and national integration,' and greatly raised the rights of the people. In particular, Article 9[369] contained the phrase that the Japanese people would renounce war and use of force as a means of settling international disputes, due to which the Postwar Constitution has also been called the Peace Constitution. Before the status of the Japanese Emperor was stipulated as the symbol of unity of the people, Emperor Hirohito announced the Declaration of Humanity (Ningen

Sengen) in January 1946 through a broadcast. Although this was also planned by SCAP, it can be said that this reduced the possibility that imperialism centered on the Japanese Emperor would newly rise. In addition, it became extremely difficult to amend the Constitution, as revision of the Constitution requires two-thirds majority of both the House of Representatives and House of Councilors respectively as well as majority public support in a referendum.

The Allied Forces put approximately 6,000 Japanese soldiers on trial in Singapore, the Philippines, Hong Kong, etc., for conventional war crimes such as abuse of war prisoners, and at least 900 soldiers were executed. At the center of attention was the International Military Tribunal for the Far East (commonly known as the Tokyo Trial), which was held from May 1946 to November 1948. In the Tokyo Trial, 28 of Japan's wartime rulers, such as Tojo Hideki (1884-1948) were tried. They were indicted for 'crimes against peace (Class A),'[370] which was first applied at the Nuremberg Trials of the Nazi leaders in 1946. They all received a verdict of guilty except for 3 people who died from disease. Thus, 7 of them including Tojo received a hanging verdict, 16 of them received a life sentence, and the remaining 2 were respectively sentenced to 20 years and 7 years of imprisonment.[371]

In August 1945, the four countries of the United States, the United Kingdom, France, and the Soviet Union concluded the London Agreement (Agreement for the 'Prosecution and Punishment of the Major War Criminals of the European Axis') and determined the ordinance of the International Court of Justice through its annex. Article 6 of this ordinance classifies criminal acts within the jurisdiction of the International Court of Justice into clause A, B, and C. Clause A includes crimes against peace, such as the planning, preparation, and execution of war of aggression. Clause B includes typical war crimes, such as violations of the laws or customs of war. Clause C deals crimes against humanity. It can be said that terms such as Class A, Class B and Class C came from the above structure. According to this classification, for instance, 'crimes against peace' was defined as a Class A war crime.[372] However, since Clause A, B, and C in the ordinance do not represent the intensity of the war crime, it is deemed more appropriate to call them Type A, Type B, and Type C. Following this logic, 'crime against peace' should be called a Type A war crime.

Type B and Type C war crime trials were interrogations on war crimes such as massacre and cruel abuse on local civilians and prisoners of war committed by the Japanese forces during the war. So China, the United States, the United Kingdom, the Netherlands, Australia, France, and the Philippines set up each country's respective courts and carried out the trials. China, the country that had suffered from the greatest damage, set up courts in ten different locations and tried 605 cases against 883 people, but only 4 people were sentenced to the death penalty. This was because the Chinese Nationalist Party (Kuomintang) led by Jiang Jieshi adopted the policy of mild punishment from the beginning, and the trials came to a close in haste due to the expansion of a civil war against the Chinese Communist Party. The People's Republic of China, which was newly established after the Chinese Communist Party led by Mao Zedong won a victory, adopted an even milder policy than the Jiang Jieshi Administration. As a result of the trials for Type B and Type C war crimes in each country, a total of 5,700 people were prosecuted, 984 of which were sentenced to the death penalty. Among the people who received a guilty sentence were approximately 300 Korean and Taiwanese people. These people were prisoner watchmen, who performed their duties pursuant to the training and orders of the Japanese military to 'treat prisoners of war as beasts.' Although they had no other choice, they ended up becoming tragic victims that were falsely accused of the crime of abusing prisoners.[373]

SCAP pushed ahead with extensive reforms to overthrow authoritarianism and build a democratic order. An important measure taken before the revision of a relevant section in the constitution was the Civil Liberties Directive of 1945. First of all, freedom of speech, the press and assembly as well as the right to organize labor or farmer unions were secured through this directive, and women's civil rights and suffrage were expanded. Through this measure, all political prisoners, including communists, were freed. SCAP made the new constitution specify the separation of the state and Shinto, the freedom of religion, and the principle of division of religion and state. It became prohibited to worship the shrine as a public figure as well as to make public expenditures for specific religious organizations. The shrine was downgraded as a private religious corporate body, and the clergy lost their status as public officials. School textbooks became targets of SCAP censorship, and the curriculum was modified in the direction of pursuing democracy. Therefore, figures that did not match with democracy were deleted from textbooks. The American education system of 6-3-3-4 was introduced, and local school boards were newly established to avoid excessively centralized and standardized education. Schools now taught peace and democracy instead of war and loyalty, and there was an innovation in education, such as extension of compulsory education and expansion of college education opportunities for women. While SCAP secured democracy and democratic rights such as freedom of speech, it implemented rigorous censorship, which shows the paradox of occupation policy.[374]

SCAP carried out a reform on the *zaibatsu* which had played the role of locomotive under the Japanese militarism system. Also, SCAP deprived ownership of holding companies dominated by the *zaibatsu* and dismantled some of the larger firms within each *zaibatsu*. In April 1947, the Anti-Monopoly Law was passed, regulating approximately 325 companies that ran the risk of excessive concentration of power in the industrial and service sectors. [375] In addition, as a counterbalance to the *zaibatsu* and large companies, SCAP promoted the organization of labor unions. Furthermore, SCAP conducted farmland reform by expropriating the land owned by big landowners and redistributing it to former tenants, in order to build small family farm systems.[376]

The various reformatory measures as mentioned above changed the values of the Japanese people as well as the distribution of socioeconomic power, causing a fever of 'democratization' in Japanese society. Yet, although the United States' occupying policies in Japan through SCAP were powerful, there was still room for the Japanese people to somewhat modify the reforms of the occupiers. This was because SCAP chose the indirect rule method, in which reforms were implemented through the Japanese bureaucracy which was formed in the time of imperialism. SCAP gave work instructions to Japan's relevant government institution through a liaison office consisting of Japanese officials fluent in English. Under this structure, the bureaucrats and elites of the Japanese government could demonstrate flexibility by artfully disobeying or modifying the directives of SCAP.

3. Advent of the Cold War and Lopsided Postwar Settlements in Favor of Japan

As symbolized in Winston Churchill's speech in March 1946 in which he stated that an Iron Curtain was descending in Europe, the Cold War began to gradually emerge in international politics. In 1947, American Secretary of State, George Marshall announced the Marshall Plan, which promised massive economic aid to Europe, in order to prevent the expansion of communist forces. In China, the Chinese Nationalist Party (Kuomintang) government, which the United States had considered as the supporter of a postwar Asian order, was being pushed out by communist forces. In Japan, the Society Party greatly expanded its influence in the elections and the Communist Party also exercised immense influence on labor unions. Therefore, in early 1948, the United States government sent George Kennan from the State Department to Japan to figure out the situation. George Kennan advised that as the occupation policy was not acting as a bulwark of the Free World but paving the way for Communists, the emphasis should now be shifted from reform to economic recovery.[377] Thus, the so-called 'reverse course' of the occupation policy came to emerge.

Therefore, SCAP downsized its plan to dismantle the *zaibatsu* in 1948, and actually relinquished requests for war reparation in 1949. Considering Japan's stagnant economy, reparations for victim nations were to be made in the form of services or industrial machinery rather than money. SCAP illegalized strikes by workers in the public sector and eased labor standards for the protection of workers. In 1950, in accordance with the recommendations of

SCAP, the Japanese government banished approximately 13,000 people from the public or private sector by accusing them of being Communist Party members, which was named the so-called Red Purge. On the other hand, many public officials, who had been in exile for taking a leading role in wartime activities, made a comeback to key positions. As conservative forces, that had temporarily left the arena after the war, seized control of the Japanese newspaper industry again, newspapers failed to thoroughly punish shameful acts of journalists during the war. Furthermore, the media, which can be regarded as the 'fourth force,' did not play its role in protecting democratic values.

In the initial stages of the occupation, the urgent priority was to eliminate Japan's capacity for war execution, so SCAP did not implement policies to help Japan's economic revival. However, as inflation surged and the Cold War advanced, SCAP set a policy to turn Japan into Asia's bulwark against communism and made various efforts to revitalize Japan's economy. In this effort, the United States dispatched Joseph Dodge, a Detroit banker and economist who hated government regulations, to Japan as a special financial advisor in February 1949. According to Joseph Dodge's advice, SCAP pushed ahead with several policies, including the pursuit of a balanced budget, discontinuation of government loans to industries, and abolition of government subsidies. The so-called 'Dodge line' managed to contain inflation, but the Japanese economy did not escape from recession as the industrial sector suffered from lack of funds. Amidst this difficult situation, Japan encountered the great fortune of the Korean War.

Due to the advent of the Cold War and the breakout of the Korean War, Japan was able to rapidly conclude the Treaty of San Francisco with the Allied Forces in a favorable way and make an early comeback to the international arena. At the San Francisco Conference, 54 countries which had directly or indirectly participated in the war against Japan during World War II were invited, but China and Korea, the biggest victim countries, were excluded. Eventually, the San Francisco Conference overlooked the issue of Japan's responsibility for Chinese invasion and Korean colonization, and the treaty was concluded, withholding the problem of substantial war responsibility amidst the absence of socialist countries and some Asian countries. Thus, the countries that suffered from the biggest damage due to Japan's colonial rule and war of aggression – China, Taiwan, Korea, etc. – were not able to speak for their interests at the San Francisco Conference. Accordingly, these countries neither received indemnity or compensation for their loss nor were they able to clearly determine territory of surrounding regions, which is causing Japan's territorial disputes today. The conclusion of the treaty was interlocked with the termination of the war as well as the Cold War structure pursued by the United States. In order to prevent the expansion of communist forces, the United States aimed to boost Japan's economic revival, push ahead with Japan's rearmament, and secure the use of a military base within Japan to station American troops. Therefore, in the midst of the Korean War, Japan established a National Police Reserve of 75,000 men in July 1950 under MacArthur's instructions, which was expanded and reorganized into the Self Defense Forces (自衛隊, Jieitai) in 1954. This brought about the controversy on rearmament, which was prohibited by the Postwar Constitution. In addition, Japan was able to significantly cut the burden of war reparations due to the initiative of the United States to use Japan as the bulwark against communism in East Asia. Based on reparations in kind and in the form of services as well as economic support of companies, Japan turned Southeast Asia into a region playing a semi-colonial role as the customer purchasing Japanese goods and the source of raw materials. Southeast Asian countries condemned Japan's predatory trading and investment, which did not allow any substantive benefits to Southeast Asian countries, despite the reparation agreements and reinforcement of economic relations.[378]

The Cold War influenced the military trial held in Japan and there was public sentiment that those who received punishments through the trial were scapegoats in a sense, as figures that most necessarily should have been interrogated escaped trial. A foremost example of figures who escaped trial were members of Unit 731, who conducted numerous biological and chemical experiments on civilians and prisoners of war. However, the United States overlooked the whole business of Unit 731 under the condition of taking over the scientific data obtained from these experiments which were prohibited by the United States laws.[379] In addition, a vast amount of loot that the Japanese military had seized in Asia was siphoned off by the conspiracy of figures in the Japanese Emperor's family and the United States military authorities.[380] Furthermore, the indiscriminate air raids that Japan committed in Chongqing and Nanjing of China were not brought to trial. In addition, the Lushun Massacre during the First Sino-Japanese War, as well as slaughters and various acts of cruelty toward civilians in colonized Taiwan and Korea were overlooked as well. In these cases, the United States consciously avoided bringing the issues to trial, due to its own air raids toward Japan as well as acts of cruelty toward Native Americans.[381] Also, Japan's special organizations, which played the role of advance guard in Japan's colonization and war of aggression and acted as the foothold of maintaining the system, were decriminalized. Furthermore, no punishment was given to the *zaibatsu*, which had supported the economy of modern Japan, by providing the material basis for the commencement and development of colonization and war of aggression, and plucking the fruit of foreign expansion. As the *zaibatsu*, who had actively cooperated with war efforts, were not prosecuted, Japan was able to retain the leading force to guide Japan's postwar economic revival.

At the center of controversy was Emperor Hirohito himself for being excluded from the trials. Many people in the United States, Australia, and other countries in the Allied Forces believed that Emperor Hirohito should be put to trial, be found guilty and be hanged.[382] However, the United States government took a prudent position toward bringing down the emperor system itself, as it held the view that the Japanese Emperor could play a useful role in keeping the nation together and legitimizing the occupation policy.[383] In other words, the United States considered that if the Emperor were to be killed or the emperor system were to be obliterated, Japan could fall into a state of anarchy and communist forces could dominate. There were some voices within the United States government that even if Emperor Hirohito was not convicted through a trial, he should step down from the throne for the sake of beginning a new era. Many Japanese people also thought that Emperor Hirohito should at least abdicate the throne.[384] In addition, many anonymous letters were sent to MacArthur and SCAP (GHQ, General Headquarters), asserting the abolition of the emperor system and prosecution against Emperor Hirohito as a war criminal, which were long and extremely logical.[385] However, Emperor Hirohito claimed that he had only been misguided by the military authorities, that he had not participated in the war, and that he did not know the atrocities of the war. Also, he asserted that an Emperor could not carelessly give up one's position and that he needed to maintain his position in order to help reconstruct Japan. To Emperor Hirohito, who was thus in a troubled situation, MacArthur was as good as a savior. MacArthur believed that keeping Emperor Hirohito in his place would act as a safety valve against anarchism and communism. In January 1946, in a memorandum sent to advisors in Washington, MacArthur warned that if Emperor Hirohito were put to trial, the occupation policy would not run smoothly, and appealed for Emperor Hirohito.[386] Thus, Emperor Hirohito was able to avoid not only a trial and hanging verdict but also disenthronement.[387]

Since the Meiji Constitution granted the Japanese Emperor the highest power to administer the affairs of the state, the Emperor should assume the heaviest legal responsibility toward all significant affairs of the state, including war. In other words, pursuant to the Constitution at the time, the commencement and termination of war was under the governing power of the Japanese Emperor and it was necessary to require an imperial rescript for the commencement of war. For instance, even in the Pacific War, there was a Royal edict on the commencement of the war against the United States at the meeting before the Emperor held on December 1, 1941. Therefore, if the Emperor had not bent to the pressure of the military authorities to pursue foreign invasion, based on his own authority, and had not granted the Royal edict to start the war, then such a war would not have taken place. In addition, even in the perspective of the International Law at the time or after the war,

Emperor Hirohito's exemption of war responsibility ran counter to legal principles.[388] Although the Tokyo Trial was led by the United States, the leaders of Japan intervened, and the United States and Japan collaborated to create a scenario in which the war responsibility was entirely shifted to the army, and fabricated an image of the Emperor as a pacifist. In other words, Emperor Hirohito was left with no other choice but to commence war due to pressure from the military authorities, and he made a declaration of surrender to terminate the war and avoid greater agony of the Japanese people.[389] Therefore, it can be said that war responsibility was imputed on the army, and in place of putting responsibility on the others, Article 9, the clause on the renunciation of war, was inserted in the new constitution, to appease the strong backlash of Asian countries.[390]

Originally, the abolition of the emperor system had been brought up by President Roosevelt of the United States at the Cairo Conference in November 1943. However, China's Jiang Jieshi not only was from a pro-Japanese family but held a special respect for Japan's emperor system, and therefore, strongly disagreed to the abolition of the emperor system and prevented it from being included in the conference. This position of the Chinese Nationalist Party's leader was linked with the relinquishment of war reparations and this position continued even after stepping into socialist China. Therefore, Japan was able to enter into diplomatic relations with not only postwar Republic of China (Taiwan) but also the People's Republic of China in the 1970s without spending a penny in war reparations.[391] In addition, the efforts of the United States and MacArthur enabled Emperor Hirohito to avoid being tried at the Tokyo Trial and escape war responsibilities, but this result was also influenced by the Emperor's attitude toward the United States. In a letter that Emperor Hirohito sent to MacArthur through Political Advisor, William Joseph Sebald (1901-1980), he wrote, "I wish that the United States will continue military occupation over Okinawa. It will be necessary also in order to respond to the threat of the Soviet Union."[392] This can be seen as a prime example of Emperor Hirohito's efforts to dispel the United States' negative view of the emperor system at the time, by announcing the Declaration of Humanity himself and even attending to the United States' military interests.

Delfin Jaranilla, a Filipino who participated in the preparation of judgment papers of majority opinion at the Tokyo Trial, submitted an 'opinion of consent' of a 35-page document in English, criticizing that the sentence was excessively lenient compared to the magnitude of the crime. Radhabinod Pal, a judge who participated as the representative of India suggested the minority opinion that it was not reasonable to prosecute all of the Type A war criminals, but Jaranilla intensely criticized him that it was a betrayal against the Court of International Justice.[393] It seems probable that Radhabinod Pal's opinion came about because India barely suffered any harm from Japan compared to other Asian countries. Meanwhile, as in the Nuremberg Trials, war crimes committed by the Allied Forces were not treated in the Tokyo Trial which was led by the Allied Forces. For instance, the United States' responsibility for dropping atomic bombs, though raised by the lawyers, was excluded from the subject of inquiry under the pretext that it was beyond the jurisdiction of the Tokyo Trial. Consequentially, the omission of a trial on the acts of the Allied Forces created a sentiment within Japanese society that the trial against war criminals was a 'trial of the victor' and that Japan was a victim that was unilaterally punished.[394] However, since Japan promised to 'accept the Tokyo Trial' in the Treaty of San Francisco in 1951 and made a comeback to international society by freeing itself from the restraints of occupation ruling accordingly, denying the Tokyo Trial would only make Japan lose credibility within international society.

One of the war crimes that Japan escaped responsibility for in the Tokyo Trial was the practice of cannibalism by the Japanese military, which was not widely known. At the final stage of the Pacific War, when the Japanese military ran out of supplies in the war fronts of the Philippines and New Guinea, the Japanese military struggled with starvation and was driven to cannibalism. The victims of the Japanese military's cannibalism were Australian soldiers captured as prisoners of war, Asian captives that were brought as workers, and the natives of New Guinea. As collective madness caused by starvation became a daily routine, the Japanese military's cannibalism was considerably prevalent in the war front in New Guinea. Australia was the only place where cannibalism was a subject of interrogation in the trials against war criminals, but even in Australia, the trials ended in smoke, taking into consideration the shock it would cause to the families of victims. Thus, the issue of cannibalism committed by the Japanese military was hushed without being brought up at all at the Tokyo Trial, and accordingly, the responsibility of Japanese commanders to victims, such as Australian soldiers, Indian and Pakistani prisoners of war, and the natives of New Guinea, disappeared as well. Furthermore, the Japanese people lost the opportunity to properly become aware of the fact that Japan drove numerous Japanese soldiers to starvation, made them commit the inhumane act of cannibalism, and many soldiers did in fact die of hunger.[395]

In addition, the International Military Tribunal for the Far East put the acts of aggression committed by the Japanese military toward the Asian colonies of the United Kingdom, the United States, the Netherlands, and France as well as China to trial, but did not prosecute Japan's colonization of Taiwan and Korea. In the trials against Type B or Type C war crimes, the Netherlands punished the person in charge for the acts of forcefully using Dutch women as comfort women. On the other hand, the sexual slavery that the Japanese military forced on the comfort women from Taiwan or Korea was not put to trial at all. Furthermore, people from Taiwan and Korea, who were forcefully mobilized and obliged to be assigned to the Japanese military or to civilian groups attached to the military as prisoner watchmen, were treated as Japanese and were convicted and sentenced to the death penalty.[396] Among the 11 countries that participated in the Tokyo Trial were countries that held colonies, making it difficult to put the act of colonization itself in a subject of trial. Consequently, Japan's colonization and its cruel acts were excluded from the trial from the outset.[397] Many Asian countries were able to have an opportunity to settle some of their hard feelings due to war damage through the trial against war criminals, but this was not at all the case for Korea and Taiwan. To make matters worse, there were some unfair cases in which some Korean or Taiwanese people, who had no choice but to collaborate with Japan, were punished as war criminals. Furthermore, as the United States focused on its own interests while implementing policies regarding Asian countries, such as Korea, Taiwan, the Philippines, etc., it also had a negative effect on the interests and future of Asian countries.

CHAPTER 8

JAPAN'S GROWTH IN THE COLD WAR ERA AND THE LATENCY OF 'JAPAN'S WAR PROBLEMS'

1. Favorable International Environment and Japan's Remarkable Economic Growth

In Europe, the Cold War was under stable control through the operation of collective security systems, such as the North Atlantic Treaty Organization (NATO) and the Warsaw Treaty Organization (WTO), under the hegemony split between the United States and the Soviet Union. On the other hand, in East Asia, there was a limit in the Soviet Union's influence, and even the United States, a country that had overwhelming power, was able to form alliances with Japan, Taiwan, and Korea only after the Korean War under the flag of anti-communism. Even an attempt to establish a collective security system in the East Asian region was difficult because Taiwan and Korea had a strong repulsion against conceiving common security with Japan which had colonized the two countries. In postwar East Asia, there were strong national and social movements to escape the domination of imperialism, establish an independent state, and carry out political and economic reform. These movements were radicalized by combining with socialist ideology, and opposition forces grew stronger as well. The United States and the Soviet Union supported the forces that would speak for their respective interests, thereby accelerating conflict and division in the East Asian region. Therefore, in Europe, Germany took responsibility for the war and was divided, but in East Asia, the defeated nation of Japan escaped division, and rather China (People's Republic of China, Taiwan), Korea (Republic of Korea, Democratic People's Republic of Korea), and Vietnam (Republic of Vietnam, Democratic Republic of Vietnam) suffered the tragedy of division, which led to gruesome wars. The United States used Japan as a base for anti-communism through sole occupation, and Japan was able to make a comeback to the international stage under the protection of the United States. Taking advantage of the global situation of the Cold War and the irony of East Asia, Japan was able to advance straight toward economic development without repenting on past affairs such as colonization and invasion.[398] In this sense, Japan was the greatest beneficiary of the postwar Cold War system.

When the Korean War broke out in June 1950, the United States ordered massive military procurements from Japan's industrial world as it was the closest. This was a stroke of luck for Japan which had been experiencing difficulties due to a severe recession after the war. From 1951 to 1953, Japan's war procurements amounted to approximately USD 2 billion, which made up roughly 60% of Japan's total exports.[399] Then Prime Minister Yoshida referred to increased demands resulting from the Korean War as a 'gift of the gods,' and businessmen, who benefited the most, went as far as to call it 'blessed rain from heaven.'[400] As a result, from 1949 to 1951, exports increased by almost 3 times and production increased by approximately 70%. Corporations started to make profits for the first time after the war and began to increase investment in equipment. Accordingly, the GNP (Gross National Product) increase rate started to record double-digit growth, and Japan stepped into the path toward active economic revival.[401]

During the decades from 1950 up until the oil shock, Japan's GNP increased by more than 10% in average annual rate. Through open international trade, the world economy grew by an annual increase rate of 5% in the 1950s and 1960s, and the international environment worked to Japan's advantage. Thanks to the stationing of the American forces and the constitutional limitation on possession of military power, Japan was able to retrench defense costs and invest it in economic development. In particular, the Korean War, which broke out when Japan was suffering from economic difficulties after the war, enabled Japanese companies to increase exports through military procurement, acting as a flare of economic revival. During the Korean War, Japan concluded the Treaty of San Francisco[402] with the Allied Forces, normalizing international relations and lowering the burden of war reparations. In addition, shortly after the conclusion of the Treaty of San Francisco, Japan entered into the US-Japan Security Treaty with the United States, lowering the burden of defense costs and concentrating only on economic revival. Furthermore, a favorable yen-dollar exchange rate in the 1950s and 1960s also played a part in promoting exports. In addition, as the Vietnam War progressed, Japan's war profits from undertaking the role as a rear logistical base with the US army base in Okinawa was a catalyst for economic development.[403]

It is true that aside from such international factors, domestic factors, such as high-spirited younger managers, a good quality of human capital, and active saving and consumption, played a critical role in Japan's postwar economic development. In particular, the role of the Japanese government was immense. The Japanese government directly intervened in business activities, selectively supporting prospective businesses and deterring certain businesses. As time went by, the government guided businesses through an informal method called 'administration guidance (kanri gyosei)' rather than through direct intervention. The government created an atmosphere in which businessmen could engage in business activities to the full, by taking on the role of supporting and promoting the economy. More substantially, state institutions actively protected and fostered nascent industries, limiting imports through the imposition of tariffs. The government enabled businesses to borrow required funds at a low interest rate and granted tax breaks to businesses in fields that were supported by government policies.

The Japanese economy, which enjoyed annual average growth rates of at least 10% since the 1950s, began to slow down after the oil shock occurred in the fall of 1973. When the oil-producing countries of the Middle East limited the supply of oil toward countries that supported the position of Israel in the Middle East War that broke out earlier that year, oil prices skyrocketed. Oil price surge caused a recession and brought forth severe inflation. In 1974, Japan's consumer prices increased by 25%, and GNP decreased by 1.4% for the first time since the late 1940s. In response, the Japanese government injected funds into projects to develop alternative energy, such as nuclear energy, water power, solar power, tidal power, etc., and led an 'energy conservation' movement which was suggestive of energy-saving campaigns during the war. In addition, the Japanese government promoted energy-saving industries, such as service and high-tech industries.

The Japanese economy soon recovered, after experiencing economic recession until 1974 which resulted from the first oil shock in the fall of 1973. From 1975 to the late 1980s, the Japanese economy showed an annual average GNP growth rate of 4-5% and continuously developed. During this period, most of the powerful countries in the West were struggling from low growth rates, high unemployment rates, and high inflation rates. On the other hand, Japan's economy was not only growing, but the unemployment rate was less than 2% and inflation was not severe. Business leaders deployed the movement for Quality Control (QC), which was an American business method of enhancing quality and reducing costs by innovating production management. As economic abundance continued all throughout the 1980s, the voices of militant unionists or citizen activists almost disappeared without a trace. Foreign businessmen continuously visited Japanese companies to learn the managerial systems of Japanese businesses, and Japanese consultants newly created the 'Total Quality Control (TQC)' program and exported it to the United States. Now Japan had turned into a corporate-centered society, and most of the people thought that if something was beneficial to companies, then it was also beneficial to the country and society. Many scholars glorified the success of the Japanese management system, and various 'theories of the Japanese' (*Nihonjinron*) emerged. When the Japanese economy continuously grew to the point of threatening the United States in the 1980s, the cultural industry, which produced such 'theories of the Japanese' came to become more active. During this time, one of the most famous bestsellers on Japan available abroad was *Japan as Number One*,[404] by

Harvard professor, Ezra Vogel. This book held the perspective that the Japanese people had created a successful social and economic system, and people in other countries, including Americans, could learn a lesson from the Japanese case. Meanwhile, a European Community Commission report in 1979 illustrated the Japanese as workaholics living in rabbit hutches.[405] This was because the Japanese worked approximately 400 more hours each year than the typical Western workers, and their living space was merely half the size of a typical American house. Despite such negative evaluations, the general assessment of Japan in other countries was of high regard for Japan up until the 1980s, and it can be said that this encouraged the self-conceit of the Japanese people and made them become enraptured with their own achievements.

The opening of the Shinkansen (Bullet Train) in 1961, the hosting of the Tokyo Olympics in 1964, and the holding of the Osaka World Exposition in 1970 symbolically showed Japan's development. The brilliant economic growth of Japan heightened Japan's status in the global economy. In 1964, Japan joined the Organization for Economic Cooperation and Development (OECD), which can be called the club of advanced countries and which discusses the common issues of advanced industrial economies and their relationship with other countries. Japan also participated in the periodic summit meetings of the heads of state of the seven leading capitalist countries,[406] which first started in 1975. The purpose of these summit meetings, which came to be known as the G-7 (the 'group of seven nations'), was to discuss the direction of macroeconomic policies to restrain inflation and promote economic development and trade. In the 1980s, Japan was also part of the G-7 Finance Ministers Meeting (Finance Ministers and Central Bank Governors) and the G-5 meeting of 5 key nations (the United States, the United Kingdom, Japan, France, West Germany). Such heightened status of Japan was an element that made the Japanese people take pride in themselves, but on the other hand, it also became the source of pressure for Japan to hold fast to its national interests.

On the hidden side of Japan's outstanding growth were ethnic and racial minorities within Japan. Koreans who had moved or more often forcefully brought to Japan during the colonization period reached approximately 2 million by the end of the war. Most of the Koreans returned to Korea after the war, but approximately 540,000 people remained for various reasons by the end of the American occupation. Their legal status was changed from the subjects of the Japanese Emperor to resident aliens, which deprived them of benefits such as relief recipients. These people were confronted with all sorts of discrimination, were not able to share the fruit of abundance by the growth of the Japanese economy, and maintained their livelihood by engaging in jobs with hard work and little pay, such as day-labor on construction sites. Another group of people who were discriminated against were the *burakumin*

(部落民). Even though the status system was abolished in the Meiji Period, these people still suffered from discrimination after the war. In particular, the large companies of Japan excluded *buraku* applicants by investigating the household register of job applicants. In the late 1960s, after a law was established to limit outsider access to a person's household register, companies continued discrimination by obtaining the list of *buraku* addresses through private agencies. In opposition to such discrimination, the *burakumin* deployed reform movements through the Buraku Liberation League, and succeeded in making the Japanese government provide subsidies, assign construction projects and bring about improvements in schools. From this point on, the living standards of the *buraku* was largely improved, drawing near the level of mainstream society, but subtle discrimination continues to this day.[407]

2. Japan's Domestic Politics and Foreign Relations after World War II

Japan's political map, which had been unfolding in a complex manner after the war, came to be organized into a considerably simple structure in 1955, after the legal issues were settled with the conclusion of the Treaty of San Francisco. First of all, the two sects of the Socialist Party reunited, and in response to this, the Liberal Party and the Democratic Party were integrated into a massive party called the Liberal Democratic Party (LDP, 自由民主党, Jiyu Minshuto). Part of the reason was that business elites encouraged the merger of the two conservative parties, using their influence as the source of political funds for conservative politicians, as they were concerned with the new integration and increasing support of the Socialist Party, which influenced labor movements. The Liberal Democratic Party dominated Japanese politics for the next 40 or so years, with close ties with business leaders and bureaucrats. Based on their policy expertise, bureaucrats drafted legislative bills and passed them over to the Liberal Democratic Party. Also, prominent bureaucrats sometimes entered the political world through the Liberal Democratic Party, some of whom later became Prime Ministers. Businesses acquired privileges by providing political funds to the Liberal Democratic Party and supporting bureaucrats. These elite groups of statesmen, businessmen, and government officials, who formed close ties, were known as Japan's 'iron triangle' and led postwar Japanese society.

However, a controversy arose even within the conservative party regarding foreign policy strategies in the 1950s. During his office as Prime Minister from 1954 to 1956, Hatoyama Ichiro (鳩山一郎, 1883-1959) attempted to keep a distance with the United States and push ahead with an independent course, and achieved some good results in 1956 by promoting normalization of relations with the Soviet Union. Yoshida Shigeru (吉田茂,

1878-1967), who had served as Prime Minister when the Treaty of San Francisco was concluded, along with his faction, were dissatisfied with the United States' attitude, but strived to cooperate with the United States to contain the communist bloc. Domestically, the majority of politicians in the Liberal Democratic Party criticized the new constitution as the 'MacArthur Constitution' which was forcefully imposed on Japan and they made an attempt to revise it. Prime Minister Hatoyama attempted to elevate the status of the Emperor from the symbol of national unity to the 'head of state' and remove Article 9, which prohibited the use of military force. In addition, by creating a clause in the Constitution that enabled the government to exercise emergency executive powers during a time of crisis, he attempted to limit civil liberties. And so, Hatoyama established a review committee of the Constitution, consisting of 30 members of the Diet and 20 experts, but faced opposition from the Socialist Party, which actively supported the new constitution, as well as from some members of the Liberal Democratic Party. Most important of all, the majority of the Japanese people, who had experienced the horrors of war, were against the revision of the Constitution, and in the 1960s, the driving force behind the revision of the Constitution became weaker.

Wartime bureaucrats played a key role not only in Japan's postwar economic policymaking but also in politics. Six wartime bureaucrats became Prime Ministers after the war, notably Yoshida Shigeru (吉田茂, incumbency: 1946-1947, 1948-1954), Kishi Nobusuke (岸信介, incumbency: 1957-1960), and Sato Eisaku (佐藤榮作, incumbency: 1964-1972) [408] and so forth. [409] Wartime bureaucrats played a leading role in economic revival by designing postwar economic policies on the basis of their wartime experiences, and executed various policies in each field of society. These bureaucrats turned the decentralized education system of the American occupation period back to the centralized system as in the period before the war. [410] In 1956, the election system for local school board members was abolished and instead the mayor or governor directly appointed school board members. In addition, the local school board was to be under the control of the Ministry of Education. The education curriculum was changed so that the free elective system was removed and the curriculum was censored by the central government.

Postwar peace movements were actively deployed in the 1950s and 1960s, with the participation of unions, Socialist and Communist Parties, and various civic, female, and student groups. The sharpest issues that came to the fore in the peace movements were the American military bases, nuclear weapons, and the US-Japan Security Treaty. As of 1960, the U.S. forces in Japan amounted to approximately 46,000 troops in hundreds of military facilities all around mainland Japan and approximately 37,000 troops in Japan's southernmost Okinawa. From 1952 up into the 1970s, criminal cases such as rape and murder occurred incessantly. However, many of these crimes were lightly punished by the American forces through extraterritoriality, which evoked the rage of the Japanese people. Atomic damages of Hiroshima and Nagasaki and the presence of tens of thousands of atomic bomb survivors (*hibakusa*) who still lived in pain, granted a significant meaning to Japan's anti-nuclear movement. In particular, in 1954, when an atomic experiment was conducted by the United States on Bikini Atoll in the central region of the Pacific Ocean, a Japanese fishing boat called the Lucky Dragon was completely exposed to radiation. As a result, at least 30 million Japanese people signed a statement opposing nuclear bomb tests.[411]

The most dramatic event related to peace movements occurred due to the revision of the US-Japan Security Treaty in 1960. Since the term of validity for the US-Japan Security Treaty was 8 years, it was necessary for the United States Congress and the Japanese National Diet to ratify the treaty by June 1960. Therefore, the United States government and the Japanese government agreed on the draft of a new security treaty in early 1960. The basic structure was similar to the previous treaty, but in order to appease the opposition of the Japanese people, the new treaty draft stipulated that the United States should notify Japan in advance if nuclear weapons were brought into Japan. In order to avoid the difficulty in extending the treaty in the future, the draft also stipulated that the treaty was to be automatically renewed unless one of the parties demanded revision or annulment. Starting from April 1960, ten protesting demonstrations were held in opposition to the new security treaty, but on the late night of May 19, while a demonstration was still going on, the Kishi Nobusuke (岸信介, 1896-1987) Cabinet suddenly ratified the new security treaty at the National Diet. As a result, the rage of the Japanese people reached its climax, and massive demonstrations were held every day for the following few weeks nearby the National Diet Building. Initially, President Eisenhower of the United States intended to participate in the signing ceremony to be held on June 19 in Tokyo, but as the demonstrations intensified, his visit was cancelled for the sake of his safety. Eventually, Prime Minister Kishi Nobusuke resigned, but he accomplished his goal of laying the foundation of a long-term US-Japan Alliance. When the new security treaty officially came into effect on June 19, the demonstrations gradually dwindled.

In late 1960, a large-scale and intense labor dispute occurred at the Miike Coal Mine of Mitsui (三井) Corporation in the southwestern end of Kyushu. Also, a horrific incident occurred in which a fanatical right-wing youth murdered Asanuma Inejiro (淺沼稻次郎, 1898-1960), the chairman of the Socialist Party, during a panel discussion among the party leaders which was being broadcasted live on television. After experiencing such hardship and pain in the 1960s, the sociopolitical atmosphere became somewhat more relaxed. During the high growth period, a new type of politics emerged which was oriented toward reconciliation and compromise, as each of the political factions restrained themselves in order to avoid conflict as much as possible. After the resignation of Prime Minister Kishi, the Liberal Democratic Party brought about a turn of affairs by concentrating on full employment and improvement of living standards based on 'Income Doubling Plan' of Prime Minister Ikeda Hayato (池田勇人, 1899-1965). Now the Liberal Democratic Party was turning into a party that embraced various political opinions, and the political world was changing from politics of confrontation to politics of compromise.

After the mid-1960s, new conflicts came to surface and new types of political movements appeared in response. This was sometimes called the politics of 'citizen movements.' First of all, this emerged as an opposition movement against Japan's involvement in the United States' Vietnam War. In 1965, grass roots civic groups assembled to establish a loosely connected network called 'Citizen's Federation for Peace of Vietnam' (Beheiren, ベ平連). Beheiren did not have rules, list of members, and membership fees, but its role was large enough that hundreds of thousands of people participated in anti-war protests. Beheiren disintegrated in 1974 when the Vietnam War came to an end.

Just as university students all over the world held fierce and violent resistance movements in the late 1960s, Japanese students also unprecedentedly went on unified student strikes and boycotted classes. In the spring of 1969, numerous universities were virtually closed, but by the summer of the same year, such student movements gave way, because these movements were out of step with the new trends of civic movements and at odds with public sentiment. By contrast, environmental movements emerged as the most effective and new sphere of civic movements. In the 1950s, many people died of pollution-related diseases such as mercury or cadmium poisoning. These diseases were called 'Itai-itai byo' (Itai-itai disease, It hurts-it hurts disease) in Japan. In the 1950s, as the contributors of pollution evaded their responsibility and interrupted investigation, and as the central and local governments took on a passive attitude, reparations for these victims were not properly made. However, from the mid-1960s to the early 1970s, pollution victims and local organizations of citizens formed a nationwide network in a similar manner as in antiwar movements. They boycotted products manufactured by businesses that caused pollution, and purchased small quantities of company stock to participate in stockholder's meetings to bring up the problems. Furthermore, they filed lawsuits at courts and received verdicts for compensation through various trials. Therefore, the government strengthened environment-related legislation and companies reinforced prevention measures.

These new types of citizens' movements had a big influence on orthodox politics from the late 1960s to the 1970s. In cities all over the nation, small and big, citizens which were organized around environmental problems, improvement of public housing, anti-base protests, and peace movements, supported politicians in the Socialist Party or Communist Party. In 1975, left-wing politicians occupied the positions of mayors or governors in 159 local governments, including Japan's 7 major cities (Tokyo, Yokohama, Osaka, Nagoya, Kobe, Kyoto, and Kawasaki). Thus, local governments seized the initiative in a broad domain, such as environmental regulations and social welfare systems. A representative figure was Minobe Ryokichi (美濃部亮吉, 1904-1984), a former professor who assumed the post of Governor of Tokyo from 1967 to 1980, and he received a great amount of support by pushing ahead with pioneering plans such as free health insurance for low-income citizens. Eventually, the Liberal Democratic Party referred to the various reformative plans promoted by local governments, reviewed them as national tasks, and launched various innovative policies.[412]

In 1968, the U.S. President Lyndon Johnson promised to return Okinawa, which was under the United States' rule, back to Japan, but the actual retrocession occurred in 1972 during President Richard Nixon's office. However, the American forces did not leave and Okinawa remained a massive military base. Even today, 20% of the fertile farmland in the central and southern region of Okinawa is occupied by the American forces.[413] Although the United States bases continued to exist, restoration of Japan's sovereignty over Okinawa opened a possibility for a more equal relationship between the United States and Japan. However, the announcement of United States President Richard Nixon's plan to visit the People's Republic of China (PRC) in July 1971, and the declaration to relinquish the gold standard in August was so shocking to the Japanese people that it was called the 'Nixon Shock.' In February 1972, President Nixon visited China, and in 1979, the United States and China established diplomatic ties at the ambassador level. Also, the United States abandoned the gold standard and adjusted the dollar price to be linked to other currencies, bringing about a big impact on the price of Japanese export goods. The fact that the United States, which Japan had considered an ally, made such a heavy announcement without consultation or prior notice, enraged the Japanese people. It was an extremely perplexing situation for the Japanese government which had faithfully followed the United States' strategy to isolate the communist regime in China despite opposing opinions within the nation. Accordingly, Japan established official diplomatic relations with China even earlier than the United States in 1972 and expanded economic cooperation.

The only country that Japan could not manage to establish diplomatic relations with up until the mid-1960s within the capitalist sphere led by the United States was the Republic of Korea. Japan and Korea had been unable to normalize diplomatic relations for a long time due to sediment of emotion that had built up over the years as well as opposition forces within both countries. Then, a new political power in Korea which seized power through a military coup rapidly advanced relations with Japan in order to make up for their weak legitimacy through economic development. There was also the United States' intention to pressure Japan to normalize diplomatic ties between Japan and Korea and provide economic aid to Korea, as the United States needed to reduce aid toward Korea due to the burden of war expenditure in the Vietnam War. Finally, in 1965, the two countries officially established diplomatic ties, and the resulting Treaty on Basic Relations declared that the 1910 Japan's annexation of Korea and all other prior treaties were 'already null and void.'[414] Thus, Japan recognized South Korea as the sole legitimate government on the Korean Peninsula, and South Korea received economic aid from Japan amounting to USD 800 million in kind or services.[415] Hereafter, the economic relationship between Japan and Korea became closer. In the early 1980s, Prime Minister Nakasone Yasuhiro (中曾根康弘, 1918-2019) expanded economic aid and attempted to further strengthen ties with Korea. In particular, he arranged a meeting in which Emperor Hirohito expressed his regrets regarding the brutality of the colonial era to South Korean President Chun Doo-hwan who visited Japan in 1984.

Furthermore, Japan made efforts to improve its diplomatic relations with ASEAN countries, and in the 1980s, Japan sharply increased Official Development Assistance (ODA) and enabled Southeast Asian countries to benefit from foreign aid. Thus, in 1991, Japan became the world's largest ODA country. Despite such efforts, Japan was still unable to resolve the distrust of many Asian people. It seems that the attitude of the Japanese people toward historical issues had a negative influence on Japan. In 1982, the Ministry of Education gave instructions to minimize the illustration of Japan's acts of aggression in Asia in history textbooks for public schools. For instance, it was recommended that 'invasion' (侵略, shinnyu) should be written as 'advance' (進出, shinshutsu), and Japanese atrocities should be deleted or toned down. This triggered fierce protests on the part of Asian countries, including China and Korea. In 1985, Prime Minister Nakasone Yasuhiro visited the Yasukuni Shrine where war criminals were enshrined, which was greatly criticized by China and Korea. In addition, in 1986, Education Minister Fujio Masayuki played down the Nanjing Massacre and asserted that the 1910 Japanese annexation of Korea was something that the Koreans had consented to. This evoked the rage of the Chinese and the Koreans, and Fujio Masayuki ended up resigning. After the mid-1980s, there was a repetition of situations in which Japan's major figures made absurd remarks such as denying the Nanjing Massacre or claiming that the colonization of Korea was through Korean people's voluntary consent, and ended up resigning when the rage and protests of the Asian people became intense.

From the 1950s, the United States made Japan play the role of lessening the burden of the United States in Asia, and this policy brought forth the consequence of aggravating the subordination of Asian countries to Japan. Normalization of diplomatic relations between Japan and Taiwan in 1952 and establishment of diplomatic relations between Japan and Korea in 1965 were driven by such policies of the United States. After normalization of diplomatic relations, Japan reinforced economic relations with Taiwan and Korea, which was accompanied by the subordination of the two countries in the technology field in the process. From 1965, Japan's exports to the United States started to surpass its imports, which was a consequence that Japan's home appliances industry expanded its market share in the US market while US industries were focused on producing war supplies to conduct the Vietnam War. In the mid-1980s, Japan's exports to the United States became more than twice the United States' exports to Japan, further increasing trade deficits of the United States. As a consequence, American executives and labor unions strongly voiced complaints, and the United States government mobilized various political means to check Japan's trade advantages. In particular, the United States Congress passed a trade bill in 1988, and in the case where the domestic markets of Japan and other countries were closed to the point of being unfair, it became possible for the United States to take retaliatory action toward the export goods of these countries pursuant to 'Super 301 clause.' Japan responded by strongly criticizing that it was a reenactment of the gunboat diplomacy of the United States and the United Kingdom in the 19th century.

As Japan succeeded in economic revival in the 1950s and continued to enjoy rapid growth in the 1960s, its economic size in 1968 in terms of GDP surpassed West Germany and ranked No. 2 in the world after the United States. As Japan continued to grow despite the oil shock in the 1970s, advanced countries started to check Japan in diverse ways. The United States' significant efforts to keep in check Japan's rapid progress in international trade became obvious in the G-5 (the United States, the United Kingdom, France, West Germany, and Japan) Finance Ministers Meeting held in Plaza Hotel of New York in September 1985. The decision made in this meeting was called the Plaza Accord, the main contents of which was to lower the value of the US dollar to the Japanese yen and Deutsche mark. In particular, the finance ministers demanded that the Japanese yen be raised in value and Japanese imports be increased in order to alleviate the adverse trade balance with Japan, and also demanded for domestic demand to be boosted in Japan. Japan's Ministry of Finance accepted these agreements and executed low interest and fiscal expansion policies. In order to boost domestic demands, the Japanese government provided large grants to local governments to be invested in roads, bridges, amusement facilities, museums, etc. Also, the low interest policy helped Japanese businesses to overcome unfavorable trade environments due to the rise in yen, by enabling them to invest in state-of-the-art technology and reduce production costs. Later, however, this became a factor that caused the bubble economy followed by asset inflation in the late 1980s.

In the late 1980s, Japan's iron triangle of elite groups of politicians, businessmen, and bureaucrats that had towed Japan's growth started to crack. The Recruit Scandal, a serious scandal that enraged the Japanese people, had occurred. The Recruit Company, which initially started as a recruiting agency, had expanded into various industries, including real estate, by spending a tremendous amount of lobby funds through financed funds which was easy to access in the Bubble Era. In this process, more than 150 bureaucrats, politicians, and other influential people had received political funds, cheap loans, stocks, etc., from this company. As a result of being involved in this scandal, 20 members of the Diet, most of whom belonged to the Liberal Democratic Party, including Cabinet members, resigned from their positions in mid-1989. Among the people who resigned were then Prime Minister Takeshita Noboru (竹下登, 1924-2006) and his predecessor Nakasone.

3. The Cold War and the Latency of 'Japan's War Problems'

After the Pacific War came to an end in August 1945, Asia's international relations and order was newly reshuffled. In particular, ideological conflicts and the Cold War split Asian countries along the two prominent countries of the United States and the Soviet Union. These circumstances blocked Asian countries and people from having opportunities to converse and communicate, which naturally buried the various problems that arose from modern Japan's invasion and colonization of Asian countries (so called 'Japan's War Problems' - abbreviation: 'Japanoblems'). China was not in a situation to bring into question 'Japan's War Problems', since it was busy building a new socialist country after experiencing a long-term anti-Japanese war and civil war. Vietnam had no time to think about Japan's War Problems, either, due to wars against France and the United States, as well as a civil war between the North and South of Vietnam. Korea, which was divided into South Korea and North Korea in Japan's stead, Jiang Jieshi's Republic of China, which barely remained in existence in Taiwan after being pushed back by Mao Zedong's Communist Party, and many Southeast Asian countries had neither the power nor will to raise the issue of Japan's War Problems, as they were struggling from economic difficulties after the war and searching for ways to survive amidst the Cold War. In particular, in capitalist bloc countries, which relied on the United States for security and economic aid, coercive governments continued to hold power under the flag of anti-communism. In these countries, the voices of the victims of Japan's invasion and colonization were also muffled in order to receive aid from the United States and Japan.

In this situation, Japan accomplished economic revival and rapid growth. Asian countries had to wait until democracy advanced and the Cold War ended for the victims by modern Japan to voice their opinions and raise the issue of the so-called Japan's War Problems. In short, the Cold War and Hot Wars in the East Asia region after the Pacific war prevented Asian people from having the opportunity to search for conversation and cooperation regarding Japan's War Problems (Japanoblems), and Japan used this situation to its advantage.[416]

If the influence factors behind the formation of Japanese society after the war and the latency of Japan's War Problems (Japanoblems) were to be analyzed in a structural aspect, it can be summarized into four aspects. The four aspects include the global structure of the Cold War centered on the United States and the Soviet Union, the structure of Cold War and Hot Wars in East Asia, the joint security system between Japan and the United States, and the long-term rule of the conservative Liberal Democratic Party. Under this structure, Japan failed to resolve the problems which needed to be solved in order to start anew after the war. The first issue that could be raised was self-reflection, apology, and compensation for war of aggression and colonization. Since the late 19th century, when Japan faced coercive incorporation into an international order driven by the Western powers, Japan did not attempt to stand up to the Western powers through Pan-Asian solidarity, but used the '*Datsua Nyuo*' (Leave Asia, enter Europe) strategy to imitate the West, accomplish rapid modernization, and dominate as the leader of Asia. After losing the war, instead of repenting on the historical wrongdoings and returning as a member of Asia, Japan adopted the 'Leave Asia, enter America' strategy and acquired various national profits by occupying the upper echelon of the capitalist economic bloc, under the umbrella of security provided by the United States. As a consequence, it was only after the collapse of the Cold War structure that Japan's War Problems (Japanoblems), which had been lying dormant during the Cold War period, came to surface.[417]

Aside from the above mentioned structural factors in which Japan failed to resolve historical issues with Asian countries and devoted itself to economic development after the war, several other important factors came to play. In the early stages of occupation rule by the Allied Forces, SCAP took various measures to remove Japan's capacity to execute war and carried out a massive banishment of figures in the government and business world that had played important roles in the execution of war. However, as the global Cold War arrived and the Chinese Nationalist Party (Kuomintang), which had been regarded as the bulwark against communism in Asia, was losing ground against the attacks of the Communist forces, the United States came to consider Japan as an important partner in Asia. Accordingly, SCAP reinstated a large number of figures who had been ousted from key positions in the public office and the economic world and kicked out numerous left-wing figures through probes of ideology in each field. Thus, as the leaders from the militaristic period of war came to lead each field again, it became even more difficult for Japanese society to harbor a sense of repent or responsibility for driving the Japanese people to war and having damaged Asian countries. In a sense, it can be said that the fact that those who came to lead Japanese society again, refused to acknowledge and repent on their past wrongdoings was natural when considering Japan's social and cultural characteristics. Therefore, postwar settlements led by these figures could be not at all satisfactory for Asian countries. These figures continued to engage themselves in negotiations with Asian countries based on the sense of contempt and discrimination toward Asians, but Asian countries were left with no other choice than to accept the unjust and insufficient negotiations as they were placed in economic difficulties and political instability.

In the Treaty of San Francisco, most countries relinquished their right to demand compensation from Japan, under the pressure of the United States, but the Philippines and South Vietnam did not give up, and Indonesia did not even ratify the treaty. In addition, the compensation issues regarding China, South Korea, Taiwan, and North Korea, which were not invited to the conference, and Myanmar, which did not attend the conference, were not settled. Therefore, Japan restored diplomatic relations with Myanmar, Indonesia, the Philippines, and South Vietnam through individual negotiations and settled reparation issues from 1955 to 1959. The war reparations issues of Cambodia, Laos, Malaysia, and Singapore were handled through Japan's economic and technological cooperation from the late 1950s to the 1960s. The war reparations issue with Korea (South Korea) was handled by concluding the Treaty on Basic Relations in 1965 and providing economic cooperation. Furthermore, in the case of China, China clarified its position of relinquishing war reparations in the declaration of Japan-China Joint Communique in 1972, and the issue was resolved through Japan's economic aid to China.[418] In the case of Vietnam, when North Vietnam and South Vietnam was reunified in 1975, Japan engaged in economic cooperation with the reunified government free of charge. In this way, Japan restored diplomatic relations and handled the issue of war reparations with almost all Asian countries. Asian countries, which lagged behind economically and were largely dominated by pro-American dictatorial regimes, had weak bargaining power and were under strong pressure from the United States, which compelled them to participate in the negotiations. Thus, Japan, backed by the United States, was able to lightly resolve the issue of war reparations toward Asian countries and was also able to achieve its economic revival and promote the expansion of Japanese companies in Asia through compensation in the form of economic aid and technological cooperation. However, such payments of war reparations or economic aid were outrageously small compared to the damage that Asian countries had suffered. Furthermore, it did not lead to compensation for the people who had been directly or indirectly victimized through war or colonization, thus failing to win their consent at all. The dissatisfaction of the victims could not be expressed during the Cold War, because the governments under the influence of the United States and Japan, suppressed these voices. Thus, Asian governments could have carried through their demands for their own national interests, supported by the opposition parties or voices of the people, but instead, in the circumstances of the Cold War, they suppressed these forces and took actions that corresponded to the interests of the United States or Japan.[419]

While Japan's War Problems (Japanoblems) thus lay dormant during the Cold War, Japan accomplished outstanding economic growth, and several other Asian countries also achieved surprising economic development. Thus, in the 1980s, the World Bank referred to such results of development as 'the miracle of East Asia,' and Korea, Taiwan, Hong Kong, and Singapore were called the Four Asian Dragons or 'Newly Industrializing Economies (NIEs).' There were several factors behind the development of these regions, two common factors of which were as follows. First, the United States actively provided aid for economic development in order to prevent the expansion of communist forces in these regions, which were situated at the forefront of Asia's Cold War and conflict of ideology. Second, placed in the situation of division or as a neighboring country of a powerful nation, there was a strong need to rapidly push ahead with economic modernization so as not to be absorbed by the counterpart or a powerful nation. Thus, the Cold War conflict between the United States and the Soviet Union, as well as pursuit of economic development of small and medium-sized capitalist nations in Asia based on aid from the United States and Japan, muffled the voices raising the issue of Japan's War Problems (Japanoblems) which occurred due to Japan's war of aggression and colonization.

CHAPTER 9

THE END OF THE COLD WAR AND RISE OF 'JAPAN'S WAR PROBLEMS' (JAPANOBLEMS)

1. The End of the Cold War, Japan's Economic Depression and Political Change

The period before and after 1990 was a huge turning point not only in world history but also in Japanese history. In 1989 the Berlin Wall that had divided Berlin into East and West collapsed, and in 1990 the two Germanys were unified. In 1989 the communist countries in Eastern Europe collapsed, and even the Soviet Union was dissolved in 1991. In Japan, Emperor Hirohito died in January 1989 and his son Crown Prince Akihito (明仁) succeeded to the throne as the new Emperor in November 1990. In 1990 a long-term recession began in Japan as the bubble economy burst.

Japan's economic growth and continued abundance during the 1980s gradually made the Japanese people become indifferent to politics and fall into complacency. However, on the opposite side of this complacency, there was a lurking danger that the bubble might burst at any moment. In late 1989 the Nikkei (日經) Stock Index had tripled in just three years, and the total value of companies listed on the Tokyo stock exchange made up 40% of the total value of stock markets worldwide. Real estate prices skyrocketed and it was estimated that the total value of real estate in Tokyo surpassed the total value of real estate in the United States in 1989. Also, the Japanese people bought up European arts in large quantities, exorbitantly increasing their prices.

However, Japan's long period of dazzling economic growth ended with the start of the 1990s. Following the Plaza Accord among the Finance Ministers of the G5 in 1985, a program launched to boost investment and domestic consumption in Japan led to stock and land prices to skyrocket. As a response, the Japanese government limited credit loans to suppress speculative investment and to deflate the bubble. Therefore, from the autumn of 1989 to the summer of 1990, the Ministry of Finance more than doubled the borrowing interest rate from 2.5% to 6%. When investors detected this movement and reacted, the Nikkei Index of the Tokyo stock market plummeted from approximately JPY 40,000 in December 1989 to JPY 20,000 in October 1990.[420] Individuals and institutional investors who could not repay their loans, due to the fall in stock prices, experienced great difficulties. Also, as real estate developers could not bear borrowing costs due to high interest rates, real estate development plans were cancelled or real estate companies went bankrupt in succession. The bankruptcy of these companies further fueled the drop in land prices, and markedly depreciated the value of real estate that had been provided as collateral. Literally, the bubble that had built up over time had burst.

Of course, the Japanese economy did not immediately fall into chaos even though stock prices and real estate prices fell. Japan was still gaining tens of billions of dollars in trade surplus from the United States and European countries. Japan's GNP maintained a high growth rate of an annual average of 4% in 1990 and 1991. Due to this, trade negotiation representatives from the United States and other G7 nations during the Uruguay Round pressured Japan to further open its domestic market. As a new multilateral trade negotiation reached an agreement in 1993, Japan had no choice but to allow the imports of rice and other agricultural products. Through these multilateral negotiations, the World Trade Organization (WTO) was established to enhance free trade and resolve disputes among countries. In bilateral negotiations, the United States made a step that ran counter to its own attitude of praising free trade by forcing Japan to set a trade quota on automobiles and steel. The United States also pressured Japan to play a more active role in the Gulf War in 1991 as a military ally. In response to this, Japan eventually offered massive war expenses amounting to USD 13 billion, since it could not dispatch troops due to the clause in the Peace Constitution that prohibits the use of military power as well as public opposition within the country.

As stock prices plunged following the burst of the speculative bubble in the early 1990s, eventually the real economy of Japan also suffered a heavy blow. Literally, a depression began and the indices representing industrial production, construction business, and wholesale price plummeted. In addition, unemployment increased, and prices continued to fall. This was interlocked with a further decline in stock prices. In response to this, the Japanese financial authorities considered that their monetary policy was too tight and lowered interest rates at an attempt to revive the economy. However, this was not effective due to the 'bad loan problem' and insolvency of banks. Furthermore, Japan's exports became sluggish as the value of the US dollar depreciated against the Japanese yen, making it difficult for exports to lead economic recovery. Meanwhile, two incidents (the Kobe earthquake and the sarin gas attack) that occurred in 1995 put the Japanese society into great chaos and further thickened the dark clouds cast over its economy. In January 1995, a great earthquake hit Kobe and nearby areas, killing approximately 6,400 people and leaving approximately 300,000 people homeless. In the morning of March 20, 1995, the followers of a new religion called Aum Shinrikyo (Aum Religion of Truth) sprayed fatal sarin gas at a subway station in Tokyo, killing 12 passengers and harming several thousands of people.

Prime Minister Hashimoto Ryutaro (橋本龍太郎, 1937-2006), who judged that there was a necessity to manage increasing budget deficits, increased the consumption tax from 3% to 5% in 1997 in order to revive the current economy and prepare for an aging society and future social safety costs. This policy further constricted the consumer sentiment and slowed down consumption expenditures, lowering the possibility of reviving the economy even more. The economic recession continued with Japan's real GDP recording minus 2% in 1997 and 1998, and zero growth in 1999. Hence, in 1998 the Newsweek magazine described the economic situation of Japan in the 1990s as 'the lost decade.' [421] To overcome this difficult economic situation, some companies employed CEOs from the West. For example, in 1999, Nissan made Carlos Ghosn from France its CEO.[422]

As the 1990s went by and the world entered a new millennium, the Japanese economy began to slowly recover. It can be said that the deregulation and privatization policies of the Japanese government, after being implemented through trial and error, finally showed some effectiveness. Therefore, from 2003 to the spring of 2008, Japan's GDP increased by annual average of approximately 2% and the unemployment rate declined from 5.3% to 4%. During this period, the rapid growth of the Chinese economy was extremely important in trade, and in 2004, China overtook the United States as Japan's largest trade partner. From 2001 to 2006, the Bank of Japan lowered its prime interest rate to 0%, which stimulated investment and exports alongside the favorable international environment.

The reason for Japan's long-term recession was not only due to the structural problem mentioned above. Japan failed to predict and adapt to the new age brought forth by the development of information technology since the 1990s. It had become difficult to respond to the demands of a new economy and society merely through loyalty toward one's company and immersion in one field, which were the strengths of the Japanese people. As creativity was required to invent new things, people who embodied such creativity became the most essential economic resource. As symbolized by the Internet, it became extremely important to communicate extensively across borders in real time. However, the tightly knit socioeconomic system and culture of Japan made it difficult for the Japanese people to adapt to this new tide. Furthermore, the proportion of Japan in the world economy fell to 8.4% in 2010 and its status as the world's second largest economic power went over to China.[423] Also, Japan has the dishonor of being the nation with the highest percentage of national debt to GDP among the OECD countries.

According to OECD research data, Japan's general government gross financial liability as a percentage of GDP in 2019 was 224.7%, the worst level. This figure is overwhelmingly higher than the United States (108.4%), which is considered to have serious fiscal deficits, or the OECD average (109.2%). Even more problematic is that this figure is on a consistently increasing trend (130.9% in 2000, 157.9% in 2005, 186.6% in 2010, 216.5% in 2015, and 224.7% in 2019).[424] Japan has accumulated this fiscal deficit in order to overcome the economic recession and cover massive welfare expenditures. Even so, it is considered that there is almost no possibility of sovereign default since 90% or more of the Japanese government's debt is from Japanese banks or the Japanese people. However, such economic recession after the end of the Cold War has made the Japanese people lose their confidence, and there have been movements to make up for this sense of loss by taking a conservative swing or seeking to become a strong military power, bringing about concerns of intensified conflict with Asian countries.

With the end of the Cold War and the beginning of economic recession, the landscape of Japan's politics went through a massive change. Bribery scandals related to the Sagawa Express, sex scandals, and the unpopular new consumption tax impaired the political order that the Liberal Democratic Party had firmly built over the past few decades. Ozawa Ichiro (小澤一郎) left the Liberal Democratic Party and created the Japan Renewal Party (新生黨), and so the solidarity among factions within the Liberal Democratic Party could no longer last. Hosokawa Morihiro (細川護熙), whose maternal grandfather was the wartime Prime Minister Konoe Fumimaro, founded the reformative Japan New Party (日本新黨). In the general election held after the general resignation of the Miyazawa Kiichi (宮澤喜一, 1919-2007) Cabinet, following a vote of no-confidence in the Cabinet in 1993, the Liberal Democratic Party secured less than half of the seats. Hence, Ozawa's Japan Renewal Party and Hosokawa's Japan New Party collaborated with the Japan Socialist Party and Clean Government Party, launching the first non-Liberal Democratic Party government since the 1950s. The Prime Minister of this coalition cabinet was Hosokawa. However, Hosokawa Morihiro stepped down after eight months in office and two months after Prime Minister Hata Tsutomu (羽田孜) succeeded him, the coalition cabinet collapsed.

After the non-Liberal Democratic Party coalition cabinet collapsed, an extremely odd phenomenon occurred in Japan's political history. The Liberal Democratic Party created a coalition cabinet with the Japan Socialist Party, which was the largest opposition party and a party that had taken a different ideological path, and made Murayama Tomiichi (村山富市, the chairman of the Japan Socialist Party) the Prime Minister. The Japan Socialist Party received connivance and concession from the Liberal Democratic Party regarding certain agenda items, in return for participating in the coalition cabinet. Hence, Prime Minister Murayama was able to candidly apologize for the slavery of the 'comfort women' and wartime brutalities on the fiftieth anniversary of the end of World War II. However, since the supporters of the Japan Socialist Party had generally been devoted to principles such as defending the Peace Constitution, opposing the US-Japan Alliance, and rejecting collusive links between politics and business, they criticized the party for abandoning its principles to gain power and were displeased with the establishment of the coalition cabinet with the Liberal Democratic Party. It can be said that this situation later became the cause of the Japan Socialist Party's decline.

After Prime Minister Murayama resigned, the factions within the Liberal Democratic Party continued to change their alignments along with the economic recession, and many short- term Prime Ministers led the Cabinet. In spring 2001, Koizumi Junichiro (小泉純一郎), who was a non-mainstream yet popular politician in the Liberal Democratic Party, was elected as the party president and became the Prime Minister. During his incumbency over 5 years, he pushed ahead with dramatic economic reformation through deregulation and privatization. At the core of his policies was the privatization of the savings and insurance system of the post office. As for Koizumi's diplomatic policy, he gained more support from the United States than Asia by playing an active role after the terrorist attacks on September 11, 2001. However, he visited the Yasukuni Shrine every year to commemorate the war dead including war criminals, provoking opposition from China and Korea.

Prime Minister Koizumi stayed in office for five and a half years with strong leadership, and this was the longest incumbency after Prime Minister Sato Eisaku (1964-1972) since the establishment of the modern Meiji government. However, his successors failed to display such strong leadership. Shinzo Abe (安倍晋三, incumbency: 2006-2007), who was the successor of Koizumi, stepped down from the position of Prime Minister after failing to properly deal with the incident where computer records of 50 million social security pension recipients were lost and facing a disastrous defeat in the House of Councilors election in 2007. His successor, Fukuda Yasuo (福田康夫, incumbency: 2007-2008), somewhat restored Japan's relationships with Asian countries, which Abe had worsened, but failed to show strong leadership.

Around a decade after the beginning of the new millennium, Japan met a series of great crises. These were the global financial crisis triggered by the US 'subprime mortgage crisis' in 2008, and the big earthquake and radiation leak from damaged nuclear facilities in 2011. These two incidents pushed the Japanese economy, which had been gradually recovering, back into the risk of a recession and triggered rapid political change. Amid ongoing internal and external crises, the Democratic Party of Japan had an overwhelming victory against the Liberal Democratic Party, whose leadership had weakened after

Koizumi, in the House of Representatives election of August 2009. The party's chairman Hatoyama Yukio(鳩山由紀夫)[425], promised in his election campaign that if the Democratic Party of Japan won and he became the Prime Minster, he would move the US military base outside of Okinawa. This was an impossible pledge for Japan, which was dependent on the United States both in terms of economic and military strategy, and thus it later came back and hit Hatoyama like a boomerang. In the end, Prime Minister Hatoyama failed to gain support from either his party or the public, stepping down in June 2010 after less than a year in office, and was replaced by Kan Naoto. However, Prime Minister Kan lost his popularity due to his proposal to double the sales tax, and the Democratic Party of Japan failed to avoid a crushing defeat in the House of Councilors election held in July under such circumstances. Amidst this political change, district-based conservative populism emerged as another political trend. The representative figure was Hashimoto Toru (橋下徹), a charismatic young politician. He was a lawyer, born in a buraku community under disdainful treatment and a graduate of Waseda University, who had gained a reputation by providing legal advice on local television. Based on his reputation, he was elected as the Governor of Osaka in the local elections in 2008. However, he ended up chipping away at his initial popularity by showing extreme right inclination and making inexorable remarks on historical issues such as the comfort women issue.

In 2010, the GDP of China caught up with that of Japan, and China became the second largest country in the world economy. When this was reported, Japanese government officials endeavored not to place much importance on it, but it was difficult for most of the Japanese people to accept the fact that they had fallen to third place in GDP ranking. As shown in the headline ('Japan Goes from Dynamic to Disheartened') of the New York Times cover story in October 2010, Japan was faced with economic problems such as deflation and reduction in consumption, but above all a 'crisis of confidence.' Japan had been a nation full of energy and ambition to the point of seeming arrogant up until the 1980s, but was now engulfed with fear for the future.[426] If defeat in the Pacific War had deprived Japan of its sense of superiority in military terms, the burst of the bubble and the long term economic recession has made Japan lose its sense of superiority and confidence in economic terms.[427] Thus far, the Japanese government had led economic growth, particularly expanding its role when the economy was dull. However, the reality is that there is a limit in government capacity to stimulate the economy, as Japan's national debt in proportion to GDP is the highest in the world.

In the afternoon of March 11, 2011, the Japanese people experienced the most powerful earthquake in Japanese history. This earthquake of 2011 was a hundred times the destructive force of the 1923 Great Kanto Earthquake which had taken at least 100,000 lives. Fortunately, as homes or buildings were designed and built to absorb the shocks, not a lot was destroyed compared to the earthquake intensity. However, a tsunami with a height of 50 feet which followed soon after took countless lives. As of July 2012, the death toll stood at approximately 19,000 people, which included 2,906 people who were still reported as missing but were most likely to be dead. In addition, approximately 270,000 people lost their homes and had to live in temporary housing. Furthermore, the tsunami destroyed the cooling system of a nuclear facility built on the coastline of the Fukushima Prefecture in the northeastern part of Japan. This Fukushima Dai-ichi (Fukushima Number One), operated by Tokyo Electric Power Company (TEPCO), was 150 miles from Tokyo, and when the cooling capability was lost, nuclear fuel rods melted down and caused a massive radiation leak, which led to the contamination of soil and seawater. There were no immediate casualties due to this radiation exposure, but it is difficult to precisely analyze and evaluate what effect this will have in the long term. Therefore, numerous people who had lived near the Fukushima nuclear power plant were forced to leave their homes.

The then Prime Minister Kan Naoto stated on March 13 that the March 11 disaster was the most severe crisis of Japan since World War II. Emperor Akihito also sent out a message of consolation not to give up hope via national television. It was the first time the Japanese Emperor made an on-air nationwide statement since August 1945, when his father Emperor Hirohito had made the declaration of surrender to the Allied Forces via radio broadcasting and encouraged the Japanese people to persevere. There were some cases of theft from the vacant homes of evacuees and embezzlement of donation funds from relief organizations, but overall, the Japanese people in the disaster-affected area showed a systematic response to the terrible disaster by maintaining an extremely orderly manner, enduring, and helping one another, which impressed many people of the world. In contrast, politicians were criticized for failing to properly take care of the people and being selfish, and the top management of Tokyo Electric Power Company was criticized for being busy trying to avoid responsibility. Meanwhile, the Self Defense Forces (自衛隊) were considered to have played a considerable role in rescue and relief missions, and the US military in Japan, which had cooperated in the activities of the Self Defense Forces, also received positive reviews.

Prime Minster Kan Naoto, who failed to effectively respond to the large scale disaster, resigned in August 2011, and Noda Yoshihiko became the new head of the Democratic Party of Japan and new Prime Minister. As the fiscal deficit of the government was so large, it was inevitable to raise the consumption tax in order to recover from the disaster. To gain support from the Liberal Democratic Party on the tax increase, he promised to hold a new election in the near future. Fettered to this promise, Noda eventually held the election for the House of Representatives in December 2012. In this election, the Liberal Democratic Party led by Shinzo Abe[428] increased its number of seats from 118 to 294, while the Democratic Party of Japan suffered a crushing defeat that cut its number of seats from 230 to 57.[429] The Liberal Democratic Party formed a coalition government with the Clean Government Party, securing a two-thirds majority in the House of Representatives. Because Abe has a strong inclination toward nationalism even within the Liberal Democratic Party, he was noncommittal in apologizing about past wars or colonization, while having an extremely strong will to amend the Constitution and take the path of a military power. As a consequence, conflict with other Asian countries further intensified during his incumbency.

Abe, who came back into power in December 2012 after losing his position in 2007, enjoyed popularity from Japanese people, who had been in a sense of loss through the 'lost two decades,' by improving the economy through the economic policy called Abenomics[430] and emphasizing the construction of a strong Japan in response to the threat of China and North Korea. Thus, in the House of Representatives election in November 2014, the Liberal Democratic Party won 291 seats, the Clean Government Party won 35 seats, and so the ruling coalition took possession of 326 seats out of the total 475 seats. Furthermore, in the House of Representatives election in October 2017, the Liberal Democratic Party (284 seats) and the Clean Government Party (29 seats) took possession of 313 seats, which was more than two-thirds of the total 465 seats, still maintaining enough seats to make amendment of the Constitution possible. Even in the House of Councilors[431], where the quorum is 242, the number of seats possessed by the Liberal Democratic Party and parties that are in favor of constitutional amendment surpasses two-thirds (162 seats). Therefore, Japan is in a situation where constitutional amendment can be promoted at any moment. However, since there are many Japanese people that are still in favor of protecting the Constitution, the Japanese government is not hastily pushing ahead with constitutional amendment. Therefore, as a prior step, the Abe government made it possible to exercise Collective Self Defense rights by altering constitutional interpretation and passed security related legislation in the National Diet. Also, Abe had extended the presidency term from '6 years through 2 consecutive terms' to '9 years through 3 consecutive terms' by revising the party regulations of the Liberal Democratic Party in 2017. Therefore, it seemed that Abe would be the Prime Minister of Japan until September 2021. Furthermore, there was a high possibility of four consecutive terms for him, so it did not seem as though he would immediately rush forward with constitutional amendment.[432] However, due to the coronavirus (COVID-19) pandemic in early 2020, the 2020 Tokyo Summer Olympics were postponed to the next summer. Furthermore, Japan had also had many difficulties in responding to the coronavirus pandemic.

Accordingly, the extension of the Abe Administration became uncertain. Eventually, in September 2020, Shinzo Abe, who had recorded Japan's longest-serving time as Prime Minister (nearly eight years), resigned because of ill health, and Yoshihide Suga (菅義偉), Abe's longtime right-hand man, succeeded him.

2. Rise of New Tensions and 'Japan's War Problems' in the Post-Cold War Era

The most urgent social problem in Japan since the 1990s is the decrease in youth population due to aging and low birth rates. Since 2004, Japan's population has shown a stagnant or decreasing trend at around 127 million, and Japan is facing the problem of a smaller and older[433] population[434] in the 21st century. In particular, the declining population is leading to a labor shortage, while the Japanese people avoid tough manual labor called the 'three-K (kiken-dangerous, kitanai-dirty, and kitsui-difficult).' Therefore, Japan is in a situation where it cannot but accept foreigners to resolve the situation of labor shortage.[435] According to 2017 statistics, the legally registered foreigners' number in Japan was 2,561,848,[436] which was only 2.0% of the population and extremely low compared to international standards. These people are mostly from China, the Philippines, and Brazil. The number of illegal immigrants reached approximately 250,000, and these people are working in jobs with high risk of injury, without proper wages and suffering from abuse. There has been mounting negative criticism on the influx of foreigners in Japan. In April 2000, Ishihara Shintaro, the Governor of Tokyo, emphasized that the military should prepare to play a bigger role as foreigners' crimes were increasing, in his address to the Self Defense Forces. He also mentioned that 'third country persons'[437] commit many crimes and may break out in revolt, encouraging a negative sentiment toward Koreans. His remarks add to the bitter taste by reminding people of the tragic history in which innocent Koreans and Chinese were slaughtered due to groundless rumors during the 1923 Kanto Earthquake.[438]

Various social problems have turned up as the Japanese economy becomes stagnant. Sadistic bullying and school phobia have become huge social problems since the 1990s. In the 1990s, a series of horrific crimes occurred in schools. The Japanese people were appalled to learn that some of the graduates of Tokyo University Department of Engineering were found to be members of the Aum Shinrikyo and that they had helped concoct poisonous gas. In 1997, a 14-year-old student killed an 11-year-old boy for no particular reason, decapitated the victim, and put his head in front of the school he attended. In 2005, a 16-year-old school girl poisoned her mother and posted the progress on the Web. Experts analyzed that the education system that focused only on college entrance exams, while neglecting education that builds students' character, aggravated the aberration of juvenile delinquents. Another type of social problem that emerged in the 1990s was a new form of 'youth prostitution.' Teenage girls who were from abundant and good family backgrounds were engaging in prostitution with adult males at a considerable price. On the reverse side of this phenomenon, it can be said that the vestiges of Japan's male-oriented sex culture, such as red-light districts during the Tokugawa Period, the state-regulated prostitution policy after the Meiji Restoration, and the Japanese military sexual slavery (so called 'comfort women' system) during the period of militarism, have come into play.

In order to stimulate the stagnant domestic economy, Japan implemented the fiscal deficit policy in which government expenditure was expanded. This policy provided the basis for the 'new economy' based on high-tech and some manufacturing industries to actively grow, but repeated budget deficits accumulated a tremendous amount of public debt. In order to prevent the bankruptcy of the social security system, the government contributed a massive amount of funds from the general revenues, which aggravated the situation. As the young working age population decreases and the elder age group which benefits from social security increases, the fiscal deficit ratio will become even worse in the future. As Japan has increased defense expenditure in recent years, the possibility of resolving the fiscal deficit will grow even slimmer.

Japan's modern history of colonization and war of aggression has acted as an obstacle for Japan to establish stable and constructive relationships with Asian countries. Ironically, the more distant Japan's colonization and war of aggression becomes as an act of the past, the larger the conflict revolving around modern Japan's historical wrongdoings grows. The most sensitive issue related to Japan's acts during the war is the issue of the 'comfort women (ianfu).' As three former Korean 'comfort women' filed a lawsuit against the Japanese government with the assistance of Japanese civic groups in 1991, the controversy of history proliferated. There was no room to argue about the fact that brothels were operated for Japanese soldiers at the battlefield and young women provided sexual comfort to Japanese soldiers under duress, but the Japanese government insisted that the Japanese Army did not directly intervene. However, in early 1992, when a Japanese historian publicized government documents that the military authorities actively intervened in the running of brothels, the Japanese government had no choice other than to acknowledge the fact. Therefore, Prime Minister Miyazawa Kiichi, who visited Korea in 1992, apologized for the issue of comfort women in a speech at the National Diet. Furthermore, in 1993, through extensive research conducted by the government, Chief Cabinet Secretary Kono Yohei (河野洋平) officially admitted and apologized that the mobilization of comfort women and running of brothels were forced and that the Japanese government had intervened. Also, in 1995, at the 50th anniversary of the termination of the war, Prime Minister Murayama Tomiichi made a comprehensive apology regarding the forced mobilization of comfort women and other atrocities during the war.[439] However, there was no proper compensation from the Japanese government and many influential politicians denied the existence or forcibleness of comfort women, which made the issue of comfort women remain unresolved.

In 1990, Emperor Akihito, jointly with Prime Minister Kaifu Toshiki (海部俊樹) at the time, apologized to Korea, and in 1992 also expressed remorse to China. However, Asian countries which had been occupied by Japan consider that Japan needs to give a more heartfelt apology. In East Asian societies, mere statements of apology cannot move the heart of the counterpart. It must be an apology that includes kneeling or bowing one's head to the floor. However, up until now, nobody among Japan's high-ranking figures have given such a sincere and heartfelt apology. Furthermore, although general apologies have been made, the good meaning of these apologies have been counterbalanced by the words of other high-ranking figures that deny any history of Japanese aggression.[440]

All sorts of criticism on Japan's war crimes that exploded after the end of the Cold War caused the backlash of nationalist forces within Japan when stepping into the 21st century. Historians that followed the new current of 'revisionism' criticized that thus far, history education had been conducted in a 'masochist' manner, in which only the dark side of Japan's past was magnified. They even denied that the Nanjing Massacre of 1937 occurred and strongly argued that comfort women were nothing more than prostitutes. To them, history education was supposed to be a means of building pride on Japan's speedy rise into an independent modern state. Therefore, they formed the 'Association to Write New History Textbooks,' and published a textbook that took on a narrowly nationalistic approach in 2001. The Japanese Ministry of Education went through several requests to revise errors and eventually approved the textbook as a government authorized textbook. Consequently, not only Japanese historians, teachers, and citizens, but also the people and governments of China and Korea fiercely criticized the Japanese government's decision. In general, the governments and people of Asian countries severely protested when Japanese leaders visited the Yasukuni Shrine, approved textbooks that undermined the aggression and brutality of Japan, or repudiated past apologies for the war. Therefore, while many Asians praise the marvelous economic growth that Japan accomplished after the war, they still do not forgive the acts of brutality committed by Japanese soldiers and bureaucrats on their territory during the war of aggression and period of colonization.[441] This historical issue makes it difficult for Japan to play a leading role in East Asia.

After the war, Japan has continued territorial disputes with three East Asian countries regarding several islands. These are the four northern islands (Russia), Dokdo/Liancourt Rocks/Takeshima (South Korea), and the Senkaku/Diaoyu Islands (China and Taiwan). These islands inherently have the possibility to trigger international conflict at any moment. An incident occurred in August 2012, in which some Chinese activists swam all the way to the Senkaku Islands escaping Japanese patrol boats. They were caught and taken into custody, but were eventually freed. A few days later, a few Japanese people came ashore on this island and claimed the sovereignty of Japan. Thus, the conflict of the two countries of China and Japan surrounding this island was sharply expressed. Later, the Noda Administration, considering the idea of Ishihara Shintaro[442], purchased the island from individual owners under the name of the national government. The Chinese government strongly protested, and the Chinese people criticized Japanese people and Japanese companies severely in various regions of China and held anti-Japanese demonstrations.

Through the end of the Cold War, the United States became the world's only superpower and posed as the police that maintained international order of globalized capitalism. However, due to accumulated fiscal deficits and trade deficits, the United States has been employing the method of intervening in regional disputes by mobilizing the military and economic power of various countries through the United Nations. Every time the United States made such interventions, they demanded Japan's active military and economic support.[443] The United States' demand for Japan to play a more active military role and Japan's ambition to become a strong military power are causing anxieties on the part of Asian countries. Thus, in 1998, the United States and Japan agreed on 'New Guidelines' to expand the regions covered by the US-Japan Security Treaty, and accordingly, Japan passed the Regional Incidents Law and the Anti-Terrorism Law. Pursuant to these laws, Japan dispatched its Self Defense Forces to Iraq from 2003 to 2007 and executed noncombatant duties.

Three-quarters of total US forces in Japan are stationed in Okinawa, and American bases occupy about 20% of the main island. In 1995, there was an incident in which three US soldiers kidnapped a twelve-year-old girl and committed gang rape. In response to this incident, strong anti-base protests arose, and approximately 85,000 people participated in the largest demonstration. Therefore, the governments of the United States and Japan agreed to slightly reduce American soldiers and move some of the military facilities to places that were less populated. Up to this point, the stationing of American forces in Japan based on the US-Japan Alliance had been under the pretext of protecting Japan from communist forces such as the Soviet Union, China, and North Korea. In addition, there was also the expectation of neighboring countries that the United States would keep the possibility of

Japan's rearmament in check. However, the end of the Cold War weakened the cause the American bases were protecting Japan from the threat of communist forces.

Despite these circumstances, the United States has kept American bases in Japan as the headquarters that oversee the whole of Asia, ranging from the western region of the Pacific Ocean to the Indian Ocean and the Persian Gulf. Furthermore, the United States has pursued the unification of the United States and Japan in terms of military, by integrating the military headquarters between the American bases in Japan and Japan's Self Defense Forces. Interlocked with Japan's right-turn and pursuit of a strong military power, these types of action by the United States are heightening tension in the Asia region. In the 1980s when Japan was at its peak as a major economic power, Japanese businesses asserted that Japan needed to become a strong country equipped with military power in order to protect its foreign assets all over the world, and political leaders actively sympathized with these views. Even after the collapse of the Cold War, East Asia is faced with the division of South Korea and North Korea on the Korean Peninsula and the separation of China and Taiwan is continuing, which means there still remains a situation of tension. And as China has risen as a strong military power based on rapid economic growth, a sense of crisis is also mounting regarding China. These circumstances have made Japan build a strong desire to strengthen its military power, and Japan's political leaders have used North Korea's nuclear tests and kidnapping of Japanese people as the pretext to become a strong military power. Furthermore, as Japan went through long-term economic recession, the two causes that have sustained postwar Japan, economic power through rapid economic growth and pacifism pursuant to the Peace Constitution, have been tarnished. Due to these turns of events, the Japanese people have lost self-confidence and Japan's future has become extremely insecure. Therefore, Japan's political leaders have presented the goal of becoming a strong military power and have been receiving a lot of support from the Japanese people who have lost a sense of direction and goal. This atmosphere within Japan has been clearly expressed through movements to revise the Constitution to enable war, revision of history textbooks to glamorize the history of modern Japan, and the visits of political leaders to the Yasukuni Shrine. Consequently, these events have triggered protests of Asian countries.

Japan's movements pursuing a strong military power based on its alliance with the United States and its strong economic power has caused vigilance on the part of not only China and Korea but also other Asian countries. Even though the Cold War ended, China, Japan, and Korea have not been able to form a close relationship like the United Kingdom, Germany, and France in Europe. This is partly due to the fact a trust relationship has not yet been established among the countries, as Japan has not properly settled its historical wrongdoings of aggression and colonization of Asian countries in the early 20th century. Rather, Japan has strongly refuted that education and railway construction in Japan's colonies or occupied territories were the driving force of modernization in these regions and enabled economic prosperity. However, this is merely an analysis based on the outcome, in which Japan attempts to evaluate its acts through the result of economic success in these countries. Since today's economic prosperity of Korea is something that the Koreans cultivated from the ruins of the Korean War,[444] it is extremely unconvincing to link Korea's economic success to the influence of Japan's colonization. Rather, when considering that the Korean Peninsula was divided instead of Japan and furthermore the Korean War broke out during the process of settling Japan's colonization and the Pacific War, Japan's assertions are absolutely ridiculous and shameful.

Most of Japan's war reparation issues with Asian countries were resolved by the 1960s pursuant to the Treaty of San Francisco and bilateral treaties. As mentioned above, these negotiations were settled without properly reflecting the intentions of the people of each country, due to pressure from the United States amidst the conflict of the Cold War, economic difficulties of the countries in question, lack of legitimacy of government regimes and so forth. Therefore, after the Cold War ended and each country became democratized, demands for reparation arose from the victims. Japan's war reparation issue with China was legally resolved when Prime Minister Tanaka Kakuei visited China in September 1972 and signed the Japan-China Joint Communique and when the two countries officially concluded the Japan-China Treaty of Peace and Friendship in August 1978. Accordingly, from 1979, the Japanese government provided various types of aid for economic cooperation, contributing to China's reform, opening, and economic development. Thus, the inter-reliance between Chinese and Japanese economies became deeper and the Japanese people came to have a more favorable opinion of China as China relinquished its war reparations from Japan when the two countries established diplomatic relations. However, after the Cold War ended, Chinese people started to express strong dissatisfaction and criticism against the Chinese government's renunciation of war reparations from Japan during the Cold War era, claiming that it was not based on national consensus. Accordingly, the Chinese government took the stance that China had only relinquished its war reparations from Japan on the state level, not the right of claim of individuals who had directly suffered from the war.

Currently, the only country with which Japan has not been able to establish diplomatic relationships among Asian countries is North Korea. In the early 2000s, there was an opportunity for the relationship between Japan and North Korea to be improved as a result of Japanese Prime Minister Koizumi's active actions, but it fell apart due to worsened public opinion within Japan. [445] In September 2002, Japanese Prime Minister Koizumi Junichiro suddenly visited North Korea and announced the 'Pyongyang Declaration of Japan and North Korea' through a meeting with Kim Jong-il, North Korea's President. When the issue of North Korea's abduction of Japanese people was clarified (8 dead, 5 living) through the summit meeting, voices rose within Japan that 'discussions on diplomatic relations between Japan and North Korea should not proceed without resolving the abduction issue'. Japan's press and mass media also amplified this opinion. The five surviving victims of the abduction temporarily returned to Japan in October, but Japan annulled its promise and made their return permanent. North Korea protested Japan's breaking of its promise and declared that the abduction issue was settled. With this, discussions on diplomatic relations between the two countries did not resume for one and a half years. In August 2003, the Six Party Talks to resolve the North Korean nuclear issue was held in Beijing for the first time. In this backdrop, Prime Minister Koizumi revisited Pyongyang in May 2004, held a meeting with Kim Jong-il, and recommenced discussions on diplomatic relations between Japan and North Korea. In the process of these negotiations between Japan and North Korea, Japan showed self-contradictory and antinomic behavior. In other words, Japan went on the rampage about the abduction of some Japanese citizens, yet chose to shut its eyes to the fact that it did not properly repent or apologize and failed to make reparations or compensations for its crimes of committing every possible brutality during the early 20th century, not only causing pain to hundreds of millions of Asians, but killing or injuring tens of millions of people and sexually abusing hundreds of thousands of women.

As seen above, as the Cold War came to an end and Asian countries became democratized, Japan's war problems (Japanoblems), which had been hidden under the surface during the Cold War, started to erupt in many ways. In the following sections, Japan's war problems (Japanoblems) will be dealt with in more detail by categorizing issues into war responsibilities, post war reparations and compensations, comfort women, territory disputes, perception of history, remembering and healing damages, and apology and repulsion nationalism.

3. War Responsibilities

Japan's war responsibility in a narrow sense refers to responsibility for human, material, and mental damage that Japan caused not only to the Allied Forces, which were the belligerency countries, but also to occupied territories and colonies in Asia over the 15 years since the Manchurian Incident in 1931 to the end of the Pacific War in 1945. Considering Japan's war responsibility in a wider sense, it includes compulsive incorporation of the bases of Ainu people and the Ryukyu Kingdom, the First Sino-Japanese War and colonization of Taiwan, and the annexation of the Korean Peninsula including Dokdo (Liancourt Rocks), which had been carried out according to Japan's external expansion policy after the Meiji Restoration. Those who should bear war responsibility are the leaders of each sector, such as military, politics and the economy, as well as the general public. Not only the military and political leaders who were the ringleaders of the war, but also the ordinary Japanese people who cooperated in war of aggression and shared the spoils of war are responsible. The postwar generation, which is enjoying the benefits of enhanced national wealth through the external invasion and colonial ruling of its ancestors, automatically inherit the responsibility of prior generations. However, what the Allied Forces questioned through the Tokyo Trials [446] was the responsibility of starting the war of aggression, so no judgment has been made on Japan's entire war responsibility. In addition, apart from the army leaders and some politicians, the Emperor, politicians, government officials, and *zaibatsu* were exempted from the war responsibility. Furthermore, the fact that they continued to play significant roles after the war became a major reason why the issue of Japan's war responsibility continues to be controversial even to this day.

Today's Japan has the legal responsibility for the historic faults of the former Japanese Empire invading and colonizing Asian countries. The Japanese people born after the war also have a political and moral responsibility to ensure that the Japanese government fulfills this legal responsibility properly. This is because a considerable part of the benefits that today's Japan and Japanese people enjoy is based on the fruits of the former colonization and war of aggression, but they did not pay for these benefits nor did they properly compensate for the damages inflicted on the other countries. Postwar Japan and its people had been able to use the Cold War situation as a shield against being held accountable by countries and their people that had suffered from Japan's war of aggression and colonization.

Among today's Japanese people, there may be persons who retort why they should take responsibility for the historical wrongdoings of their ancestors of the past. Tesa Morris-Suzuki explains this through the concept of 'involvement (連累),' which means that as a being with a conscious relation with the past, one recognizes that one is an accessory after the fact (as a legal term).[447] This means that even if one did not directly persecute or cause pain to 'the other,' one cannot be free from the responsibility since he or she is living in the present society which was built on the benefits gained from persecutions or exploitations of the past, at which point no reasonable actions were taken.[448]

The word responsibility means that one can respond to someone, meaning that one is ready to respond when there is a call or request from 'the other'. At the basis of all societies and all human relationships, there is a kind of social agreement that one should respond when 'the other' calls out, as the minimal trust relationship for individuals to coexist. In the case where an individual or group hears the call of 'the other', the individual or group is given the responsibility to choose whether or not to respond. Responding to the call of 'the other' is a plus to the image, making it possible to maintain or renew the human relationship. Through this, one can confirm one's basic trust relationship with 'the other'. In this sense, Japan had dismissed the calls of 'the other', namely Asian countries or Asian people, by using the situation of the Cold War, and Japan has not responded head-on to the demands that have exploded after the end of the Cold War. In short, Japan has not taken the legal, political, or ethical responsibility for Asian countries and Asian people who had suffered from Japan's colonization and war of aggression.[449]

Approximately 27% of the Allied prisoners of war captured by the Japanese troops died, which is a great contrast with the fact that 4% of UK and US prisoners of war who were captured by German or Italian troops died. The cause of death of prisoners who were detained by Japanese troops was mostly disease, malnutrition, and brutal abuse. As the Japanese military's abuse toward captives from the Allied Forces became more severe in the Pacific War, the government representatives of the Allied Forces announced the St. James Declaration on the punishment of Japanese war criminals in 1942.[450] The Potsdam Declaration of July 26, 1945 explicitly presented that legal responsibility would be imposed not only on the abusers of captives from the Allied Forces but also on those with war responsibility. On January 19, 1946, SCAP (Supreme Commander for the Allied Powers) proclaimed a charter on the establishment of an International Military Tribunal for the Far East. The International Military Tribunal for the Far East was mainly in charge of punishing war criminals at the leader level. However, the International Military Tribunal for the Far East did not prosecute Emperor Hirohito, who had the biggest war responsibility. When opinions on how to treat the problem of Emperor Hirohito were split even within the United States government, the State-War-Navy Coordinating Committees (SWNCC) sent a letter (SWNCC 55/6) to SCAP in October 1945, asking his opinion on the prosecution of Emperor Hirohito. In MacArthur's reply to Army Chief of Staff Eisenhower on January 25, 1946, he expressed an objecting opinion in the aspect that in the case where Emperor Hirohito were to be prosecuted, military troops of a million men would be necessary to rule over Japan. Thus, the issue of prosecuting Emperor Hirohito was concluded. Apart from the war criminal trials, there were views within the ruling class of Japan that Emperor Hirohito should be abdicated from the throne to take moral responsibility of war,[451] but even this movement failed due to the intervention of SCAP.

The Japanese ruling class also not only prevented Emperor Hirohito from being brought to trial as a war criminal but put the blame of war on the few leading members of the Japanese Army in the Tokyo Trial, and ended up evading responsibility. One of the reasons why this was possible was that during the two weeks after Emperor Hirohito made a declaration of surrender on August 15, 1945, before the Allied Forces landed on Japan, the Japanese government and military authorities incinerated all the documents that could be used in war criminal trials. [452] Therefore, the Japanese government's assistance was necessary during the Tokyo Trial, and in this process, the Japanese people were able to drive the trials toward their desired direction.[453] As the Tokyo Trial was conducted poorly, the investigation on and punishment for the crimes against humanity that Japan committed against Asian people was not properly realized. In other words, crimes against humanity, such as medical experiments and chemical warfare against Asian people, and mobilization of forced labor and sexual slavery for the Japanese military, etc., were hardly handled. In particular, brutalities such as medical experiments conducted by Unit 731 were not brought to trial even though the American forces acquired pertaining material due to the opposition of the leading members of the American forces. The detailed contents of the medical experiments and biological warfare committed by Unit 731 came to light when the Soviet Union put 12 apprehended members of Unit 731 on trial in December 1949 in Khabarovsk and published the records the following year.[454]

After the end of the war, Japanese leaders did their utmost to maintain the emperor system, which was the frame of modern Japan, and to advocate for the Emperor, who was the one with the greatest responsibility for the war of militarism. Eventually, they retained the emperor system by creating a distorted image of history in which the entire responsibility of war was on the Japanese Army, and enabled the Emperor to escape from all the responsibility. Tojo Hideki, who was tried as a Type A war criminal in the war crimes trial, testified in the Tokyo Trial in December 1947 through the statement that 'No Japanese person would be able to disobey the will of the Japanese Emperor, and he had not taken any action against the will of the Japanese Emperor.' Thus, the authorities of the American forces and the leaders of the Japanese government, who had been pushing for the exemption of the Emperor, put all sorts of pressure on him to change his testimony. Eventually, one week later, Tojo stated in the court that 'The Emperor desired and loved peace.'[455] In the case of Konoe Fumimaro, who was the Prime Minister of the cabinet during the Second Sino-Japanese War, was responsible for the occupation and massacre of Japanese troops in Nanjing and the expansion of the Chinese front, but the US exempted him from responsibility as it was recognized that he made efforts to end the Pacific War against the US in the early stages. Thus, not only did most of the ruling class, including the Emperor, escape from war responsibility through the Tokyo Trial, but they played an active part as leaders in postwar conservative politics. Japan's conservative politicians including Yoshida Shigeru turned all war responsibilities to the leading members of the Japanese Army and solidified their position by cooperating with the United States during the Cold War. Therefore, they could not criticize the United States for dropping atomic bombs and carrying out indiscriminate bombings against Japan and refused to repent for their own invasion and colonization of Asian countries.

Since Japan's ruling class, who were largely responsible for the war, escaped war crimes trials and interrogation on war responsibility by using the Japanese Army as the scapegoat, it was even more difficult for the ordinary Japanese people, who had been mobilized to war by the military authorities and the Japanese government, to have any sense of responsibility for the war. Since brutal colonization and the atrocious acts of the Japanese military on the battlefield were committed in other Asian countries, most of the ordinary Japanese people were not even aware of the actual circumstances. The government's censorship played a part, but there was also the fact that most of the media outlets only praised victories in war and refrained from covering the negative side of war. Furthermore, the Japanese people harbored a victim's mentality rather than a perpetrator's mentality, due to the atomic bombings of Hiroshima and Nagasaki, indiscriminate air raids by the American forces, and shortage of daily necessities. In addition, the strict dual structure of the ruling class and the subjugated class which was fixed during the Tokugawa Period was still deeply rooted. This meant that the ordinary Japanese people did not have sovereign power and were mere subjects of rule. Therefore, it was difficult for the ordinary Japanese people to have an independent sense of responsibility for the sovereign actions of the ruling class.

In fact, the issue of war responsibility of ordinary Japanese people did come up right after losing the war. The then Higashikuni Naruhiko Cabinet asserted the 'All 100 Million People Repent,' which did not mean responsibility toward victim countries, but meant that all of the Japanese people should regret and repent toward the Emperor for losing the war, shifting the responsibility of defeat to the ordinary people. It was through the book *War Responsibility* (戰爭責任) published by Ienaga Saburo (家永三郎, 1913-2002) in 1985 that the issue of the war responsibility of the ordinary Japanese people came to be discussed in earnest. He asserted that the ordinary Japanese people had the responsibility of engaging actively in the country's acts of violence or failing to prevent it from happening, and that the Japanese people had a joint responsibility in a moral sense toward the people of victimized countries. On the other hand, he admitted that the ordinary Japanese people were in a way victims themselves in the relationship with the state power, because they were always mentally and physically under the control of power, as they were deprived of the right to know and the freedom of expression at the time.[456] Meanwhile, Takahashi Hikoroshi (高橋彦博) asserted that the direct performers of inhumane acts of atrocity were soldiers who originated from the people, and emphasized that it was necessary to self-consciously question the war responsibility of the ordinary Japanese people, since they accepted the existence of war leaders and went on to actively support them.[457] Thus, he pointed out the fact that the Japanese people's questioning of their own war responsibility was slight, and asserted that the perpetrator's responsibility as the actual performers of war needed to be discussed. Despite these discussions, the Japanese people reinforced their awareness of themselves as victims rather than perpetrators, based on the fact that Japan was the sole victim country of atomic bombings in the world, that they suffered from shortage of daily necessities and air raids of the American forces at the final stage of the Pacific War, and that at least 3 million Japanese soldiers and civilians died in the battlefield. It is true that the dual structure of perpetrator and victim has doubled the difficulties of questioning the war responsibilities of the Japanese people. Of course, the political leaders and the press have a lot to answer for the fact that a victim's mentality was strengthened within the Japanese people.

However, it must not be overlooked that the suffering and sacrifice of the Japanese people arose from the wrong strategy and choice of Japan's leaders. The misfortune of the Japanese people was sufficiently predictable, as Japanese troops were repeatedly defeated by US troops, who had overwhelming military force in the Pacific War. If Japan's leaders could not predict this, it falls under gross negligence, and if they continued war despite having had predicted this, then it falls under willful negligence. If this were to be approached by law, this would be murder or at least involuntary homicide resulting in death. Despite the fact that Japan's leaders had several opportunities to prevent the calamity to be suffered by its people in advance, they were not able to take a new turn due to the militarist strategy that they had pursued so far and the deified Japanese Emperor System. First, when Saipan was captured in July 1944 and senior statesmen joined their efforts to force the Tojo Cabinet to undergo general resignation, Japan could have established a Cabinet headed by a Prime Minister who was a civilian politician rather than a military officer and stopped the war. If so, Japan would not have had to suffer the sacrifices by the Okinawa Battle, air raids on mainland Japan, atomic bomb attacks, and Soviet participation in the war. There were several suggestions, in political and diplomatic channels such as former Prime Minister Konoe Fumimaro's Memorial to the throne on February 1945, to stop the war at an early stage in order to protect the country and lessen the sacrifice. Therefore, it could have been possible to end the war through a resolution of Japan's leaders including the Japanese Emperor, using these suggestions as momentum. Later, Japan had other opportunities to end the war in May 1945 when Germany surrendered or in July when the Potsdam

Declaration was proclaimed. However, Japan missed all these opportunities and ended up facing the worst situation.

The Tokyo Trial put the responsibility of war mainly on the leading members of the Japanese Army. On the other hand, the Emperor, politicians, economic figures, and ordinary Japanese people were able to evade responsibility. Therefore, there was sympathy toward those who underwent trial and a perception that those people were the victims. Furthermore, as the Tokyo Trial was initiated by the Allied Forces and especially by the American forces, the Japanese people criticized that it was a victor's trial and had the perception that it was an unjust trial. However, the biggest problem was that the Japanese people went on building a new government and society without clearly revealing the criminal nature of the war waged by Japan. As bureaucrats of the Tojo Cabinet, such as Kishi Nobusuke (岸信介), who used to be the ruling class during the war, continued to play key roles after the end of the war, Japan could not go through exposure and interrogation of war crimes by itself. Therefore, the Japanese people's repentance on the war ended at the self-reflection of initiating a reckless war in which they had no chance of winning, and failed to arrive at the understanding that it was a war of aggression and this action posed immense agony and damage to Asian countries.

The foreign expansion and invasion of modern Japan can be viewed as the result of pursuing an expansion of survival space for the entire Japanese people, so it is difficult to say that the war responsibility lies only with the leading members of the military authorities or political leaders. The Japanese are a people with a strong sense of group consciousness based on the family, and this family consciousness expands into the society and country, emphasizing loyalty and affiliation toward groups. In the early 20th century, Japan's military authorities and ruling class used this group consciousness of the Japanese people to create a totalitarian garrison state and to concentrate on invasion and domination of Asia. Therefore, the significant responsibility of modern Japan's war of aggression and colonization of Asia lies with the Emperor, the leading members of the military, and political leaders but the ordinary Japanese people, who actively sympathized and spontaneously or semi-spontaneously participated in the war, need to assume responsibility as well. As all countries consist of people, it can be said that the substantial liability of compensation for a country's actions lies with all the people of the country.

It can be said that Japanese people have an accomplice consciousness of having directly and indirectly cooperated and participated in the implementation of the war, even though they say they were deceived by the military authorities. Therefore, as Emperor Hirohito who was the sovereign ruler and head of state at the time did not take responsibility for the war under the grounds that he was deceived by the military authorities, then the

Japanese people could also escape the responsibility, and both the Japanese Emperor and the people could position themselves as victims. Consequentially, as the Japanese Emperor was exempted from responsibility at the Tokyo Trials, Japanese people also became unconscious of their war responsibilities and rather, their historical awareness degenerated into regarding themselves as the victims.

One of the arguments for exempting the Japanese Emperor from war responsibility is that he was a pacifist and was against war. Put in another way, it means that the Japanese Emperor was against the war because the war went against peace and could not be justified. If this is true, then, the Japanese Emperor, who was the sovereign ruler and head of state at the time, becomes responsible for not preventing a war that went against peace from happening. Likewise, the Japanese people cannot escape from the responsibility of having cooperated and implemented substantive military operations in this wrongful war.

When one party harms another party and damages are made, if the perpetrator is not punished or the damages made by the perpetrator are not compensated for, this goes against the principle of justice. Not only in Japan, but in any country, if somebody is murdered or raped, the criminal is supposed to be arrested and given severe punishment. Nobody considers this revenge. The same logic applies when a country causes damage to another country or its people. Therefore, Japan must take responsibility for invading and colonizing Asian countries and causing immense pain to Asian people through killings, rape, plunder, economic exploitation, etc. Those who had taken the lead must necessarily be punished and those who cooperated must receive corresponding punishment. Furthermore, ordinary soldiers or civilians who participated in the war of aggression and colonization, voluntarily or semi-voluntarily, and committed acts of brutality, must take their responsibility as well. In addition, they should apologize and provide sufficient compensation to victim countries and their people. However, aside from some of the leading members of the Japanese Army, most Japanese war leaders escaped punishment and ordinary Japanese people have spent 75 years or more after the end of the war without a sense of responsibility. Thus, by failing to restore historical justice, Japan has regrettably failed to establish a future-oriented relationship with Asian countries in the new century and only shows a backward-looking attitude.

4. Postwar Reparations or Compensations

If Japan had made the declaration of surrender at an earlier point, then the Hiroshima and Nagasaki bombings would not have occurred. At any rate, the United States, which succeeded in an atomic bomb test in July 1945, dropped atomic bombs on Japan in order to rapidly bring an end to the war. Due to the might of the atomic bombs, Japan suffered from horrendous damages on human lives and property, which made the Japanese people consider themselves as the victims of war. Therefore, under the self-awareness that Japan was the only country in the world to suffer from atomic bombings, the ordinary Japanese people of postwar Japan came to hold the view that they should never be caught up in war again, emphasizing anti-nuclearism and pacifism. This made the Japanese people become insensitive to self-reflection or awareness as a perpetrator in Japan's war of aggression which was the root cause of the bombings. In addition, in order to give symbolic prominence to their damage, the Japanese people have made Hiroshima into a sacred place, which covers up an important fact. In other words, it has been overlooked that more than 10% of all victims of the atomic bombings were Koreans drafted by the Japanese,[458] and there were numerous Chinese victims as well. The reason that these Asian people were victimized was that Hiroshima, which became the symbol of pacifism after the war, was a major military base and center for the munitions industry, and these Asians were forcefully mobilized and brought to Hiroshima. These Asian victims were excluded from the postwar GI Bill of Rights for the reason of not being Japanese citizens. However, it is a violation of the general principles of International Human Rights Law to discriminate people according to their nationality in the implementation of relief policies. In addition, it has been pointed out that the GI Bill of Rights, which was only applied to Japanese people and even applied to those who can be seen as war criminals, contributed to implanting the sense within Japanese society that the Japanese were the only victims of the war.[459]

One of the reasons why postwar Japan's war reparations were not sufficiently carried out was that along with the Japanese government's diplomatic efforts, the United States alleviated Japan's war responsibility. This was partly due to the fact that excessive demands for war reparations to Germany after World War I triggered the appearance of the Nazi Party. The Potsdam Declaration of July 1945 included contents that war reparations should be made within the extent of maintaining the Japanese economy and should not reach the point of triggering rearmament.[460] In a similar context, in order to limit the scope of war reparations, the first half of Article 14 of the Treaty of San Francisco of 1951 diagnosed that Japan's economic level was not high enough to make complete war reparations.[461] Furthermore, the second half of Article 14 of the treaty stipulated the relinquishment of war reparations on the part of the Allied Forces,[462] dramatically reducing Japan's burden of war reparations. Since China and Korea suffered from the greatest damage in the war but were excluded from the conference, it can be said that the outcome of the treaty turned out to be indulgent toward Japan. John Foster Dulles (1888-1959), the United States negotiator at the Treaty of San

Francisco, admitted that 'As Japan's war of aggression brought about a great amount of loss and agony, each country is entitled to billions of dollars in war reparations,' but pleaded that 'Japan does not have the ability to make war reparations, since it needs to import rations and resources for survival.'[463]

Amid the Korean War, on November 24, 1950, the U. S. Department of State announced the 'Seven-point Memorandum' with basic principles for formulating a Japanese peace treaty, which stipulated the relinquishment of war reparations of all the belligerent powers. The United States viewed that if Japan made payments for war reparations and Japan's economic revival were to be delayed, then the United States would be obliged to make larger amounts of foreign aid to Japan. Therefore, the United States devised a method in which war reparations could be made to increase Japan's productivity and expand its global markets. Thus, the treaty was concluded by changing the demands of Asian countries for war reparations in cash to provision of services and products, which led the reparation amounts to be drastically cut. Although the wording of war reparations was used, compensations in cash was not realized at all. This method of war reparations was greatly beneficial to Japan's economic revival. In this respect, it is generally reasonable to bear the burden of war reparations, but Japan's postwar reparations turned out to be a benefit instead of a burden. In other words, Japan's postwar reparations cannot be called war reparations in its true sense.

Japan made a comeback to international society by drastically reducing the burden of war reparations through the Treaty of San Francisco with the Allied Forces. But Japan still adhered to a colonial or racist attitude when concluding bilateral treaties with neighboring countries in Asia. While Japan assumed the position of taking legal responsibility as a defeated country toward the Western countries of the Allied Forces, Japan held fast to the attitude of giving benefits to Asian countries, which were the subjects of colonization and war of aggression. Therefore, in treaties with Korea and Malaysia, for instance, Japan used expressions such as 'economic cooperation', which is devoid of the sense of responsibility or reparations, and 'unfortunate incidents', which avoids the sense of apology. On the other hand, in treaties with the Netherlands and Sweden, Japan utilized expressions such as regret and sorrow, responsibility pursuant to International Law. Thus, Japan showed the attitude of taking responsibility toward Western countries that had relatively less damage, while refusing to use any expressions of apology or responsibility toward Asian countries that suffered from substantial damage.

When taking a closer look at the background and contents of the Treaty of San Francisco, it was based on the perception that Japan could not make sufficient reparations toward victim countries under the pretext of 'the maintenance of a viable economy for Japan.'[464] As a consequence, Japan was able to minimize the size of war reparations, and actual war reparations were made in the form of in kind and services, which was actually beneficial to Japan's economic development. Furthermore, Japan succeeded in economic revival by taking advantage of the Korean War and accomplished brilliant economic development by depending on the safe market of the capitalist bloc centering on the United States, which provided an umbrella of national security during the Cold War era. Especially when Asian countries were divided and suffered from civil wars because of Japan's colonization and invasion, Japan distanced itself from these wars by using the Peace Constitution as a shield and hiding under the protection of the US-Japan Security Treaty. Furthermore, Japan fully capitalized on these circumstances to build the foundation of economic revival and prepared to take off through increased demands resulting from the wars. Thus, if Japan had risen to become an economic power surpassing the level of maintaining a viable economy, it is only natural to make war reparations on this basis. If Japan had gone through these steps in the 1970s and 1980s, Japan would have been able to exercise political leadership in Asia and Japan would have become a respected leader of the world in the 21st century.

After the late 1980s, the dictatorial governments of Asian countries collapsed and democratization was in progress. Furthermore, the Cold War came to an end through the falls of the socialist regimes of Eastern Europe, the reunification of East and West Germany, and the dissolution of the Soviet Union. Thus, the voices of war victims in Asia, which had been suppressed under the dictatorial governments of the Cold War era, began to be expressed. Korean women, who were comfort women for Japanese soldiers, demanded compensation from the Japanese government, and starting with the filing of lawsuits in the Tokyo District Court, various reparation lawsuits followed. However, the Japanese government continues to assume the position that such demands for reparation 'had already been settled diplomatically.' However, it is judged that this is not the position of a normal country. When the Pacific War started with Japan's surprise attack on Pearl Harbor, the United States sent Japanese immigrants and Japanese Americans born in the United States to concentration camps for the reason of being enemy aliens. Therefore, Japanese Americans made movements for reparation after the war, and the United States government enacted a law in 1988 and made apologies and compensations. The United States' forward-looking attitude shows a striking difference from the behavior of the Japanese government. Shortly before Japan surrendered in World War II, the Soviet Union forces stationed in Manchuria, the northern region of the Korean Peninsula, and the southern region of Sakhalin sent approximately 640,000 Japanese prisoners of war and some civilians to concentration camps located in various regions of the Soviet Union, such as Siberia. These people suffered from forced labor amidst a shortage of food and bitter cold for a span of two to three years up to 11

197

years, during which approximately 60,000 people died. The Soviet Union, which did not participate in the Treaty of San Francisco, announced the Soviet-Japanese Joint Declaration in 1956, normalizing diplomatic relations and relinquishing demands for war reparations between each other. However, when the demands of the victims erupted after the end of the Cold War, the Japanese government clarified in 1991 that 'The Declaration of 1956 merely relinquished the war reparations between the countries, not the individual rights of claim of the people.'[465] Compared to Japan's refusal to compensate for the civilian victims in Asia by stating that it was 'an issue that had been diplomatically concluded among the countries,' it cannot but be pointed out as a logical inconsistency and antinomic behavior.[466]

On the surface, of course, the Japanese government had expressed its opinion in the early 1990s through the Chief of the Treaties Bureau or the Section Chief of Northeast Asia Division in the Ministry of Foreign Affairs that, by the Treaty on Basic Relations in 1965, only Korea's diplomatic custody was relinquished and that the individual rights of claim did not dissipate.[467] However, Japanese courts have dismissed individual claims for various reasons. Many Japanese people and people from victim countries have attempted to receive compensation for their damage through the Japanese courts after the war, but it has never been properly resolved. The position of Japanese courts regarding war responsibility has been presented through the 19th century legal reasoning of 'a state without responsibility (國家無答責)' in which individuals cannot make claims for damages inflicted by government authorities, denial of individual rights of claim pursuant to International Law, logic of resolution en bloc through the interpretation of postwar treaties, and denial of claim according to extinctive prescription of Japanese Civil Law. Also, the legal remedy movements of the Japanese people, which achieved a certain degree of success by being deployed based on the GI Bill of Rights, ironically caused the side-effect of reinforcing the perception that only the Japanese people were the victims of war. In other words, Korean people and Taiwanese people living in Japan were excluded from the benefits of the GI Bill of Rights under the pretext that they were alien residents.[468] The legal principle of 'a state without responsibility' is a principle evading the responsibility of unlawful acts of the government or bureaucrats, which was valid up until the war because Japan did not have regulations on the liability of a country's unlawful act and the exercise of government power was not subject to Civil Law. In addition, Japanese courts have dismissed claims for reparation by applying the latter part of Article 724 of the Civil Law, which stipulates that claims for damages cease to exist when 20 years have lapsed since the occurrence of the unlawful act. Recently, however, there have been some rulings that even if claims have been ultimately dismissed due to the lapse of extinctive prescription, the responsibility itself of a country's unlawful act exists.[469] It seems reasonable to increase the responsibility of the Japanese government since damage reliefs have been delayed by failing to take measures such as actively informing victims of means of relief. In comparison to Japan's evasion of reparations, Germany has made payments of more than EUR 70 billion as reparations for Nazi crimes since 1952.[470]

Since treaties do not relinquish individual rights of claim, it should be considered that victims have rights of claims. Some rulings in this direction had been released in some courts, such as the Toyama District Court in Japan. However, the problem is that Japanese courts generally judge that rights of claim have ceased to exist due to extinctive prescription pursuant to domestic Japanese law. The Japanese government, the party implementing the treaties, has obligations pursuant to the Forced Labor Convention (indemnification liability pursuant to Article 15 and Article 16, and punishment liability pursuant to Article 25). Therefore, dissipating rights and obligations pursuant to international law by applying the extinctive prescription regulation pursuant to domestic law is an act of prioritizing domestic law over international law, which results in harming stable international order. In 1946, the Japanese government requested that businesses 'deposit' unpaid wages for Taiwanese and Korean people, but did not inform the creditors or families of the deceased of the fact, and the deposits ceased to exist after the extinctive prescription of 10 years lapsed. Likewise, colonials who were forcefully drafted were unable to claim their properties, such as savings deposits, installment savings, reserves for retirement, and welfare pension insurance due to such extinctive prescription.[471] In other words, the proper rights of victims by modern Japan were infringed due to the negligence of the state or company under the circumstances of termination of war and deprivation of citizenship, with no reasons attributable to the individuals. Therefore, it is not reasonable to apply the extinctive prescription to these proper rights of colonial victims and it goes against the principle of justice.

In the process of settling the issues after the war, internationally, Japan evaded responsibilities for reparations to Korean and Taiwanese people who were forcefully drafted to Japan during the war by considering them as Japanese during the war, but domestically, Japan applied a new Nationality Act which considered these people as aliens and excluded them from the beneficiaries of the GI Bill of Rights. Even the data possessed by Japan shows that there were 449,524 (207,183 of which were from Taiwan and 242,341 of which were from Korea) ex-colonial soldiers and civilians attached to the military, and that 724,722 people from Korea and 51,190 people from China were forcefully mobilized.[472] Initially, in the draft version of the constitution represented by the Allied Forces, there was a phrase 'foreigners are equal before the law,' but the Japanese government deleted this phrase and inserted a nationality clause that 'the requirements of Japanese nationals should be determined by law' in Article 10 of the new Constitution, sticking to the old tradition of Article 18 in the Imperial Constitution. Furthermore, shortly before the new Constitution came into effect, the Japanese government proclaimed the 'Alien Registration Odinance,' and starting from the day the Treaty of San Francisco came into effect (April 28, 1952), Japan officially renounced the nationality of ex-colonials.[473] As a result, ex-colonials from Taiwan and Korea were considered as foreigners and were excluded from the benefits of the GI Bill of Rights. They were unable to benefit from reparations if they did not become naturalized as Japanese citizens. These people, who had been forcefully included and assimilated as subjects of the Japanese Empire during the war, had become the subjects of discrimination and exclusion in postwar Japan. This shows a stark contrast with the cases of the United States, the United Kingdom, France, Italy, and Germany, where pensions or lump sum allowances are granted to old soldiers of foreign nationalities. In addition, among the people who were found guilty of Type B or Type C war crimes and sentenced to death or prison labor, approximately 300 people were from Taiwan and Korea. Under the situation of colonization, these people were forced to work and be incriminated as prisoner watchmen, and were thoroughly excluded from the postwar compensation system.[474] Furthermore, Taiwanese and Korean people who were executed as war criminals were treated as Japanese people and enshrined together at the Yasukuni Shrine. Thus, the Taiwanese and Korean people who were forced to work as Japanese soldiers or civilians attached to the military were treated as Japanese people and received punishment such as the death penalty. However, Taiwanese and Korean people who should have been subject to benefits, such as the Soldier Pension Law and GI Bill of Rights, were excluded from such reparations under the pretext that they were not Japanese nationals. In other words, they were the victims of the irony of being included in the subjects of war responsibility but being excluded from the subjects of postwar reparation benefits. In addition, it is a contradiction and an insult to the deceased that Japan excluded them from the beneficiaries of the Soldier Pension Law and the GI Bill of Rights but enshrined them in the Yasukuni Shrine.

Although there were many rulings in which individual damage suits were dismissed due to extinctive prescription, there have been 'reconciliations' between victims and companies. Of course, the claims of individuals have continued to be rejected due to the Supreme Court's mindset of 'a state without responsibility' pursuant to the Meiji Constitution and the mindset of Jyuninron (受忍論)[475] that the people must accept and bear the sacrifices of war together. Whereas many of the court rulings have rejected individual claims under the pretext of 'a state without responsibility' and the theory that the people must endure, by stating that the indemnification legislation is 'the discretionary judgment of the legislative branch', a new opportunity to resolve the indemnification issue can be explored to some degree. Therefore, claims for trial have been dismissed, but there have been rulings that have added additional remarks that acknowledge the fact of damage and suggest indemnification legislation. In October 1999, the Osaka High Court mentioned that it seemed to be an unlawful act pursuant to the State Tort Liability Act that the state had continued discrimination under the pretext of nationality and refused to put the matter right. As a consequence, the Japanese government and National Diet proclaimed in June 2000 a law, offering "condolence money" for foreign nationals killed or injured while serving with the Imperial forces and temporarily enabled these people to receive condolence money for 3 years from April 2001, even though the beneficiaries were few. In the trials against NKK Corporation, Nippon Steel Corporation and Fujikoshi, the companies acknowledged that the plaintiffs had engaged in labor, thus accomplishing reconciliation. Regarding the incident of forced labor at the Hanaoka Mine, Kajima Corporation acknowledged that even though the forced labor was based on government policy, the company also had 'responsibility,' thereby enabling reconciliation. The company left JPY 500 million in trust to China's Red Cross to establish the 'Hanaoka Fund for Peace and Friendship,' which was used as a self-support fund or scholarships for victims and bereaved families.[476]

As victims of forced labor in the 1940s were unable to receive any indemnity or compensation legally or economically from Japan, they filed a lawsuit at the Korean court. Four Korean plaintiffs, Lee Chun-sik, Yeo Wun-taek, Shin Cheon-su, and Kim Kyu-su, went to Japan after being appeased by the former Nippon Steel Corporation (sufficient wages and food, acquisition of skills, guarantee of a stable job after going back to Korea), suffered from forced labor in places such as Osaka, and did not receive proper pay. Among these four, Yeo Wun-taek and Shin Cheon-su filed a claim for payment of overdue wages and indemnification for damages against the new Nippon Steel Corporation at the Osaka District Court in Japan in December 1997, but eventually lost the case on the grounds of the lapse of extinctive prescription and absence of individual rights of claim. Thus, the four people filed a lawsuit at the Korean court in 2005. However, both the first trial and the second trial ruled against the plaintiff, under grounds that Japan's final ruling did not be seen as reversing the morality and other social orders in Korea, and that the extinctive prescription had lapsed. However, in 2012, Division 1 of the Supreme Court (presiding judge: Chief Justice Kim Neung-hwan) in Korea overturned the lower court rulings and sent the case back to Seoul High Court in the meaning that indemnity payments should be made. The intent of the judgment was that 'it is clear that the acts of Japanese companies violated the morality and other social orders in Korea, and since the Japanese government has denied the existence of unlawful acts and liability for damages, it is difficult to interpret that the liability for damages has been fulfilled or individual rights of claim have been relinquished.

Accordingly, Seoul High Court ruled that 'payments of KRW 100 million should be made to the plaintiffs.' Since then, the final ruling of the Supreme Court had been delayed for over 5 years, and only one survivor, Lee Chun-sik, remained among the four plaintiffs. After the launch of the new government, it turned out through prosecutors' investigation that the Supreme Court (Chief Justice: Yang Seung-tae) and the Park Geun-hye government intervened in the lawsuit and deliberately delayed the trial. After this issue of delaying the trial came to the surface, the Supreme Court submitted the case to Supreme Court decision in July 2018, and the final ruling was made in three months that the judgment of Seoul High Court was correct. However, as the Japanese government is opposing such ruling of Korea's Supreme Court, it is yet to be seen whether the indemnity payments will actually be made to the victims. Furthermore, since the summer of 2019, the Japanese government has been inflicting economic retaliation against Korea in opposition to the Korean Supreme Court's ruling regarding the compensation for forced labor victims during the Japanese colonial rule, and since then, the diplomatic relationship between Japan and Korea has deteriorated.

The Japanese government strongly insists that there cannot be any indemnity for forced labor because Korea relinquished its right of claim through the Treaty on Basic Relations in 1965. However, this assertion lacks justification because it runs counter to announcements made by the Japanese government itself. First, the Japanese government itself recognized that what perished through the Treaty on Basic Relations was 'diplomatic protection,' and that individual rights of claim still remain. In a House of Councilors meeting in August 1991, Congresswoman Shimizu Sumiko (清水澄子) of the Social Democratic Party of Japan asked the Japanese government 'whether individual rights of claim perished with the Treaty on Basic Relations between Japan and Korea.' To this, Yanai Shunji (柳井俊二), Director General of the Treaty Bureau of Japan's Ministry of Foreign Affairs, replied that 'The Treaty on Basic Relations means that the two countries relinquished diplomatic protection as a state, but that it did not extinguish individual rights of claim pursuant to domestic law'. When Japanese Canadians filed a lawsuit against the Japanese government regarding individual rights of claim, the Japanese government also unfolded the same argument that they could file a lawsuit in Canada because individual rights of claim do not extinguish through treaties between countries. [477] Second, the Japanese government enacted legislation in 1965 to extinguish the individual rights of claim of Koreans. If the individual rights of claim had been extinguished with the Treaty on Basic Relations, then it would have been unnecessary to enact such a law. Then it should be considered that Japan made this law because it is not so. Third, the nature of the economic support that Japan provided pursuant to the Treaty on Basic Relations was called 'congratulatory payment for independence' by

Japan itself, and there was no room to use this money as indemnity for individuals. Japan's economic support did not consist of any cash but was rather provided in installments over approximately 10 years in the form of products and services. What it would be used for and how it would be used was determined at a joint committee consisting of government representatives of each country, and there were no reparations for individual victims. Thus, the Japanese government, which was involved in this matter at the time, cannot claim that individual indemnity was realized.

Making reparations for damages due to war of aggression or colonization means that Japan clarifies its responsibility as a perpetrator toward Asian countries and Asian people and makes collective and individual compensation. These reparations will not simply end in settling historical wrongdoings but will become a crucial foundation in determining the direction of what kind of relationship Japan and the Japanese people will form with Asian countries and Asian people in the future.

5. Modern Japan's Abuse of Human Rights: Japanese Military Sexual Slavery Issues

Japan, which had actually evaded war responsibility for nearly 50 years within the structure of the Cold War, had also neglected the issue of sexual slavery during the war which was an unprecedented collective infringement of women's rights in the history of the world. However, due to the end of the Cold War, as issues that lay dormant during the structure of the Cold War erupted and international concerns on human rights increased, the issue of Japanese military sexual slavery arose as a matter of global attention. In particular, after the end of the 1980s, as political democratization advanced in Asian countries and the influence of feminism became greater, many former comfort women began to reveal their painful past as sexual slaves of the Japanese military.[478] It can be said that Japan neglected the issue of comfort women due to the Cold War, but there were other important factors such as the Japanese people's sexual consciousness and view of war, refusal to repent on colonization, exemption of the Japanese Emperor's war responsibility, etc. Most of all, at the foundation of the Japanese people's sexual consciousness was the big influence of creating a modern system of state-regulated prostitution during the Meiji Period, treating women as sexual objects and making sexuality as something controlled by the government. This led to connivance and even encouragement of overseas prostitution, as Japan expanded toward the continent. Even worse, a representative intellectual of the Meiji Period, Fukuzawa Yukichi (福澤 諭 吉) actively recommended 'exportation of prostitutes' by contributing an article[479] called "Emigration of the people and money-making of prostitutes (娼婦)" in the

Jiji Shinpo on January 18, 1896. As a reflection of this social atmosphere, Japan introduced the state-regulated prostitution system in Taiwan after the First Sino-Japanese War and in Korea after the Russo-Japanese War, invigorating the overseas prostitution of Japanese women. Under this national system of sexual violence, Japanese women who were confronted with economic difficulties went abroad and engaged in prostitution. The state power of Japan, which utilized Japanese women within this system against humanity, could not have respected the human rights of women of other countries, particularly women who were under colonial rule. Therefore, during the Pacific War, the Japanese military raped and institutionally forced not only women under colonial rule but also women in occupied territories into sexual slavery as comfort women without any qualms of conscience.[480]

The problem is that such acts of violation of human rights by the Japanese military was not properly dealt with in the International Military Tribunal for the Far East or the Type B and C war crime trials held in each country after the war. It is especially problematic that the fact that women from Korea and Taiwan, which were under Japan's colonial rule, were mobilized as comfort women and exploited as sexual slaves was not mentioned at all in all trials. Even the Tokyo Trial rulings acknowledged that the Japanese military routinized plunder and rape in China, and Japan revised the Army Criminal Law to prevent these acts during the war. According to the former Army Criminal Law (1907), there was a problem that when one raped a woman while plundering, he was subject to imprisonment for life or at least 7 years, but when one only committed rape, it would be a rape offense, a crime requiring a complaint from the victim, and could not be punished unless the victim files a lawsuit. In response, Japan revised the Army Criminal Law in February 1942 to abolish the clause of an offense subject to complaint and made it possible to enable punishment of imprisonment for life or at least 1 year, in the case of a rape offense. Aside from this legal device, another device to prevent rape in occupied territories was the system of comfort women, but the acts of violation of human rights related to the recruitment and transportation of comfort women and running of brothels were not substantially treated in trials after the war. As a result, half a century went by while the representative act of violation of human rights committed by the Japanese military was buried during the Cold War era after the war.[481]

Since the early 1990s, the issue of Japanese military sexual slavery surfaced in the façade of history. These war crimes committed by the Japanese military were almost completely hidden from the public sphere of history for nearly half a century after the end of the war. After Korea's Kim Hak-sun stepped forward as the first woman to confess that she had been a victim of sexual slavery, approximately 160 women in Korea and thousands of women worldwide came forward as well. Some of these people were forcefully mobilized by the military or the police, but a considerable number of them were tricked into becoming comfort women for the Japanese military. Mobilizing women through employment fraud or human trafficking was an unlawful act according to Japanese Criminal Law and international treaties to which Japan was a signatory. The research report of the International Court of Justice (1994), the Coomaraswamy report of the United Nations Commission on Human Rights (1996), and the recommendation of the expert committee of the International Labor Organization (1996) have consistently pointed out the forced sexual services and sexual slavery at military brothels. Some Japanese people have denied the illegality of the Japanese military comfort women system by putting forward that there was no forced mobilization such as 'human hunting' and there are no public documents to act as evidence. However, the essence on the issue of comfort women is that it was an organized system of sexual violence by the Japanese military, not whether there was forcibleness in the form of mobilization. Even if forced mobilization was publicly conducted, it would be unimaginable for the Japanese military or government authorities to keep record of forced mobilization in the form of public documents because they were aware of the illegality of 'forced mobilization.' In addition, even if there were records in the form of public documents, it would be difficult to find material remaining in the present, since Japan conducted an extensive incineration of public documents in order to destroy traces of evidence after the war. In a sense, it seems that an era of negation is continuing even during the 21st century. In other words, if the Cold War era after the war was a period during which the perpetrators attempted to push the victims into a 'cave of oblivion,' intentionally covered up traces of crime, and desired for witnesses to disappear, the era after the end of the Cold War is a period during which living witnesses are silenced and testimonies of witnesses who revealed their names are disregarded. Many Asian people were brutally killed by the Japanese military that called themselves imperial troops under the name of the Japanese Emperor. Likewise, comfort women for the Japanese military, who were referred to as 'gifts to the imperial troops,' were placed in the situation of sexual slavery. For this reason, the surviving comfort women came to demand the apology from the Japanese Emperor.[482]

Even though the Japanese government and military attempted to remove public documents or specific materials related to the comfort women system, which was uncomfortable even to themselves, detailed materials serving as proofs have been discovered recently. The most decisive documentary evidence is the material on comfort women that Professor Yoshimi Yoshiaki (吉見義明) found in the Defense Agency Library and publicized through the *Asahi Shimbun* on January 11, 1992. The material titled 'the directions related to the recruitment of comfort women for military comfort stations,' which was a note from the adjutant of the Department of the Army on March 4, 1938, is documentary evidence of the Japanese authorities' intervention.[483] In addition, there is a document titled 'the matter of women sailed over to China,' which was written by the Police Bureau (National Police Agency of today) of the Home Ministry in 1938, which was submitted by the Japanese government by the request of Yoshikawa Haruko, a member of the House of Councilors. This material shows the structure in which Japan mobilized comfort women at the time.[484] Furthermore, in the early 1990s public documents written by the American forces and Japanese Defense Agency, which showed that comfort women were under the control of the Japanese military, were discovered at the Hoover Institute at Stanford University.[485] Due to the discoveries of such public documents, the Japanese government started to change their attitude in the early 1990s, acknowledging the facts and making apologies. Aside from these, various proofs were discovered afterward and the most important evidence is the agonizing testimonies of numerous women who were sexually abused as sexual slaves of the Japanese military.

Even after the end of the Cold War, Japan insisted that the 'comfort women system' was conducted by 'private businessmen' and refused to acknowledge that the Japanese government or Japanese military played any part at all. Enraged by this, Korea's Kim Hak-sun (金學順) went public in August 1991 as the first woman to reveal herself a former comfort woman, and filed a lawsuit in the Japanese court with two other victims in December of the same year. Afterward, many victims who had spent years in mental and physical torment, came to reveal their existences as comfort women, due to their rage toward the attitude of the Japanese government, changes in social circumstances, and their strong will that they could not die in silence. As mentioned above, in 1992 Professor Yoshimi Yoshiaki discovered a public document which was evidence of the government's intervention, clarifying that the Japanese military played a part in the conscription of comfort women as well as the opening, management, and operation of brothels. Therefore, the Japanese government had no choice other than to apologize for the forced mobilization and victimization of comfort women through 'Kono Statement.'[486] In spite of this fact, regarding the various trials filed by former comfort women, the Japanese government has continued to hold the stance that it is an issue that was already diplomatically resolved among the countries, and has refused to take a faithful attitude in acknowledging the fact or making compensation. Since the late 1990s, as the power of the rightwing forces, which criticize that the existing history textbooks are grounded on a self-tormenting view of history, has become stronger, the Japanese government has undermined or deleted the illustration of the issue of 'comfort women' through textbook screening. While this attitude of Japan continues, people who were former comfort women are living with deep mental and physical wounds. There were many extreme cases of Post-traumatic Stress Disorder (PTSD) and these former comfort women are still spending agonizing days due to strong anxiety, insomnia, fear, and depression.[487]

In 1995, at the 50th anniversary of the end of the war, Prime Minister Murayama Tomiichi's Cabinet, which made a historical statement on Japan's colonization and war of aggression, decided to establish the Asian Women's Fund (AWF) to resolve the issue of comfort women. The Murayama Cabinet was considering four specific policies.[488] The first policy was to send a letter of apology to each of the individual victims in the name of the Prime Minister. The second policy was for the Japanese government to implement medical and welfare programs by providing JPY 1,200,000 to Filipino victims and JPY 3,000,000 to Korean and Taiwanese victims. The third policy was to make payments of atonement money amounting to JPY 2,000,000 to each of the victims by raising funds among the Japanese citizens. The fourth policy was to conduct historical research on comfort women. The Japanese government presented such an ambiguous policy, as it had taken the position that Japan's war responsibility of colonization or war of aggression had been legally resolved through the Treaty of San Francisco and individual treaties with each country. This was not a desirable and genuine attitude for Japan to approach the issue of comfort women, but it would have been better if Asian countries, comfort women victims, and civic groups had accepted Japan's offer and strived to induce a more forward-looking attitude of Japan. This is because the Japanese society and government took a more conservative swing afterward, and their will and attitude to resolve historical issues and the issue of comfort women have continued to step backwards. In the end, it can be said that the Murayama Statement and its action plan was the best possible outcome the Japanese government could offer regarding the issue of comfort women.

The lawsuits that comfort women filed against Japan were eventually all dismissed or overruled. Nevertheless, some rulings in lower courts acknowledged the damage and urged legislative resolution. On April 27, 1998, the Shimonoseki branch of the Yamaguchi District Court pointed out the political negligence of the congressmen and urged resolution by rapidly pushing ahead with legislation for compensation. The Shimonoseki ruling indicated that the comfort women system was a stark manifestation of discrimination against women and ethnicity, violating the dignity of female personalities from the roots, and committing ethnic discrimination. Furthermore, it mentioned that the issue of comfort women was not an issue of the past but a fundamental issue of human rights that must be overcome in the present. Among the trials related to comfort women, this was practically the only ruling in which the Japanese judicial court took a major step forward. In the end, the ruling of the Hiroshima High Court on March 29, 2001 admitted room for fathoming the feelings of comfort women, but dismissed the accusation of the plaintiffs, under the judgment that specific methods of compensation should be subject to the discretion of the legislative body.[489]

Since the Abe government came into office, Chief Cabinet Secretary Kono Yohei's Statement of August 1993, which recognized the forcibleness of recruitment and management of comfort women and expressed apology and resolution to prevent its recurrence, started to be denied. As a result, the contents on Japanese military sexual slaves started to be extensively deleted from middle school and high school history textbooks. Meanwhile, in 2011, Korea's Constitutional Court ruled that it was unconstitutional that the Korean government did not actively come forward to resolve the issue of the right of Japanese military comfort women to request for indemnification, despite the situation that Korean and Japanese governments have different interpretations on the matter. A few years later, Korea's Park Geun-hye government came to a sudden agreement in December 2015 after discussions with Japan's Abe government. The core of the agreement at the time was the idea of launching a project to cure the wounds of the victims by establishing a foundation with the Japanese government's budget. However, there was strong opposition from living former Japanese military comfort women as well as the Korean people, as the agreement was made without reflecting the voices of the Japanese military sexual slavery victims themselves and because the contents of the agreement were insufficient. The UNOHCHR (Office of the United Nations High Commissioner for Human Rights)'s Committee Against Torture (CAT) pointed out in a report on Korea published in May 2017 that they 'welcome the agreement between the two countries, but the contents of the agreement are insufficient in terms of compensation for and reputation recovery of the victims, and clarification of truth and commitment to prevention of recurrence.' This can be viewed as actually calling upon a renegotiation. Since May 2017 when the new government stepped into office in Korea, a task force for review on the comfort woman issue agreement was formed and managed under the control of the Minister of Foreign Affairs. In December 2018, this task force announced that the Park Geun-hye government had reached an agreement with Japan without reflecting the voice of the Japanese military sexual slavery victims. Korea's Minister of Foreign Affairs, Kang Kyung-wha, said that 'an agreement that has not reflected the intention of the victims cannot be a true solution to a problem.' Also, Minister Kang said that the Reconciliation and Healing Foundation fund would be covered by the Korean government budget and the 1 billion yen that the Japanese government had contributed would be returned. Furthermore, Korea's Ministry of Gender Equality and Family accepted the opinions of the Japanese military sexual slavery victims and began dissolution procedures for the Reconciliation and Healing Foundation. Of course, Korea's Moon Jae-in administration did not cancel the agreement or request for a renegotiation. However, as the foundation which had been established through contributions from the Japanese government budget and which was the core of the agreement between Japan and Korea was dissolved, it can be considered that the agreement between Japan and Korea has been incapacitated. Such results may have been due to the fact that the two governments at the time only considered the political situation of their own country and tried to rapidly come to an agreement regarding a crucial issue that had remained unsolved for decades, secretly without the sexual slavery victims knowing about it.

It has been more than 75 years since the war caused by modern Japan came to an end. Almost all the victims of Japan's war of aggression and colonization have passed away and now only a few remain. In particular, there are only a few hundred women left among the numerous Asian women who were forced to spend their blooming youth as comfort women (sexual slaves) of the Japanese military. In around 10 more years, even most of these few remaining women will have left this world. Japan might inwardly think that everything will be buried when these few women pass away, but that will most certainly not be the case. If that happens, Japan will lose the subjects to whom it truly needs to apologize and leave the liability of the past to its descendants forever. Even if all the victims disappear, and thus the witnesses of the past disappear, the stain that Japan left on history will never be erased, and the dishonor of attempting to hide the history of disgrace and turning away from the voices of the victims will heavily weigh upon it.

6. Territorial Disputes by Japan in East Asia

After the Meiji Restoration, Japan developed into a modern state by securing human and material resources through imperialistic expansion of territory and by developing new capitalist markets. Thus, in response to the pressure and threat of Western powers, modern Japan sought to achieve national prosperity and military power and form a nation state through the Meiji Restoration, expanding its territory through annexation, colonization, invasion and occupation of neighboring regions. Even after the war, Japan achieved economic revival and rapid growth by taking advantage of the favorable international environment of the Cold War, based on resources, technology, management, and knowhow that it had acquired while implementing the national development strategy of external expansion until the end of the war. After the war, Japan lost most of the territory that it had acquired during the militaristic expansionism era, but it continues to create territorial disputes with countries in the East Asia region, such as China, Russia, and Korea. All the regions that have such disputes share the common feature of being places that were incorporated into Japanese territory based on the territory expansion policy according to modern Japan's national development strategy of external expansion.

In general, each country claims sovereignty by using the concept of indigenous territory, when approaching the issue of territory. 'Mainland Japan,' which means the place where Japanese people started living in the beginning, can be roughly translated as 'Japan proper;' which ultimately means 'indigenous territory.' In the sense of indigenous territory, Hokkaido or Okinawa, which differs in terms of history, ethnicity, and race, is not included in 'mainland Japan.'[490] Japan's reclamation and incorporation of Hokkaido and Okinawa occurred after the modern Meiji government came into power. Also, it was only at the end of the 19th century and beginning of the 20th century that Taiwan was colonized and Dokdo (Liancourt Rocks) and the Korean Peninsula was incorporated into Japanese territory. Therefore, the only region that can be called Japan's indigenous territory is restricted to the territory before the Meiji Restoration. In spite of this, if Japan claims that other territory pertains to its indigenous territory, then it is the same as claiming that it has been 'illegally taken over' or 'illegally occupied' by the counterpart country. The fact that Japan claims sovereignty over Dokdo (Liancourt Rocks, Takeshima), Senkaku Islands (Diaoyu Islands), and the four northern islands in terms of indigenous territory shows that Japan has yet to escape the historical awareness of the past period of imperialism.

On July 26, 1945, the Allied Forces of the United States, the United Kingdom, the Soviet Union and the Republic of China announced the Potsdam Declaration, which demanded Japan's unconditional surrender. In the Potsdam Declaration of the Allied Forces, it is stipulated that 'The sovereignty of Japan is limited to Honshu, Hokkaido, Kyushu, Shikoku, and the island area determined herein.' On August 14, Japan notified embassies and legations in the United States, the United Kingdom, China, and the Soviet Union that the Emperor had announced an imperial rescript accepting the Potsdam Declaration. By accepting the Potsdam Declaration, Japan agreed that its sovereignty was limited to the regions stipulated in the Declaration. The surrender documents were signed by Foreign Minister Shigemitsu Mamoru and Army Chief of Staff Umezu Yoshijiro on September 2 aboard the American warship, the Missouri docked on Tokyo Bay. It stipulated that 'Japan will faithfully fulfill the articles and clauses of the Potsdam Declaration.' The Far Eastern Commission of the Allied Forces, which was established in December 1945, determined the 'Basic occupation policy of Japan after surrender' in June 1947' and stipulated that 'Japan's sovereignty is limited to Honshu, Hokkaido, Kyushu, Shikoku, and island areas.' The Directives of the Supreme Headquarters for the Allied Powers in January 1946 also stipulated that Japan's territory consists of 'approximately 1,000 islands, including the four major islands, Tsushima Island, and the Ryukyu Islands north of latitude 30° and excluding Dokdo (Liancourt Rocks), the Kuril Islands (Chishima Islands), the Habomai Islands, Iturup Island, and Shikotan Island.' Postwar Japan was clearly aware of the range of territory in which Japan's sovereignty lay. On August 17, 1951, Japan's Prime Minister Yoshida confirmed at the general meeting of the House of Representatives that 'As written on the surrender documents, Japan's territory is restricted to the four main islands and their annexed islands, and all other territory has been relinquished, and this is the solemn fact.'[491]

Since it was decided as above after the war with respect to the territory that modern Japan acquired through its foreign expansion policy, it can be understood that there are no grounds for Japan to arouse territorial disputes in the East Asia region. Thus, it is inappropriate for Japan to trigger disputes with neighboring countries with respect to Dokdo (Liancourt Rocks, Takeshima), Senkaku Islands (Diaoyu Islands), the four northern islands (Kuril Islands: Kunashir Island, Iturup Island, Habomai Islands, Shikotan Island). Furthermore, such behaviors toward Korea and China, which Japan had posed a tremendous amount of pain through colonization and war of aggression for decades in the early 20th century, are inconsistent with the characteristics of the Japanese people to consider causing inconvenience to others as a dishonor. If Japan continues territorial disputes, there is a high possibility of triggering a new conflict in East Asia, where economic interdependence has grown deeper after the war. In particular, in a reality where East Asian countries become more conservative and show stronger trends of nationalism, intensification of territorial disputes caused by Japan has a high possibility of creating military conflicts. Especially, excessively raising its voice with respect to Senkaku Islands (Diaoyu Islands) or Dokdo (Liancourt Rocks, Takeshima), which Japan has a weak cause for claiming its dominium both in terms of geography and history, will only provoke the counterpart countries. Therefore, when it comes to territorial disputes, it is very important to prevent the status quo from changing for the worse instead of drastic change in status quo.

Let us first examine the four northern islands (Kuril Islands: Kunashir Island, Iturup Island, Habomai Islands, and Shikotan Island) that Japan's indigenous people, the Ainu people, used to live and have considerable links with Japan in terms of geography and history. These islands were incorporated as Japanese territory when Meiji Japan reclaimed Hokkaido. The Russian Empire, which was the predecessor of the Soviet Union, had no choice but to transfer the southern Sakhalin region to Japan when it was defeated in the Russo-Japanese War in 1905. It also had to relinquish the northern region of Hokkaido and the four northern islands, over which it had attempted to exercise consistent influence since the 19th century. It appears that this historical grudge had an influence on the treatment process of World War II. In the Yalta Conference in February 1945, during the final stages of World War II, the United States allowed the Soviet Union to occupy the southern region of Sakhalin and the Kuril Islands (Chishima Islands) in order to induce the Soviet Union's participation in the war against Japan, which later became the cause of the territorial dispute. Based on the Yalta Conference, the postwar affiliation of these islands was determined. In other words, these islands completely became the Soviet Union's territory when the Treaty of San Francisco concluded in September 1951 stipulated in Article 2 Clause C that 'Japan will relinquish all rights and claims to the Kuril Islands.' Japan had no choice but to accept such decisions of the Allied Forces right after being defeated in the war but did not abandon its aspiration towards these islands. Not only did some Japanese people cultivate these islands as their home, but the islands are also geographically adjacent to Hokkaido, which became mainland Japan. It can then be said that there is a reasonable side to Japan's demands. Unlike Yoshida Shigeru, who adopted pro-American policies, the new Prime Minister Hatoyama Ichiro actively worked toward normalizing diplomatic relations with the Soviet Union, taking into account not only economic profits but also the return of the four northern islands. Therefore, he announced the Soviet-Japanese Joint Declaration with Khrushchev during his visit to the Soviet Union in October 1956. In the territorial section of the Joint Declaration, it is stated that 'Taking into account the interests of Japan, the Soviet Union agrees to transfer the Habomai Islands and the Shikotan Island to Japan, but these islands will be transferred after a peace treaty is settled between the countries.'[492] After the Soviet-Japanese Joint Declaration, the Soviet government hastened the conclusion of a peace treaty with Japan, and actually started to close down businesses and relocate residents from the Habomai Islands and the Shikotan Island in 1957. However, as the United States created conflict between the two countries to prevent Soviet and Japanese relations from rapidly advancing, Japan came to show a desire toward the remaining two islands. This eventually thwarted the conclusion of a peace treaty between Japan and the Soviet Union, making even the half-way resolution go down the drain. If Japan had accepted the Habomai Islands and the Shikotan Island as the first step and maintained a close economic relationship with the Soviet Union, there might have been a high possibility that Japan could have received the other two islands (Kunashir Island, Iturup Island) as a benefit in return for providing large scale economic support when Russia experienced difficulties during the period of transformation after the dissolution of the Soviet Union. Japan has lost an opportunity of a lifetime and it has become a matter to be regretted for years to come.[493]

Among the three regions that Japan claims as its territory, the only place that Japan has effectively ruled over is the Senkaku Islands (尖閣列島, Diaoyu Islands (釣魚島) in Chinese). The Senkaku Islands, which are uninhabitable islands, were not part of Japan's territory prior to the 1880s. After several field surveys starting from 1885, the Japanese government considered it ownerless land and incorporated the islands as Japanese overseas territory in 1895. However, historical references show overwhelming evidence that the islands belonged to China. Therefore, it can be said that Japan's claim of dominium based on preoccupancy of ownerless land is unreasonable.[494] The Senkaku Islands are not only extremely far away from mainland Japan, but are much closer to Taiwan than Okinawa.[495] Japan forcefully incorporated Ryukyu Kingdom, which could be considered a tributary of China, as Japanese territory, and by using this island as a starting point, Japan incorporated the surrounding islands and Taiwan into its territory or colony. It is hard to say that these acts of imperialism, in which Japan invaded and colonized even regions that were far away from mainland Japan, is justifiable. Therefore, for the future of East Asia, Japan's attitude should be reconsidered and converted. In this aspect, it can be said that the tacit agreement of the two countries to keep the issue of the Senkaku Islands as an unsettled issue in the mid-1970s when China and Japan were improving their relationship was a wise act of conflict management. China needed Japan's economic support or cooperation and did not have to create conflict for a small island. However, when the Cold War came to an end and the long suppressed dissatisfaction in China erupted, the issue of the Senkaku Islands started to rise to the surface. Even so, in order not to aggravate the relationship between China and Japan, which came to have greater economic interdependencies, the two countries entered into the Japan-China Fishery Agreement in 2000 and agreed to each exercise control over the fishing boats of their own country in the regions surrounding the Senkaku Islands. In other words, the two countries prepared a system to prevent disputes surrounding private fishing boats from being expanded into tensions between the two countries. However, in September 2010, there was an incident in which a Chinese fishing boat collided into a patrol boat of Japan's Maritime Safety Agency and the Japanese government arrested the captain and intended to bring the case to trial for obstruction of performance of official duties. But eventually, the captain was released due to China's pressure. Up to that point, the governments and public opinion of the two countries were considerably quiet with respect to the issue of the Senkaku Islands. However, after this incident, the issue of the Senkaku Islands completely rose to the surface. Japan had adopted the policy of raising its legal status by increasing the effective occupation period of the Senkaku Islands, but now Japan ended up weakening its own favorable position. The issue of the Senkaku Islands is a case that clearly shows that such territorial disputes must be adequately managed not only for the national interest of Japan but also for stability and peace in East Asia.

At the Cairo Conference of 1943, the United States' President Roosevelt had the intention to return Okinawa (Ryukyu), which Japan merged in 1879, to China. However, as the conflict of the Cold War intensified after the war, considering the strategic importance of the Okinawa region, the United States desired to be stationed for a long term and selected the country that would satisfy such needs. The United States considered that rather than China, where the Communist Party government had already come to power, Japan, which belonged to the capitalist bloc and was part of the security system between the United States and Japan, would secure the long-term stationing of the American forces. Therefore, the United States handed Okinawa over to Japan. The Senkaku Islands (Diaoyu Islands), which had never been part of Okinawa and originally was Chinese territory, was included in this transfer. When the Chinese government protested, the United States government declared that Japan had been given only administrative authority (施政權), not sovereignty, and clarified that 'if the two countries hold different views with respect to sovereignty, then they may discuss and resolve the issue.' This decision of the United States left room for conflict and dispute between China and Japan.[496]

Among the three regions in East Asia where Japan is triggering territorial disputes, Dokdo (Liancourt Rocks, Takeshima)[497] is a group of islands where the odds are most against Japan in terms of justification and substance. Historical sources and material presented by Korea are more abundant and convincing, and Korea is currently effectively ruling over the island. In the case of Dokdo, Japan quietly incorporated the island into its territory in February 1905 based on the logic of preoccupation of ownerless land in order to install watchtowers amidst the Russo-Japanese War. However, such action lacked justification because Joseon Korea was already ruling over the island.[498] After Japan won the Russo-Japanese War and secured control over the Korean Peninsula, Japan forcefully merged the entire Korean Peninsula in August 1910, ruling over the land for 35 years until August 1945. It is reasonable to say that Dokdo was excluded from Japanese territory, since the Potsdam Declaration of the Allied Forces, which demanded Japan's surrender, limited Japan's sovereignty to Honshu, Hokkaido, Kyushu, Shikoku, and island areas determined by the Allied Forces, and Japan surrendered and accepted this declaration. Furthermore, the Directives (SCAPIN No. 677)[499] of the Supreme Commander for the Allied Powers (SCAP) on January 29, 1946 listed Ulleung Island, Dokdo, and Jeju Island as regions excluded from Japanese territory.[500] Therefore, after the war, Korea's fishermen were engaged in fisheries on Dokdo and its adjacent seas under the protection of the MacArthur line. And in April 1951, Korea's President Rhee Syngman established the Peace Line, which was 8 nautical miles from Dokdo, and externally declared that Dokdo was Korean territory. Since then, Korea has continued legal and effective occupation of Dokdo within the extent of the Peace Line (Syngman Rhee Line). The Treaty of San Francisco, which was concluded during the Korean War without Korea's presence, stipulates that 'Japan recognizes Korea's independence and relinquishes all rights, jurisdiction, and claims over Korea, including Jeju Island, Geomun Island, and Ulleung Island.' Japan uses this regulation as a basis for claiming that it did not relinquish Dokdo, but following this logic, Japan could even make the claim that Geoje Island and Kanghwa Island of Korea belong to Japan as well, since these islands were not mentioned as relinquished. Since the Treaty of San Francisco did not include Korea, the victim country that was held as Japan's colony and forcefully mobilized and exploited in the Pacific War, if territorial issues were determined to Korea's disadvantage, that itself is enough to question its legitimacy. Despite Japan's diplomatic efforts, however, the issue of Dokdo had been settled in a way that it was not out of step from historical justice. Therefore, the United States Board on Geographic Names (BGN, established pursuant to Presidential decree in 1890 and legislation in 1947), which handles policies regarding geographic names home and abroad, has marked Dokdo (Liancourt Rocks) [501] as belonging to Korea. Then in late July 2008, BGN changed the classification of Dokdo, which had been continuously marked as Korean territory, to a region affiliated to no country. However, when President Bush visited Korea, Korea raised objections, and President Bush directed Secretary of State Rice to review the matter, and accordingly the BGN classification of Dokdo was changed back to Korean territory.[502] It was only proper for Japan to return other countries' territories which it had acquired through foreign expansion after the war. Especially in the case of Dokdo, it is a symbol of the Korean people's independence after suffering 35 years of agony under Japanese colonial rule and further disputes by Japan cannot but be shameless acts. As examined above, it is undeniable that Dokdo is Korean territory, both in terms of history and International Law. Despite this fact, Japan has incessantly attempted to cause conflict since the end of the war by claiming that Dokdo belongs to Japan. A prime example is that the Shimane Prefecture Council passed the 'Takeshima Day' bill in March 2005 to commemorate the day (February 22, 1905) that Dokdo of Korea was incorporated into Japan under the name of 'Takeshima'. Commemorative events have been held every year, and recently, the Japanese government has sent high-level figures to the events, aggravating Korea's opposition.

In 1948 on the Korean Peninsula, which was put under colonial rule by imperialist Japan and then divided and ruled by the United States and the Soviet Union, the Republic of Korea was established in the south and the Democratic People's Republic of Korea in the north. Rhee Syngman, who became the President of South Korea, strongly demanded the cession of Tsushima Island.[503] In the New Year's address in 1949, President Rhee Syngman announced a statement demanding the transfer of Tsushima Island as a form of compensation for colonization by Japan. Taken aback, Japan's Ministry of Foreign Affairs sent a 33-page written report on Tsushima Island to the United States on July 1949 and actively defended their position. In other words, Japan strongly insisted that Tsushima played an important role in the exchanges and cooperation between Japan and Korea, but it had belonged to Japan from the beginning to the present day.[504] When Japan's Shimane Prefecture Council adopted the ordinance to enact Takeshima Day on March 18, 2005, Korea's Masan City Council adopted an ordinance on March 18 to determine June 16, the day when General Yi Jongmu departed from Masanpo to conquer Tsushima Island (Daemado in Korean) in the early days of the Joseon Dynasty of the Korean Peninsula, as Daemado Day. Initially, the Masan City Council made discussions to adopt a resolution to urge Japan's Shimane Prefecture to discard the ordinance for Takeshima Day, but in a turn of events, the council came to push ahead with the enactment of an ordinance for Daemado Day. In response, Korea's Ministry of Foreign Affairs and Trade, through a spokesperson's remark, demanded that the council refrain from arousing unnecessary controversies between the countries. Masan City Council's position of claiming that Daemado (Tsushima Island) is Korean territory and enacting Daemado Day is not entirely groundless. There is a public document housed in the Tsushima Museum that says that the 'So (宗)' family, which ruled over Tsushima Island, was a subject of the Tokugawa Shogunate and an official of the Joseon Kingdom of the Korean Peninsula.[505] Therefore, Tsushima Island had been part of the regional history of both Japan and Korea. However, in Korea, the issue of Daemado Day has not been highlighted to the point of causing diplomatic issues with Japan as Takeshima Day in Japan.

Japan has been forming international relations in East Asia centered on the United States, based on the US-Japan Security Treaty. Therefore, even in territorial disputes between Japan and East Asian countries, the United States has always been involved in some way. The United States has always attempted to attain strategic interests in Asia with Japan as a key partner. Therefore, it can be said that the United States and Japan have taken joint steps even in territorial disputes. However, the degree of intervention has varied depending on the relationship between the United States and the counterpart of the territorial disputes. For instance, in the case of the Soviet Union, since it was the United States' greatest competitor during the Cold War, the United States created conflict and made territorial disputes meet a deadlock, once Japan reconciled with the Soviet Union in the late 1950s by normalizing diplomatic relations and attempted to resolve territorial disputes. Even in the case of socialist China, when returning sovereignty over Okinawa back to Japan in the early 1970s, the United States handed over administrative authority of Senkaku Islands (Diaoyu Islands) as well, keeping China in check and securing its own convenience in utilization. In the case of Korea, which stands face to face with socialist North Korea, although the United States had temporarily wavered due to Japan's diplomatic efforts in the process of concluding the Treaty of San Francisco, the United States has substantially recognized Dokdo (Liancourt Rocks, Takeshima) as Korean territory, faithful to the Cairo Declaration, Potsdam Declaration and the Directives of the Allied Forces shortly after the war. Pursuant to the US-Japan Security Treaty, if Japan's administrative control area were to be attacked by another country, the United States is to intervene according to its own constitution. In this sense, the four northern islands (Kuril Islands) occupied by the Soviet Union are not subject to the US-Japan Security Treaty, since they are not under Japan's administration. Since the Senkaku Islands (Diaoyu Islands) are currently under Japan's control, the United States can intervene pursuant to the US-Japan Security Treaty, in the case of external invasion. Since Dokdo (Liancourt Rocks, Takeshima) is occupied by Korea and not under the control of Japan, there is no room for the intervention of the American forces pursuant to the US-Japan Security Treaty even if another country attacks the island. However, in this case, the United States can intervene pursuant to the US-Korea Security Treaty. Therefore, with respect to Japan's territorial disputes, Senkaku Islands are the only area where the American forces can intervene pursuant to the US-Japan Security Treaty.[506] However, even in this case, the United States needs consent from Congress, pursuant to the regulations of the Constitution, so the United States cannot automatically intervene. As examined above, it is not as though Japan can attain assistance in resolving territorial disputes just by strengthening its alliance with the United States. Therefore, Japan should no longer make territorial disputes an element of conflict not only for its own interest but for coexistence and co-prosperity with East Asian countries.

7. Issues of Historical Awareness, Remembering and Healing Damages

When considering the origins of civilization and the path of mankind, pre-modern civilization in Japan could not but be later than China and Korea, but even so, there were many cases in which the Japanese people presented distorted theories on history. Such tendencies of Japan frequently occurred during modern Japan after the Meiji Restoration. Even in recent days, although a considerable length of time has lapsed since modern Japan collapsed due to defeat in the war, there was an incident in which the Paleolithic Age was fabricated, shaking the roots of the credibility of Japanese archeology. In 1992, Fujimura Shinichi (藤村新一), the deputy director at the Tohoku Paleolithic Institute, consecutively excavated stone artifacts from 400,000 to 600,000 years ago at the hilly areas of Kamitakamori, and such discoveries were included in high school textbooks from 1998. However, video tapes in which Fujimura Shinichi secretly dug holes and buried stone artifacts were disclosed to the *Mainichi Shimbun* (毎日新聞), confirming that his excavations were faked. Japan's history circles, and furthermore, Japan's society had a complex that its Paleolithic period was later than Korea's, and accordingly, the atmosphere that attempted to extend Japanese history was created, which resulted in such bold fabrication.[507] Even before the modern period, Japanese people attempted to lift themselves as superior people through Japanese studies and the notion of a divine country. Particularly after the Meiji Restoration, Japan solidified its 'Leave Asia' mindset and became obsessed with the thought that it must precede China and Korea in terms of civilization and history. This obsession created Japan's sense of superiority and contempt toward Asian countries and Asian people, and made the Japanese people claim that war of aggression and colonization was justifiable.

Because the Japanese people have harbored such perceptions of history, they minimize or cover up wrongdoings such as war of aggression and colonization of Asian countries when describing modern history in postwar textbooks, and rather attempt to remember it as a glorious history centered on its resistance against the Western powers. During the occupation rule of the Allied Forces after the war, democratization came to the center of education and the Japanese people had a notion of self-reflection on colonization and war of aggression to some extent. However, as the Cold War surfaced in the late 1940s and the occupation policy of the Allied Forces changed, the Japanese people came to reinforce war victims' mentality, rather than reflecting on the war of aggression. Furthermore, from the late 1950s, Japan introduced the textbook screening system and began to undermine illustrations on invasion war or colonization. In the textbook screening of 1982, Japan attempted to distort its historical wrongdoings by changing the expression 'invade' to 'advance,' which caused strong backlash from China and Korea. From the late 1990s, historical revisionism arose, and Japan has showed stronger movements to minimize or delete illustrations on war of aggression or colonization in textbooks. Of course, it would not be fair to say that Japanese society advanced only toward the direction of completely hiding or distorting historical facts as mentioned above. While criticisms continued toward the Japanese Ministry of Education's control over the contents of textbooks, Ienaga Saburo, then Professor at Tokyo University of Education, wrote a high school textbook of Japanese history containing the facts of Japan's war of aggression and applied for authorization in 1963. The Japanese Ministry of Education requested that illustrations on the recklessness and horrors of war be revised or deleted, but as Ienaga Saburo refused, the textbook failed to receive authorization. In response, Ienaga Saburo filed for a trial against the government on the history book in June 1965, claiming that textbook screening violated the freedom of expression pursuant to the Constitution and infringed upon prohibition to intervene in educational contents pursuant to the Fundamental Education Law. The trial continued for a long time amidst the support of not only many teachers and citizens but also civic groups. Finally, in August 1997, the Supreme Court acknowledged the illegality of textbook screening which attempted to delete from the textbook the facts of Japan's war of aggression, such as the Nanjing Massacre and Unit 731. Based on such textbook trials, Japan's history textbooks after the mid-1980s have greatly improved toward the direction of conveying the historical facts of war. Despite this, as the activities of historical revisionism became animated after the late 1990s, Japan's history textbooks have been changing toward minimizing or rather glamorizing modern Japan's historical wrongdoings. In particular, after the emergence of the Abe government, this tendency is becoming stronger. The Japanese government is diffusing distorted history education by revising the Fundamental Education Law and strengthening government guidelines for teaching in middle and high schools as well as the textbook screening system. Because of this, matters related to Japanese military sexual slavery are disappearing from elementary, middle, and high school textbooks. Even the Dokdo (Liancourt Rocks, Takeshima) and the four northern islands (Kuril Islands), which Korea and Russia are respectively governing legally and effectively, are indicated as Japan's indigenous territory.

During the Cold War era, China and Korea could not afford to ponder on historical issues, as they were preoccupied with economic development and maintenance of their own regimes, under the restraint of ideology. However, Japan's history textbook issue in 1982 brought forth a change in the attitudes of China and Korea. With the history textbook issue as momentum, China launched nationwide projects to excavate and preserve remains related to the anti-Japanese war. China restored the Japanese Kwantung Army's fortress site in the northeastern region of China and built monuments and memorials at places where the Japanese military had committed genocide. Furthermore, China consecutively established large-scale anti-Japanese history memorial halls, such as the Memorial Hall of the Victims in Nanjing Massacre by Japanese Invaders (1985) and the Museum of the War of Chinese People's Resistance against Japanese Aggression (1987). Through approximately 80 memorial facilities, China is publicizing the horrors of the war of aggression caused by imperialist Japan and the brave anti-Japanese resistance of the Chinese people. These memorials are being used as an educational mechanism for patriotism in order to secure a collective identity, in place of the socialist ideology that has declined due to Chinese economic reform. In Korea, due to the issue of history textbooks, several memorial facilities have been built based on the topic of the agony of Japanese colonial rule and anti-Japanese resistance. Thus, the Independence Hall opened in 1987, the Seodaemun Independence Park was built in 1992, and the Japanese Colonial Government Building, which was the symbol of Japan's colonial rule, was torn down in 1995. In particular, the Independence Hall construction was carried forward through donations from the people, as the issue of Japanese history textbooks became controversial at home and abroad in 1982. The Chun Doo-hwan government had weak legitimacy as it had come into power through a military coup d'état and in an effort to somewhat make up for its weak legitimacy, the government used the issue of Japanese history textbooks to establish the Independence Hall by collecting public opinion and raising funds. Now China and Korea are trying to escape from suppressing the expression of painful experiences of Japan's invasion and colonization due to ideology and anti-communism respectively, and to remember their pasts as the history of victory in war and independence. In response to Japan's distortion of history textbooks, China and Korea came to emphasize victory in war and independence, thereby going through a change in history education. Modern history came to make up half of China and Korea's history education, with special emphasis on patriotism and nationalism.[508]

As the Cold War intensified and Asian countries came to concentrate on economic developments in the situation of heightening ideological conflicts and long-lasting dictatorial governments, memories of Japan's invasion war and colonization were pushed out into the distance or suppressed. Despite the fact that Asian countries and Asian people suffered from tremendous agony and damage due to modern Japan's invasion and colonization, several decades have passed since the war as though nothing had happened. Then such historical scars came to be exposed when the Japanese government recommended that Japan's 'invasion' to Asian countries be revised to 'advancement' in the process of its history textbooks screening in 1982, and China and Korea fiercely resisted in response. In particular, after the late 1980s, as democratization advanced in Asian countries and the Cold War came to an end, victims who had been silent started to raise their voices, exposing the atrocious acts that modern Japan committed in Asia. Thus, amidst the pain of reliving agonizing memories of the past, victims came to demand Japan's apology and appropriate compensation. Now the issue on how to heal the pain of the victims and historical scars of the Asian people arose as a key task.

During the period when China (People's Republic of China) was established, the Cold War between the capitalist bloc, led by the United States, and the socialist bloc, led by the Soviet Union, was starting to intensify. As China's regime shifted from the Nationalist Party government to the Communist Party government, the United States aimed to make Japan its partner to fight against socialist forces in East Asia, instead of China. Consequently, the newly emerged People's Republic of China suffered economic blockade from the capitalist bloc led by the United States. The Chinese people were still suffering from the horrific memories of Japan's invasion war and domination but did not have a proper opportunity to express the deep scars of the war and anti-Japanese sentiments while in the situation of the Cold War. History education in China during the 1950s and 1960s was conducted through socialist revolution and struggle, including the brutalities of imperialist Japan during the anti-Japanese war as a part of the education curriculum. After the Japan-China Joint Communique was announced in 1972 and the relations between Japan and China were restored, the Chinese leaders adhered to the position that it was Japan's militarists that had a responsibility for causing the war and ordinary people were dragged to war with no other choice. Furthermore, China relinquished its claims for war reparations, under the premise that if Japan was excessively burdened with claims for war reparations, then the Japanese people would have to bear the burden, which would then have an influence on the friendly relations between the two countries. Meanwhile, the Chinese leaders controlled their people so that Chinese people's claims for compensation or anti-Japanese sentiments would not be expressed at any time. At the time, China's relationship with the Soviet Union had taken a turn for the worse, and China strove to improve its relationship with the United States and Japan, which made China prevent the ordinary Chinese people from expressing memories of the war and refrain from actively questioning Japan's responsibility for the war.

To the Korean people who were forced to suffer from all sorts of hardships during the war as Japan's colony, the vestiges of the Japanese Empire were primarily something that had to be erased. The shrines which had been built in many parts of Korea were rapidly destroyed after liberation in 1945. The statue of Ito Hirobumi and the Hirobumi-tera (博文寺), built to commemorate him at the foot of Namsan Mountain in Seoul, were destroyed at once. The Korean people attempted to build various monuments of liberation in these locations but failed to achieve distinguished outcomes due to economic difficulties and ideological conflict. As Korea gradually recovered from the calamities of the Korean War, in order to expand its political influence, the then Rhee Syngman government raised anti-communism and anti-Japan as the flags of nationalism and pushed ahead with symbolization processes such as the erection of the statue of Ahn Jung-geun, who shot Ito Hirobumi in 1909. However, the situation turned upside down after the democratic government that was formed through the April 19 Revolution was overthrown by a military coup d'état and a suppressive government oriented toward anti-communism was created. Korea's military government placed more emphasis on establishing facilities that propagandized or advocated the state-led anti-communism policy rather than building memorial monuments that disclosed collective memory related to Japan's colonization and resistance against it.

Thus, in China and Korea, the agonizing memories of Japan's invasion and colonization were never significantly expressed by either individuals or organizations until the early 1980s. This was because political suppression continued in these countries within the system of the Cold War, and the two countries were barely making ends meet due to poverty. However, as the

Japanese government triggered the issue of history textbooks in 1982, China and Korea built various memorial facilities related to Japan's invasion and colonization. Now the two countries were starting to revive the painful memories of the past by escaping from the ideological restraints of class struggle and anti-communism and by pursuing nationalism and anti-Japanese histories. Furthermore, the dissolution of the Cold War further accelerated such movements of the two countries. As the Cold War came to an end, the Chinese people started to voice their dissatisfaction. The Chinese government did not actively restrain this situation, as in the Cold War era, and sometimes even used it as a political and diplomatic means toward Japan. As political democratization was accomplished in the late 1980s and the Cold War came to an end, the Korean people started to pull out painful memories of the past and request Japan's repentance and apology.

However, there are some factors to take into consideration when looking at China and Korea's remembrance of war and colonization, in the perspective of creating a future-oriented history. The memorial facilities of China and Korea, with respect to Japan's invasion or colonization, shares commonalities in that they both highlight the memories of pain and damage, while praising anti-Japanese heroes. Such monuments, which act as records of invasion and resistance, leave something to be desired in expressing messages of peace that can support the realization of peace beyond the country-level throughout Asia and the world. In other words, by sticking to the theme of anti-Japan and independence, these monuments have a difficulty in escaping much from the country-specific and ethnocentric approach. Under the circumstances where Japan is not showing thorough self-reflection and apology and furthermore not making necessary reparations for the suffering that it caused to Asian countries and Asian people during the early 20th century, the above mentioned aspects are somewhat inevitable for the victim countries. Even so, in the future, if Asian countries design and implement programs that include future-oriented values such as peace, reconciliation, and co-existence, then it may be somewhat helpful in bringing about a change in Japan's attitude.

In the pre-modern era, Korea played a role as the intermediary of Chinese civilization, and in the modern era, Japan acted as the intermediary of Western civilization. Even so, the two countries of Japan and Korea are called 'countries that are close, but at the same time far,' which is because there is a psychological distance compared to the geographical and cultural proximity of the two countries. Due to the humiliation of being dominated by Japan, which was considered the beneficiary of culture and an underdeveloped country during the pre-modern era, Koreans came to harbor an even stronger antipathy toward Japan. Thus, the Japanese strengthened their superiority and contempt through the history of ruling over Korea, and Koreans strengthened their victim mentality and animosity due to the memories of being dominated by Japan. Therefore, as the Japanese lack a perpetrator's mentality and the Koreans have a strong victim's mentality, the two countries show conflicting aspects of 'lack or excess of historical consciousness.'[509] However, the perpetrator can easily forget the fact of perpetration by believing perpetration was committed due to its superior ability and being captivated by a sense of superiority. On the other hand, the victim continues to go through difficulties since the victim who suffered from the damage cannot easily forget it.

The scars of war were not only left on China, Korea, and Asian countries. As it was a modern war in which all the people were involved, the Japanese people had no choice but to be sucked into the whirlpool of war. Okinawa, which was forcefully incorporated as Japanese territory after the establishment of modern Japan through the Meiji Restoration, was a site of tragedy beyond measure. The most intense and gruesome battle in the Pacific War took place in Okinawa in 1945. The Japanese military fought with its back against the wall in order to defend mainland Japan and was nearly wiped out, and the United States military also suffered enormous casualties in the process. More tragic was that approximately 120,000 Okinawans were killed by both the Japanese and the United States military due to the ferocious battle between the two. Furthermore, Okinawa was under the occupation rule of the United States for nearly 30 years after the war and then was returned to Japan in 1972. However, even to this day, American bases occupy approximately 10% of the Okinawa Prefecture (approximately 20% of the Okinawa main island) and 70% or more of all American bases in Japan are located in Okinawa. As a result of such circumstances, the Okinawans are experiencing not only inconvenience in life but also many socioeconomic problems. Therefore, Okinawans still have a deep-rooted antipathy and sense of alienation toward the mainland Japanese and a resistance toward the Americans. In particular, at the end of the Pacific War, when the United States began a broad scale attack on Okinawa, the Japanese military forced the Okinawans to commit mass suicide, which was too big of a scar. Therefore, in March 2007, when the Japanese government made instructions to delete or revise illustrations of 'mass suicide' in high school textbooks, Okinawa Prefecture strongly opposed and adopted a resolution demanding the withdrawal of the government guideline.

As a consequence of Japan's war of aggression, more than 3 million Japanese soldiers and civilians died. The spirit tablets of the Japanese soldiers who died in the war are enshrined in the Yasukuni Shrine and are worshiped as gods. Shortly after Japan's defeat in the war, when the occupying authorities separated Shinto from the state, there were concerns that the enshrinement of the war dead could become difficult in the future. Therefore, the Yasukuni Shrine (靖國神社) enshrined together at least 2 million war dead since the Manchuria Incident through a temporary memorial ceremony held in November 1945. Furthermore, in the case of colonials, Japan enshrined approximately 21,000 Koreans and 27,000 Taiwanese, under the logic that since they were Japanese at the point of death, they should be considered Japanese even after death. Such enshrinement of these souls faced objection in various aspects in the days to come. In June 2001, Korean families of the deceased demanded that their kin be removed from the shrine, since the Korean families of deceased soldiers and civilians attached to the military were deprived of the benefits pursuant to the GI Bill of Rights (援護法) and the Soldier Pension Law (恩級法) under the pretext of having a different nationality. The Taiwanese also demanded that the souls of the war dead be commemorated in Taiwan's own way, as they could not leave the souls of the war dead to roam around in a foreign land. The Okinawans also insisted that it was unacceptable for victims who were driven to death with no choice to be enshrined together with the Japanese military. Thus, the Yasukuni Shrine deprived the families of the deceased of the mind and right to commemorate their dead families in their own way, and some politicians are taking advantage of this for political purposes.

Today, the Yasukuni Shrine is called into question in several aspects. First of all, among the approximately 2.3 million Japanese soldiers that died starting from the Manchurian Incident until the end of the Pacific War, more than half starved to death. If Japan's leaders had surrendered earlier, it would have been possible to avoid their starvation or annihilation. The Japanese military soldiers were trained to fight to the death for the Japanese Emperor and commit suicide if they were defeated. Furthermore, they were eventually driven to death due to the wrong judgment of the leaders. By establishing a formality of worshipping for the soldiers who died so absurdly, the leaders made the families of the deceased easily accept the death of their loved ones and be comforted. Therefore, the leaders who drove the innocent soldiers to death were not even properly questioned about their actions. Yasukuni Shrine can indeed be considered a clever tool employed by modern Japan and the Japanese military authorities to conceal the fact that the authorities made good Japanese people die and to prevent anyone from questioning the responsibility of the authorities.[510] Also, Yasukuni Shrine commemorates Japanese soldiers who died while executing ruthless suppression operations in the process of colonizing the Korean Peninsula and Taiwan. Furthermore, it also commemorates approximately 1,000 people who were condemned to the death penalty during war crime trials for Type B and Type C war criminals. Most problematic of all is the fact that 14 war criminals, including Tojo Hideki, the Prime Minister at the time of war, were enshrined together in Yasukuni Shrine in 1978. The 14 war criminals also included Matsui Iwane, the Commander in Chief at the Nanjing Massacre, but worshipping such leaders who planned and executed the war of aggression as gods means that Japan does not recognize them as war criminals. Furthermore, the practice

224

of the Japanese political leaders to visit the Yasukuni Shrine cannot but trigger opposition by Asian countries that suffered from the damages of Japan's war of aggression, since it is viewed as an act of remembering invasion and domination as a history of glory rather than showing self-reflection and repentance on the war. As a result, Emperor Hirohito did not visit the Yasukuni Shrine after 1978 when the Type A war criminals were enshrined, and the Emperors that followed have not done so either. Another reason why the Yasukuni Shrine is problematic is that the exhibit hall inside the shrine and the Yushukan Museum glamorizes the history of aggression, and excludes Japan's war of aggression, colonization, and the resulting damages of neighboring countries and their people. By excluding critical introspection on the historical context and justifying the war of aggression, the Yasukuni Shrine makes it impossible to realize the pain and damage of war. The Yasukuni Shrine had also played a key role in applauding the death for the Emperor and accordingly mobilizing people in the war in modern Japan. The reality in which today's Japanese leaders, who are taking a rightward shift, are visiting the Yasukuni Shrine without hesitation may sound like a prelude to another conflict and war in East Asia in the 21st century.

In general, a state demands 'sacrifice' from its people. If people die from war, the state glorifies and extols this death as 'sacred sacrifice' for the country and demands other people to sacrifice in such way for the country.[511] However, there is a condition under which death at war can be a 'sacred sacrifice.' It needs to be a death at a justifiable war. It may seem irrational to discuss justice in a war where it is inevitable to kill people, but it is still possible to have a discussion about it. American political scientist Michael Walzer, in his book *Just and Unjust War* (1977)[512], defines a war for invasion (assault) as unjust and a war for self-defense (for self-protection) as just. A state exists for the purpose of protecting the lives and property of its people, and furthermore, to protect its community. If one state invades another state, the invaded people are demanded to risk their lives to save their rights. In other words, if a state is invaded, some people lose their lives while fighting for these rights. Walzer asserts that this type of death can be called a sacrifice. Thus, it has to be a death from self-defensive war, not a war of invasion, in order for the members of a community to willingly accept and appreciate it as a valuable sacrifice. However, in the case where someone loses one's life while being mobilized in a war of aggression, to call such death a sacred sacrifice is to falsely package the legitimacy of that war and compel other innocent sacrifices. Therefore, the act of Japan's political leaders paying their respects at the Yasukuni Shrine and saying that they are commemorating the sacred sacrifice of Japanese soldiers who had been mobilized in the war of aggression and met violent deaths, is not only an act of concealing an unrighteous war but also deceiving the Japanese people. Also, this means that Japan can invade Asian countries again in the future, and that it would mobilize Japanese people again and make them into offerings of innocent sacrifice in the process.[513]

Japan initiated the Pacific War, experienced repeated defeat, and finally surrendered as a result of the broad scale attacks and atomic bombings of the Allied Forces (United States). Despite the fact that Japan was the warmonger and perpetrator, Japan harbored a victim's mentality due to damages from air raids and atomic bombings by the American forces in the final stages of the war. Thus, Japan became negligent in questioning its own war responsibility and responsibility as a perpetrator. Of course, the Japanese, who had directly suffered from the atomic bombing, came to protest war itself and cherish peace after the war. And so, Japan built the Hiroshima Peace Memorial Park, which has played a role as the key hub of peace movements in Japan and the world. However, this memorial park only focuses on the atomic bombing itself, not on why Japan caused the war and why Japan did not avoid the atomic bombing although it could have. Furthermore, this park does not show how much damage was caused to Asian countries and Asian people as a result of this war. For instance, even though Okunoshima (大久野島), where the poison gas used to kill people in China was manufactured, is located in Hiroshima Prefecture, the exhibition hall within this memorial park does not show this fact. Therefore, Hiroshima Peace Memorial Park is turning into a hub that consistently reproduces the victim's mentality in the Japanese people and dilutes their sense of responsibility as the people of the perpetrator country.

The Okinawa Prefectural Peace Memorial Park is a place where the memorial methods of the Yasukuni Shrine and the Hiroshima Peace Memorial Park coexist. Within the Okinawa Prefectural Peace Memorial Park, there are commemorative spaces similar to the method of the Yasukuni Shrine, such as the Okinawa National Cemetery Park for the War Dead (國立沖繩戰歿者墓苑) established in 1979 and cenotaphs and memorial towers erected by various local institutions of Japan. These monuments focus on the courageous acts of the Japanese military and the Battle of Okinawa itself, but disregards the damage of the Okinawan people. Unlike this, the Okinawa Prefectural Peace Memorial Museum, which opened in 1977, exhibits materials that show how Okinawans were controlled during the war as well as oral materials vividly informing people how the Japanese military slaughtered civilians. In particular, during the mid-1990s, when a conservative governor of Okinawa Prefecture exercised pressure to newly reconstruct the museum toward the direction of glamorizing the patriotic actions of the Japanese military, the Okinawans opposed and instead newly opened the museum based on the damage of the Okinawans. However, the 'Cornerstone of Peace', which was erected in 1995, was engraved with the names of 241,000 people who died at the Battle of Okinawa without distinguishing between the Japanese military perpetrators and the victims, which thereby erased the perpetrator's mentality of the perpetrator and rather disguised perpetrators as victims. In the Ministry of Education's history textbook screening, Japan has generally glamorized its war against the United States, while minimizing or distorting the fact of perpetration in the form of war of aggression and colonization. Of course, there are many Japanese people who reject war and love peace due to the atomic bombing, but ironically, Japanese people came to have a victim's mentality as well, thereby becoming oblivious to the fact of perpetration or negligent toward making apologies to the victims or helping them heal.

8. Issues of Apology, Reconciliation, and Resistant Nationalism

Owing to the Cold War situation and the United States' strategy, Japan focused on postwar recovery and economic growth, while neglecting its responsibility for invasion and colonization of Asian countries. As the Cold War progressed, belonging to the capitalist bloc led by the United States, Japan functioned as the bastion against the proliferation of communism in Asia and took economic benefits which enabled Japan to rise as an economic power in the 1980s. However, even Japan needed to improve its relationships with Asian countries in order to promote greater national interest, which led to some diplomatic efforts and Japan made some expressions of apology to Asian countries in the name of Prime Ministers. Nonetheless, some influential politicians dashed cold water on such efforts of self-reflection and apology by making improper remarks, which caused Asian countries to protest and went against reconciliation and peace in Asia. It can be said that the behavior of Japanese political leaders after the war has been literally a cyclical repetition of apologies and absurd remarks.

Through the Treaty of San Francisco, Japan normalized relations with capitalist countries after the war, but was not able to resume diplomatic relations with Korea. As a result of Kubota Kanichiro (久保田貫一郎)'s statement[514] that 'Japan's colonial rule of Korea was beneficial to Korea' during the third round of talks between Japan and Korea in October 1953, the two countries did not have a chance to negotiate for approximately 10 years. The new Korean government that came into power through a military coup d'état in the early 1960s was eager to normalize diplomatic relations with Japan in order to complement its weak political legitimacy through economic development. In other words, the new government had a strong intention to push ahead with economic development plans through Japan's economic aid and cooperation. The United States, which was sinking into a pit in the Vietnam War, urged the two countries to normalize diplomatic relations, with the anticipation that Japan would bear the burden of providing economic aid to Korea. In Korea, students and the opposition party intensely protested against the Korean government's humiliating diplomacy, asserting that 'Normalization of diplomatic relations between Korea and Japan should only be progressed under the premise Japan makes apologies and compensation for its colonial rule.' Since it was necessary to appease the opposing sentiment within Korea in the process of normalizing relations between Japan and Korea, the diplomatic lines of Japan and Korea prepared a statement by the Japanese Foreign Minister. When Japanese Foreign Minister Shiina Etsusaburo (椎名悦三郎, 1898-1979) arrived at Gimpo Airport to visit Korea on February 17, 1964, he announced a statement that 'Japan genuinely regrets that there was a period of misfortune between the two countries, and deeply reflects on it.' This was the first statement of apology made by a high-level official of Japan after the war, and the negotiations between Japan and Korea advanced with more ease afterward.

It was difficult for China, which belonged to the socialist bloc, to get along with Japan due to ideological differences during the Cold War era. During the Cold War era, Japan had to play a role as the bulwark against communism in Asia according to the United States' strategy. Therefore, Japan had to function as an opposing power against communist countries by establishing diplomatic relations with Jiang Jieshi's Taiwan, which was still part of the capitalist bloc. However, Japan was shocked when the United States' President Nixon announced plans to visit China, and in response, Japan's Prime Minister Tanaka Kakuei (田中角栄, 1918-1993) visited China in September 1972, announcing the Japan-China Joint Communique and normalizing relations with China earlier than the United States. The advancement of these diplomatic relations was influenced by Japan's sense of betrayal from the United States as well as the urgency of Japan's economic world to seek China's vast market. Japan had no choice but to apologize for its war of aggression toward China, and the Japan-China Joint Communique included the phrase that 'Japan feels deep responsibility for inflicting significant damage to the Chinese people by waging war in the past and deeply reflects upon it.' It can be viewed that this was a much more advanced statement than the statement announced by Foreign Minister Shiina Etsusaburo in 1964 in the negotiation process of normalizing diplomatic relations between Japan and Korea. In response, China relinquished its claims for war reparations on the state level, and the fundamental content of this joint communique was included in the preamble to the Japan-China Treaty of Peace and Friendship concluded in 1978.

After the Treaty of San Francisco, throughout the 1950s, Japan was unable to restore diplomatic relations in East Asia, not only with the socialist countries of China and North Korea but also with Korea (South Korea). Therefore, Japan attempted to avoid isolation in Asia by entering into favorable relations with Southeast Asian countries. Japan had resumed diplomatic relations with Southeast Asian countries through the Treaty of

San Francisco and bilateral treaties and further attempted to establish favorable relations through compensations in the form of economic cooperation. However, as this method of compensation took on the form of economic aid toward developing countries, Japan became the benefactor of aid and Southeast Asian countries became the beneficiaries and such relationship hurt the pride of Southeast Asian countries. Of course, Southeast Asian countries had scars from the invasion and domination of the Japanese military, but it can be said that the degree was relatively less intense compared to China or Korea, which suffered for decades. In addition, the degree of damage from war varied from country to country. In the case of India, which barely suffered any damage, there were relatively active efforts to advance economic cooperation with Japan after the war. However, most Southeast Asian countries did not receive the visits of Japanese Prime Ministers all that hospitably. Protests of Southeast Asian people continued believing that Japan's economic expansion under the pretext of economic aid gave immense profits to Japan but did not benefit the economic development of Southeast Asian countries all that much. When Prime Minister Tanaka Kakuei visited the five countries of the Philippines, Thailand, Singapore, Malaysia, and Indonesia in January 1974, fierce anti-Japanese protests arose in various parts of the countries. In Indonesia, the anti-Japanese protest developed into a riot with slogans such as 'We oppose to Japan's economic invasion,' 'Economic beast, go away,' and Tanaka had to return to Japan after travelling to the airport on an air force helicopter. In August 1977, Prime Minister Fukuda Takeo strove to appease the antagonism of the Southeast Asian people during his visit to several Southeast Asian countries, and in particular, announced the 'Fukuda Doctrine' in Manila, Philippines, which was the last place on his itinerary. This doctrine contained contents that 'Japan will not become a military power, will recognize diversity of ethnic groups and cooperate on an equal footing, and will actively cooperate with ASEAN.' It can be said that this doctrine was made for the purpose of placating Southeast Asian countries, which were being shaken up by the threat of communization after South Vietnam fell, and expressing self-reflection on unilateral economic relationships by Japan.

As we have seen above, Japan showed extremely varying behaviors in the process of normalizing relations with Asian countries during the Cold War era. In other words, Japan determined whether to make an apology or not and to what extent the apology should be made, depending on the gap of national power and the degree of damage of the country in question. In the cases of China and Korea, which suffered the greatest damage of Japan's war of aggression and colonization, Japan had no choice but to normalize diplomatic relations individually, as the two countries were unable to participate in the Treaty of San Francisco. Therefore, a long period of time elapsed before Japan was able to normalize diplomatic relations with China and Korea, and the process was extremely difficult and the expressions of apology were made with great difficulties. In the case of China, Japan included the phrase 'feel deeply responsible for' and 'self-reflection' in the Japan-China Joint Communique. This was because Japan had a great possibility of obtaining economic benefits through China's vast market, China had suffered the greatest damage from Japan's invasion, and Japan had a great need to escape from the dismay of the Nixon Shock. In the case of Korea, despite the fact Japan inflicted the agony and suffering of colonial rule which lasted for 35 years, Japan still possessed a sense of superiority over Korea which was its former colony. Furthermore, as Korea had weak national power, Japan only showed a gesture of self-reflection through a statement by the Foreign Minister prior to establishing diplomatic relations and did not include any words of apology or self-reflection in the Treaty on Basic Relations between Japan and Korea. In the case of Southeast Asia, not only had Japan already restored basic relations through the Treaty of San Francisco, but the degree of damage was not as big as China or Korea, and the national powers of the countries were not very strong, so Japan did not feel the need to repent or apologize at all. Southeast Asia was merely a passage through which Japan could enter into Asia after the war and a source of resources and a market that could bring economic benefits to Japan.

Up until the 1970s, Japan had normalized relations with almost all Asian countries, and during the last 10 years of the Cold War, there were no particular conflicts aside from Japan's history textbook screening issue (1982), Prime Minister Nakasone's visiting the Yasukuni Shrine (1985), and Japanese Minister of Education Fujio Masayuki's remark that agitated China and Korea (1986). Fujio Masayuki (藤尾正行, 1917-2006), the Minister of Education of Prime Minister Nakasone's Cabinet, contributed to the October 1986 edition of the *Bungeishunju* that 'Not only is massacre a part of war but the number of causalities in Nanjing was exaggerated, and since the Japanese annexation of Korea was agreed upon mutual arrangement, Korea has a certain degree of responsibility.' There were extremely intense protests on the part of China and Korea regarding his remark. Prime Minister Nakasone Yasuhiro, who had striven to improve the relations between Japan and Korea, managed the difficult situation by eventually firing Fujio Masayuki, who refused to withdraw his remarks and also refused to resign from his position as minister.[515] Prime Minister Nakasone had advanced relations between Japan and Korea by choosing Korea as the first overseas country to visit after his inauguration as Prime Minister, inviting Korea's President Chun Doo-hwan to Japan for the Emperor to personally give a statement of regret over colonial rule, and giving a statement of apology himself as Prime Minister. However, Minister of Education Fujio Masayuki had dampened all his efforts. After a Prime Minister or key leader created momentum for reconciliation through self-reflection and apology, another political leader would make a remark causing resistance from China or Korea, messing up the relations among the countries and ending up resigning. This type of behavior repeatedly happened into the 1990s.

As the Cold War came to an end between the late 1980s and the early 1990s, Asian countries began to show dissatisfaction toward Japan's lukewarm attitude on its invasion and colonization, and the individual victims started to raise their voices as well. Due to this atmosphere, Japan started to take on a more active gesture even toward Southeast Asian countries which it had neglected thus far. Prime Minister Kaifu Toshiki stated that 'Japan solemnly reflects upon Japan's acts which gave unbearable suffering and pain to people in the Asia Pacific region' through a statement in Singapore in May 1991. In particular, as there was an outpour of testimonies of the former Japanese military comfort women and documentary evidence that the Japanese military had actually been involved were presented, the Japanese government conducted an investigation. Eventually, on August 4, 1993, Chief Cabinet Secretary Kono Yohei of Miyazawa Kiichi's Cabinet acknowledged the forcefulness by stating that 'Recruitment, transportation, and management were mostly conducted against the will of the women, through deceit and coercion' and also announced a statement of apology. Prime Minister Hosokawa Morihiro who visited Korea in November 1993, apologized in the Gyeongju Conference with President Kim Young-Sam saying that 'Japan would like to genuinely repent and offer a deep apology as a perpetrator on the fact that Korea experienced suffering and pain in various forms, such as being prohibited from speaking Korean at school, being forced to change their names to Japanese names, and being drafted as comfort women, due to Japan's colonial rule.' The highlight of apologies by Japan's highest political leaders was the statement on 'the 50th anniversary of the end of war' given by Prime Minister Murayama Tomiichi on August 15, 1995. Murayama Tomiichi expressed a keen self-reflection and sincere apology by saying that 'It was wrong to give immense damage and pain to Asian countries and Asian people through Japan's invasion and colonization.' Based on such apology by the Japanese Prime Minister, Japan and Korea, and China and Japan created a framework for reconciliation and future-oriented relationships in the late 1990s. This was realized in October 1998, when Japan clearly apologized about the past and Korea promised a future-oriented reconciliation through the Japan-South Korea Joint Declaration by Korea's President Kim Dae-jung and Japan's Prime Minister Obuchi Keizo. In addition, the Japan-China Joint Declaration between China's President Jiang Zemin and Japan's Prime Minister Obuchi Keizo in November 1998 was announced with similar contents as the Japan-South Korea Joint Declaration, though some expressions were toned down. Prime Minister Koizumi, who powerfully led Japan during the early to mid-2000s, came into conflict with Asian countries regarding the issue of visiting the Yasukuni Shrine, but repeatedly apologized about Japan's historical issues. Prime Minister Koizumi actively apologized through his remarks after visiting Lugouqiao (盧溝橋, the Marco Polo Bridge) in the outskirts of Beijing and the Museum of the War of Chinese People's Resistance against Japanese Aggression in Beijing in October 2001, his remarks after visiting the site of Seodaemun Prison which used to be a prison during the Japanese colonial period in Korea, his remarks during the Pyongyang Declaration on September 17, 2002, and his statements as Prime Minister on the '60th anniversary of the end of war' in 2005 which was similar to Prime Minister Murayama's statements.

As Japan was on the defensive due to historical issues, the opposing forces within Japan began to raise their voices as well. Therefore, from the 1990s on, some political leaders continued the so-called 'absurd remarks' regarding historical issues. The persons directly involved with such absurd remarks were unable to defend their position and had to resign due to the oppositions of Asian countries. Nagano Shigeto, the Justice Minister of Prime Minister Hata Tsutomu's Cabinet which was formed after the resignation of Prime Minister Hosokawa, stated in May 1994 that 'The definition of the Pacific War as a war of aggression is incorrect, and the Nanjing Massacre is a fabricated story.'[516] This statement triggered strong opposition from China, and he eventually stepped down from his position in the Cabinet. Sakurai Shin, who became Minister of Environment after the Murayama Cabinet stepped into power in June 1994, resigned from his position in August after making a controversial remark that 'Japan's war was inevitable, and Japan did not wage a war of aggression but fought for the independence of Asia.'[517] In June 1995, Watanabe Michio, former Deputy Prime Minister and Foreign Minister, stated in a lecture and press conference in his hometown of Utsunomiya that 'The Japanese annexation of Korea was an amicable international treaty,' which triggered strong opposition from Korea and some students threw firebombs at the Japan Culture Center in Seoul. In November 1995, Minister of Government Administration of the Murayama Cabinet, Eto Takami stated that 'It was wrong for the Prime Minister to make an apology, and Japan did good deeds during the colonial rule.' Around this time, Korea's President Kim Young-sam held a joint press conference with China's President Jiang Zemin, who was visiting Seoul, criticized Eto's statement and showed strong emotions by saying that 'This time, we will teach the Japanese some manners.' However, the 'absurd remarks' of Japanese politicians regarding historical issues seldom appeared from 1996 to 2002. The reason was that spirits of cooperation were highly elated between Japan and Korea because it was decided in 1996 that Japan and Korea would jointly host the 2002 FIFA World Cup. Nevertheless, in May 2003, Taro Aso, the grandson of former Prime Minister Yoshida from his mother's side, stated in a lecture at Tokyo University as the Chairman of the Policy Research Council of the Liberal Democratic Party that 'Koreans wanted to change their names to

Japanese names in order to not experience disadvantages in finding employment,' provoking the Koreans once more. In October 2003, Governor of Tokyo, Ishihara Shintaro, stated that 'The Japanese annexation of Korea was realized through the collective opinion of the Korean people who chose Japan.' However, as cultural and economic exchanges between Japan and Korea have become more vigorous after the co-hosting of the World Cup, the response of the Korean people toward such remarks were not as vehement as it used to be.

Since the late 1990s, Japanese society had been seized with a sense of crisis due to approximately 10 years of economic recession and requests of Asian countries to settle historical issues. As a consequence, the activities of groups such as the 'Association for the Advancement of the Liberal View of History' and the 'Tsukuru Kai (Japanese Society for History Textbook Reform),' which claim to advocate a view of history centered on Japan and the Japanese people, started to become active. These groups criticize that middle and high school textbooks only highlight Japan's dark history, and view this as a self-disparaging illustration of history. As such perceptions are spreading into generations which did not experience the war and grew up during the period of economic prosperity, there are concerns that when these generations come to lead Japan, it will become even more difficult to realize reconciliation and cooperation with Asian countries. They have come to harbor strong feelings such as 'Until when are we going to discuss war responsibilities?' and 'There ought to be no more apologies.' Furthermore, since the Abe government stepped into office, politicians have been visiting the Yasukuni Shrine nonchalantly and denying or even glorifying Japan's history of colonizing and invading Asian countries without hesitation.

CHAPTER 10

GERMANY'S POSTWAR SETTLEMENTS AND
JAPAN'S ATTITUDE

1. Germany's Post World War II Settlements and Advancement of European Integration

Germany and Japan, the principal offenders of the war in Europe and Asia, have always been compared in terms of postwar settlements. In particular, the fact that Japan has not only never shown heartfelt repentance and apology but has not given war reparations or compensations properly, comes in stark contrast with Germany which has made postwar settlements in a relatively exemplary manner. While the historical issue of invasion and resistance has been a stepping stone toward reconciliation, cooperation, peace, and integration in Europe, it has been a seed of conflict and dispute in Asia. It was necessary for Germany to thoroughly overcome historical issues in order to be recognized as a sovereign state and revive its economy through cooperation with European countries. Therefore, Germany, or the then West Germany, made political and historical efforts to make settlements for World War II. The necessary war reparations and compensations were made accordingly. In particular, the emergence of neo-Nazism came as a shock to Israel and Western countries and naturally led to pressure against Germany, which was one of the important factors that triggered Germany to earnestly begin efforts to overcome historical issues.

The fundamental policy of the Allied Forces in dealing with postwar Germany was specified in the declaration of the Yalta Conference which was held in February 1945, and the major contents can be summarized as the so-called 4D policies of denazification, demilitarization, decartelization and democratization.[518] However, the West German society had not been active in overcoming historical issues from the very beginning after the end of the war. After the war came to an end, the denazification policies, such as war criminal trials and broad scale purge, were pushed ahead by the Allied Forces, particularly the American forces. Such policies led to the resistance of many Germans who were still nostalgic about Nazi Germany. Furthermore, this denazification policy was not thoroughly advanced as the Cold War became serious. Thus, up until the 1950s, it can be said that the German society literally became a community that kept silent about historical issues. Then in 1959, neo-Nazism abruptly made a salient appearance committing a series of anti-Semitic acts, and in 1961, the German society was pressured and provoked when Israel held a public trial against Adolf Eichmann, the main culprit of the Holocaust. Through the Eichmann Trial, the Germans started to realize that their dark history, which they believed had been settled, was still nearby. Furthermore, a new interest on the past spread through German society as they experienced the Auschwitz Trial which revealed the true picture of the Nazi's horrendous crimes against the Jews, and the controversy on extinctive prescriptions of Nazi crimes in the mid-1960s. This interest was widely diffused, along with the social reform movement that swept through Europe in the late 1960s, and in 1969 when the progressive regime of the Social Democratic Party came into power, Germany adopted 'Ostpolitik' (Eastern Policy) and made efforts to improve relations with the Soviet Union and Eastern European countries in the communist bloc, marking a turning point in Germany's change. Willy Brandt, the Chancellor of West Germany, knelt before a monument in a Jewish ghetto in Warsaw, Poland in 1970, which was a symbolic incident that moved not only the Germans but the Europeans.

It was not only due to Germany's own will and efforts that Germany was successful in overcoming its historical issues. The influence of the international society on the German government and the Germans cannot be overlooked. West Germany's government could not disregard international pressure, as it was desperate to reconcile and improve relations with European countries and the world in order to secure its existence as a country and revive its economy. As mentioned above, it was primarily Israel that played a key role in constantly exposing the memories of the Nazi's brutal past and arousing the public opinion of the international society. As Hannah Arendt pointed out through the Eichmann Trial, not particularly evil people but extremely ordinary people took part in the national goal of exterminating the Jews without a pang of conscience. The Germans and Europeans shuddered at the fact. Germany had a chance to self-reflect by recollecting the period when the banality of evil was literally rampant.[519] Furthermore, video clips related to the Holocaust, which were produced in countries abroad, such as the United States where the Jews had strong influence and brought into Germany, also had a great impact on German society. Thus, not only the central government but also the local governments of West Germany deployed various projects to uncover records on Nazi crimes and refreshed the memories of the citizens. Historians contributed to the formation of a culture of remembrance through publications and various cultural activities. In fact, Germany was active toward reparations for the brutal Holocaust led by the state but had refused compensations for foreigners who had engaged in forced labor in German companies. However, due to the pressure of international public opinion and the establishment of a coalition government of the Social Democratic Party and the Green Party in 2000, Germany's major companies decided to compensate for the damage of foreigners who had engaged in forced labor. Consequently, the Memory, Responsibility and Future (EVZ, Erinnerung, Verantwortung und Zukunft) Foundation was established, by raising funds amounting to DM 10 billion (approximately 5.2 billion euro), based on the funds from companies that had employed forced laborers during the Nazi period and government subsidies (DM 5 billion). [520] In addition, the regime competition between East Germany and West Germany as a result of the Cold War acted rather as an impetus for West Germany to make efforts to overcome historical issues. East Germany refused Israel's claims for reparations, under the pretext that it did not inherit the responsibilities of the Nazi regime. Unlike West Germany, such attitude of East Germany after the war has been pointed out as the reason why East Germany failed to implant a genuine sense of self-reflection on Nazism to the postwar generation.[521]

Germany has adhered to the principle that all the Germans take the responsibility for war reparations together, for the pain and damage that Germany inflicted on European countries and their people during World War II. Here, all the Germans refer not only to war criminals that committed the brutalities of the Nazi regime but include even the Germans who were against the war and include not only the Germans during the war but also the postwar generations. The Germans have made compensations to the victims of World War II in various methods, and the compensations have been made through the assets that have been created by Germans who do not have a direct relationship with the war as time goes on. Therefore, it can be said that in the case of Germany, almost all Germans have taken part in assuming the responsibility for war reparations.[522] In West Germany, more than 90,000 Nazi figures were brought to trial not only through the International Military Tribunal of the Nuremberg Trials but trials conducted by the Germans themselves, and approximately 7,000 cases reached a guilty verdict. Furthermore, through a resolution of the parliament in 1979 that 'The extinctive prescription of Nazi crimes is abolished and will be questioned forever,' Germany has been consistently punishing Nazi crimes.[523]

Among the reasons as to why it was possible for Germany to repent and reconcile with neighboring countries in this manner, were the remarks of influential figures as follows. [524] Karl Jaspers, a renowned philosopher confessed that 'I committed the crime of failing to risk my life to block the acts of killing others and only watching with my arms crossed, and the fact that I am still alive even after such acts have been committed becomes a crime that weighs on me.' His stance was that even though it was difficult for all German people to be punished under criminal charges for war crimes, since everybody was a tacit accomplice, nobody could escape from a political and ethical sense of guilt.[525] On May 8, 1985, in a speech commemorating the 40th anniversary of the end of the war, President Weizsäcker of West Germany stated with the following meaning. 'Whether one is guilty or innocent, whether one is old or young, all Germans must assume responsibility over the past. One who shuts his eyes toward the past eventually becomes blind in the present. One who refuses to take inhuman acts to heart is vulnerable to falling into such dangers again.' A German journalist Ralph Giordano pointed out in his book *The Second Guilt or The Burden of Being German*[526] in 1987 that 'If the crimes committed by the Germans during the Hitler era were the 'first guilt,' then the 'second guilt' is the psychological denial and suppression of the 'first guilt' after the war.' Giordano claimed that 'The majority of Germans are guilty of such 'second guilt,' and it has become one of the fundamental characteristics of West Germany's political culture, but the Germans must assume this burden even from now on.' Chancellor of reunified Germany, Gerhard Schröder, stressed that the lesson of history should not be forgotten, at a rally in Berlin on January 25, 2005, the 60th anniversary of the liberation of the Auschwitz concentration camp. He mentioned that 'Remembering the history and violence of the Nazi era is a sort of moral obligation, and this responsibility is not only toward the victims and survivors of the Nazis's violence and their families but also toward ourselves.'[527]

European countries, including Germany and France, that had experienced two World Wars, which had brought about devastating results, strove to prevent war by reinforcing economic ties and interdependency. People thought that if Germany, the warmonger of two World Wars, were to be organically integrated in industrial fields with France, Germany's major counterpart in war, and economic interdependency between the countries were to be promoted, then Germany would not be able to wage war due to such ties. Thus, cooperation which first occurred in the steel production industry led to cooperation in other industrial fields, and eventually resulted in the overall economic integration of today. Furthermore, a considerable degree of integration has been accomplished in the aspects of politics and administration as well. In 1951, the six countries of Germany, France, Italy, Belgium, the Netherlands, and Luxembourg signed the Treaty of Paris and established the European Coal and Steel Community (ECSC). In 1957, European countries concluded the Treaty of Rome, creating a customs union and establishing the European Economic Community (EEC) and the European Atomic Energy Community (EURATOM). As economic cooperation and integration advanced in Europe, the European Economic Community (EEC) was changed into the European Community (EC). As the European Community (EC) showed a successful appearance, various other European countries such as the United Kingdom joined in the 1970s. The European Community (EC) expanded its geographical range, and based on the outcomes of economic integration, the European Community (EC) adopted the Single European Act in 1986. Furthermore, European countries concluded the Maastricht Treaty in 1992 and formed the European Union (EU), integrating not only currency and monetary policy but also various other policies.[528] In these advancements of European integration, Germany's attitude of being born again as a member of Europe and as a peaceful nation after the war, by thoroughly repenting on the wrongdoings of Nazi Germany and actively making the necessary compensations, played a crucial part. This attitude of postwar Germany implanted trust in neighboring European countries and enabled mutual cooperation and reconciliation. This is a stark contrast with the situation after World War I, when European countries showed distrust toward Germany, attempted to put a heavy economic burden on Germany, and triggered another conflict which led to World War II.

2. Comparison of Germany and Japan in Postwar Settlements

In comparison with Germany, various factors have been pointed out as reasons why the Japanese society was unable to properly settle historical issues such as war responsibilities, the most noteworthy of which was the difference in the occupation system experienced by the two countries. The United States, which led postwar occupation policy, adopted a multilateral cooperation policy in Europe and a bilateral unilateralism in Asia.[529] The reality is that while Germany formed the European Union (EU) by establishing strong ties based on reconciliation and cooperation with European countries after the war, Japan is isolated to some extent by pushing ahead with pro-American policies while setting aside East Asian countries. In the process of forming a modern country, Japan learned many things from Germany, such as the constitution and various institutions. The two countries were defeated in the war at similar times and successfully underwent postwar restoration in similar methods. However, with respect to the area of settlement of historical issues, Japan has taken a path that varied from the path that Germany took after the war. Germany was active in making settlements for the past by apologizing and compensating for the pain that Germany inflicted on neighboring European countries as a result of World War II, but Japan has shown regressive behavior, denying and distorting its past history of war of aggression. Even though Japan set Germany as its model in the process of forming a modern country, why is it that Japan has not followed the exemplary footsteps of Germany after the war?

After its defeat, Germany was directly ruled by the Allied Forces for approximately 4 years, and unlike Japan, Nazi leaders did not play key roles after the war, because the Nazi government had collapsed and the Allied

Forces had excluded the government leaders at the time. In the case of Japan, it was not divided as in the case of Germany because it was under sole occupation of the American forces. Furthermore, as the American forces adopted an indirect occupation rule structure, the emperor system was maintained and almost all of the wartime bureaucrats and political leaders reemerged to carry out major roles. Instead of sole occupation of the American forces, if Japan had been divided and ruled by several countries of the Allied Forces, as in the case of Germany, Japan would not have been able to avoid division. However, as Japan managed to avoid division, tragically, the countries that Japan had colonized and invaded, such as Korea, China, and Vietnam were divided. In addition, owing to increased demands as a result of wars in these countries that broke out in the process of division, Japan prepared a foundation for economic revival and rapid growth.

Both Japan and Germany had a high possibility of progressing toward wide scale democratization amidst the situation of a power vacuum after the war, but the actual consequences differed according to the circumstances of each country. In the case of Germany, the occupying forces suppressed democratization movements such as popular movements and party reconstruction movements, and took the initiative in pushing ahead with reforms. The most representative among these reforms was the policy called denazification, which banished figures that had played major roles in the Nazi government from public positions. Shortly after being defeated in the war, there still remained an atmosphere in which the German people supported Nazism ideology and Hitler, and political elites were in an agreement with the occupying forces in that such political culture should be cut off after the war. The American forces which occupied Japan was free from the responsibility of maintaining public order due to indirect rule, and in this situation, concentrated on reforms and performed the role of improving political freedom and rights, until the advent of the Cold War. Unlike the elites of Germany, after losing the war, the political elites of Japan did not reflect on the fascist emperor system which had propelled the war, and rather considered retaining the imperial family as the greatest task. Therefore, a reform led by the Japanese could not be expected, and without a strong reform led by the American forces, even the restructuring of economic institutions or political democratization that was accomplished, would have been difficult.

The commonality of the post occupation policies on Japan and Germany is that whereas there were strict restrictions militarily, economic policies were extremely lenient. While making certain that Japan and Germany could never become empires that would pursue militarism or fascism, economic reforms and political democratization were strongly propelled. This is a stark contrast with the situation after World War I when the Allied Forces imposed powerful economic sanctions such as requesting massive war reparations from defeated Germany, while controlling Germany's military activities relatively loosely.

After the war, Japan signed the Treaty of San Francisco with the Allied Forces, but in the case of Germany, neither was a treaty conference held nor was a peace treaty concluded. Because Germany was divided and ruled by the Allied Forces and then divided into the two countries of East Germany and West Germany, a peace treaty could not be concluded. Therefore, it can be said that the Treaty on the Final Settlement with Respect to Germany (September 1990) among the six nations (East Germany, West Germany, the four powers that occupied Germany after the end of the war), which was concluded shortly before East Germany and West Germany reunified (October 1990), replaced a peace treaty. Therefore, Germany, which did not conclude a peace treaty, concentrated on economic compensations rather than legal reparations, whereas Japan, which did sign a peace treaty, tried to conclude everything with the treaty and reparations and made postwar settlements without harboring the concept of compensations.

Unlike Japan's Tokyo Trial, Germany's Nuremberg Trials prosecuted not only individuals but also groups and organizations. Germany's trials against war criminals and postwar settlements included not only the fact of waging war but also the illegalities and criminal acts committed by the Nazis, but Japan's trial attempted to minimize the range to only the war itself. In Japan, the ruling class and subjugated class alike tried to avoid responsibility by blaming the war for all problems. Therefore, even the war criminals who were tried and punished were recognized as the scapegoats of war. And so, in 1956, when the last Type A war criminal was released from the Sugamo Prison, where Type A war criminals who had been tried at the Tokyo Trial were imprisoned, no more prisoners from the Tokyo Trial remained.

It is a stark contrast that there was no case in which war criminals were investigated or prosecuted by the Japanese government or Japanese people after the war, whereas in the case of Germany, the Allied Forces made the Germans try the war criminals of the Nazi regime pursuant to Germany's Criminal Act. Germany extended the extinctive prescription on Nazi crimes several times and eventually abolished it. In this process, German people had the opportunity to become clearly aware of the fact of perpetration. On the other hand, there were discussions to include Japanese prosecutors or judges in the Tokyo Trial, but it was not realized. Had Japanese prosecutors and judges been included in the Tokyo Trial, then it would have avoided the controversy of being a 'victor's trial,' or 'victor's justice,' which may have acted as momentum for the Japanese people to push ahead with the prosecution of war criminals themselves, as in the case of Germany.[530]

Europe went through the calamities of two World Wars by Germany in the early 20th century. However, in the late 20th century, Europe had formed the European Union (EU) centering on Germany and France, and is promoting common interests. The background behind integration in the European society, which could not but have had misgivings toward Germany, was that Germany exhaustively punished the wrongdoings of the Nazi era and made heartfelt apologies and compensations to neighboring countries after the war, and such genuineness of the Germans was accepted by other European countries. Even after the end of the occupation rule after the war, Germany continued to chase and punish Nazi war criminals, and legally punishes those who praise the Nazis or use the Nazi symbol even to this day. Meanwhile, after the end of the occupation rule of the Allied Forces, Japan has never even once prosecuted and given a guilty sentence to war criminals on its own. Even worse, Japan has a greater tendency to deny or dilute the responsibility of war and colonization. There are no restraints even if the extreme right wing strides down the streets waving the Rising Sun Flag (旭日旗) that fluttered at the forefront of the Japanese military during the war. The Hinomaru (日の丸) and Kimigayo (君が代), which were the symbols that restrained and distressed the Japanese people under the system of a totalitarian garrison state, have officially emerged again as Japan's national flag and national anthem. This is Japan's reality today. Even though it has been over 20 years since the 21st century began, Japan is rather showing the behavior of reverting back to the early 20th century.

Various reasons can be mentioned as factors that prevented Japan's postwar settlements from progressing as thoroughly as Germany's. As mentioned above, there was a difference in the occupation system, and the United States, which had sole occupation over Japan adopted policies to its own interest. This led to the indirect rule of using the Japanese Emperor and wartime ruling class, triggering the result in which the actual figures responsible for the war were exempted from punishment. In comparison to Japan which surrendered in mid-August of 1945 and had the American forces stationed in early September, Germany which was occupied in early May of 1945, was able to finish trials for war criminals before the advent of the Cold War, which brought about better results. Unlike the case of Germany in which the documents of the Nazi government were immediately confiscated by the Allied Forces after the war and submitted as evidence in the trials on war crimes, in the case of Japan, documents that would be disadvantageous for Japan in trials were massively destroyed or forged during the two weeks from its surrender to the arrival of the US military. Due to the advent of the Cold War and consequent changes in the United States' occupation policy, Japan's major war criminals were exempted and Japan's responsibility for war reparations was lightened. Furthermore, Japan was able to conclude its peace treaty in a favorable way during the Korea War. Germany made diversified efforts, such as apologies and compensations, as cooperation with European countries was essential for postwar settlement and economic revival. On the other hand, Japan turned its back on Asian countries to which it had inflicted pain and damage through war of aggression and colonization and concentrated on achieving economic and security interests through an alliance with the United States. The incidents that had an immense impact on the Germans and the Japanese were the tragedies of Auschwitz and Hiroshima. Whereas the former formed a perpetrator's mentality on the Germans, the latter formed a victim's mentality on the Japanese. Postwar Germany thoroughly reflected on its 'Germanification of Europe' policy, namely 'deeuropeanization' policy, and made a declaration to return to Europe and restart as a peaceful country, which was accepted by European countries. During the late 19th century and early 20th century, Japan proceeded toward the path of war of aggression and colonization of Asia, by pursuing Western modernization based on the strategy of '*Datsua Nyuo*' ('Leave Asia, enter Europe'). However, instead of reflecting upon such historical wrongdoings and returning as a member of Asia after the war, Japan had chosen to achieve economic revival and solve security issues through the strategy of 'Leave Asia, enter the United States.'[531]

Japan made compensations mainly to people who directly participated in the war, such as Japanese soldiers and civilians attached to the military. Consequently, no compensations were made to Japanese civilians (excluding atomic bomb victims), people from colonies, and other Asian victims. In other words, postwar Japan limited the target of war relief to 'those who were under the employment of the state,' such as soldiers and civilians attached to the military, and thus, not only the Japanese victims of air raids but victims of Asian countries were thoroughly excluded from compensations. Thus, in a sense, Japanese soldiers, the leading force of perpetration, have lived on government pension benefits, whereas numerous victims have lived hard lives in poverty, shame, and physical and mental suffering. This clearly goes against not only human rights and morality but historical justice. On the contrary, Germany, France, and the United States try to make exhaustive compensations without distinguishing between the beneficiaries in such a way. The Federal GI Bill of Rights of West Germany which was established in 1950 included the victims of air raids as the beneficiaries of the same type of relief and did not discriminate against soldiers depending on rank or nationality. Germany's war relief shows a tremendous difference with Japan's in terms of quality.[532]

Another factor that brought forth differences of postwar settlement between Germany and Japan was the difference in the education system. Due to the experience of abuse during the Nazi era, West Germany strictly restricted the state's intervention in educational issues after World War II. The major principle with respect to Germany's history textbooks was that a broad scale consensus in terms of society, politics, and historical science had to be reflected. Therefore, strict censorship of textbooks by the government, as in Japan, was unthinkable in Germany. In comparison to Germany, Japan made a different approach by making political interventions in the education field, especially history and social sciences. In Japan, the influence of politics on history textbooks is extremely strong. The Ministry of Education has had the opportunity to delete illustrations or criticisms of Japan's wrongdoings during the colonial rule or invasion through the textbook screening system. Accordingly, history textbooks, such as the book written by Japan's renowned historian Ienaga Saburo, which are deemed as extremely critical by the government, can easily be rejected through the approval process. Therefore, as the Japanese society and government take a more conservative swing in recent days, illustrations of Japan's historical wrongdoings are fading away.[533]

3. Criticism of Japan's Postwar Settlements

Japan's modern history from the late 19th century to the early 20th century had been a history of invasion and domination of Asian countries. Due to the Cold War and the occupation policy of the United States, postwar Japan did not have a chance to settle such history and concentrated only on economic development to become an economic power while turning a blind eye to Asia. However, as the Cold War and the conflict between the United States and the Soviet Union came to an end, Asian countries looked back on their relationships with Japan and came to demand a settlement of the past from Japan. In response to such demands of Asian countries, Japan searched for a new relationship, and up until the early 1990s, there had been some degree of efforts, as in the Kono Statements and the Murayama Statements. However, as a long-term recession and uncertainty toward the future overlaps, historical revisionists are raising their voices and rightwing forces are getting stronger, which is pushing away into the distance a genuine settlement of the past on the part of Japan. As necessary follow-up measures, such as repentance, apology, and reparations for historical wrongdoings, are not being made by Japan, distrust and criticism have been expressed by not only Asian countries but also international society for a long period of time. If Japan wishes to take on the roles and responsibility of a leader in Asia, it has become urgent to at least now start to establish mutual trust through a settlement of the past.

Fundamentally, the responsibility of the war of aggression caused by Japan in the early 20th century lies with Japan's ruling class at the time, in other words, the Japanese Emperor, the military authorities, the Cabinet, and the underpinning *zaibatsu*. However, even the ordinary Japanese people cannot escape from the responsibility. This is because Japan's foreign expansion and war of aggression was the result of pursuing an expansion of the entire Japanese people's survival space. In particular, as modern warfare is called total war that includes all civilians and mobilizes all of the resources, Japan's invasion of China and the Pacific War would have been impossible to execute without the participation of the Japanese people. In fact, most of the mass slaughters and rape that occurred in China were carried out by the spontaneous choice of the Japanese soldiers, not by the orders of a Japanese ruler. Therefore, it is quite natural for the key figures in charge of war to receive criminal punishment through trials for their war criminals and ordinary Japanese people should not only bear the responsibility to make reparations for victim countries but also take moral responsibility. However, most of the key figures in charge did not so much as be questioned for their responsibilities in the midst of the Cold War, with the exception of a small portion of people who were hanged or imprisoned. In particular, seeing that Emperor Hirohito, who was thought to have the biggest responsibility, did not take any responsibility at all, many Japanese people were unable to feel that they were an accomplice to the act of giving inexpressible pain to Asians through massacres, rape, economic exploitation, etc.[534] Therefore, Japanese people managed to escape the issue of war responsibility by not making war reparations and concentrating on economic development under the shelter of the United States during the Cold War.

Furthermore, the issue of how to view the responsibility of Japan's postwar generation is another problem. Of course, Japan's postwar generation could say that it is inappropriate to discuss war responsibility, since they did not cause the war or participate in it. However, it can be said that a considerable portion of the fruits of modernization that present day Japanese people are enjoying were borne on the foundation achieved through Japan's expansion into Asia, colonization, and war of aggression. It was through the invasion and domination of Asia that Modern Japan eventually achieved the primitive accumulation of capital and succeeded in modernization. And so, the Japanese people lived in the glory of being the strongest nation in Asia before the defeat of the war, and even after the war, Japan took a new leap on the foundation of resources accumulated in this manner to become an economic power. In spite of the fact that Japan was the party that exploited Asian countries through colonization and caused the war, Japan made a comeback to international society without paying a proper price taking advantage of the Cold War and the Korean War. And so, the pain of the Asian people, who have continued to groan after the war from the wounds that modern Japan's colonization and war of aggression left in various regions of Asia and the elimination of a possibility for these countries to accomplish self-supporting development, shows a stark contrast with the comfort and abundance that today's Japanese people have enjoyed. Therefore, in the case of a Japanese person, whether a member of the generation that took part in the war or a member of the generation that was born after it, all Japanese people must assume the responsibility for war reparations as well as a moral responsibility toward the people of the victim countries. If the Japanese people at the least do not show an attitude of taking responsibility for the war in the form of such war reparations, then Japan, as a member of international society in the 21st century, will never be able to rise into a position of a leader due to such heavy psychological liabilities. Like the Germans, if the new Japanese people who have not experienced the war can courageously face up to the historical wrongdoings of their ancestors, and make war reparations through moral bravery, Japan will be able to put down its historical liability, and furthermore, become the leader to open a new era of peace in Asia.

After the war, Japan was incorporated into international society without properly apologizing to Asian countries and Asian people and omitting the process of making reparations. This was partly due to the circumstances of the times with the occupation of the American forces after the war as well as the advent of the Cold War, but the main reason was that Japan was not prepared for self-reflection. First of all, Japan hitched on the logic of America's occupation policy and easily escaped from a sense of responsibility toward Asia. And it was difficult for Japan to have a sense of responsibility toward Asia, because Japan, as the only non-Western country to successfully modernize by pursuing the *Datsuaron* (Escape from Asia), thought that it was reasonable that Asian countries should be its targets of domination. It seems that Japan inwardly thought that since Japan had been defeated by the United States, it had no choice other than to be occupied by and accept the reform policies of the United States, but there was no need to apologize to or make reparations for Asian countries. Therefore, Japan adhered to a dignified posture in the negotiations to normalize diplomatic relations with Korea and made certain that expressions of self-reflection or responsibility on historical issues would not be included in the Treaty on Basic Relations. In particular, it was impossible to punish those who were responsible for the past wrongdoings, because wartime bureaucrats, politicians, and businessmen seized the initiative once more in the process of restoring the economy and forming a political order after the war. Even though these forces made a strong movement to revise the Peace Constitution in the 1960s, it failed due to opposition from the majority of the Japanese people who had directly experienced the war. However, the postwar generation, who have been educated by these ruling forces who did not repent on the past, will have a stronger sense of feeling that colonial rule and war of aggression have nothing to do with them as time goes by, which arouses concerns that movements to revise the Constitution and the conservative swing will be accelerated in the future. In this sense, it has become more important for Japan to reflect upon its historical wrongdoings in the past and provide well-informed history education to the new generation.

As seen in Chapter 2, according to Ruth Benedict, Western culture has been formed based on sin, whereas Japanese culture is based on typical shame (*haji*, 恥), or humiliation. Ruth Benedict analyzed that the Japanese were much more fearful of tarnishing their honor by committing a crime rather than committing a crime itself. In other words, as long as their wrong deeds do not come into the view of others, the Japanese do not need to be shameful, and do not think it necessary to reveal or acknowledge it. In addition, *sekentei* (世間体, saving face) is a word that expresses the mindset of the Japanese to place importance on how one is viewed in the eyes of others, which is closely related to the concept of shame (*haji*) as analyzed by Ruth Benedict. Japan's distortion of history and bold attitude toward victim countries can be identified on the basis of this cultural and psychological understanding. In conclusion, it seems that the Japanese people consider it a national humiliation to acknowledge the historical wrongdoings of colonization and invasion in the early 20th century, and regard it as tarnishing the country's honor. This is particularly why Japan flatly denies the major case of its violation of human rights during the war, namely, mobilization and sexual enslavery of military comfort women. Even worse, there are some rightwing figures that strongly claim that the Nanjing Massacre in China was fabricated. However, the Japanese are overlooking the fact that people around the world consider the act of refusing to acknowledge clear historical wrongdoings as far more dishonorable. Denying historical facts, in order not to feel humiliated and therefore to protect one's honor is ultimately causing the result of demeaning one's honor even more. The problem is that Japan's ruling class does not even realize this and is pursuing a history of denial and oblivion about past wrongdoings. In short, a considerable number of Japanese people are denying their original sin of being the perpetrator of invasion or colonization and only emphasize the wretchedness and tragedy of war. Consequently, they are inverting values by turning sense of guilt into a victim mentality and falling into a pit of oblivion where they do not recognize the responsibility of a perpetrator.

While Japan glamorizes and yearns for the fruits of the colonization and invasion by the foreign expansion policy of imperialism, Japan denies and tries to conceal the severe treatment and exploitation toward other countries that occurred consequentially in the process. What is the true honor of the country of Japan? Thoroughly reflecting upon and introspecting its past of incredible wrongdoings and preparing a new milestone toward the future - isn't this the genuine way to regain Japan's honor? However, it seems that Japan places importance on the honor of the family (家) and small groups, but makes light of genuine national honor. The people of the world are expecting Japan to recognize its historical wrongdoings and truly repent, but Japan is going contrary to these expectations. Japan's distortion of history is an insult to countless Asian people who were brutally killed and raped by Japanese soldiers in Nanjing and various other regions of Asia. This is an act of stealing even the rightful spot entitled to the sacrificed souls, and furthermore, it may extend to disgracing all Japanese people.

The reason that Japan fails to properly understand the situation and position of Asian countries and Asian people and cannot make healthy relationships with them is that Japan does not have a critical mind towards itself. In other words, Japan and the Japanese people lack a serious introspection and self-reflection on how they treated Asian countries and Asian people in its history. Even though it is impossible to turn back the wrongdoings of the past, what is important is how one views them and what efforts are made to heal the wounds. If such efforts are not made, it is inevitable that the shame of not knowing that one has committed a humiliating act is added to the list of shameful acts. It is because Japan does not realize such national humiliation that it cannot stand straight in Asia and the whole world.

No matter which country, the role of the press or media is very important in forming the political attitude or historical values of its people. Depending on whether the press and media is conservative or progressive, it can be said that the general public, which accesses it on a daily basis, is strongly influenced. On the other hand, it can be said that the primary reason why Japanese people cannot have a proper view of history today is due to the screening of elementary, middle, and high school textbooks conducted by the Japanese Ministry of Education. The government minimizes or deletes the contents that give an unfavorable impression of Japan or can be disadvantageous to Japan by screening history textbooks. Even though the Japanese government's historical awareness is regressive, the press and media should play their role as a balancing weight, so that ordinary people are not buried in state-led history education. However, the reality in Japan is not the case. When examining the media coverage of the Women's International War Crimes Tribunal on Japan's Military Sexual Slavery held in December 2000 in Tokyo, most of the mass media of Japan, except for the *Asahi Shimbun* and some local newspapers (*Ryukyu Shimpo*, *Okinawa Times*), were passive in reporting the news and showed an attitude that was close to concealment. In addition, ETV, an educational television channel affiliated to NHK, covered the Women's International War Crimes Tribunal, but pursuant to the top management of NHK, the original intent was distorted and key messages of the trial was entirely shattered. The title of the program itself was changed from 'Questioning wartime sexual violence by the Japanese military' to 'Questioning wartime sexual violence,' the testimony of a Japanese soldier was deleted from the aired version, and the scene where a court sentence acknowledged the responsibility of the Japanese government and Emperor Hirohito was deleted. In short, the actual message that the Women's International War Crimes Tribunal sought to convey was entirely deleted as it was considered disadvantageous to Japan and the Japanese people. The reason why such mainstream press shifted toward becoming passive in covering Japan's war responsibility or the issue of Japanese military sexual slavery was that after the late 1990s, historical revisionism movements that pursued nationalism became stronger, and there was a conspicuous tendency of giant mass media outlets to follow this trend. In the case of *Yomiuri Shimbun* and NHK, which are Japan's greatest media outlets in the newspaper and television sectors respectively, power is concentrated on conservative top management, and these media have diversified and expanded its market after the late 1980s. Along with these giant media outlets, almost all the mass media outlets in Japan showed a strong tendency to place diversification of markets in response to globalization and the attitude of nationalism at the forefront after the 1990s.[535] In short, in Japan the Ministry of Education exercises control over elementary, middle, and high school textbooks through the screening system, and the mass media, which took the lead in praising militarism during the war, still has a conservative rightwing nationalistic view of the press even after the war, so it seems difficult to expect the Japanese people to form a desirable historical awareness through school or mass media education.

Japan, the perpetrator, came to harbor a victim's mentality due to the air raids and atomic bombings of the American forces and shortage of daily necessities at the final stages of the war. In addition, the Japanese people refused to assume their responsibility by shifting the war responsibility on a certain few leaders of the military authorities. Figures who were hanged after the trial were enshrined together in the Yasukuni Shrine and are worshipped as gods, and even the figures who were imprisoned were all released by the mid-1950s. In this sense, nobody among the Japanese people had actually taken the responsibility of war. This has rather acted as a factor behind the bold attitude of Japan within international society. Furthermore, by turning all responsibilities towards the war itself, Japan has not acknowledged the responsibilities of individuals who committed horrendous crimes and has granted exoneration. Therefore, it has become even more difficult to expect the ordinary Japanese people, who did not participate actively in the war, to have a sense of responsibility toward the war. Consequently, since nobody had taken the responsibility, postwar Japanese people could easily say that the war was bad and show the appearance of pursuing peace in their own way. In this sense, one may call postwar pacifism in Japan 'pacifism with no responsibility.'[536]

There are many cases where Japanese people make extremely important decisions depending on the atmosphere of the occasion without undergoing rational discussions. And then later on, even if the decision proves to have been a mistake, they habitually make the excuse that 'At the time, it was not an atmosphere in which one could oppose to.' Therefore, even if one has been involved in an important political decision, one keeps making excuses and no one tries to take responsibility for the merits and demerits caused by the decision. The Japanese war leaders who were brought to the Tokyo Trial seriously repeated excuses such as 'It had no ill intentions,' 'I did not do it intentionally.' Thus, the then Japanese people kept making excuses and refused to take responsibility for their own acts, so how can the Japanese people of today be expected to take the responsibility of the war that they did not wage, in other words, the war that the previous generation caused? To this day, many conservative rightwing figures in Japan still make excuses such as 'Japan's domination of Asia was to lead underdeveloped neighboring countries into the right path,' 'Japan was cornered to the point of no choice other than war.'[537]

In Japan, people are taught not to cause *meiwaku* (迷惑), in other words, to trouble or cause inconvenience to others. Causing trouble to others is something that Japanese people are very reluctant to do. Causing trouble to others is a humiliating act and something that tarnishes one's honor and becomes a laughingstock to others. Therefore, it is the etiquette of Japanese people to conduct oneself extremely prudently, with concerns about the impact and injury that not only words that are used in broadcasting and newspapers, but a trivial word in daily life might bring forth. However, it seems as though such attitude in life only applies domestically within Japan and fails to be applied to other countries and their people beyond borders. If trouble caused by an individual becomes a humiliation, then trouble, or even worse, pain and great damage, caused to other countries and their people certainly should be an even greater humiliation, but this does not seem to be the case at all. In addition, while the Japanese people are careful about even trivial words among themselves, they habitually spit out absurd remarks toward and rub salt into the wounds of Asians to whom they caused tremendous pain and damage in the early 20th century.

Shinzo Abe, who represents the rightwing political forces of Japan, had continued to visit the Yasukuni Shrine directly and indirectly during his service as the Prime Minister, where the war criminals were enshrined. While claiming to advocate freedom and democracy, Abe had shown the contradiction of visiting the Yasukuni Shrine. Max Boot, the United States' major columnist of Neocon mentioned the shock that he felt when he visited the Yasukuni Shrine in 2003 in a contribution to *The Weekly Standard*, the publication of Neocon. In his contribution titled 'Japan's memory lapses,' Boot revealed that he was greatly shocked by the exhibitions in the Yushukan Museum, which is the war museum inside the Yasukuni Shrine. Boot showed his astonishment and rage, as the contents of the exhibition tried to justify all of Japan's military actions up to Japan's defeat in 1945.[538] Meanwhile, Japan views China and North Korea as countries that have problems with respect to human rights and democracy. However, it is necessary to examine whether Japan has the qualifications to discuss the human rights issues of China or

North Korea. If Japan wishes to discuss the human rights issues of these countries, Japan must first seriously reflect upon its own acts of violation of human rights toward China, the Korean Peninsula, and Asian countries, and make the necessary apologies and compensations. Furthermore, Japan must rethink compulsory education on patriotism, such as the flag raising of the Hinomaru and the chanting of the Kimigayo in unison, which is similar to dictatorship.

While the Japanese claim to love beauty, why had they habitually committed such hideous and evil acts in various regions of Asia without a moment's hesitation in the early 20th century? The Japanese are known to be considerate toward others, but why have they so easily blurted out remarks that are no different from rubbing salt in the wounds of Asian people rather than soothing them after the war? The Japanese are famous for being clean, but how come their actions make Asians feel sick and nauseous? Humans discover the vitality of their souls and prove the value of their existence when they reflect upon their faults, big or small. Likewise, countries and people have a bright future and can create peace with other countries and people when they plainly reveal their historical wrongdoings and repent. An adequate compensation should be made for Japan's forced labor and sexual slavery issues, but what is more important is how to resolve the issue of past wounds and emotions. Japanese military sexual slavery victims have been holding demonstrations every Wednesday in front of the Japanese embassy in Korea for nearly 30 years, but the situation can change immensely if Japan's Prime Minister or leading figures hold their hands and give one word of apology. Furthermore, if the Japanese Emperor comes in person to make that apology, it will be enough to assuage the hard feelings.

Modern Japan has pursued an imperialist policy in order to become an empire, like the United Kingdom, in Asia. Thus, Japan went to war with Qing (China) and Russia, colonized Taiwan and the Korean Peninsula which were neighbors in East Asia, and swallowed up China's Manchuria. Furthermore, Japan invaded mainland China and even occupied Southeast Asia, and waged the Pacific War against the United States which was emerging as the strongest state in the world. Such greed of Japan eventually brought forth a gruesome outcome for not only Japan itself but also Asian countries. The image of an empire that can generally be envisioned is exploitation and plundering of the periphery. Accordingly, the periphery becomes poorer and poorer, and the core becomes richer and richer. In reality, many such empires had existed, but they did not last long. This is because after a while, resistance against the core increases, so the costs of domination exceed the profits gained from the periphery. However, on the other hand, empires that made the periphery interested in the subsistence of the empire, by not discriminating and actively investing in the periphery, were able to last for a much longer period of time.[539] Even when viewed from this general theory perspective, modern

Japan's imperialist experiment could only end in failure. This is because Japan discriminated against, exploited, and suppressed Asian countries, which were the periphery, based on military power, only for the interests of mainland Japan, which was the core. If Japan had meditated on this lesson from history, Japan's footsteps after the war would have been different than the way it unfolded. Japan revived its economy through the Korean War and also made a comeback to the international stage through the Treaty of San Francisco during this war. Japan also boosted its economy even more through war profits from the Vietnam War, and stepped up as the world's second largest economic power in 1968. Of course, even such an outcome was largely achieved through the pain and economic subordination of the periphery. Even so, Japan would have been able to newly position itself as the leading state of Asia if it had helped the growth of the periphery since the 1970s as the second largest economic power in the world and devoted efforts to heal historical wounds instead of bringing about territorial disputes. If so, Japan would have been able to construct an imperial order in a new dimension and coexist with other peripheral countries as the core of Asia.

4. Japan's Historical Wandering

When the Western powers started to plunder China, which was the leading power of Asia during the mid-19th century, Japan came to set *Datsuaron* (Escape from Asia), the idea of escaping from Asia and pursuing the West, as its national strategy. This *Datsuaron* was conceptualized by Fukuzawa Yukichi, who defined China as a negative subject, the Oriental absolute monarchy, and he presented *Datsua Nyuo* (Leave Asia, enter Europe) as the strategy for modern Japan's civilization and survival. Of course, there were discussions of a Pan-Asian solidarity in response to the pressures of the West on Asia, but the Pan-Asian solidarity was crowded out by *Datsuaron* (Escape from Asia), as China helplessly handed over various kinds of concessions to the Western powers and Korea failed in the Gapsin Coup. However, while pushing ahead with Western modernization through the Western methods of imperialism and colonialism, Japan did also advocate Asianism. Thus, Japan needed justification for expanding markets and accumulating capital through colonization and invasion of Asian countries. Therefore, modern Japan imitated and followed the West, while consistently stressing that it was a member of Asia. Such strategy and world view of Japan made Japan harbor superiority over and contempt for Asia but also feel a sense of belonging and homogeneity. This contradiction of awareness of modern Japan made Japan propound the narrative justification of liberating Asians in the Pacific War while colonizing and invading Asia as a national development strategy.

This attitude of Japan toward Asia can be examined through the Western-oriented perspective of othering and belittling the East, in other words, through the prism of Orientalism. To the Westerners, 'Orient' referred to people or cultures that were less advanced, regressive, and stagnant. This is based on the fictional belief that Western society was more advanced and progressive. Traditional Orientalism was an imperialist world view that stressed the stagnancy, backwardness, and heteronomy of the Eastern people. In his book *Orientalism*, Edward Said limited the range to the Middle East, but in *Culture and Imperialism*, he expanded the concept to refer to all other regions in contrast to the West, the vast center of modernity. This indicates that Western imperialism and colonialism exercised overwhelming power and influence even in the realm of culture, beyond the realms of military, politics, and economy.[540] If this concept is expanded even more, in the perspective of a certain center or advanced region, the periphery or less advanced regions are pictured as pre-modern, stagnant, and unstable. Therefore, it can be said that the attitude of modern Japan toward Asian countries is a projection of such Orientalism.

In this concept of Orientalism, modern Japan was an advanced society that had succeeded in the Meiji Restoration and became a modern country, whereas Asian countries were societies that were still less advanced and unable to escape from stagnancy. Some conservative historians of the United States, such as John Fairbank, evaluated Japan's development of capitalism after the Meiji Restoration as a success, while evaluating other Asian countries, which failed to achieve modernization, as less advanced regions in contrast to Japan.[541] This can be seen as a typical form of historical awareness in which the idea of Orientalism has been projected. Such historical awareness can be excessively one-sided. This is because on the other side of success, the pain and frustration of numerous people is inherent. It can only be considered a true success if such aspects are included in making the evaluation. In this regard, modern Japan could be viewed as a massive altar on which the health, lives, and happiness of the majority of the people were offered for the ambition of the few rulers who strove to accomplish national prosperity and military power in a short period of time. For instance, Meiji Japan recorded an annual average growth rate of 5%, but 80-90% of the factory workers in the cotton industry, which was the key industry at the time, were female workers under the age of 25. The daughters of poor farmers who were sweet-talked into working at the factories were forced to endure heavy labor for 14-17 hours a day while resting only two days a month. Due to chronic fatigue, deficiency of nutrition, and unsanitary living conditions, there were cases where diseases such as pneumonia spread and infected hundreds of female workers in the same factory. Even if Japan succeeded in accumulating capital in the Meiji Period, what awaited the workers who actually underpinned this success was not success but deficiency of nutrition, disease, and a shortened life.[542] This structure eventually accompanied the pain and sacrifice of Asian countries in the process of strengthening foreign expansion by Japan.

To pre-modern Japan, China was always a model to imitate and an object of reverence. However, after succeeding in the Meiji Restoration, Japan's new leading force considered China as an object to overcome and dominate based on the *Datsuaron* (Escape from Asia). Thus, Japan actively accepted the modern institutions and technologies of the West in order to build the foundation for modernization and initiated the First Sino-Japanese War after augmenting its military and eventually achieved victory. In the background, the perception of modern Japan's ruling class or intellectuals on China, namely their perception as 'oriental despotism' or 'oriental stagnation' acted as a logic that justified and legitimized its invasion and domination of China as the dismantling and renewal of the old Chinese society. China was an object that was necessary for Japan's existence but also a mountain and enormous 'other' to overcome. In this sense, Japan's modernization was a process through which Japan formed its self-awareness by showing that Japan was different from China and that it was superior. Furthermore, Japan emphasized the independent existence of Japan and Japanese culture by highlighting its cultural heterogeneity with China and by 'othering' China. Despite the fact that China and Chinese culture was the premise on the existence of Japan and Japanese culture, it was so enormous that modern Japan invaded the Chinese continent and committed atrocious acts without hesitation based on superiority and contempt in order to deny and overcome such gigantic 'other'.[543]

Under this ideological background, imperialist Japan showed a collective madness that invoked a fundamental skepticism on humans. It can be said that basically the entire Japanese society was intoxicated with collective madness as follows: the Japanese people during the First Sino-Japanese War who laughed and smiled happily while reading newspapers showing pictures of Japanese soldiers stabbing Chinese people to death, the Buddhist monks during the Russo-Japanese War who volunteered for the military saying that 'If one kills the enemy without fear or guilt, one becomes a Buddhist saint,' and the liberal writers or philosophers such as Akutagawa Ryunosuke (芥川龍之介, 1892-1927) or Uchimura Kanzo (内村鑑三, 1861-1930) who joined the vigilante groups that mercilessly killed Korean and Chinese people during the Great Kanto Earthquake of 1923. However, some comfort can be found in the fact that in the midst of such collective madness, there was a small minority of conscientious Japanese people. Some examples are Kotoku Shusui (幸德秋水, 1871-1911), an anarchist who opposed the annexation of Korea, and Yanaihara Tadao (矢内原忠雄, 1893-1961), a Christian humanist who strongly raised his voice against the Second Sino-Japanese War. The people who were not bewitched under collective madness were an extremely small minority. Sometimes, these people had to pay a big price for their resistance as in the case of Kotoku Shusui, who ended up being executed.[544]

Various research findings show that the roots of the Japanese people originated from people on the Korean Peninsula. Professor Kohama Mototsuku of Osaka University investigated the skull morphology of the Japanese and found that the origins of modern Japanese people were the Ainu people (descendants of the Jomon people) and the people on the Korean Peninsula. Through a computer simulation, Professor Hanihara Kazuro (埴原和郎) of Tokyo University, came to the conclusion that the proportion of direct descendants of the Jomon people and immigrants of the 7th century was 1:9.6. Accordingly, he revealed that the Japanese were not homogenous but consisted of mixed-blood from a minority of natives and majority of immigrants from the Korean Peninsula. In particular, Hanihara's view was that today's Japanese people have a higher degree of similarity with today's Korean people, rather than the Ainu people who are the descendants of Jomon people.[545] Based on archaeological research findings, Professor Jared Diamond of the University of California, Los Angeles, claimed that Japanese people are descendants of people who immigrated from the Korean peninsula with rice farming technologies around B.C. 400. There are theories that the Japanese people evolved from people who settled during the Ice Age around B.C. 20000, and that horse-riding people of Central Asia came through Korea and conquered Japan around A.D. 4, but the most influential theory in Western academia is that the Japanese originated from the Korean Peninsula.[546] Of course, even if the roots are the same, it is undeniable that thousands of years in different living environments and cultures produced totally different people. However, in order to maintain its groundless pride as a country of the gods and a superior people, Japan tries not to acknowledge such scientific results and even invaded Asian countries in the early 20th century so as to prove its fictional belief.

Amidst the whirlpool of global change after the 19th century, it seems that there were two occasions where Japan well-grasped the situations, established national strategies, and put them into practice. The first occasion was that around the end of the Tokugawa Shogunate era, after Japan felt a sense of crisis due to the pressure of the West, it brought the Meiji Restoration to success and pushed ahead with modernization. The second occasion was that after being defeated in the Pacific War, Japan enacted the Peace Constitution under occupation rule, concluded the Treaty of San Francisco to its own favor during the Korean War, and became an economic power by concentrating on economic development under the umbrella of national security provided by the United States. However, such success arouses concern when recollecting the lesson that history may repeat itself. This is because among non-Western countries, Japan was the only country to succeed in Western modernization in the late 19th and early 20th century, and based on this success, Japan went ahead with colonization and invasion of

Asia and even waged war against the United States. Japan's recent movements of taking a conservative swing and seeking to become a military power after overcoming the postwar crisis and succeeding in economic development overlaps with the historical experiences that Japan actively showed the ambitions of colonization and invasion of Asian countries since the late 19th century on the basis of advanced modernization after the Meiji Restoration. Of course, the circumstances could be different if Japan were to make a resolution not to repeat the same mistake through self-reflection and introspection, and actually show such attitude in international relations. However, considering the movements of today's Japanese government and Japanese society which have shifted to the rightmost side since the end of the war, Asian countries cannot but feel concern and fear once again. The reason why we learn history and place importance in history is to refrain from repeating historical wrongdoings and to change human society into a more peaceful and improved state. Yet, Japan refuses to learn the meaning of history and is rather making the mistake of distorting history and moving toward repeating historical wrongdoings of the past.

Of course, the reason why Japan was unable to properly understand the historical lessons and showed such attitudes was partly due to the situational circumstances of that particular period. Japan, which had formed a vast empire, surrendered due to the massive air raids and atomic bombings of the Allied Forces and degenerated into an occupied country of the United States, which made Japan develop the victim mentality instead of the perpetrator mentality. Due to this situation, Japan failed to have an opportunity to make settlements on the negative history and form a new relationship with Asian countries which it had colonized and invaded in the past. Also, Asian countries which were less advanced in terms of politics and the economy, did not have the capabilities to ask Japan to take responsibility and induce Japan's self-reflection and introspection. Therefore, postwar Japan evaded the resolution of historical issues with Asian countries and devoted itself only to economic revival and growth in its national interest. In particular, during the Cold War, Japan provided a military base for the United States pursuant to the US-Japan Security Treaty, and left the issues of defense and military to the United States with the promise that the United States would maintain Japan's security. However, the burden of security in Asia ended up being borne by countries such as Korea and Taiwan, which were much less advanced in terms of the economy, and within Japan, Okinawa made the sacrifice of accommodating most of the United States' military bases.

Postwar Japan has influenced the world economy as a member of advanced countries after becoming an economic power without properly establishing relationships with Asian countries after the war. Rather, Japan has evaded self-reflection and future-oriented efforts to restore its relationships with Asian countries that it barbarously dominated. Modern

Japan had pushed ahead with foreign expansion under the rationale that it had to protect adjacent countries and regions, namely its zone of interest, in order to protect its own territory, namely its zone of sovereignty. In this process, Japan colonized Taiwan and Korea, ruled over Manchuria by establishing Manchukuo (the Empire of Manchuria) which was no different from a colony, and even invaded China. Furthermore, after heightening a sense of crisis by claiming that the Allied Forces was besieging Japan (ABCD encirclement)[547], Japan occupied the Indochina Peninsula amidst the power vacuum due to the war in Europe, under the pretext of liberating Asia. Under the logic of protecting its zone of sovereignty and zone of interest, breaking the siege for survival, and liberating Asia, Japan went as far as to make a surprise attack on the United States' Pearl Harbor, causing the Pacific War. In order to justify the 'liberation of Asia' as its cause for war, Japan should have liberated Taiwan and Korea which it had already colonized, returned Manchuria to China, and furthermore, withdrawn from China. In addition, Japan should have helped Southeast Asian countries establish their governments immediately after pushing away the Western forces from Southeast Asia, and should have withdrawn as soon as possible. Also, Japan claims that it was compelled to engage in war due to the besiegement of the Allied Forces, but it was merely to protect not only the regions it had occupied through the Second Sino-Japanese War but also Manchuria and the colonies, Korea and Taiwan. In other words, since it would be impossible to continue its war and occupation in China if the supply of resources from the United States, such as oil, was cut, Japan attempted to solve the issue of lack of resources by occupying Southeast Asia. Furthermore, Japan thought that if it withdrew from China, then it would be forced to give up all the foreign territories it had strived to acquire over the years.[548] Although it was a war that was executed under a fictional logic and belief, the Japanese have believed it was legitimate, which is why they do not feel any sense of perpetration against the Asian people and do not even think of making any proper apologies. Therefore, even the gestures of self-reflection and apology that were displayed by somewhat conscientious political leaders in the early 1990s after the end of the Cold War are on the verge of being denied by the rightist nationalist government and rightwing forces of recent days.

Historically, Japan barely has any experience in which the ordinary people became the main agent to bring forth revolutions in society systems. In the general development of human history, the power of the subjugated class grew stronger in opposition to the overwhelming power of the few members of the ruling class, and there were frequent occurrences of so-called revolutions to overthrow this power relationship. However, revolutions, in which the relationship of rulers and subordinates is changed in a violent way, accompany other side-effects and damage. This is why representative democracy, in which the ruling forces are regularly replaced through elections came to settle. Even in countries adopting representative democracy, the formation of the public's subjective and independent consciousness depends considerably on historical experiences of the past. The Japanese people prior to 1945 obeyed the militarist system unconditionally,[549] and even after the war, the Japanese people conformed to the new system and failed to show independent attitudes. More problematic is the fact that the ruling class, which had been governing such people, neither made a thorough self-reflection on its history nor took on an attitude of trying to prevent the Japanese people, along with the Asian people, from being in misery again. The greatest change in Japanese history was manifested through the Meiji Restoration of 1868 and modernization which followed. However, Japan's modernization was limited to material modernization oriented on practical aspects such as industrialization, and the values and ideologies of democracy, fundamental human rights, civil liberties, and rights to equality were nothing more than ornaments. Therefore, prior to 1945, Japan formed 'subjects' under an authoritarian militarist system, but failed to nurture 'citizens' in a democracy. As these subjects were the fruits of the militarist system led by the emperor, there was no chance for these subjects to become the principal agents of a republican political system. In Japan prior to surrendering to the Allied Forces in 1945, democracy was merely an object of rule and suppression by the Japanese Emperor and the ruling class.[550] After the war, democratization and demilitarization was strongly propelled by the United States' occupation rule. Along with it, the Peace Constitution, which degraded the Japanese Emperor into a symbolic figure, was established and enacted. Accordingly, Japan finally prepared a foundation to form a democratic system. However, since this was not initiated by the Japanese but heteronomously granted by the occupation army, after the occupation rule came to an end, the consciousness of the Japanese people showed a considerable tendency to return to the period before the war. Despite the fact that 20 years have passed since the beginning of the 21st century, the historical awareness and independent identity of Japanese society has become rather weaker.

Up until the 1980s, Japan recorded enormous surpluses in its trade with the United States. Such profits were refluxed to the United States in the form of bond investments, which consequentially covered the fiscal deficits of the United States. In addition, due to the adjustment of exchange rates according to the Plaza Accord, the yen value increased dramatically and Japan had to bear tremendous losses. This was the price that postwar Japan had to pay in return for having saved an enormous amount on defense spending by being provided with an umbrella of national security pursuant to the US-Japan Security Treaty and for achieving economic development by relying on the United States after the war. As Japan only cared for the United States and failed to make any effort toward Asia, Asian countries became dissatisfied with Japan, which eventually led Japan to rely on the United States even more. Since 2010, Japan has been pushed behind by China in terms of economic size, but it is still a global economic power. However, when historically considering the fact that almost all countries that dominated the world through military power or economic power eventually declined without lasting more than one century, it cannot be guaranteed how long Japan will be able to keep its current level of economic development. Therefore, while it still has sufficient economic power, if Japan uses its power in a useful way for the Asian countries, which it inflicted tremendous damage and pain upon, it will be favorable for the future of Japan and Asian countries alike.

On August 9, 1999, 54 years after the atomic bombing of Nagasaki (長崎), a bill to stipulate the Hinomaru (日の丸) and the Kimigayo (君が代) as the national flag and national anthem was passed by the Japanese National Diet with an overwhelming number of votes. Also, this bill stipulates Kigensetsu (紀元節) before the defeat in war, a fictitious day (February 11), namely the enthronement day of Emperor Jimmu from a mythical past, as the 'national foundation day.' During the early 20th century when Japan's militarism was rampant in the name of being loyal to the Japanese Emperor, and when Japan colonized and invaded Asian countries, Hinomaru and Kimigayo always existed in the background. Therefore, the fact that Japan enacted a bill on its national flag and national anthem in the last year of the 20th century leaves behind an ominous premonition in that it can be comprehended as a will to repeat once again the nationalistic delusion and consequent tragedies of neighboring countries that modern Japan created in the early 20th century.[551] The country name of Japan and the title of Japanese Emperor were created during the late 7th century and early 8th century and have been used since then, but it was only after the Meiji Restoration that the presence of Japan or the Japanese Emperor was settled more deeply in the consciousness of the ordinary people.[552] Even so, there are many Japanese people that believe as a fact the fictitious assertion that the popular consciousness about Japan as a state and the history of worshipping the Japanese Emperor as a god[553] have existed long before written history. Furthermore, the act of Prime Ministers and influential politicians visiting the Yasukuni Shrine, where war criminals are enshrined, as well as the nationalistic history textbook screening, which refuses to recognize Japan's past war of aggression or fault of colonization, are all evoking opposition and concern from neighboring Asian countries.

Japan's Prime Minister Koizumi abruptly visited Pyongyang in September 2002 and announced the Japan-North Korea Pyongyang Declaration with Supreme Leader of the Democratic People's Republic of Korea, Kim Jong-il, and decided to enter diplomatic relations at an early point. In this declaration, Japan expressed 'sincere repentance and heartfelt apology' for colonial rule. In response, North Korea agreed to make efforts to resolve the issue of Japanese people who had been kidnapped, and to accept economic cooperation instead of making claims for reparations for colonization. Through such high-level meetings between Japan and North Korea, normalization of diplomatic relations between the two countries was anticipated, but it failed to advance due to the containment of the United States and aggravating public opinion within Japan. The United States, which had defined Iran, Iraq, and North Korea as the 'axis of evil' after the 9.11 terrorist attacks and strengthened economic blockade against them, held Japan in check by raising the issues of North Korea's nuclear weapon development. Even within Japan, as voices that instigated national sentiment regarding the issue of kidnapped Japanese people became louder, Japan's relations with North Korea became rather aggravated. However, it can be said that Japan's attitude of violently criticizing North Korea on the issue of kidnapped Japanese people without properly reflecting upon or apologizing for Japan's colonization of the Korean Peninsula and the unjust discrimination and suppression of Korean people residing in Japan after the war, is the height of self-centered nationalism. North Korea's acts of violating human rights should be heavily criticized by international society. However, as for Japan, the task of looking back on how many Korean people they killed, forcefully drafted and conscripted, and even used as comfort women enforcing sexual slavery in the early 20th century, should come first.

Japan shows the contradictory attitude of recognizing its modern history as a history of resistance against Western powers, while refusing to justly accept the criticism of Asian countries and Asian people against the invasion and colonization by Japan. The Japanese people even criticize such criticism by Asian people by defining it as 'evil nationalism.' This is a criticism that rather the Japanese people themselves should receive. If Japan wishes to criticize the nationalism of Asian countries, Japan must first properly respond to the requests of Asian countries to hold responsibility for war of aggression and colonization. The reason why Japan is criticized by Asian countries and faces opposition from Asians is that Japan refuses to reflectively introspect on its own history and neglects making apologies and reparations for the pain and damage that it caused to neighboring countries. Furthermore, as the economic abundance that it has enjoyed for years is starting to become unstable, Japanese society today is showing the aspect of wandering about aimlessly with no sense of direction in respect to itself and others, the world and history, and life itself.

CHAPTER 11

RESPONSE OF INTERNATIONAL SOCIETY AND SUGGESTIONS FOR JAPAN AND ASIA

1. Response of International Society and Necessity of Solidarity

It is said that the number of people sacrificed by 'political and military violence' by one state to another state and by one human to another human, such as wars, revolutions, civil wars, and persecution, in the 20th century reaches 170 million. Representatively, the death toll was approximately 10 million in World War I and 50 million in World War II. In the Pacific War, the death toll was approximately 3 million for Japan and 20 million in other Asian countries. In our world, which has already greeted the 21st century, there are roaming spirits of those who were not able to live out their lives and were unjustly sacrificed.[554]

After World War II, Germany was directly occupied by the United States and neighboring countries, whereas Japan was solely occupied by the United States, which made Asian countries lose the opportunity to impose their intentions on Japan. Germany's neighboring countries were all strong nations that had substantial influence on Germany. On the other hand, in the case of Japan, the neighboring Asian countries were nascent countries with a weak awareness of human rights as they were ruled by dictatorships. These countries also strived to maintain their systems and achieve economic development by relying on the economic powers of the United States and Japan and as a result, the voices of the victims of colonization or war were silenced. At first, just like Japan, Germany was unable to punish war criminals properly due to the unusual situation of the Cold War, especially since Germany was divided into East Germany and West Germany. Eventually, Germany changed its attitude as the Holocaust started to receive more attention and as international society started to put pressure on Germany. Behind Germany's change in attitude, were the leading role taken on by Israel, a Holocaust victim country, and active activities of Jewish people around the world. However, China, Korea, Vietnam and other Southeast Asian countries that suffered from Japan's colonization and invasion did not have the ability or the will to exercise influence on or pressure Japan, as they were caught up in civil wars or economic difficulties amidst the Cold War situation. Germany could only survive through reconciliation and cooperation with neighboring countries. On the other hand, Japan was able to develop without reconciliation and cooperation with neighboring Asian countries, as it used the Cold War situation to its advantage by becoming one axis of the hierarchical capitalist system under the security umbrella of the United States. Due to the various reasons mentioned above, the outcomes of postwar settlements of Japan and Germany were considerably different. Most of the Nazi war criminals of Germany, who had caused severe pain to Jewish and European people, disappeared after being sentenced for their crimes or lived shameful lives in hiding. On the other hand, most of the war criminals of Japan were not prosecuted, with the exception of a few, and rather they assumed important posts in the government and business world after the war, living prosperous lives revered as heroes. When considering the above situation, between Germany and Japan, which is a more just society? Now, people all around the world who love justice and peace should come together to stop the history-denying and inhumane footsteps of Japan. These people must continue to reveal the true face of Japan's crimes and inform the world about Japan's acts of covering up and denying historical wrongdoings, and furthermore, make international society bring Japan into judgment. It is necessary to make all the people of the world see and feel the atrocities of modern Japan by erecting memorials in various places around the world, such as the United States, Europe, China, Korea, Japan, Taiwan, Vietnam, the Philippines, Indonesia, Singapore and Australia. These activities would not be revenge against Japan, but an attempt to make Japan realize on its own what it had done and to protect the universal values of world history such as justice and peace.

As seen above, Germany's exemplary settlement of historical wrongdoings was fundamentally based on its own will and efforts, but it cannot be overlooked that behind it was the strong and persistent pressure and efforts of international society, such as the Allied Forces, Israel, and the Jewish society.[555] In this sense, it can also be said that the reason why Japan's settlement of historical wrongdoings is insufficient is that there was a lack of pressure and effort from both the victim countries in Asia, including China and Korea, and the Allied Forces at the time. Even when taking into account the fact that the situation of postwar Asia was different from Europe and that there were adroit efforts on Japan's part to avoid war responsibility, it can be said that international society played an extremely meager role in pressuring Japan and making efforts to resolve the issue. Therefore, if Asian countries simply interpret Japan's failure to settle its historical wrongdoings through the narrow framework based on the conservativeness and irresponsibility of Japanese society and respond with national sentiment, this may arouse opposition in the unprepared Japan and even has the risk of being used as a political tool by conservative right wing forces within Japan. Considering this situation, it is necessary to have the wisdom and patience to let Japan realize for itself what kind of behavior corresponds to true national interest as a member of international society and wait for Japan to change on its own.

Whatever form it was conducted in, colonization and invasion of other countries cannot be justified in any case. In this sense, colonization and war of aggression conducted by Japan's imperialism should be dealt with apology and reparation based on deep self-reflection. Furthermore, the Japanese people of today live in a nation that benefited from the past colonization and war of aggression conducted by Japan's imperialism. Therefore, as long as they do not give up their nationality, they hold the political and moral responsibility of the acts of their past generation. Also, even if one is not a Japanese national, if one is interested in human history and justice, one holds a responsibility to fight against Japan's distortion and denial of history.

Various human rights treaty commissions, such as the United Nations Human Rights Council (UNHRC) and the Convention on the Elimination of All Forms of Discrimination against Women, and the International Labor Organization (ILO), all recommended the Japanese government to resolve the 'comfort women' issue as soon as possible.[556] In February 1996, Radhika Coomaraswamy submitted a report to the UNHRC urging the Japanese government to make an official apology and compensation, and this report included recommendations to punish people who were in charge. In other words, this report considered the comfort women system a crime against humanity and recommended the Japanese government to restore the human rights of the victims and make compensation to them, issue a written apology, and punish those who were involved with comfort stations. The report of Gay J. McDougall of the UNHRC Sub-Commission on Discrimination in August 1998, also recommended the Japanese government to ask for the responsibility of the perpetrators in collaboration with the UNHRC High Commissioner. In other words, this report stated that it was necessary to hold the perpetrators responsible for their actions and give sufficient compensation to the victims in order to sever the vicious circle of wartime sexual crimes evading punishment, and that the Japanese government should take legal responsibility. There can be no statute of limitations for war crimes and 'crimes against humanity' in international law.[557]

As the Japanese government continued to refuse to make an official apology and compensation for Japanese military sexual slavery victims, the US House of Representatives, the EU Parliament, and the parliaments of several other countries adopted resolutions in 2007 urging the Japanese government to make an official apology and compensation for the sexual slavery of comfort women. While discussions were underway in the US House of Representatives regarding the resolution on comfort women,

Japan's Prime Minister Shinzo Abe (安倍晋三) denied in 2007 that the Japanese military had forcefully mobilized comfort women, which caused a public uproar in the United States. Then Prime Minister Abe apologized that his remarks had been a mistake, making it difficult to submit the motion of the comfort women resolution to the House. However, when 45 members of the Japanese National Diet and leading figures of Japanese society put an advertisement in *The Washington Post* that stated 'there was no forcibleness regarding Japanese military comfort women by the government and they were treated well,' it received strong backlashes from the public again. Consequently, the US House of Representatives unanimously adopted the Japanese military comfort women resolution on July 30, 2007, officially urging the Japanese government to make an apology. Following the example of the US House of Representatives, the Dutch Parliament, the Canadian House of Representatives, and the EU Parliament passed their respective comfort women resolutions as well. These resolutions define that 'Japanese military sexual slavery was an unprecedented sexual abuse as well as an exploitation of women's rights in the mid-20th century, and the Japanese government has an obligation to educate its people accurately on this matter and to apologize to the victims.'

Thus, the reason the Japanese military 'comfort women' issue caught the attention of international society was that solidarity actions were taken beyond borders by women and various women's organizations and civic groups, not only from the victim countries of Korea and China but also from the perpetrator country of Japan. Since January 1992, the Korean Council for Women Drafted for Military Sexual Slavery by Japan has held demonstrations in front of the Japanese Embassy in Korea every Wednesday, and the number of gatherings has already exceeded 1,400. These demonstrations have requested the Japanese government apologize and make compensations to Japanese military 'comfort women,' punish the people who are responsible, and properly describe the truth about comfort women in Japanese history textbooks. The participation of civic groups from home and abroad has increased over the years, and on December 14, 2011, the Statue of Peace (Sonyeosang – literally 'Statue of Girl' in Korean, Comfort Woman Statue) was erected in front of the Japanese Embassy in Korea in order to commemorate the 1,000th 'Wednesday Demonstration.' With this as momentum, numerous Statues of Peace were later erected all over the country in Korea. Furthermore, despite Japan's obstruction by every possible means, in July 2013, a 'Comfort Woman Statue', symbolizing damage due to Japanese military sexual slavery, was erected for the first time outside Korea in a city park in Glendale of California, the United States, which is a city with a population of approximately 200,000. Later, Statues of Peace related to comfort women were erected in Michigan and New York in the United States, as well as Australia, China, and the Philippines. At the same time, 'monuments to commemorate comfort women' were established at various locations around the world to remember the victims who suffered as Japanese military sexual slaves.

After Korea's Kim Hak-sun (died in 1997) filed the first lawsuit related to the Japanese military comfort women issue, there have been ten lawsuits by 93 victims from Korea, China, Taiwan, the Philippines, and the Netherlands. These lawsuits were supported by the citizens of victim countries and the perpetrator country through joint cooperation. The joint cooperation between the citizens of victim countries and the perpetrator country of Japan during the process of the lawsuit can become a model to overcome historical obstacles and lay the groundwork for reconciliation and peace. However, all the lawsuits related to the Japanese military comfort women issue were lost. Despite the defeat, some verdicts acknowledged the fact that damage was inflicted on the Japanese military comfort women victims. This is in contrast to other types of damage claim lawsuits regarding war damages caused by the Japanese military, in which individual rights of claim were rejected based on the legal principle of 'a state without responsibility (國家無答責).'[558] In other words, the court pointed out the liability for the legislative omission of the Japanese government related to the damage relief of comfort women, and made a ruling with a suggestion attached that the executive and legislative branches should prepare a relief plan for the victims. Through such efforts, almost all of Japan's middle school history textbooks included a description of Japanese military comfort women in 1997. However, this change heightened a sense of crisis for the rightwing conservatives, and since the 2000s, descriptions related to Japanese military comfort women are gradually disappearing from textbooks due to the pressure of rightwing conservatives and the screening system by the Ministry of Education.

In December 2000, the 'Women's International Criminal Court to Try the Sexual Slavery of the Japanese Troops' was held in Tokyo, proposed by Japanese civil women's groups and with participants such as the war victims around the world, NGOs, jurists and researchers acting internationally. The final verdict was made in December 2001 in the Hague, Netherlands, after hearing the testimonies of former Japanese military comfort women who had not been able to tell anyone about their painful experience out of shame, and examining the evidence at court according to international law.[559] As the Japanese government, Emperor Hirohito, and ten former Japanese military commanders were found guilty, the verdict was a supplement to the postwar Tokyo Trial which had excluded the Japanese military comfort women issue. This Women's International Criminal Court ruled that the Japanese military 'comfort women' system was sexual slavery and a 'crime against humanity.' In addition, this court reexamined international laws of war (jus in bello, international humanitarian law), such as Convention with Respect to the Laws and Customs of War on Land which was additional clauses to the

Hague Conventions, in order to guarantee women's human rights, and emphasized that the Post-traumatic Stress Disorder (PTSD) of the female victims should also be considered.[560]

Colonialism can be considered a crime against humanity. Since the 1980s in the United States, apologies and compensations were made to American Indians, Japanese Americans, and the Aleutians. In particular, the United States made payments of USD 20,000 (equivalent to JPY 2,000,000 at the time) with a letter of apology from the President to Japanese immigrants[561] who were sent to internment camps during the Pacific War. As it was the US government that had committed the fault, the government was responsible for locating those who were eligible for compensation, and the victims were able to receive compensation regardless of their current nationality or residence. Also, Canada has been paying a check of CAD 21,000 (approximately JPY 2,000,000) with a letter of apology to the Japanese Canadians who were sent to concentration camps during the Pacific War.[562] In Australia, apologies have been made to the Aborigines, and in the United Kingdom, apologies have been made to the Maori people in New Zealand. From August to September in 2001, the 'World Conference against Racism, Racial Discrimination, Xenophobia and Related Intolerance,' namely the so-called Durban Conference, was held in South Africa. Various governments and NGOs participated in this conference and confirmed that colonization is a crime against humanity and that it deserves criticism. An inter-governmental declaration stated that 'Colonialism caused racism, racial discrimination, xenophobia and related intolerance,' and that 'Africans, African immigrants, Asians, and Asian immigrants, and Aborigines were victims of colonization and still are victims of the results of colonization.'[563] Near the end of the 20th century, in a Mass held in the St. Peter's Basilica in Rome, Pope John Paul II asked for God's forgiveness and apologized for all the sins committed by the Catholic Church over the past 2000 years. It was an official apology for the many wrongdoings in Catholic history committed under the name of religious truth, such as the Crusades, forced conversions, the Inquisitions, and persecution of the Jewish.

As we have examined above, there is a considerable number of Japanese immigrants in the United States and Canada, who had been deported and had their properties confiscated during World War II under the grounds of being from the enemy country, and only after 1988 did they receive apologies and compensations from the two governments respectively. They had become the scapegoats of Japan's original sin of the war of aggression, not by their own wrongdoings. Also, there are many Japanese immigrants in various countries in South America. They have also settled down in various countries, facing discrimination and suppression as minorities. Since they have experienced sacrifice and suffering for being Japanese or being minority immigrants, they can show compassion for other victims or suppressed people. In other words, they can speak for innocent Asians who had suffered from terrible acts of invasion and brutal colonization which modern Japan, their motherland, had inflicted on Asian countries in the early 20th century. Japanese Canadians were assisted by Chinese, Korean, Filipino, Jewish Canadians as well as Aboriginal Canadians in eliciting an apology and compensation from the Canadian government. Furthermore, these people and Japanese Canadians promoted a petition to support Ienaga's textbook lawsuit which took place in Japan in 2001, and actively participated in the movement to recommend Ienaga as a Nobel Peace Prize candidate. Therefore, if Japanese Americans and Japanese Canadians cooperate, there is a chance of bringing about change in Japan. This is because what they truly wish for is for their motherland to candidly reveal and apologize for the shameful historical wrongdoings rather than covering up and denying them. Furthermore, these people also hope for Japan to become a leading country, both in name and reality, that steps toward the morally correct direction in international society.

Postwar Japan was characterized by high economic growth, parliamentary democracy based on the confrontation and co-existence of conservative and progressive ideas, and pacifism upheld by the Peace Constitution and the US-Japan Alliance. This, in a sense, was a benefit for Japan, as Japan could drastically reduce the burden of military expenditure through the US-Japan security system and the shouldering of military risks by neighboring countries (Korea, Taiwan). While the young men of neighboring countries had to serve in the military through the draft system, the young men of Japan were able to enjoy the benefit of not serving in the military. However, the situation began to change as the Cold War came to an end and democracy advanced in neighboring countries. As the United States' demand for Japan to shoulder military expenditure became stronger and Asian countries' demands for Japan to settle historical wrongdoings exploded, Japan started to walk down the path of a rightward shift interlocked with a long-term economic recession. After the Cold War was dismantled, there were two seemingly contradictory flows in East Asia, that is, the advancement of globalization based on neoliberalism and the reinforcement of nationalistic tendencies. In particular, due to the development of information technology and the Internet, the boundaries of non-government entities such as individuals or corporations will become wider and mutual contact and dependency is expected to become stronger. However, in East Asia, despite the expansion of economic and cultural interactions, new conflicts are on the rise due to the strengthening of nationalistic characteristics of countries. In particular, as Japanese society is becoming more conservative and the Japanese government has been led by rightward political leaders such as Shinzo Abe and Yoshihide Suga, who refuse historical reconciliation, there are increasing concerns that the feud and conflicts will escalate among Asian countries.[564]

Greece, which is a member of the European Union and uses the Euro currency, has been experiencing lasting economic difficulties, receiving relief loans from the IMF for the past 8 years due to national debt. The situation of Greece has been having a significantly harmful influence on the economy of the European Union. Japan, which is suffering from a long-term economic recession, has a larger national debt than Greece but has not arrived at the level of having to receive relief loans. The reason is that in the case of Greece, most of the national debt is from abroad, but in the case of Japan, most of the national debt is from the Japanese people. Therefore, however large the national debt of Japan may be, there is barely any concern that Japan will encounter sovereign default through large amounts of money leaking outside the country. This situation has allowed Japan to not need much help from international society despite its economic difficulties and to adhere to its arrogant and shameless attitude toward Asian countries over the years. However, the national debt needs to be repaid someday and works as a factor that limits the fiscal policy of a country, and therefore it is a huge burden to the national economy. The reason Japan came to bear such a tremendous debt is that welfare expenditures drastically increased as it stepped into a super aged society and that expenses increased to provide rice subsidies and establish infrastructure in rural areas where the main voters of the ruling party reside. Furthermore, as the Japanese society is taking a rightward shift and the Japanese government is aiming to become a military power, military expenditures are gradually increasing, further resulting in increasing Japan's national debt, and this is expected to aggravate the limitations of managing fiscal policies.

Although it varies depending on society or region, personal grudges and group or national grudges are usually resolved through revenge or reconciliation. For the Japanese people, taking revenge when humiliated is recognized as an obligation and is often passed on to the next generation. The Aitsu (會津) domain, which had stood opposed to the Choshu domain that led the Meiji Restoration, were defeated and the Aitsu people were branded as rebels. Due to this, the harsh feelings that the Aitsu people collectively shared did not easily fade away even after many generations. The one who strikes may easily forget it, but the one who is struck cannot forget easily. This is true among individuals and groups, but also in relationships between countries. As a nation, even though Japan had gained the Liaodong Peninsula after the First Sino-Japanese War, it had been forced to yield this peninsula through the Tripartite Intervention led by Russia, but eventually took revenge by winning in the Russo-Japanese War. If Japan considers it to be natural to take revenge for the humiliation it suffered as an individual, group, or nation, then it should allow revenge from Asian countries and their people for the humiliation and damages that were caused by Japan and its people. If Japan does not want to be revenged, it should at least make a heartfelt apology and compensate for the damage. If Japanese people pass down their revenge for humiliation from generation to generation, apology and compensation should also be passed down to the next generation as well. Japan should have begun new international relationships with Asian countries in the 21st century by resolving the grudges harbored in Asian people from imperialist Japan's historical wrongdoings in the early 20th century. However, Japan screened movies such as 'Pride'[565] which glorified war criminals like the former Prime Minister Tojo Hideki, and denied and even beautified the atrocities committed by Japanese troops during the war. Furthermore, Japan reinstated the Hinomaru and Kimigayo which had been the symbols of Japan's militarism and Japanese Emperor System that had caused great pain to Asians, and Japan is viewing the Nanjing Massacre and the Japanese military sexual slavery issue as a fabrication or exaggeration. If such footsteps of Japan's rightwing forces continue in this direction, it will be inevitable for Japan to become more and more isolated from not only Asian countries but also from various countries around the world.

As the use of the Internet has spread globally since the 1990s, it has had an immense influence on all sectors, such as politics, the economy, society, and culture. Recently, as the use of social networking services (SNS) or YouTube has increased drastically on the Internet, positive functions and dysfunctions have appeared at the same time. With respect to the topic of this book, the harmful consequences of YouTube or social networking services raise heightened concerns. For instance, videos that deny the historical fact that there were Japanese military comfort women and insult such victims, are uploaded on YouTube sometimes. When such fake information spreads as if they are true without being filtered, victims suffer once again with a wound that cannot be erased. Therefore, it is necessary for Google which operates YouTube, to equip the system to autonomously sort through and delete such videos. If this is not enough, Google could consider creating a system that handles the problem by receiving reports from trustworthy YouTube users. If such self-purification is not at play, YouTube and the Internet will overflow with trashy news and users may eventually turn away from them. Furthermore, neglecting the situation where some people distort and deny history and insult victims is committing a 'third crime'. According to Ralph Giordano's logic, the 'first crime' is modern Japan's crime of inflicting immense suffering and damages to Asian countries and their people, the 'second crime' is psychologically suppressing and denying the 'first crime,' and the 'third crime' is neglecting the 'second crime' and not taking any measures about it. Therefore, in order not to commit the 'third crime,' when YouTube videos and fake news that distort history and insult victims are uploaded, it is necessary to actively respond beyond borders and the interests of companies.

2. Lessons for Change and Sustainable Development in Japan

Even if the Japanese muster up the courage to thoroughly repent and apologize for Japan's past wrongdoings and make sufficient compensations this very moment, and even if they continue to live in atonement, it cannot but be insufficient. This is because there were numerous people who died in agony during Japan's war of aggression and colonization, and also people who died while waiting for Japan's apology and compensation after the war. Above all, there were countless number of people who forever disappeared into the abyss of history in some corner of Asia without anyone to remember their names. Yet, however insufficient it may be, if the Japanese repent for Japan's historical wrongdoings and apologize to the victims, and continue to live in atonement in the future, then the historical debt to be borne by future generations may be relieved to that extent. Therefore, if Japan truly cares about its nation and has regard for its future generations, then its urgent priority would be to escape from the attitude of trying to cover up its historical wrongdoings of the previous century and attempting to remember them as a history of glory.

Japan's colonization and war of aggression toward Asian countries originated from its ambition to become an empire in Asia by learning the behavior of Western imperialistic countries. Moreover, Japan succeeded in modernization through such expansion policy toward Asia. Such colonization and war of aggression, which became the foundation of modern Japan, created the tragic history of causing human and material damage in Asian countries and destroying the possibility of enabling self-generating modernization and construction of nation states in Asia. However, what is more worrying is that the present and future depends on how this tragic history is viewed. In other words, the choice of one's historical path of the present and future depends on how one's history is remembered. One pessimistic example can be examined through how Japan distorted the historical truth of the Imjin War (Japanese invasions of Korea, 1592-1598) and misused it in the modern age. *The Jingbirok (The Book of Corrections: Reflections on the National Crisis During the Japanese Invasion of Korea, 1592-1598)*, written by a Korean nobleman Yoo Seong-ryong (柳成龍, 1542-1607) during the Imjin War, clearly recorded not only the victories but also the defeats and internal disorder of Korean troops. On the other hand, most of Japan's records on the Imjin War portrayed the war as if Japan had been victorious. Japan's fundamental memory of the Imjin War was compiled based on these distorted records, and when modern Japan was about to proceed with its external expansion policy after the Meiji Restoration, Toyotomi Hideyoshi's invasion of Korea received attention as a precedent of 'taking a great leap to the continent.' This clearly shows not only that Japan was oblivious of the fact that it did not win the Imjin War and that it caused great suffering to Korea, but also that Japan lacked a sense of criticism toward history.[566] In addition, this ultimately means that another tragedy may occur in the future if Japan fails to form an accurate historical consciousness based on criticism and self-examination on the historical wrongdoings committed by modern Japan. It is worrying that the tragic history may be repeated once again in that some forces within Japan today are trying to conceal all the faults and brutalities committed by modern Japan and attempting to beautify the period when they dominated Asian countries as a history of glory.

It is an animal's instinct to survive by any means necessary. However, even the world of beasts is not dominated by the principle of 'unconditionality' beyond survival. Lions hunt to escape hunger, but only eat what they need. Lions do not eat or save more than they need. However, human beings try to take more than they need out of greed. Then other people cannot have it, which leads them to live in difficulty. This appears in societies or countries in which people are involved, as well as relationships between the societies or the countries. Especially, in the case of a country which legitimately holds violent measures, all groups and individuals within its sovereignty can be strongly regulated. When the power of a country goes beyond its borders and tries to influence or dominate another country, uncontrollable conflicts occur and sometimes lead to war. In this sense, modern Japan attempted to take possession of territories and economic interests beyond what was necessary and tried to exercise control, causing indescribable suffering and damages to many Asian countries and their people. Japan claimed to learn from the Western world, but did not learn properly. As a second mover, Japan could have avoided the trials and errors of Western imperialist countries. By the late 19th century, most of the Western powers had already been modifying their imperialistic external strategies.

By giving up something small, it is possible to gain something bigger. On the other hand, by coveting something small, it is likely to lose something bigger. Let us say there is a child. In front of the child, there is a jar with a narrow opening that can barely fit one hand. This jar has some candy in it. Due to the structure of the jar, the candy will not pour out merely by flipping or tilting the jar. The child puts his hand in the jar and grasps a handful of candy. However, the opening of the jar is just wide enough for an open hand to pass through, but too narrow to pull out a fist. When the child cannot take out his fist full of candy, he starts to cry, even though he can enjoy the candy by only grabbing a couple of candies with the tip of his fingers. In the end, the child breaks the jar with a hammer to take possession of all the candy. However, this jar happens to be a piece of porcelain which his parents cherish. When his parents come home and see what happened, they are furious. The child is scolded and can no longer have any more candy. It is possible to understand modern Japan through this simple story. Japan established a modern state system through the Meiji Restoration, incorporated Hokkaido and Okinawa into Japanese territory, and colonized Taiwan after winning the First Sino-Japanese War. In the 20th century, Japan quietly incorporated Dokdo (Liancourt Rocks) into Japanese territory under the name of Takeshima during the Russo-Japanese War, and turned the entire Korean Peninsula into its colony after winning the Russo-Japanese War. In addition, taking advantage of World War I, Japan quickly occupied the regions in Asia that Germany had dominated. In 1931, Japan triggered the Manchurian Incident to occupy Manchuria, and established a puppet government called Manchukuo (the State of Manchuria, the Empire of Manchuria). Moreover, in 1937, Japan full-fledgedly invaded China, occupying many regions and killing a countless number of people. Japan's binge did not stop here, so it started to invade Southeast Asian countries and take possession of many islands in the Pacific. Against the United States which disapproved of Japan's acts, Japan launched a surprise attack on Pearl Harbor, Hawaii, and started the Pacific War. However, Japan was continuously defeated by the Allied Forces centered on the United States, and finally surrendered after losing numerous soldiers and suffering from bombing raids as well as atomic bombings on its mainland. Thus, Japan lost almost all of the territories it had acquired after the Meiji Restoration. It was the greed of modern Japan that brought about this catastrophe, and Asian countries do not have trust in such Japan even to this day.

According to Hannah Arendt, if one country is to settle a history such as the Holocaust, this country cannot escape from the responsibility of making a sentence on itself regarding the matter. Likewise, if Japan is to settle the historical wrongdoings of colonization and war of aggression, it is necessary for Japan to take measures such as making a sentence, judgment, adjudication, and trial on itself. This sentencing must initially be performed by the Japanese government, and the Japanese government must take legal responsibility, such as compensation from the government budget or punishment of those who are responsible. If the Japanese government does not properly fulfill this legal responsibility, the Japanese people should take the political and moral responsibility to make their government fulfill it. This is because the Japanese people hold political sovereign power over the country of Japan pursuant to the Constitution, and are Japanese citizens according to the Nationality Act. Therefore, if, for example, the Japanese government stages the politics of oblivion by denying or obfuscating Japan's responsibility for colonization and war of aggression through the textbook screening system, the Japanese people have the political responsibility to put a stop to this. Furthermore, assuming war responsibility as Japanese people means transforming Japan into a new country by changing the structure and culture of the Japanese society which made colonization and war of aggression possible. If Japanese people do not wish to take on this responsibility as Japanese nationals, they only need to give up the benefits of the national wealth accumulated through Japan's colonization and war of aggression as well as the privileges they have enjoyed as Japanese nationals over the years. In other words, they may acquire nationality of another country or voluntarily become refugees by giving up their Japanese passports. This is because being liberated from political responsibility is the same thing as losing political rights. If Japan and the Japanese people avoid taking war responsibility, it will be impossible to restore the trust relationship with Asian countries and their people, which Japan had destroyed in the past, and Japan and the Japanese people will not be able to avoid isolation from Asia and the world. On the other hand, if Japan and the Japanese people take the responsibility to respond to the calls of Asian countries and Asian people from the past, present, and future, Japan will be able to restore the trust relationship which Japan had destroyed in the past and go on in building a new relationship.[567]

According to Arendt, evasion of judgment was the mental structure under the totalitarian system that made Eichmann's large-scale massacre of Jewish people possible.[568] When a crime is committed, there is a call for judgment of justice for the criminal. If no judgment takes place for this criminal, the most fundamental sense of justice which constitutes the conditions of human society will be destroyed. It is only after this judgment on the demand of justice is made that it becomes possible to seek reconciliation related to the wounded past. Unless one looks squarely at the history that one does not want to look back on and wants to suppress and also makes a judgment on it, the history will remain unresolved forever. This judgment is accompanied by punishment and forgiveness, which becomes a condition that can sever the endless loop of evasion and revenge between the perpetrator and the victim and eventually elicit reconciliation. Therefore, the people responsible for modern Japan's Nanjing Massacre and Japanese military sexual slavery should necessarily have received judgment through this sense of justice. Japan were not punished and failed to punish itself through making a judgment in the shoes of the Asian victims that it had caused great harm by colonization and war of aggression. Therefore, Japan is still unable to overcome its negative heritage to this day. As no judgment and punishment based on a sense of justice has been initiated by Japan and the Japanese people in the first place, Japan is not in a situation where it can expect forgiveness from the victim countries and their people. According to Arendt's logic, by evading judgment and punishment based on the universal sense of justice, Japan and the Japanese people are failing to promote true reconciliation with Asian countries and are degenerating themselves into an unjust country and people.

Japan is a country with great historical debt to Asian countries such as China and Korea, and to other countries around the world. In the ancient times, Japan accepted the products of civilization from the then advanced civilized societies of China and Korea, and in the medieval times, Japan gained all kinds of benefits from trade with neighboring countries while maintaining a closed society within its self-regulating feudal system. Of course, even at that time, Japan looted the shores of the Korean Peninsula and China through piracy, and in the late 16th century, invaded Joseon Korea, killing many people and devastating the land over many years. In the modern age, Japan became the first non-Western country to accomplish modernization by accepting Western civilization and institutions. Japan, which achieved Western modernization, created an empire and held supremacy in Asia through colonization and war of aggression against neighboring Asian countries. The fact that modern Japan was on the fast track to immense growth means that Asian countries and their people lived in proportionate pain. Some Japanese people say that during colonial rule, the construction of infrastructure such as railroads and roads boosted modern industrial development in the colonies. However, the intent behind this was to efficiently execute colonial rule and exploitation and to facilitate its expansion to the continent and invasion of Asian countries. Furthermore, Japan's brutal and suppressive colonial rule obstructed the self-generating development of the colonized countries. Also, Japan claims that its domination of Asia through war of aggression was an act of liberating Asia from the Western powers. However, this is also merely rhetoric to sugarcoat Japan's acts of invasion and colonization which were strategies and tools to achieve Japan's imperialistic ambitions. Rather, Japan's rule over occupied territories was much more brutal than that of the Western powers.

The driving forces of various social activities in China, Korea, and Southeast Asia today are currently playing those roles because their ancestors fortunately survived the period of modern Japan's colonization and invasion. If the people who were sacrificed by modern Japan had not experienced such brutality, they would have had descendants, left their footprints in their respective societies, and contributed to the development of each respective country. Furthermore, their descendants would have left some legacy, be it small or large, in the development of humanity. However, due to Japan's colonization and invasion, many people were brutally killed in front of their families, and countless people died in various regions of Asia without anyone to remember them. Furthermore, people who survived but had suffered physical wounds or mental damage lived their lives in agony, and now most of them have already passed away and only a few remain. No matter how appropriately Japan makes apologies or reparations, it can be no compensation or consolation to those who have already passed away. Nevertheless, the Japanese are attempting to deny Japan's historical wrongdoings and trying to remember those days as a history of glory, even more so in recent days. This is an act of committing another crime against history. It is imperative that Japan clears the faults of the past century in the earlier part of this century. This is the only way for Japan to literally become a true global leader. Otherwise, Japan will forever live in an ever increasing debt to Asia and the world. In no way can history be concealed or glorified, no matter how hard one may try.

After its defeat in war, using the Cold War situation, Japan lightened its responsibility to make war reparations and made a comeback to international society through the Treaty of San Francisco, under the protection of the United States. On the other hand, the Asian countries that suffered from Japan's colonization or invasion went through the immense pain of having their territories divided or experiencing civil wars as a consequence. In the midst of all this, Japan established the foundation for economic revival through the Korean War and prepared to take off through the Vietnam War. Furthermore, Japan joined the ranks of economic power by minimizing its military expenditure and focusing only on economic development, under the military security umbrella of the United States. As Japan became an economic power, a door opened for Japan to repay the debt it owed to Asian countries and their people, but Japan lost its opportunity to become a global leader befitting its status as an economic power by being oblivious to its historical responsibility and turning away from a political solution. In other words, after Japan became the second largest economic power in the world, during the 1970s and 1980s it could have genuinely recovered its relationships with Asia and the world through thorough self-reflection and apology as well as sufficient compensations, but Japan lost this great opportunity. However, if Japan begins a new course at least now, then there is still hope.

Erich Fromm (1900-1980) analyzes the individual human's life through the proposition 'To have or to be.'[569] He considers the life style of 'being' to be more desirable than the life style of 'having', and recommends the former to us. This analysis on the individual can be applied to the society and even the country. A country's point of direction can be divided into 'having' and 'being'. In other words, will it pursue imperialistic expansion of territory or expansion of dominance captivated by the desire to conquer and dominate, or will it pursue a relation-oriented existence headed towards coexistence and co-prosperity of nations? This can be used as a criterion to compare Japan and Germany of the past and Japan and Germany of the present. To own something is to be bound to it. This applies to countries as well. The desire to expand its territory leads to tragedies such as conflicts between countries and even war. This means that even though possession is necessary for individuals and countries, if it is used as a tool for excessive desire it will lead to a tragic ending. The fact that Japan has recently been claiming dominium over some islands and causing conflicts among countries shows that Japan has yet to escape from the desire of territorial possession which falls in the dimension of 'to have.'

Japan's historical debt to Asian countries and their people is becoming larger like a snowball as time goes by. This tells us that it is extremely difficult for Japan to resolve this debt at this point. Nonetheless, if Japan acknowledges all of its wrongdoings from its expansion policy since the Meiji Restoration, conducts a thorough investigation and announces the findings of it, takes time for a heartfelt self-reflection and apology, and takes compensatory and future-oriented measures, then the world will praise Japan's courage and look up to Japanese people. The first task would be to lay down the territories that it acquired after the Meiji Restoration and fully give up the disputed areas. It would not be easy for the rightist Japanese government or political leaders to push ahead with this. This is especially so in a situation where the right wing groups, which try to deny Japan's history of faults and rather remember it as a history of glory, are becoming more powerful day by day. However, beyond our expectations, there is a chance that this may be solved easily. This is because Japan has a Japanese Emperor who used to have absolute power and authority equivalent to a god in the modern age and who continues to have great influence as the symbolic monarch after the war. In other words, if the Japanese Emperor who desires peace can stand up, various problems may be solved easily. During World War II when militarism was rampant at its peak and all the soldiers were ready to continue the war at the risk of their lives, it was the Japanese Emperor who put an end to it by making the declaration of surrender. Therefore, if the Japanese Emperor and the Japanese people band together and take measures to promote peace in East Asia, then 'Japan's war problems' ('Japanoblems'), which have been aggravated over the years, can be solved easily. If so, the Japanese Emperor may be able to win a Nobel Peace Prize and will gain the respect of the world, and Japan will be able to become one of the leading nations in the world, both in name and in reality.

What influence did Japan's militarism and imperialism have on art and literature, and what role did these areas play? Artists literally need to enjoy freedom of creation in its original sense in order to come up with a proper work of art, but what was the reality of modern Japan? How come in Japan there were no enlightened artists, such as Picasso during Spain's militarism? Why were there no works of art accusing the atrocities of Japan, such as Picasso's Guernica? When the Dreyfus affair took place, Emile Zola pointed out the extensive criminal acts committed to conceal the truth, through his correspondence 'I accuse.'[570] If a country's intellectual power is alive, it is possible to see such courageous actions of conscientious intellectuals in every quarter. Yet, how many courageous intellectuals like Emile Zola would there be among Japanese people, who have an incomplete perception of history and furthermore, who distort the history without hesitation? Morality cannot exist in a society where there is no 'the other'. This is because morality only comes into play in a relationship with 'the other'. If 'the other nations' are not acknowledged, there can be no such thing as morality in international society. If Japan disregards the pain Asian countries suffered from Japan, it cannot be treated as a true member of international society.

There are also voices of criticism concerning the rightward shift of the Japanese political leaders and their acts of aggravating relationships with neighboring countries. Right before Shinzo Abe served his first term as Prime Minister in 2006, Nishimura Masao, the former president of the Nihonkokyo (日本興業) Bank, contributed an article titled 'An Outspoken Statement to the Next Prime Minister' in the July 2006 edition of *Ronza* (論座). Nishimura is the half-brother of Abe Shintaro (who is the father of Shinzo Abe), and therefore, the uncle of Shinzo Abe. In his article, he sharply pointed out the harms of populist and nationalistic politics, and strongly criticized the enshrinement of Type A war criminals in the Yasukuni Shrine as well as the Prime Minister's act of paying respects to the shrine.[571] It is a relief that there are people who have balanced thoughts in Japan. However, it seems that Japanese society lacks the ability to control the activities of political leaders who are trying to gain popularity by taking a rightward shift and putting forward the banner of a 'strong Japan.' In this situation, it is imperative to instill a desirable and sound perception of history into the new generations which will lead the future. However, even this young generation is being captivated by the conservative forces and the political leaders who lean on these forces. Consequently, it seems that the settlement of history and reconciliation with Asian countries is becoming farther and farther from reach.

Henry David Thoreau (1817-1862) declared that before being a citizen of a country, he is an 'individual' and a 'human being' who has the duty to do what he thinks is right. Therefore, he considered the government as a system of expediency which enables people to coexist without disturbing one another, and claimed that it is the minimum duty of a citizen to not accept something that the government imposes unreasonably.[572] Did the Japanese people lack this sense of citizenship when Japan stepped into the path of militarism and dragged the Japanese people into the gust of war? Meanwhile, John Stuart Mill (1806-1873) called into question the 'tyranny of the majority,' which can appear in a society that has achieved democracy against the tyranny of power.[573] The problem with this violence, that a group or society imposes upon an individual, is that it penetrates into the detailed areas of individual life and controls the mind and soul, offering no way out. Therefore, we often witness the phenomenon of social dictatorship in which the power of the majority suppresses an individual's freedom of thought and emotion, which is just as bad as political dictatorship. In the case of the past militarist Japan, it was impossible for the people to stop colonization and war of aggression and they rather showed alignment and enthusiasm toward these acts, as the political dictatorship of the Japanese Emperor and the social dictatorship of the majority came into play. In present-day Japan, political dictatorship has weakened but ideological and social dictatorship is in full swing on the wave

276

of the rightward shift toward conservatism.

Some Japanese political leaders and conservative forces take the stance that Japan cannot apologize for its past invasions or colonization, as it is irrelevant to the Japanese people of today. This attitude is grounded on libertarian thought, which claims that all human beings should only take responsibility for the results of actions based on their own free choice and that it is inappropriate to take responsibility for others or a community, as each individual is a free and independent being. From this point of view, there is no room for a collective sense of responsibility. However, unlike the thoughts of libertarians who argue that individuals only take moral and legal responsibility over the consequences of their voluntary choices, Michael Sandel argues that human beings living in a community cannot but rely on the moral power of a citizen's obligation and responsibility as an individual's identity lies on the premise of a community. [574] To Sandel, solidarity obligation is connected to this aspect of human existence. According to communitarianism, living as a member of a community means understanding and accepting even the moral and political obligations that one did not set up for oneself. Sandel considers these people as members of communities such as families, countries, and nations as well as people who undertake responsibility over the history of those communities. This communitarianist identity means that affiliation is accompanied by responsibility and that a human being can only feel pride for a country's history and tradition when one acknowledges collective responsibility for one's country. This is precisely why the Japanese people of today must take responsibility for the colonization and invasion by modern Japan.

Immanuel Kant (1724-1804) argued that in determining certain principles of action, one's own principles must also be applicable to other people's principles. He called this the categorical imperative (kategorischer imperativ), and it was sometimes modified into the absolute categorical imperative of 'human beings should be treated as an end in themselves and not as a means to something else' as a principle in treating people. This categorical imperative is an imperative that one should act in a certain way, not because it is beneficial to oneself but because it is the morally correct thing to do. In addition, this is not an order imposed by another person but an order that one imposes on oneself. Postwar Japan and the Japanese people need to criticize themselves based on the principle of categorical imperative regarding their lack of self-reflection, apology, and responsibility, and start walking down a new path.

From the end of World War II to the early 1990s, the Japanese military sexual slavery issue was treated as if it had not existed in history and was withdrawn into distant memory. Japan operated the Japanese military comfort women system during the war, making Asian women into sex slaves, which was in itself a crime. Furthermore, the fact that Japan excluded information about such a system in its postwar public education, mass media, and in the process of orchestrating national memory, also constituted a crime that was no different from an accessory after the fact. However, the Japanese military sexual slavery issue, which had thus far been treated as such, suddenly rose to the surface in the early 1990s. Rising from the pain of oblivion and disgrace, the Korean victims of Japanese military sexual slavery exposed Japan's crime to the world. This call of the victims of Japanese military sexual slavery was a voice of 'the other' that sharply accused the deceitfulness of Japan that lost sight of its responsibility for invasion and colonization and was even oblivious of the fact that it had lost sight of it. Emmanuel Levinas (1906-1995) takes the view that if one does not pay attention to the voice of 'the others' who lived in a tragic history and does not feel 'shame' when looking into their eyes, then there can be no awakening to one's moral responsibility. The morality of Levinas pursues non-in-difference for the death, wounds and pain of 'the other.'[575] According to the perspective of Levinas' morality and philosophy, Japan lost the opportunity to feel ashamed and take moral responsibility, by turning away from the sorrowful voices and desperate eyes of 'the other'. If Japan feels shame for its historical wrongdoings, it means that it accepts that its colonization and invasion in the 20th century caused pain to Asian countries and that it ceaselessly makes it a mission of the present and the future not to forget its responsibility. Therefore, if Japan faces from now on the past, present, and future with this attitude, then there is hope for not only Japan but also Asia.

Japan is the first country in the world to oppose war and ban the use of military force in its Constitution. This Peace Constitution is a promise to Asian countries and the world that Japan will not engage in war. Based on this, Japanese people have expressed their desire for peace that they will not again experience the calamities of the war. Thanks to the existence of this Peace Constitution, Japan was able to focus only on economic growth while being less suspected by Asian countries over the years, and eventually managed to become a global economic power. Thus, one Japanese woman started a movement to recommend this Peace Constitution as a candidate for the Nobel Peace Prize in 2014. As a response to this, some members of the National Assembly in Korea conducted a signature-seeking campaign to recommend Japan's Peace Constitution (Article 9) and Japanese figures and groups supporting it as a candidate for the 2015 Nobel Peace Prize. However, Japan's conservative politicians are trying to cast away this meaningful and precious Peace Constitution. They are attempting to modify Article 9 of the Peace Constitution, which prohibits the use of military force, to take on the path of a great military power. This is an expression of Japan's will to once again head towards a warfare country rather than a peaceful country. However, if Japan properly recalls what great loss and pain the war in the early 20th century caused to Japan itself and Asian countries, can it really make that choice? Now it is time for Japan to properly show Asia and the world that it is no longer a warfare country but a peaceful country.

As Japanese politics and society become conservative and rightwing forces gain power, efforts to amend the Peace Constitution in order to have military power legitimately and become a country that can wage war, are becoming even stronger. In particular, such movements have accelerated since the Abe government stepped into office. However, Japan is not at all learning from its history. Modern Japan, which accomplished modernization after the Meiji Restoration, made reinforcement of military power and external expansion its core strategy and invaded Asian countries and trampled on them through colonial rule. However, Japan triggered the Pacific War and it was only after Japan was bombarded with extensive air raids and atomic bombing from the United States that it surrendered. Japan wishes to remember its victory in external wars based on military power and domination of Asian countries as a history of glory, but ultimately, it caused immeasurable pain and damage to Asian people and Japan itself suffered from bitter defeat and pain. After the war, Japan learned a lesson from this defeat and focused on economic growth rather than holding and expanding military power based on the Peace Constitution, and emerged as an economic power. Through these experiences, Japan is able to acutely learn just as well as any other country the harms of external expansion and war of aggression based on military power as well as the benefits of pursuing peace. Holding military power and engaging in war is something that requires immense economic cost. With the advent of high-tech weapons in recent years, these costs are increasing even more. In the 21st century, the United States spent an astronomical amount of money in the Iraq War but was not particularly effective. It was accompanied by human sacrifice and damage in the United States' leadership. Due to the Iraq War, the United States led by President Bush went into a massive deficit finance in contrast to the balanced finance during the Clinton Administration, and consequently, the United States faced the situation of having to coax allies into providing war expenditure or participating in the war. If Japan amends the Peace Constitution, drastically expands its current military expenditure[576], and becomes a country capable of war, then Japan would be making itself a dangerous country. By dispatching the Self Defense Forces overseas and participating in war, Japanese troops may die or get injured on the battlefield, and above all, it will add to the massive fiscal deficit that Japan currently holds, which may lead to bankruptcy. Therefore, the path that Japan should take is not that of a military power but that of a peaceful country. Japan should give up the ambition to become a great military power and take the path towards Asia's peaceful coexistence and co-prosperity on the foundation of the Peace Constitution. Japan's mainstream forces of today are following the footsteps down the same path taken by modern Japan in the early 20th century, the journey's end of which is crystal clear. Japan needs to learn from its past experiences and make a wiser choice.

Today's Japan is striving to take the path of a military power commensurate with the status of an economic power, paying no attention to the concerns of other Asian countries. Above all, Japan is trying to legalize the possession of military power by amending the Constitution and also pushing ahead with overseas deployment of armed forces under the pretext of international contribution and active pacifism. However, the rightward shift of the Japanese society cannot but be a burden to Japan itself. First of all, amidst the ongoing long-term economic recession, increased military expenditure will make the finances of the Japanese government even more difficult alongside rising welfare expenditure. Furthermore, in a situation where Japan's relationship with Asian countries is aggravated by historical issues, such as Japanese military sexual slavery and Yasukuni Shrine tribute visits, Japan's pursuit of a military power will further isolate it in Asia. In 2005, Japan engaged in active diplomacy, such as promising aid to underdeveloped countries in Africa, in order to become a permanent member of the United Nations Security Council, but it ended in failure. The Abe government had also made efforts for Japan to become a permanent member of the United Nations Security Council, but it had not turned out as Japan wished due to various reasons.[577] This mainly stems from the fact that Japan has not gained the trust of Asian countries and international society, as Japan has not shown genuine and sufficient self-reflection, apology, and reparations for its historical wrongdoings in the early 20th century. In a situation where the world is becoming connected like a web due to the development of the Internet and information technology, and the formation of regional communities is accelerating with the intensification of mutual dependence in each field, Japan's rightward shift and pursuit of military power are causing a waste of unnecessary money and energy in Asia. Therefore, if Japan and Asia are to nourish hope for the future, Japan needs to first and foremost escape from the undesirable path it is currently taking.

In the Pacific War, the Japanese people became one with the Japanese Emperor and the military authorities, being fanatical over invasion of Asia and victories in war and becoming the foundation to uphold the militarist system. After being defeated in the war, by passing their responsibilities on to some military leaders that were punished as war criminals in a trial driven by the Allied Forces, the Japanese people freed themselves of war responsibility and did not question themselves of their responsibilities. Japan failed to undergo the process of drastically parting with the concept of external expansion and militarism under rigorous self-reflection on colonization and war of aggression and vowing to push forward peace and friendship in Asia. Rather, the sense of unity in Japanese society during the period of war continued in a new form by establishing 'Corporate Japan' focused on economic growth after the war. Keeping pace with the strategy of economic revival and high economic growth led by the state and capital, Japan's ordinary people felt a new sense of unity in which they perceived loyalty and devotion to their company as patriotism. However, in the 1990s, when the bubble of Japan's economy burst and global competition intensified with the end of the Cold War, Japan began to feel a new sense of crisis. Furthermore, with the advancement of democracy in Asian countries and the end of the Cold War, the voices of war victims which had been suppressed over the years began to spurt out and historical issues which had not been resolved after the war rose to the surface, increasing the need for Japan to establish new international relationships. As Japan's long-term economic recession began and demands by Asians for Japan to resolve historical issues increased, the Japanese people thought that they needed a sense of unity with their country and companies in order to overcome the crisis and maintain the position of a strong Japan. Therefore, after the mid-1990s, many Japanese people integrated their own fates with government policies to restore the global competitiveness of companies as well as policies to reinforce military power to strengthen Japan's self-defense power, and regarded this as underpinning their identities as Japanese people. However, this attitude of the Japanese people only shows that they have not learned any lessons from history. This is because the current behavior of the Japanese people is extremely similar to the image of their ancestors during the past period of war. If Japan moves forward with the strategy of confrontation and domination instead of reconciliation and cooperation with its neighboring countries in Asia, the tragedy of war may be reproduced once again. Therefore, the current Japanese government should first and foremost come forward and take responsibility for the colonization and war of aggression that the past Japanese government committed against Asian countries. The Japanese people of today should also take the attitude of assuming responsibility for the immense suffering and damage that the Japanese people of the early 20th century caused to Asians. In order for this to happen, Japan must recognize its responsibility for historical facts and establish a foothold to restore trust with victim countries, by extensively disclosing public documents related to colonization and war of aggression, which it has been reluctant to do so far. In addition, Japanese people should create a momentum for looking back on their history, by disclosing diaries that were kept by themselves or their ancestors.[578] Furthermore, they should vow that they will acquire the will to prevent such reckless government from coming into power again in the future, as well as the capability to build a new Japan that seeks international peace and reconciliation.

However, stepping into the 21st century, new history textbooks have been introduced by the conservative forces, and history books such as *History of the People* (國民の歷史)[579], which glorify Japan's history, are overflowing.

Regarding Japan's colonization of the Korean Peninsula, *History of the People* argues that the act of Japan at that time was a natural act that emerged from international dynamics and was conducted by the inevitability of world history, and thus, there is no need for ethical judgment. If a murderer defends his act of murder as an inevitable action due to the circumstances at the time, he is giving himself an indulgence and killing the victim twice. Likewise, if *History of the People* justifies Japan's colonization of the Korean Peninsula by saying that it was 'an inevitability of world history,' this is the same as colonizing the Korean Peninsula (both North Korea and South Korea) once again.[580] In the end, these books are being published by some scholars or are based on their own theories. The behaviors of some Japanese scholars, who are dumping their scholarly conscience and developing their ideologies or studies only for the interests of their country, are being projected in these books. In particular, the fact that some historians are showing this type of conduct is a big problem and a sin to history itself. Even so, it is a relief that most historians are sharing a sound historical consciousness and history textbooks written by these historians are being adopted in the educational field for the most part. Of course, ever since the Abe government came to power, rightist voices have become louder in political circles and Japanese society, and so it is a concern that the narration of history textbooks is being influenced as well.

In any country, the sources through which ordinary people absorb information and knowledge and form public opinion are school education and the mass media. In particular, the role of the press or mass media is extremely big in forming a view of history or social values. Newspapers directly and indirectly influence the values and actions of the readers through news and editorials, and also play a part in indirectly forming national sentiments or views through entertainment or educational functions. However, the newspapers of modern Japan played the role of advocating and propagating colonization and war of aggression under the oppressive militarist system, and even after the war were not able to play the role of sparking self-reflection on such acts or questioning the war responsibility of Japanese society. Most of Japan's radio and television broadcasting stations also developed based on the newspaper companies, showing similar patterns to the newspapers. In particular, there are no limitations in corporate ownership between industries in Japan, so national television broadcasting stations are being monopolized by newspaper companies, enabling newspapers and television broadcasting stations to become gigantic mass media with dominant positions and infringe upon the diversity of public opinion. Even if there is nothing that can be done immediately about such governance structure, there is a necessity for Japanese journalists to set a new direction for the better future of Japan. There is a high possibility that Japan's future will head towards a worse direction if Japan's mass media narrowsightedly looks only in one way and leads the Japanese people in that manner. The mass media of modern Japan did not properly depict the calamities of war and rather became the spearhead of the line that glorified the war, blocking the Japanese people from establishing an upright consciousness. Taking this into account, it appears as though today's mass media in Japan is not properly functioning as a public institution of the society. The current situation in which the mass media is mindful of the social or political forces that are taking a conservative swing and fails to properly criticize the government that disregards the Peace Constitution and pursues military expansion, overlaps with the Japanese mass media of the 1930s and 1940s. In a situation where the Japanese government and society are about to become the epicenter of conflict in East Asia once again, the reality of Japan's mass media instigating the situation and being immersed in gaining commercial profits causes great concern.

Pursuant to the Peace Constitution, Japan cannot officially hold military force, but the current scale of Japan's Self Defense Forces is enough to call Japan a military power. Nevertheless, Japan is currently trying to become a military power commensurate with its economic power to intervene in international disputes and expand its national interest to the utmost. However, this causes alarm to many Asians because of the history in which Asian countries experienced the agony and damages of colonization and invasion for decades as Japan took the path of external expansion based on military force in the early 20th century. In particular, such concerns are heightening since the Abe government came into office and openly showed its ambition to become a military power by amending the Constitution. Now Japan is standing at the crossroads of whether to take the path of peace and reconciliation or the path of confrontation and conflict. First, Japan can take the path of mutual peace and common prosperity with Asia by settling past affairs without any statute of limitation with Asian countries and their people to whom Japan had caused human, physical, and mental damage in the early 20th century. Otherwise, by following the footsteps of its militarist behaviors of the early 20th century and attempting to become a military power and pursuing external expansion, Japan can continue down the path of causing friction and conflict with Asian countries and harming world peace. If the Japanese people make a more rational and wise decision, they will take the former path rather than the latter. Since continuing conflict and enmity with neighboring countries, by concealing the crimes that Japan committed in the past and expanding military expenditure, is a shortcut to committing its historical crimes once again, Japanese people who truly love Japan should avoid this at all costs. One who learns a lesson from history but does not live up to it is foolish and will once again leave a huge stain on history.

After the Meiji Restoration, Japan was obsessed with catching up with countries more advanced than itself and was successful to a certain degree.

In other words, modern Japan willingly accepted the institutions and civilization of the Western powers, and after it succeeded in industrial modernization, Japan aimed to strengthen its military and externally expand, committing acts of colonization and invasion against Asian countries. After being defeated in the war, Japan introduced the advanced technology and management techniques of the Western world and focused on economic development, stepping among the ranks of economic powers. This strategy of Japan was effective when there was a 'global standard' to follow. Yet, although Japan can conform to a global standard, it is weak in leading the path to set a global standard. When radical social change was needed in Europe, people with the strong will to actualize an ideal society that had never been realized before emerged, and it was only after treading on the ideological corpses begotten from their painful experiments that a sound social theory was born. In Japanese history, Sakamoto Ryoma (坂本龍馬, 1836-1867) is often mentioned as a figure who portrayed a picture of the desirable society in his own words and attempted to realize it during the turbulent period at near end of the Tokugawa Shogunate.[581] For Japan, which has gone through historical wandering since the 20th century, it is necessary for more such leading figures to appear. Furthermore, it is hoped that more figures who can set the global standard will emerge among these people. Thus, it is hoped that Japan can lead the world not only economically but also culturally and morally. In order for this to happen, Japan will need to settle its past affairs at a level beyond the demands of Asian countries and the world and at a level equal to or surpassing Germany's example. If Japan undergoes such change, it will be able to build a foundation to take the leap into becoming a genuine superpower in the 21st century, where soft power rather than hard power is becoming increasingly important.

The degree of an individual's moral maturity depends upon the ability to see oneself objectively. The act to reflect on and examine oneself to become a better person is a unique ability given only to human beings. Likewise, a society can only become a mature society when it reflects on and criticizes its own acts and makes efforts to improve. An intellectual is a person who examines the society to which he belongs in an objective manner, identifies and changes problematic aspects, and makes efforts to create a better society.[582] From this point of view, it is doubtful whether the Japanese society and the individuals and intellectuals within it are striving to properly alter the society in a more desirable direction based on critical reflection. The barometer of it is in what way Japan reflects and apologizes for the brutalities it committed to Asian countries and their people in the early 20th century, but the general view is that Japanese society has yet to do that. Scholars who had provided the ideological basis of modern Japan borrowed Hegel's concept of 'oriental despotism' or 'oriental stagnation', unfolding the logic that Asian countries could be regarded as another 'Orient', or in other words, a subject to dominate and suppress. Lévi Strauss points out that it is arrogance for one society to monopolize 'all the meaning and dignity which human beings can enjoy' and belittle the other society for lacking it.[583] This arrogance formed the conceptual basis of all the evil deeds and historical wrongdoings committed by modern Japan. Breaking this down will be the shortcut for Japan to create a society based on more rational and universal thoughts and ideologies.

However painful it may be to look back on the past, there is a necessity to maintain a critical distance by making a judgment on the past history. It is important to have the courage to look squarely at what faults there were in the past and make a critical judgment under one's own responsibility. Only by going through this process can one escape from the dark past, and only when the responsibility of the perpetrator is clarified does it become possible to cure the scars of the victim. However, it seems that the atmosphere of militarist invasion after the Manchurian Incident in the early 1930s is permeating the base of Japanese society today. Since 1999, not only were laws solidifying the US-Japan security system passed, but also the emblems that symbolized former Militarist Japan brazenly appeared. The national flag (Hinomaru) and national anthem (Kimigayo) of modern Japan were inseparable with the nationalism, external wars of aggression, and imperialistic history of modern Japan. It is necessary to be cautious about the pressure of 'nationalization' and the violence of unity caused by the national flag and anthem and tighten guards against the politics of symbols by the nation state. Postwar Germany and Italy both changed their national flags and pursued reconciliation with neighboring countries. As the Hinomaru and Kimigayo were symbols of colonization and invasion against Asian countries in the past, Japan should have changed them in view of reconciling with Asia through self-reflection.[584]

Nationalism is created with the internal factor of self-identity and the external factor of relationships with 'the others'. Modern Japan internally pursued homogeneity through the principle of integration, and externally made 'the others' subjects of domination and suppression through the principle of exclusion. This postwar assessment of modern Japan is going through a change by glorifying or relativizing the past with the advent of historical revisionism.[585] Historical revisionism emphasized the superiority of Japan and the backwardness and stagnancy of Asian countries in order to justify imperialistic Japan. Therefore, to modern Japan, inferior Asian countries deserved to be dominated and were nothing but incapable existences lacking modernization capabilities. In other words, the argument is that not only did Japan have to help the incapable Asian countries achieve modernization, but it had to protect them from the Western imperialist countries. However, if Japan truly wished to help modernize Asian countries, it would have been possible through exchange and cooperation rather than through colonization or war of aggression. Causing pain by unilaterally merging and invading Asian countries against their free will and blocking the opportunity for these countries to push ahead with modernization and develop on their own is the ultimate in arrogance and a crime to history. In this sense, the argument of historical revisionism is mere sophistry. Historical revisionism claims that there were many colonial people who regarded Japanese rule in a positive manner and volunteered to become Japanese officials or soldiers in order to rise to success. However, in a dismal situation where there was no prospect of liberation and independence due to the continuation of oppressive colonial rule, it might have been an inevitable choice for survival for individuals. In addition, historical revisionism strongly denies the coerciveness of Japanese military sexual slavery, and claims that self-disparaging history education is a sin as students who learn about this through textbooks are made to think that 'Japan is the worst country in the world.' However, a country that denies war crimes, such as the Nanjing Massacre and the operation of the Japanese military sexual slavery system, disregards the pain of the victims by these crimes, and refuses to apologize or make reparations for these crimes, may be the worst country in the world. It is bad enough to have committed a heinous crime, but it is even worse to deny it and fail to repent for it. If such attitude and behavior of historical revisionism continues and expands, it would be an act of creating an imaginary and fictitious history only for Japan and the Japanese people and an act of confining themselves in an 'island of history or isolated island of history.'

When Emperor Hirohito died in 1989, Japanese society was overwhelmed in a solemn mood of mourning. Emperor Hirohito was the symbol and actual leader of Japan's militarist system in the early 20th century, but he was exempted from war responsibility due to the US occupation policy and the Cold War situation and received respect as the symbolic emperor after the war and lived a full life. As he was such an influential figure, it is a pity that he did not resolve the historical wrongdoings of modern Japan before he died. If Emperor Hirohito himself had actively played such role, he could have lightened the historical debt placed upon the succeeding emperors as well as the Japanese people. The Japanese people were only humanly sorrowful about Emperor Hirohito's death, and did not make any effort to settle their historical wrongdoings and to reconcile with Asian countries. Japan did not manage to make the death of Emperor Hirohito into momentum to end its war responsibility once and for all. When Japanese society was overwhelmed by the atmosphere of lamentation for the emperor's death, the Asian people, who suffered immense pain and damage from Japan that had been ruled by that very emperor, were silently assuaging their historical wounds. If Japanese society continues to turn away from the voices of the Asians who suffered from modern Japan and makes excuses to international society only in their own interest, it will be difficult for Japan ever to be born again as a respectful country. Meanwhile, it can be said that Emperor Akihito, who had shown a much sounder historical consciousness and flexible attitude compared to Japan's rightwing forces, had played the role of a counterweight to some degree. Although he witnessed militarist Japan in his youth, he also experienced Japan's postwar growth as well as Japan's awkward relations in international society. Therefore, he was in a position to bring an end to an era. Unfortunately, he abdicated the throne in April 2019, without being able to continue such a role. His eldest son Naruhito became the new Japanese Emperor. It is fortunate that Emperor Naruhito is also assessed to be an opponent of war or a pacifist. Therefore, even though former Emperor Akihito has reached an old age of late 80s, it is expected that he, as the father of the Emperor (上皇), plays a crucial role in settling Japan's historical wrongdoings and establishing peace in Asia along with the new Emperor.

In April 2015, there was an incident that was completely different from what Prime Minister Abe and politicians had denied or even glorified Japan's historical wrongdoings. Kyushu University School of Medicine in Fukuoka of Japan opened the Medical History Museum which showed the School of Medicine's history of over 100 years. The museum honestly revealed the 'Kyushu University's vivisection of US prisoners of war' incident which occurred near the end of the Pacific War. This museum, which was opened through alumni donations, showed the historical achievements of Kyushu University School of Medicine through various displays such as medical records and medical instruments, but also revealed its shameful faults without hiding anything. Considering Japan's current political situation, which is rushing into extremes through distortion of history and rightward shift, it seems that Kyushu University's action would have required considerable courage and determination. What Asia and the world wish from Japan is this kind of attitude.[586] Despite the fact that there are many politicians that shout for amendment of the Peace Constitution and gaining international status as a military power, Japanese society continues to be maintained without strong agitation. This is probably because there are many Japanese people who think and act based on sound common sense and universal human rights. This is why the world cannot give up hope on Japan and why the world still desires for Japan to change on its own.

3. Lessons for Cooperation, Coexistence and Co-prosperity in Asia

Historically, Asian countries developed through exchange and cooperation at times and conflict at other times, but the history of cooperation was much longer than the history of conflict. The history of conflict was primarily formed during the modern and contemporary age, in the center of which was

Japan. The modern and contemporary history of Asia can roughly be divided into three periods. The first period is when Japan tore down the traditional regional order that was centered on China and gained hegemony by using military power based on the successful Western modernization. The second period is when Japan exposed its ambition for imperialistic expansion and went on colonizing and invading Asian countries, making them go through a history of agony and ordeals. The third period is after the war, in which the Cold War was formed, transformed, and dissolved, and when Japan stood up once again as an economic power. Japan is a country that historically developed through relationships with East Asian countries. However, Japan caused agony and damage to Asians by disdaining and dominating Asian countries based on the modernization it accomplished by copying the Western powers through the '*Datsua Nyuo* (Leave Asia, enter Europe)' strategy. Furthermore, after the war, Japan became an economic power by turning away from Asia and focusing on economic growth amidst the Cold War situation through the 'Leave Asia, enter the United States' strategy. After the Cold War system collapsed, Europe strengthened ties in economic, social, cultural and political fields by accomplishing the unification of Germany and launching the European Union. On the other hand, in Asia, especially in East Asia, the Korean Peninsula continues to be divided and tension is mounting with the rise of China and Japan's movements to become a military power.

Japan's imperialistic expansion in the early 20th century and postwar economic growth can be seen as a result of the Japanese people responding to changes in the international environment, devising their own strategies, and enhancing their abilities. However, Japan's historic development was not accomplished only based on its own capacities. There was a bit of luck in each historical step. First of all, during the ancient times, China and Korea which were the advanced regions at the time, were not much interested in dominating Japan. It can also be said that it was lucky for Japan that Mongolia, which had been a powerful world empire, did not try to invade Japan any further after two failed attempts due to typhoons in the 13th century. Furthermore, during the 16th and 17th centuries, the Western powers were more interested in the new continent discovered by Columbus, and during the 19th century, they were more interested in China than Japan. In particular, after World War II ended with the victory of the Allied Forces, as the US occupation policy of Japan became less punitive and more focused on economic development due to the influence of the Cold War, Japan was able to focus on its path to economic growth. The Korean War and the Vietnam War which broke out in the Cold War situation acted as a catalyst for Japan to revive its economy and accomplish rapid growth.

Despite the fact that many Asian countries have a negative perception of Japan due to the rape, looting, and murder committed by Japan during its period of colonization and invasion, they have pushed ahead with economic development by using Japan's postwar economic miracle as their model.[587] In this situation, if Japan had shown an exemplary attitude in settling postwar issues like Germany, in addition to achieving economic growth, it would have been reborn as a respected nation. Japan, which is an island country with a considerable distance from the continent, historically showed strength in learning what they needed from other countries and converting what they learned into something practical. Therefore, Japan was the first among non-Western countries to succeed in modernization, and even after the war, Japan revived its devastated economy to grow into an economic power. However, Japan's success was focused on material and practical aspects, showing extreme vulnerability in aspects such as desirable values or ideologies. It appears to be due to this imbalance in the development of modern and contemporary Japan that it is failing to show political and ethical leadership in international society even though Japan is now an economic power. One thing to note here is the fact that modern Japan achieved economic development mainly through colonization and invasion of other countries, but Asian countries successfully achieved industrialization in another way after the war. In other words, the capitalist countries such as Korea, Taiwan, Hong Kong, and Singapore succeeded in achieving rapid industrialization by using the situation of the Cold War, and the socialist countries such as China and Vietnam did so through the reform and opening policy after the end of the Cold War. Of course, it is also true that there is a thread of connection with the industrialization policy that Japan pursued, in that both categories of countries pushed ahead with state-led developmental dictatorship in order to achieve industrialization.

Looking back on the history of Asia related to Japan, international relationships were stabilized and neighboring countries were able to enjoy peace when Japan implemented the 'closed country (鎖國, sakoku)' policy. The most representative period was during the Tokugawa Period, when Japan implemented a strong closed country policy and peace was maintained for over 250 years both internally and externally. From the 1600s to the mid-1800s, Japan established the most stable political order in its history and enjoyed a period of peace for over 250 years based on its closed country policy. The most evident characteristic of this period was that there was no war, which is a stark contrast with the periods before and after this period.[588] In other words, this period clearly contrasts with the warring states period from the late 1400s to the late 1500s, as well as the period of continental expansion and militarist wars from the late 1800s to the early 1900s. Of course, after Japan lost the war in 1945, Japan also opened an age of peace based on the Peace Constitution and accomplished brilliant economic growth. But this has only been going on for 75 years and, in a sense, it was an inevitable choice due to its defeat in the war and the Cold War situation. Furthermore, as Japan has been denying its historical wrongdoings and has been taking the path of endlessly pursuing to become a military power since the late 1990s, a shadow is being cast upon the peace that the Japanese and Asian people have enjoyed over the years.

There is an 'asymmetry' between the invading country and the invaded country which cannot be discussed along the same lines, and there is also an asymmetry between the perpetrator and the victim. This asymmetry of power relationships accumulates contrasting experiences of 'coercion' and 'resistance.' Experiences that have been accumulated thus are reflected and represented in present day lives and ways of thinking. Therefore, if the asymmetry of power relationships continues, the asymmetry of experiences that comes from it further intensify. The way to sever this link is for the invading country or the perpetrator, which is in the superior position in the power relationships, to acknowledge its own faults and apologize as well as make reparations or compensations towards the invaded country or the victim. Therefore, there still exists an asymmetry between Japan and Asian countries as well as between Japanese people and Asian people, and Japan has in its hand the key to resolve this asymmetry. Recognizing a country's history through objectification begins by acknowledging historical wrongdoings of the past the way they are. Acknowledgement of historical wrongdoings brings about the issue of responsibility and leads to the expression of the will to never again repeat the same mistakes of the past by apologizing and making reparations with a sense of responsibility. If this perception of history comes into play in Japan, the asymmetric relationship with the victims of Japan's historical wrongdoings will be corrected and a proper self-identity will be reestablished. Therefore, a resolution of this asymmetry is absolutely critical not only for the future of Asian countries that suffered damage due to Japan but also for that of Japan itself.

Even after Japan's colonial rule ended with Japan's defeat in the war, Japanese people still had a sense of contempt and discrimination against Korean people. Therefore, during the negotiations to normalize diplomatic relations between Japan and Korea, Japan showed no sign of self-reflection and rather showed a high-handed and bold attitude by abusing Korea's economic vulnerability and weakness in the legitimacy of the Korean government. It seems that this is a stark example of the nature of Japanese people being strong to the weak and weak to the strong. Due to such nature of Japan, when Korea achieved considerable economic development, hosted the 1988 Summer Olympics, and co-hosted the 2002 FIFA World Cup with Japan, it might have hurt the self-esteem of Japan. It is questionable whether Japan truly acknowledged Korea at the time. But one thing for certain is that unless Japan acknowledges and respects its counterpart country and forms a partnership, be it Korea or another country, weak or strong, Japan cannot become a true member of international society. Unless Japan does so, it will make it difficult for Japan to exert leadership in international society, and ultimately, it will be forever impossible for Japan to become a respected country.

As seen already, China and Korea respectively emphasize the history of damage due to war and colonization and have memorial halls in various places for this. It is natural for Asian countries to record and commemorate the history of pain that modern Japan unilaterally inflicted on them for the coming generations to learn from. However, it is not desirable for these memorial halls to be used to cultivate hatred and intensify a sense of confrontation against Japan. It is effective enough to let Japan, which is attempting to conceal its historical wrongdoings, know the truth, and inform all the countries and nations in the world of these facts. It is entirely up to Japan whether to properly reflect on and apologize for the past and create an international society in which it reconciles and peacefully co-prospers with neighboring countries. However, this does not mean international society should stand by idly and watch Japan abandon the fulfillment of its historical responsibility. International society should give advice at times, express criticism at other times, and exercise pressure when necessary, so that Japan takes the right path. In this sense, Japan is active in extensively operating memorial facilities showing the damage done by atomic bombings in Hiroshima and Nagasaki, but it is difficult to find memorial facilities commemorating Asian countries and their people, or even Japanese people, who also suffered from Japan's colonization and war of aggression. Furthermore, Japan is getting rid of evidence related to the tormenting sites where Asians were forcefully mobilized. Rather, as can be seen in the case of the Yushukan Museum, a memorial hall in the Yasukuni Shrine, Japan is openly exhibiting war facilities and making its people feel proud of its past history of standing up against the powerful country of the United States. In addition, Japan is reinforcing mechanisms that strengthen its consciousness as a victim rather than a perpetrator and making its people remember its history of invasion as a history of glory. This attitude of Japan is reflected in the narration and screening of elementary, middle and high school history textbooks. This will prevent the growing young generation of Japan from properly perceiving the historical brutalities committed by their ancestors and instill in them a wrong attitude towards Asia and the world. In this case, conflicts in Asia surrounding Japan may be reproduced on an enlarged scale and this will ultimately bring about an outcome that hampers Japan's true national interest.

If Japan wishes to truly reconcile and cooperate with Asian countries, it must first regain the trust of neighboring countries and create the perception that Japan's economic power can help foster prosperity in the Asia region. For this to happen, Japan needs to sincerely apologize and make maximum efforts to compensate for the numerous loss of lives and property that it caused through the Nanjing Massacre, Unit 731's medical experiments on living bodies, mobilization and sexual slavery of military comfort women, colonization, and invasion. Unless these issues are settled, Japan will sound hypocritical even if it propagates the damages of atomic bombings in Hiroshima and Nagasaki and cries out for protecting peace. It has been consistently pointed out that Japan lacks the attitude of self-reflection and sense of responsibility for its past colonization and invasion, so Japan is in stark contrast with Germany's example. Therefore, despite the fact that Japan is an economic power, Japan's political leadership has not been acknowledged by Asia as well as the world, and furthermore, Japan has been seriously distrusted by neighboring countries. Now Japan must take the attitude of 'One who has tied a knot must untie it (Solve the problems you yourself create, 結者解之)' and properly settle the negative historical affairs of the 20th century. This is necessary in order for Japan to make a new start in the 21st century and to exert international leadership befitting its economic status. Above all, this is urgently needed for the Japanese people to enjoy freedom and liberation as human beings, and furthermore, to share mature interactions with Asians and citizens of the world. It is a childish and incorrect perception to think that making an apology will be disadvantageous and acknowledging a fault will dishonor the ancestors. Rather, this attitude puts the country of Japan and its people under a larger yoke of shame and dishonor by denying a historical fact that clearly existed. It is a much more honorable and mature attitude to candidly acknowledge and reflect on its historical wrongdoings and ask for the understanding of other countries and their people.

An examination of East Asian history shows that weak countries were forced to comply with the hierarchical order imposed by the empire in the region. In other words, a dominant-subordinate relationship was formed by China's Sinocentrism prior to the modern era and by Japan's colonialism and regional hegemonic policy during the modern era. However, after World War II, a hierarchy was created under ideological blocs represented by the United States and the Soviet Union. Especially, in the capitalist bloc, a system was formed in which the United States and Japan were at the center and the rest of the countries was peripheral. After the dissolution of the Cold War, a new axis appeared with the rise of China, but the hierarchical system centered on the United States is still exerting its power. In this situation, Japan's position is becoming ambiguous. In terms of economic trade relationships, mutual dependence with China and Asian countries is intensifying, but Japan's political and military relationship continues to be centered on the US-Japan Alliance, so Japan is unable to form a new framework in the aspect of political relationships. In other words, Japan is returning to Asia in the economic aspect but continuing to take the stance of *Datsuaron* (Escape from Asia) in terms of politics. This imbalance of international relationships may ultimately work as an obstacle for Japan to seek true national interest.

Modern Japan first invaded and colonized the Korean Peninsula, using Korea's weakness as a lever, and then expanded on to invade China based on this foothold. This means that if the two strong countries of Japan or China are to achieve peace and cooperation in the future, rather than expansion and collision, then Korea's weakness needs to be overcome. It is primarily the responsibility of (South and North) Korea to overcome its weakness, but Japan and China should help and collaborate in order for Korea, which was divided in the tragic history of East Asia, to be reunified and enjoy prosperity and stabilization. Therefore, both the Sinocentric order of great-power chauvinism centered on China and Japan's expansionism based on the sense of superiority of *Datsuaron* (Escape from Asia) should be denied. In this sense, the reunification, stability, and prosperity of the Korean Peninsula is not only the business of Korea but absolutely necessary for peace and prosperity in the whole region of East Asia.[589] In other words, in order for genuine peace and coexistence to be realized in East Asia, it is necessary to resolve confrontation and conflict between North Korea and South Korea on the Korean Peninsula, which was divided in Japan's stead in the competitive process between the Allied Powers after 35 years of colonization. More precisely, after World War II when the United States and the Soviet Union were in the process of occupying Japan and the regions that Japan had previously conquered, unlike the case of Germany, Korea was divided into two countries in Japan's stead. Therefore, the primary cause of Korea's division is attributable to the United States and the Soviet Union's decision to divide and rule the Korean Peninsula, which had been Japan's colony, instead of dividing and occupying Japan as a means of holding Japan responsible for the war as in the case of Germany. This also went against the common goal of the Allied Forces to hold Japan and Germany responsible for causing the war and to establish a new postwar order. In particular, this was overly harsh on the Korean people on the Korean Peninsula, who had groaned under Japan's colonial rule for 35 years and wished for a reunified unitary state. Therefore, the United States and Russia should play an active role, under the principle of solving the problems that they themselves created, so that the brutal and innocent punishment inflicted on the Korean Peninsula by the wrong choices of the United States and Russia can be lifted as soon as possible. In particular, it can be said that the responsibility and role of the United States is great, as it had been one of the axes during the Cold War era and has become the world's strongest nation in the post-Cold War era. Therefore, the United States should significantly advance the recently progressing United States-North Korea summit in order to bring an end to the armistice stalemate. The United States should furthermore conclude a peace treaty and normalize diplomatic relations with North Korea in order to bring peace on the Korean Peninsula. If the President of the United States accomplishes this task, he or she would likely be awarded the Nobel Peace

Prize and would be remembered as the historical figure who ended the last remaining Cold War situation. Of course, Japan has a more fundamental responsibility in that it annexed and colonized the Korean Peninsula and provided the cause of Korea's division. Therefore, Japan, which has not properly shown self-reflection, nor offered an apology, nor provided reparations after the war with respect to the current situation of division between North Korea and South Korea, should do its best to carry out its responsibility earlier rather than later.

Japan was Asia's central country for more than a century but is now standing at the crossroads of gradually stepping down into the status of a peripheral country. The early 20th century in Asia was literally the age of Japan. By proceeding with Western modernization at an early stage and accomplishing national prosperity and military power, Japan transformed into an imperialistic country that colonized or invaded Asian countries. Despite the fact that Japan experienced the bitterness of defeat in war as a result of a reckless external invasion war, it was able to maintain its central status in Asia as a subordinate ally of the United States, amidst international relations in the Cold War. However, as the Cold War came to an end and as China rose up to become the second largest economy in the world and even surpassed Japan in military power, it seems increasingly possible that Japan will become a peripheral country. In terms of economic power, which was postwar Japan's biggest strength, not only has Japan been overtaken by China but the gap with Korea and other major Asian countries has been narrowed. Also, Japan's pride and honor of being the only country in the world with a Peace Constitution has recently been threatened by the rightwing forces that seek to make Japan a military power. Considering the fact that soft power, such as culture, institutions, and moral influence, is growing more in importance compared to hard power, such as political and military power, Japan is falling behind some of its neighboring countries.

After being defeated in the war, it appears to be extremely abnormal for Japan to have continued substantial territorial disputes with its neighboring countries, such as Russia, China, and Korea, for over 75 years, considering that it really should have opened a new era. The fact that Japan agreed to the Potsdam Declaration and surrendered meant that it accepted the decision to limit Japan's territorial sovereignty to Honshu, Hokkaido, Kyushu, Shikoku and their annexed islands. Starting from the First Sino-Japanese War, Japan had taken the territories of other countries and incorporated them into Japanese territory through various wars and forced annexations. After the First Sino-Japanese War, Japan acquired Taiwan through the cession and made it into its colony, and after the Russo-Japanese War, it gained South Sakhalin through the cession. During the Russo-Japanese War, Japan incorporated Dokdo (Liancourt Rocks, Takeshima) of Korea into its territory after which it forcefully annexed the entire territory of Korea. Taking advantage of World War I, Japan occupied Germany's leased territory in China's Shandong Peninsula and several islands in the South Pacific. In the early 1930s, Japan triggered the Manchurian Incident and colonized Manchuria. Taking a step further, since the late 1930s, Japan invaded China, occupied Southeast Asia, and even attacked the US territory of Pearl Harbor in Hawaii, triggering the Pacific War. Therefore, after Japan's reckless war was over, it was reasonable to return the territories it had extorted thus far and it would have been obliged to accept it even if it was forced to additionally give up its original territory.[590] From this point of view, it can be considered that postwar Japan benefitted from not losing any more of its territory.

During the early stages after the end of the war, Japan did not strongly vocalize territorial issues, considering normalization of international relations. In particular, as it was urgent for Japan to make a comeback to international society, Japan took the stance of willingly acquiescing to the demands of the Allied Forces. The then Prime Minister Yoshida announced that he readily agreed to the Treaty of San Francisco in that sense. In the process of forming the treaty, as the shadow of the Cold War lay heavy and the Korean War broke out, China and Korea were not able to participate in the treaty and the Soviet Union did not sign it. Of course, Japan made the most out of this situation to attain its interests. Furthermore, after Japan succeeded in economic revival through profits from the Korean War and accomplished outstanding economic growth during the mid-1950s and 1960s, Japan began to vocalize its opinion on territorial issues.[591] Hence, even though the Soviet Union suggested a reasonable solution (transfer of two of the four islands when signing the peace treaty) during the negotiation process to normalize diplomatic relationships between Japan and the Soviet Union in the mid-1950s, Japan insisted on the retrocession of all four islands. Eventually, the territorial dispute between the Soviet Union and Japan was left in the same state as it had been immediately after the war. Furthermore, even in its diplomatic negotiations with China and Korea, Japan stuck to the attitude of not ceding its point on territorial disputes. In particular, after signing the Japan-Korea Basic Treaty in 1965, Japan wrote in its Foreign Policy Blue Book a lame explanation that 'Dokdo (Liancourt Rocks, Takeshima) is subject to future dispute negotiations as long as there is no special agreement to exclude Dokdo,' showing an obsession over territorial issues and pushing aside larger national interests or national objectives as well as peace and mutual interests in Asia.

Dokdo (Liancourt Rocks, Takeshima) has been effectively governed by Korea after the war for a period of nearly twice as long as the period during which Japan took possession of it. Of course, Dokdo was historically Korea's territory for over several hundred years before Japan illegally possessed it. During the period of war with Russia, Japan quietly incorporated Dokdo into

Japanese territory without the consent of Korea for military purposes and as a prerequisite step to forcefully annex Korea. When considering this situation, it is contrary to conscience or morality for Japan, which caused great pain to Korea through colonization, to claim that Dokdo is 'Japan's inherent territory' and that Korea is 'illegally dominating.' In the early 20th century, Japan illegally dominated Dokdo and the entire Korean Peninsula,[592] but then had no choice but to return it 35 years later. Now there is no other course of action for Japan to take but to abandon its claim for dominium over Dokdo, which is now effectively governed by Korea. The faster this decision is made, the better it is for both Japan and Korea. Continuing to claim something that cannot ever be accomplished is a foolish act that not only worsens relations between Japan and Korea but also aggravates emotions between the Japanese and the Koreans. Of course, it would be beneficial for the future-oriented development of the relationship of the two countries to provide opportunities for Japanese fishermen of Shimane Prefecture to engage in fishing operations in the seas near Dokdo for the harmonization of interests between Japanese and Korean people and to declare that Korea will not set this island as the starting point of the economic zone, despite the fact that Dokdo is Korean territory.[593] However, these actions could be taken, only if Japan changes its attitude.

It is necessary for Japan to follow the attitude taken by postwar Germany in settling territorial issues. After the war, Germany made a drastic concession to France regarding territorial issues, overcoming its long-standing conflict with France. In the process of settling postwar issues, the Soviet Union included the eastern part of Poland into its territory, causing Polish territory to move westward so that Poland's border with Germany changed to the Oder-Neisse line. In spite of this, Germany yielded the Alsace-Lorraine region to France. As reconciliation and cooperation between Germany and France advanced, the European Union was formed and the EU Parliament was established in Strasbourg, the central city of Alsace-Lorraine. Germany yielded to Poland an area larger than Kyushu, Shikoku, and Chukoku of Japan put together. Germany offered this land despite the fact that it used to be the land of the former Preussen Kingdom, which was the key region of the past German Empire. Furthermore, the Alsace-Lorraine region, which Germany yielded to France, is a large piece of land equivalent to 70% of Kyushu of Japan. Germany changed its national goal from the traditional mindset of considering the protection of territory as the top priority to expanding influence as its top priority. Adenauer, who was the Prime Minister of West Germany at that time, aimed to provide a more lasting security system to European countries by designing a Germany that would coexist with European countries in the future. Therefore, according to the plans of Jean Monnet (1888-1979) and Robert Schuman (1886-1963), efforts to bind Europe together as one were made and finally the European Union was born.[594] The situation that unfolded in Europe after the war shows a stark contrast with the situation in East Asia. Whereas Germany yielded such a vast amount of land to Poland and France and deepened mutual cooperation with European countries, Japan has been claiming dominium over some small islands that are inappropriate for human inhabitance and heightening the waves of conflict in East Asia. Taking the case in which Germany drastically yielded lands to its adjacent countries in Europe, what if we were to replace Germany with Japan, and Poland and France with Korea and other Asian countries? If Japan had taken the same path as Germany, would not mutual dependence in East Asia have been deepened and would not Asian people be living in an atmosphere enjoying more peace and co-prosperity? What if Japan were to do that in the future? What would be required to make Japan take such actions?

Although Germany had to give up a considerable amount of land after the war, it did not attempt to demand for retrocession in its peace talks. Setting aside the territorial issues as unsolved, Germany focused on developing relationships with neighboring countries and the Soviet Union (Russia). On the other hand, Japan has considered even the islands that are uninhabitable and not geographically big as territory that it had to recover, and has made these islands its major diplomatic agenda. Thus, Japan was not able to improve its relationships with not only neighboring countries but also the Soviet Union (Russia) to that extent. As of 2009, Russia's major trade partners were Germany, the Netherlands, and China in order of scale, and Japan marked 11th place. It did improve a bit, but Japan's trade volume with Russia in 2017[595] ranked 8th, after China, the Netherlands, Germany, Belarus, the United States, Italy, and Korea[596]. If Japan had made rapid progress in its relationship with the Soviet Union and even signed a peace treaty, rather than making territorial issues its core task since the late 1950s, trade and economic collaboration between Japan and Russia would have developed further.[597] Japan has failed to promote true national interest by making the territorial issues that cannot be easily solved into a diplomatic agenda. The problem is that Japan is continuing to maintain that attitude and even making a stronger voice in territorial issues by pursuing to become a military power, raising concerns that conflict and enmity in East Asia will intensify.

The University of Maryland's Professor Thomas Schelling, a Nobel Prize winner in Economics, stressed in his publication *The Strategy of Conflict*[598] that 'Victory does not only mean taking something away from the other party, and it is necessary to identify what is most important among many national goals.' From this point of view, Germany set peace, coexistence, and co-prosperity in Europe as more important goals over territory and strived for those goals. Through such actions, Germany was reborn into a completely new country after the war and has become the most influential country in the European Union. Therefore, it is necessary for Japan to benchmark Germany's successful model and set up a new national goal. Furthermore, Japan should learn from the postwar history of Germany and France, which created a steadfast relationship of interdependence, and promote the formation of an East Asian community with China and Korea. Moreover, in the situation where China has emerged not only as an economic power but also as a military power, Japan's acts of arousing tension will do much more harm than good. China surpassed Japan in terms of GDP in 2010, now being three times the size of Japan, and also overwhelming Japan in terms of military power both qualitatively and quantitatively.[599] Now it is more realistic and desirable for Japan to pursue economic interests as well as various tangible and intangible interests by deepening the relationship of mutual dependence and peace rather than trying to start an arms race in East Asia. If Japan refrains from harming the interests of neighboring countries and rather shows efforts and consideration to help them gain major interests instead, then the international order in East Asia will unfold in favor of Japan.

It is important for Japan to bravely face the acts which it had committed in the past and make a critical judgment on its historical wrongdoings based on its own responsibility. In other words, Japan should first make the judgment that Japan's colonization and invasion was a crime in the perspective of victim countries, which suffered from the severe agony of losing countless lives and property, as well as the judgment that Japanese people were also perpetrators. Japan was able to enjoy many things by causing pain and damage to neighboring countries in the past, and this was a foundation on which Japan built its prosperity of today. Therefore, in the situation that Japanese people are enjoying various rights and receiving protection by holding Japanese nationality, they cannot claim that the historical wrongdoings committed by modern Japan have nothing to do with them. If Japan assumes clear responsibility for its invasion as well as colonization, and in particular, takes obvious responsibility for the Japanese military sexual slavery issue at the national level, the citizens of the world will think highly of such an attitude of Japan. Japan will then be able to establish moral superiority over the Western powers and demand them to take responsibility for their respective colonial histories.

A survey on the war waged by modern Japan, conducted by Professor Sanuki Hiroshi of Hosei University of Japan every year for over a decade on the first day of his course on Education Laws of the Department of Society and Citizens, reveals shocking results. In the wars waged by modern Japan during the early 20th century, Japan lost 3.1 million people and China lost over 10 million people. Yet, more than one-third of the respondents of the survey over the past decade have replied that Japan suffered a greater death toll than China. Regarding the number of Chinese deaths, more than half of the respondents replied that China lost less than 1 million people and 10% of the respondents replied that China lost less than 100,000 people. The same survey conducted in study meetings for adults in the region showed similar results as the university students. Most of the students vaguely thought that the deaths of the Chinese people were caused by the collision of armies and were not properly aware of the fact that Japanese troops attacked villages and slaughtered local residents pursuant to the policy of procuring rations locally. In addition, as they understood the war through the framework of the Pacific War, they had a strong impression that it had been a war against the United States and overlooked Japan's invasion against China. Thus, as they have only learned mostly about the atomic bombings and air raids by the United States, they understand the war from the victim's point of view and it is difficult for them to form the perception that Japan had been a perpetrator in Asia.[600]

In parallel with its unconditional surrender, Japan had to abruptly give up its occupied territories and colonies. The Japanese people living on mainland Japan were not able to properly witness or realize the misery of the people living in colonies or occupied territories. With a few exceptions, most of the war leaders were not properly interrogated for their responsibility. Rather, due to the US occupation strategy of using the Japanese Emperor System and the Japanese government, the war leaders were able to preserve their status as the ruling class of Japanese society and conceal the fact of perpetration. When the Korean War broke out, a treaty that was 'lenient' toward Japan was signed through the San Francisco Peace Conference. Furthermore, the Japanese people formed a consensus of protesting against war due to the damages done by the atomic bombings and broad scale air raids by the United States and came to have a victim mentality, rather than awareness as a perpetrator. Japan did not clarify why it began the war or how much pain and damage it caused to neighboring countries and their people through the war, nor did it properly pass it on to posterity through history education. In the end, even though the majority of the Japanese people have opposed war and pursued peace, they have spent over 75 years without having a sense of responsibility as nationals of a perpetrating country. Such an attitude of Japan will not be tolerated for people with a sense of universal justice and will have a negative impact on the future of Japan. The truth of historical wrongdoings cannot be concealed even if one tries. The more one tries to hide it, the shabbier one becomes, and one only ends up blocking the path to restore one's true honor. Japan is throwing itself into a 'collective memory loss' and strengthening its sense of 'collective irresponsibility.' In order for Japan to recover its historical conscience, it must escape from this 'collective memory loss' and actively face the historical wrongdoings that it committed in the past. Based on this awareness, Japan should show the attitude of making sincere apologies and assuming responsibility. Despite the fact that it triggered the horrors of World War I and World War II, the reason why Germany has been accepted as a member of the international society and has gained respect, is that its thorough self-reflection on the past, heartfelt apology, and efforts to take its responsibility were accepted by neighboring countries and the international society.

In various Asian countries, many people are loudly voicing their criticism against Japan's distortion of history and rightward shift. Such criticism is correct, but its continuance is increasing Japan's fatigue and repulsion against it. Japan's distortion of history and rightward shift has reached a dangerous level, and there is a need for a deep analysis on why Japan seeks to take such a dangerous path. Perhaps Japan is taking this path as it cannot properly find the correct path to go down. Therefore, when Asian countries such as China or Korea criticize Japan, it is necessary to guide Japan towards a productive direction and a correct path. The values of trust, solidarity, good will, and participation are intangible capital that determine the safety and happiness of the members of a community. In other words, these assets that form and support a society and community are social capital, which was used by Robert D. Putnam, James S. Coleman and so forth.[601] If we expand this concept and apply it to international society, it appears that this social capital is necessary for the safety of countries and the formation of a peaceful international community. East Asian countries are required to make efforts to form a regional community by strengthening this social capital.

In 2001, Japan's rightwing forces produced a history textbook that distorted modern Japan's history of perpetration through 'the Group for a New History Textbook.' When the new history textbook passed the screening of the Ministry of Education, it caused strong opposition from Asian countries. As a consequence, historians, teachers, and civic groups of China, Japan, and Korea criticized New History Textbook[602] of Hushosa, and they have engaged in active joint activities, such as holding the 'Forum for Recognition of History and East Asian Peace' in Nanjing, China in March 2002. In particular, they engaged in activities to publish a joint history textbook for the students and general public of the three countries of East Asia, and A History to Open the Future[603] was published in 2005 as the first outcome of their joint research. As more than 75 years have passed since the end of the war and the number of people with first-hand experience of the war has significantly diminished, the postwar generation, which makes up the majority of the population, only has an abstract perception of the war, raising the risk of falling into narrow nationalism. To avoid this risk, it is necessary to jointly conduct a wholesome history education so that the generation that did not experience the war can comprehensively understand Asian history in the 20th century, which was marked by wars. However, a joint history education does not mean that historical awareness is unified into one. It is not desirable for one country to force its historical awareness upon another country to overcome the gap in historical awareness. Above all, it is important to build a relationship of mutual trust and continue conversations regarding history, by autonomously changing one's own attitude while also waiting for the other party to change its attitude as well. It is not a 'self-torment' to critically reflect on one's own history. On the other hand, it is a process of advancing one's history and growing one step further. In Asia, where the scars of Japan's colonization and invasion in the early 20ᵗʰ century still remain, it has become an urgent task to share historical perceptions beyond borders and implement joint history education. [604] Considering the fact that the reconciliation of Germany and other European countries regarding their history made integration and peace in the European region possible, it is important for Japan and its neighboring countries to settle their historical issues and reconcile in the East Asian region. In this sense, there is a need for the East Asian countries to benchmark Europe's history education and efforts to create a common perception of history.

Three major trends since the mid-1990s surrounding Japan's war crimes and postwar responsibilities can be summarized as follows. The first is China's change. Despite the fact that China suffered the most loss of lives from Japan's war of aggression, Mao Zedong and Zhou Enlai only placed responsibility on few military personnel rather than on the Japanese people and therefore relinquished their requests for war reparations. However, after the end of the Cold War, a considerable number of Chinese people began to question this lenient attitude, and government-level actions have been strengthened since the Xi Jinping government came into office. Second, as protection of human rights gained more attention in the realm of international politics, the problem of Japan's war crimes grew into an international issue. In other words, the problem of Japan's war crimes came to be characterized as an issue of human rights infringement committed by the Japanese government and military during the period of war and colonization. In particular, the issue of former Japanese military comfort women became a matter of great interest in the international society, which raised awareness on the importance of human rights. Third, a kind of 'apology fatigue' has increased in Japan since the late 1990s. Among the advanced countries, Japan has been considered as the only country to evade responsibility for imperialistic wars and colonization. Despite this situation, numerous Japanese people are showing reactions such as 'Why does only Japan have to apologize?' or 'How many times do we have to apologize?'[605]

Japanese people have been reluctant to acknowledge their historical wrongdoings for various reasons. One reason would be that China and the United States – the former having suffered the greatest damage from the war and the latter having exercised the greatest influence after the war – showed incredible leniency towards Japan. Therefore, the Japanese have not been able to place much meaning on war responsibility. Second, considering that even the Western powers conducted acts of invasions and colonization, Japanese people wonder why only Japan should receive criticism. Third, Japanese people think that while their acts are clearly wrong based on present-day standards, these acts originated from an inevitable war and were not problematic according to the standards and international laws of that time. Fourth, Japanese people consider themselves as victims, as they suffered severe damage from the extensive air raids and atomic bombings of the United States during the final stages of the war. Fifth, the Japanese government has been claiming that matters related to reparations or compensation for invasion and colonization have already been settled with the relevant countries through treaties, with the exception of North Korea.[606]

However, Japan's refusal to acknowledge its historical wrongdoings for these reasons is not justifiable in various aspects. The reason China and the United States showed a lenient attitude in settling Japan's war responsibility was that the Cold War, as well as the internal and external situations of each country, came into play. Therefore, the leniency of the two countries did not mean an exemption of modern Japan's war responsibility. In addition, the fact that Western powers committed similar faults does not mean Japan can escape from its crimes. It should also be taken into consideration that Western powers made postwar efforts to solve issues related to war and colonization much more actively than Japan, as seen in the example of Germany. Also, Japan does not deserve to raise the issue of applicable standards, in that it indiscriminately committed crimes and condemnable brutalities even through the lens of international law and humanity of that time. The damage inflicted on Japan during the final stages of the war was brought upon itself by failing to surrender earlier. Furthermore, since the war itself was caused by Japan and Japan inflicted even greater damage to Asian countries, it is an unabashed claim to bring up its own damage. In addition, although Japan claims that it settled the issues on war of aggression and colonization through treaties, there were many issues that were not actually covered in the treaties, such as the Japanese military comfort women issue. Also, Asian countries were not able to properly receive war reparations from Japan due to the pressure from the United States. Considering these facts, the attitude of the Japanese government and the Japanese people hesitating to acknowledge their historical wrongdoings and failing to properly repent, apologize, and make reparations can only be called extremely shameless.

It is not in the least desirable for Japan to fail to acknowledge its historical wrongdoings and rather try to deny or reduce them, with reasons that are not valid in international society. If Japan continues to disregard the criticism and reasonable requests of Asian countries that suffered great damage caused by Japan, it will be inevitable that Japan faces opposition and resistance from Asian countries in other various fields. Furthermore, unless Japan takes on the attitude of acknowledging and repenting for its historical wrongdoings, it will be difficult for Japan to gain trust and respect in international society. Japan has already solidified its reputation as a country and nation that does not fulfill its own responsibility in comparison to Germany. This negative assessment from international society will harm the overall national interest of Japan in the future. Although it is impossible to change the past history, it is extremely important to resolve not to commit the same faults again in the future, by acknowledging and self-reflecting on historical wrongdoings. Only with such an attitude can Japan truly become a member of Asia and be reborn as a leading country that receives trust and respect from international society.

It is fully understandable and reasonable that Asian countries, such as China and Korea, have a negative assessment of and critical attitude towards Japan, since they unilaterally suffered from the damages of Japan's invasion and colonization in the early 20th century. Nonetheless, it needs to be commented on some points that could have been improved regarding the attitude of the Asian countries over the years. First, the Chinese and Korean people have a tendency to criticize Japan from a moral point of view, and there have even been cases where the Chinese and Korean people think they are morally superior and that Japanese people are morally inferior. However, just because they are victims, it is not desirable to think that they are morally superior and to morally belittle Japan. Second, China and Korea often use the historical issues of Japan as a diplomatic card. This is sometimes necessary for national interest, but in a situation where mutual dependence in economy and other fields is deepening, it may rather be a loss for both sides when this aspect becomes a diplomatic obstacle. Third, it needs to be taken into account that the ruling class that is leading Japan today, as well as the majority of Japanese people today, are postwar generations that do not have a proper self-awareness on invasion and colonization. It was difficult for the postwar generation to have a sense of responsibility, because the forces that had led Japan to war retained their positions and also led postwar Japan, which worked as a factor to dilute Japan's war responsibility in the Cold War situation. It may be for this reason that the Japanese people are failing to understand when Asian countries are criticizing Japan for its past history issues. Therefore, when Asian countries deal with Japan's historical issue, they need to take a more strategic and sophisticated approach by taking these aspects into account. There is a need for patience, guiding and waiting for Japan's new generations to gradually realize the faults of their past generations and develop a sense of responsibility. Furthermore, Korea and China must show a different aspect from that of Japan in dealing with the damages and sufferings inflicted on neighboring countries by them in the past, so that their demands for Japan to change its stance on historical wrongdoings are justified. Therefore, South Korea needs to provide a sincere apology and sufficient compensation for the massacre of Vietnamese people carried out by the Korean troops during the Vietnam War. China also needs to reflect and apologize for historically reigning over its neighboring countries.

East Asian countries have built and operated monuments and facilities mainly reflecting their own view of the past in order to remember the past and to utilize them in history education. Especially in the case of Japan, it tries to not reveal as much as possible any evidence or item that can expose the faults and shame of the militarist era. This method has a limitation in that it cannot bring about genuine historical reconciliation. Even so, efforts to overcome these problems still exist among East Asian countries. One example would be the case in which the lawsuits of Chinese and Korean people, requesting Japan's self-reflection, apology, and compensation after the end of the Cold War, gained support from local Japanese people and continue to be supported to this day. Also, the fact that Korean and Japanese citizens and civic groups collaborated in 2008 to erect a memorial monument commemorating Japanese military 'comfort women' on Miyako Island (宮古島) in Okinawa has an important meaning. The fact that it was a voluntary movement from the people to commemorate the victims and pass down the bitter memories of the past to the future generations, showed the possibility to prevent the comfort women issue from being buried by the distorted and nationalistic collective memory encouraged by the state and local governments.[607]

One country that Japan has been unable to normalize diplomatic relationships with to this day is North Korea. North Korea was born when the Korean Peninsula, which used to be a colony of Japan, was put under the divided occupation of the United States and the Soviet Union after the war. The United States suggested the occupation plan to divide the Korean Peninsula at the 38th parallel north, in order to prevent the Soviet Union from participating in the occupation of Japan, as well as to prevent the Soviet Union from occupying the entire Korean Peninsula. The Soviet Union agreed to this, as it had already occupied Manchuria and considered it to be profitable to occupy the northern part of the Korean Peninsula. The division of the Korean Peninsula was carried out firsthand by the powerful countries of the United States and the Soviet Union, but it can be considered that Japan also has a large responsibility, as it was Japan that provided the cause for the division. Utsunomiya Tokuma (宇都宮德馬, 1906-2000), who was a conservative politician that acted as a mediator between Japan and North Korea, considered that 'Because Japan annexed Korea and used it as a military base, the Soviet Union which declared participation in the war against Japan occupied the northern part of the Korean Peninsula with the intent to disarm the Japanese troops, which led to the division of North and South Korea.'[608] Thus, if Japan had not colonized the Korean Peninsula, and Japan had not waged war against the United States, the Korean Peninsula would not have been divided into the two countries of North Korea and South Korea. The defeated country of Japan, which had colonized the Korean Peninsula, managed to avoid being divided by occupation as the Korean Peninsula was divided into North and South Korea in Japan's stead. All the more, Japan formed the basis for economic revival through profits from the Korean War. However, South and North Korea lost countless lives and suffered immense property loss due to the Korean War, and as the ideological gap widened from the war, the two Koreas have borne tremendous costs in an arms race and regime competition. The Korean Peninsula, which had been colonized for 35 years, experienced the tragic history of being divided and occupied instead of Japan and even suffered damages from the war. How can Japan, the United States, and the Soviet Union (Russia), which made this tragedy happen, be held responsible? At the very least, these countries should make more active efforts to help resolve the war situation and establish a peace regime on the Korean Peninsula. Japan and the United States should establish diplomatic relations with North Korea as soon as possible and induce North Korea to develop as a normal country, so that peace can come to settle in the Korean Peninsula and Asia.

In 2005, Japan actively strived to become a permanent member of the United Nations Security Council but failed. The United Nations is an international organization established by the Allied Powers that fought against Nazi Germany and militarist Japan in World War II. If Japan and Germany were to become permanent members of the Security Council, which plays a key role in the UN, this would literally mean the end of the postwar structure. However, many countries are raising questions on whether Japan should gain such status, as not only does Japan leave much to be desired in self-reflection, apology, and compensation for its colonization and war of aggression but it is attempting to deny or make little of its atrocities during the war. Furthermore, Japan is openly showing its ambition to become a military power by amending its Peace Constitution in the 21st century. Even now, Japan holds extremely strong military power in Asia. Only the fact that the Peace Constitution prohibits Japan from having military force has made it difficult for Japanese people to discuss out in the open on how to manage the democratic control of its military power. If Japan were allowed to have military force, it is necessary to place strong devices that can prevent Japan from provoking a war or becoming a perpetrator. However, considering the current atmosphere of the Japanese society, it seems difficult to hope for such mechanisms.[609] If Japan wishes to become a permanent member of the UN Security Council and play a role as a true leading country of international society, it is an urgent priority to restore the trust of Asian countries based on sincere self-reflection and apology for its historical wrongdoings.

Since the Japanese Emperor of modern Japan was a figure with absolute power and divine authority, he can be considered to have the greatest responsibility for the war of aggression and colonization against Asian countries. However, due to the US occupation policy and the Cold War situation, Emperor Hirohito escaped responsibility, announced the Declaration of Humanity, and became the symbolic monarch pursuant to the

Peace Constitution. Even so, it is difficult to neglect the influence the Japanese Emperor has on the Japanese people due to the characteristics of Japanese society. Emperor Hirohito made an effort to refrain from playing a political role in the newly changed circumstances of the times, and such attitude was succeeded by his son, Emperor Akihito. This attitude of the Japanese Emperor seems to be functioning somewhat as a braking device in Japanese society, which is tilting more to the right. At the very least, it is preventing the extreme right forces from voicing their political views using the Japanese Emperor. Emperor Hirohito visited seven European countries in 1971 and the United States in 1975, following visits to Southeast Asian countries in the 1960s, in order to promote amity and friendship among countries. Immediately after Emperor Hirohito returned from the United States, he expressed his will that he would be 'very glad if a Japan-China peace treaty were signed so that he could have an opportunity to visit China.' It seems that a sense of responsibility for the fact that the Manchurian Incident, the Second Sino-Japanese War, and the Nanjing Massacre happened during his time came into play to a certain degree. In addition, Emperor Hirohito felt uncomfortable with the fact that war criminals who had been punished in the Tokyo Trial were co-enshrined in the Yasukuni Shrine in 1978, and he stopped paying his respects at the shrine afterwards. This became known to the world when a notepad of Court Minister Domida was disclosed in August 2006. Domida's memo was written when Emperor Hirohito told him personally on April 28, 1988. Emperor Hirohito had occasionally visited the Yasukuni Shrine after the war but did not visit the shrine any longer after the co-enshrinement of war criminals. It was in 1985 that China first protested against Prime Minister Nakasone's visits to the Yasukuni Shrine, so it can be said that the Japanese Emperor had quit his visits to the shrine at his own discretion earlier than 1985. His son, Emperor Akihito, followed the footsteps of his father. In this sense, it seems that the Japanese Emperors have had a much sounder perception of history and international mindset compared to the rightist politicians that claim to care for Japan's ancestors and national interest.[610]

Emperor Akihito, the successor of Emperor Hirohito, showed even more active movements to promote amity and friendship with Asian countries, in the difficult situation of Japanese society after the Cold War. Japan's efforts to pursue Reconciliation and peace with Asian countries after the end of the Cold War were undermined due to the acceleration of the conservative swing since the late 1990s. By enacting various laws, Japan revived the national flag and national anthem, which used to symbolize militarist Japan, and started to use a national foundation day. In April 2004, when the compulsory use of Japan's national flag and national anthem became an issue, Kishi (棋士), a member of the Tokyo Metropolitan Government Board of Education, was invited to a garden party of the Imperial family and mentioned to the

Japanese Emperor that he 'wished to hoist the national flag in all of the schools in Japan and make students sing the national anthem.' To this remark, the Japanese Emperor expressed his opinion that 'Indeed that which is not forced is desirable.' Such a stance of the Japanese Emperor may have been reflected, in that there was no mood to force the national flag on national holidays. In a press conference prior to his visit to Southeast Asia in June 2006, when Emperor Akihito mentioned acts of terror, such as the May 15 Incident or the February 26 Incident committed by the so-called 'patriotic soldiers' in the 1930s, he expressed a feeling of wariness towards distorted 'patriotism.' Furthermore, Emperor Akihito visited Southeast Asia and China, seeking amity and friendship as well as reconciliation between Japan and each of these countries. In 1994, he made a memorial visit to Iojima (硫黄島), which used to be a ferocious battlefield. In 1995, he visited Hiroshima and Nagasaki, which suffered from atomic bombings as well as Okinawa, where brutal battles took place and many civilians were killed. In June 2005 which was 60 years after the war, he visited the island of Saipan, where many civilians were forced to commit suicide, and on his way back, he laid flowers at the 'Cornerstone of Peace in Okinawa' and paid a silent tribute to the 'Pacific Korean Memorial Peace Tower.' In 2009, he visited Hawaii which the Japanese troops attacked, and in April 2015, he visited Palau, despite Prime Minister Abe's opposition.[611] Among the countries which modern Japan invaded or colonized, the Japanese Emperor has not visited the closest country, Korea. Emperor Akihito had once mentioned the Japanese royal family's 'connection with Korea' saying that 'It is written in the *Shoku Nihongi* (續日本紀) that the birth mother of Emperor Kanmu (桓武) was a descendant of King Muryeong of Baekje.' It can be considered that he had indirectly expressed his desire to visit Korea, by emphasizing the ties that the ancestors of the Japanese royal family had with Korea. Although it would not have been easy in a situation where the rightwing forces were gaining power in Japan, it seems that Emperor Akihito would have advanced reconciliation and friendship between Japan and Korea by visiting Korea if conditions had been created, considering his attitude and features.[612] However, regrettably, he officially announced on August 8, 2016 that he would abdicate the throne during his lifetime[613] due to his old age and health issues, and indeed he abdicated the throne on April 30, 2019.[614] His throne was succeeded by his eldest son, Crown Prince Naruhito. Japan selected 'Reiwa (令和, れいわ, meaning beautiful peace or harmony) as the era name of the new Emperor Naruhito's period. It is hoped that Emperor Naruhito, who has been considered just as much of a pacifist as his father, will play the role of a new rudder in Japanese society, which is taking a rightist swerve.

It is a contradiction for Japan to claim it supports liberty, democracy, and peace, and at the same time pay respects to the Yasukuni Shrine where war criminals are enshrined. In addition, Japan reacts extremely sensitively about the criticism of Asian countries in terms of its present-day national interests, while being lenient about its past wrongdoings. Japan strives to close its eyes to the brutalities it committed to neighboring countries in the past, and the resulting agony and damage from it. When China, Korea, and other Asian countries point out this attitude of Japan, Japan appears to be sick of being preached at. This attitude leads to 'detesting China (嫌中)' and 'detesting Korea (嫌韓).' However, it would be desirable for Japan to think that thanks to the presence of China, Korea and other Asian countries, Japan has an opportunity to look back on the historical wrongdoings that it has become oblivious to and negligent of. Otherwise, it would be difficult for Japan to realize what it had done wrong in the past, what it is lacking at the moment, and what it needs for the future.

Globally, there has been the end of the Cold War, the advancement of democratization, and deepening of mutual dependence in an economy based on informatization. But in East Asia, escaping from the Cold War still remains a task to solve. In a situation where the hegemony of the United States is becoming stronger in the post-Cold War era, East Asian countries are not making active efforts to mutually understand one another. Rather, as the influence of the United States is increasing, mutual enmity is expanding among East Asian countries. Amidst such international relations in East Asia, Japan focuses only on military diplomacy based on the US-Japan Security Treaty and is negligent of diplomacy with East Asian countries. Rather, with the United States on its back, Japan has been turning away from the demands and wishes of East Asian countries. Therefore, Japan does not have self-awareness as a member of Asia, nor is it able to provide a vision for the future of Asia. In East Asia, the wounds caused by the imperialistic invasion and colonization of modern Japan have remained without a chance to be healed. Japan has now arrived at the stage where it should actively consider normalization of diplomatic relations with North Korea and a breakaway from diplomatic policies biased towards the United States. Furthermore, Japan should make efforts to actualize a multilateral security system that encompasses the entire region of East Asia or a community such as the European Union. The Japanese government shows a tendency to approach foreign relations by highlighting the military aspect, such as the threat of China or the nuclear issue of North Korea. However, unlike other countries, it is the greatest strength of Japan that it has a Peace Constitution, and that it has longed for peace after the war. It was also a wise choice on the part of Japan to focus on economic growth on this basis. Now that Japan has become an economic power, it is trying to become a military power. However, this movement is an insult not only to the Peace Constitution but also to the Japanese people who have made efforts to protect it and a betrayal to the Asian countries which have desired for Japan to be a country of peace. Therefore, Japan should keep in mind that it can gain control of moral and political hegemony in East Asia based on the Peace Constitution and its postwar history of pursuing peace.

For a regional community to come into existence, it is essential to connect traffic and communication facilities. In this sense, Asia is equipped with a certain level of infrastructure for the creation of a regional community, since Asia is connected through a railroad network. 18 member countries of the UN Economic and Social Commission for Asia and the Pacific (ESCAP) gathered in Busan, South Korea in 2006 to sign the 'Intergovernmental Agreement on the Pan Asia Railway Network.' According to this agreement, the Pan Asia Railway Network includes the North Railway which connects the Korean Peninsula, Russia, China, Mongolia, and Kazakhstan, the South Railway which connects southern China, Myanmar, India, Iran, and Turkey, the North-South Railway which connects Russia, Central Asia, and the Persian Gulf, and the China-ASEAN Railway which connects China and the ASEAN countries. The 'Intergovernmental Agreement on the Pan Asia Railway Network' took effect in June 2009, and the UN Economic and Social Commission for Asia and the Pacific held a commemoration ceremony in Bangkok of Thailand. Based on the existing railways of each country, this Pan Asia Railway Network was opened by connecting these railway networks. As a railway network spreading across 114,000 km and connecting 28 countries and regions, it came to be called the 'Iron Silk road.' When the operation of this Pan Asia Railway Network becomes active, it will stimulate economic development and co-prosperity in the Asia region as well as promote cultural exchange and international trade between Asia and Europe.[615] In this context, the fact that North Korean leader Kim Jong-un took this railway from Pyongyang to Vietnam to attend the United States-North Korea summit in Hanoi, Vietnam in late February, 2019, provides clear implications. In this situation, if Japan continues its current diplomatic and economic relationships centered on the United States and hesitates to become a member of Asia, Japan may end up being isolated in Asia when mutual dependence deepens among continental countries based on railway connections. The ASEAN+3 (ASEAN Plus Three, APT) Convention, which began with ASEAN's invitation of the heads of China, Japan, and Korea in December 1998, was a momentum to create a great-sphere economic zone in East Asia, encompassing Northeast Asia and Southeast Asia. In December 2005, the East Asia Summit (EAS) was held with the participation of Australia, New Zealand, and India in the ASEAN+3. The EAS signed the basic FTA among countries in the region and declared to make efforts to establish an East Asian community. Despite the fact that the United States was displeased with the concept of an FTA in East Asia, it has been participating in the EAS since 2010 so as not to be isolated in the process of regional cooperation in East Asia. Japan has reluctantly participated in this current of regional cooperation but shows an extremely passive attitude in forming critical agendas, as it is making use of military and diplomatic strategies based on the US-Japan Alliance. Furthermore, Japan rather works as an obstacle in the creation of an economic community, as it fails to gain the trust of Asian countries due to the fact that it has not been making proper efforts to overcome modern Japan's historical wrongdoings of invasion and colonization. The political and emotional gap between Japan and Asian countries surrounding historical issues is a problem which must necessarily be tackled for the creation of a regional community in Asia.

In particular, the structure of conflict, which is a remnant of the Cold War, and the structure of cooperation, which is a characteristic of the new age, coexists in international relations surrounding East Asia. The structure of conflict between North Korea and the three countries of the United States, Japan, and South Korea has not gone through qualitative changes, but the structure of conflict related to China and Russia collapsed with the end of the Cold War and a new form of structure has emerged. The structure of cooperation is taking the form of strengthening bilateral economic cooperation, while heading towards the direction of multilateral economic cooperation or regional integration.[616] Furthermore, there are two tides at the basis of East Asia - Neoliberalism at a global scale and agitative nationalism with the overtones of a nation-state. These two tides are working together in entanglement to create new and complicated relations. In particular, the national defense expenditure of East Asian countries continues to increase, and military forces are maintained on a large scale. The reason behind this is interpreted that the mode of confrontation from the Cold War era, such as the division of the Korean Peninsula continues to exist despite reform and opening in East Asia, and this has a synergistic effect as it is interlocked with a new crisis. Furthermore, as Japan tries to justify its history of colonization and invasion and avoid apology or responsibility of perpetration, this attitude stimulates the nationalism of East Asian countries, such as China and Korea. As a response, the voices of Japan's rightwing forces get louder and nationalism gets stronger, resulting in an endless vicious circle. As long as this situation continues, peace, co-existence, and mutual prosperity in East Asia will likely have a long way to go. Fortunately, in the case of the Korean Peninsula, since a new government stepped up in South Korea in May 2017 to replace the previous government which had an uncompromising stance toward North Korea, there has been a change of mood. Starting with the PyeongChang Olympic Winter Games in February 2018 as momentum, the two Koreas stepped into conversation mode, and there had been three Inter-Korean summits as well as one United States-North Korea summit (Singapore) in 2018 alone. Through these talks, a new discussion has begun to resolve North Korea's nuclear issues and to establish peace on the Korean Peninsula. There was another United States-North Korea summit in Vietnam in late February 2019, but the parties failed to reach a concrete agreement, making many people realize that it is difficult to settle decades of hostile relations in a short period of time. Compared to 2017, when North Korea and the United States strongly criticized each other, it is true that the circumstances surrounding the Korean Peninsula have considerably improved within the three years, but there is still a long way to go. Not only the United States and North Korea, but also parties of the Korean War, such as South Korea and China, should cooperate even more, end the armistice situation as soon as possible, and double efforts to establish a new system of peace.

Due to the nature of state power, it is not easy for one country to spontaneously recognize, repent for, apologize for, and fulfill its responsibility for an act of perpetration toward another country. However, if that country is formed and operated democratically, and there are many citizens who repent for their history of invasion and perpetration and pursue peace and co-existence, then the leadership of that country may shift from unilateral pursuit of national interests and conflict to the pursuit of peace and mutual prosperity. In the case of Germany, the members of civil society such as history teachers made the move to open the door to conversations on history. In addition, the leadership of Chancellor Konrad Adenauer and Chancellor Willy Brandt expedited reconciliation with European countries. Under this peacemaking atmosphere, UNESCO led the progress in conversations, and in 1992 when the European Union was founded, authors from 12 countries published a joint history textbook. In this aspect, the activities promoted by the History Educationalist Conference of Japan, which was founded in July 1949, with 'peace and democracy' as the goal of education, are meaningful. Centered on these educationalists, exchanges with Chinese and Korean scholars became more active since the 1990s. In 2005, the three countries of China, Japan, and Korea jointly published *A History to Open the Future*, which dealt with East Asia's modern and contemporary history. In particular, in 2010, which was the one hundredth anniversary of Japan's annexation of Korea, a joint declaration was announced by approximately 1,000 intellectuals, including Korean and Japanese historians.[617] This joint declaration stated that Japan's annexation of Korea 100 years ago was fundamentally invalid, as the contents and procedures were unfair and forceful. In a situation where confrontation is becoming rather stronger in East Asia, direct government intervention in historical and cultural issues may expand to diplomatic issues, so the role of civil society is extremely important.

As the United States and China are becoming the central axis of the world in terms of economy and military in the 21st century, Japan, which has over the years made use of a diplomacy strategy biased towards the United States based on the US-Japan Alliance, is required to make a choice on which country to place more importance in the future. However, for Japan, which has a strong sense of rivalry with China, it would not be easy to choose China at the moment, since it would mean being incorporated into a system of East Asian regional order centered on China. Hence, as long as China does not attain national power that overwhelmingly exceeds that of the United States, Japan will continue to use the strategy of keeping China in check through its solidarity with the United States. China already surpassed Japan in terms of GDP in 2010, becoming the second largest economy in the world. In addition, the size of China's economy exceeded twice that of Japan in 2014, and the gap is consistently increasing every year. According to the *World Economic Trends* published by the Japanese Cabinet in May 2010, the proportion of each country's GDP to world aggregate GDP in 2030 is foreseen to be 23.9% for China, 17.0% for the United States, and 5.8% for Japan.[618] Furthermore, China has a far larger military force than Japan and its level of weaponry is much more advanced. China is spending much more in military expenditure than Japan, and as foreign capital and technology are being combined to this, China's military power may be strengthened to the level of matching the strength of the United States in the future. In this situation, it seems to be impossible for Japan to build the capacity to stand up against China in terms of economy and military. Therefore, it would be a much wiser choice for Japan to strengthen peaceful relationships with China and promote the enhancement of Japan's practical national interests.

In East Asia, as the two countries of pre-modern superpower China and the modern superpower Japan were both exceedingly impatient in pursuing the new tasks of the era, they made an extremely breathless competition in the time of history. This impatience caused the abnormality in the development of East Asian history. In particular, modern Japan pursued militaristic external expansion policies based on its success in Western modernization, leaving a deep scar in the history of Asia.[619] During the 1920s before Japan's militarism was in full swing, Ishibashi Tanzan (石橋湛山, 1884-1973), Japan's representative liberalist, argued that Japan should dismiss the illusion of being a 'Big Japan (military expansionism)' and return to being a 'Small Japan.'[620] He claimed that 'If Japan abandons the ambition to exercise dominion over China and gives up Manchuria, Taiwan, Korea, and Sakhalin, there will be no need for national defense regarding possession, and thus war will not occur at all.' He presented these arguments long before the Manchurian Incident, which was extremely analytic and contained wisdom with insights into the future. If modern Japan had executed its Asian policies based on this logic, there would not have been such tragedy that put Asian history in the early 20th century into a vortex. Likewise, this lesson from history applies to the future as well. Therefore, the directing point of Japan should not be focused on heading towards another tragedy. The world eagerly waits for a Japanese politician like Ishibashi who can provide a clear analysis on the worrisome steps that present-day Japan is taking and be able to present a desirable direction for the future.

The knowledge we have about the past influences the creation of our emotions, awareness, and actions in almost every field. In addition, the scope and level of this knowledge is sometimes determined by our emotions, awareness, and actions. In the end, people choose a side between love and hatred, happiness and sadness, and reconciliation and conflict, depending on what perspective and knowledge they have on history. Therefore, history education is important to that extent, and when that history reaches beyond the scope of one country, it should necessarily be accompanied by consideration towards other countries.[621] A wall of mutual hostility and distrust remains tall among Asian countries, due to the modern history marked by invasion and resistance, as well as perpetration and victimization, and the insufficient self-reflection, apology, and compensation from Japan's part. In a situation like this, what is important is history education for the future generation. History education should teach students to what degree each country acknowledges its past faults or crimes and how much it empathizes with the pain of other countries. It would be a shortcut to self-reflection and reconciliation for the perpetrator to personally see and experience the site of agony. Especially, a frank history education on the part of the perpetrator would be a cornerstone for peace in Asia. Even if Asia's modern and contemporary history is stained with pain and disgrace, it is a common history, and the settlement of this history as well as the construction of a new future is also a common task.[622] In this sense, Europe's experience will be a most useful reference and lesson. France and Germany as well as Germany and Poland have created organizations for mutual cooperation to make efforts to publish joint history and geography textbooks in order to reduce conflicts from disparities in historical perception. Based on these efforts, present-day Europe has created a community called the European Union and is pursuing co-prosperity and development. Asian countries should learn from Europe's experience and create a community that engages in mutual cooperation and development.

REFERENCES

A Joint Declaration by Japanese and Korean Intellectuals – On the Centennial of the Japanese Annexation of Korea, Seoul and Tokyo, May 10, 2010.

Amino, Yoshihiko, *Rethinking Japanese History*, Tokyo: Chikumashobo Ltd., 2005 (Translated by Gyeong-taek Lim, Seoul: Dolbegae, 2015).

Amino, Yoshihiko, *What is Japan? - History of Japan*, Tokyo: Kodansha Ltd., 2000 (Translated by Hun Park, Seoul: Changbi Publishers, 2003).

Arendt, Hannah, *Eichmann in Jerusalem: A Report on the Banality of Evil*, New York: Penguin Books, 1963.

Awaya, Kentaro et al., *War Responsibility and Postwar Responsibility – How are Japan and Germany Different?*, Tokyo: The Asahi Shimbun Company, 1994.

Bartlett, Bruce R., *Cover-Up: The Politics of Pearl Harbor, 1941-1946*, New York: Arlington House, 1978.

Bary, William Theodore De, Ryusaku Tsunoda, and Donald Keene, *Sources of Japanese Tradition*, vol. 2, New York: Columbia University Press, 1964.

Beauchamp, Edward, "Foreign Employees of the Meiji Period", *Kodansha Encyclopedia of Japan*, vol. 2, 1983.

Behr, Edward, *Hirohito: Behind the Myth*, New York: Villard Books, 1989.

Benedict, Ruth, *The Chrysanthemum and the Sword: Patterns of Japanese Culture*, Boston: Houghton Mifflin Company, 1946 (Mariner Books edition 2005).

Bergamini, David, *Japan's Imperial Conspiracy*, New York: William Morrow and Company, 1971.

Bix, Herbert P., "Inventing the 'Symbol Monarchy' in Japan, 1945-52", *Journal of Japanese Studies*, vol. 21, no. 2, Summer 1995.

Bix, Herbert P., "The Showa Emperor's Monologue and the Problem of War Responsibility", *The Journal of Japanese Studies*, vol. 18, no. 2, Summer 1992.

Bix, Herbert P., *Hirohito and the Making of Modern Japan*, New York: HarperCollins, 2000.

Blacker, Carmen, *The Japanese Enlightenment: A Study of the Writings of Fukuzawa Yukichi*, Cambridge, England: Cambridge University Press, 1964.

Borton, Hugh, *Japan's Modern Century*, New York: Ronald Press, 1955.

Buruma, Ian, *Inventing Japan 1853-1964*, New York: The Modern Library, 2003.

Buruma, Ian, *The Wages of Guilt: Memories of War in Germany and Japan*, New York: Farrar Strauss & Giroux, 1994.

Cabinet Office of Japan, *2017 White Book on Aging*, 2017.

Calman, Donald, *The Nature and Origins of Japanese Imperialism: A Reinterpretation of the Great Crisis of 1873*, London: Routledge, 1992.

Chang, Iris, *The Rape of Nanking: The Forgotten Holocaust of World War II*, Harmondsworth: Penguin, 1997.

Cho, Baek-gi, "The Solution to Japan's Sexual Slavery Issue in International Law – the Past, Present, and Future of Japan-Korea Relations," *Journal of Law*, vol. 31, no. 1, 2011.

Cho, Myeong-cheol et al., *The Choice of the Japanese*, Seoul: Dareun Sesang, 2002.

Choi, Eun-mi, "Research on the Effect of US Foreign Policy on Postwar Settlements – Focusing on Germany's and Japan's Cases of War Criminal Treatment and War Reparations among States," *Donga Research* (58), 2010.

Choi, Jang-geun, "Pending Issues and Prospects of Japan's Territorial Disputes", Tae-ho Park, and Cheol-hee Park (eds.), *East Asia's Localism, Nationalism, and Regionalism – Focusing on the Growth of the Japanese State and the Evolution of International Order in East Asia*, Seoul: Ingan Sarang, 2007.

Cohen, Theodore, *Remaking Japan: The American Occupation as New Deal*, New York: Free Press, 1987.

Coleman, James S., "Social Capital in the Creation of Human Capital", *American Journal of Sociology*, vol. 94, 1988.

Cook, Haruko Taya and Theodore Failor Cook, *Japan at War: An Oral History*, New York: New Press, 1992.

Coox, Alvin, "The Pacific War", Peter Duus (ed.), *The Cambridge History of Japan*, vol. 6 (The Twentieth Century), Cambridge, England: Cambridge University Press, 1989.

Coox, Alvin, *Nomonhan: Japan against Russia 1939*, Stanford, California: Stanford University Press, 1985.

Cortazzi, Hugh, *The Japanese Achievement*, London: Sidgwick and Jackson, 1990.

Dallek, Robert, *Franklin D. Roosevelt and American Foreign Policy, 1932-1945*, New York: Oxford University Press, 1979.

Daniels, Gordon, "Japan at War", Richard Bowring and Peter Kornicki (eds.), *Cambridge Encyclopedia of Japan*, Cambridge, England: Cambridge University Press, 1993.

Daws, Gavan, *Prisoners of the Japanese: POWs of World War II in the Pacific*, New York: William Morrow, 1994.

Diamond, Jared, *Guns, Germs and Steel: The Fates of Human Societies*, New York: W.W. Norton & Company, 2005.

Dore, Ronald Philip, *Land Reform in Japan*, London: Oxford University Press, 1959.

Dower, John W., "The Useful War", Carol Gluck and Stephen R. Graubard (eds.), *Showa: The Japan of Hirohito*, New York: Norton, 1992.

Dower, John W., *Embracing Defeat: Japan in the Wake of World War II*, New York: W.W.Norton & Company, 2000.

Dower, John W., *Empire and Aftermath: Yoshida Shigeru and the Japanese Experience*, Cambridge: Harvard Council on East Asian Studies, 1980.

Dower, John W., *War without Mercy: Race and Power in the Pacific War*, London and Boston: Faber and Faber, 1986.

Edwards, Walter, "In Pursuit of Himiko: Postwar Archeology and the Location of Yamatai," *Monumenta Nipponica*, vol. 51, no. 1, Spring 1996.

Elison, George, "Oda Nobunaga (1534-1582)", *Kodansha Encyclopedia of Japan*, vol. 6, Tokyo: Kodansha, 1983.

Fackler, Martin, "Japan Goes from Dynamic to Disheartened: Retrenchment Offers the West a Grim View of the Future", *New York Times*, October 17, 2010.

Fairbank, John King, Edwin O. Reischauer, and Albert M. Craig, *East Asia: Tradition and Transformation*, Boston: Houghton Mifflin, 1973.

Farris, W. Wayne, *Japan to 1600: A Social and Economic History*, Honolulu: University of Hawaii Press, 2009.

Field, Norma, *In the Realm of a Dying Emperor: A Portrait of Japan at Century's End*, New York: Vintage Books, 1991.

References

Fogel, Joshua A., *The Nanjing Massacre in History and Historiography*, Oakland, CA: University of California Press, 2000.

Foreign Language Publishing House (ed.), *Materials on the Trial of Former Servicemen of the Japanese Army Charged with Manufacturing and Employing Bacteriological Weapons*, Moscow: Foreign Language Publishing House, 1950.

Francks, Penelope, *Japanese Economic Development: Theory and Practice*, London: Routledge, 1992.

Fromm, Erich, *To have or to Be?*, New York: Harper & Row, 1976.

Gerschenkron, Alexander, *Economics Backwardness in Historical Perspective*, Cambridge: Harvard University Press, 1962.

Gibney, Frank, *The Pacific Century: America and Asia in a Changing World*, New York: Scribners/Macmillan, 1992.

Giordano, Ralph, *Die Zweite Schuld oder Von der Last Deutscher zu sein* (*The Second Guilt or the Burden of Being German*), Hamburg: Rasch und Röhring, 1987.

Global Trade Information Services, *World Trade Atlas*.

Gluck, Carol, *Japan's Modern Myths: Ideology in the Late Meiji Period*, Princeton: Princeton University Press, 1985.

Gordon, Andrew, *A Modern History of Japan: From Tokugawa Times to the Present* (Third Edition), New York: Oxford University Press, 2014.

Gordon, Andrew, *Labor and Imperial Democracy*, Berkeley: University of California Press, 1991.

Ha, Jae-hwan, Kwang-jun Choi, and Chang-rok Kim, "Legal Liability to Korea and Koreans – A Review of the Issue of 'Japanese Military Sexual Slavery' in International Law" *Journal of Law*, vol. 37, no. 1 (Serial Number 45), December 1996.

Ha, Woo-bong, *Japan and Korea – History and Future of Mutual Awareness*, Seoul: Salim, 2005.

Hadley, Eleanor M., "Zaibatsu Dissolution", *Kodansha Encyclopedia of Japan*, vol. 8, Tokyo: Kodansha, 1983.

Han, Yeong-woo, *Empress Myeongseong and the Korean Empire*, Seoul: Hyohyung Publishing, 2001.

Hane, Mikiso, *Modern Japan: A Historical Survey*, Boulder and London: Westview Press, 1992.

Harris, Sheldon, *Factories of Death: Japanese Biological Warfare, 1932-1945, and the American Cover-up*, London: Routledge, 1994.

Hasegawa, Tsuyoshi, *Racing the Enemy: Stalin, Truman, and the Surrender of Japan*, Cambridge: Belknap Press, 2005.

Havens, Thomas R. H., *Fire across the Sea: The Vietnam War and Japan, 1965-1975*, Princeton, N. J.: Princeton University Press, 1987.

Hayashi, Hirofumi, *Questioning Japan's Pacifism – Focusing on War Crimes Trial, Peace Constitution, and East Asian Relations*, Tokyo: Kamogawa Co., Ltd., 2008.

Heinrichs, Waldo, "World War Ⅱ", *Kodansha Encyclopedia of Japan*, vol. 8, Tokyo: Kodansha, 1983.

Henshall, Kenneth, "From Sedan Chair to Aeroplane: The Meiji Period Tokyoite Transported through Time and Place", *Journal of the Oriental Society of Australia*, vol. 20-21, 1988-89.

Henshall, Kenneth, *A History of Japan: From Stone Age to Superpower* (Third Edition), Hampshire: Palgrave Macmillan, 2012.

Heo, Tae-su, "A Brief View on Japan's Postwar Responsibilities," Secretariat of the National Assembly of Korea, *National Assembly Research Service Monthly*, vol. 206, February 1992.

Hicks, George, "The Comfort Women", Peter Duus, Ramon H. Myers, and Mark R. Peattie (eds.), *The Japanese Wartime Empire 1931-1945*, Princeton, N.J.: Princeton University Press, 1996.

Hicks, George, *The Comfort Women: Japan's Brutal Regime of Enforced Prostitution in the Second World War*, New York: Norton, 1995.

Hirakawa, Sukehiro, "Japan's Turn to the West", Marius B. Jansen (ed.), *The Cambridge History of Japan*, vol. 5 (The Nineteenth Century), Cambridge, England: Cambridge University Press, 1989.

History Educationalist Conference of Japan (ed.), *East Asian World and Japan*, Tokyo: Aoki Shoten Publishing Co., 2004.

Honda, Katsuichi, *Studies of the Nanking Massacre*, Tokyo: Bansei Sha Publishing, 1992.

Honda, Katsuichi, *The Nanjing Massacre: A Japanese Journalist Confronts Japan's National Shame*, New York: M. E. Sharpe, 1999.

Hong, Seong-pil, "An Assessment of Japan's Perception and Fulfillment of Postwar Responsibilities in the Perspective of International Law," Chungnam

University, *Chungnam Law Review*, vol. 23, no. 1, June 2012.

Howard, Chris Perez, *Mariquita: A Tragedy of Guam*, Suva: Institute of Pacific Studies of the University of the South Pacific, 1986.

Howell, David L., *Geographies of Identity in Nineteenth Century Japan*, Berkeley: University of California Press, 2005.

Hu, Hua-Ling, *American Goddess at the Rape of Nanking: The Courage of Minnie Vautrin*, Illinois: Southern Illinois University Press, 2000.

Hunter, Janet, *The Emergence of Modern Japan: An Introductory History since 1853*, London: Longman, 1989.

Hyun, Daesong, *Birth of Territorial Nationalism: The Politics of the Dokdo/Takeshima Issue*, Kyoto: Minerva-Shobo, 2006.

Ienaga, Saburo, *War Responsibility*, Tokyo: Iwanami Shoten, 1985.

International Monetary Fund, *World Economic Outlook Database*.

Ishikawa, Shoji and Kazuomi Hirai (eds.), *The Unfinished Twentieth Century - Political History of East Asia 1894 ~*, Tokyo: Horitsu Bunka Sha, 2003.

Ital, Heiko, "Coping with the past in Germany and Japan - or why Japan is downplaying its war crimes in history textbooks in contrast to Germany", *Korean Journal of Social Sciences*, vol. 22, no. 4, December 2012.

Ito, Chosei, *Rediscovering Collectivism: Driving Force of Growing Economy*, Tokyo: Diamond Inc., 1969.

Jang, In-seong, *Meiji Restoration – the Starting Point of Modern Japan*, Seoul: Salim, 2007.

Japan-Korea Common History Textbook Production Team, *Japan and Korea, the History in Between*, Seoul: Humanist Books, 2012.

Jaspers, Karl, *Die Schuldfrage*, Heidelberg: L. Schneider, 1946 (*The Question of German Guilt*, translated by E. B. Ashton, New York: The Dial Press, 1947).

Jeong, Geun-shik, *History of Suffering: Memory and Testimony of the Atomic Air Raid*, Seoul: Seonin, 2005.

Jeong, Hye-seon, *Japanese History Digest 100*, Seoul: Garam Planning Publisher, 2011.

Johnson, Chalmers, *Blowback: The Costs and Consequences of American Empire*, New York: Metropolitan Books, 2000.

Kang, Sang-jung and Shunya Yoshimi, Translated by Seong-mo Lim and Kyeong-won Kim, *Perspective of Globalization*, Seoul: Yeesan Publishing, 2004.

Kato, Shuichi et al., *Hidden Form of Japanese Culture*, Tokyo: Iwanami Shoten, 1991.

Kazuko, Watanabe, "Militarization, Colonialism, and the Trafficking of Women: 'Comfort Women' Forced into Sexual Labor for Japanese Soldiers", *Bulletin of Concerned Asian Scholars*, vol. 26, no. 4, Oct.-Dec. 1994.

Kidder, J. Edward, "The Earliest Societies in Japan", Delmer M. Brown (ed.), *The Cambridge History of Japan*, vol. 1 (Ancient Japan), Cambridge, England: Cambridge University Press, 1993.

Kim, Choong-seek, *Sorrowful Islands*, Seoul: Hyohyung Publishing, 2005.

Kim, Pil-dong, *Japan's Identity*, Seoul: Salim, 2005.

Kim, Yong-deok, *An Insight on Japanese Modern History*, Seoul: Jisik-Sanup Publications, 1991.

Kim, Yong-woon and Soon-shin Jin, *Speaking of the History and Future of Korea-China-Japan*, Seoul: Literature & Thought, 2000.

Kim, Yong-woon, *The Mindsets of the Japanese and the Koreans*, Seoul: Hangilsa, 1985.

Klug, Foster, "US backtracks on name of disputed Asian islands," July 30, 2008, Associated Press (AP).

Korea Times, July 28 & 31, 2008.

Korean Association for Japanese History, *Atlas Japanese History*, Seoul: Sakyejul, 2011.

Korean Council for Women Drafted for Military Sexual Slavery by Japan, Association for Research on Japanese Military Sexual Slavery, *Korean Comfort Women Taken by Force*, Seoul: Hanul Publishing Group, 1993.

Kosaka, Masataka, "The Showa Era", Carol Gluck and Stephen R. Graubard (eds.), *Showa: The Japan of Hirohito*, New York: Norton, 1992.

Koyasu, Nobukuni, *How Asia has been depicted: Orientalism in Modern Japan*, Tokyo: Fujiwara Shoten, 2003.

Kristof, Nicholas, "A Japanese Generation Haunted by Its Past", *New York Times*, January 22, 1997.

Kwon, Seong-wook, *The Second Sino-Japanese War*, Seoul: Miji Books, 2015.

Large, Stephen, *Emperor Hirohito and Showa Japan: A Political Biography*, London: Routledge, 1992.

Ledyard, Gari, "Horse-Rider Theory", *Kodansha Encyclopedia of Japan*, vol. 3, Tokyo: Kodansha, 1983.

Lee, Changsoo and George Devos, *Koreans in Japan*, Berkeley: University of California Press, 1981.

Lee, Gye-hwang, *War of Memory – Historical Perception of Contemporary Japan and the Japan-Korea Relations*, Seoul: Ewha Womans University Press, 2003.

Lee, Jin-mo, "West Germany's Process of Overcoming the past after the War (1945-1990) – Focusing on the Roles of the Allied Powers and the Civil Society," *Research on Eastern and Western Culture* (7), 2000.

Lee, Kyu-shu, "Japan's War Responsibility Issues and Neo-nationalism," Gachon University Institute of Asian Culture, *Asian Culture Research*, vol. 29, March 2013.

Lee, Seong-hwan, *Warfare State Japan*, Seoul: Salim, 2005.

Lévi Strauss, Claude, *The Savage Mind* (French: *La Pensée Sauvage*, 1962), Chicago: University of Chicago Press, 1966.

Levinas, Emmanuel (tr. Alphonso Lingis), *Totality and Infinity*, Hague: Martinus Nijhoff Publishers, 1979.

Lie, John, *Multiethnic Japan*, Cambridge: Harvard University Press, 2001.

Lockwood, William, *The Economic Development of Japan: Growth and Structural Change*, Princeton, N.J.: Princeton University Press, 1968.

Los Angeles Times, "A Royal Denunciation of Horrors: Hirohito's Brother - an Eyewitness - Assails Japan's Wartime Brutality", July 9, 1994.

MacArthur, Douglas, *Reminiscences*, New York: McGraw-Hill, 1964.

Maga, Tim, *Judgment at Tokyo: The Japanese War Crimes Trials*, Lexington: University Press of Kentucky, 2001.

Magosaki, Ukeru, *Japan's Territorial Disputes – Senkaku, Dokdo (Takeshima), Northern Islands*, Tokyo: Chikumashobo Ltd., 2011.

Mainichi Daily News, August 13, 1994.

Maruyama, Masao, *Thoughts and Behaviors of Contemporary Politics*, Tokyo: Mirai-Sha, 1964.

Massarella, Derek, *A World Elsewhere: Europe's Encounter with Japan in the Sixteenth and Seventeenth Centuries*, New Haven, Connecticut: Yale University Press, 1990.

Matsumoto, Katsumi, *Current Status and Tasks of Postwar Compensation Lawsuits in Japan*, Seoul National University, BK21 Legal Study Group, Public Interest and Human Rights Law Research Center, *Public Interest and Human Rights*, vol. 4, no. 1, February 2007.

McClellan, Edwin, *Two Japanese Novelists: Soseki and Toson*, Chicago: University of Chicago Press, 1969.

McCormac, Gavan and Satoko Oka Norimatsu, *Resistant Islands: Okinawa Confronts Japan and the United States*, Lanham, Maryland: Rowman & Littlefield Publishers, 2012 (Translated by Yeong-shin Jeong, Seoul: Changbi Publishers, 2014).

Meiroku Zasshi: Journal of the Japanese Enlightenment, translated by William Reynolds Braisted, Cambridge: Harvard University Press, 1976.

Metzler, Mark, *Lever of Empire: The International Gold Standard and the Crisis of Liberalism in Prewar Japan*, Berkeley: University of California Press, 2006.

Mill, John Stuart, *On Liberty*, London: John W. Parker & Son, 1859.

Miller, Frank O., *Minobe Tatsukichi: Interpreter of Constitutionalism in Japan*, Berkeley: University of California Press, 1965.

Min, Doo-gi, *Competition with Time*, Seoul: Yonsei University Press, 2000.

Miyajima, Hiroshi, *Criticizing Japan's View of History*, Seoul: Changbi Publishers, 2013.

Moffet, Sebastian, "Japan Justice Minister Denies Nanking Massacre", *Reuters*, May 5, 1994.

Morris-Suzuki, Tessa, "An Integral part of Our National Territory: Frontiers and the Image of the Nation in Japanese History", a thesis of International Symposium to Commemorate Establishment of Hanyang University's Research Institute of Comparative History and Culture ('Frontiers or Borders?', 23-24 April, 2004), Edited by Ji-hyeon Lim, *Modern Borders, Changes in History*, Seoul: Humanist Books, 2004.

Morris-Suzuki, Tessa, *In Search of Critical Imagination: Japan in an Age of Globalization*, Tokyo: Heibonsha, 2013.

Münkler, Herfried, *Imperien*, Berlin: Rowohlt·Berlin Verlag GmbH, 2005 (Translated by Jin-seong Kong, Seoul: Chaeksesang Publishing Co., 2015).

Murphy, Richard Taggart, *The Weight of the Yen: How Denial Imperils America's Future and Ruins an Alliance*, New York: Norton, 1996.

Najita, Tetsuo and Harry Harootunian, "Japanese Revolt against the West", Peter Duus (ed.), *The Cambridge History of Japan*, vol. 6 (The Twentieth Century), Cambridge, England: Cambridge University Press, 1989.

Najita, Tetsuo, "Some Reflections on Idealism in the Political Thought of Yoshino Sakuzo", Bernard S. Silberman, Harry D. Harootunian and Gail Lee Bemstein (eds.) *Japan in Crisis: Essays on Taisho Democracy*, Princeton, N.J.: Princeton University Press, 1974.

New York World, November 28, 1894.

Newsweek, "The Lost Decade", July 27, 1998.

Nishi, Toshio, *Unconditional Democracy: Education and Politics in Occupied Japan 1945-1952*, Stanford: Hoover Institution Press, 1982.

Nishio, Kanji (ed.), *The History of the People*, Tokyo: Sankei Simbun Co, 1999.

Nishio, Kanji et al. (eds.), *New History Textbook*, Tokyo: Hushosa, 2001.

OECD, *Global Economic Outlook*, June 2017.

Oguma, Eiji, *The State of Japan*, Tokyo: Shinyosha, 2018.

Oh, Ji-yeong, *Tonghak History*, Seoul: Yeongchang Publishing Company, 1940.

Okakura, Yoshisaburo, *The Life and Thought of Japan*, Tokyo: Dentosha, 1913 (Published script of lecture titled "The Life and Thought of Japan" in Boston, US in 1910).

Park, Hun, *How was the Meiji Restoration Possible?*, Seoul: Minumsa Publishing Group, 2014.

Park, No-ja, *Empire of White Masks – Orientalism, Moving Beyond Western-centric History*, Seoul: Hangyeorae Press, 2003.

Park, Seong-su, *Research on Independence Movement History*, Seoul: Changbi Publishers, 1980.

Park, Yeong-jae et al., *Dissecting Today's Japan*, Seoul: Hangilsa, 1987.

Patrick, Hugh T., "The Economic Muddle of the 1920s", James William Morley (ed.), *Dilemmas of Growth in Prewar Japan*, Princeton, N.J.: Princeton University Press, 1971.

Pearson, Richard, *Ancient Japan*, New York: George Braziller, 1992.

Piccigallo, Philip R., *The Japanese on Trial: Allied War Crimes Operation in the East, 1945-1951*, Austin: University of Texas Press, 1980.

Pitman, Joanna, "Repentance: Tokyo-Postcard", *The New Republic*, February 10, 1992.

Putnam, Robert D., *Bowling Alone: The Collapse and Revival of American Community*, New York: Simon & Schuster, 2000.

Rasteiro, Rita and Lounès Chikhi, "Revisiting the Peopling of Japan: An Admixture Perspective," *Journal of Human Genetics*, no. 54(6), June 2009.

Reischauer, Edwin O. and Albert M. Craig, *Japan: Tradition and Transformation*, London, Boston, and Sydney: George Allen & Unwin, 1979.

Reischauer, Edwin O., *Japan: Past and Present*, New York: Knopf, 1964.

Rickert, Erwin (ed.), *The Good German of Nanking: The Diaries of John Rabe*, New York: Knopf, 1998.

Riesman, David and Evelyn Thompson Riesman, *Conversations in Japan: Modernization, Politics and Culture*, New York: Basic Books Inc., 1967.

Rummel, Rudolph. J., *China's Bloody Century: Genocide and Mass Murder Since 1900*, London: Routledge, 2007.

Ruoff, Kenneth J., *The People's Emperor: Democracy and the Japanese Monarchy, 1945-1995*, Cambridge: Harvard University Press, 2001.

Said, Edward W., *Culture and Imperialism*, New York: Vintage Books, 1994.

Said, Edward W., *Orientalism*, New York: Pantheon, 1978.

Sandel, Michael, *Justice: What's the Right Thing to Do?*, New York: Farrar, Straus and Giroux, 2009.

Sanuki, Hiroshi, "Sixty Years since Bombing and War Defeat, Thinking about Japan's Responsibility toward Peace in East Asia", Korean Association of History Education, *History Education Research*, June 2005.

Schelling, Thomas C., *The Strategy of Conflict*, Cambridge: Harvard University Press, 1980.

Schoenberger, Karl, "Japan Aide Quits over Remark on WW II ", *Los Angeles Times*, May 5, 1988.

Schoppa, Leonard James, *Education Reform in Japan: A Case of Immobilist Politics*, London: Routledge, 1993.

Seagrave, Sterling and Peggy Seagrave, *The Yamato Dynasty: The Secret History of Japan's Imperial Family*, London and New York: Bantam Press, 1999.

Seidensticker, Edward, *Low City, High City, Tokyo from Edo to the Earthquake*, New York: Knopf, 1983.

Shabshina, Fania Isaakovna, Translated by Myeong-ho Kim, *In Colonial Korea*, Seoul: Hanul Publishing Group, 1996.

Sheff, David, "Shintaro Ishihara-candid conversation", *Playboy*, vol. 37, no. 10, October 1990.

Shim, Gi-jae, *Japan's Past and Present Read through Historical Trends*, Seoul: Dankook University Press, 2009.

Smith, Thomas C., *Native Sources of Japanese Industrialization, 1750-1920*, Berkeley: University of California Press, 1989.

Soh, Chunghee, "Human Rights and the 'Comfort Women'", *Peace Review*, vol. 12, no. 1, 2000.

Song, Choong-gi, "Germany's Belated Historical Settlement – Focusing on Compensation to Forced Laborers under Nazi Rule," *History Criticism* (73), 2005.

Suzuki, Yuko, *War Responsibility and Gender: 'Liberalist View of History' and the Issue of Japanese Military 'Sex Slaves'*, Tokyo: Mirai-Sha, 1997.

Takahashi, Hikohiro, *War Responsibility on the Part of the People*, Tokyo: Aoki Shoten Publishing Co., 1989.

Takahashi, Tetsuya, *Postwar Responsibility Argument of Japan*, Tokyo: Kodansha, 2005.

Takahashi, Tetsuya, *State and Sacrifice*, Tokyo: Japan Broadcast Publishing Co., 2005 (Translated by Mok Lee, Seoul: Chaekgwahamge, 2008).

Takashiro, Koichi, *Japan's Dual System of Power – Shogun and the Emperor*, Seoul: Salim, 2006.

The Asahi Shimbun, November 1, 1975.

The Asia Peace and History Research Institute, *Perception of History beyond Borders in East Asia*, Seoul: Seonin, 2008.

The Association for the Verification of Inhuman Conduct by Japanese Researchers and Health Care Professionals during the War, Translated by Akira Suzuki, *Unit 731 and the Doctors: War and Medical Ethics*, Seoul: Media

Health Cooperative, 2014.

The China-Japan-Korea Common History Text Tri-National Committee, *Modern and Contemporary History of East Asia Jointly Written by China, Japan and Korea 1 - Understanding East Asian History through Changes in International Relations*, Seoul: Humanist Books, 2012.

The China-Japan-Korea Common History Text Tri-National Committee, *A History to Open the Future*, Seoul: Hangyeorae Press, 2005.

The China-Japan-Korea Common History Text Tri-National Committee, *Modern and Contemporary History of East Asia Jointly Written by China, Japan and Korea 2 - Understanding the History of People and Interaction by Theme*, Seoul: Humanist Books, 2012.

The Japan Times (weekly international edition), "Nanjing Testament," August 22-28, 1994 & July 18-24, 1994.

The Ministry of Finance of Japan, *Japanese Public Finance Fact Sheet*, each year.

The Ministry of Foreign Affairs of Japan, *100 Years of the Ministry of Foreign Affairs*, Tokyo: Hara-Shobo, 1969.

The Ministry of Internal Affairs and Communications (Statistics Bureau), *Statistical Handbook of Japan 2019*.

The National Institute on Social Security and Population Issues, *The Future Population Estimation of Japan – 2017*.

The Northeast Asian History Foundation (ed.), *Historical Narration and Peace in East Asia*, Seoul: Northeast Asian History Foundation, 2011.

The Weekly Standard, December 1, 2003.

The Yomiuri Newspaper (Yomiuri Shimbun), June 8, 1976 & July 6, 1994.

Thoreau, Henry David, *Resistance to Civil Government*, 1849 (Norwalk, Connecticut: Easton Press, 1993).

Tian, Nan, et al., "Trends in World Military Expenditure, 2019", *SIPRI Fact Sheet* (April 2020), Stockholm International Peace Research Institute, 2020.

Toyo Keizai Shinpo, Editorials on July 30, August 13, and September 23, 1921.

Trefalt, Beatrice, "Living Dead: Japanese Prisoners-of-War in the Southwest Pacific", *New Zealand Journal of East Asian Studies,* vol. 3, no. 2, December 1995.

Tsurumi, Shunsuke, *A Cultural History of Postwar Japan 1945-1980*, London and New York: Kegan Paul International, 1987.

Uchida, Tatsuru, *Japan as a Peripheral Country*, Tokyo: Shinchosha, 2009.

Ukai, Satoshi et al., Translated by the Translation Network of Study Space 'Suyuneomeo,' *Anti-Japan and East Asia*, Seoul: Somyong Publishing, 2005.

UN Comtrade, *The International Trade Statistics Year Book 2018*.

United Nations, National Accounts Main Aggregate Database.

Upham, Frank, "Unplaced Persons and Struggles for Place", Andrew Gordon (ed.), *Postwar Japan as History*, Berkeley: University of California Press, 1993.

Utsumi, Aiko, *Reflection of Japan and Asia in Terms of Postwar Compensation*, Tokyo: Yamakawa Shuppansha Ltd., 2002.

Vogel, Ezra F., *Japan as Number One*, Cambridge: Harvard University Press, 1979.

Wada, Haruki, *How to Solve Territorial Issues*, Tokyo: Heibonsha, 2012.

Wakamiya, Yoshibumi, *Reconciliation and Nationalism – East Asian World View of Postwar Conservatives*, Tokyo: The Asahi Shimbun Company, 2006.

Walzer, Michael, *Just and Unjust: A Moral Argument with Historical Illustrations*, New York: Basic Books, 1977.

Ward, Robert Edward, "Presurrender Planning: Treatment of the Emperor and Constitutional Change", Robert Edward Ward and Yoshikazu Sakamoto (eds.), *Democratizing Japan: The Allied Occupation*, Honolulu: University of Hawaii Press, 1987.

Wilkinson, Endymion Poter, *Misunderstanding: Europe versus Japan*, Tokyo: Chuokoronsha, 1981.

Williams, Peter and David Wallace, *Unit 731: The Japanese Army's Secret of Secrets*, London: Hodder & Stoughton, 1989.

World Bank, *World Development Indicators*.

World Trade Organization (WTO), *World Trade Statistical Review 2019*.

Yasuaki, Onuma, "Japanese War Guilt and Postwar Responsibilities of Japan", *Berkeley Journal of International Law*, vol. 20, issue 3, 2002.

Yoshida, Yutaka, *Japanese People's View of the War*, Tokyo: Iwanami Shoten, 1995.

Yoshimi, Yoshiaki, "The Achievements and Tasks of Research on the Japanese Military Sexual Slavery Issue," *The Violence of Japanese Colonization and Japanese Military Sexual Slavery* -International Seminar Booklet on the Japanese Military Sexual Slavery Issue, 2007.

Yoshimi, Yoshiaki, *Military Comfort Women*, Tokyo: Iwanami Shoten, 1995.

Yoshimi, Yoshiaki, *What is Japanese Sexual Slavery System?*, Tokyo: Iwanami Shoten, 2010 (Translated by Sang-gu Nam, Seoul: Yeoksa Gonggan, 2013).

Young, Louise, *Japan's Total Empire*, Berkeley: University of California Press, 1998.

Zhu, Cheng Shan (ed.), *The Memorial Hall of the Victims in Nanjing Massacre by Japanese Invaders*, Hong Kong: London Editions (HK) Ltd, 2010.

NOTES

[1] Hua-Ling Hu, *American Goddess at the Rape of Nanking: The Courage of Minnie Vautrin*, Illinois: Southern Illinois University Press, 2000, p.97.

[2] Cheng Shan Zhu (ed.), *The Memorial Hall of the Victims in Nanjing Massacre by Japanese Invaders*, Hong Kong: London Editions (HK) Ltd, 2010, pp.22-23.

[3] Andrew Gordon, *A Modern History of Japan: From Tokugawa Times to the Present* (Third Edition), New York: Oxford University Press, 2014, p.114.

[4] Here, zone of sovereignty refers to the scope (territory) in which the sovereignty of governmental power has effect. Sovereignty means exclusive and absolute control over territory.

[5] During the 60 or so years from the Meiji Restoration until the defeat in the war, 15 of the 28 prime ministers were from the military, holding office for 30 years and 11 months.

[6] Seong-hwan Lee, *Warfare State Japan*, Seoul: Salim, 2005, pp.8-11.

[7] War reparations of 200 million taels of silver (approximately 400 million yen) at the time amounted to 3 times the budget of China, more than 4 times the budget of Japan, and approximately 2 times the war expenses at the time.

[8] Eiji Oguma, *The State of Japan*, Tokyo: Shinyosha, 2018, p.63.

[9] The China-Japan-Korea Common History Text Tri-National Committee, *Modern and Contemporary History of East Asia Jointly Written by China, Japan and Korea 1 - Understanding East Asian History through Changes in International Relations*, Seoul: Humanist Books, 2012, pp.143-144.

[10] Myeong-cheol Cho et al., *The Choice of the Japanese*, Seoul: Dareun Sesang, 2002, pp.196-197.

[11] Eiji Oguma, *The State of Japan*, Tokyo: Shinyosha, 2018, pp.29-38.

[12] Kenneth Henshall, *A History of Japan: From Stone Age to Superpower* (Third Edition), Hampshire: Palgrave Macmillan, 2012, p.139.

¹³ Japan returned Liaodong Peninsula to China due to the intervention of Russia, Germany, and France (Tripartite Intervention), and this Tripartite Intervention acted as momentum for Japan to be more cautious in diplomacy and strengthen its will to become a 'rich country, strong army.' Thus, Japan gained victory in the Russo-Japanese War 10 years later.

¹⁴ Now China became 'a sleeping pig rather than a sleeping lion' due to the Japanese, and the Japanese referred to the Chinese as pigs and started calling the country 'Shina (支那).'

¹⁵ Seong-hwan Lee, *Warfare State Japan*, Seoul: Salim, 2005, p.24; The China-Japan-Korea Common History Text Tri-National Committee, *Modern and Contemporary History of East Asia Jointly Written by China, Japan and Korea 1 - Understanding East Asian History through Changes in International Relations*, Seoul: Humanist Books, 2012, p.83.

¹⁶ *New York World*, which heard of this massacre severely criticized that 'Japan is a barbaric monster under the mask of civilization' in its news article published on November 28, 1894.

¹⁷ Japan called these forces 'Shina occupation forces.'

¹⁸ Doo-gi Min, *Competition with Time*, Seoul: Yonsei University Press, 2000, pp.1-7, p.9.

¹⁹ Andrew Gordon, *A Modern History of Japan: From Tokugawa Times to the Present* (Third Edition), New York: Oxford University Press, 2014, p.223.

²⁰ According to data released by Japan's Ministry of International Trade and Industry, direct Vietnam War demands toward Japan amounted to 320 million dollars in 1965, 470 million dollars in 1966, 500 million dollars in 1967, 590 million dollars in 1968, 640 million dollars in 1969, and 660 million dollars in 1970. Also, economic gains due to increased exports to countries that profited from the Vietnam War or exports to the US that had higher demands for consumer goods due to the war boom were not small. Japan's exports to the US exceeded imports in 1965 and rapidly grew by an average annual rate of 21% until 1975 (The Northeast Asian History Foundation (ed.), *Historical Narration and Peace in East Asia*, Seoul: Northeast Asian History Foundation, 2011, pp.274-275).

²¹ Shoji Ishikawa and Kazuomi Hirai (eds.), *The Unfinished Twentieth Century -*

Political History of East Asia 1894 ~, Tokyo: Horitsu Bunka Sha, 2003, pp.184-186.

22 Hirofumi Hayashi, *Questioning Japan's Pacifism – Focusing on War Crimes Trial, Peace Constitution, and East Asian Relations*, Tokyo: Kamogawa Co., Ltd., 2008, pp.94-95.

23 Seong-hwan Lee, *Warfare State Japan*, Seoul: Salim, 2005, p.93.

24 Yeong-jae Park et al., *Dissecting Today's Japan*, Seoul: Hangilsa, 1987, p.68.

25 Aiko Utsumi, *Reflection of Japan and Asia in Terms of Postwar Compensation*, Tokyo: Yamakawa Shuppansha Ltd., 2002, p.10.

26 John W. Dower, *War without Mercy: Race and Power in the Pacific War*, London and Boston: Faber and Faber, 1986, p.48.

27 George Hicks, "The Comfort Women", Peter Duus, Ramon H. Myers, and Mark R. Peattie (eds.), *The Japanese Wartime Empire 1931-1945*, Princeton, N.J.: Princeton University Press, 1996; Watanabe Kazuko, "Militarization, Colonialism, and the Trafficking of Women: 'Comfort Women' Forced into Sexual Labor for Japanese Soldiers", *Bulletin of Concerned Asian Scholars*, vol. 26, no. 4, Oct.-Dec. 1994.

28 Eiji Oguma, *The State of Japan*, Tokyo: Shinyosha, 2018, pp.89-96.

29 Andrew Gordon, *A Modern History of Japan: From Tokugawa Times to the Present* (Third Edition), New York: Oxford University Press, 2014, p.223.

30 Second lieutenants Noda Tsuyoshi (野田毅) and Mukai Toshiaki (向井敏明) had a 'Contest to decapitate 100 people' and pictures of these soldiers standing proudly with the swords they used for the accomplishments made the headlines in Japanese newspapers and magazines at the time (Joshua A. Fogel, *The Nanjing Massacre in History and Historiography*, Oakland, CA: University of California Press, 2000, p.82; Seong-wook Kwon, *The Second Sino-Japanese War*, Seoul: Miji Books, 2015, p.284).

31 George Hicks, *The Comfort Women: Japan's Brutal Regime of Enforced Prostitution in the Second World War*, New York: Norton, 1995, p.43.

32 Nicholas Kristof, "A Japanese Generation Haunted by Its Past", *New York*

Times, January 22, 1997.

33 History Educationalist Conference of Japan (ed.), *East Asian World and Japan*, Tokyo: Aoki Shoten Publishing Co., 2004, pp.165-166.

34 Andrew Gordon, *A Modern History of Japan: From Tokugawa Times to the Present* (Third Edition), New York: Oxford Univ. Press, 2014, pp.202-203.

35 The China-Japan-Korea Common History Text Tri-National Committee, *Modern and Contemporary History of East Asia Jointly Written by China, Japan and Korea 1 - Understanding East Asian History through Changes in International Relations*, Seoul: Humanist Books, 2012, p.197.

36 The China-Japan-Korea Common History Text Tri-National Committee, *A History to Open the Future*, Seoul: Hangyeorae Press, 2005, pp.148-159.

37 George Hicks, *The Comfort Women: Japan's Brutal Regime of Enforced Prostitution in the Second World War*, New York: Norton, 1994, p.32.

38 David Bergamini, *Japan's Imperial Conspiracy*, New York: William Morrow and Company, 1971, p.45.

39 John W. Dower, *War without Mercy: Race and Power in the Pacific War*, London and Boston: Faber and Faber, 1986, pp.45-46.

40 Janet Hunter, *The Emergence of Modern Japan: An Introductory History since 1853*, London: Longman, 1989, p.58; *The Japan Times* (weekly international edition), "Nanjing Testament," August 22-28, 1994.

41 Joanna Pitman, "Repentance: Tokyo-Postcard", *The New Republic*, February 10, 1992, pp.14-15.

42 Ian Buruma, *Inventing Japan 1853-1964*, New York: The Modern Library, 2003, p.106.

43 *The Yomiuri Newspaper*, July 6, 1994; *The Japan Times* (weekly international edition), July 18-24, 1994.

44 Iris Chang, *The Rape of Nanking: The Forgotten Holocaust of World War II*, Harmondsworth: Penguin, 1997; Katsuichi Honda, *The Nanjing Massacre: A Japanese Journalist Confronts Japan's National Shame*, New York: M. E. Sharpe, 1999; Erwin Rickert (ed.), *The Good German of Nanking: The Diaries of John Rabe*,

New York: Knopf, 1998.

[45] Kenneth Henshall, *A History of Japan: From Stone Age to Superpower* (Third Edition), Hampshire: Palgrave Macmillan, 2012, p.123.

[46] David Sheff, "Shintaro Ishihara-candid conversation", *Playboy*, vol. 37, no. 10, October 1990, p.63.

[47] Iris Chang, *The Rape of Nanking: The Forgotten Holocaust of World War II*, Harmondsworth: Penguin, 1997.

[48] Sheldon Harris, *Factories of Death: Japanese Biological Warfare, 1932-1945, and the American Cover-up*, London: Routledge, 1994, pp.102-112.

[49] The China-Japan-Korea Common History Text Tri-National Committee, *Modern and Contemporary History of East Asia Jointly Written by China, Japan and Korea 1 - Understanding East Asian History through Changes in International Relations*, Seoul: Humanist Books, 2012, p.199.

[50] The China-Japan-Korea Common History Text Tri-National Committee, *A History to Open the Future*, Seoul: Hangyeorae Press, 2005, pp.152.

[51] Rudolph. J. Rummel, *China's Bloody Century: Genocide and Mass Murder Since 1900*, London: Routledge, 2007, p.139.

[52] The China-Japan-Korea Common History Text Tri-National Committee, *A History to Open the Future*, Seoul: Hangyeorae Press, 2005, p.133, pp.152-153.

[53] Yoshibumi Wakamiya, *Reconciliation and Nationalism – East Asian World View of Postwar Conservatives*, Tokyo: The Asahi Shimbun Company, 2006, pp.103-106.

[54] History Educationalist Conference of Japan (ed.), *East Asian World and Japan*, Tokyo: Aoki Shoten Publishing Co., 2004, p.184. (The Association of Returnees from China eventually disbanded in 2002 when the original membership of 1,000 shrank to 300 and average age of members reached the mid-80s. However, younger activists who were moved by the activities of the Association of Returnees from China launched 'the Association Succeeding the Miracle of Fushun Society (Succession Association).')

[55] Isii Shiro, who was promoted to Major after becoming a professor of immunology at the Army Medical School in Tokyo, reported to superior

authorities that biological weapons were the inexpensive next generation weapons, resulting in the establishment of the virus and chemical weapon institute in 1932. Furthermore, he requested a research team to be dispatched to Manchuria to experiment the findings of germ research and develop new weapons, which resulted in the establishment of an exclusive unit in Pingfang, Harbin.

56 Edward Behr, *Hirohito: Behind the Myth*, New York: Villard Books, 1989, p.172.

57 The Association for the Verification of Inhuman Conduct by Japanese Researchers and Health Care Professionals during the War, Translated by Akira Suzuki, *Unit 731 and the Doctors: War and Medical Ethics*, Seoul: Media Health Cooperative, 2014.

58 The China-Japan-Korea Common History Text Tri-National Committee, *A History to Open the Future*, Seoul: Hangyeorae Press, 2005, pp.154-155.

59 History Educationalist Conference of Japan (ed.), *East Asian World and Japan*, Tokyo: Aoki Shoten Publishing Co., 2004, pp.182-183.

60 "A Royal Denunciation of Horrors: Hirohito's Brother - an Eyewitness - Assails Japan's Wartime Brutality", *Los Angeles Times*, July 9, 1994.

61 History Educationalist Conference of Japan (ed.), *East Asian World and Japan,* Tokyo: Aoki Shoten Publishing Co., 2004, pp.160-161.

62 The China-Japan-Korea Common History Text Tri-National Committee, *Modern and Contemporary History of East Asia Jointly Written by China, Japan and Korea 1 - Understanding East Asian History through Changes in International Relations*, Seoul: Humanist Books, 2012, pp.118-121.

63 The China-Japan-Korea Common History Text Tri-National Committee, *Modern and Contemporary History of East Asia Jointly Written by China, Japan and Korea 1 - Understanding East Asian History through Changes in International Relations*, Seoul: Humanist Books, 2012, pp.108-109.

64 The China-Japan-Korea Common History Text Tri-National Committee, *A History to Open the Future*, Seoul: Hangyeorae Press, 2005, pp.46-47; Japan-Korea Common History Textbook Production Team, *Japan and Korea, the History in Between*, Seoul: Humanist Books, 2012, p.68.

65 Japan-Korea Common History Textbook Production Team, *Japan and Korea, the History in Between*, Seoul: Humanist Books, 2012, p.70.

66 Qing made an additional payment of 30 million taels of silver as reparations in return for taking back Liaodong Peninsula from Japan through the Tripartite Intervention of Russia, France, and Germany.

67 Saburo Ienaga, *War Responsibility*, Tokyo: Iwanami Shoten, 1985, pp.65-66.

68 Aiko Utsumi, *Reflection of Japan and Asia in Terms of Postwar Compensation*, Tokyo: Yamakawa Shuppansha Ltd., 2002, pp.19-20. (However, Dulles insisted that 'Japan needs to import food and raw materials for survival, but even 2 trillion dollars is not enough for such payments' and tried to diminish the intensity of China's and each Asian country's claims for compensation).

69 History Educationalist Conference of Japan (ed.), *East Asian World and Japan*, Tokyo: Aoki Shoten Publishing Co., 2004, p.240.

70 Baek-gi Cho, "The Solution to Japan's Sexual Slavery Issue in International Law – the Past, Present, and Future of Japan-Korea Relations," *Journal of Law*, vol. 31, no. 1, 2011, pp.417-419.

71 Jae-hwan Ha, Kwang-jun Choi, and Chang-rok Kim, "Legal Liability to Korea and Koreans – A Review of the Issue of 'Japanese Military Sexual Slavery' in International Law" *Journal of Law*, vol. 37, no. 1 (Serial Number 45), December 1996, p.86.

72 History Educationalist Conference of Japan (ed.), *East Asian World and Japan*, Tokyo: Aoki Shoten Publishing Co., 2004, p.241.

73 Yoshiaki Yoshimi, *What is Japanese Sexual Slavery System?*, Tokyo: Iwanami Shoten, 2010 (Translated by Sang gu Nam, Seoul: Yeoksa Gonggan, 2013, pp.22-25).

74 Scholars varyingly estimate that approximately a minimum of 50,000 to a maximum of 400,000 women were mobilized, and recent studies present that the latter (approximately 400,000 women) is more convincing. (Chunghee Soh, "Human Rights and the 'Comfort Women'", *Peace Review*, vol. 12, no. 1, 2000, pp.123-129).

75 Yoshiaki Yoshimi, "The Achievements and Tasks of Research on the Japanese Military Sexual Slavery Issue," *The Violence of Japanese Colonization and*

Japanese Military Sexual Slavery – International Seminar Booklet on the Japanese Military Sexual Slavery Issue, 2007, pp.22-24.

[76] Baek-gi Cho, "The Solution to Japan's Sexual Slavery Issue in International Law – the Past, Present, and Future of Japan-Korea Relations," *Journal of Law*, vol. 31, no. 1, 2011, pp.424-425.

[77] History Educationalist Conference of Japan (ed.), *East Asian World and Japan*, Tokyo: Aoki Shoten Publishing Co., 2004, p.242.

[78] The China-Japan-Korea Common History Text Tri-National Committee, *A History to Open the Future*, Seoul: Hangyeorae Press, 2005, pp.158-159.

[79] History Educationalist Conference of Japan (ed.), *East Asian World and Japan*, Tokyo: Aoki Shoten Publishing Co., 2004, p.243.

[80] Yoshiaki Yoshimi, *Military Comfort Women*, Tokyo: Iwanami Shoten, 1995, pp.27-28.

[81] The China-Japan-Korea Common History Text Tri-National Committee, *Modern and Contemporary History of East Asia Jointly Written by China, Japan and Korea 2 - Understanding the History of People and Interaction by Theme*, Seoul: Humanist Books, 2012, pp.321-322.

[82] Korean Council for Women Drafted for Military Sexual Slavery by Japan, Association for Research on Japanese Military Sexual Slavery, *Korean Comfort Women Taken by Force*, Seoul: Hanul Publishing Group, 1993.

[83] Baek-gi Cho, "The Solution to Japan's Sexual Slavery Issue in International Law – the Past, Present, and Future of Japan-Korea Relations," *Journal of Law*, vol. 31, no. 1, 2011, pp.427-428.

[84] Kentaro Awaya et al., *War Responsibility and Postwar Responsibility – How are Japan and Germany Different?*, Tokyo: The Asahi Shimbun Company, 1994. p.214.

[85] The China-Japan-Korea Common History Text Tri-National Committee, *Modern and Contemporary History of East Asia Jointly Written by China, Japan and Korea 1 - Understanding East Asian History through Changes in International Relations*, Seoul: Humanist Books, 2012, pp.93-94.

[86] The China-Japan-Korea Common History Text Tri-National Committee,

A History to Open the Future, Seoul: Hangyeorae Press, 2005, p.81.

[87] History Educationalist Conference of Japan (ed.), *East Asian World and Japan*, Tokyo: Aoki Shoten Publishing Co., 2004, pp.143-146.

[88] The China-Japan-Korea Common History Text Tri-National Committee, *Modern and Contemporary History of East Asia Jointly Written by China, Japan and Korea 1 - Understanding East Asian History through Changes in International Relations*, Seoul: Humanist Books, 2012, pp.210-211.

[89] Tetsuya Takahashi, *State and Sacrifice*, Tokyo: Japan Broadcast Publishing Co., 2005 (Translated by Mok Lee, Seoul: Chaekgwahamge, 2008), p.45.

[90] Edward Seidensticker, *Low City, High City, Tokyo from Edo to the Earthquake*, New York: Knopf, 1983, pp.3-7.

[91] Changsoo Lee and George Devos, *Koreans in Japan*, Berkeley: University of California Press, 1981; Ian Buruma, *Inventing Japan 1853-1964*, New York: The Modern Library, 2003.

[92] Hye-seon Jeong, *Japanese History Digest 100*, Seoul: Garam Planning Publisher, 2011, pp.382-386.

[93] Hashima is approximately 18.5km southwest of Nagasaki Port, and approximately 4.5km from the Nagasaki Peninsula by the shortest distance.

[94] The draft indication presented at the time was Koreans and others 'were brought against their will and forced to work under harsh conditions.'

[95] History Educationalist Conference of Japan (ed.), *East Asian World and Japan*, Tokyo: Aoki Shoten Publishing Co., 2004, p.249.

[96] The China-Japan-Korea Common History Text Tri-National Committee, *Modern and Contemporary History of East Asia Jointly Written by China, Japan and Korea 2 - Understanding the History of People and Interaction by Theme*, Seoul: Humanist Books, 2012, pp.316-318.

[97] The China-Japan-Korea Common History Text Tri-National Committee, *A History to Open the Future*, Seoul: Hangyeorae Press, 2005, p.188.

[98] In the 1970s, Titi Village, near Jelulung, demanded the Japanese Embassy apologize for this incident and to bear the cost of erecting a monument in

memory of the victims (*The Yomiuri Newspaper*, June 8, 1976).

[99] Hirofumi Hayashi, *Questioning Japan's Pacifism – Focusing on War Crimes Trial, Peace Constitution, and East Asian Relations*, Tokyo: Kamogawa Co., Ltd., 2008, p.57.

[100] The China-Japan-Korea Common History Text Tri-National Committee, *Modern and Contemporary History of East Asia Jointly Written by China, Japan and Korea 2 - Understanding the History of People and Interaction by Theme*, Seoul: Humanist Books, 2012, pp.323-324.

[101] Kenneth Henshall, *A History of Japan: From Stone Age to Superpower* (Third Edition), Hampshire: Palgrave Macmillan, 2012, p.135.

[102] Aiko Utsumi, *Reflection of Japan and Asia in Terms of Postwar Compensation*, Tokyo: Yamakawa Shuppansha Ltd., 2002, pp.17-22.

[103] The China-Japan-Korea Common History Text Tri-National Committee, *A History to Open the Future*, Seoul: Hangyeorae Press, 2005, p.189.

[104] Aiko Utsumi, *Reflection of Japan and Asia in Terms of Postwar Compensation*, Tokyo: Yamakawa Shuppansha Ltd., 2002, pp.18-19.

[105] John W. Dower, *War without Mercy: Race and Power in the Pacific War*, London and Boston: Faber and Faber, 1986; Gavan Daws, *Prisoners of the Japanese: POWs of World War II in the Pacific*, New York: William Morrow, 1994.

[106] Beatrice Trefalt, "Living Dead: Japanese Prisoners-of-War in the Southwest Pacific", *New Zealand Journal of East Asian Studies*, vol. 3, no. 2, December 1995, pp.118-120.

[107] Andrew Gordon, *A Modern History of Japan: From Tokugawa Times to the Present* (Third Edition), New York: Oxford University Press, 2014, p.209.

[108] Hirofumi Hayashi, *Questioning Japan's Pacifism – Focusing on War Crimes Trial, Peace Constitution, and East Asian Relations*, Tokyo: Kamogawa Co., Ltd., 2008, pp.88-89.

[109] Chris Perez Howard, *Mariquita: A Tragedy of Guam*, Suva: Institute of Pacific Studies of the University of the South Pacific, 1986.

[110] After the 16th century, armed merchants organized by the wealthy class in

China's southeast region (present day Zhejiang Province, Fujian Province regions) would participate in the activities of these Japanese raiders.

[111] History Educationalist Conference of Japan (ed.), *East Asian World and Japan*, Tokyo: Aoki Shoten Publishing Co., 2004, p.77.

[112] Gye-hwang Lee, *War of Memory – Historical Perception of Contemporary Japan and the Japan-Korea Relations*, Seoul: Ewha Womans University Press, 2003, pp.187-188.

[113] Yong-woon Kim, *The Mindsets of the Japanese and the Koreans*, Seoul: Hangilsa, 1985, p.20.

[114] Choong-seek Kim, *Sorrowful Islands*, Seoul: Hyohyung Publishing, 2005, pp.74-75, pp.91-93.

[115] History Educationalist Conference of Japan (ed.), *East Asian World and Japan*, Tokyo: Aoki Shoten Publishing Co., 2004, pp.122-124.

[116] Ji-yeong Oh, *Tonghak History*, Seoul: Yeongchang Publishing Company, 1940.

[117] The China-Japan-Korea Common History Text Tri-National Committee, *Modern and Contemporary History of East Asia Jointly Written by China, Japan and Korea 1 - Understanding East Asian History through Changes in International Relations*, Seoul: Humanist Books, 2012, pp.85-86.

[118] Yeong-woo Han, *Empress Myeongseong and the Korean Empire*, Seoul: Hyohyung Publishing, 2001.

[119] Japan-Korea Common History Textbook Production Team, *Japan and Korea, the History in Between*, Seoul: Humanist Books, 2012, p.79.

120 However, for some reason, perhaps due to a feeling of discomfort about such measures, the Japanese government did not disclose the incorporation of Dokdo into Japanese territory in the official gazette, but instead issued an order to Shimane Prefecture to announce it in the Report of Shimane Prefectural Government (島根縣報). In recent days, Japan has designated the announcement date of February 22 as 'Takeshima Day' and holds ceremonies every year, resulting in continuous conflicts between Japan and Korea.

[121] The China-Japan-Korea Common History Text Tri-National Committee,

Modern and Contemporary History of East Asia Jointly Written by China, Japan and Korea 1 - Understanding East Asian History through Changes in International Relations, Seoul: Humanist Books, 2012, pp.118-121.

[122] The China-Japan-Korea Common History Text Tri-National Committee, *Modern and Contemporary History of East Asia Jointly Written by China, Japan and Korea 1 - Understanding East Asian History through Changes in International Relations*, Seoul: Humanist Books, 2012, pp.129-131.

[123] The China-Japan-Korea Common History Text Tri-National Committee, *Modern and Contemporary History of East Asia Jointly Written by China, Japan and Korea 2 - Understanding the History of People and Interaction by Theme*, Seoul: Humanist Books, 2012, p.148.

[124] The merger treaty can be considered illegal in various aspects: i) the fact that the treaty was realized forcefully against the intention of the Emperor of the Korean Empire and the general public, ii) the fact that there was no signature of the Emperor on the treaty document and that the seal was not the seal of the state that represents a country, iii) the fact that Japanese Resident-General of Korea, who participated as the Japanese party to the treaty, lacked legitimacy because the Office of Resident General was installed through the illegal Japan-Korea Treaty of 1905 (Eulsa Treaty).

[125] The China-Japan-Korea Common History Text Tri-National Committee, *Modern and Contemporary History of East Asia Jointly Written by China, Japan and Korea 2 - Understanding the History of People and Interaction by Theme*, Seoul: Humanist Books, 2012, p.150.

[126] The China-Japan-Korea Common History Text Tri-National Committee, *Modern and Contemporary History of East Asia Jointly Written by China, Japan and Korea 1 - Understanding East Asian History through Changes in International Relations*, Seoul: Humanist Books, 2012, pp.156-157.

[127] Seong-su Park, *Research on Independence Movement History*, Seoul: Changbi Publishers, 1980; Ian Buruma, *Inventing Japan 1853-1964*, New York: The Modern Library, 2003, pp.65-66.

[128] Shoji Ishikawa and Kazuomi Hirai (eds.), *The Unfinished Twentieth Century - Political History of East Asia 1894 ~*, Tokyo: Horitsu Bunka Sha, 2003, p.71.

[129] History Educationalist Conference of Japan (ed.), *East Asian World and*

Japan, Tokyo: Aoki Shoten Publishing Co., 2004, pp.140-141.

[130] The China-Japan-Korea Common History Text Tri-National Committee, *Modern and Contemporary History of East Asia Jointly Written by China, Japan and Korea 1 - Understanding East Asian History through Changes in International Relations,* Seoul: Humanist Books, 2012, p.160.

[131] The China-Japan-Korea Common History Text Tri-National Committee, *Modern and Contemporary History of East Asia Jointly Written by China, Japan and Korea 1 - Understanding East Asian History through Changes in International Relations,* Seoul: Humanist Books, 2012, pp.161-163.

[132] The China-Japan-Korea Common History Text Tri-National Committee, *Modern and Contemporary History of East Asia Jointly Written by China, Japan and Korea 1 - Understanding East Asian History through Changes in International Relations,* Seoul: Humanist Books, 2012, pp.201-202.

[133] Fania Isaakovna Shabshina, Translated by Myeong-ho Kim, *In Colonial Korea,* Seoul: Hanul Publishing Group, 1996.

[134] The China-Japan-Korea Common History Text Tri-National Committee, *A History to Open the Future,* Seoul: Hangyeorae Press, 2005, pp.160-171.

[135] The China-Japan-Korea Common History Text Tri-National Committee, *Modern and Contemporary History of East Asia Jointly Written by China, Japan and Korea 2 - Understanding the History of People and Interaction by Theme,* Seoul: Humanist Books, 2012, pp.158-159.

[136] The China-Japan-Korea Common History Text Tri-National Committee, *Modern and Contemporary History of East Asia Jointly Written by China, Japan and Korea 1 - Understanding East Asian History through Changes in International Relations,* Seoul: Humanist Books, 2012, pp.210-211.

[137] The China-Japan-Korea Common History Text Tri-National Committee, *A History to Open the Future,* Seoul: Hangyeorae Press, 2005, pp.166-167.

[138] Gye-hwang Lee, *War of Memory – Historical Perception of Contemporary Japan and the Japan-Korea Relations,* Seoul: Ewha Womans University Press, 2003, pp.280-281.

[139] Hirofumi Hayashi, *Questioning Japan's Pacifism – Focusing on War Crimes Trial, Peace Constitution, and East Asian Relations,* Tokyo: Kamogawa Co., Ltd., 2008,

Notes

p.146.

[140] Yong-woon Kim and Soon-shin Jin, *Speaking of the History and Future of Korea-China-Japan*, Seoul: Literature & Thought, 2000, p.30.

[141] Japan's conservative politician Utsunomiya Tokuma's perspective is that Japan is responsible for the division of the Korean Peninsula into north and south in that the Soviet Union, which proclaimed its participation in the war against Japan in August 1945, stationed troops on the Korean Peninsula under the pretext of disarming the Japanese army, because Japan annexed Korea and used it as a military base (Yoshibumi Wakamiya, *Reconciliation and Nationalism – East Asian World View of Postwar Conservatives*, Tokyo: The Asahi Shimbun Company, 2006, pp.210-213.).

[142] Aiko Utsumi, *Reflection of Japan and Asia in Terms of Postwar Compensation*, Tokyo: Yamakawa Shuppansha Ltd., 2002, pp.16-21.

[143] Thus, the forces that led the South Korean government after the war were people who cooperated with Japan under Japanese colonial rule, the so-called pro-Japanese collaborators. This is similar to postwar Japan, where the wartime ruling power came to lead the society at large again under the indirect rule of the US troops (Hirofumi Hayashi, *Questioning Japan's Pacifism – Focusing on War Crimes Trial, Peace Constitution, and East Asian Relations*, Tokyo: Kamogawa Co., Ltd., 2008, pp.125-129.).

[144] Japan-Korea Common History Textbook Production Team, *Japan and Korea, the History in Between*, Seoul: Humanist Books, 2012, p.196, p.199, p.203.

[145] History Educationalist Conference of Japan (ed.), *East Asian World and Japan*, Tokyo: Aoki Shoten Publishing Co., 2004, p.192.

[146] The China-Japan-Korea Common History Text Tri-National Committee, *Modern and Contemporary History of East Asia Jointly Written by China, Japan and Korea 2 - Understanding the History of People and Interaction by Theme*, Seoul: Humanist Books, 2012, pp.170-171.

[147] Aiko Utsumi, *Reflection of Japan and Asia in Terms of Postwar Compensation*, Tokyo: Yamakawa Shuppansha Ltd., 2002, p.64.

[148] If the word 'operation' refers to the act of treating a live patient, the word 'dissection' refers to the act of making an incision in a dead body to understand the structure or investigate the cause of death, etc. Therefore, the

act of creating the word 'vivisection' by performing the act of dissection on a living person is utterly beyond ethical connivance.

149 The China-Japan-Korea Common History Text Tri-National Committee, *Modern and Contemporary History of East Asia Jointly Written by China, Japan and Korea 2 - Understanding the History of People and Interaction by Theme*, Seoul: Humanist Books, 2012, pp.247-249.

150 Due to the atomic bomb attack of the US armed forces, 140,000 people died in Hiroshima and 70,000 people died in Nagasaki, but foreign national victims, such as Koreans and Chinese, who were known to be approximately 70,000 in number, were excluded from the GI Bill of Rights policy of the postwar Japanese government, did not receive proper treatment, and suffered from economic destitution until their death.

151 More than 100 Japanese military comfort stations were installed in Okinawa alone, and numerous sexual slaves dragged from Japan, Korea, Taiwan, China, and Southeast Asian countries died in the midst of the battles.

152 Pilots of suicide planes were called Kamikaze or Shinpu, mostly consisting of teenagers who were trained for only a few weeks and deployed into mission.

153 The China-Japan-Korea Common History Text Tri-National Committee, *A History to Open the Future*, Seoul: Hangyeorae Press, 2005, pp.172-183.

154 As Japan went through repeated defeats in the Pacific War, there were many such incidents in which civilians committed suicide in the Pacific and Southeast Asian regions. In particular, in the summer of 1944, when the US troops attacked Saipan where there were many Japanese residents, many Japanese women spontaneously fell off the cliff at Marpi Point on the northern part of the island. In the case of people hesitating before the leap, Japanese soldiers even shot at them to make them fall off the cliff.

155 Gavan McCormac and Satoko Oka Norimatsu, *Resistant Islands: Okinawa Confronts Japan and the United States*, Lanham, Maryland: Rowman & Littlefield Publishers, 2012 (Translated by Yeong-shin Jeong, Seoul: Changbi Publishers, 2014, p.64).

156 The US military base occupies approximately 20% of Okinawa's main island, which includes fertile farmland (Gavan McCormac and Satoko Oka

Norimatsu, *Resistant Islands: Okinawa Confronts Japan and the United States*, Lanham, Maryland: Rowman & Littlefield Publishers, 2012 (Translated by Yeong-shin Jeong, Seoul: Changbi Publishers, 2014, p.148).

157 Gi-jae Shim, *Japan's Past and Present Read through Historical Trends*, Seoul: Dankook University Press, 2009, pp.142-151.

158 The China-Japan-Korea Common History Text Tri-National Committee, *Modern and Contemporary History of East Asia Jointly Written by China, Japan and Korea 2 - Understanding the History of People and Interaction by Theme*, Seoul: Humanist Books, 2012, pp.310-312.

159 Japan-Korea Common History Textbook Production Team, *Japan and Korea, the History in Between*, Seoul: Humanist Books, 2012, p.140.

160 Eiji Oguma, *The State of Japan*, Tokyo: Shinyosha, 2018, pp.79-89.

161 Myeong-cheol Cho et al., *The Choice of the Japanese*, Seoul: Dareun Sesang, 2002, p.246.

162 Aiko Utsumi, *Reflection of Japan and Asia in Terms of Postwar Compensation*, Tokyo: Yamakawa Shuppansha Ltd., 2002, pp.76-77.

163 Japan-Korea Common History Textbook Production Team, *Japan and Korea, the History in Between*, Seoul: Humanist Books, 2012, pp.79-83.

164 Ian Buruma, *Inventing Japan 1853-1964*, New York: The Modern Library, 2003, pp.58-59.

165 Edward Behr, *Hirohito: Behind the Myth*, New York: Villard Books, 1989, p.366.

166 Kenneth Henshall, *A History of Japan: From Stone Age to Superpower* (Third Edition), Hampshire: Palgrave Macmillan, 2012, p.1.

167 Yong-deok Kim, *An Insight on Japanese Modern History*, Seoul: Jisik-Sanup Publications, 1991, pp.54-55.

168 Andrew Gordon, *A Modern History of Japan: From Tokugawa Times to the Present* (Third Edition), New York: Oxford University Press, 2014, pp.3-6.

169 As a keyword that represents Japan, people sometimes choose

'Shimaguni-konjo (島國根性, island country mentality)' which can be found in the Japanese dictionary. In the dictionary, it is defined as "the property of being short-sighted, closed, and narrow-minded because interaction with other countries is limited," "a disposition often found in people of island countries, who are short-sighted and lack tolerance, while having strong unity, independence, and exclusiveness." Shimaguni-konjo is a collective sentiment which mixes emotion and illogic. It is apprehended that this type of country may have defiance, strengthen exclusivity and unite the more when a neighboring country points out a flaw. The reason why modern Japan is resistant toward neighboring countries' request for self-reflection and apology in relation to historical issues is probably not unrelated to this type of attribute (Choong-shik Kim, *Sorrowful Islands*, Seoul: Hyohyung Publishing, 2005, pp.5-8).

[170] Yong-deok Kim, *An Insight on Japanese Modern History*, Seoul: Jisik-Sanup Publications, 1991, pp.12-14.

[171] Myeong-cheol Cho et al., *The Choice of the Japanese*, Seoul: Dareun Sesang, 2002, p.281.

[172] David Riesman and Evelyn Thompson Riesman, *Conversations in Japan: Modernization, Politics and Culture*, New York: Basic Books Inc., 1967.

[173] Edwin O. Reischauer and Albert M. Craig, *Japan: Tradition and Transformation*, London, Boston and Sydney: George Allen & Unwin, 1979.

[174] Yong-deok Kim, *An Insight on Japanese Modern History*, Seoul: Jisik-Sanup Publications, 1991, pp.17-18.

[175] Therefore, this can be considered as a country name made in consciousness of an empire on the continent (Amino Yoshihiko, *Rethinking Japanese History*, Tokyo: Chikumashobo Ltd., 2005 (Translated by Gyeong-taek Lim, Seoul: Dolbegae, 2015, p.166.)).

[176] Tatsuru Uchida, *Japan as a Peripheral Country*, Tokyo: Shinchosha, 2009, p.44, pp.114-117.

[177] Chosei Ito, *Rediscovering Collectivism: Driving Force of Growing Economy*, Tokyo: Diamond Inc., 1969.

[178] Pil-dong Kim, *Japan's Identity*, Seoul: Salim, 2005, pp.24-28.

179 Ruth Benedict, *The Chrysanthemum and the Sword: Patterns of Japanese Culture*, Boston: Houghton Mifflin Company, 1946 (Mariner Books edition 2005), pp.98-113.

180 Yoshisaburo Okakura, *The Life and Thought of Japan*, Tokyo: Dentosha, 1913 (Published script of lecture titled "The Life and Thought of Japan" in Boston, US in 1910).

181 Ruth Benedict, *The Chrysanthemum and the Sword: Patterns of Japanese Culture*, Boston: Houghton Mifflin Company, 1946 (Mariner Books edition 2005), pp.145-176.

182 Yong-woon Kim and Soon-shin Jin, *Speaking of the History and Future of China-Japan-Korea*, Seoul: Literature & Thought, 2000, pp.117-118.

183 Shuichi Kato et al., *Hidden Form of Japanese Culture*, Tokyo: Iwanami Shoten, 1991.

184 Pil-dong Kim, *Japan's Identity*, Seoul: Salim, 2005, pp.35-39.

185 Yong-deok Kim, *An Insight on Japanese Modern History*, Seoul: Jisik-Sanup Publications, 1991, p.19.

186 Hannah Arendt, *Eichmann in Jerusalem: A Report on the Banality of Evil*, New York: Penguin Books, 1963.

187 Koichi Takashiro, *Japan's Dual System of Power — Shogun and the Emperor*, Seoul: Salim, 2006, p.85.

188 Yong-woon Kim and Soon-shin Jin, *Speaking of the History and Future of China-Japan-Korea*, Seoul: Literature & Thought, 2000, pp.118-120.

189 Yong-woon Kim, *The Mindsets of the Japanese and the Koreans*, Seoul: Hangilsa, 1985, p.147.

190 A mania refers to an expert in a certain field, and an otaku refers to a person who is obsessed with a certain field beyond the level of mania to the point of being crazy.

191 Yong-woon Kim, *The Mindsets of the Japanese and the Koreans*, Seoul: Hangilsa, 1985, pp.10-63.

[192] Ruth Benedict, *The Chrysanthemum and the Sword: Patterns of Japanese Culture*, Boston: Houghton Mifflin Company, 1946 (Mariner Books edition 2005), pp.222-225.

[193] Yong-woon Kim, *The Mindsets of the Japanese and the Koreans*, Seoul: Hangilsa, 1985, pp.165-207.

[194] Pil-dong Kim, *Japan's Identity*, Seoul: Salim, 2005, pp.29-34.

[195] Yeong-jae Park et al., *Dissecting Today's Japan*, Seoul: Hangilsa, 1987, pp.175-176.

[196] Ruth Benedict, *The Chrysanthemum and the Sword: Patterns of Japanese Culture*, Boston: Houghton Mifflin Company, 1946 (Mariner Books edition 2005), pp.253-273.

[197] Yong-woon Kim and Soon-shin Jin, *Speaking of the History and Future of China-Japan-Korea*, Seoul: Literature & Thought, 2000, pp.67-68.

[198] Yong-woon Kim and Soon-shin Jin, *Speaking of the History and Future of China-Japan-Korea*, Seoul: Literature & Thought, 2000, p.88.

[199] Yong-woon Kim, *The Mindsets of the Japanese and the Koreans*, Seoul: Hangilsa, 1985, pp.122-141.

[200] Pil-dong Kim, *Japan's Identity*, Seoul: Salim, 2005, pp.6-23.

[201] Masao Maruyama, *Thoughts and Behaviors of Contemporary Politics*, Tokyo: Mirai-Sha, 1964.

[202] Myeong-cheol Cho et al., *The Choice of the Japanese*, Seoul: Dareun Sesang, 2002, p.59.

[203] Yong-woon Kim and Soon-shin Jin, *Speaking of the History and Future of China-Japan-Korea*, Seoul: Literature & Thought, 2000, p.35.

[204] Yong-woon Kim, *The Mindsets of the Japanese and the Koreans*, Seoul: Hangilsa, 1985, p.129.

[205] Tatsuru Uchida, *Japan as a Peripheral Country*, Tokyo: Shinchosha, 2009, pp.173-175.

[206] Myeong-cheol Cho et al., *The Choice of the Japanese*, Seoul: Dareun Sesang,

2002, p.61.

[207] David Bergamini, *Japan's Imperial Conspiracy*, New York: William Morrow and Company, 1971, p.16.

[208] Tatsuru Uchida, *Japan as a Peripheral Country*, Tokyo: Shinchosha, 2009, p.114.

[209] Ruth Benedict, *The Chrysanthemum and the Sword: Patterns of Japanese Culture*, Boston: Houghton Mifflin Company, 1946 (Mariner Books edition 2005), pp.277-278.

[210] Yong-woon Kim, *The Mindsets of the Japanese and the Koreans*, Seoul: Hangilsa, 1985, pp.97-98, p.119.

[211] Tatsuru Uchida, *Japan as a Peripheral Country*, Tokyo: Shinchosha, 2009, pp.218-221.

[212] Yeong-jae Park et al., *Dissecting Today's Japan*, Seoul: Hangilsa, 1987, p.163.

[213] The China-Japan-Korea Common History Text Tri-National Committee, *Modern and Contemporary History of East Asia Jointly Written by China, Japan and Korea 2 - Understanding the History of People and Interaction by Theme*, Seoul: Humanist Books, 2012, pp.23-24.

[214] Korean Association for Japanese History, *Atlas Japanese History*, Seoul: Sakyejul, 2011, p.156.

[215] Koichi Takashiro, *Japan's Dual System of Power – Shogun and the Emperor*, Seoul: Salim, 2006, p.61.

[216] Taisho Democracy is a term that symbolically summarizes Japan's political democratization which unfolded from after the Russo-Japanese War in 1905 to the late 1920s centering on popular election and party politics.

[217] The China-Japan-Korea Common History Text Tri-National Committee, *Modern and Contemporary History of East Asia Jointly Written by China, Japan and Korea 2 - Understanding the History of People and Interaction by Theme*, Seoul: Humanist Books, 2012, p.29.

[218] Heian (Kyoto, 京都) was Japan's capital for approximately 1,000 years until the Meiji government transferred the capital to Tokyo (東京) in 1890, and the

400 or so years until the Kamakura Shogunate came into power in 1192 is called Heian (平安) Era.

[219] There was a similar attempt during the Muromachi Shogunate, in which the third Shogun, Ashikaga Yoshimitsu (足利義滿, 1358-1408) was raised to Japanese King by yielding submission to China's Ming Emperor as a subject. Furthermore, he made his son Yoshimochi (義持) into a shogun, and then as the abdicated emperor (Daijo Tenno, 太上天皇), attempted to make his other son Yoshisuku (義嗣) into the Japanese Emperor. If Ashikaga Yoshimitsu or Oda Nobunaga had lived longer, there would have been a high possibility that the Japanese Emperor System would have been abolished or a new family of Japanese Emperor would have come into power (Yoshihiko Amino, *Rethinking Japanese History*, Tokyo: Chikumashobo Ltd., 2005 (Translated by Gyeong-taek Lim, Seoul: Dolbegae, 2015, pp.186-187.).

[220] Koichi Takashiro, *Japan's Dual System of Power – Shogun and the Emperor*, Seoul: Salim, 2006, pp.3-5.

[221] Gi-jae Shim, *Japan's Past and Present Read through Historical Trends*, Seoul: Dankook University Press, 2009, pp.96-98.

[222] Gi-jae Shim, *Japan's Past and Present Read through Historical Trends*, Seoul: Dankook University Press, 2009, pp.164-167.

[223] Article 1 of the Meiji Constitution stipulates 'The Empire of Japan shall be reigned over and governed by a line of Emperors unbroken for ages eternal,' and Article 3 stipulates 'The Emperor is sacred and inviolable.'

[224] Koichi Takashiro, *Japan's Dual System of Power – Shogun and the Emperor*, Seoul: Salim, 2006, pp.60-61, pp.85-86.

[225] Gye-hwang Lee, *War of Memory – Historical Perception of Contemporary Japan and the Japan-Korea Relations*, Seoul: Ewha Womans University Press, 2003, pp.58-59.

[226] Pil-dong Kim, *Japan's Identity*, Seoul: Salim, 2005, pp.47-51.

[227] *The Asahi Shimbun*, November 1, 1975.

[228] Ian Buruma, *The Wages of Guilt: Memories of War in Germany and Japan*, New York: Farrar Strauss & Giroux, 1994, pp.249-250.

[229] Norma Field, *In the Realm of a Dying Emperor: A Portrait of Japan at Century's End*, New York: Vintage Books, 1991, pp.233-234.

[230] Andrew Gordon, *A Modern History of Japan: From Tokugawa Times to the Present* (Third Edition), New York: Oxford University Press, 2014, pp.309-310.

[231] Richard Pearson, *Ancient Japan*, New York: George Braziller, 1992, p.64.

[232] This period has been named after the pattern (jomon, cord-pattern) discovered on pottery presumed to be from this period.

[233] Kenneth Henshall, *A History of Japan: From Stone Age to Superpower* (Third Edition), Hampshire: Palgrave Macmillan, 2012, p.10.

[234] Rita Rasteiro and Lounès Chikhi, "Revisiting the Peopling of Japan: An Admixture Perspective," *Journal of Human Genetics*, no. 54(6), June 2009, pp.349-354.

[235] Kenneth Henshall, *A History of Japan: From Stone Age to Superpower* (Third Edition), Hampshire: Palgrave Macmillan, 2012, pp.6-7.

[236] Here Wa or Wo refers to dwarf, or the land of dwarfs.

[237] Here Wei refers to one of the three kingdoms of China at the time, and Eastern Barbarians include not only Japan, but also Korea, and the people of Manchuria.

[238] Most experts consider Yamatai to be the same place as Yamato (大和), in the Nara basin region, which became the first capital of the Japanese state hundreds of years later, but some consider it to have been located in the northern region of Kyushu (Walter Edwards, "In Pursuit of Himiko: Postwar Archeology and the Location of Yamatai," *Monumenta Nipponica*, vol. 51, no. 1, Spring 1996, pp.53-79.).

[239] She lived in a fort protected by 100 men and was waited on by approximately 1,000 women and one single man, and it was through this man that she communicated with the outside world. It is said that she was only involved in spiritual matters, and the administrative matters related to governance was delegated to her younger brother.

[240] J. Edward Kidder, "The Earliest Societies in Japan", Delmer M. Brown

(ed.), *The Cambridge History of Japan*, vol. 1 (Ancient Japan), Cambridge, England: Cambridge University Press, 1993, pp.48-107.

[241] Gari Ledyard, "Horse-Rider Theory", *Kodansha Encyclopedia of Japan*, vol. 3, Tokyo: Kodansha, 1983, pp.305-307.

[242] Edwin O. Reischauer, *Japan: Past and Present*, New York: Knopf, 1964, p.18.

[243] W. Wayne Farris, *Japan to 1600: A Social and Economic History*, Honolulu: University of Hawaii Press, 2009, p.148.

[244] The title *Seiitai-shogun* is usually shortened to *shogun*.

[245] Kenneth Henshall, *A History of Japan: From Stone Age to Superpower* (Third Edition), Hampshire: Palgrave Macmillan, 2012, pp.34-38.

[246] Derek Massarella, *A World Elsewhere: Europe's Encounter with Japan in the Sixteenth and Seventeenth Centuries*, New Haven, Connecticut: Yale University Press, 1990, p.32.

[247] Nowadays, *samurais* are described as having absolute loyalty to one's lord to the point of risking one's life, but in the middle ages, it was rather a more general phenomenon to serve a different lord and meet and part depending on the circumstances.

[248] Hugh Cortazzi, *The Japanese Achievement*, London: Sidgwick and Jackson, 1990, p.130.

[249] There is a well-known story in Japan about these three people that goes like this: If a song bird does not sing, Nobunaga will kill it right away, Hideyoshi will persuade the bird to sing, and Ieyasu will wait until the bird sings. It can be said that this symbolically shows that the three people have different personalities and manner of handling work (Hugh Cortazzi, *The Japanese Achievement*, London: Sidgwick and Jackson, 1990, p.121).

[250] George Elison, "Oda Nobunaga (1534-1582)", *Kodansha Encyclopedia of Japan*, vol. 6, 1983, pp.61-65.

[251] William Theodore De Bary, Ryusaku Tsunoda, and Donald Keene, *Sources of Japanese Tradition*, vol. 2, New York: Columbia University Press, 1964, pp.319-322.

252 Kenneth Henshall, *A History of Japan: From Stone Age to Superpower* (Third Edition), Hampshire: Palgrave Macmillan, 2012, pp.61-65.

253 Andrew Gordon, *A Modern History of Japan: From Tokugawa Times to the Present* (Third Edition), New York: Oxford University Press, 2014, pp.43-44.

254 Andrew Gordon, *A Modern History of Japan: From Tokugawa Times to the Present* (Third Edition), New York: Oxford University Press, 2014, pp.19-20.

255 History Educationalist Conference of Japan (ed.), *East Asian World and Japan*, Tokyo: Aoki Shoten Publishing Co., 2004, p.83.

256 In-seong Jang, *Meiji Restoration – the Starting Point of Modern Japan*, Seoul: Salim, 2007, pp.14-31.

257 Hun Park refers to this as 'exaggerated sense of crisis.' According to Park, this 'intense and exaggerated sense of crisis' played a big role in speedy system reform and maintenance of the country's independence. On the other hand, this immediately led to harsh attacks toward other countries. Thus, it eventually boiled down to tireless invasion of Asian countries. (Hun Park, *How was the Meiji Restoration Possible?*, Seoul: Minumsa Publishing Group, 2014).

258 In 19th century Japan, the resistance of farmers was not large scale as in China or Korea, but dispersed and temporary riots requesting lower taxes or replacement of corrupt officials frequently occurred. Extremely rare for Japan, there was Oshio Heihachiro (大鹽平八郎)'s rebellion in 1837, which is considered as a riot, in which poor people gathered together under the slogan of 'killing despotic officials and extravagantly wealthy merchants' and attempted to seize Osaka Castle, but it was immediately suppressed.

259 Kenneth Henshall, *A History of Japan: From Stone Age to Superpower* (Third Edition), Hampshire: Palgrave Macmillan, 2012, pp.69-70.

260 Andrew Gordon, *A Modern History of Japan: From Tokugawa Times to the Present* (Third Edition), New York: Oxford University Press, 2014, pp.52-53.

261 Yeong-jae Park et al., *Dissecting Today's Japan*, Seoul: Hangilsa, 1987, p.52.

262 The most famous people among Yoshida's pupils were Ito Hirobumi (伊藤博文) and Yamagata Aritomo (山縣有朋).

263 Sakamoto was an anti-foreign assassin who shouted for expulsion of foreigners, and one day in 1862, he set out to kill Katsu Kaishu (勝海舟), a central figure who was trying to modernize the naval forces of the Tokugawa Shogunate into the Western style. However, Sakamoto abandoned his plan to kill Katsu and transformed into an open-the-country reformer after being persuaded all afternoon by Katsu, who convinced him to first hear him out, about the inevitability of modern reform. (Andrew Gordon, *A Modern History of Japan: From Tokugawa Times to the Present* (Third Edition), New York: Oxford University Press, 2014, pp.54-59).

264 Donald Calman, *The Nature and Origins of Japanese Imperialism: A Reinterpretation of the Great Crisis of 1873*, London: Routledge, 1992, pp.90-93.

265 Major figures who helped the Meiji Emperor lead the new government included Saigo Takamori (1827-1877), Okubo Toshimichi (1830-1878), and Matsukata Masayoshi (1835-1924) among those from Satsuma, and Kido Koin (1833-1877), Inoue Kaoru (1835-1915), Yamagata Aritomo (1838-1922), and Ito Hirobumi (1841-1909) etc., among those from Choshu.

266 Thomas C. Smith, *Native Sources of Japanese Industrialization, 1750-1920*, Berkeley: University of California Press, 1989.

267 Andrew Gordon, *A Modern History of Japan: From Tokugawa Times to the Present* (Third Edition), New York: Oxford University Press, 2014, pp.61-62.

268 Through this reform, 260 domains were abolished and 77 prefectures were established, which were integrated into the present day count of 47 in 1889.

269 Ian Buruma, *Inventing Japan 1853-1964*, New York: The Modern Library, 2003, pp.54-55.

270 The primary reason for dispatching the delegation was to amend the unequal treaty signed in 1858, but every time the Japanese delegation tried to raise the issue, Western countries applied restraint and requested that Japan raise its legal system and politics to their level before asking for amendments in the treaty.

271 Kenneth Henshall, "From Sedan Chair to Aeroplane: The Meiji Period Tokyoite Transported through Time and Place", *Journal of the Oriental Society of Australia*, vol. 20-21, 1988-89, pp.70-80.

272 *Meiroku Zasshi: Journal of the Japanese Enlightenment*, translated by William

Reynolds Braisted, Cambridge: Harvard University Press, 1976, p.125.

273 Fukuzawa visited the US and Europe and became the spearhead of Japan's westernization, and also established an educational facility (Keio Gijyuku, 慶 應義塾), which later developed to Keio University, in order to spread his ideas. At first, Fukuzawa took the stance of emphasizing human rights, but later advocated Japan's imperialistic Asian invasion and asserted the Datsuaron (脱 亞論, Escape from Asia), which meant that Japan should resist being a part of Asia anymore, as the logic actively supporting it (Carmen Blacker, *The Japanese Enlightenment: A Study of the Writings of Fukuzawa Yukichi*, Cambridge, England: Cambridge University Press, 1964.).

274 Sukehiro Hirakawa, "Japan's Turn to the West", Marius B. Jansen (ed.), *The Cambridge History of Japan*, vol. 5 (The Nineteenth Century), Cambridge, England: Cambridge University Press, 1989, p.468.

275 Edward Beauchamp, "Foreign Employees of the Meiji Period", *Kodansha Encyclopedia of Japan*, vol. 2, 1983, pp.310-311.

276 This *Imperial Rescript on Education* was prepared by Motoda Eifu (元田永孚, 1818-1891) and Yamagata Aritomo (William Theodore De Bary, Ryusaku Tsunoda, and Donald Keene, *Sources of Japanese Tradition*, vol. 2, New York: Columbia University Press, 1964, pp,139-140). To Yamagata Aritomo, education was to teach loyalty, discipline, and obedience, and to cultivate people who did not have 'selfish' individualism (Ian Buruma, *Inventing Japan 1853-1964*, New York: The Modern Library, 2003, p.53).

277 Carol Gluck, *Japan's Modern Myths: Ideology in the Late Meiji Period*, Princeton: Princeton University Press, 1985, p.151.

278 The first local civil rights movement group was organized by Itagaki Taisuke (板垣退助) at the old Tosa domain in early 1874. He is a person who left the government when the plan to invade Korea miscarried, and unlike Saigo Takamori who led the armed uprising, he submitted a petition to establish a Parliament (民選議院設立建白書) to the government. Itagaki's organization was soon to collapse, but in the late 1870s, there was a growing interest for a constitution and parliament which expanded into a popular movement for political participation.

279 The Jiyu Minken Undo was a political resistance or pro-democracy movement to check the new Meiji government led by leaders of Satsuma and

Choshu, but it was also a political movement for the ruined *samurai* class and people from the Tosa domain and Hizen (肥前) domain, who were excluded from the new government, to secure their political position (In-seong Jang, *Meiji Restoration – the Starting Point of Modern Japan*, Seoul: Salim, 2007, p.71).

[280] Andrew Gordon, *A Modern History of Japan: From Tokugawa Times to the Present* (Third Edition), New York: Oxford University Press, 2014, pp.84-86.

[281] Penelope Francks, *Japanese Economic Development: Theory and Practice*, London: Routledge, 1992, pp.38-189.

[282] Alexander Gerschenkron, *Economics Backwardness in Historical Perspective*, Cambridge: Harvard University Press, 1962, pp.5-30.

[283] Andrew Gordon, *A Modern History of Japan: From Tokugawa Times to the Present* (Third Edition), New York: Oxford University Press, 2014, pp.87-89.

[284] In this Yasukuni Shrine, the ancestral tablets of Japanese soldiers who died in the Pacific War, etc., were later set up, and after the ancestral tablets of war criminals were enshrined together in the late 1970s, various Asian countries have strongly resisted Japanese government officials paying their respects at the Yasukuni Shrine.

[285] Andrew Gordon, *A Modern History of Japan: From Tokugawa Times to the Present* (Third Edition), New York: Oxford University Press, 2014, pp.106-112.

[286] In-seong Jang, *Meiji Restoration – the Starting Point of Modern Japan*, Seoul: Salim, 2007, pp.8-91.

[287] Shoji Ishikawa and Kazuomi Hirai (eds.), *The Unfinished Twentieth Century - Political History of East Asia 1894 ~*, Tokyo: Horitsu Bunka Sha, 2003, pp.244-246.

[288] Andrew Gordon, *A Modern History of Japan: From Tokugawa Times to the Present* (Third Edition), New York: Oxford University Press, 2014, pp.18-19.

[289] Gi-jae Shim, *Japan's Past and Present Read through Historical Trends*, Seoul: Dankook University Press, 2009, pp.131-140.

[290] Andrew Gordon, *A Modern History of Japan: From Tokugawa Times to the*

Present (Third Edition), New York: Oxford University Press, 2014, pp.74-75.

[291] Gi-jae Shim, *Japan's Past and Present Read through Historical Trends*, Seoul: Dankook University Press, 2009, pp.142-147.

[292] Andrew Gordon, *A Modern History of Japan: From Tokugawa Times to the Present* (Third Edition), New York: Oxford University Press, 2014, pp.73-74.

[293] History Educationalist Conference of Japan (ed.), *East Asian World and Japan*, Tokyo: Aoki Shoten Publishing Co., 2004, p.113.

[294] Such imperialistic manner of Japan was similarly demonstrated in the process of annexing Joseon of the Korean Peninsula in the early 20th century.

[295] Gi-jae Shim, *Japan's Past and Present Read through Historical Trends*, Seoul: Dankook University Press, 2009, pp.148-151.

[296] Andrew Gordon, *A Modern History of Japan: From Tokugawa Times to the Present* (Third Edition), New York: Oxford University Press, 2014, pp.74-75.

[297] Jang-geun Choi, "Pending Issues and Prospects of Japan's Territorial Disputes", Tae-ho Park and Cheol-hee Park (eds.), *East Asia's Localism, Nationalism, and Regionalism – Focusing on the Growth of the Japanese State and the Evolution of International Order in East Asia*, Seoul: Ingan Sarang, 2007, pp.81-87.

[298] History Educationalist Conference of Japan (ed.), *East Asian World and Japan*, Tokyo: Aoki Shoten Publishing Co., 2004, pp.255-256.

[299] Nobukuni Koyasu, *How Asia has been depicted: Orientalism in Modern Japan*, Tokyo: Fujiwara Shoten, 2003, pp.19-70.

[300] The China-Japan-Korea Common History Text Tri-National Committee, *Modern and Contemporary History of East Asia Jointly Written by China, Japan and Korea 1 - Understanding East Asian History through Changes in International Relations*, Seoul: Humanist Books, 2012, p.21.

[301] The well-known journalist Tokutomi Soho (德富蘇峰) reminisced that the return of the Liaodong Peninsula was an incident that dominated the rest of his life. His perspective was that honesty and justice was useless without strength, and therefore, Japan's advancement ultimately depended on military power (David L. Howell, *Geographies of Identity in Nineteenth Century Japan*,

Berkeley: University of California Press, 2005, p.117).

[302] Shoji Ishikawa and Kazuomi Hirai (ed.), *The Unfinished Twentieth Century - Political History of East Asia 1894 ~*, Tokyo: Horitsu Bunka Sha, 2003, pp.7-56.

[303] However, the judgment of the judicial branch was life imprisonment.

[304] As the United Kingdom, an ally of Japan, refused to allow Russia's Baltic Fleet to use the Suez Canal, this fleet had no choice but to make a long voyage around the southern tip of South Africa.

[305] The China-Japan-Korea Common History Text Tri-National Committee, *Modern and Contemporary History of East Asia Jointly Written by China, Japan and Korea 2 - Understanding the History of People and Interaction by Theme*, Seoul: Humanist Books, 2012, pp.99-121.

[306] Edwin McClellan, *Two Japanese Novelists: Soseki and Toson*, Chicago: University of Chicago Press, 1969, p.37.

[307] Kenneth Henshall, *A History of Japan: From Stone Age to Superpower* (Third Edition), Hampshire: Palgrave Macmillan, 2012, p.108.

[308] William Lockwood, *The Economic Development of Japan: Growth and Structural Change*, Princeton, N.J.: Princeton University Press, 1968, pp.38-39.

[309] Tetsuo Najita, "Some Reflections on Idealism in the Political Thought of Yoshino Sakuzo", Bernard S. Silberman, Harry D. Harootunian and Gail Lee Bemstein (eds.) *Japan in Crisis: Essays on Taisho Democracy*, Princeton, N.J.: Princeton Univ. Press, 1974, p.56.

[310] Andrew Gordon, *A Modern History of Japan: From Tokugawa Times to the Present* (Third Edition), New York: Oxford University Press, 2014, pp.172-174.

[311] Tatsuru Uchida, *Japan as a Peripheral Country*, Tokyo: Shinchosha, 2009, pp.73-82.

[312] Andrew Gordon, *A Modern History of Japan: From Tokugawa Times to the Present* (Third Edition), New York: Oxford University Press, 2014, pp.174-179.

[313] Kenneth Henshall, *A History of Japan: From Stone Age to Superpower* (Third

Edition), Hampshire: Palgrave Macmillan, 2012, p.112.

[314] Hugh T. Patrick, "The Economic Muddle of the 1920s", James William Morley (ed.), *Dilemmas of Growth in Prewar Japan*, Princeton, N.J.: Princeton University Press, 1971, pp.252-255; Mark Metzler, *Lever of Empire: The International Gold Standard and the Crisis of Liberalism in Prewar Japan*, Berkeley: University of California Press, 2006, Part 3.

[315] Zhang Zuolin was a figure who collaborated with Japan, which tried to block the northern expedition of the Nationalist government led by Jiang Jieshi (also known as Chiang Kai-shek), but as the Nationalist government expanded its influence, he tried to show allegiance to the National government.

[316] Edwin O. Reischauer and Albert M. Craig, *Japan: Tradition and Transformation*, London, Boston, and Sydney: George Allen & Unwin, 1979, p.249.

[317] Stephen Large, *Emperor Hirohito and Showa Japan: A Political Biography*, London: Routledge, 1992, p.49.

[318] The China-Japan-Korea Common History Text Tri-National Committee, *Modern and Contemporary History of East Asia Jointly Written by China, Japan and Korea 1 - Understanding East Asian History through Changes in International Relations*, Seoul: Humanist Books, 2012, pp.183-185.

[319] Seong-hwan Lee, *Warfare State Japan*, Seoul: Salim, 2005, p.66.

[320] Andrew Gordon, *Labor and Imperial Democracy*, Berkeley: University of California Press, 1991, pp.266-267.

[321] Louise Young, *Japan's Total Empire*, Berkeley: University of California Press, 1998, pp.55-114.

[322] Janet Hunter, *The Emergence of Modern Japan: An Introductory History Since 1853*, London: Longman, 1989 p.124.

[323] John W. Dower, "The Useful War", Carol Gluck and Stephen R. Graubard (eds.), *Showa: The Japan of Hirohito*, New York: Norton, 1992, p.53.

[324] Masataka Kosaka, "The Showa Era", Carol Gluck and Stephen R.

Graubard (eds.), *Showa: The Japan of Hirohito*, New York: Norton, 1992, p.32.

[325] Elder military men such as General Tojo Hideki (東條英機) were affiliated to the Control Faction. They opposed terroristic violence and tried to cooperate with existing elites. Furthermore, they tried to fully mobilize the society in the imminent full-scale war with the West.

[326] At the time, Minobe was appointed as a representative of the House of Peers.

[327] Frank O. Miller, *Minobe Tatsukichi: Interpreter of Constitutionalism in Japan*, Berkeley: University of California Press, 1965.

[328] Herbert P. Bix, *Hirohito and the Making of Modern Japan*, New York: HarperCollins, 2000.

[329] Gi-jae Shim, *Japan's Past and Present Read through Historical Trends*, Seoul: Dankook University Press, 2009, p.27.

[330] Yong-deok Kim, *An Insight on Japanese Modern History*, Seoul: Jisik-Sanup Publications, 1991, pp.50-51, pp.135-138.

[331] The Xian Incident (西安事變) is an incident which occurred on December 12, 1936 where Zhang Xueliang (張學良, also known as son of Zhang Zuolin (張作霖) who died in 1928 due to a train explosion caused by the Japanese troops) detained the president of the Chinese Nationalist Party (Kuomintang) government, Jiang Jieshi in Xian (西安), demanding an end to the civil war with the Chinese Communist Party and a joint struggle against Japanese imperialism.

[332] That day, when a Japanese soldier did not return from a walk to the Marco Polo bridge area, his superior presumed that he was missing and asserted that the area should be searched. The Chinese troops suggested a joint search, but the commander of the Japanese troops took this as an insult. A violent event occurred between the two parties and escalated into a battle. (Ian Buruma, *Inventing Japan 1853-1964*, New York: The Modern Library, 2003, p.101).

[333] Seong-hwan Lee, *Warfare State Japan*, Seoul: Salim, 2005, p.69

[334] Alvin Coox, *Nomonhan: Japan against Russia 1939*, Stanford, California: Stanford University Press, 1985.

335 Mikiso Hane, *Modern Japan: A Historical Survey*, Boulder and London: Westview Press, 1992, p.297.

336 Seong-hwan Lee, *Warfare State Japan*, Seoul: Salim, 2005, p.4, p.71.

337 Bruce R. Bartlett, *Cover-Up: The Politics of Pearl Harbor, 1941-1946*, New York: Arlington House, 1978, pp.19-20.

338 Robert Dallek, *Franklin D. Roosevelt and American Foreign Policy, 1932-1945*, New York: Oxford University Press, 1979, p.307.

339 Hye-seon Jeong, *Japanese History Digest 100*, Seoul: Garam Planning Publisher, 2011, pp.368-373.

340 Nobukuni Koyasu, *How Asia has been depicted: Orientalism in Modern Japan*, Tokyo: Fujiwara Shoten, 2003, pp.36-38.

341 Yoshibumi Wakamiya, *Reconciliation and Nationalism – East Asian World View of Postwar Conservatives*, Tokyo: The Asahi Shimbun Company, 2006, pp.96-98.

342 Gi-jae Shim, *Japan's Past and Present Read through Historical Trends*, Seoul: Dankook University Press, 2009, pp.275-277.

343 Katsuichi Honda, *Studies of the Nanking Massacre*, Tokyo: Bansei Sha Publishing, 1992, p.129.

344 Kenneth Henshall, *A History of Japan: From Stone Age to Superpower* (Third Edition), Hampshire: Palgrave Macmillan, 2012, p.117.

345 The China-Japan-Korea Common History Text Tri-National Committee, *Modern and Contemporary History of East Asia Jointly Written by China, Japan and Korea 2 - Understanding the History of People and Interaction by Theme*, Seoul: Humanist Books, 2012, pp.244-251.

346 Gordon Daniels, "Japan at War", Richard Bowring and Peter Kornicki (ed.), *Cambridge Encyclopedia of Japan*, Cambridge, England: Cambridge University Press, 1993, p.103.

347 Andrew Gordon, *A Modern History of Japan: From Tokugawa Times to the Present* (Third Edition), New York: Oxford University Press, 2014, pp.209-

213.

[348] Andrew Gordon, *A Modern History of Japan: From Tokugawa Times to the Present* (Third Edition), New York: Oxford University Press, 2014, p.215.

[349] Tetsuo Najita and Harry Harootunian, "Japanese Revolt against the West", Peter Duus (ed.), *The Cambridge History of Japan*, vol. 6 (The Twentieth Century), Cambridge, England: Cambridge University Press, 1989, pp.758-767.

[350] Hirofumi Hayashi, *Questioning Japan's Pacifism – Focusing on War Crimes Trial, Peace Constitution, and East Asian Relations*, Tokyo: Kamogawa Co., Ltd., 2008, pp.100-102. (From this point of view, the reasoning for evasion of responsibility, that the war expanded because of the leaders of the military authorities, and the Japanese Emperor and citizens were all victims who were deceived by the leaders of the military authorities, loses persuasive power).

[351] The China-Japan-Korea Common History Text Tri-National Committee, *Modern and Contemporary History of East Asia Jointly Written by China, Japan and Korea 2 - Understanding the History of People and Interaction by Theme*, Seoul: Humanist Books, 2012, pp.278-283.

[352] Seong-hwan Lee, *Warfare State Japan*, Seoul: Salim, 2005, pp.76-78.

[353] Kenneth Henshall, *A History of Japan: From Stone Age to Superpower* (Third Edition), Hampshire: Palgrave Macmillan, 2012, pp.134-135.

[354] John W. Dower, *Empire and Aftermath: Yoshida Shigeru and the Japanese Experience*, Cambridge: Harvard University Council on East Asia Studies, 1979, p.265.

[355] Alvin Coox, "The Pacific War", Peter Duus (ed.), *The Cambridge History of Japan*, vol. 6 (The Twentieth Century), Cambridge, England: Cambridge University Press, 1989, p.369.

[356] Waldo Heinrichs, "World War II", *Kodansha Encyclopedia of Japan*, vol. 8, Tokyo: Kodansha, 1983, p.276.

[357] Haruko Taya Cook and Theodore Failor Cook, *Japan at War: An Oral History*, New York: New Press, 1992.

[358] Hugh Borton, *Japan's Modern Century*, New York: Ronald Press, 1955,

pp.485-486.

[359] Article 8 of the Potsdam Declaration stipulates that the conditions of the Cairo Declaration have to be fulfilled. This Cairo Declaration stipulates that Japan should return the Pacific islands that it occupied and the territory that it extorted from China, such as Manchuria and Taiwan, etc., during World War I. Furthermore, it stipulates that Japan will be expelled from all other lands that Japan took through violence and greed. Thus, only the territory from when the Meiji Period started was recognized, and Japan's sovereignty was not recognized for the lands that Japan violently and greedily occupied afterwards. Therefore, the Senkaku/Diaoyu Islands that Japan took from China after the First Sino-Japanese War in 1895 or Dokdo (Liancourt Rocks, Takeshima) that Japan incorporated into Japanese territory without notice to Korea in 1905 should naturally be restored to Chinese (or Taiwanese) and Korean territory. (Potsdam Declaration - 8. The terms of the Cairo Declaration shall be carried out and Japanese sovereignty shall be limited to the islands of Honshu, Hokkaido, Kyushu, Shikoku and such minor islands as we determine. The Cairo Declaration – Japan shall be stripped of all the islands in the Pacific which she has seized or occupied since the beginning of the first World War in 1914, and all the territories Japan has stolen from the Chinese, such as Manchuria, Formosa, and the Pescadores, shall be restored to the Republic of China. Japan will also be expelled from all other territories which she has taken by violence and greed.)

[360] Andrew Gordon, *A Modern History of Japan: From Tokugawa Times to the Present* (Third Edition), New York: Oxford University Press, 2014, pp.221-222.

[361] Andrew Gordon, *A Modern History of Japan: From Tokugawa Times to the Present* (Third Edition), New York: Oxford University Press, 2014, p.225.

[362] Seong-pil Hong, "An Assessment of Japan's Perception and Fulfillment of Postwar Responsibilities in the Perspective of International Law," Chungnam University, *Chungnam Law Review*, vol. 23, no. 1, June 2012, p.391.

[363] Tsuyoshi Hasegawa, *Racing the Enemy: Stalin, Truman, and the Surrender of Japan*, Cambridge: Belknap Press, 2005, pp.295-298.

[364] Theodore Cohen, *Remaking Japan: The American Occupation as New Deal*, New York: Free Press, 1987, pp.58-61.

³⁶⁵ In general, the administrative organization of the Supreme Commander is called GHQ (General Headquarters).

³⁶⁶ Frank Gibney, *The Pacific Century: America and Asia in a Changing World*, New York: Scribners/Macmillan, 1992, p.182.

³⁶⁷ Through the instruction SCAPIN-677, Governmental and Administrative Separation of Certain Outlying Areas from Japan, SCAP defined Japanese territory as the four major islands, the approximately 1,000 adjacent islands, Tsushima Island, some islands of the Ryukyu Islands above latitude 30 degrees, and excluded all other islands. As such, Japanese territory was returned to the state before the initiation of the First Sino-Japanese War. Therefore, when putting together the Cairo Declaration, Potsdam Declaration, and SCAP's instruction, Japan's territory is limited to mainly the territory of the four major islands, so Japan has no grounds for engaging in territorial disputes with neighboring countries, such as China, Korea, etc., regarding islands it acquired violently and greedily after the First Sino-Japanese War of 1895.

³⁶⁸ Douglas MacArthur, *Reminiscences*, New York: McGraw-Hill, 1964, pp.286-287.

³⁶⁹ Article 9 reads: Aspiring sincerely to an international peace based on justice and order, the Japanese people forever renounce war as a sovereign right of the nation and the threat or use of force as a means of settling international disputes. In order to accomplish the aim of the preceding paragraph, land, sea, and air forces, as well as other war potential, will never be maintained. The right of belligerency of the state will not be recognized.

³⁷⁰ This refers to planning and actively executing warfare.

³⁷¹ Tim Maga, *Judgment at Tokyo: The Japanese War Crimes Trials*, Lexington: University Press of Kentucky, 2001.

³⁷² Hirofumi Hayashi, *Questioning Japan's Pacifism – Focusing on War Crimes Trial, Peace Constitution, and East Asian Relations*, Tokyo: Kamogawa Co., Ltd., 2008, p.29.

³⁷³ History Educationalist Conference of Japan (ed.), *East Asian World and Japan*, Tokyo: Aoki Shoten Publishing Co., 2004, pp.178-180.

³⁷⁴ Toshio Nishi, *Unconditional Democracy: Education and Politics in Occupied Japan*

Notes

1945-1952, Stanford: Hoover Institution Press, 1982, pp.90-105.

375 Eleanor M. Hadley, "Zaibatsu Dissolution", *Kodansha Encyclopedia of Japan*, vol. 8, Tokyo: Kodansha, 1983, p.365.

376 Ronald Philip Dore, *Land Reform in Japan*, London: Oxford University Press, 1959.

377 Frank Gibney, *The Pacific Century: America and Asia in a Changing World*, New York: Scribners/Macmillan, 1992, p.201.

378 Therefore, when Prime Minister Tanaka Kakuei (田中角榮, 1918-1993) visited Bangkok and Jakarta in 1974, there were large-scale anti-Japanese riots.

379 Peter Williams and David Wallace, *Unit 731: The Japanese Army's Secret of Secrets*, London: Hodder & Stoughton, 1989, p.286.

380 Sterling Seagrave and Peggy Seagrave, *The Yamato Dynasty: The Secret History of Japan's Imperial Family*, London and New York: Bantam Press, 1999, p.216.

381 Hirofumi Hayashi, *Questioning Japan's Pacifism – Focusing on War Crimes Trial, Peace Constitution, and East Asian Relations*, Tokyo: Kamogawa Co., Ltd., 2008, pp.60-62.

382 Herbert P. Bix, "Inventing the 'Symbol Monarchy' in Japan, 1945-52", *Journal of Japanese Studies*, vol. 21, no. 2, Summer 1995, pp.320-321.

383 Stephen Large, *Emperor Hirohito and Showa Japan: A Political Biography*, London: Routledge, 1992, pp.136-139; Robert Edward Ward, "Presurrender Planning: Treatment of the Emperor and Constitutional Change", Robert Edward Ward and Yoshikazu Sakamoto (eds.), *Democratizing Japan: The Allied Occupation*, Honolulu: University of Hawaii Press, 1987, pp.3-18.

384 Kenneth J. Ruoff, *The People's Emperor: Democracy and the Japanese Monarchy 1945-1995*, Cambridge: Harvard University Press, 2001, p.135; Shunsuke Tsurumi, *A Cultural History of Postwar Japan 1945-1980*, London and New York: Kegan Paul International, 1987, p.26.

385 Kentaro Awaya et al., *War Responsibility and Postwar Responsibility – How are Japan and Germany Different?*, Tokyo: The Asahi Shimbun Company, 1994. pp.112-116.

386 Robert Edward Ward, "Presurrender Planning: Treatment of the Emperor and Constitutional Change", Robert Edward Ward and Yoshikazu Sakamoto (eds.), *Democratizing Japan: The Allied Occupation*, Honolulu: University of Hawaii Press, 1987, p.16.

387 Stephen Large, *Emperor Hirohito and Showa Japan: A Political Biography*, London: Routledge, 1992, pp.141.

388 The Northeast Asian History Foundation (ed.), *Historical Narration and Peace in East Asia*, Seoul: Northeast Asian History Foundation, 2011, pp.216-219.

389 Emperor Hirohito's exemption from charges of war crimes acted as a factor that hindered the formation among Japanese citizens of an independent sense of war responsibilities and overcoming of the past history.

390 Hirofumi Hayashi, *Questioning Japan's Pacifism – Focusing on War Crimes Trial, Peace Constitution, and East Asian Relations*, Tokyo: Kamogawa Co., Ltd., 2008, pp.81-83.

391 Aiko Utsumi, *Reflection of Japan and Asia in Terms of Postwar Compensation*, Tokyo: Yamakawa Shuppansha Ltd., 2002, pp.23-24.

392 The Northeast Asian History Foundation (ed.), *Historical Narration and Peace in East Asia*, Seoul: Northeast Asian History Foundation, 2011, p.18.

393 History Educationalist Conference of Japan (ed.), *East Asian World and Japan*, Tokyo: Aoki Shoten Publishing Co., 2004, pp.177-178.

394 Kentaro Awaya et al, *War Responsibility and Postwar Responsibility – How are Japan and Germany Different?*, Tokyo: The Asahi Shimbun Company, 1994, pp.105-106.

395 Kentaro Awaya et al., *War Responsibility and Postwar Responsibility – How are Japan and Germany Different*, Tokyo: The Asahi Shimbun Company, 1994, pp.102-104.

396 Aiko Utsumi, *Reflection of Japan and Asia in Terms of Postwar Compensation*, Tokyo: Yamakawa Shuppansha Ltd., 2002, p.53-54.

397 Kentaro Awaya et al., *War Responsibility and Postwar Responsibility – How are*

Japan and Germany Different?, Tokyo: The Asahi Shimbun Company, 1994, p.87.

398 The China-Japan-Korea Common History Text Tri-National Committee, *Modern and Contemporary History of East Asia Jointly Written by China, Japan and Korea 1 - Understanding East Asian History through Changes in International Relations*, Seoul: Humanist Books, 2012, pp.226-229.

399 Thomas R. H. Havens, *Fire across the Sea: The Vietnam War and Japan, 1965-1975*, Princeton, N. J.: Princeton University Press, 1987, p.93.

400 John W. Dower, *Empire and Aftermath: Yoshida Shigeru and the Japanese Experience*, Cambridge: Harvard Council on East Asian Studies, 1980, p.316.

401 Andrew Gordon, *A Modern History of Japan: From Tokugawa Times to the Present* (Third Edition), New York: Oxford University Press, 2014, pp.239-240.

402 As the Cold War intensified and some countries were not able to attend, this treaty failed to reflect the interests of non-attending countries. Among the invited countries, the three countries of Yugoslavia, India, and Burma refused to attend, and the three countries of the Soviet Union, Poland, and Czechoslovakia attended but refused to sign the treaty as they opposed the contents of the treaty. As for China, the biggest victim nation, neither the People's Republic of China in Beijing nor the Republic of China in Taiwan were invited to the conference due to conflict of opinions between the United Kingdom and the United States. Furthermore, neither South Korea nor North Korea, which suffered through Japan's colonization and were at war at the time, were invited.

403 Japan not only paved the way for economic revival through the Korean War, but also accelerated high growth through profits from the Vietnam War. Korea also established a foothold for economic development by gaining economic profits from dispatching troops to the Vietnam War. Such memories also acted as motives for Japan and Korea to actively participate in the Iraq War. Therefore, the legacy of such distorted memories of war raise concerns that East Asia may be swept away in a vortex of another war. Economic profits gained from the damages of war amongst other countries is never desirable.

404 Ezra F. Vogel, *Japan as Number One*, Cambridge: Harvard University Press,

1979.

[405] Endymion Poter Wilkinson, *Misunderstanding: Europe versus Japan*, Tokyo: Chuokoronsha, 1981, p.221.

[406] The United States, Japan, West Germany, the United Kingdom, France, Italy, and Canada.

[407] Frank Upham, "Unplaced Persons and Struggles for Place", Andrew Gordon (ed.), *Postwar Japan as History*, Berkeley: University of California Press, 1993, pp.327-332.

[408] Prime Minister Kishi was originally born in the Sato family and was Prime Minister Sato's elder brother, but was adopted by the Kishi family.

[409] Some other examples of wartime officials who became Prime Ministers after the war include Ikeda Hayato (1960-1964), Fukuda Takeo (1976-1978), and Ohira Masayoshi (1978-1980).

[410] Leonard James Schoppa, *Education Reform in Japan: A Case of Immobilist Politics*, London: Routledge, 1993, chapter 5.

[411] Andrew Gordon, *A Modern History of Japan: From Tokugawa Times to the Present* (Third Edition), New York: Oxford University Press, 2014, p.272.

[412] Andrew Gordon, *A Modern History of Japan: From Tokugawa Times to the Present* (Third Edition), New York: Oxford University Press, 2014, p.284.

[413] Chalmers Johnson, *Blowback: The Costs and Consequences of American Empire*, New York: Metropolitan Books, 2000, p.36.

[414] Here, the timing of 'already (もはや)' is interpreted by the Korean government as the time when the illegal treaties were signed, whereas it is interpreted by the Japanese government as the time when the government of the Republic of Korea was established on August 15, 1948, and so the opinions of scholars are not unified. However, since an invalid legal act does not generate legal effect accordingly, the Japan-Korea Annexation Treaty and other treaties prior to that are fundamentally invalid, and therefore it is reasonable to consider that it was invalid from the time when the treaty was signed. However, in the case where subsequent actions have actually been taken as a result of an invalid legal act, restitution becomes an issue, and if unfair profits have been generated to the counterpart, they need to be

returned. Therefore, even if restitution for the Japanese annexation of Korea pursuant to invalid treaties and colonization is impossible, it is reasonable to make appropriate compensations for profits that Japan made, or in contrary, damages that Korea suffered from.

415 It can be said that this was the result of a compromise between the Japanese government, which attempted to avoid official compensation for colonization, and the Korean government, which needed funds for economic development. Regarding this economic aid, Korea's view is that it was a sort of compensation, and Japan's view is that it was a type of fund for economic cooperation or congratulatory money for independence.

416 The Asia Peace and History Research Institute, *Perception of History beyond Borders in East Asia*, Seoul: Seonin, 2008, pp.394-401.

417 Shoji Ishikawa and Kazuomi Hirai (eds.), *The Unfinished Twentieth Century - Political History of East Asia 1894 ～*, Tokyo: Horitsu Bunka Sha, 2003, pp.242-243.

418 Through the Japan-China Joint Communique, Japan stated that it took to heart its responsibility for causing grave damage to Chinese citizens through the past war and deeply regretted it, and based on this, the Chinese government relinquished war reparations on the government level. Regarding relinquishment of the claim for war reparations, Premier Zhou Enlai reasoned that the Jiang Jieshi government had already relinquished claims for reparations and the Communist government could not be comparatively narrow-minded. Furthermore, he explained that if China makes demands for reparations to Japan, the burden would ultimately be borne by the Japanese citizens, which is not desirable for promotion of friendship between China and Japan.

419 Eiji Oguma, *The State of Japan*, Tokyo: Shinyosha, 2018, pp.141-149.

420 Richard Taggart Murphy, *The Weight of the Yen: How Denial Imperils America's Future and Ruins an Alliance*, New York: Norton, 1996, Part 3.

421 *Newsweek*, "The Lost Decade", July 27, 1998. As Japan was unable to escape from the state of economic recession even into the 2000s, it is sometimes referred to as the 'lost two decades,' including this period.

422 Ghosn is a figure who was sent as a troubleshooter when France's Renault

entered into a capital partnership with Nissan, which was facing financial difficulties, in 1999. He revived the company through large scale cost cutting and intensive restructuring. In 2005, he became the CEO of Renault, and in 2016, when Nissan acquired a 34% share in Mitsubishi Motors and created the Renault-Nissan-Mitsubishi Alliance, he became the chairman. However, on November 19, 2018, he was suddenly arrested by the special branch of the Tokyo District Prosecutor's Office on charges of embezzlement and malpractice, etc., as soon as he arrived at Haneda Airport on his private jet to enter Japan. He was released on bail in March 2019 and placed under house arrest, but he secretly escaped from Japan and fled to Lebanon in December 2019.

[423] The proportion of Japan in world GDP (nominal GDP, converted into dollars) is consistently on the decline (15.2% in 2000, 10.1% in 2005, 8.4% in 2010, 5.9% in 2015, and 5.8% in 2018). This is in clear contrast with China (3.5% in 2000, 5.1% in 2005, 9.1% in 2010, 15.0% in 2015, and 15.9% in 2018), which is showing a consistently increasing trend, and the US (31.4% in 2000, 27.4% in 2005, 22.8% in 2010, 24.3% in 2015, and 23.9% in 2018), which still makes up the largest proportion (World Bank, *World Development Indicators*; International Monetary Fund, *World Economic Outlook Database*; United Nations, *National Accounts Main Aggregate Database*).

[424] OECD, *Global Economic Outlook*, November 2019.

[425] His grandfather (Hatoyama Ichiro) had been prime minister in the 1950s.

[426] Martin Fackler, "Japan Goes from Dynamic to Disheartened: Retrenchment Offers the West a Grim View of the Future", *New York Times*, October 17, 2010.

[427] Kenneth Henshall, *A History of Japan: From Stone Age to Superpower* (Third Edition), Hampshire: Palgrave Macmillan, 2012, p.188.

[428] Abe showed tremendous political growth, in the halo of his mother's father Kishi Nobusuke, who had been a previous Prime Minister, and his father Shintaro Abe, who had been a previous Foreign Secretary, and finally became Prime Minister in 2006. However, he lost his position in 2007 due to immature political response and health issues, etc. However, he succeeded in coming back to power in 2012, by restoring his health and expanding his personal connections on the one hand and presenting a vision to resolve economic issues and strengthen Japan's external status. The Yamaguchi

Prefecture, which is Abe's election district, is the Choshu domain which cultivated the leading figures of Japan's modernization. Since the Prime Minister system was introduced in the late 19th century, as many as 9 prime ministers are from Yamaguchi Prefecture. Yoshida Shoin (吉田松陰), who emphasized in the mid-19th century the necessity of development through imperial restoration and external invasion and cultivated numerous leading figures of modernization, was also from this region. Ideologically, Abe respects Yoshida Shoin from Yamaguchi Prefecture the most. Although Abe was born in Tokyo, he took over his father's election district in Yamaguchi Prefecture, and visits this region very often and regards it as his hometown, so it would be reasonable to consider him a Yamaguchi person. Therefore, due to this regional and ideological influence, it can be explained that Abe demonstrates a strong nationalistic and rightwing manner in terms of politics.

429 Another thing to focus on in the 2012 elections is that the Osaka Mayor Toru Hashimoto allied with Tokyo's Governor Shintaro Ishihara, creating the Japan Restoration Party (Nihon Ishin no Kai) to take 54 seats. This Restoration Party takes a more conservative stance than Abe, active about the amendment of the Constitution and claiming that Japan should have nuclear weapons.

430 Abenomics (アベノミクス) had been described as initially being comprised of 'three arrows.' The first arrow was to realize the inflation target (2%) through bold monetary policies. The second arrow was to increase public investment through 'maneuvering fiscal policies.' The third arrow was to attempt long-term invigoration of the economy from the supply side as a growth strategy. The Abe Cabinet proposed three new arrows in September 2015, namely, 'strong economy that gives birth to hope (nominal GDP of 6 trillion yen),' 'childcare support that realizes dreams (birth rate of 1.8%),' and 'social security that gives relief.'

431 The term of House of Councilors is 6 years, in which one-half of the seats are selected through elections every 3 years. Currently, the quorum of the House of Councilors is 242 seats, in which 121 seats are elected every 3 years.

432 Even though more than a year still remained in Abe's term, there had been the view that Abe might serve four consecutive terms. Therefore, unless a strong candidate to replace Abe emerged soon, Abe's presidency term for the Liberal Democratic Party might have possibly been extended to 2024. As Japan follows a Parliamentary Cabinet System, if the Liberal Democratic Party continues to stay in power and the presidency term of the Liberal

Democratic Party is extended again, then the Prime Minister's term is automatically extended as well.

433 In measuring the degree of aging, a widely used measure is the percentage of aging population (percentage of population aged 65 years or older to total population). A society is considered an 'aging society' if this percentage of aging population exceeds 7%, 'aged society' if this percentage exceeds 14%, and 'super-aged society' if this percentage exceeds 21%. In the case of Japan, it entered into an 'aging society' in 1970, 'aged society' in 1994, and 'super-aged society' in 2007. The percentage of aging population in Japan in 2015 reached 26.6%, and is on the rise every year (Cabinet Office of Japan, *2017 White Book on Aging*, 2017).

434 According to the data of the National Institute on Social Security and Population Issues, it is forecast that Japan's population will fall below the 100 million line in 2053 at 99.24 million, and will mark 88.08 million in 2065. (The National Institute on Social Security and Population Issues, *The Future Population Estimation of Japan – 2017*).

435 John Lie, *Multiethnic Japan*, Cambridge: Harvard University Press, 2001.

436 The Ministry of Internal Affairs and Communications of Japan (Statistics Bureau), *Statistical Handbook of Japan 2019*.

437 Third country person is a term that refers to East Asian people excluding Japan, and was particularly widely used to refer to Koreans.

438 Andrew Gordon, *A Modern History of Japan: From Tokugawa Times to the Present* (Third Edition), New York: Oxford University Press, 2014, pp.311-312.

439 Ahead of this, on August 23, 1993, Prime Minister Hosokawa Morihiro (細川護熙) stated at his first speech expressing his convictions after his inauguration that he "expresses anew deep self-reflection and apology for the fact that Japan's past acts of aggression and colonization, etc., gave rise to unbearable suffering and sadness to many people." (Yutaka Yoshida, *Japanese People's View of the War*, Tokyo: Iwanami Shoten, 1995).

440 Kenneth Henshall, *A History of Japan: From Stone Age to Superpower* (Third Edition), Hampshire: Palgrave Macmillan, 2012, p.199.

441 Kenneth Henshall, *A History of Japan: From Stone Age to Superpower* (Third

Edition), Hampshire: Palgrave Macmillan, 2012, p.2.

442 In April 2012, Shintaro Ishihara released a statement that Tokyo, of which he was governor, would purchase the Senkaku Islands, which was under private possession.

443 Shoji Ishikawa and Kazuomi Hirai (eds.), *The Unfinished Twentieth Century - Political History of East Asia 1894 ～*, Tokyo: Horitsu Bunka Sha, 2003, pp.206-207.

444 In 1953, which was right after the Korean War, Korea was one of the world's poorest nations with per capita GDP of only USD 67. However, from the 1960s, Korea managed to achieve compact economic growth through efforts of the government, businesses, and the people, and in 2018, per capita GDP amounted to USD 33,622 (UN, *National Accounts Main Aggregate Database*).

445 History Educationalist Conference of Japan (ed.), *East Asian World and Japan*, Tokyo: Aoki Shoten Publishing Co., 2004, pp.251-253.

446 The Tokyo Trials were conducted by judges representing a total of 11 countries, including the United States, the United Kingdom, the Soviet Union, France, China, Australia, Canada, the Netherlands, New Zealand, India, and the Philippines. No judges were present to represent countries that suffered from severe damage due to Japan's occupation, such as Malaysia, Singapore, Indonesia, Burma, Vietnam, etc., and countries that were colonized by Japan, such as Korea and Taiwan. Therefore, the interests of countries that suffered from acts of invasion and colonial exploitation were not properly represented.

447 Tessa Morris-Suzuki, *In Search of Critical Imagination: Japan in an Age of Globalization*, Tokyo: Heibonsha, 2013, pp.60-67.

448 Shoji Ishikawa and Kazuomi Hirai (eds.), *The Unfinished Twentieth Century - Political History of East Asia 1894 ～*, Tokyo: Horitsu Bunka Sha, 2003, pp.253-255.

449 Tetsuya Takahashi, *Postwar Responsibility Argument of Japan*, Tokyo: Kodansha, 2005, pp.29-40.

450 Philip R. Piccigallo, *The Japanese on Trial: Allied War Crimes Operation in the East, 1945-1951*, Austin: University of Texas Press, 1980, pp.3-5.

[451] High-ranking figures within Japan who took this view include Konoe Fumimaro (近衛文麿), who had been a Prime Minister during the war, and Higashikuninomiya Naruhiko (東久邇稔彦), who was the first Prime Minister after the war and also Hirohito's uncle from the Imperial family. Vice-chamberlain Kido Koichi (木戸幸一), who was found guilty as a war criminal in the Tokyo Trial, made efforts to prevent the prosecution of Hirohito, and sent a letter to Hirohito from prison setting forth his views that after Japan restored sovereignty by signing a Peace Treaty, it would be desirable for the Emperor to take responsibility for being defeated in the war and abdicate the throne (John W. Dower, *Embracing Defeat: Japan in the Wake of World War II*, New York: W.W.Norton & Company, 2000, pp.320-326.).

[452] According to the data of Japan's Ministry of Foreign Affairs, there are records that the incineration of documents began due to a decision that 'The written documents of the Ministry of Foreign Affairs must not be used by a third party in any situation regardless of what the contents are' on August 7, 1945 (The Ministry of Foreign Affairs of Japan, *100 Years of the Ministry of Foreign Affairs*, Part 2, Tokyo: Hara-Shobo, 1969).

[453] John W. Dower, *Embracing Defeat: Japan in the Wake of World War II*, New York: W.W.Norton & Company, 2000, pp.482-484.

[454] Foreign Language Publishing House (ed.), *Materials on the Trial of Former Servicemen of the Japanese Army Charged with Manufacturing and Employing Bacteriological Weapons*, Moscow: Foreign Language Publishing House, 1950.

[455] Ian Buruma, *Inventing Japan 1853-1964*, New York: The Modern Library, 2003, pp.146-147.

[456] Saburo Ienaga, *War Responsibility*, Tokyo: Iwanami Shoten, 1985, pp.281-282.

[457] Hikohiro Takahashi, *War Responsibility on the Part of the People*, Tokyo: Aoki Shoten Publishing Co., 1989, p.49.

[458] In August 1945, there were approximately 50,000 Koreans living in Hiroshima and approximately 20,000 Koreans living in Nagasaki. Approximately 40,000 Koreans died from the bombings and among the survivors, approximately 23,000 Koreans went to South Korea and approximately 2,000 Koreans went to North Korea (Geun-shik Jeong, *History of Suffering: Memory and Testimony of the Atomic Air Raid*, Seoul: Seonin, 2005,

pp.14-15).

459 Kentaro Awaya et al., *War Responsibility and Postwar Responsibility – How are Japan and Germany Different?*, Tokyo: The Asahi Shimbun Company, 1994. pp.6-7, p.48.

460 The Potsdam Declaration states the relevant details as follows: Japan shall be permitted to maintain such industries as will sustain her economy and permit the exaction of just reparations in kind, but not those which would enable her to re-arm for war.

461 The first half of Article 14 of the Treaty of San Francisco states as follows: It is recognized that Japan should pay reparations to the Allied Powers for the damage and suffering caused by it during the war. Nevertheless, it is also recognized that the resources of Japan are not presently sufficient, if it is to maintain a viable economy, to make complete reparation for all such damage and suffering and at the same time meet its other obligations.

462 The second half of Article 14 of the Treaty of San Francisco states as follows: Except as otherwise provided in the present Treaty, the Allied Powers waive all other claims of the Allied Powers and their nationals arising out of actions taken by Japan and its nationals in the course of the prosecution of the war, and claims of the Allied Powers for direct military costs of occupation.

463 Aiko Utsumi, *Reflection of Japan and Asia in Terms of Postwar Compensation*, Tokyo: Yamakawa Shuppansha Ltd., 2002, pp.19-20.

464 Aiko Utsumi, *Reflection of Japan and Asia in Terms of Postwar Compensation*, Tokyo: Yamakawa Shuppansha Ltd., 2002, p.87.

465 Deputy Director General Takashima of the Europe and Asia Division of the Ministry of Foreign Affairs, who attended the House of Councilors meeting on March 26, 1991, explained that in Article 6 of the Soviet-Japanese Joint Declaration, the two nations mutually relinquished claims for reparations, but this did not include the claims by individual Japanese citizens towards the Soviet Union or its citizens (Aiko Utsumi, *Reflection of Japan and Asia in Terms of Postwar Compensation*, Tokyo: Yamakawa Shuppansha Ltd., 2002, p.8.).

466 Eiji Oguma, *The State of Japan*, Tokyo: Shinyosha, 2018, pp.150-155.

467 Aiko Utsumi, *Reflection of Japan and Asia in Terms of Postwar Compensation*, Tokyo: Yamakawa Shuppansha Ltd., 2002, pp.61-62.

468 Seong-pil Hong, "An Assessment of Japan's Perception and Fulfillment of Postwar Responsibilities in the Perspective of International Law," Chungnam University, *Chungnam Law Review,* vol. 23, no. 1, June 2012, pp.418-422.

469 Katsumi Matsumoto, *Current Status and Tasks of Postwar Compensation Lawsuits in Japan*, Seoul National University, BK21 Legal Study Group, Public Interest and Human Rights Law Research Center, *Public Interest and Human Rights*, vol. 4, no. 1, February 2007, pp.39-45.

470 Kyu-shu Lee, "Japan's War Responsibility Issues and Neo-nationalism," Gachon University Institute of Asian Culture, *Asian Culture Research,* vol. 29, 2013.3, p.238.

471 Aiko Utsumi, *Reflection of Japan and Asia in Terms of Postwar Compensation*, Tokyo: Yamakawa Shuppansha Ltd., 2002, pp.65-66.

472 Kentaro Awaya et al., *War Responsibility and Postwar Responsibility – How are Japan and Germany Different?*, Tokyo: The Asahi Shimbun Company, 1994, pp.46-48.

473 On April 19, 1952, it was notified under the name of the Civil Case Division Head of the Ministry of Justice that all ex-colonials would lose their Japanese nationalities with the effectuation of the Peace Treaty (Aiko Utsumi, *Reflection of Japan and Asia in Terms of Postwar Compensation*, Tokyo: Yamakawa Shuppansha Ltd., 2002, p.45).

474 History Educationalist Conference of Japan (ed.), *East Asian World and Japan*, Tokyo: Aoki Shoten Publishing Co., 2004, p.180.

475 Regarding the claim for compensation made by Japanese victims who were detained in Siberia, the Supreme Court of Japan dismissed the lawsuit in 1997 on the grounds that 'Citizens must endure the pain together.'

476 Aiko Utsumi, *Reflection of Japan and Asia in Terms of Postwar Compensation*, Tokyo: Yamakawa Shuppansha Ltd., 2002, pp.49-88.

477 In 1942, which was during the Pacific War, the Canadian government relocated approximately 22,000 Japanese immigrants to concentration camps

and confiscated their property, on the grounds that they could be a threat as they were from the enemy country. These Japanese Canadians were released only in 1949, which was 4 years after the war ended. Afterwards, they filed a lawsuit against the Canadian government to return the property that had been confiscated, but as it became difficult to exercise the rights of appeal due to the Treaty of San Francisco, they filed a lawsuit against the Japanese government. Thus, as this treaty, which Japan entered into with countries of the Allied Forces, included content that rights of claim between the countries of the Allied Forces and Japan related to the war were considered to have extinguished, the claims of Japanese Canadians against the Canadian government could not be recognized. To this, the Japanese government clarified that 'what was extinguished through the treaty was diplomatic protection, not individual rights of claim, so plaintiffs should file a lawsuit against the Canadian government.'

[478] Tessa Morris-Suzuki, *In Search of Critical Imagination: Japan in an Age of Globalization*, Tokyo: Heibonsha, 2013, p.81.

[479] In this article, Fukuzawa Yukichi asserted that 'prostitutes' were necessary in order to satisfy the needs of men who get appointed overseas by themselves pursuant to Japan's emigration and colonization policies and to boost the morale of soldiers deployed overseas, and also claimed that the 'prostitutes' themselves could earn money abroad.

[480] Yuko Suzuki, *War Responsibility and Gender: 'Liberalist View of History' and the Issue of Japanese Military 'Sex Slaves'*, Tokyo: Mirai-Sha, 1997.

[481] Aiko Utsumi, *Reflection of Japan and Asia in Terms of Postwar Compensation*, Tokyo: Yamakawa Shuppansha Ltd., 2002, pp.80-82.

[482] Tetsuya Takahashi, *Postwar Responsibility Argument of Japan*, Tokyo: Kodansha, 2005, pp.136-158.

[483] Yoshiaki Yoshimi, *Military Comfort Women*, Tokyo: Iwanami Shoten, 1995, pp.6-36.

[484] Hirofumi Hayashi, *Questioning Japan's Pacifism – Focusing on War Crimes Trial, Peace Constitution, and East Asian Relations*, Tokyo: Kamogawa Co., Ltd., 2008, pp.114-115.

[485] Tae-su Heo, "A Brief View on Japan's Postwar Responsibilities,"

Secretariat of the National Assembly of Korea, *National Assembly Research Service Monthly*, vol. 206, February 1992, p.13.

[486] In August 1993, Kono Yohei (河野洋平), Japan's Chief Cabinet Secretary, disclosed the findings of the investigations that started since December 1991 and announced a statement (the so-called Kono Statement). Secretary Kono Yohei not only recognized the forcibleness of the mobilization (conscription) of comfort women, but also admitted that such acts were a significant violation of human rights and apologized.

[487] History Educationalist Conference of Japan (ed.), *East Asian World and Japan*, Tokyo: Aoki Shoten Publishing Co., 2004, pp.240-244.

[488] Onuma Yasuaki, "Japanese War Guilt and Postwar Responsibilities of Japan", *Berkeley Journal of International Law*, vol. 20, issue 3, 2002, pp.606-607.

[489] Aiko Utsumi, *Reflection of Japan and Asia in Terms of Postwar Compensation*, Tokyo: Yamakawa Shuppansha Ltd., 2002, pp.83-84.

[490] Haruki Wada, *How to Solve Territorial Issues*, Tokyo: Heibonsha, 2012, pp.22-23.

[491] Ukeru Magosaki, *Japan's Territorial Disputes – Senkaku, Dokdo (Takeshima), Northern Islands*, Tokyo: Chikumashobo Ltd., 2011, pp.96-99.

[492] Ukeru Magosaki, *Japan's Territorial Disputes – Senkaku, Dokdo (Takeshima), Northern Islands*, Tokyo: Chikumashobo Ltd., 2011, pp.112-113.

[493] In December 2016, Russia's President Putin visited Japan and adopted an economic cooperation plan between the two countries with Japan's Prime Minister Abe. The details included an idea to develop the Kuril Islands, which has been an object of territorial dispute between the two countries for a long time, into a cruise port of call. With Putin's visit to Japan and such discussions as momentum, the Japanese media created an atmosphere in which Japan could soon get back the so-called 'northern territory' and the Abe Cabinet also attempted to actively push ahead with the return of territory. However, this atmosphere within Japan has provoked the Russian government and its people, and so the situation is that it is difficult to expect advances in negotiations.

[494] Ukeru Magosaki, *Japan's Territorial Disputes – Senkaku, Dokdo (Takeshima),*

Northern Islands, Tokyo: Chikumashobo Ltd., 2011, pp.58-67.

495 The Senkaku Islands are approximately 1,000km from mainland Japan (Kyushu), 410km from Okinawa, 330km from mainland China, and 170km from Taiwan.

496 The Northeast Asian History Foundation (ed.), *Historical Narration and Peace in East Asia*, Northeast Asian History Foundation, 2011, pp.123-124.

497 Dokdo (Liancourt Rocks) is located in the middle of the sea between Japan and Korea (211km from the main island of Japan (Honshu), 216km from the mainland of Korea), approximately 87km from Korea's Ulleung Island and 157km Japan's Oki Islands. Dokdo consists of two large rocky islands. Currently, Korea's guards are stationed at the islands, and as for civilians, only a minimum number of Koreans with authorized access can reside on the islands as the whole of Dokdo is a Natural Reserve.

498 Dokdo (Liancourt Rocks), along with the adjacent Ulleung Island, has belonged to the nation on the Korean Peninsula for over 1,000 years. There had been policy measures related to Dokdo in terms of national administrative management of the nation on the Korean Peninsula even in the modern era. At the time, the government of the Korean Empire registered Dokdo (at the time, called Seokdo) under the administrative district of Ulleung Island on October 25, 1900 pursuant to Emperor Gojong's Imperial Order No. 41.

499 Governmental and Administrative Separation of Certain Outlying Areas from Japan.

500 Article 5 stipulates that Japan as defined in this directive will continue to be applied as long as there are no particular regulations in the future (5. The definition of Japan contained in this directive shall also apply to all future directives, memoranda and orders from this Headquarters unless otherwise specified therein). Therefore, since there are no articles in any of the regulations of the Supreme Headquarters of the Allied Forces or the Treaty of San Francisco that stipulates that Dokdo is to be included into Japanese territory, there is no change in the status of Dokdo as Korean territory.

501 In the United States, Dokdo is called Liancourt Rocks, which was named after a French whale catcher boat that discovered the island in 1849.

502 *Korea Times*, July 28 & 31, 2008; Foster Klug, "US backtracks on name of disputed Asian islands," July 30, 2008, Associated Press (AP).

503 Tsushima (對馬, つしま) is an island located in the Korea Strait (Tsushima Strait) between Japan and Korea, the size of which is 695.9 km². The shortest distances from Japan and Korea are 82 km and 50 km respectively.

504 Daesong Hyun, *Birth of Territorial Nationalism: The Politics of the Dokdo/Takeshima Issue*, Kyoto: Minerva-Shobo, 2006.

505 Tessa Morris-Suzuki, "An Integral part of Our National Territory: Frontiers and the Image of the Nation in Japanese History", a thesis of International Symposium to Commemorate Establishment of Hanyang University's Research Institute of Comparative History and Culture ('Frontiers or Borders?', 23-24 April, 2004), Edited by Ji-hyeon Lim, *Modern Borders, Changes in History*, Seoul: Humanist Books, 2004, p.204.

506 Ukeru Magosaki, *Japan's Territorial Disputes – Senkaku, Dokdo (Takeshima), Northern Islands*, Tokyo: Chikumashobo Ltd., 2011, pp.153-164.

507 Hye-seon Jeong, *Japanese History Digest 100*, Seoul: Garam Planning Publisher, 2011, pp.16-17.

508 The China-Japan-Korea Common History Text Tri-National Committee, *Modern and Contemporary History of East Asia Jointly Written by China, Japan and Korea 2 - Understanding the History of People and Interaction by Theme*, Seoul: Humanist Books, 2012, pp.344-347.

509 Woo-bong Ha, *Japan and Korea – History and Future of Mutual Awareness*, Seoul: Salim, 2005, pp.5-79.

510 Hirofumi Hayashi, *Questioning Japan's Pacifism – Focusing on War Crimes Trial, Peace Constitution, and East Asian Relations*, Tokyo: Kamogawa Co., Ltd., 2008, pp.69-70.

511 Tetsuya Takahashi, *State and Sacrifice*, Tokyo: Japan Broadcast Publishing Co., 2005 (Translated by Mok Lee, Seoul: Chaekgwahamge, 2008), p.15.

512 Michael Walzer, *Just and Unjust: A Moral Argument with Historical Illustrations*, New York: Basic Books, 1977.

513 World War II broke out due to Germany's and Japan's invasion of

neighboring countries, and almost all of the ordinary people of the two countries were dragged to war. This war was designed and promoted by the elitist leading class that led the countries at the time, and ordinary people were mobilized under the grounds of serving their countries. Eventually, most of the good people came to participate in a war in which they were killing people of other countries without even knowing the reason and they themselves were innocently killed.

514 In Korea, this is referred to as the so-called 'absurd remark of Kubota.'

515 Karl Schoenberger, "Japan Aide Quits over Remark on WWⅡ", *Los Angeles Times*, May 5, 1988.

516 Sebastian Moffet, "Japan Justice Minister Denies Nanking Massacre", *Reuters*, May 5, 1994.

517 *Mainichi Daily News*, August 13, 1994.

518 Jin-mo Lee, "West Germany's Process of Overcoming the past after the War (1945-1990) – Focusing on the Roles of the Allied Powers and the Civil Society," *Research on Eastern and Western Culture* (7), 2000, p.214.

519 Hannah Arendt, *Eichmann in Jerusalem: A Report on the Banality of Evil*, New York: Penguin Books, 1963.

520 Choong-gi Song, "Germany's Belated Historical Settlement – Focusing on Compensation to Forced Laborers under Nazi Rule," *History Criticism* (73), 2005, pp.287-288.

521 Kentaro Awaya et al., *War Responsibility and Postwar Responsibility – How are Japan and Germany Different?*, Tokyo: The Asahi Shimbun Company, 1994. pp.205-206.

522 The Northeast Asian History Foundation (ed.), *Historical Narration and Peace in East Asia*, Seoul: Northeast Asian History Foundation, 2011, p.232.

523 Kentaro Awaya et al., *War Responsibility and Postwar Responsibility – How are Japan and Germany Different?*, Tokyo: The Asahi Shimbun Company, 1994. pp.6-8.

524 Kentaro Awaya et al., *War Responsibility and Postwar Responsibility – How are Japan and Germany Different?*, Tokyo: The Asahi Shimbun Company, 1994.

pp.10-12.

[525] Karl Jaspers, *Die Schuldfrage*, Heidelberg: L. Schneider, 1946 (*The Question of German Guilt*, translated by E. B. Ashton, New York: The Dial Press, 1947).

[526] Ralph Giordano, *Die Zweite Schuld oder Von der Last Deutscher zu sein* (*The Second Guilt or the Burden of Being German*), Hamburg: Rasch und Röhring, 1987.

[527] The Northeast Asian History Foundation (ed.), *Historical Narration and Peace in East Asia*, Seoul: Northeast Asian History Foundation, 2011, p.235.

[528] The European Union had consisted of 28 member countries in 2019. Until 2019, there had not been any countries that withdrew from the European Union, but in June 2016, the United Kingdom decided to leave (so-called Brexit, compounding the words Britain and exit) as the result of a referendum, and in the end, the UK officially left the European Union on 31 January 2020 after 47 years of membership.

[529] Eun-mi Choi, "Research on the Effect of US Foreign Policy on Postwar Settlements – Focusing on Germany's and Japan's Cases of War Criminal Treatment and War Reparations among States," *Donga Research* 58, 2010, p.65.

[530] John W. Dower, *Embracing Defeat: Japan in the Wake of World War II*, New York: W.W.Norton & Company, 2000, pp.475-476.

[531] Shoji Ishikawa and Kazuomi Hirai (eds.), *The Unfinished Twentieth Century - Political History of East Asia 1894 ~*, Tokyo: Horitsu Bunka Sha, 2003, pp.242-243.

[532] Kentaro Awaya et al., *War Responsibility and Postwar Responsibility – How are Japan and Germany Different?*, Tokyo: The Asahi Shimbun Company, 1994, p.40.

[533] Heiko Ital, "Coping with the past in Germany and Japan - or why Japan is downplaying its war crimes in history textbooks in contrast to Germany", *Korean Journal of Social Sciences*, vol. 22, no. 4, December 2012, pp.229-230.

[534] Herbert P. Bix, "The Showa Emperor's Monologue and the Problem of War Responsibility", *The Journal of Japanese Studies*, vol. 18, no. 2, Summer 1992, p.330.

[535] Sang-jung Kang and Shunya Yoshimi, Translated by Seong-mo Lim and

Kyeong-won Kim, *Perspective of Globalization*, Seoul: Yeesan Publishing, 2004, pp.157-170.

536 Hirofumi Hayashi, *Questioning Japan's Pacifism – Focusing on War Crimes Trial, Peace Constitution, and East Asian Relations*, Tokyo: Kamogawa Co., Ltd., 2008, pp.66-68.

537 Tatsuru Uchida, *Japan as a Peripheral Country*, Tokyo: Shinchosha, 2009, p.44, pp.44-57.

538 *The Weekly Standard*, December 1, 2003.

539 Herfried Münkler, *Imperien*, Berlin: Rowohlt·Berlin Verlag GmbH, 2005 (Translated by Jin-seong Kong, Seoul: Chaeksesang Publishing Co., 2015).

540 Edward W. Said, *Orientalism*, New York: Pantheon, 1978; Edward W. Said, *Culture and Imperialism*, New York: Vintage Books, 1994.

541 John King Fairbank, Edwin O. Reischauer, and Albert M. Craig, *East Asia: Tradition and Transformation*, Boston: Houghton Mifflin, 1973.

542 No-ja Park, *Empire of White Masks – Orientalism, Moving Beyond Western-centric History*, Seoul: Hangyeorae Press, 2003, pp.276-278.

543543 Nobukuni Koyasu, *How Asia has been depicted: Orientalism in Modern Japan*, Tokyo: Fujiwara Shoten, 2003, pp.141-155.

544 No-ja Park, *Empire of White Masks – Orientalism, Moving Beyond Western-centric History*, Seoul: Hangyeorae Press, 2003, pp.107-108.

545 Hye-seon Jeong, *Japanese History Digest 100*, Seoul: Garam Planning Publisher, 2011, pp.34-35; Yoshihiko Amino, *Rethinking Japanese History*, Tokyo: Chikumashobo Ltd., 2005 (Translated by Gyeong-taek Lim, Seoul: Dolbegae, 2015, pp.249-250).

546 Jared Diamond, *Guns, Germs and Steel: The Fates of Human Societies*, New York: W.W. Norton & Company, 2005.

547 Here, ABCD refers to America, Britain, China, and Dutch (Ian Buruma, *Inventing Japan 1853-1964*, New York: The Modern Library, 2003, pp.115-116).

548 However, Japan is existing as a state and enjoying prosperity as an

economic power, even though it does not possess occupied regions in China or Manchuria and does not have colonies such as the Korean Peninsula and Taiwan. According to Japan's logic in the early 20th century, Japan can only exist and achieve prosperity by colonizing Taiwan and Korea again, establishing a puppet government in Manchuria, and furthermore, occupying not only China but also Southeast Asia.

549 On the contrary, in Germany under the rule of Hitler who caused World War II, numerous German people risked their lives and resisted the Nazis. In Italy, the people rose up and overthrew the Mussolini government and liberated northern Italy from the Fascists before the Allied Forces arrived.

550 Shoji Ishikawa and Kazuomi Hirai (eds.), *The Unfinished Twentieth Century - Political History of East Asia 1894 ~*, Tokyo: Horitsu Bunka Sha, 2003, pp.244-247.

551 Yoshihiko Amino, *What is Japan? - History of Japan*, Tokyo: Kodansha Ltd., 2000 (Translated by Hun Park, Seoul: Changbi Publishers, 2003, pp.18-27).

552 Yoshihiko Amino, *What is Japan? – History of Japan*, Tokyo: Kodansha Ltd., 2000 (Translated by Hun Park, Seoul: Changbi Publishers, 2003, pp.87-105, pp.229-256).

553 The forces that led the Meiji government merely tried to use the Japanese Emperor in forming a centralized modern state, and it was not as though they worshipped the Japanese Emperor from the beginning. They enacted a constitution that defined the Japanese Emperor as the only sovereign power in Japan and a sacred being, and internalized this through the Imperial Rescript on Education and Shinto, through which the idea of worshipping the Japanese Emperor came to take root. In particular, the Japanese Emperor became even more deified through the First Sino-Japanese War, Russo-Japanese War, merger of the Korean Peninsula, occupation of Manchuria, the Second Sino-Japanese War, and the Pacific War.

554 Tetsuya Takahashi, *Postwar Responsibility Argument of Japan*, Tokyo: Kodansha, 2005, pp.91-92.

555 Taking a look at how Israel and the Jewish acted as the driving force for international pressure for postwar Germany to properly make historical settlements, the following questions can be raised. China suffered the greatest damage from modern Japan, but why was it that Chinese people living abroad

all over the world could not play a role similar to the Jewish? Was it because Chinese people living abroad, such as in Singapore, etc., did suffer damage, but not to as severe a degree as the Jewish? Are Chinese people and Chinese people living abroad even properly aware of the fact that approximately 10 million Chinese people were sacrificed through the Nanjing Massacre, etc.? What should be done in order to make these people play a similar role to the Jewish? Furthermore, one way for these people to play a role would be to build solidarity with other Asians living all around the world, but how can we make these people play such role?

556 Aiko Utsumi, *Reflection of Japan and Asia in Terms of Postwar Compensation*, Tokyo: Yamakawa Shuppansha Ltd., 2002, pp.85-86.

557 Tetsuya Takahashi, *Postwar Responsibility Argument of Japan*, Tokyo: Kodansha, 2005, p.50.

558 This means that even if an individual suffered from damages due to state action under the old Constitution which did not allow compensation for damages from state institutions, the government under the new constitution does not take responsibility for it.

559 Aiko Utsumi, *Reflection of Japan and Asia in Terms of Postwar Compensation*, Tokyo: Yamakawa Shuppansha Ltd., 2002, pp.78-80.

560 The China-Japan-Korea Common History Text Tri-National Committee, *Modern and Contemporary History of East Asia Jointly Written by China, Japan and Korea 2 - Understanding the History of People and Interaction by Theme*, Seoul: Humanist Books, 2012, pp.358-360.

561 Due to the Japanese military's air raid on Pearl Harbor in Hawaii in 1941, approximately 120,000 Japanese immigrants who lived on the west coast of the United States were treated as 'spies' or dangerous people. Eventually, the United States government evacuated them to temporary 'relocation centers' which were established on barren land in the inland through the President's Administrative Order No. 9066. The United States government had actually deported Japanese immigrants to 'incarceration camps.' Approximately two-thirds of these people were pure American citizens who had been born in the United States.

562 Aiko Utsumi, *Reflection of Japan and Asia in Terms of Postwar Compensation*,

Tokyo: Yamakawa Shuppansha Ltd., 2002, pp.1-2.

563 Hirofumi Hayashi, *Questioning Japan's Pacifism – Focusing on War Crimes Trial, Peace Constitution, and East Asian Relations*, Tokyo: Kamogawa Co., Ltd., 2008, pp.148-150.

564 Satoshi Ukai et al., Translated by the Translation Network of Study Space 'Suyuneomeo,' *Anti-Japan and East Asia*, Seoul: Somyong Publishing, 2005, pp.345-361.

565 The movie 'Pride' portrays history as if the US and Britain waged war against Japan and Japan only responded to protect itself. This cannot be further from the truth and is merely fiction. Japan expanded the war step by step by fabricating various opportunities and excuses, and at each phase, the Japanese executed the war by devising the scenario and directing the scenes.

566 Hiroshi Miyajima, *Criticizing Japan's View of History*, Seoul: Changbi Publishers, 2013, p.157.

567 Tetsuya Takahashi, *Postwar Responsibility Argument of Japan*, Tokyo: Kodansha, 2005, pp.46-64.

568 Hannah Arendt, *Eichmann in Jerusalem: A Report on the Banality of Evil*, New York: Penguin Books, 1963.

569 Erich Fromm, *To have or to Be?*, New York: Harper & Row, 1976.

570 When Alfred Dreyfus (1859-1935), a Jewish officer in France was falsely accused and received a verdict of guilty in the late 19th century, in a situation where everybody was keeping silent, Emile Francois Zola (1840-1902), who had no connection with him, showed a strong sense of justice and compassion in his well known article 'J'Accuse.' 'I will say the truth. I swore that I would say it if the judicial branch, which has legal authority, does not say the absolutely perfect truth. This is also my obligation. If I do not do this, the spirit of a person suffering from a crime that he did not commit will haunt me every night from a faraway place that has lost the world.'

571 Yoshibumi Wakamiya, *Reconciliation and Nationalism – East Asian World View of Postwar Conservatives*, Tokyo: The Asahi Shimbun Company, 2006, pp.38-39.

572 Henry David Thoreau, *Resistance to Civil Government*, 1849 (Norwalk,

Connecticut: Easton Press, 1993).

573 John Stuart Mill, *On Liberty*, London: John W. Parker & Son, 1859.

574 Michael Sandel, *Justice: What's the Right Thing to Do?*, New York: Farrar, Straus and Giroux, 2009.

575 Emmanuel Levinas (tr. Alphonso Lingis), *Totality and Infinity*, Hague: Martinus Nijhoff Publishers, 1979.

576 The military expenditure of the Japanese government has made up 5-6% of all general accounting expenditure since the mid-1970s, but as the total budget size of the government has increased, the amount has consistently increased every year. The current amount of Japan's total military expenditure is 10% larger than South Korea, which is responding to a situation of division of the Korean Peninsula (The Ministry of Finance of Japan, *Japanese Public Finance Fact Sheet*, each year; Nan Tian, et al., "Trends in World Military Expenditure, 2019", *SIPRI Fact Sheet* (April 2020), Stockholm International Peace Research Institute, 2020).

577 In order to become a permanent member of the United Nations Security Council, it is necessary to have a unanimous vote of the existing 5 permanent member states, majority vote of 10 non-permanent member states, and furthermore, two-thirds support of United Nations member states. It would be difficult to gain such approval and support due to the disappointing conduct that Japan has demonstrated after the war as a war criminal state, but it is also difficult to be realized because the current UN system would have to be torn down in order for Japan to become a permanent member of the United Nations Security Council. In other words, the current UN system has been formed and maintained centering on the Allied Forces at the time of World War II, and the UN Charter stipulates that Japan, which was an Axis Power in the war, is an object to be held in check.

578 Since there are barely any Japanese people left that personally experienced the war and it would be difficult for them to write about their experiences themselves even if they are alive, people from civic groups could record these if the survivors dictate their stories.

579 Kanji Nishio (ed.), *The History of the People*, Tokyo: Sankei Simbun Co, 1999.

580 Nobukuni Koyasu, *How Asia has been depicted: Orientalism in Modern Japan*,

Tokyo: Fujiwara Shoten, 2003, pp.253-255.

[581] Tatsuru Uchida, *Japan as a Peripheral Country*, Tokyo: Shinchosha, 2009, p.44, pp.93-99.

[582] In this sense, there needs to be more intellectuals like Uchida Tatsuru, who has a critical view of and tries to improve Japanese society which continues to be economically rich but not mature (Tatsuru Uchida, *Japan as a Peripheral Country*, Tokyo: Shinchosha, 2009).

[583] Claude Lévi Strauss, *The Savage Mind* (French: *La Pensée Sauvage*, 1962), Chicago: University of Chicago Press, 1966.

[584] Tetsuya Takahashi, *Postwar Responsibility Argument of Japan*, Tokyo: Kodansha, 2005, pp.260-269.

[585] The concept of historical revisionism refers to a reactionary movement that attempted to destroy the existing historical awareness by denying or minimizing historical facts themselves in relation to Germany's actions of starting World War II. In the case of Japan, historical revisionism manifests itself through movements to deny the existence or minimize the scale of the Nanjing Massacre or Japanese Military Sexual Slavery. Japan's historical revisionism holds fast to the position of denying responsibility for colonization and war of aggression.

[586] The recent conduct of Kyushu University School of Medicine is the type of universal attitude that human society expects. The German Medical Association already adopted a resolution to convict doctors who took part in war crimes in 1947, and announced a statement of apology in 1950. The Berlin Medical Association announced in 1988 a statement that asked responsibilities of the doctors who were involved in Nazi crimes and lamented the victims. Since then, many medical organizations have commemorated victims and apologized to victims and their families.

[587] Kenneth Henshall, *A History of Japan: From Stone Age to Superpower* (Third Edition), Hampshire: Palgrave Macmillan, 2012, p.2.

[588] Andrew Gordon, *A Modern History of Japan: From Tokugawa Times to the Present* (Third Edition), New York: Oxford University Press, 2014, pp.11-14.

[589] Doo-gi Min, *Competition with Time*, Seoul: Yonsei University Press, 2000,

pp.49-50.

590 Haruki Wada, *How to Solve Territorial Issues*, Tokyo: Heibonsha, 2012, pp.60-61.

591 Ukeru Magosaki, *Japan's Territorial Disputes – Senkaku, Dokdo (Takeshima), Northern Islands*, Tokyo: Chikumashobo Ltd., 2011, pp.201-204.

592 Dokdo (Liancourt Rocks, Takeshima) was incorporated into the Shimane Prefecture on February 22, 1905 by the Meiji government, and at around the 100th anniversary of the incorporation, Shimane Prefecture decided to commemorate this day as 'Takeshima Day' and has held events every year. Recently, Japan's central government has been dispatching Assistant Minister level figures to the commemoration ceremony. The reason Shimane Prefecture designated this day was because of discontentment that Japanese fishing boats could not go near Dokdo for fishing activities due to the interference of Korea. However, Japan's commemoration of February 22, 1905 as the day it incorporated Dokdo into its territory is no different from acknowledging that it incorporated Dokdo due to ambitions to expand its territory during modern Japan's expansion period. This is because Dokdo was under the rule of Joseon, which governed the Korean Peninsula, until then.

593 Haruki Wada, *How to Solve Territorial Issues*, Tokyo: Heibonsha, 2012, pp.228-236.

594 Ukeru Magosaki, *Japan's Territorial Disputes – Senkaku, Dokdo (Takeshima), Northern Islands*, Tokyo: Chikumashobo Ltd., 2011, pp.48-55, pp.206-209.

595 Global Trade Information Services, *World Trade Atlas;* World Trade Organization (WTO), *World Trade Statistical Review 2019;* UN Comtrade, *The International Trade Statistics Year Book 2018.*

596 Compared to Korea, which is a neighbor in the East Asian region, Japan's population is 2.5 times bigger and Japan's economic size is at least 3 times bigger.

597 Ukeru Magosaki, *Japan's Territorial Disputes – Senkaku, Dokdo (Takeshima), Northern Islands*, Tokyo: Chikumashobo Ltd., 2011, pp.200-201.

598 Thomas C. Schelling, *The Strategy of Conflict*, Cambridge: Harvard

University Press, 1980.

[599] Ukeru Magosaki, *Japan's Territorial Disputes – Senkaku, Dokdo (Takeshima), Northern Islands,* Tokyo: Chikumashobo Ltd., 2011, pp.215-221.

[600] Hiroshi Sanuki, "Sixty Years since Bombing and War Defeat, Thinking about Japan's Responsibility toward Peace in East Asia", Korean Association of History Education, *History Education Research,* June 2005, pp.258-262.

[601] Robert D. Putnam, *Bowling Alone: The Collapse and Revival of American Community,* New York: Simon & Schuster, 2000; James S. Coleman, "Social Capital in the Creation of Human Capital", *American Journal of Sociology,* vol. 94, 1988, pp-95-120.

[602] Kanji Nishio et al (eds.), *New History Textbook,* Tokyo: Hushosa, 2001. The problem is that historians are creating such distorted historical consciousness and furthermore they are trying to instill this into Japan's adolescents through a government authorized textbook. When adolescents who have been educated based on this distorted historical consciousness become the main characters in the history of the future, there will be a higher possibility of aggravating confrontation and conflict, rather than reconciliation and cooperation, among East Asian countries.

[603] The China-Japan-Korea Common History Text Tri-National Committee, *A History to Open the Future,* Seoul: Hanibook (Hangyeorae Press), 2005.

[604] The China-Japan-Korea Common History Text Tri-National Committee, *Modern and Contemporary History of East Asia Jointly Written by China, Japan and Korea 2 - Understanding the History of People and Interaction by Theme,* Seoul: Humanist Books, 2012, pp.368-371.

[605] Onuma Yasuaki, "Japanese War Guilt and Postwar Responsibilities of Japan", *Berkeley Journal of International Law,* vol. 20, issue 3, 2002, pp.601-602.

[606] Onuma Yasuaki, "Japanese War Guilt and Postwar Responsibilities of Japan", *Berkeley Journal of International Law,* vol. 20, issue 3, 2002, pp.604-615.

[607] The China-Japan-Korea Common History Text Tri-National Committee, *Modern and Contemporary History of East Asia Jointly Written by China, Japan and Korea 2 - Understanding the History of People and Interaction by Theme,* Seoul: Humanist Books, 2012, pp.347-349.

608 Yoshibumi Wakamiya, *Reconciliation and Nationalism – East Asian World View of Postwar Conservatives*, Tokyo: The Asahi Shimbun Company, 2006, pp.211-213.

609 Kentaro Awaya et al., *War Responsibility and Postwar Responsibility – How are Japan and Germany Different?*, Tokyo: The Asahi Shimbun Company, 1994, pp.175-180.

610 Yoshibumi Wakamiya, *Reconciliation and Nationalism – East Asian World View of Postwar Conservatives*, Tokyo: The Asahi Shimbun Company, 2006, pp.299-320.

611 Palau is a place where Japanese troops were almost annihilated (only 34 survivors among approximately 11,000 Japanese troops) due to the attack of US troops from September to November 1944. Even though Emperor Akihito had reached an old age of 81 years, he pushed ahead with a visit to Palau in 2015 at the seventieth anniversary of the end of the war. However, Prime Minister Abe was of the position that Japan should refrain from recalling past historical issues because he wanted to emphasize Japan's new future-oriented role in commemoration of the seventieth anniversary of the end of the war. So Abe requested that the Emperor reconsider the visit to Palau under the grounds that 'there were no accommodations in Palau that would be suitable for the Japanese Emperor.' When the Japanese Emperor responded by saying that 'he did not mind sleeping out in the open,' Abe had no choice but to reluctantly consent to the Emperor's visit to Palau. Abe's statement at the seventieth anniversary of the end of the war was made without deviating much from the Murayama Statement in 1995, due to the checks of the Japanese Emperor who takes the pacifist line.

612 Yoshibumi Wakamiya, *Reconciliation and Nationalism – East Asian World View of Postwar Conservatives*, Tokyo: The Asahi Shimbun Company, 2006, pp.321-328.

613 In the history of Japan, there had been a considerable number of Emperors who had abdicated the throne during their lifetime, but there has been no such case for over 200 years after Emperor Koukaku abdicated the throne to his son Ninko in 1817.

614 On June 9, 2017, the Japanese National Diet passed the Special Law for the Japanese Emperor's Abdication, and Emperor Akihito officially

abdicated the throne on April 30, 2019.

615 The China-Japan-Korea Common History Text Tri-National Committee, *Modern and Contemporary History of East Asia Jointly Written by China, Japan and Korea 2 - Understanding the History of People and Interaction by Theme*, Seoul: Humanist Books, 2012, pp.136-137.

616 The Northeast Asian History Foundation (ed.), *Historical Narration and Peace in East Asia*, Seoul: Northeast Asian History Foundation, 2011, p.122.

617 A Joint Declaration by Japanese and Korean Intellectuals – On the Centennial of the Japanese Annexation of Korea - (May 10, 2010. Seoul/Tokyo).

618 Ukeru Magosaki, *Japan's Territorial Disputes – Senkaku, Dokdo (Takeshima), Northern Islands*, Tokyo: Chikumashobo Ltd., 2011, pp.216-217.

619 Doo-gi Min, *Competition with Time*, Seoul: Yonsei University Press, 2000, pp.1-31.

620 *Toyo Keizai Shinpo*, Editorials on July 30, August 13, and September 23, 1921.

621 Tessa Morris-Suzuki, *In Search of Critical Imagination: Japan in an Age of Globalization*, Tokyo: Heibonsha, 2013, pp.101-104.

622 The Asia Peace and History Research Institute, *Perception of History beyond Borders in East Asia*, Seoul: Seonin, 2008, pp.234-242.

ABOUT THE AUTHOR

Charles Park

The Director of East Asian History and Peace Institute

Seoul National University, Bachelor of Arts (Asian History)
Seoul National University, Bachelor of Arts (International Relations)
University of Leuven, Master of European Politics and Policies
Seoul National University, Master of Policy Studies
State University of New York at Stony Brook, Master of Science in
                                        Technology Management
Seoul National University, Ph.D. in Engineering (Technology Management)
University of Seoul, Ph.D. in Policy Studies

All proceeds from this book will be used to help the victims of modern Japan's colonization and invasion as well as to promote peace in Asia.

Made in the USA
Las Vegas, NV
27 February 2024

86324177R00236